Serial Murderers and Their Victims

SERIAL MURDERERS AND THEIR VICTIMS

SIXTH EDITION

ERIC W. HICKEY

California School of Forensic Studies
Alliant International University

WADSWORTH
CENGAGE Learning

Australia • Brazil • Japan • Korea • Mexico • Singapore • Spain • United Kingdom • United States

***Serial Murderers and Their Victims*, Sixth Edition**
Eric W. Hickey

Publisher: Linda Ganster

Senior Acquisitions Editor: Carolyn Henderson Meier

Developmental Editor: Rachel McDonald

Assistant Editor: Virginette Acacio

Editorial Assistant: Casey Lozier

Media Editor: Andy Yap

Marketing Manager: Michelle Williams

Marketing Assistant/Associate: Jack Ward

Marketing Communications Manager: Heather Baxley

Art and Cover Direction, Production Management, and Composition: PreMediaGlobal

Manufacturing Planner: Judy Inouye

Rights Acquisitions Specialist: Roberta Broyer

Cover Designer: Riezebos Holzbaur/Yenny Yulianny

Cover Image: ULKASTUDIO/ Shutterstock

Library of Congress Control Number: 2012936020

ISBN-13: 978-1-133-04970-8

ISBN-10: 1-133-04970-2

Wadsworth
20 Davis Drive
Belmont, CA 94002-3098
USA

Cengage Learning is a leading provider of customized learning solutions with office locations around the globe, including Singapore, the United Kingdom, Australia, Mexico, Brazil, and Japan. Locate your local office at **www.cengage.com/global**.

Cengage Learning products are represented in Canada by Nelson Education, Ltd.

To learn more about Wadsworth, visit **www.cengage.com/wadsworth**

Purchase any of our products at your local college store or at our preferred online store **www.cengagebrain.com**.

Printed in the United States of America
1 2 3 4 5 6 7 16 15 14 13 12

For my son Chad P. Hickey, who is always in my heart.

To the victims, both the living and the dead—may their suffering not be ignored nor forgotten.

To every person who has a passion for the study and application of forensics.

And to Col. Robert Ressler, retired FBI, who never really retired, and for that I am grateful.

Eric W. Hickey, Ph.D.

A Special Dedication

Twenty-two years have passed since one of the founding fathers of modern criminal profiling and behavioral analysis retired from the FBI's Behavioral Analysis Unit. But no matter. Robert Ressler still finds himself in demand around the world for his knowledge and expertise in analyzing and interpreting the most complex and unusual of violent criminals and their crimes. As Robert's current partner, I know firsthand that hardly a day passes where we don't receive an email, letter, or telephone call seeking Robert's advice in solving an extremely difficult homicide case or imploring him to lecture at some well-known university around the world. There is always an audience anxious to learn from one of the pioneers in criminal behavioral analysis who had the foresight and research acumen to understand that there was much that we, as a society, could learn from the most violent of offenders, the serial killer.

In fact, Robert has been given credit for coining the term "serial killer" in its modern iteration. But those intimately involved in the field know that Robert's contribution goes well beyond nomenclature: his groundbreaking research and unique approaches to understanding violent offenders' behaviors has paved the way for law enforcement agencies around the world to organize and develop their own profiling units. In addition, Robert's creation of ViCAP, the computerized Violent Criminal Apprehension Program database, is responsible for helping police and sheriff departments nationwide link what previously would have been viewed as individual murder cases, leading to the successful capture of serial offenders who undoubtedly would have continued plying their trade, undetected, across the country.

In his long FBI career, Robert worked tirelessly to push the boundaries of his research into violent criminal behavior in order to understand the psychological and behavioral attributes and crime scene dynamics of serial killers, mass murderers, and offenders who commit sexual homicide. He shared that knowledge through the publication of numerous articles and books that have assisted law enforcement agencies around the world in helping to solve their previously unsolved cases. Robert's life work has also helped to soften the sharp edges of the traumatic wounds left in the lives of the families of so many of the men, women, and children who fell victim to these violent offenders. He remains a hero, mentor, teacher, and problem solver to tens of thousands who have learned from his research and followed in his footsteps.

Despite his well-deserved reputation and fame, Robert has always remained accessible to those who have asked for his assistance. And he has always been humble in providing it. I am honored to call Robert my friend, mentor, and partner. He has had a significant impact on the direction my career has taken, and years down the line, when I look back on all I've accomplished, I hope I will find I have honored his legacy. The truth, however, is that his shoes are exceptionally large, and I doubt that anyone will ever be able to fill them.

Mark E. Safarik M.S., V.S.M. (FBI Ret.)
Executive Director
Forensic Behavioral Services International
Fredericksburg, Virginia

Eric W. Hickey is the dean of the California School of Forensic Studies at Alliant International University, where he oversees the growth and development of the largest clinical forensic studies program in the United States. At Alliant he often teaches seminars in profiling psychopaths, sex offenders, and sexual predators. Dr. Hickey has taught many courses in criminal personalities, sex crimes and paraphilia, homicide, and psychopathology in several universities and colleges, as well as for jail and prison staff. He supervises theses and dissertations involving forensic and criminal psychology. Dr. Hickey has considerable field experience working with the criminally insane, psychopaths, sex offenders, and other habitual criminals. He has also served as an adjunct instructor for the American Prosecutor's Research Institute at the National Advocacy Center in Columbia, South Carolina, profiling stalkers and cyberstalkers.

He publishes books and articles and lectures extensively on the etiology of violence and serial crime. His book, *Serial Murderers and Their Victims*, sixth edition (Wadsworth), is used as a teaching tool in universities and by law enforcement in studying the nature of violence, criminal personalities, and victim–offender relationships. Another of his books, *The Encyclopedia of Murder and Violent Crime* (Sage Publishers), explores the phenomenon of murder and violence through the eyes of some of the world's most noted experts. In 2006 he published his edited book *Sex Crimes and Paraphilia* (Prentice Hall Publishers), a comprehensive examination of sexual perversions, sex offending, and sexual predators. A coauthored book, *The Myth of a Psychiatric Crime Wave* (Carolina Academic Press), examines the misperceptions and reality of the mentally ill and mentally disordered as criminals. His current research focuses upon the development of his theory of *relational paraphilic attachment* (RPA) and sexual predators. His expertise is regularly sought by the media, including appearances on CNN, History Channel, NPR, *Larry King Live*, *20/20*, A&E *Biography*, *Good Morning America*, CBC, True TV, Discovery, and TLC.

He consults with private agencies and testifies as an expert witness in both criminal and civil cases. He is a court-qualified expert in paraphilia including pedophilia, child molestation, and fetishes; stalking; adult rape and sexual assault; and violent criminal behavior including robbery, burglary, and homicide (solo and serial). A former consultant to the FBI's UNABOM Task Force, Dr. Hickey currently assists local, state, and federal law enforcement in training and investigations. He also conducts seminars for agencies involving the profiling and investigating of sex crimes, arson, robbery, homicide, stalking, workplace violence, and terrorism as well as workshops for mental health practitioners. Dr. Hickey is a member of an FBI Threat Assessment Regional Evaluation Team that addresses campus violence and potential threats. He is internationally recognized for his research on multiple-homicide offenders and has conducted seminars in countries throughout Europe, Asia, and North America. He has also trained VIP protection specialists in Israel in profiling stalkers, threat assessment, and interventions.

Contents

Preface

Serial Murderers and Their Victims was the first scholarly, comprehensive, empirical examination of serial murder in the United States. Chapter 1 examines the emergence of serial and mass killing in the United States and the many problems involved in adequately defining the phenomenon. Chapters 2–4 explore cultural, biological, psychological, and sociological frameworks as explanations for serial murder and present a model for understanding serial killing as a process.

Chapter 5 explores criminal paraphilia, fantasy, and sex offenders and predators, some of whom attach themselves to their victims through a process of *relational paraphilic attachment.* Chapters 6 through 9 sort out the demographic, social, and behavioral characteristics of male and female offenders, those who murder with accomplices, and others who find their victims as healthcare providers. The role of stalking in serial murder is also examined and placed into a classification system.

Chapter 10 examines the victims and victim–offender relationships in cases of serial murder as well as certain more vulnerable populations including prostitutes, young women, gay men, teens, children, and the elderly. Chapter 11 explores serial killing around the world and compares serial murder in the United States with its occurrences in other countries such as Canada, Japan, Germany, Russia, and South Africa.

Chapter 12 examines how society responds to serial murder. This includes the role and utility of forensics as a science in studying and investigating serial crime, current issues faced by law enforcement officials such as detection and apprehension of offenders using a variety of emerging profiling techniques and the challenges of cold case files, and the role of NCAVC and ViCAP. Chapter 12 also explores the process of interviewing serial killers and includes an interview with an incarcerated serial killer. The chapter concludes by exploring sentencing, punishment, treatment, and prevention tactics in cases of serial murder.

This book is intended for students interested in understanding multiple homicide, the nature of serial killing, the offenders, and their victims. It is designed to supplement a variety of college and university courses covering a wide spectrum of forensic studies including criminology, criminal justice, deviant behavior, sex crimes, victimology, abnormal psychology, and penology. Students using this book will be exposed to concepts and information that will help prepare them to understand society's most dangerous criminals. For those currently working in law enforcement, this book should serve as a useful reference and in-service tool.

THE SIXTH EDITION

This new sixth edition has received considerable updates, with new cases, current demographic analysis of serial killers in the United States, and the restructuring of two chapters. All chapters now have a set of Learning Objectives to assist readers and instructors as to the overarching features of each chapter.

Chapter 1: Current homicide data updates were added, and I moved the Columbine High School Massacre profile to Chapter 4, where there now is a significant new section on school shootings. To emphasize the differences between mass and serial murder in Chapter 1, I included Andrew Kehoe, the worst case of mass murder of children in the United States. I also included the lone wolf terrorist case of Nidal Hasan, the Ft. Hood mass murderer, and Amy Bishop, the university professor who shot six of her departmental colleagues in a shooting rampage. These cases underscore the intellectual level of some mass murderers and their ability to plan and execute with deadly precision. To this end I also included a section on bifurcated mass murders, or cases where offenders commit their murders in more than one location within the same day or time frame. I expanded the examination of the myths of serial murder and moved the section on myths from Chapter 7 to Chapter 1. Finally, in Chapter 1 I added the case of Elias Abuelazam, who murdered several adult male strangers by walking up to them in public locations and stabbing them to death. The serial stabbing case emphasizes the variety of ways serial killers can target their victims.

Chapter 2: I did a small reorganization in Chapter 2 by moving the section on ritualism, cults, and child victims in Chapter 8 to Chapter 2. This section includes the Robin Gecht and associates case of ritualistic serial murder and underscores that a small percentage of serial killers do engage in cult-like or self-styled satanic killings.

Chapter 3: I made many edits, changes, and updates that begin with a restructuring of the presentations of insanity, neurosis, mental illness, and personality disorders. This new structuring includes the examination of serial killers who were insane during their murders. I added the cases of Joseph Kallinger, the Shoemaker, and Ed Gein, the American Psycho. While cases of insane serial killers are rare, they rank among the most depraved killers in American history. This chapter includes significant updates regarding psychopaths and how they prey upon unsuspecting victims. The case of Bernard Madoff has been added to emphasize the scope of psychopathic behaviors and the various Ponzi-scheme offenders who victimize American citizens. A new section on female psychopaths and how they operate should be of interest to readers. I also added in Chapter 3 a new type of profile, which will be seen in later editions as well, that explores current research in a specific topic by reviewing a prominent researcher in the field. "Focus on Psychopathy" highlights the career, current research, and publications of Dr. Chris Patrick, a prominent scholar at Florida State University. I also reexamined Dr. Hare's PCL-R Factors 1 and 2 and presented them as tools and deficits of psychopaths. I identified a prominent tool of the psychopath, often difficult to see, which makes the tool very effective in controlling his/her victims. Readers will also be challenged to think about how they would respond to the "trolley problem," a new addition to this chapter.

Chapter 4: I added a new section on American school shooters and multiple-homicide offenders who began their careers in murder as juveniles. This new section includes current studies on juvenile serial violence. I moved the Columbine case from Chapter 1 to Chapter 4 as well as the Edmund Kemper case from Chapter 7. I added a new profile on Craig Price, the Warwick Slasher, one of the most brutal teenage serial killers in the annals of American crime.

Chapter 5: This chapter has several updates regarding sexual predators, paraphilia, female sex offenders, and homicide. New case studies in paraphilic behavior, including pedophile clergy, are added to assist the reader in understanding the development of paraphilia. Typologies of female sex offenders are examined, including treatment outcomes. I also added a new section on the myths and realities of predator priests, including current research. Thanks to police I also have been able to include the case of the Banana Man. This case emphasizes the psychopathology of paraphilic predators and how they are able to successfully stalk and prey upon unsuspecting child victims.

Chapter 7: I moved the "Myths of Serial Murder" to Chapter 1 and added some very important updates and analysis in Chapter 7. Current data of all new serial killers in the United States from 2004 to 2011 are provided in a very readable format. Analysis of these data reveal some very significant trends and changes in the demographics of serial murder. This is one of the most important updates in this sixth edition not only because it debunks stereotypes of serial killers, but it also underscores the fact that many victims of serial murder are being ignored by the media. The significant increase in serial killers who are black in the United States is contrary to the stereotype that the majority are white offenders. I have included the case of Samuel Dixon along with several well-documented cases of black serial killers to emphasize that society needs to recalibrate its thinking about serial murder. I also added a new section on highway or truck-stop serial killers who use our interstate highways to find, abduct, murder, and dispose of hundreds of victims, many of whom are prostitutes.

Chapter 8: The most important part of the changes in Chapter 8 is the updated information regarding serial killers in the United States from 2004 to 2011. Readers can compare these most recent data to prior studies on team killers and note similarities and changes in their trends. One section on ritualism, cults, and child victims was moved to Chapter 2 for better organization of material.

Chapter 9: The most important part of the changes in Chapter 9 is the updated information regarding serial killers in the United States from 2004 to

2011. Readers can compare these most recent data to prior studies on the female serial killers and note similarities and changes in their trends.

Chapter 10: This important chapter focuses upon victims of serial murder and provides updated information on victimization from 2004 to 2011. I include current scholarly research by Dr. Quinet, who addresses the ignored problem of the "missing missing" and the many prostitutes who are mere statistics in the study of serial murder. I make recommendations to readers regarding books to read by former FBI personnel and provide updates on agencies that deal with missing and murdered children. These updates include NCMEC data as well as Department of Justice information on missing and murdered children. I also include scholarly research by Dr. Alexander, who posits Routine Activities Theory and Life-Course Theory as ways to understand victim–offender relationships in target selection.

Chapter 11: Although murders overall in the United States are at 40-year lows, serial and mass murders continue to slowly increase. Multiple homicide worldwide also continues to attract international attention. I have included the notorious case of Anders Breivik, the Norwegian mass murderer who bifurcated his attacks. I also included the incredible case of Russell Williams, the former commander of the largest air force base in Canada. I document his ability to lead a double life while he progressed from voyeurism to fetishes to serial murder. The section on serial murder in South Africa has also been updated and now includes a rare case of muti murder of a family member.

Chapter 12: Chapter 12 of the fifth edition was merged with Chapter 13 from the fifth edition to add more order and process to serial-murder case management. The final chapter is now titled "Responding to Serial Killers." I have provided many updates in restructuring this final chapter. I included the tragic case of the Frog Boys to illustrate the complexity of crime scene analysis that can require persons with expertise in many fields including anthropology, orthodontics, criminal justice, criminology, culture, sociology, psychology, weaponry, DNA, etc. A new section on cold case files is introduced along with several new cases that encourage reader participation in explaining offender behavior, fantasies, and paraphilic interests. I discuss the role of cold case review teams and provide two disturbing new cases for consideration: Larry Hall, who is now in prison for the murder of one college student but is believed by investigators to have murdered over 30 other female victims, and the case of Joseph Naso, "the Alphabet Killer," who liked to kill prostitutes with first and last names beginning with the same initial. In addition, several research updates are provided. I also merged and edited the section on interviewing serial killers to make the chapter compatible with the process of responding to serial murder investigations. Finally, under disposition of serial killers, I included Dr. Welner's Depravity Scale, which allows students to go online and decide for themselves how certain crimes of violence should be categorized in terms of their levels of violence. I trust that you will find this sixth edition to be current, provocative, informative, and useful in understanding the phenomenon of serial murder.

Serial Murderers and Their Victims debunks the myths and stereotypes that have evolved from public efforts to find easy explanations for the relatively rare yet horrifying phenomenon of serial murder. It also raises many questions about serial killers and their behavior. The research for this book has included visits to prisons, police departments, and numerous university libraries across the United States, as well as extensive Internet searches and interviews with numerous sexual predators such as pedophiles, child molesters, stalkers, paraphiliacs, and several serial murderers, their spouses, ex-spouses, lovers, and friends. I explored the lives of dead victims and victims who survived the attacks, and I communicated with families and relatives of the victims. Despite the extensive social, psychological, physiological, and financial devastation inflicted by serial murderers on their victims and the victims' families, the victims are often reduced to little more than crime statistics. The etiology of victimization and the continued suffering of survivors must not be forgotten or neglected.

SUPPLEMENTS

To further enhance the use of this textbook, the following supplements are available to qualified adopters. Please consult your local sales representative for details.

Instructor's Resource Manual with Test Bank

Prepared by Amy Hembree, the manual includes learning objectives, key terms, a detailed chapter outline, a chapter summary, discussion topics, student activities, and a test bank. Each chapter's test bank contains questions in multiple-choice, true/false, fill-in-the-blank, and essay formats, with a full answer key. The test bank is coded to the learning objectives that appear in the main text, and includes the page numbers in the main text where the answers can be found. Our Instructor Approved seal, which appears on the front cover, is our assurance that you are working with an assessment and grading resource of the highest caliber.

The manual is available for download on the password-protected Website and can also be obtained by e-mailing your local Cengage Learning representative.

PowerPoints

Prepared by the author, Eric W. Hickey, these handy Microsoft PowerPoint slides, which outline the chapters of the main text in a classroom-ready presentation, will help you in making your lectures engaging and in reaching your visually oriented students. The presentations are available for download on the password-protected Website and can also be obtained by e-mailing your local Cengage Learning representative.

ACKNOWLEDGMENTS

I wish to recognize and thank the many people who helped during the course of my research and publication of this sixth edition. I was very fortunate to have very talented forensic doctoral students passionate about conducting research on predators and their victims. Those who assisted me in varying stages of my sixth edition were Blake Harris (my project coordinator), Alison Carlile, Dena Legari, Cody Charette, Melissa Murphy, Michele Wysopal, Arava Halevi, Karina Wong, Rina Norris, Julie Mizera, Xarina Chen, and Toni Ognibene (Fresno State University).

Some of these students will graduate in June 2012, while the rest are still facing their dissertation and/or their forensic internship year. As I worked with this dedicated group, I realized that these are they who will one day replace me and my fellow colleagues who have been engaged in multiple-homicide research. I think their work will not only be significant in the eyes of the scientific community but also be instrumental in helping others. Jason Crow, also one of our stellar students with a passion for dissecting the nature of sexuality and sex offending, was always willing to engage me as I updated my research on sexual predators.

Working with doctoral students is a great experience for me. They bring fresh ideas, enthusiasm, excitement, and promise to our California School of Forensic Studies (CSFS) programs. This is especially true of Dr. Blake Harris, who was one of our doctoral students and became my teaching and research assistant. Blake did it all. He was nothing less than phenomenal in his productivity, organizational skills, punctuality, and enthusiasm. I have never met a more determined or dedicated person. Blake volunteered for every task and project I engaged in during the three years he worked with me. He served as my project manager for the sixth edition and coordinated the other graduate students. I cannot thank him enough for his loyalty and assistance. He and his spouse, Celesta, also one of our top CSFS doctoral students, are going to be incredible forensic psychologists wherever their careers take them.

Each of these doctoral students researched specific areas of multiple homicide that could possibly be included in this sixth edition. And a special thanks to Alison (Aly) Carlile and Cody Charette for their extra time and willingness to serve as sounding boards for me as I engaged in structuring the sixth edition. Our discussions were timely and most helpful in starting and completing the revision. I express my many thanks to each and every one of these doctoral students for their time and effort.

Every once in a while I come across someone in my career who seems to appear on my doorstep wanting to help and collaborate. Enzo Yaksic did just that and offered to collect serial murder cases for me to use in updating my tables for 2004–2011 found in Chapters 7–10. A special thanks to Dr. Mike Aamodt of Radford University, Virginia, and Dr. John White of Richard Stockton College Center for Public Safety and Security, New Jersey, for their help in identifying the race of specific serial killers who appear in the sixth edition updates constructed by Enzo. He also prepared the original profile for the Samuel Dixon case that was facilitated by the use of the Serial Homicide Expertise and Information Sharing Collaborative. Enzo, thank you so much for your assistance. Your passion for the field of forensics is exactly what is needed to further the work. Working with you has been most enjoyable, and I am sure that we will collaborate for many years to come. Also, a special thanks to James A. Reavis, Psy.D., Director of Forensic Services at the Relationship Training Institute in San Diego,

California, for his assistance in developing the profile of Samuel Dixon. Your collaboration is much appreciated.

I deeply appreciate the assistance of Dr. Gérard Labuschagne, Brigadier of the Investigative Psychology Unit of the Forensic Science Services Division of the South African Police Service, and Dr. Charisse T. M. Coston, at the University of North Carolina at Charlotte, in helping me better understand ethnic, racial, and cultural differences in serial murder. Indeed, there are many sensitive issues discussed in this book. In no way do I mean to be critical or disparage any group, regardless of nationality, race, ethnicity, culture, religion, socioeconomic class, or sexual orientation. My goal is always to expose the truth in order to help reduce victimization, provide greater understanding of the nature of multiple homicide, and better identify the perpetrators. I also want to thank Cathy C. Petchel, visiting professor of psychology at Washington and Jefferson University, Pennsylvania, and Dr. Susan Williams of Kansas State University, Kansas, for their friendship and passion for teaching. Their enthusiasm is contagious.

In addition, my profound gratitude goes to my colleagues and my lifelong friends Dr. John R. Fuller, a noted scholar and my best critic (the guy who tells you when you have egg on your face), Lloyd A. Mackenzie (my Canadian childhood, hell-raiser buddy), whose counsel, encouragement, and true friendship will never be forgotten, and Steven W. Opager, mon ami, bien-aimé, a man of soul who has walked in my shoes and understands.

Special thanks to Alliant International University and the faculty and staff of California School of Forensic Studies for supporting me in following my dreams. Thanks also to Roberta Roper of the Stephanie Roper Committee for her willingness to share her personal tragedies and her efforts to be more than a mere survivor; and to Mike Reynolds, author of the "Three Strikes" and the "10-20-Life" laws. Neither of these fine people expected their daughters to be brutally murdered, but as a result, each of these social justice champions have spent many years fighting to establish victims' rights and justice for violent offenders. We are safer because of them. And to Nadia Fezzani, my journalist friend in Montreal, Canada, who decided, after being a victim of violent crime, to walk into the lions' den and interview serial killers.

In addition, my appreciation goes to the entire Wadsworth team, especially to my more-than-patient, wonderful chief editor, Carolyn Henderson Meier. I deeply appreciate her support and guidance for both the fifth and sixth editions. I especially want to thank Rachel McDonald, assistant editor responsible for overseeing this project and for her vigilance, thoroughness, and professionalism in seeing this sixth edition to fruition. And of course, Rathi Thirumalai, my production manager, who caught all of my errors and kept me on task, Isabel Saraiva, permissions editor, who dogged me for permissions, Virginette Acacio, assistant editor, who handled the Instructors Manual and Test Bank development, and Michelle Williams, senior marketing manager and Webinar coordinator. Never could an author expect to find a more competent, professional team of editors than those at Wadsworth.

I would like to thank the reviewers for this sixth edition, who include: Kevin Barrett, SUNY/Rockland Community College; Kevin Beaver, Florida State

University; Denise Bissler, Randolph-Macon College; Martha Bray, Fort Hays State University; Diana Bruns, Southeast Missouri State University; David A. Camp, Blackburn College; Robert Carroll, East-West University; Russ Cheatham, Cumberland University; Enid Conley, Johnson & Wales University, North Miami Campus; Julie Cowgill, Oklahoma City University; Martha Earwood, University of Alabama at Birmingham; Phyllis B. Gerstenfeld, California State University at Stanislaus; Sandra Grant, Midwestern State University; Christopher Hensley, University of Tennessee at Chattanooga; Stacey Hervey, Metro State College; David Horiuchi, Troy University; Andy Johnson, Bethel University; Natalie Johnson, University of North Texas; Soraya K. Kawucha, University of North Texas; Edward C. Keane, Housatonic Community College; David D. Legere, New England College; Joel Lundstrom, Barton Community College; Darlene Mallick, Anne Arundel Community College; Dennis F. Mazone, Bloomfield College; LaVarr McBride, Weber State University; Dyan McGuire, Saint Louis University; Tracy L. Newvine, Troy University; Dr. Brian Ogawa, Washburn University; Daniel Osborne, Empire State College; Cornel Plebani, Husson University; Dennis Powell, Middle Tennessee State University; Brad Reyns, Southern Utah University; Jennifer Riggs, Eastern New Mexico University at Ruidoso; Leeanna Rossi, Western New Mexico University; Ken Salmon, Arizona State University; Natalee Segal, Paradise Valley Community College; Mary Shenouda, University of Arkansas at Fort Smith; Donna M. Sherwood, Macomb Community College; James Sparks, University of Alabama at Birmingham; Lesley Stevens, CUNY, Queens College; Barbara Tipton, Chemeketa Community College; Dennis Williams, Arkansas Tech University; and James Wright, Chattanooga State Community College.

Finally, and most importantly, I want to thank my family: first, my dearest friend and spouse, Holly Peacock-Hickey, for her contributions, encouragement, corrections, and assistance on my behalf. You are my constant sounding board and guide. Your patience and insights are valuable beyond measure. Thank you for reminding me that my greatest resource is the Lord Almighty. And to my four beautiful children, Trevor, Erin, Alicen, and Chad, my two step-sons, Ben and Chad, and my twelve adorable grandchildren: Joshua, Melissa, Samantha, Aidan, Ethan, Megan, Lauren, Katie, Andrew, Abbie, Kennington, and Adeley. As they journey through life, I will always hope that they might think of their dad and granddad with kindness and always know that I will love them, unconditionally, forever and ever. They stand for all that is good and worthwhile in this world, and I have never been more proud of them. And in memory of my dear parents, Wes and Shirley Hickey. Their devotion and support was constant and their love unconditional. I miss them.

Eric W. Hickey

The tragedy of life is what dies inside a man while he lives.
—Albert Schweitzer

Now ask yourself this question and see if by the time you have finished reading this most horrifying book, you have discerned the answer:

What is required to live the life of one's own image?

The answer is within…

Introduction

LEARNING OBJECTIVES

- To understand the many myths surrounding the phenomenon of serial murder and how society perpetuates those myths
- To explore the definition of homicide and the various classifications of murder in American society
- To explore the extent of mass and serial murder in the United States
- To examine the definitions and differences between mass and serial murder
- To evaluate case studies of mass and serial murder as they relate to the reality and frequency of multiple homicide in modern society

THE PHENOMENON OF SERIAL MURDER

Multiple murder is undoubtedly one of the most terrifying and fascinating phenomena of modern-day crime. We are frequently reminded of how vulnerable we can be when persons who decide to kill us can do so with relative ease. No one ever imagined a military psychiatrist going on a shooting rampage at Fort Hood, Texas, in 2009, killing 13 military personnel and wounding many others; a female college professor in 2010 in Alabama shooting six members of her department; a college student in 2011 in Arizona walking into a grocery store and shooting to death six people and seriously wounding many others, including a congresswoman; or a man walking into an IHOP restaurant in Nevada and shooting several people before ending his own life. As of 2011, investigators in Long Island, New York, have unearthed or located in wooded areas ten victims believed to be those of a serial killer. Other serial killers include the Craigslist Ripper or Gilgo Killer Joel Rifkin, an unemployed landscaper who confessed to murdering 17 prostitutes; and Robert Shulman, responsible for the deaths of 5 other prostitutes. Multiple murder is one of the most sensationalized areas of research within the fields of criminology, psychology, and sociology. Getting down to the "real facts" of a case rather than getting caught up in the inevitable media barrage has become a task difficult for even the most stringent, reputable researchers. The problems are many and interrelated. Philip Jenkins (1994), in his book *Using Murder: The Social Construction of Serial Homicide*, provides a scholarly examination of how serial killing has been dealt with by the media, law enforcement personnel, and the public. Indeed, much of what we know, or claim to know, about serial murder is based on misinformation and myth construction. Nearly 20 years later many of those misperceptions continue, fueled by our interest in forensics and violent crime. One of the primary confounding myths of serial murder is that they are all, by definition, sexual. Schlesinger (2004) in his seminal work, *Sexual Murder*, notes that many seemingly sexual murders are not sexually motivated and that many sexual homicides are not overtly sexual (pp. 2–6). As a result of the sensational nature of this form of murder, the aura surrounding it has assumed a life of its own as it filters throughout both the public and private sectors of society.

SERIAL MURDER: FACT AND FICTION

In the summer of 1981 in Atlanta, Georgia, Wayne Williams, a young African American male, was arrested for his involvement in multiple homicides of young African American males. He was believed, at that time, to be one of the nation's more prolific serial killers. This case brought increased focus on serial murder and the fact that not all serial killers are white, nor are the victims, and even children could be targets. Technology, specifically hair-fiber evidence, became a critical factor in convicting Williams, and forensic science became prominent in explaining why such evidence ultimately played a key role in linking Williams to the crimes. Over 20 homicides were attributed to Williams, most of them children, although he was actually convicted of murdering just two of his victims. The horror and fascination of this case focused media attention on Atlanta both during the homicides and after Williams's capture. Within the next three years several more accounts of serial murder appeared in newspapers around the country. The American public had been invaded by a new criminal type, the serial murderer. Lurking in our communities, preying on hapless victims, serial murderers had suddenly emerged from the criminal underground—perhaps a product of the Vietnam War or possibly a by-product of technology and the moral decay of our society. In the past, most citizens simply assumed serial killers must be insane. No one knew for sure. But as the cases of serial murder increased, as did the body counts, the ever-growing reality of multiple murders began to intrude on public awareness. Something had to be done to stem the tide of homicides with no apparent motive.

In 1984 the Federal Bureau of Investigation (FBI; 1984a, 1984b; Ninety-Eighth Congress, 1984) appeared before the U.S. Senate to seek funding for the development of a program specifically targeting violent criminals. According to news accounts of the hearing, as many as 5,000 people per year were believed to be killed by serial murderers. Although this was factually not true, the numbers used to describe the victims in all categories of violent crime were, nonetheless, shocking and incredible. The public and public officials alike were horrified, and funding was procured for the program. For the next several years the incidence of serial murder was considered by the public to be pervasive in our society, though in fact this remained far from the truth. No one knew how many serial killers actually existed at any one time, but it was clear that the number of victims killed by such offenders did not even begin to approach 5,000. Where that inflated figure first originated is still a mystery. Perhaps a piece of information exchanged during an interview between the media and law enforcement personnel had been misinterpreted. What is important is not who started the rumors but that they were so quickly disseminated without ever being verified.

Such forms of disinformation are not new or uncommon. For example, when marijuana came into public view during the 1940s, a film, *Reefer Madness*, was distributed, depicting the powerfully destructive forces of the illegal substance. Clean, upstanding young men and women, on experiencing the effects of just one reefer, were transformed into raving, sex-crazed lunatics. Though amusing to us now, such exaggeration is disturbing in light of the film's original purpose and effects.

Much of the proliferation of disinformation is a result of public pressure to know more about a specific subject. In some respects, a symbiotic relationship has developed among law enforcement personnel, the media, and the public that serves, in fact, to encourage disinformation in regard to certain types of issues. Realizing this, some researchers, such as Philip Jenkins and others, began questioning the actual extent of serial murder. We do not question that serial murder occurs, but to what quantifiable and qualitative extent? This is the role of the social scientist: to objectively examine phenomena to determine their origin, nature, and impact on society.

Members of the community also want to understand the phenomnenon of serial murder. A very popular and interesting radio program *Behind the Yellow Tape*, founded by Joey Ortega, can be found on www.blogtalkradio.com/behindthetellowtape as well as their companion blog www.behindtheyellowtape.wordpress.com. National and international forensic experts discuss investigative techniques, criminal psychology, current research in behavioral analysis, violent crimes, profiling, victimology and other relevant topics. Ortega is also the co-founder of the Ullemeyer group, a company that offers forensic and investigative services, training in forensic disciplines, investigative specialties and crime scene investigations to both private and public agencies. Their company, located in Santa Barbara, California can be found online at www.ullemeyer.com. Nadia Fezzani, an investigative journalist in Montreal, Canada, herself a victim of violent crime, decided to interview serial killers and publish her findings. Her compelling book, *My Serial Killers*, (2011) documents the face to face interviews she conducted with these men. The apparent or perceived increase in the modern serial, or multiple, murder has incited interest among social scientists in several areas. Researchers have begun to explore the social, psychological, and biological makeup of the offenders in order to establish accurate profiles. In spite of their efforts, during the 1980s the body of knowledge about serial murders remained small compared to the number of unanswered questions—especially concerning the extent of the phenomenon. In more recent years law enforcement personnel and academicians have come closer to understanding the dynamics of serial killing and its etiology, or causation.

The pure sensationalism and horror of serial murder have also spawned a plethora of novels about such murders, and the figure of the cold-blooded and senseless serial killer has been exploited by the media: for example, in television documentaries and prime-time shows—such as those that depicted California's Hillside Strangler, the BTK Strangler case, and the infamous Ted Bundy *(The Deliberate Stranger)*—and in various box-office thrillers. Because of the wide publicity given to serial murderers, a stereotype of this type of killer has formed in the mind of American society. The offender is thought of as a ruthless, bloodthirsty sex monster who lives a Jekyll-and-Hyde existence—probably next door to you. Increasingly, crime novels and movies have focused on multiple-homicide offenders. Consider the steady proliferation of multiple-homicide films in which serial killing occurs (see Table 1.1).

Although the list in Table 1.1 is not exhaustive, it is representative of each decade. It does not include films involving mass murder (the killing of a number of people all at one time) or horror films depicting vampires and murderous zombies, but only films portraying real people murdering other people. Notice the explosion of serial-murder themes between the early 1990s and 2008. More than half of those never made it to theaters but went straight to home-video release. In the privacy of one's home, viewers are bombarded with graphic

TABLE 1.1 Increase in Films with Serial Killing, 1920–2008

Decade	Number of Serial Murder–Themed Films
1920s	2
1930s	3
1940s	3
1950s	4
1960s	12
1970s	20
1980s	23
1990s	150+
2000s	300++

SOURCE: © Cengage Learning, 2013.

killings, mutilations, and sexual torture. Clearly, this cinematic emphasis has added credibility to the notion of high body counts at the hands of ubiquitous serial-killer monsters.

In his 1987 book *The Red Dragon*, Tom Harris gave a fictional account of a serial killer who took great pleasure in annihilating entire families. Later his work was made into the movie *Manhunter*, an engrossing drama of psychopathology, blood, and carnage. At that time Hollywood was only beginning to realize the huge market for multiple-murder movies. Some years later, the next book by Harris and the derivative movie, both titled *Silence of the Lambs*, caught the American imagination. By 2001, movies such as *Copycat, Kiss the Girls*, the Scream trilogy, *Along Came a Spider, Hannibal*, the Saw series, *Hostel*, and *The Bone Collector* continued to exploit the public's fascination with serial murder without yielding much insight about the offender. Filmmakers, unable to adequately navigate the minds of serial offenders, resorted to technology and special effects to draw in viewers, as seen in the film *The Cell*. Other films, such as *Seven*, a dark, disturbing movie, attempted to offer some understanding of the murdering mind but confused viewers with the concepts of psychopathy, psychosis, and murder. By late 2003, a remake of the classic horror film *Texas Chainsaw Massacre* appeared in theaters just a few weeks before the confession and conviction of the Green River Killer, Gary Leon Ridgway, in the murders of 48 young women (see Profile 1.7). Serial-murder movies are now rivaled by a plethora of television and cable serials such as *CSI, Profiler, Forensic Files, Criminal Minds, Cold Case Files*, and *Dexter*. Viewers can now examine, from the comfort of their homes, theaters, computers, Kindles, and iPods, the minds and crimes of violent predators.

Novelists such as Easton Ellis, with his exploration of psychopathy, narcissism, sadism, and murder in *American Psycho* (later made into a movie by the same name), and Caleb Carr, author of the acclaimed serial-murder thriller *The Alienist*, clearly indicate that writers are familiarizing themselves with the topic of serial murder and have begun to inject some insightful and historical perspectives into their narratives. The fictional accounts of serial killing, however, often fail to surpass the horror described in nonfictional accounts of serial murder by writers such as Ann Rule, a former acquaintance of the serial killer Ted Bundy; Bundy was executed in January 1989. Besides her work on Bundy (*The Stranger Beside Me*, 1980), she has written about Jerry Brudos (*Lust Killer*, 1983), Randy Woodfield (*The I-5 Killer*, 1984), and Harvey Carnigan (*The Want-Ad Killer*, 1988).

MYTHS OF SERIAL MURDER

The result of such an array of cases of serial murder as well as media focus has given rise to several general myths surrounding the phenomenon. With every myth, just as in every stereotype, there is a measure of truth. The following are long-held myths surrounding serial killers.

Myth	*Fact*
1. They are nearly all white.	One in five serial killers is black.
2. They are all male.	Nearly 17% are female.
3. They are insane.	Insanity is a legal term. Very few offenders (2%–4%) are legally insane.
4. They are all lust killers.	Many are, but several cases do not involve sexual assaults, torture, or sexual mutilations.
5. They kill dozens of victims.	A few have high body counts but most kill under 10 victims.
6. They kill alone.	About one in four have one or more partners in murder.
7. Victims are beaten, stabbed, strangled, or tortured to death.	Some victims are poisoned or shot.
8. They are all very intelligent.	Most are of average intelligence.
9. They have high mobility in the United States.	Most offenders remain in a local area.
10. They are driven to kill because they were sexually abused as children.	Many kill as a result of rejection and abandonment in childhood.
11. Most serial murderers cannot stop killing.	Some serial killers stopped killing for several years before they killed again or until they were caught, including Dennis Rader (BTK), Jeffrey Gorton, Jeffrey Dahmer, and Theodore Kaczynski. Such offenders often substitute paraphilic behaviors or other diversions in lieu of killing.
12. Most serial killers want to be caught.	Like anyone, they learn and gain confidence from experience. Many want-to-be serial killers end up in prison after their first murder. Some become very adept at concealing their identities and may feel as if they will never be caught.

Throughout the 1990s, dozens of novels and nonfiction accounts of multiple homicide were published for the entertainment and sometimes enlightenment of the general public. Amid this proliferation, female serial killers were given increased attention in true-crime accounts of "black widows" (women who, for various reasons, kill their husbands, then remarry only to carry out the cycle of homicide again and again); nurses who kill their elderly, young, or otherwise helpless patients; mothers who murder their children; females who assist men in serial killing; and a few women who have stalked and murdered men.

Researchers who have been examining the phenomenon of serial murder to promote greater understanding—and, they hope, develop intervention strategies—have also been busy. Case study analysis of serial murder has begun to provide researchers with insightful information, however tenuous. For example, Elliott Leyton (1986a) in his book *Hunting Humans* provides in-depth examinations of the lives and minds of a few contemporary U.S. serial killers and their relationships with their victims. In *Mass Murder: The Growing Menace* (1985), *Overkill* (1994), and *Extreme Killing* (2011), Jack Levin and James Fox assess some of the dynamics of serial and mass murder. Fox, Levin, and Quinet in *The Will To Kill* (2011) analyze the circumstances in which people kill one another and provide insights to family and school homicides. Ronald Holmes and James DeBurger, in their work *Serial Murder* (2010), formulate typologies based on material gathered from interviews with serial murderers. Holmes's second work, *Profiling Violent Crimes: An Investigative Tool* (2009), has become a useful tool in the investigation of serial murder. Steve Egger's work *Serial Murder: An Elusive Phenomenon* (1990) and his *The Killers Among Us* (2001) underscore several critical problems encountered by researchers and law enforcement investigators of serial murder. Robert Keppel, a law enforcement officer who has investigated several cases of serial killing, published his observations in *Serial Murder: Future Implications for Police Investigations* (1989). Jenkins (1994) has examined societal forces such as law enforcement, the media, and public interest, which have acted as catalysts in the emergence of the serial-murder phenomenon as a social construct. Also in recent years, a number of documentaries, such as CNN's *Murder by Number*, have critically examined the extent and impact of serial murder. In 1994, British television produced an award-winning documentary *To Kill and Kill Again* (Optomen Television, 1994). As a result of the case of Jeffrey Dahmer and other cases, serial murder began to be explored not merely as an act, but as a *process*. In 1996, several books examining serial murder, including *Serial Murderers and Their Victims*, first edition, were placed on the compact disc *Mind of a Killer*. This "serial-murder library" allowed researchers, students, and law enforcement personnel to access a vast amount of information, including biographies, photographs, and the investigative tools used to track serial killers. By 2001, other scholarly documentaries including *Understanding Murder* (the Learning Channel) aired on television and sought to examine the roles of psychology and biology in serial murder; in 2002 Court TV explored the careers of criminal profilers in *The Elite: The New Profilers*; in 2002 WE Channel examined female serial killers in *Black Widows: Explaining Women Who Kill Their Husbands*; and in 2010 CNN revisited the Wayne Williams case in *The Atlanta Child Murders*.

Many other people associated with research on serial murder have also contributed to the body of knowledge on the subject. For instance, Dr. Katherine Ramsland, a prolific author and professor of forensic psychology and criminal justice at DeSales University in Pennsylvania, has published scholarly articles and books involving serial murder. Two of her books I highly recommend are *The Human Predator: A Historical Chronicle of Serial Murder and Forensic Investigation* (Berkley, 2005) and *The Mind of a Murderer: Privileged Access to the Demons that Drive Extreme Violence* (Praeger, 2011). Philip Jenkins, at Pennsylvania State

University, has explored the social environments of serial murderers, whereas Candice Skrapec, a forensic psychologist in the Department of Criminology, California State University, Fresno, has gathered data on the psychogenic status of serial offenders. Al Carlisle, a psychologist at the Utah State Prison and Provo Canyon Boys School, has explored dissociative states and other forces that may affect the mind of a serial killer. David Canter and Donna Youngs at the University of Huddersfield, England, have organized the International Research Centre for Investigative Psychology, an impressive program that, among other things, emphasizes the application of science in geographic profiling of crimes and offenders. D. Kim Rossmo, formerly of the Vancouver Police Department, in his 1995 dissertation made a substantial contribution to the field of forensics through his geographic profiling of serial murderers. Now a senior research professor at the Center for Geospatial Intelligence and Investigation, Texas State University, he is considered to be one of the top geographic profilers in the world. Increasingly, both academicians and law enforcement personnel are becoming involved in the study and exploration of violent serial crime. While all of this research is critical in establishing a knowledge base, Haggerty (2009) notes that focusing on the etiology and biography of offenders is only part of the equation in understanding serial murder. He argues that serial killers are distinctively modern and that thus far "broader social, historical and cultural context have been largely ignored" (p. 168). He outlines six important preconditions for serial murder that have their roots in modernity:

- Mass media and the rise of celebrity status. Be a serial killer and appear in *TIME* magazine, have movies made about you, and gain a following of murder groupies.
- A society populated with strangers.
- A society void of value considerations that encourages extreme rationalization. Depersonalization of others and perceiving relationships as instrumental makes killing others so much easier and pleasurable.
- A cultural framework that through processes of denigration positions specific groups for increased predation, such as the elderly, children, prostitutes, homeless, and homosexuals.
- Opportunity structures that afford serial killers more access to certain victims such as females who now often work outside their homes, and, of course, prostitutes.
- Society can be engineered, and for some serial killers, they provide a service in ridding society of certain undesirable types of people. (pp. 168–187)

Haggerty has indeed provided a broader platform from which researchers can investigate and study serial murder. These structural and cultural frameworks may have significant utility in explaining multiple homicide and even help us understand how we might detect, investigate, prosecute, and categorize these forms of murder and murderers.

Law enforcement officials have been dealing with serial murders for many, many years. By the 1990s, however, the nature and sophistication of investigation techniques had changed. Computer technology, especially the development of the Internet, expedited data collection and analysis. During the mid-1980s, the FBI established, at its Behavioral Science Unit in Quantico, Virginia (now referred to as the Investigative Support Unit), the Violent Criminal Apprehension Program (VICAP). VICAP is designed to collect detailed information on homicides throughout the United States. Investigators such as former FBI agents Robert Ressler and John Douglas, both pioneers in the investigation and classification of serial killers, collectively interviewed many notorious serial killers in the United States. Ressler and colleagues published their findings in *Sexual Homicide* (1988), which became a standard reference text for this form of murder. In addition, the U.S. government continues to develop programs such as the National Center for the Analysis of Violent Crime (NCAVC) to focus specifically on repetitive offenders, including serial murderers.

NUMBERS AND TYPES OF MASS MURDERS AND SERIAL KILLINGS IN THE UNITED STATES

The number of murders in the United States fluctuated around 25,000 per year by the early 1990s. By that time, we had witnessed a 20-year period of murder and manslaughter rates increasing 300% while police clearance rates for these crimes had declined from 93% in 1962 to 74% in 1982 and to about 65% by 1995 (FBI, 1995). Homicide rates in the United States during this period appeared to be one of the highest of any Westernized nation. In recent years, however, we have seen a remarkable decline in violent crime. The last several years have seen fewer violent and property crimes. By 2003, areas of the United States were reporting 30-year lows in crime rates. The Centers for Disease Control (2001) found that in 1997, of the 5,285 workplace deaths, 14% were homicides, far behind deaths caused by mining and agriculture accidents. By 2002 the number of murders in the United States had dropped to just over 14,000, with a 1.1% increase in 2003 (see Table 1.2) and almost equal numbers of white and black residents being victimized, even though blacks constitute only 13% of the U.S. population (see Homicide Facts 2010). By 2007, murders in the United States had slowly continued to rise to over 17,000, but these were still nearly half the murder rates of the early 1990s. Between 1991 and 2010 murder rates dropped by 51%.

Homicide Facts 2010*

- An estimated 14,748 persons were murdered nationwide in 2010, a 4.23% decline from 2009.
- For homicides in which the age of the victim was known
  - 9.94% of murder victims were under 18
  - 32.86% were between the ages of 20 and 29

*National Center for Victims of Crime, 2011.

TABLE 1.2 United States Homicide Rates, 1987–2010 (Murder and Nonnegligent Manslaughter)

Year	Number of Murders	Rate per 100,000 Population
1987	20,096	8.3
1989	21,500	8.7
1991	24,703	9.8
1993	24,526	9.5
1995	21,606	8.2
1997	18,208	6.8
1999	15,522	5.7
2000	15,586	5.5
2001	16,037	5.6
2002	16,229	5.6
2003	16,528	5.7
2004	16,148	5.5
2005	16,740	5.6
2006	17,030	5.7
2007	16,929	5.6
2008	16,442	5.4
2009	15,399	5.0
2010	**14,748**	**4.8**

SOURCE: © Cengage Learning, 2013.

- 20.35% were between the ages of 30 and 39
- 13.39% were between 40 and 49
- 11.55% were between 50 and 64;
- 4.55% were ages 65 and older.

- Homicides of teenagers ages 13 to 19 accounted for 12.41% of murder victims.
- Males accounted for 77.4% of murder victims and 22.5% were female.
- The sex of the offender was known in 73.19% of homicide cases. Among those cases, 90.27% of offenders were male and 9.73% were female.
- In the majority of homicide cases 92% were 18 or older.
- Whites accounted for 46.5% of homicide victims while 49.8% were black. For 3.7% of victims, race was classified as "other" or "unknown."
- Homicide was generally intra-racial: white offenders murdered 83% of white victims, and black offenders murdered 90% of black victims.
- Homicides in which the type of weapon was specified, 68% of the offenses were committed with firearms.

The lower rate in violent crime, especially murder, is explained by several contributing factors. First, the U.S. economy, bolstered by new advances in technology, had been in a strong growth period for several years. Although an economic slowdown occurred after 2001 and was affected by the September 11 attack on the World Trade Center and subsequent war with Iraq, unemployment remained relatively low. Second, the victim's movement acted as a catalyst for many new legal reforms. For example, Mike Reynolds, the father of Kimberly Reynolds, who was gunned down while leaving a restaurant in Fresno, California, became the father of three-strikes laws, along with many other laws requiring harsher punishments for repeat offenders. Some states, such as New York, have seen a dramatic increase in the number of police officers on duty. Some argue that violent offenders eventually "age out" because they become too old to commit violent crimes. For whatever reasons, most likely a combination of factors, crime dropped dramatically and steadily until 2000. Behind the statistics is the reality that crime rates will inevitably rise again given the growing rates of unemployment, disasters such as Hurricane Katrina in New Orleans in 2005, and significant increases in the cost of living.

Though murder rates have been declining in general, it is clear from the data that certain types of homicides are occurring more frequently. While the majority of murders result from domestic and community conflicts, many murders are perpetrated by strangers. Because of a marked increase in stranger-to-stranger homicides, in some cities, such as Los Angeles, as many as 60% of all murders go without being prosecuted each year. The increasing number of serial murders is believed by some experts, including your author, to account for some of these unsolved cases.

Mass Murder

Serial murders, however, are not the only type of killings attracting considerable public attention. Mass murders, in which several victims are killed within a few moments or hours, seem to be occurring with greater frequency. In this context, the term *mass murder* does not refer to institutional mass murder as ordered by dictators or ethnic cleansing of groups of people as seen in Europe and Africa but rather the individually motivated and carried-out mass murders in the workplace or in private residences. The current frequency of mass murder in the United States has increased from approximately one case per month to approximately one case every 10 days (author's files). Part of the increase can be attributed to how we define mass murder. Although mass murders were once considered to involve public displays of violence (school attacks, for instance), we now must include domestic mass murders (the killing of some or all of one's family members and/or acquaintances). According to the FBI, killing four or more persons at one time is considered to be a *mass murder*. Over half of all attempted and/or completed mass murders in the United States involve domestic homicides. Other cases of mass murder involve offenders walking into schools, shopping malls, restaurants, or government offices and randomly shooting bystanders—as in April 1990, when a man released only the day before from a psychiatric institution walked into a crowded shopping mall in Atlanta, Georgia, and began shooting everyone in his path.

PROFILES IN MODERN MASS MURDER IN THE UNITED STATES

- Jared L. Loughner, a 22-year-old pot-smoking army and college reject, was considered by the police to be angry and mentally unstable when he entered a shopping center in Tucson, Arizona, in 2011 and shot twenty people, killing six. His primary target was congresswoman Gabrielle Giffords, who was also critically wounded.
- Dr. Amy Bishop, a Harvard trained neurobiologist, shot six faculty members in a department meeting at the University of Alabama in 2010, killing three of them. She had been denied tenure (see Profile 1.1).
- Dr. Nidal M. Hasan, a psychiatrist and major in the military, shot over 40 military personnel, killing 13, at Fort Hood, Texas, in 2009. He had become a radicalized Muslim who viewed the United States as an aggressor nation (see Profile 1.2).
- Omar Thornton, 2010, shot and killed eight coworkers and himself at a beer distribution company in Manchester, Connecticut. He had just been terminated for stealing beer from the company.

In other cases a troubled parent or sibling has annihilated entire families. In recent years there have also been several instances of assailants walking into elementary or secondary schools, or sometimes just standing by the playground, and randomly shooting children (see Profile 1.3).

As mentioned, another type of mass murder includes the killing of family members. Based on the number of victims in each case, some domestic mass murders are viewed as *mini-mass murders* because relatively few victims (three to four) are killed. Consider the perpetrators under *Profiles in Modern Mass Murder in the United States*. There is not a *distinctive* profile of such killers. Some are mentally ill while others are just angry. Many are males but some are females. Some kill because they subscribe to political or religious ideologies at variance with the community in which they reside. Some are white, others black. Some are Asian, Hispanic, or African American while many are Caucasian. Some are very well educated in professional careers while others have high school educations in blue-collar jobs. Some do not work. Some kill at school or on college campuses, others where they work or live. Some kill their families while others kill coworkers or strangers. Some kill both relatives and strangers. Many use guns, but some use knives, fire, or bombs.

When combining all mass murders, mini-mass murders, and attempted mass murders, the incidence of such murders remains very high. Although the reality is that the United States is experiencing relatively low homicide rates (the actual

PROFILE 1.1 Dr. Amy Bishop, 2010

Although women are far less likely than men to commit mass murder, especially in the public sector, they can be just as deadly as men. Dr. Amy Bishop, 46, wife and mother of four children, had a long history of violent outbursts, but most people did not want to be involved or were not in a position to make the connections that linked her violent behavior. Those who did know her were able to witness some of her mood swings. So often her brilliance was diluted by her sudden bouts of rage when she felt ignored or treated unfairly. When she was 21, following a dispute at her parent's home, Amy loaded her father's shotgun and shot and killed her 18-year-old brother, Seth. She claimed it was an accident. Amy came down the stairs with the loaded shotgun saying that she wanted to see how it worked and now was trying to unload it. Told not to point the weapon at Seth, she did so anyway and shot him. She fled with the shotgun in hand to a car dealership, and when confronted by police refused to surrender the weapon. An officer had to disarm her. The family supported their daughter, saying that the shooting was accidental, and ultimately the investigation deemed the killing accidental. Twenty-six years later, following her assault on her university colleagues, the investigation into her brother's death was reopened and Dr. Bishop was also charged with his murder.

Amy continued throughout her life to act out in fits of rage. In 2002 she was charged with assault after screaming and hitting a woman in the head at a local IHOP restaurant because the woman had taken the last available booster seat for her child and Amy wanted to use it for one of her children. In 1994 she was questioned in a mail bomb plot against a doctor at Harvard University, where Amy had earned her doctorate and had worked sporadically in post-doctoral research. Eventually the investigation closed without charges against anyone. Her neighbors reported that she did not handle criticism from others well at all. Another person noted that she embellished her resume to indicate that she had worked at Harvard two years longer. Her students feared her at times, as she would move from empathy to anger in a moment. Her volatility caused several of her graduate students to leave her labs permanently. She was outraged when not placed as first author on a scientific article for publication even though she had no right to that position. She yelled at other people's children and could be extremely unfriendly.

She joined the University of Alabama as an assistant professor in the biology department. Her husband found work as a computer engineer at a start-up company. She and her husband had developed a special method of cell preservation that could change the way biomedical research is done. In 2009 she appeared on the cover of *The Huntsville R&D Report*. All seemed to be going well until she was turned down for tenure due to a weak research and publication record. She appealed the decision but was encouraged by her chair and others to start looking for work elsewhere. The family was under increasing financial stress, so Amy hired an attorney. She also started practicing with a firearm. In November 2009 her appeal was denied. February 12, 2010, Dr. Bishop attended a departmental faculty meeting, and after sitting quietly for about 30 minutes pulled out a handgun and shot six faculty members, killing three of them.

number of murders per 100,000 population), public perception, fueled by infrequent yet horrific mass murders such as Columbine, Virginia Tech, Fort Hood, Texas, and Tucson, Arizona, leads citizens to feel that murder is more common than ever (see Profile 1.4).

School mass murders, as a result of copycats, access to weapons, global media attention, and increased socialization to violence, have become a prominent

PROFILE 1.2 Nidal M. Hasan, the Ft. Hood Shooter, 2009

On November 5, 2009, Major Nidal Malik Hasan, 39, an American-born Muslim of Palestinian descent and a U.S. Army psychiatrist, entered Ft. Hood, the largest army base in the United States, near Killeen, Texas, and shot 45 military personnel at a medical clinic. Thirteen of those victims died from their wounds. Hasan was shot by a female civilian army police officer and is now paralyzed from the chest down. He currently awaits a court martial where he will face either life in prison with no possibility of parole or receive the death penalty. Hasan has been used as an example of persons sympathetic to radical Islam who have been radicalized to carry out acts of terror on American soil. However, Hasan may not have developed ties to any specific terrorist group, but may have become a lone wolf with sympathies toward radical Islam. Hasan was very stressed because he did not want to be deployed and be in a war zone involving other Muslims. Was Hasan experiencing cognitive dissonance in trying to deal with this conflict of interest between his sworn duty to the United States and his dedication to his faith? Or, perhaps he was disgruntled with his poor job performance review he received after working at Walter Reed Army Medical Center for six years. The investigation continues.

societal concern. There have been several major school attempted or completed mass murders in the United States in recent years (see Chart 1.1).

MASS MURDERER CLASSIFICATIONS

Several mass murderer typologies developed by Holmes and Holmes (2000) at the University of Louisville are presented here, including three typologies from other authors. Their thorough classification of mass murderers identifies behavioral and psychological characteristics of these offenders:

1. **Family Slayer or Annihilator**—a person who kills his family and commits suicide.
2. **Murderer for Profit**—a person who kills in order to profit materially. Murderers for profit may kill their family or other groups of people such as coworkers or friends. In 2000, Joseph Kibwetere, leader of the Ugandan cult members of the Movement for the Restoration of the Ten Commandments of God, murdered over 700 followers to avoid having to return money and possessions they had entrusted to him.
3. **Murderer for Sex**—a person with the primary goal to sexually torture, rape, and murder the victims; a comparatively rare typology. Richard Speck forced his way into a nurses' residence and raped and tortured eight nurses to death (Levin and Fox, 1985).
4. **Pseudo-Commando**—a person with an obsession for guns and a fantasy for murder. James Huberty walked into a McDonald's restaurant, shot 21 people to death, and wounded another 19 victims (Dietz, 1986).

PROFILE 1.3 Marcus Wesson, 2003

Wesson, 57, a quirky man with dreadlocks, was a cult leader of his own family who controlled how, when, and where they would live their lives. He told them that he saw himself as God and they better see him in that light as well. When he walked to a store his wives walked several paces in the rear. He held contempt for women and used them to satisfy his wants and needs. His daughters and nieces bore him children as he moved his "family" to various locations in California. At one point Wesson kept his family sequestered in a large tent for 12 years in the Santa Cruz Mountains. They finally settled in Fresno, where the family lived quietly and the sexual abuse was kept secret. One of his wives, Elizabeth, married Wesson when she was 8 years of age, was pregnant by 14, and by 26 years of age had given birth 11 times. The children were "home schooled" and were seldom seen by the general public. Wesson kept nine coffins in his small home as a reminder of what could happen to them.

Two nieces who fled his control decided to go back for the children he had fathered by them. He had warned his family for many years to be prepared for the devil in a blue uniform and wearing a badge. The end was near, and now that day had come. When Wesson saw police and his two nieces standing outside his home, he said that he would cooperate and give them the children. Instead, he gathered all his children/wives together in their suicide pact. The eldest was 25, followed by a 17-year-old. The remaining seven were all under the age of nine. Wesson shot each one in the temple and tossed the bodies in a pile in a bedroom. Of course Wesson, being the coward he was, did not kill himself, but instead surrendered to police and blamed the killings on his 25-year-old daughter/wife who also had been shot and killed. Some of his own sons later defended Wesson, stating that their father was a wonderful man who loved his children and would never harm any of them. Other accounts offered more insight: Wesson abused his family emotionally, physically, and sexually and manipulated them using fear for his own gain. Years later, and with more clarity on how they had all been victimized by Wesson, some of the surviving children and Elizabeth related how he was a master manipulator and at times extremely violent. Being with him was like being in prison where punishments for even minor infractions of his rules could lead to 30 days of physical abuse. The violence and threat of violence was only one of his forms of control. He held prayer sessions and Bible studies that lasted hours. He wrote his own version of the Bible to meet his vision. When the boys were old enough to work they turned all they earned over to Wesson. The sexual abuse for the girls started around age seven or eight.

Marcus Wesson now resides on death row in San Quentin State Prison.

5. **Set-and-Run Killer**—a person who plans an escape route following the killing aftermath. An example is the bombing of the Federal Building in Oklahoma City, Oklahoma, where 168 people, including 19 children, perished. Other set-and-run killers may use poisons or set fires.
6. **Psychotic Killer**—a person suffering from acute or chronic psychosis who is considered to be legally insane.
7. **Disgruntled Employee**—a person who seeks revenge for real or imagined wrongs at the hands of coworkers or employers. During the 1990s, several incidents of postal workers killing coworkers and supervisors spawned the phrase *going postal.*

PROFILE 1.4 Andrew Kehoe, America's Mass Murderer of Children: The Bath School Disaster, 1927

Born in 1872 and raised by a stepmother following the early death of his mother, Andrew Kehoe bore much resentment about his mother being replaced. Working at the oil stove one day the stepmother accidentally caught herself on fire. Andrew, now 14, threw a bucket of water on the fire that caused it to spread even further and as a result, the stepmother died from her burns. This event may have been a harbinger for his mass murder.

Kehoe married in 1912 and bought a farm in the Bath Township, Michigan. He was known to be a controlling man with a quick temper against those who disagreed with him. A member of the local school board, Kehoe was angered by a property tax levied to fund a new school building. This tax, he believed, was a financial hardship as his wife, Nellie, was suffering from tuberculosis that required extensive medical care. In truth, Kehoe had an extensive collection of farm machinery and tools that could have been sold to cover his mortgage, but he was not about to compromise. Ultimately the financial strains caused Kehoe's farm to go into foreclosure.

Approximately one year prior to the school attack Kehoe began purchasing over a ton of pyrotol, an incendiary explosive used for excavation. He also purchased boxes of dynamite in small enough quantities so as not to draw attention and conducted practice explosions on his farm. Because Kehoe was a school board member and a handyman, he had full access to the school and spent many hours installing his explosives. Kehoe not only had a plan to blow up the school but he also planned to kill anyone who came to their rescue after the explosion. He filled his car with metal tools, nails, piping, and other pieces of metal and packed the trunk with dynamite. He also placed pyrotol firebombs throughout his farm. A day or two prior to the school attack Kehoe killed his wife by blunt force trauma to her head. On May 18, 1927, Kehoe detonated the firebombs at his home, destroying his farm animals and his wife's body. The large fire drew many volunteer firefighters from the area. An hour later, at 9:45 A.M., the school bombs were detonated in the north wing of the building, killing 38 elementary school children and 2 teachers. Another injured child died a few months later. About one hour later Kehoe arrived amid the chaos and rescue efforts. Summoning the school superintendent to his car, Kehoe detonated his vehicle, killing himself, the superintendent, an 8-year-old boy, the postmaster, and his father-in-law. Investigators later found another 500 pounds of bombs hidden in the school's south wing. Final death toll: 45.

Kehoe had left a note on his fence that read: Criminals are made, not born.

8. **Disciple-Type Killer**—a person who commits murder at the behest of a charismatic leader such as Charles Manson.
9. **Ideological Mass Murderer**—a person, especially a cult leader, who is able to persuade others to kill themselves or each other, as in the cases of Jim Jones (Jonestown Massacre), Herff Applewhite (Heaven's Gate), and David Koresh (Waco Massacre).
10. **Institutional Mass Murderer**—a person who commits mass murder as a crime of obedience when ordered to by his or her leader. This often is manifested in the form of genocide, "ethnic cleansing," and religious bigotry as occurred in the Kosovo region, the Stalin farm collectivization, Armenian and Nazi Holocausts, and the Crusades (Hickey, 2000).

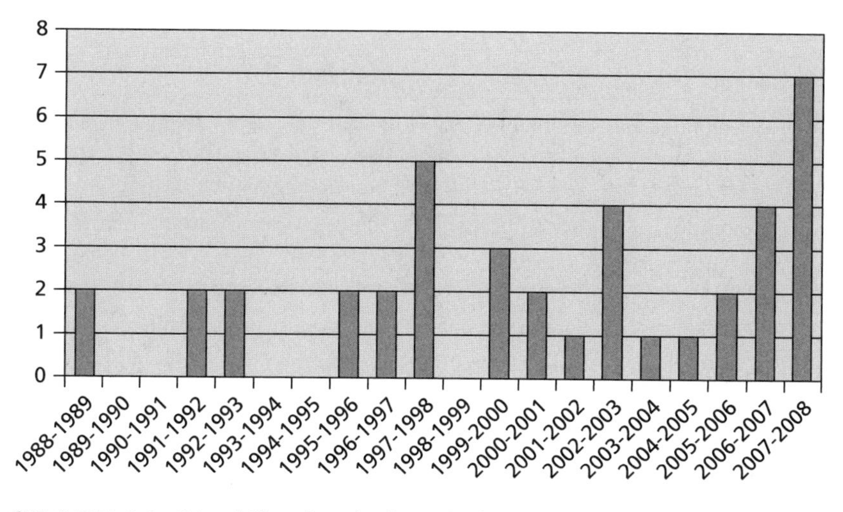

CHART 1.1 School Shootings in the United States, 1988–2008
SOURCE: © Cengage Learning, 2013.

Although researchers have barely begun to collect data on such crimes, certain commonalities emerged from their findings that offenders are primarily white, male, and encompass a wide age range. Invariably, handguns, semiautomatic guns, and rifles are the weapons used to kill suddenly and swiftly. But when we control for gender, race, ethnicity, victim preference, mode of killing, and other variables, we also see that there are nearly as many exceptions as there are those who "fit" the general stereotype.

Although victims are often intentionally selected by the killer (for example, a former boss, an ex-wife, or a friend), other persons who happen to be in the area also become collateral prey. Some offenders, simply frustrated by perceived injustices and inequities, lash out at groups of victims who bear no relationship to them. Table 1.3 gives a brief listing of modern-day mass murderers.

Unlike serial killers, the mass murderer appears to give little thought or concern to his or her inevitable capture or death. Some are killed by police during the attack, whereas others kill themselves once they have completed the massacre. In some cases offenders surrender to police and offer no resistance. With the exception of those who murder their families, most appear to commit their crimes in public places. In cases in which families are murdered, the killer, if he does not commit suicide, usually leaves ample evidence to lead to his or her arrest.

As stated earlier, some mass murders appear to be premeditated—as in the case of Charles Whitman, who fired on unsuspecting victims from the bell tower at the University of Texas at Austin. He carried a footlocker full of supplies, including food and ammunition, to the top of the tower in preparation for his attack. Conversely, some cases of multiple homicide may be sparked by what could be viewed as a trivial remark, simply a minor insult or provocation. However, in both cases, those who engage in multiple homicide appear to do so in an effort to regain, even for a brief moment, a degree of control over their lives. To the observer, this motivation may not appear rational. To the killer, however, it may make perfect sense, given his or her psychological disorientation.

TABLE 1.3 A Sampling of Modern Mass Murderers

Year	State	Offender	Death Toll
1927	Michigan	Andrew Kehoe	Bombed a school—37 children, 8 adults dead
1949	New Jersey	Howard B. Unruh	Shot neighbors—13 dead
1955	Colorado	Jack G. Graham	Bombed a plane with his mother on it—44 dead
1966	Illinois	Richard F. Speck	Stabbed/strangled nurses—8 dead
1966	Texas	Charles Whitman	Shot students and bystanders—16 dead
1966	Arizona	Robert B. Smith	Shot women in beauty salon—5 dead
1974	Louisiana	Mark Essex	Shot police officers—9 dead
1975	Ohio	James Ruppert	Shot family members—11 dead
1976	California	Edward Allaway	Shot coworkers—7 dead
1977	New York	Fred W. Cowan	Shot coworkers—6 dead
1982	California	Humberto de la Torre	Revenge arson against uncle—killed 25 in hotel blaze
1982	Pennsylvania	George Banks	Shot family and acquaintances—13 dead
1984	California	James O. Huberty	Shot patrons at McDonald's—21 dead
1985	Pennsylvania	Sylvia Selgrist	Shot several in mall—2 dead
1986	Oklahoma	Patrick Sherrill	Shot coworkers—14 dead
1987	Florida	William B. Cruse	Shot persons at a mall—6 dead
1987	Arkansas	Ronald G. Simmons	Shot family—16 dead
1988	California	Richard Farley	Shot workers in a computer company—9 dead
1988	Minnesota	David Brown	Axed family—4 dead
1988	Illinois	Laurie Dann	Shot, poisoned many—1 dead
1988	North Carolina	Michael C. Hayes	Shot neighbors—4 dead
1989	California	Patrick Purdy	Shot several children in school yard—5 dead
1990	Florida	James E. Pough	Shot 13 in an auto loan company—8 dead
1990	New York	Julio Gonzalez	Set fire to a nightclub—87 dead
1991	Michigan	Thomas McIlvane	Shot 9 at post office—4 dead
1991	Iowa	Gang Lu	Shot 6 people at the University of Iowa—5 dead
1991	Texas	George Hennard	Shot 45 people in Luby's restaurant—23 dead
1992	California	Eric Houston	Shot 14 at high school—4 dead
1993	Texas	David Koresh	Fire/shooting, murder/suicide pact—101 dead

TABLE 1.3 Continued

Year	State	Offender	Death Toll
1993	California	Gian L. Ferri	Shot 14 at a law firm—8 dead
1993	New York	Colin Ferguson	Shot 25 in commuter train—6 dead
1993	Arizona	Jonathan Doody	Shot several in Buddhist temple—9 dead
1995	New York	Michael Vernon	Shot 8 in a store—5 dead
1995	Oklahoma	Timothy McVeigh, Terry Nichols	Bombed federal building in Oklahoma City—168 dead, including children in day-care center
1996	California	Joshua Jenkins	15-year-old allegedly beat/stabbed family—5 dead
1997	Kentucky	Michael Carneal	14-year-old shot students—3 dead
1997	South Carolina	Arthur Wise	Shot several workers in a parts plant—4 dead
1997	California	Daniel Marsden	Shot 2 coworkers—wounded 4 and killed himself
1997	California	Arturo Torres	Shot ex-boss and 3 others— killed by police
1998	Arkansas	Mitchell Johnson, Andrew Golden	13-year-old and 11-year-old shot students—5 dead
1998	Connecticut	Matthew Beck	Shot 3 supervisors and president of Connecticut Lottery Corp., then killed himself—4 dead
1998	Oregon	Kip Kinkel	15-year-old shot 28 students—2 dead—after killing his parents
1999	Georgia	Mark Barton	Shot 22 at stock trading companies—9 dead—after beating his wife and two children to death
1999	Hawaii	Bryan Uyesugi	Shot and killed 7 coworkers at Xerox office
1999	Colorado	Eric Harris, Dylan Klebold	Two seniors at Columbine High School shot and killed 12 students, 1 teacher. Killers committed suicide.
2000	Florida	Dexter Levingston	Mildly retarded man kills 4 relatives and a 12-year-old girl by shooting and stabbing them with machete and screwdriver
2000	Kansas	Reginald and Jonathan Carr	Assaulted, raped and shot, execution style, 5 young adults
2000	Pennsylvania	Richard Baumhammers	A former immigration lawyer, who hated non-whites, shot and killed 5 men in Pittsburgh: 1 Jew, 2 Asians, 1 African American, and 1 man of Indian descent
2001	Texas	Andrea Yates	Drowned her 5 children, one at a time
2003	Illinois	Salvadore Tapia	Shot former coworkers at an auto parts factory—6 dead
2004	California	Marcus Wesson	Charged with shooting and killing his 9 children

(continued)

TABLE 1.3 Continued

Year	State	Offender	Death Toll
2004	Florida	Troy Victorino and 3 teens	Charged with beating 6 adults to death while they slept
2005	Minnesota	Jeffrey Weise	Student at Red Lake High School shot and killed his grandfather, grandfather's girlfriend, 5 students, 1 teacher, and 1 security guard—9 dead. Killer committed suicide.
2005	Wisconsin	Terry Ratzman	Churchgoer shot 11 people at a church service in a hotel—7 dead. Killer committed suicide.
2006	Pennsylvania	Charles Roberts	Milk truck driver shot 6 Amish girls in a schoolroom—4 dead. Killer committed suicide.
2006	Indiana	James Stewart, Desmond Turner	Shot 4 adults and 3 children—7 dead
2006	Washington	Kyle Huff	Shot 8 people at a rave party—6 dead. Killer committed suicide.
2007	Virginia	Seung-Hui Cho	Student at Virginia Tech shot 57 people—32 dead. Killer committed suicide.
2008	Ohio	Michael Davis	Set fire to a house, killing 2 women and 4 children—6 dead
2008	Kentucky	Wesley Higdon	Killed 5 coworkers before killing himself
2009	California	Ervin Lupoe	Shot his wife, 5 children, and himself
2009	Ohio	Devon Crawford	Shot his wife, sister-in-law, 3 young children, and himself
2009	Alabama	Michael McLendon	Shot 5 family members and 5 others before killing himself
2009	North Carolina	Robert Stewart	Shot 8: an employee and 7 patients in a nursing home
2009	California	Devan Kalathat	Shot his 2 children and 3 relatives before killing himself
2009	New York	Jiverly Wong	Killed 13 at an immigration center before committing suicide
2009	Washington	James Harrison	Killed his 5 children before killing himself
2009	Texas	Nidal M. Hasan	Shot and killed 13 military personnel at Ft. Hood, TX, and wounded 30 others
2010	Connecticut	Omar Thorton	Shot dead 8 coworkers before killing himself
2011	Michigan	Rodrick Dantzler	Killed 7 including his daughter and ex-girlfriend before killing himself
2011	New York	Maksim Gelman	Killed 4 in a stabbing rampage and attempted to kill others

TABLE 1.3 Continued

Year	State	Offender	Death Toll
2011	Arizona	Jared L. Loughner	Shot 6 to death in a store, including a young girl, and wounded several others
2011	Arizona	Carey H. Dyess	Shot 5 to death, including the attorney representing his fifth wife in divorce settlement. He then shot himself
2011	Indiana	David E. Ison	Shot and killed 4 members of a family and a neighbor shot to death
2011	Ohio	Michael Hance	Shot and killed 7 victims: his girlfriend, her relatives, and some neighbors

SOURCE: Authors files, 2011.

It would appear that not all mass murderers are motivated by similar circumstances, yet the final outcome is the same. Feelings of rejection, failure, and loss of autonomy create frustrations that inevitably overwhelm them, and they experience a need to strike back. And for many killers the best way to lash out against a cold, forbidding society is to destroy its children. Gunning down children in a schoolyard not only provides the needed sense of power and control but is also a way of wreaking vengeance where it hurts the community the most. According to a 2000 *New York Times* study of 100 "rampage" mass murders,* where 425 people were killed and 510 injured, the killers:

1. Often have serious mental health issues
2. Are not usually motivated by exposure to videos, movies, or television
3. Are not using alcohol or other drugs at the time of the attacks
4. Are often unemployed
5. Are sometimes female
6. Are not usually Satanists or racists
7. Are most often white males, although a few are Asian or African American
8. Sometimes have college degrees or some years of college
9. Often have military experience
10. Give pre-attack warning signals
11. Often carry semiautomatic weapons obtained legally
12. Often do not attempt escape
13. Half commit suicide or are killed by others
14. Most have a death wish (Fessenden, 2000)

White (2000), in her study of mass murderers, found that most offenders who kill in the workplace do not attempt suicide and do not force authorities

*These murders were generally not domestic, robbery, or gang related.

to kill them or try to evade arrest. In contrast, domestic mass murderers usually commit suicide or are killed by police. The single most salient factor in such rampage mass murders is mental disorder and/or mental illness. Some mass murderers, so deeply depressed, become schizophrenic or psychotic. Others suffer from severe anxiety and personality disorders. These are not rational people at the time of the murders, even when their behaviors are calculated and decisive. Many of them are not legally insane but suffer from severe psychological dysfunctioning as a result of both chronic and acute stress (see Profile 1.5).

The social impact of mass murders tends to be restricted to the communities in which they occurred. Increased security at schools, office buildings, and shopping malls is the usual response, including improved social services to better identify potentially dangerous individuals. However, the track record in predicting criminal behavior thus far has been dismal. Recognizing potential mass murderers is usually a matter of hindsight; we are quick to attach motivating factors and personality defects to offenders once they have vented themselves on their victims. The fact remains, however, that mass murders, in relation to other crimes—even other forms of homicide—are relatively rare, and they appear to occur as randomly as serial killings do.

PROFILE 1.5 Mark Barton, Portrait of a Mass Murderer, 1999

He was a stock day trader at the All-Tech Investment Group in Atlanta, Georgia. On July 29, 1999, Barton armed himself with over 200 rounds of ammunition and with his Glock 9mm and Colt .45 went to Momentum Securities, a brokerage firm. After some small talk he shot and killed four people. He then calmly drove over to All-Tech and killed five more people. As he left he was overheard saying, "I hope this won't ruin your trading day." Barton would later shoot himself in the head as police cornered him in Atlanta. He was angry over the loss of $100,000 in day trading in recent weeks. The money he was investing had been collected from a life insurance policy that he had taken out on his first wife, Debra, in 1993. Only a month after the policy was in force, Debra and her mother Eloise Spivey were found chopped to death with a hatchet. Police believed that Barton was the killer but lacked evidence to arrest him. Barton eventually was given $450,000 of the life insurance money, but by then he had already found his new wife, Leigh Ann, a woman with whom he was having an affair while still married to Debra. His new life, however, was far from peaceful. Barton, once suspected of molesting his daughter Mychelle as a small child, underwent a court-ordered evaluation. The psychologist noted during testing that Barton was capable of committing homicide. More insightful words would be hard to find. In one of his final notes he wrote, "I don't plan to live very much longer, just long enough to kill as many of the people that greedily sought my destruction."

Just prior to the mass murder in Atlanta, Mark Barton, 44, murdered his second wife, Leigh Ann, 27, his son, Matthew, 12, and daughter, Mychelle, 8. Barton would later write on his suicide note that his sweetheart (Mychelle) and buddy (Matthew) died "with little pain." Each of the children died from hammer blows to the head while they slept, then were placed underwater in the bathtub to be sure they were dead. He wrapped sheets and towels around each of the three bodies to only allow their faces to show and placed a teddy bear on Mychelle and a video game on Matthew.

Bifurcation in Mass Murder

Within cases of mass murder there are some important distinctions worth noting. One of these is *bifurcation*. Most mass murders usually occur at or around one distinct location such as a school, an office building, or a private residence. In some mass killings an offender begins his/her murders in one location and then moves to another building or address to continue the killing (see Profile 1.4). These bifurcated attacks, although not common, continue to occur periodically.

Public to public events that are deemed mass murders are extremely rare, such as Seung-Hui Cho, the Virginia Tech mass murderer who began his killings in one campus location, waited a period of time, then went to another location and killed many more students and faculty (see Profile 1.6). In 2011 another mass murderer in Norway, Anders Breivik, bombed government buildings in downtown Oslo, killing seven. Two hours later and many miles away on Utoya Island he shot and killed another 69 victims. The same year in Carson City, Nevada, a 32-year-old Mexican immigrant walked up to a man sitting on a motorcycle outside an IHOP restaurant and shot him with a rifle. He then entered the restaurant and shot several national guardsmen, killing two of them. Upon exiting the IHOP the gunman walked into the parking lot and took aim at various stores close by and began shooting at them before finally killing himself.

Private to public mass murders, however, are much more likely to occur when mass murder events are bifurcated. These events usually involve an individual who kills family members and/or friends at a private residence, after which they proceed to enter a public place such as a business or school and kill more victims. Several offenders killed their spouse, parent(s), and/or children before traveling to public locations to continue the killings. Michael McLendon shot his mother and her four dogs before going to other private and public locations to continue his killings.

Bifurcation of mass murder events may help in understanding the mind-sets of such killers. Indeed, mental illness is commonly found in mass murderers, yet there are some who are not suffering from severe cognitive distortions, hallucinations, hearing voices, and paranoia. Others exhibit a spectrum of personality disorders, such as James Huberty, who told his wife one day that he was "going to hunt humans" and then proceeded to shoot 35 victims, killing 21, at a McDonald's restaurant. Charles Whitman carefully planned his mass murder by first killing his wife and mother, then climbed the bell tower at the University of Texas, Austin, and shot 46 people, killing 16. In some cases the offender bifurcates the events because he does not want to leave his family members to endure the aftermath of his murders. Others kill their family members because they are the primary targets and then proceed to other public or private locations to kill more. Usually these events involve rifles or handguns.

A Sampling of Bifurcated Mass Murders in the United States 1950–2011

1927 Andrew Kehoe—45 dead, 58 wounded

1950 Ernest Ingenito—9 dead, 1 wounded

1966 Charles Whitman—16 dead, 32 wounded

PROFILE 1.6 Virginia Tech Massacre, 2007

"You forced me into a corner," said Seung-Hui Cho. "You had a hundred billion chances and ways to have avoided today. ... But you decided to spill my blood. You forced me into a corner and gave me only one option. The decision was yours. Now you have blood on your hands that will never wash off."

On April 16, 2007, 23-year-old Seung-Hui Cho left his dormitory on the Virginia Tech campus armed with a 9mm pistol and a .22-caliber handgun. He entered a coeducational residence hall that housed 895 people and shot to death a 19-year-old female freshman and a 22-year-old male resident assistant. About two hours later, Cho entered an engineering classroom building about a half mile from the initial shootings. He chained the front doors locked from the inside and made his way to the second floor. Cho killed another 30 people in four different classrooms before turning the gun on himself. At least 15 other people were wounded in the shootings. Another 60 students were injured as they ran or leapt to safety from the windows of their classrooms.

Cho's underlying psychological diagnosis at the time of the shootings remains a matter of speculation. In the ensuing investigation, police found a suicide note in Cho's dorm room that included comments about "rich kids," "debauchery," and "deceitful charlatans." On April 18, 2007, NBC News received a package from Cho time-stamped between the first and second shooting episodes. It contained an 1,800-word manifesto, photos, and 27 digitally recorded videos in which Cho likened himself to Jesus Christ and expressed his hatred of the wealthy. Various sources concluded that because of Cho's inability to handle stress and the "frightening prospect" of being "turned out into the world of work, finances, responsibilities, and a family," Cho chose to engage in a fantasy where "he would be remembered as the savior of the oppressed, the downtrodden, the poor, and the rejected."

Looking over his life, one can see a long history of psychological problems. Cho, a South Korean who had moved to the United States at age eight, was a senior English major at Virginia Tech. At the age of three, he was described as shy, frail, and wary of physical contact. In the eighth grade, Cho was diagnosed with depression as

1971 Douglas Dean—5 dead

1987 Ronald G. Simmons—16 dead, 4 wounded

1989 John M. Taylor—4 dead, 1 wounded

1991 Andrew Brooks Jr.—6 dead, 2 wounded

1991 Joseph M. Harris—4 dead

1998 Kip Kinkle—4 dead, 22 wounded

1999 Mark O. Barton—9 dead, 13 wounded

1999 Lawrence Hensley—4 dead, 1 wounded

2005 Jeffrey Weise—10 dead, 5 wounded

2006 Jennifer San Marco—7 dead

2009 Michael McLendon—11 dead

2010 Christopher Speight—8 dead

well as selective mutism, a social anxiety disorder that inhibited him from speaking. Cho's family sought therapy for him, and he received help periodically throughout middle school and high school. High school officials worked with his parents and mental health counselors to support Cho throughout his sophomore and junior years. However, he eventually chose to discontinue therapy.

When he applied to Virginia Tech, school officials did not report his speech and anxiety-related problems or special education status because of federal privacy laws that prohibit such disclosure unless a student requests special accommodation. However, his psychological problems continued.

During the fall semester of 2005, one of Cho's professors expressed concern over his "sinister" writings. He was asked by the professor to either change his writing style or leave his poetry class. Cho responded, "You can't make me." The co-director of the Creative Writing program removed him from the class and tutored him one on one. He was again asked to attend counseling, but refused.

In November and December of 2005, Cho was investigated by the university for stalking and harassing two female students. After the investigation, he was ordered to have no contact with them. After this order, Cho sent a suicidal instant text message to a roommate. His message was reported to campus authorities and he was taken by campus police to a local community services center where he received a voluntary counseling evaluation. He was determined to be "mentally ill and in need of hospitalization." This evaluation, declaring him "an imminent danger to self or others," was sent to court. Cho was taken to a psychiatric hospital and evaluated by a psychologist. The psychologist concluded that Cho "presents an imminent danger to himself as a result of mental illness." The court ordered that Cho receive follow-up outpatient treatment, but reports indicate he did not seek out services. In February, Cho began purchasing weapons and ammunition and began videotaping his manifesto. In a few weeks Cho carried out the largest school massacre in the history of the United States.

SOURCE: NYTimes, MSNBC, CNN, ABC News, Roanoke Times.

2011 Rodrick S. Dantzler—7 dead, 2 wounded

2011 Eduardo Sencion—5 dead, 7 wounded

Differences among Mass, Serial, and Spree Murderers

In both mass and serial murder cases, victims die as the offender momentarily gains control of his or her life by controlling others. But the differences between these two types of offenders far outweigh the similarities. First, mass murderers are generally apprehended or killed by police, commit suicide, or turn themselves in to authorities. Serial killers, by contrast, usually make special efforts to elude detection. Indeed, they may continue to kill for weeks, months, and often years before they are found and stopped—if they are found at all. In the case of the California Zodiac Killer, the homicides appeared to have stopped, but an offender was never apprehended for those crimes. Perhaps the offender was incarcerated for only one murder and never linked to the others, or perhaps he or she was imprisoned for other crimes. Or the Zodiac Killer may have just decided to stop killing or to move to a new location and kill under a new modus operandi, or method of committing the crime. The killer may even have become immobilized because of an accident or an illness or may have died without his or her story ever being told. Speculation exists that the Zodiac Killer has stalked victims in the New York City area. The Zodiac case is only one example of unsolved serial murders, many of which will never be solved.

Second, although both types of killers evoke fear and anxiety in the community, the reaction to a mass murder will be much more focused and locally limited than that to serial killing. People generally perceive the mass killer as one suffering from mental illnesses. This immediately creates a "they versus us" dichotomy in which "they" are different from "us" because of mental problems. We can somehow accept the fact that a few people go "crazy" sometimes and start shooting others. However, it is more disconcerting to learn that some of the "nicest" people one meets lead Jekyll-and-Hyde lives: a student by day, a killer of coeds by night; a caring, attentive nurse who secretly murders sick children, the handicapped, or the elderly; a building contractor and politician who enjoys sexually torturing and killing young men and burying them under his home. When we discover that people exist who are not considered to be insane or crazy but who enjoy killing others for "recreation," this indeed gives new meaning to the word "stranger." Although the mass murderer is viewed as a deranged soul, a product of a stressful environment who is just going to "explode" now and then (but of course somewhere else), the serial murderer is seen as much more sinister and is more capable of producing fear.

The third difference is that the mass murderer kills groups of people at once, usually within a few minutes or hours, whereas the serial killer individualizes his or her murders. The serial killer continues to hurt and murder victims, whereas the mass murderer makes his or her "final statement" in or about life through the medium of abrupt and final violence. We rarely, if ever, hear of a mass murderer who has the opportunity to enact a second mass murder or to become a serial killer. Similarly, we rarely, if ever, hear of a serial killer who also enacts a mass murder.

The mass murderer and the serial killer are quantitatively and qualitatively different, and disagreement continues about their characteristics just as it does about the types of mass and serial offenders that appear to have emerged in recent years. White (2000) thoroughly examined the differences between mass and serial murderers and summarized the differences as shown in Table 1.4. An important change from White's findings is that the current number of murders required in a case to be classified as serial murder is two (FBI, 2008).

Researchers also distinguished *spree* murders from mass and serial murders as being three or more victims killed by a single perpetrator within a period of hours or days in different locations. They often act in a frenzy, make little effort to avoid detection, and kill in several sequences. Offenders may kill more than one victim in one location and travel to another location. There appears to be no cooling-off period even though the murders occur at different places (Greswell and Hollin, 1994). These murders, sometimes called *cluster killings*,

TABLE 1.4 Differences Between Mass and Serial Murderers

	Mass	Serial
Murder is means of control over life	✓	✓
Usually arrested or killed at crime scene	✓	
Often commits suicide after the crime	✓	
Eludes arrest and detection		✓
Likely to travel and seek out victims		✓
Evokes long-term media/public attention		✓
Kills individuals		✓
Kills several in short period of time	✓	
Murders viewed as single incident	✓	
Minimum number of victims agreed on by researchers	4	4
Murderer is usually white male	✓	✓
Motivated primarily by material gain or revenge	✓	
Victims usually female		✓
Firearms are the common choice of weapon	✓	
Kills in spontaneous rage	✓	

SOURCE: Data from White, 2000.

tend to last a few days, weeks, or even months. In 1997, Andrew Cunanan, a 27-year-old from San Diego, California, went on a four-state killing spree that culminated in the murder of fashion designer Gianni Versace in Florida. Cunanan feared that he might be infected with the AIDS virus and vowed revenge on whomever was responsible. Some of the five men he murdered were gay and some were not. Upon killing them with guns, knives, and blunt objects, Cunanan would steal cars and money from his victims. He continued to kill as he journeyed southeastward toward his final murder and suicide. The problem with the concept of spree murder is that investigators and researchers cannot agree on how to adequately define *cooling off*. As of 2008 experts have collectively agreed that the concept of spree murder be eliminated and that such offenders be included with other cases of serial murder (FBI, 2008).

Perhaps the most critical stumbling block that today stands in the way of understanding serial murder is the disagreement among researchers and law enforcement personnel about how to define the phenomenon.

DEFINING HOMICIDE, MURDER, AND SERIAL MURDER

The reader should be clear about how we categorize various types of murders based upon familial relationships and group identification as well as how we define the taking of a person's life. Many murders are committed within families by other family members, while other murders are committed on a global scale.

- *Neonaticide:* killing of a newborn within the first 24 hours of his or her life.
- *Infanticide:* killing of an infant child who is less than one year of age.
- *Siblicide:* typical in survival behavior of animal groups, the term is also used to refer to the killing of an individual by a sibling or siblings or facilitated by the parent(s).
- *Fraticide:* killing of one's brother or sister. Often used in terms of military fratricide or the act of killing a relative(s) or countrymen. Used also to describe the killing of one's own military forces, such as "friendly fire" incidents.
- *Prolicide:* killing one's own children, including infanticide and killing of a fetus in utero. Commonly referred to as *filicide*, which usually refers to the killing of a minor, including a stepchild.
- *Parricide:* killing of a parent(s) or other relative. *Patricide* refers to the killing of one's father, while *matricide* is the killing of one's mother.
- *Genocide:* extermination of a specific racial, ethnic, religious, or national group of people.

Each state in the United States has very specific criteria for defining murder. *Justifiable homicide* is sometimes referred to as "no fault" homicide, and usually involves the killing of someone under necessity or duty. These killings lack criminal intent. This can include various forms of defense of family, self, or others. *Manslaughter* can be either *voluntary manslaughter* that involves the killing of another person(s) in the heat of passion, in the commission of another felony, or in self-defense. *Involuntary manslaughter* is sometimes referred to as negligent homicide and involves the killing of another person(s) while committing a non-felony offense such as reckless driving (also referred to as vehicular manslaughter). A person who chooses not to maintain the brakes on his car, which results in a car crash that takes the life of one or more persons, is usually determined to be guilty of negligent manslaughter. Of course, there may be exceptions depending upon circumstances and the state in which the offense occurred.

In California, to receive a death sentence an offender must be "death eligible," which means that the person must have committed a homicide, specifically murder. All homicides are not illegal, however. In some cases, such as self-defense or when the state holds an execution, the killings are viewed as homicides and are not considered illegal killings. The issuer of the death certificate of a man executed in California noted the cause of death as being a homicide, for example. Indeed, a *murder* requires an illegal taking of another's life specifically formed around intent. Such determinations are made based upon provocation, cooling off periods, and what a reasonable person would be expected to do under the circumstances leading to the killing.

From a judicial point of view the most serious of murders are those that are *capital* cases involving *premeditated murder*, or the willful, intentional killing of another person(s). Such cases may qualify a person, if convicted, for a death sentence. However, most persons convicted of *first-degree* murder find their way into lengthy prison terms rather than a death sentence. First-degree murder usually includes *felony murder*, or murder committed while in the course of committing another felony, such as killing someone while robbing a bank. Other forms of first-degree murder may involve poisoning, lying in wait, torture, use of explosives, and in some states, such as California, using armor-piercing bullets or doing a "drive-by" killing.

Usually for a sentence of death the offender must have willfully, deliberately, and with premeditation murdered another with *special circumstances*. These special or aggravating circumstances in first-degree murder may include a prior murder by the offender; multiple murders; killing of a peace officer, witness, prosecutor, or judge; lying in wait; torture with intent to kill; murder due to race, ethnicity, religion, or nationality; felony murder; and use of poison. Even when an offender does receive a death sentence, the likelihood of actually being executed is minimal. In California the average length of time for an appeals process to be completed is over 16 years. Most of the condemned in California die of natural causes, commit suicide, or are murdered by fellow inmates.

Serial murder, one of those special circumstance categories, draws a lot of media attention. In February 1989, the Associated Press released a story about a serial killer who preyed on prostitutes in the same area of Los Angeles that harbored the Southside Slayer.* He was believed to have killed at least 12 women, all with a small handgun. The news story referred to the victims as "strawberries"—young women who sold sex for drugs. Farther north, the Green River Task Force in Seattle, Washington, continued to investigate a series of murders of at least 48 young women over a 21-year span (see Profile 1.7). When the corpses of boys and young men began appearing along the banks of the Chattahoochee River in Atlanta, Georgia, during the early 1980s, police became convinced a serial killer was at work in the area.

The preceding cases are typical of murders one might envision when characterizing victims of serial killers. The media quickly and eagerly focus attention on serial killings because they appear to be so bizarre and extraordinary. They engender the kinds of headlines that sell newspapers: "The Atlanta Child Killer," "The Stocking Strangler," "The Hillside Strangler," "The Sunday Morning Slasher," "The Boston Strangler," ad infinitum. The media focus not only on how many victims were killed but also on how they died. Thus they feed morbid curiosity and at the same time create a stereotype of the typical serial killer: Ted Bundy, Ed Kemper, Albert DeSalvo, and a host of other young, white males attacking unsuspecting women who are powerless to defend themselves from the savage sexual attacks and degradations by these monsters.

Egger's (1984) global definition of serial murder attempts to create parameters for the behavior:

> Serial murder occurs when one or more individuals ... commits a second murder and/or subsequent murder; is relationshipless (victim and attacker are strangers); occurs at a different time and has no connection to the initial (and subsequent) murder; and is frequently committed in a different geographic location. Further, the motive is generally not for material gain but

---

*Identity unknown; killed 12–20 victims between September 1983 and May 1987. Offender believed to be black and to have enjoyed mutilating his young female victims.

PROFILE 1.7 Gary Leon Ridgway, the Green River Killer, 1982–1998

In 2001, a 52-year-old truck painter was arrested in connection with the murders of seven prostitutes, drug addicts, and young female runaways in the Seattle, Washington, area. DNA and microscopic paint particles linked him to most of the murders. Police also suspected him for the murders of over 40 more street women. All of his victims, except for three women in their 30s, were between 15 and 26 years of age. Most of the killings, know as the Green River Murders, occurred in the mid-1980s as bodies began surfacing along the Green River near Seattle suburbs. In 2003, Ridgway negotiated an agreement with the district attorney's office to confess to 42 of those murders as well as 6 other murders not tied to the Green River killings. In exchange for his confession he escaped the death penalty and received life in prison with no chance for parole. This ended one of the longest murder investigations ever conducted in the United States. Gary Ridgway, with 48 victims, now holds the record for the most serial-murder convictions in the history of the United States.

Ridgway did not travel around the nation in search of victims but chose them mostly from the area in which he lived. In retrospect, there were many clues that pointed to Ridgway as a suspect. In 1980, a prostitute accused him of choking her but the police let him go. In 1982, he was field interviewed by Port of Seattle police while in a parked car with prostitute Kelli McGinness, 18. McGinness disappeared in June 1983. That same year he pled guilty to solicitation of an undercover policewoman posing as a prostitute. In 1983 Ridgway became the prime suspect in the disappearance of Marie Malvar, who was last seen fighting with him in his truck. By 1984, Ridgway became the primary Green River Killer suspect but, professing his innocence, he passed a polygraph in 1985. Although semen samples had been collected from Ridgway, they were only used to determine blood types and not for identification of a specific person. Circumstantial evidence and inconclusive physical evidence kept investigators from trying Ridgway for fear that he would be acquitted. With the introduction of viable DNA evidence and a desire to avoid a trial, Ridgway decided, like so many other serial killers, to negotiate a deal that would spare his life. He led investigators on dozens of searches that yielded four more sets of remains.

The Green River Killer turned out to be, on the surface, a rather unexceptional person. Born in Utah in 1949 to Tommy Newton and Mary Rita Steinman, Ridgway graduated from high school in 1969 after being held back two grades. He joined the Navy in 1969 and was honorably discharged in 1971. His first marriage in 1970 ended in divorce in 1972. His second marriage in 1973 lasted until 1981, just one year before he would embark on his murderous career. His son Matthew was born to his second wife in 1975. He married for the third time in 1988 and legally separated in 2002. His third wife said they had a happy marriage and that he was a reliable, regular employee at the same job for 32 years.

Ridgway was a sociable man who liked to drink beer, read his Bible at work, hunt, fish, and work in his yard. He was considered by others to be meticulous, overbearing at times, but friendly. He was always careful not to talk about himself. He liked to go on vacations with his third wife and travel in their RV. He liked to proselytize to convert fellow workers to Christianity. First a Baptist and later a Pentecostal, Ridgway enjoyed doing missionary work to spread the Word of God. He watched religious television programs that often brought him to tears.

But Ridgway nurtured a dark side that included over 20 years of soliciting prostitutes. As a teen he often was the one who was getting into trouble at school and his grades were barely passing. He lived in a home dominated by his mother. He frequently watched as his father submitted to emotional and physical abuse from his mother. He became estranged from his father. He tried to hire on as a police officer but was rejected. He enjoyed telling sex-related jokes and passing on tips on how to approach streetwalkers. He found himself sexually attracted to his mother. He often sexually harassed female coworkers at his job as a painter. As a young adult he developed an attraction to prostitutes and was extremely concerned about his physical appearance. He also had a temper and in 1982 choked his second wife. Ridgway harbored immense rage toward women that he eventually unleashed on prostitutes.

Within two years after the first Green River murders began, an unsigned letter appeared that was poorly written and had most words running together. It began, "what you eedtonoaboutthegreenriverman." The next line read, "dontthrowaway," and typed at the bottom was "callmefred." The FBI profiler, at the time, was confident that the letter was not authentic. Unfortunately the analysis was wrong and 19 years later Ridgway discussed "his roadmap to his murders" letter during his confession. It was sent to throw off investigators and was the only written communication that he ever made during his nearly 21-year killing career. The letter made reference to necrophilia and fingernail clippings taken from some of his victims. Some of the letter was true, but the clues given were misread by authorities and media. Near the bottom of the letter is the line, "Oehatkindofmanisthis," or "What kind of man is this?"

Ridgway picked up many of his victims along Highway 99 south of Seattle. The Sea-Tac Strip, as it was known in the 1980s, was heavily trafficked by prostitutes. Ridgway said he strangled many of the women, mainly runaways and prostitutes, during sex, and that he left some bodies in "clusters." He noted that he quite enjoyed choking his victims and that killing prostitutes was a "career." He said he enjoyed driving by the sites afterward, thinking about what he had done. Sometimes he stopped to have sex with the bodies.

The following are excerpts of Ridgway's confession to authorities:

> I killed most of them in my house near Military Road, and I killed a lot of them in my truck, not far from where I picked them up ... I killed some of them outside. I remember leaving each woman's body in the place where she was found. ... In most cases when I killed these women I did not know their names. Most of the time I killed them the first time I met them and I do not have a good memory of their faces. I killed so many women I have a hard time keeping them straight.... I picked prostitutes as my victims because I hate most prostitutes and I did not want to pay them for sex. I also picked prostitutes as victims because they were easy to pick up without being noticed. I knew they would not be reported missing right away and might never be reported missing. I picked prostitutes because I thought I could kill as many of them as I wanted without getting caught.... I liked to drive by the [body] clusters around the county and think about the women I placed there. I usually used a landmark to remember a cluster and the women I placed there. Sometimes I killed and dumped a woman intending to start a new cluster and never returned because I thought I might get caught putting more women there....

Ridgway, in response to a detective asking him to rank himself on a scale of 1–5, with 5 "being the worst possible evil person that could have done this kind of thing," viewed himself as a 3 because, in his words, *"for one thing, ah, I killed 'em, I didn't torture 'em. They went fast."*

One interesting fact about Ridgway is that he became a prime suspect in the 1980s but still continued to murder over the next 15 years. He confessed to murders occurring in 1990 and 1998 but may have killed several others during that timeframe. In addition, he claimed responsibility for four sets of unidentified remains. Ridgway did not enter pleas to seven deaths previously attributed to the Green River Killer, though he remains a suspect in those deaths.

> is usually a compulsive act specifically for gratification based on fantasies. The key element is that the series of murders do not share in the events surrounding one another. Victims share in common characteristics of what are perceived to be prestigeless, powerless, and/or lower socioeconomic groups (that is, vagrants, prostitutes, migrant workers, homosexuals, missing children, and single and often elderly women). (p. 351)

But is this definition too restrictive? For those in law enforcement, serial killing generally means the sexual attack and murder of young women, men, and children by a male who follows a pattern, either physical or psychological. However, this definition fails to include many offenders and victims. Consider the BTK Strangler (BTK meaning bind, torture, and kill) serial killer of the mid-1970s who killed all of his victims in a 3.5-mile radius in Wichita, Kansas. He first killed a family and then went on to kill young women. This change in victim selection seems at odds with general characteristics of serial killers. The BTK Strangler resurfaced in 2004 and disclosed evidence that he had continued killing into the 1980s and beyond. Like the Zodiac Killer, the BTK enjoyed taunting police. The fact that Robert Beattie, a lawyer, was writing a book on the BTK Strangler when the killer suddenly resurfaced further supported the notion of this killer's need for recognition. Another example took place in 1988 in Sacramento, California, where several bodies of older or handicapped adults were exhumed from the backyard of a house where they were supposed to have been living. Investigators discovered that the victims had been killed for their social security checks. It was apparent that the killer had premeditated the murders, had selected the victims, and had killed at least six over a period of several months. Most law enforcement agencies would naturally classify this case as a serial killing—except for the fact that the killer was female. Because of rather narrow definitions of serial killing, females are generally not classified as serial killers even though they meet the requirements for such a label. One explanation may simply be that we rarely, if ever, hear of a female "Jack the Ripper." Women who kill serially generally use poisons to dispose of their victims and are not associated with the sexual attacks, tortures, and violence of their male counterparts (see Chapters 6 and 9).

Redefining Serial Murder

To include all types of serial killers, the definition of serial murder must clearly be as broad as possible. For instance, Hickey (1986), by simply including all offenders who through premeditation killed three or more victims over a period of days, weeks, months, or years, was able to identify several women as serial killers. However, there exists such confusion in defining serial killing that findings can also easily be distorted. In addition, current research presents some narrow operational definitions of serial murder without any documented assurances that the focus does not exclude pertinent data. To suggest, for example, that all victims of serial murder are strangers, that the killers operate primarily in pairs, or that they do not kill for financial gain is derived more from speculation than verifiable evidence, given the current state of serial-murder research.

In essence, *serial murderers* should include any offenders, male or female, who kill over time. Most researchers now agree that serial killers have a minimum of two victims (FBI, 2008). Usually there is a pattern in their killing that can be associated with the types of victims selected or the method or motives for the killing. This includes murderers who, on a repeated basis, kill within the confines of their own home, such as a woman who poisons several husbands, children, or elderly people in order to collect insurance. In addition, serial murderers include those men and women who operate within the confines of a city or a state or even travel through several states as they seek out victims. Consequently, some victims have a personal relationship with their killers and others do not, and some victims are killed for pleasure and some merely for gain. Of greatest importance from a research perspective is the linkage of common factors among the victims—for example, as Egger (1985) observed, the "victims' place or status within their immediate surroundings" (p. 3). Commonality among those murdered may include several factors, any of which can prove heuristic in better understanding victimization.

San Antonio Symposium

To that end the Federal Bureau of Investigation's Behavioral Analysis Unit at the National Center for the Analysis of Violent Crime hosted a symposium in San Antonio, Texas, in 2006 and invited 150 experts in the fields of psychiatry, forensic psychology, law, criminal investigation, and behavioral analysis. One of the general purposes of the symposium was to create a definition of serial murder that could be used by all people who investigate and research multiple homicides, specifically serial murder. Federal law passed by the United States Congress titled Protection of Children from Sexual Predator Act of 1998 (Title 18, United States Code, Chapter 51, and Section 1111) defines serial murder:

> *The term "serial killings" means a series of three or more killings not less than one of which was committed in the United States, having common characteristics such as to suggest a reasonable possibility that the crimes were committed by the same actor or actors.*

The definition was to establish criteria when the FBI could be involved in assisting local law enforcement agencies in their investigations of serial murder and was not intended to be a general definition for serial murder. Those attending the San Antonio symposium created a general definition of serial murder that would include specific factors including the requirements of one or more offenders, two or more murdered victims, the killings should be occurring in separate events at different times, and the time period between murders separates serial murder from mass murder. As a result the following definition for serial murder was crafted: ***the unlawful killing of two or more victims by the same offenders in separate events*** (FBI, 2008, p. 12).

This broad definition accomplishes two important tasks: It identifies the actual number of killings necessary to be considered as serial murder (two or more) and allows for a variety of persons who commit multiple homicides over time to be included. Indeed, this definition can include persons who kill for altruistic purposes such as gang or organized crime hit men, persons motivated primarily for financial gain, domestic terrorists, persons who illegally euthanize the elderly and dying, etc. The group noted the following categories as the primary motivations of serial killers:

- Anger: defenders are motivated by rage or hate toward society or subgroups within American society
- Criminal enterprise: offenders commit serial murder to gain status or other tangible or intangible rewards such as drugs and/or organized crime activities
- Financial gain: the primary focus of the offender is monetary gain from the killings. This often involves "black widow" killings, serial robbery homicides, and multiple homicides insurance or welfare fraud
- Ideology: serial murder to promote the goals and philosophies of specific individuals or groups including racial/ethnic attacks and murders of specific gender groups
- Power thrill: persons who commit serial murder for excitement and empowerment
- Sexual: persons who kill repeatedly for sexual purposes in attempts to gain physical sexual gratification and/or fulfill sexual fantasies
- Psychosis: persons with serious mental illness that may include visual or auditory hallucinations, delusions, and/or paranoia (p. 24)

These findings significantly expand the public perception that serial killers are synonymous with sexual predators and opens the door for researchers to explore other categories of persons who kill serially, including women who repeatedly kill their newborns, healthcare professionals who prey on patients, and serial arsonists who are willing to kill people for financial gain. Indeed, criminologist Gwenn Nettler noted that there are many roads, many whys, and many contingencies in understanding criminal behavior.

TYPOLOGIES OF SERIAL MURDER

Much of our information and misinformation about criminal offenders is based on taxonomies, or classification systems. Megargee and Bohn (1979) noted that researchers usually created typologies based on the criminal offense. This invariably became problematic because often the offense comprised one or more subgroups. Researchers then examined repetitive crime patterns, which in turn created new complexities and problems. Megargee and Bohn further noted that, depending on the authority one chooses to read, one will find between 2 and 11 different types of murderers (pp. 29–32).

Although serial murder is believed to represent a relatively small portion of all homicides in the United States, researchers are engaged in the task of classifying serial killers. Consequently, various typologies of serial killers and patterns of homicides have emerged. Not surprisingly, some of these typologies and patterns conflict with one another. Some are descriptions of causation, whereas others are diagnostic in nature. In addition, some researchers focus primarily on individual case studies of serial killers, whereas others create group taxonomies that accommodate several kinds of murderers.

Wille (1974) identified 10 different types of murderers covering a broad range of bio-socio-psychological categories: Depressive; Psychotic; Afflicted with organic brain disorder; Psychopathic; Passive aggressive; Alcoholic; Hysterical; Juvenile (a child is the killer); Mentally retarded; and Sex killers. Lee (1988) also created a variety of labels to differentiate killers according to motive, including Profit; Passion; Hatred; Power or Domination; Revenge; Opportunism; Fear; Contract killing; Desperation; Compassion; and Ritual killers.

Even before American society became aware, in the early 1980s, of serial murder as anything more than an anomaly, researchers had begun to classify multiple killers and assign particular characteristics and labels to them. Guttmacher (1973) described sadistic serial murderers as those who derive sexual gratification from killing and who often establish a pattern, such as the manner in which they kill or the types of victims they select, such as prostitutes, children, or the elderly. Motivated by fantasies, the offender appears to derive pleasure from dehumanizing his or her victims. Lunde (1976) recognized and noted distinctions between the mass killer and the serial killer, notably that the mass killer appears to suffer from psychosis and should be considered insane. In contrast, he found little evidence of mental illness among serial killers. Danto (1982) noted that most serial murderers might be described as obsessive-compulsive because they normally kill according to a particular style and pattern.

Researchers create profiles of the "typical" serial killer from the accumulating data on offenders and victims in the United States. The most stereotypic of all serial murderers are those who in some way are involved sexually with their victims. It is this type of killer who generates such public interest and alarm. Stories of young women being abducted, raped, tortured, and strangled appear more and more frequently in the newspapers.

Holmes and DeBurger (1988, pp. 55–60) have characterized four types of serial murderers and examined the motives reported to have influenced the offenders. The formation of these typologies is based on specific assumptions about the phenomenon of serial killers. These assumptions include the belief that such crimes are nearly always psychogenic, meaning that such behavior is usually stimulated not by insanity or economic circumstances but by "behavioral rewards and penalties." The "patterns of learning" are related to "significant others" who in some way reinforce homicidal behavior. A second assumption involves an "intrinsic locus of motives," whereby motives are explained as something only the offender can appreciate because they exist entirely in his or her own mind. Most "normal" people have great difficulty in fathoming why someone would want to kill other people. However, in the mind of the killer the motivations are often very meaningful. In a final assumption, Holmes and DeBurger explain that the reward for killing is generally psychological even though some killers may benefit materially from their crimes. According to these "core characteristics," Holmes and DeBurger (1988) identify the following four types of serial killers:

1. **Visionary Type**—such murderers kill in response to the commands of voices or visions usually emanating from the forces of good or evil. These offenders are often believed to be suffering from some form of psychosis.
2. **Mission-Oriented Type**—these offenders believe it is their mission in life to rid the community or society of certain groups of people. Some killers may target the elderly, whereas others may seek out prostitutes, children, or a particular racial/ethnic group.
3. **Hedonistic Type**—offenders in this category are usually stereotyped as "thrill seekers," those who derive some form of satisfaction from the murders. Holmes and DeBurger also identified subcategories in this typology, including those who kill for "creature comforts" or "pleasure of life." This would include individuals such as Dorothea Montalvo Puente of Sacramento, California, who was arrested in November 1988 for allegedly poisoning to death at least seven destitute elderly victims in order to cash their social security checks. Another subcategory Holmes and DeBurger refer to is "lust murderers," which includes offenders who become sexually involved with the victims and often perform postmortem mutilations.
4. **Power/Control-Oriented Type**—in this typology Holmes and DeBurger contend that the primary source of pleasure is not sexual, but the killer's ability to control and exert power over his helpless victim. Some offenders enjoy watching their victims cower, cringe, and beg for mercy. In one case an offender killed his young victims only after he had been able to break their will to survive. Once the victim had acquiesced, the offender would complete his task and slaughter him or her.

These general classifications of serial killers are useful in organizing existing data. Such motivational taxonomies help us to understand why certain offenders take the lives of their victims. Levin and Fox (1985) have also constructed types of serial murders including sexual or sadistic killings that appear to mirror Holmes and DeBurger's subcategory of "lust murders." Another typology similar to Holmes and DeBurger's hedonistic subtypes is described by Levin and Fox as murders of expediency or for profit (1985, pp. 99–105). Their third typology identifies "family slayings" as a major category of murder. This type does not appear to be particularly consistent with their prior two categories, which are constructed from motivational dynamics.

Although family killers could be motivated by sadism or expediency, with few exceptions they are generally blood related to their victims and kill them all in a relatively short period of time. However, the noting of this inconsistency should not be viewed as a criticism of Levin and Fox's work.*

---

*In the data set constructed by Levin and Fox, 33 cases are identified involving 42 offenders, including those who had been involved in simultaneous incidents of murder and cases of serial killing. Little differentiation is noted between simultaneous and serial murder.

PROFILE 1.8 Elias Abuelazam, the Serial Stabber, 2010

Elias Abuelazam, 34, a Christian Arab and naturalized U.S. citizen, was arrested while boarding an Israeli flight to Tel Aviv in Atlanta, Georgia. He was charged with 18 attacks on men in Ohio, Michigan, and Virginia. Fourteen of the attacks occurred in the Flint, Michigan, area. Five of the Michigan victims died from their stab wounds. Witnesses reported a man getting out of a van, walking up to men on the street, asking for help or directions, and then stabbing them before fleeing. Most of the victims were African American or had darker skin, but race has yet to be determined as a motive in this case. Abuelazam had been detained on two prior occasions for the stabbings but had been released as police determined that he was not their suspect. Since his arrest for the murders police have announced that Abuelazam also has a 2007 arrest warrant for a "family based assault."

Instead we are obliged to recognize the need for other typologies that may not be constructed solely on the basis of apparent motivations.

The FBI, through application of early profiling techniques, identified the characteristics of "organized" and "disorganized" murders (Ressler et al., 1988). Using information gathered at the scene of the crime and examining the nature of the crime itself, agents constructed profiles of the offenders, which in turn were categorized as "organized" or "disorganized." For example, an organized murderer is often profiled as having good intelligence and being socially competent, whereas the disorganized offender is viewed as being of average intelligence and socially immature. Similarly, some crime investigators often find that organized offenders plan their murders, target strangers, and demand victims to be submissive, whereas disorganized killers may know their victims, inflict sudden violence on them, and spontaneously carry out their killings (Ressler et al., 1988, pp. 121–123).

More specifically, organized killers profiled as lust murderers (an offender sexually involved with his victim) by the FBI possess many of the following personal characteristics:

1. Highly intelligent
2. High birth-order status
3. Masculine image
4. Charismatic
5. Socially capable
6. Sexually capable
7. Occupationally mobile
8. Lives with partner
9. Geographically mobile
10. Experienced harsh discipline
11. Controlled emotions during crime

12. High interest in media response to crime
13. Model inmate

The organized lust killer also exhibits fairly predictable behaviors after the crime, including a return to the crime scene, a need to volunteer information, enjoying being friendly with police, expecting to be interrogated by investigators, sometimes moving the victim's body to a new location, or exposing the body to draw attention to the crime.

The disorganized offender is characterized as follows:

1. Below-average intelligence
2. Low birth-order status
3. Socially immature
4. Seldom dates
5. High school dropout
6. Father often under- or unemployed
7. Lives alone
8. Has secret hiding places
9. Nocturnal
10. Lives/works near crime scene
11. Engages in unskilled work
12. Significant behavioral changes
13. Low interest in media attention
14. Limited alcohol consumption
15. High anxiety during crime

According to the FBI, the disorganized lust killer also exhibits a variety of predictable behaviors following a murder, including returning to the crime scene, possibly attending the funeral or burial of victim, keeping a diary, changing employment, becoming religious, experiencing changes in personality, and submitting personal advertisements in newspapers regarding his victims (FBI, 1985). Although such profiles were helpful in understanding offender behavior, the *organized-disorganized* dichotomy has proven to be a stepping-stone to more advanced profiling techniques as researchers delve inside the minds of serial murderers. To understand such offenders can help to curb their behavior both through efforts of law enforcement and most importantly by addressing the etiological roots of the crimes.

In the quest to comprehend why serial murderers treat the lives of others so callously, research usually focuses on the perceived overt motivations of the offenders. Did they kill for money? Thrills? Were they focusing on hatred, revenge, sexual pleasures, or other likely motivations? We erroneously assume that if we stare long and intently enough at a perceived motivation for homicidal behavior we will be able to comprehend the dynamics of its etiology. What we

A	Specific victims Specific methods	Variety of victims Specific methods	B
C	Specific victims Variety of methods	Variety of victims Variety of methods	D

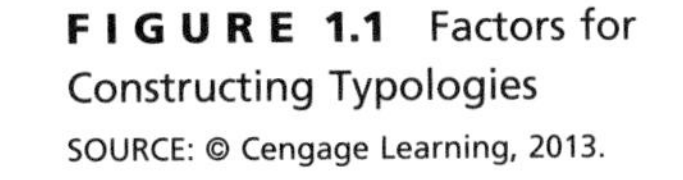

FIGURE 1.1 Factors for Constructing Typologies
SOURCE: © Cengage Learning, 2013.

must not forget is that the amount of research to date in the area of multiple homicide is limited. Recognizing this handicap, researchers, whether they are involved with the technical forensics of a case or responsible for classifying or typing offenders, must be willing to explore other factors that may contribute to motivations or to the construction of typologies. To say a serial killer murdered as a result of greed, hatred, or fantasy may easily obscure other important variables. For example, the types of victims or the methods used to kill may point to other reasons why the murders occurred.

Figure 1.1 illustrates just one of the many possible combinations of factors that may assist researchers in the construction of typologies. Because we have only begun to explore serial murder in an organized manner, we may find that matching variables may generate new ways of conceptualizing offenders' behavior or victimization patterns. In Figure 1.1, each cell refers to victims and methods of killing victims. Ted Bundy, for example, sought out young, attractive females whom he bludgeoned and tortured to death. He was particularly specific in both victim selection and method of killing. David Bullock of New York was suspected in 1982 of killing at least six victims, including a prostitute, his roommate, and several strangers, by shooting each one. In this case the killer sought out a variety of victims but used a specific method to kill them. In the case of Richard Cottingham, also known as "The Ripper," the killer hunted prostitutes in New Jersey and New York. Even though he went after specific targets, he varied his methods of killing. Finally, Herbert Mullin, of California, is believed to have killed 13 victims, including campers, hitchhikers, friends, and people in their homes, using a variety of methods. Why is it that some offenders have no specific victims as targets whereas others are extremely particular in whom they choose to murder? And why do some offenders always follow a ritualistic pattern of killing but others use different methods of killing their victims?

Some serial killers such as Ted Bundy always go hunting for their victims and, once they find a suitable person, kill and dispose of the body in remote areas. Conversely, some serial killers wait at home for their victims to walk into their traps, similar to the spider awaiting the fly. In some cases the victims are killed and buried on the offender's property. John Wayne Gacy is believed to have killed 33 young males, most of whom became buried trophies under the offender's home. In other cases offenders advertise in the newspapers for offers of employment, marriage, and so on, waiting for unsuspecting victims to ring their doorbell. Each of these modus operandi may be useful in generating particular typologies of serial killers.

Hickey (1986), in noting specific variations in the degree of mobility exercised by offenders, has delineated three distinct groups of offenders: (1) traveling serial killers, who often cover many thousands of miles each year, murdering victims in several states as they go; (2) local serial killers, who never leave the state in which they start killing in order to find additional victims (Wayne Williams, for example, operated in several different law enforcement jurisdictions in and around Atlanta, Georgia, but never had a need to move elsewhere); and (3) serial killers who never leave their homes or places of employment, whose victims already reside in the same physical structure or are lured each time to the same location. These "place-specific" killers include nurses (male and female), housewives, offenders who are self-employed, and other individuals or accomplices who prefer to stay at home rather than go out hunting for victims.

Each new typology raises the issues of motivation and etiology. We may find sometimes that typologies overlap one another or that one generates more explanations and understanding than do others. For the present, researchers continue to examine the phenomenon of serial killing from a multitude of perspectives. Different perspectives will continue to generate a variety of typologies and operational definitions of serial murder. Which typologies seem the most appropriate depends on who is applying them. What is important to remember is that the limited research done so far on serial murder leaves considerable room for new ideas.

METHODOLOGY USED IN THIS BOOK

The data for the present study were gathered through biographical case study analysis of serial murderers and their victims. Given the 200-plus-year time frame of this study and general limited accessibility of many offenders, the author interviewed several serial killers, reviewed cold case files, and completed close retrospective examinations of all serial murder cases. This form of analysis is commonly employed in examining the lives of serial killers. As Glaser and Strauss (1967) have convincingly argued, there are systematic methods in conducting qualitative research that may point toward theoretical explanations for social behavior. Their notion of "grounded" theory as a methodology includes what they refer to in their work as *constant comparisons*. By examining different groups or individuals experiencing the same process, we learn to identify structural uniformities. Grounded theory stresses a systematic, qualitative field method for research. The present study is based on cases of serial murder within the timeframe of 1800–2011. The cases were identified through as many avenues as possible, including interviews, newspapers, journals, bibliographies, biographies, computer searches of social science abstracts, and, of course, the data set from the first edition of this book, until the process became repetitive or redundant and new information ceased to be found.

Unfortunately, one can never be sure of the precise moment that data collection should be halted. Depending on one's range of definitions for serial murder, one technically could include in one's research killings committed by individuals who work as enforcers within the realm of organized crime, political and/or religious terrorists who kill repeatedly, and members of street gangs. One might also include those who repeatedly tamper with food and medicinal products, bringing death to persons who ingest them; those who practice euthanasia; or—based on a certain ideological perspective—those who carry out abortions in clinics. From a historical perspective one might also include the gunslingers of the Old West who frequently killed in order to promote themselves and their lifestyles.

Although each of these typologies and perspectives might be worth attention, this study excluded them from its overall operational definition of serial murder. Instead, only cases appearing in a text or a news report in which an offender had been charged with killing two or more individuals over a period of days, weeks, months, or years were included. In addition, patterns of conduct and victim-offender relationships were examined to determine offenders' motivations for homicide.

A few exceptional cases were also included in which offenders were reported to have killed only one victim but were suspect in other slayings or in which evidence indicated their intent to kill others. To justify inclusion, the homicides had to be deliberate, premeditated acts whereby the offender selected his or her own victims and acted under his or her own volition. Often a distinct pattern emerged in the method of killing or in the apparent motives for the murders. Usually the murders were to some degree motivated by sex, money, vengeance, hatred, or an unidentifiable impulse to kill. Each case was analyzed for specific data, including the timeframe and the geographic locations of the criminal behavior, the number of victims, the relationship of victim to offender, age and gender of particular victims, and the degree of victim facilitation (responsibility of the victim for his or her own death). Critics of this research point out the impossibility of identifying all serial murderers, thereby leaving open to question the accuracy of general profiles constructed in this study. Indeed, we can never know for sure the actual number of serial killers, but given their notoriety the chances of society not being alerted to them are few. In addition, each time this study is replicated with similar results more strength is added to the constructed profiles. As Dr. John R. Fuller, a noted criminologist, observes, one of the greatest strengths of this research is the cases themselves. Each case, properly investigated, can provide a treasure trove of information that helps researchers and investigators understand the minds and behaviors of serial killers.

This sixth edition of *Serial Murderers and Their Victims* provides more scientific analysis of offender behavior and updated coverage of serial-murder cases. Spanning the timeframe between 1800 and 2011, the data represent the approximate number of victims of over 100 female offenders and over 550 male offenders in the United States. These offenders total nearly 650 serial killers and represent over 500 cases (some cases were team killers and had more than one offender). They are responsible for a minimum range of 3,500 homicides to a maximum of 5,650 homicides. This victim range is specified because a few serial murderers killed so many people that only close approximations of the actual number can be ascertained. Difficulty occurs in accurately determining the number of victims of serial murderers, especially when one is dealing with a few offenders who have allegedly killed over a hundred people. Indeed, the majority of these particular cases occurred in the 19th century, when record keeping was not as accurate or efficient as it is today. Often data sources are not consistent in reporting figures for these "super" serial killers. In addition, some of the data on victims may have been exaggerated because of the sensational nature of the crimes. Consequently, the killers in these cases were excluded from our study, as were the killers in unsolved cases of homicide in which serial murder was suspected. Although the data do not represent an exhaustive study of serial murderers, they do form one of the largest and most varied assortments of multiple killers ever studied.

The sixth edition of this text offers much more insight into serial murder throughfrom greater exploration of the bifurcation of mass murderers and expanded classifications of murder in Chapter 1. Serial killer cult cases are examined in Chapter 2 and psychotic serial killers in Chapter 3, including two cases of persons deemed insane while they carried out their murders. In Chapter 4 we examine juvenile school shooters and serial killers who began their murders as teenagers. In Chapter 5 we explore the female sex offenders as predators, and pedophile priests/pastors. Chapter 6 introduces readers to serial killers who work in the health care industry as nurses, orderlies and doctors to and prey upon unsuspecting victims. Chapter 7 also examines highway predators who abduct victims in one state, kill them in another, and deposit their bodies along interstates. Chapter 8 examines serial killers who kill in teams of two or more and how they operate as teams to stalk and kill their victims. Updates on female serial killers are provided in Chapter 9 as well as updates of victimization in Chapter 10. Some new and fascinating cases of international multiple homicides including Anders B. Breivik of Norway, Col. Russell Williams of Canada and Muti murders in South Africa are found in Chapter 11. Finally current issues in profiling, a discussion of the gravity scale, ongoing investigations of cold case files, and an analysis of the frog boys case in South Korea complete the revision of the concluding Chapter 12. Several new cases have been selected for this new sixth edition involving sexual predators and paraphilia including The Banana Man. Also, new cases of serial murder have been included: Jerry Marcus, Anthony Sowell, Russell Williams, Elias Abuelazam (Profile 1.8), and Loren Herzog, and as well as new profiles of mass murderers: Marcus Wesson, Nidal Hasan, and Amy Bishop. More discussion again is presented exploring psychopathy and the *DSM* and the need for more research into neurobiology and its role in violent behavior.

A 2011 summary interview by your author with a recently discovered cold case serial killer, Larry Hall, is included in Chapter 12, as well as the cold case file of Joseph Naso, the Alphabet Killer is documented in Chapter 11. These additions will assist readers in understanding why serial sexual predators are victim selective and how some are able to kill for several years without detection. Updates of current literature and research have been added throughout the sixth edition. Finally, 2011 updates are provided for some tables, charts, and graphs.

In tandem with the increasing number of serial-murder typologies is the expanding literature that attempts to sort out and explain why such a phenomenon occurs with such regularity. The next three chapters examine a plethora of literature, including medical, biological, psychological, cultural, sociological, structural, philosophical, religious, and environmental perspectives.

Cultural Development of Monsters, Demons, and Evil

LEARNING OBJECTIVES

- To examine the historical connections of myth construction and murder
- To explore intersections between murder, cults, and evil
- To understand how culture contributes to the perpetuation of myths involving murderers and their victims
- To examine case studies of cult murder exemplifying evil

Saw films, *Scream, Halloween, Friday the 13th, Prom Night, Nightmare on Elm Street, The Ring*, and other "splatter" movies remind us that evil, dangerous beings reside in our communities. The notion of evil monsters, demons, ghouls, vampires, werewolves, and zombies roaming the Earth can be traced back to early civilizations. In the past, explanations for mass and serial murders were often derived from demonology or the belief that life events were controlled by external forces or spirits. The notion that life on Earth was primarily controlled by forces of good and evil has its origins in the belief in the existence of gods and devils.

In many past cultures—and in some modern ones—mental illness was generally viewed as a distinct form of possession, the controlling of a human by an evil spirit. The Gospel of St. Matthew in the Bible refers to two persons possessed with devils who were "exceedingly fierce," and when Christ bade them come out, they went immediately and entered the bodies of swine. In turn the "swine ran violently" to the sea and perished in the waters (Matthew 8:28–32). In the Gospel of St. Mark a similar experience occurs, except the man is described as a lunatic possessed with a devil. The devil, discovered to be many devils, was thus called Legion and consequently cast out into a herd of swine. In turn, the swine again "ran violently" into the sea and perished (Mark 5:1–14). In the modern-day world, David Richard Berkowitz, the "Son of Sam" or "44-Caliber Killer," who hunted 13 victims over a period of 13 months in

New York City, first claimed he did the killings because his neighbor's demonically possessed dogs commanded him to do so. Later he admitted he concocted the story to get back at his neighbor and his noisy dogs.

Historically, there seems to have been some confusion in distinguishing insane persons from those who were "possessed." Sometimes those who were mentally ill were identified as being possessed at least in the Middle East, and sometimes mentally ill or possessed people were revered as the oracles of a deity or a soothsayer. In other times and places, similarly afflicted people were stoned to death or subjected to trephining, an early form of treatment of illnesses whereby holes were drilled in the skull to allow the evil spirits to leave (Suinn, 1984, p. 32).

Some cultures also believed that a person could be "invaded" by more than one spirit at a time. In modern days we might call such a manifestation a case of multiple personalities, as described in Thigpen and Cleckley's *The Three Faces of Eve* (1957) and Flora Schreiber's *Sybil* (1973). The notion of multiple personalities has been sometimes used as a defense by serial killers. For example, Kenneth Bianchi, one of the "Hillside Stranglers" in California and also Washington, claimed that he was involved in killing 12 women because he was controlled by multiple personalities. Convincing for a while, Bianchi's defense finally came apart under close scrutiny by psychiatric experts.

People have also believed that evil spirits can inhabit the bodies of animals, causing them to act wildly. Just as many cultures have long entertained the notion that criminals can be possessed by demons, they have identified particular animals that are most likely to be possessed as well. In many legends and much folklore, wolves are singled out as being the most likely animal to have dealings with the devil. The natural enmity between wolf and man has existed for centuries, and consequently wolves have been hunted relentlessly. Given the belief that humans and animals can be demonically possessed, it is not surprising that the belief also exists that a possessed human could become a wolf. A person able to command such a metamorphosis became known as a werewolf (*were* was an Old English term for *man*). The belief in "lycanthropy," or the transformation of people into wolves, can be traced back to at least 600 B.C., when King Nebuchadnezzar believed he suffered from such an affliction. Jean Fernal (1497–1558) of France, a physician, believed lycanthropy to be a valid medical phenomenon. Many societies around the world have a term for "werewolf": France, *loup-garou*; Germany, *werwolf*; Portugal, *lob omen*; Italy, *lupo mannaro*. In Africa stories abound of "were-leopards" and "were-jackals," whereas "were-tigers" are common in India (Hill and Williams, 1967, p. 185).

To those living in the 16th and 17th centuries, witches were similar to werewolves in that one was able to experience the transformation only if a pact was made with the Prince of Darkness, or Satan. In the 16th century, Paracelsus wrote that violent, wicked men may have the opportunity to return after death as an animal, usually a wolf. The purpose of this human-to-wolf transformation was the inevitable killing of humans, particularly children, in order to eat their flesh. Recurrent throughout werewolf literature is the theme of anthropophagy, or the enjoyment of eating human flesh. Jean Grenier, a young 17th-century Frenchman, claimed to be a werewolf and confessed that he had devoured the flesh of many young girls. Another notorious werewolf was Germany's Peter Stubb, or Stump, of the 16th century. After completing a "pact" with the devil, he simply donned a wolfskin belt and was able to transform himself whenever he had the urge to kill. Naturally, he murdered those who offended him along with several women and girls, whom he raped and sexually tortured before cannibalizing. Stubbs, who fathered a child by his daughter and then ate his own son, managed to murder 13 young children and 2 expectant mothers by some of the most perverse and cruel methods imaginable (Hill and Williams, 1967, pp. 189–190).

Lycanthropy was also viewed as a form of madness in which a person believed himself or herself to be an animal, usually a wolf, and expressed a desire to eat raw meat, experienced a change in voice, and had a desire to run on all fours. To ensure the perpetuation of werewolf lore, stories of those possessed usually included reminders of how difficult it is to destroy such monsters. The werewolves were believed to be extraordinarily powerful creatures who could change back to human form at will or at the break of day. Belief in these terrifying creatures was often fueled by the occasional discovery of a mutilated corpse along a highway or brought in with the tide. Consider the story of the Sawney Beane family and how their behavior may have reinforced the belief in werewolves and other similar monsters.

> Born under the reign of James I of Scotland about 1600 A.D., in east Lothian near Edinburgh, Sawney Beane, described as idle and vicious, took up with a woman of equally disreputable character. They relocated to a large cave that was difficult to detect because the sea tide covered the entrance. Sawney and his wife took shelter in this cave and began robbing and murdering unsuspecting travelers. To avoid detection they murdered every person they robbed, and to satisfy their need for food they resorted to cannibalism. Each time they killed someone they carried him or her to their den, quartered the victim, and salted the limbs and dried them for later consumption. Each family member played a specific role in capturing and killing their victims. To ensure that no one escaped, precautions were taken to attack no more than six people on foot or two on horses. This arrangement lasted several years, during which time they sired 6 sons and 6 daughters, 18 grandsons and 14 granddaughters, most the offspring of incest.
>
> Frequently the Beane family would dispose of surplus legs and arms by throwing them into the sea. In due course many of these body parts were carried by the tides to other shores, where they were discovered by townspeople. Search parties failed to uncover any new information; they just cast suspicion on innocent travelers and innkeepers. Although dozens of persons were arrested, people continued to disappear regularly. Following several years of searching, soldiers finally discovered the cave, but they were not prepared for what they found inside. Aside from many boxes of jewels and other valuables, arms, legs, and

thighs of men, women, and children hung in rows while other body parts were soaking in pickling. The family was arrested and executed without trial, the men suffering death by extreme mutilation and the women burned at the stake (Kerman, 1962, pp. 11–15).

Vampires also took their place in the showcase of horror but not until they received the attention of writers in the 19th century. Bram Stoker's *Dracula* (1897) was modeled on the 15th-century Wallachian nobleman Vlad Tepes, also known as "Vlad the Impaler" and "Drakul" (Dragon). He was particularly known to be a vicious and depraved sadist who enjoyed torturing and murdering peasants who lived within his jurisdiction. Stories circulated about the secret horror chambers in the depths of his castle and how he was believed to be the devil or at least one of his emissaries (Hill and Williams, 1967, p. 195). Tales evolved suggesting that some vampires could also transform themselves into wolves. However, vampires usually had but one goal—to drink human blood—whereas werewolves mutilated and cannibalized. Vampires were also believed to be sexually involved with their victims, albeit discreetly, because of (for some people) the erotic nature of sucking human blood. In his book *Man into Wolf* (1951), Robert Eisler described a British "vampire" who in 1949 murdered nine victims and drank blood from each of them. By 1995, any erotic subtleties in vampirism had been replaced with direct expressions of sexual arousal, gratification, and their fusion with violence and death. In the 1994 film *Interview with a Vampire: The Vampire Chronicles*, vampires dine upon the blood of female victims, who experience orgasmic arousal and, immediately following, terror and death. Thus, the repeated implications of sexual mania in the role-creation of the vampire throughout history are clearly couched in paraphilia (see Chapter 5).

Werewolves and vampires are joined by a host of other sinister monsters all bent on the destruction of humankind, especially young women and children. Among them are zombies, or walking "corpses," and ghouls who reportedly feast on both live and dead bodies. The sexual connotation of these acts is pervasive. Some of the early European serial killers who were thought to have been vampires or other "creatures of the night" in reality were nothing more than depraved murderers. Following are brief descriptions of two such people:

Gilles de Rais, born in 1404, became heir to the greatest fortune in the whole of France. After fighting alongside Joan of Arc and being awarded the title Marshall of France, his beloved Joan of Arc was captured and put to death. Apparently he never recovered from the loss and soon lost his great wealth. Convinced that he needed to make a pact with the Devil himself in order to regain his fortunes, he murdered a young boy by slitting his throat, severing his wrist, cutting out his heart, and ripping out his eyes from their sockets. He then saved the boy's blood to write out his pact with the Devil. Having discovered his enjoyment for torturing and killing children, he began to recruit them in large numbers for his own murdering pleasure. Although documentation is not available, it is believed he killed several hundred children, drinking their blood and engaging in necrophilia. One of his many perverted pleasures was to have the heads of his child victims stuck on upright rods. De Rais would then have their hair curled by a professional beautician and have their lips and cheeks made up with rouge. A beauty contest was then held, and the "winner" was used for sexual purposes.

Countess Elizabeth Bathory of 15th-century Hungary became heavily involved in sorcery, witchcraft, and devil worship. Although she married and bore children, she maintained a predilection for young girls. With her husband off to the wars, she began to indulge herself in the torture and slaying of young girls and women. Stimulated by sado-eroticism, the countess bathed in the blood of her victims in order to maintain her fair complexion. She was believed to have been responsible for the deaths of more than a hundred victims.

Such people appear to be the forerunners of the modern serial killer. Their acts are no more disgusting or cruel than those of their 20th- and 21st-century counterparts. We have kept their legends alive by scapegoating the wolf and perpetuating the tales of vampires, witches, ghouls, and zombies.

A function of the early European church was to find ways to eradicate the problems attributed to witchcraft and sorcery. Under guidance from Pope Innocent VIII, two Dominicans, Heinrich Institor (Kramer) and Jakob Sprenger produced the first encyclopedia of demonology, the *Malleus Maleficarum (Witch's Hammer)*, in 1486. This compendium of mythology would be used for centuries to identify and destroy witches, wizards, and sorcerers. Thousands of people were "identified" through torturous means and then promptly burned at the stake (Marwick, 1970, pp. 369–377). The latent or unintended function of the great witch-hunt, or the Grand Inquisition, was the creation of a witch "craze" that cost many innocent lives. Sanctioned by government, the witch-hunt took on new meaning, and practically overnight witches were to be found everywhere. The efforts of the church and state probably did more to perpetuate the belief in sorcerers, werewolves, vampires, witches, and so on, than any other single force in society.

One more type of historical "monster" bears mentioning. In Jewish medieval legend a *golem* was a robot, or an artificial person (*golem* means a "clay figure supernaturally brought to life"). Golems were given "life" by means of a charm; occasionally they ran amok and had to be destroyed. Dr. Joshua Bierer (1976) uses the term *golem* to describe a case in which a man and his wife were having serious marital problems due primarily to his inability to develop any kind of meaningful relationship. His extramarital affairs were frequent, always in search of something he could not find. His mistresses did not sense that he was actually without love, commitment, or a desire for meaningful relationships. In reality he hated all women and wanted to kill them. To avoid this psychological truth he moved quickly from one affair to another. Dr. Bierer explained that this client had

had a difficult childhood during which his mother was incapable of showing him any affection. Both parents were absent for long periods of time, leaving him to the whims of a cruel nanny who apparently frequently forced him into emotionally stressful situations. Dr. Bierer concluded that everybody needs love, affection, and attention. Without these one can become emotionally truncated and run the risk of developing into a golem (pp. 197–199).

Although we cannot assume that people suffering from the "golem syndrome" will become murderers, the golem profile does appear to capture the essence of many serial killers. A person who can orchestrate the destruction of another human being and have no remorse, no feeling for his or her victim or external need to defend his or her actions, exemplifies the term *golem*.

For example, in one case during the late 1970s a young man was confined to a state mental hospital for the criminally insane. Alienated from others, he had dropped out of school but was still living with other students. His feelings of inferiority and fear of others fueled his journey into loneliness. Fantasy replaced reality, and soon he began indulging himself in morbid literature while his disdain intensified for those around him. He began reading a work by Dr. David Abrahamsen, *The Murdering Mind*, and quickly identified with the main character. He also began to fantasize about death and how it might feel to kill another person. One night after quarreling with a roommate over a box of detergent, this young man drifted into his fantasy world. He decided it was now time to realize his ultimate fantasy. He went to a closet and removed and loaded a shotgun and then went into his roommate's bedroom. He carefully placed the shotgun next to the head of his intended victim, and a moment later another roommate across the hall was jolted awake by the blast. The killer calmly propped the shotgun against the wall, called the police, and informed them that he had just killed his roommate and that he would be waiting for them to come and get him. People were appalled by his "coolness," his lack of remorse, his lack of feeling for what had taken place. He appeared to be devoid of emotions entirely. He was finally found guilty but mentally ill and confined to the state hospital.

Although the monsters we have discussed have their origins in demonology, witchcraft, belief in the supernatural, and folklore, modern "monsters," of course, are no longer attributed to transcendental sources. The mutilated corpses strewn in pieces along highways in California and the bodies left to rot in secluded wooded areas of Washington State or secreted under the floorboards of someone's home in Chicago are not the victims of fictional beings. Instead, they are the victims of the David Hills, the Ted Bundys, and the John Gacys of our society. Monsters in their own right, but the monster lives within and is unleashed only when the intended victim has entered his or her area of control. Are the men and women who commit such atrocities today possessed of the devil, or are they simply evil people, devils unto themselves who make their conscious choice for evil, just as others choose good? The answer may become difficult and complicated as we explore the possible explanations for serial murder.

CULTS AND THE OCCULT

Closely tied to the notions of evil and demonology are cult-related activities. In the United States it is not a crime to belong to a cult—the term means "a system of religious worship; devotion or homage to person or thing." Nor is it a crime to practice beliefs of the occult—things that are "kept secret, esoteric, mysterious, beyond the range of ordinary knowledge; involving the supernatural, mystical, magical" (Sykes, 1976, pp. 249, 755)—provided those practices occur within an accepted legal framework.

Satanic cults in the United States appear to have attracted a growing number of followers interested in the worship of Satan. The problem does not stem from the fact that people join satanic organizations but from the belief that such cults may indeed practice human sacrifices. Anton LaVey, a one-time rock musician and actor consultant for the movie *Rosemary's Baby*, founded the Church of Satan on the witches' feast day of Walpurgis Night (Walpurgisnacht), April 30, 1966, which reportedly has a membership of 20,000 (Holmes, 1990). LaVey wrote *The Complete Witch, The Satanic Rituals*, and *The Satanic Bible*. According to LaVey's bible (1969), members worship the trinity of the devil—Lucifer, Satan, and the Devil—including nine pronouncements of the devil that Satan represents:

1. indulgence, instead of abstinence,
2. vital existence, instead of spiritual pipe dreams,
3. undefiled wisdom instead of hypocritical self-deceit,
4. kindness to those who deserve it, instead of love wasted on ingrates,
5. vengeance, instead of turning the other cheek,
6. responsibility, instead of concern for the psychic vampires,
7. man as just another animal, sometimes better, more often worse, than those who walk on all fours, who because of his divine and intellectual development has become the most vicious of all,
8. all of the so-called sins, as they lead to physical, mental, or emotional gratification,
9. the best friend the church has ever had, as he has kept it in business all these years (LaVey, 1969, p. 25).

Holmes (1990), who interviewed two high priests and several coven members of satanic cults, noted that members are encouraged to fulfill their potential by advancing through different levels of "actualization" via magic, spells, rituals, and so on. They progress by holding membership in the Church of Satan and participating in traditional worship services similar to the rituals, hierarchy, and organization of other churches. They may then progress to other levels within the church. Members learn from their satanic bible various "invocations," including the Invocations Employed toward the Conjuration of Lust and Destruction. One chapter carries the title "On the Choice of a Human Sacrifice." Those who are proven devotees and have advanced in the levels of "personal affiliation" are invited to participate in human and animal sacrifices that include the use of various devices and rituals. It is important to understand that membership involvement in satanic churches depends on factors common to any church, including loyalty, knowledge, and understanding of doctrines and oaths and the degree of commitment to these covenants. Indeed, many satanic cults operate independently of the main church. For example, in 1971 the Satanic Orthodox Church of Nethilum Rite was established in Chicago in an occult bookshop. As a competitor to LaVey's church, members of the Chicago church believe in God as the creator of the universe and that Satan, as the holder of all knowledge, created God.

In the late 1980s a voodoo cult in Matamoros, Mexico, heavily involved in drug smuggling into the United States, was believed to have killed 15 to 20 victims, executing them with machetes, guns, and knives. The group had come to believe that through certain forms of witchcraft the drug smugglers could gain protection from police, bullets, and other threats to their drug trade. By cutting out and burning the brains of a victim and then mixing them with blood, herbs, rooster feet, goat heads, and turtles, the cult members believed they could operate with impunity (Associated Press, 1989).

Voodooism predates La Vey's Church of Satan by hundreds if not thousands of years and varies considerably in rituals, spells, and hoaxes. Rather than a formal organization, voodoo is the use of or belief in religious witchcraft. Persons trained in the practice of voodoo cast spells on or bewitch others as a means of protection, vengeance, and so forth. In this particular case the secret charms and hoaxes of voodoo were practiced to meet the "special" needs of the smugglers. The group, led by a "godfather" and a female witch, killed and mutilated for their own reasons, including greed and vengeance.

Indeed, serial killer cults have been documented in other countries in recent years. In 2010 a 22-year-old Kenyan male confessed to killing several women in order to belong to a cult. The killer admitted to shaving off each victim's hair as proof to the cult leader that he was carrying out his orders. The killings were not done for ransom or blood but always for the hair. The killer claimed that the cult had at least three branches that met regularly. Philip Onyancha, another Kenyan, confessed to killing between 17 and 19 victims, mostly female, and drinking their blood. He said that he too was part of a cult led by Elizabeth Wambui, and that his goal was to kill 100 people (see Muti Murder, Chapter 11). Saturn death cults (aka the infamous "Gods" industry), and vampire cults, all have links to satanic and/or cult murders. Of course, much of what is reported about such groups and their crimes is swirled in the minds of conspiracy theorists and sensationalists and has little to do with reality. Serial killers such as Henry Lee Lucas and his partner Otis Toole who claimed to be part of a national serial killer cult serve only to fuel vivid imaginations. Charles Manson and his family were viewed by some as a satanic cult, yet Manson claimed the murders carried out by his followers were to be the catalyst of a race war in the United States. In 2011 the West Memphis Three were released after serving 18 years in prison for the killing of three 8-year-old boys. At the time of the murders, one of the alleged killers claimed to be Wiccan, while the media portrayed him as a Satanist. Two of the boys had been drowned while the third had bled to death after his genitals had been mutilated and partially removed. Were the killers acting as a cult or Satanists?

Most serial murderers who are involved in cult-related homicides do not appear to be particularly advanced in Satan worship. Several appear to be self-styled Satanists who dabble in the occult, but the extent of their involvement is difficult to measure. Donald Harvey, believed to have methodically murdered 58 victims in at least three different hospitals, had books on Satan worship in his possession but refused to comment about the material. Richard Ramirez, the Night Stalker in California, ardently proclaimed his ties to Satanism by displaying his pentagram* tattooed on his left palm, shouting "hail Satan!" when leaving court, and listening incessantly to the AC/DC *Highway to Hell* album. Part of his ritualistic attacks included inscribing satanic symbols in the homes of victims. Henry Lucas, a serial killer who roamed the southern states and killed hitchhikers, confessed his involvement with Satan worship. Allegedly he and his partner Otis Toole were paid to kidnap children to be used for human sacrifices, prostitution, and black-market sales. The duo were believed to be members of the satanic group Hand of Death. Robin Gecht and three other young men terrorized Chicago in the early 1980s by abducting, mutilating, and killing several young women. In a form of Satan worship, they were believed to have cut up animal and human body parts for sacrifice on a makeshift altar and then to have cannibalized some of the remains. Robert Berdella of Kansas City publicly admitted in 1989 to the ritual tortures and homosexual murders of several young men but denied any connection to Satan worship even though evidence indicated otherwise.

Steve Daniels (1989), a specialist in ritual/cult groups, reasons that one can see that if a serial killer picks and chooses beliefs that fit his aberrant needs, mixes this with signs, symbols, and machinations of Satanism, conceives personal rituals and adds to all of this a liberal use of drugs, a frightening picture emerges: an evil, drug-lubricated butchering machine who justifies his behavior by exalting Satan.

Assessing the degree of influence of satanic worship among serial killers has begun to attract both law enforcement personnel and academic researchers. It is premature to state that serial killers in general have ties to satanic cults even though what the offenders *do* is satanic in nature. The fact remains that many serial killers have had no ties to Satan worship before or during their murder careers. In fact, less than 5% of serial murder cases are linked directly to satanic worship or cult-related activities. Perhaps offenders mention Satanism when they are captured simply to add to the already sensational nature of the homicides. Perhaps the police and the media overreact and refer to Satanism when they are confronted by the work of a serial killer. Perhaps there are certain types of serial killers who can be described as cult-driven, whereas others are influenced only superficially by Satanism. In the cases of those who do become involved in satanic worship and serial killing, we should determine which behavior started first. Does satanic worship stimulate individuals or groups of people to kill, or

---

*A five-pointed star formed by intersecting lines, used as a mystical symbol.

were they already murderers when they found Satanism to be attractive? For whatever reasons, it appears that reports of cult-related homicides continue to persist—which may provide researchers with useful research data.

RITUALISM, CULTS, AND CHILD VICTIMS

Considerable attention has been given to ritualistic crimes, including child abuse and murder. Conspiracies organized by groups of adults have been credited with using day-care centers as fronts for exploiting children. These allegations have included a litany of abuse and sexual exploitation. Finkelhor, in his book *Nursery Crimes* (1988), concluded that, although abuse does occur in daycare centers, he did not find any abnormally high rates of abuse. Instead, he pointed out that such abuse was much more likely to happen in the home, caused by parents and relatives. What this may suggest is that abuse is indeed a social concern but that it has not become as institutionalized as some people believe. Instead, abuse continues to be primarily a function of private, rather than collective, interests. However, only a few cases involving groups or organizations are needed to influence public perception because of the tremendous publicity, scandal, and arrests.

For example, in 1989, 16 Catholic priests, former priests, and other men in the Roman Catholic community in the province of Newfoundland, Canada, were charged with or convicted of sexual offenses against young boys. Because of priests' high community visibility, what started as a focus on one suspect quickly became a witch-hunt for anyone affiliated with the Catholic priesthood. In 1984, in the McMartin preschool case in Manhattan Beach, California, seven people were accused of the ritualistic torture of children. After the longest trial ever in the U.S. history, charges against most of the defendants were dropped because of insufficient evidence, and the key suspects were acquitted. Similar cases have surfaced in Bakersfield, California; Jordan, Minnesota; and Anneewakee in Douglasville, Georgia.

On April 11, 1989, a mass grave was unearthed near Matamoros, Mexico, just south of the Texas border. The grave contained 15 corpses, many of which appeared to have been ritualistically sacrificed. Cauldrons with animal remains mixed in a broth of human blood and boiled body parts were found not far from a bloodstained altar. Suspects arrested said the victims were "killed for protection." This group of drug smugglers was practicing a form of black magic in which sacrifices to the devil, both human and animal, were believed to provide protection from bullets and criminal prosecution (Fox and Levin, 1989, pp. 49–51). Kahaner, in his book *Cults That Kill* (1988), noted that Satanism and murder are increasing and that an epidemic of youth violence is sweeping the country. The Robin Gecht case supports this claim (see Profile 2.1).

Such cases continue to surface and ignite public outrage, especially those that center on families and children. Marron, in his book *Ritual Abuse* (1988), described the complexity of a case in which parents allegedly performed ritualistic tortures on their own children. By the time the courts, investigators, and

PROFILE 2.1 Robin Gecht, Edward Spreitzer, and Andrew and Thomas Kokoraleis, 1981–1982

Robin Gecht, 28, could be described as charismatic in his ability to draw others to him, especially those who were easily led. Raised on the north side of Chicago, he went to live with his grandparents after he allegedly molested his sister. He eventually became a carpenter-electrician in order to provide for himself, but his strongest skills were his abilities to manipulate and use others. Gecht also had a developing interest in Satanism, cults, and secret rituals. On one occasion he remarked to a friend that through his study of ancient torture practices, he discovered that some female victims were mutilated and their breasts removed to be used later as tobacco pouches. But Robin seemed to be a harmless individual, and no one suspected him, at least not those who knew him, to be involved with the wave of female abductions in the city.

Meanwhile Robin sought out those who might help him realize his sexual fantasies. He had already hired Ed Spreitzer to work for him and eventually met the Kokoraleis brothers, who joined his group. They were all young men: Andrew Kokoraleis, 19; Thomas Kokoraleis, 22; and Ed Spreitzer, 21. One investigator described the three as "classic followers" and "generic nobodies." Using a van belonging to Gecht, they roamed the city, usually at night, hunting for female victims.

Police confirmed eight murders carried out by the group, although some of the killers claimed between 10 and 12 victims, and others went as high as 17. The victims were raped, beaten, stabbed, or strangled to death and often sexually mutilated. Following Gecht's arrest for slashing an 18-year-old prostitute, police began to probe deeper into the assailants' backgrounds. They undoubtedly became more suspicious when they discovered that Gecht had worked for John Gacy, the killer of 33 males. Gecht had commented to a friend that Gacy's only mistake had been to bury the bodies under his house. In one place where Gecht had recently lived, police found crosses painted in red and black on the walls of the attic. Thomas Kokoraleis admitted that the room had contained an altar on which cult members dissected both animal and human parts as sacrifices.

As the probe continued, police found a common trait among the victims whose bodies had not completely decomposed. In each of the cases the victim's breasts had been mutilated and cut off with a knife or piano wire. At least one of the killers admitted that they had been told by their leader Gecht to "bring a breast back to the house." Apparently the trio wanted to do Gecht's bidding in order to please him. Once a victim had been found and killed, her breasts would be placed on the altar. Gecht would then read Bible passages while the group engaged in cannibalism.

After five years, the four were convicted of various offenses. Gecht, whom prosecutors described as being similar to Charles Manson, has yet to be convicted of any murders even though the others testified against him. Instead he received a 120-year sentence for the attack on the 18-year-old prostitute, on the evidence of one eyewitness. His lengthy sentence includes time for attempted murder, rape, deviant sexual assault, armed violence, aggravated kidnapping, and aggravated battery. Ed Spreitzer pleaded guilty to six murders and received a death sentence. Some of the victims included Lorraine Borowski, 21, a secretary; Rose Beck Davis, a housewife; Sandra Delaware; Linda Sutton, 28; Shui Mak, 30; and Rafail Tirads, 28, a male who was shot from a car. Andrew Kokoraleis also received a death sentence for his part in the murders. Thomas Kokoraleis had his murder conviction reversed on technical grounds, and after a second trial and a plea bargain he received a 70-year sentence. It is unlikely that the remains of all their victims will ever be recovered, because many of them were buried in forested areas (Baumann, 1987).

social service agencies had all been involved, affixing blame and determining culpability had become extremely difficult.

In attempting to sort out the connection, if any, between Satanism, cult activities, and serial murderers, investigators should recognize that many murders in general are carried out by non-strangers. Also, acts of Satanism or cult worship are much more likely to be self-styled than part of any organized effort. In one case, Robert Berdella, a serial killer involved in the murders of several young men, was accused of Satan worship. Indignant, Berdella requested an interview with the press and, although he admitted to the murders, he categorically denied any association with cultists, Satan worship, or occult activities (author's files). In only a few cases of team offenders who targeted children were there any hints of Satanism, rituals, or other cultlike activities.

The connection of satanic worship and child sacrifices never fails to generate near hysteria in a community. The reality, however, is that people are much more likely to be killed in a domestic argument, by an intoxicated driver, in an accident, or by disease than by Satan worshipers. The cases of those few who do fall prey to such bizarre practices generate such publicity that people believe the problem has suddenly become epidemic. To add to the confusion, some serial killers may give the appearance of killing children for cult-related purposes.

Such self-styled "Satanism," in which each offender adapts rituals to his or her own purposes, appears to be more common than organized satanic sacrifices. In a 1994 survey of 11,000 psychiatric and police workers across the United States, the National Center on Child Abuse and Neglect found more than 12,000 accusations of group cult sexual abuse using satanic ritual. Except for a few cases of solitary offenders adapting cult rituals, not one report could be substantiated. It is exactly these forms of disinformation that generate and perpetuate beliefs that satanic groups are preying on children ("Study Belies Reports," 1994). Recently, a few persons have claimed to have been ritualistically victimized or that they watched as members of satanic groups sacrificed children. Known as repressed memory syndrome, many adult patients under the care of psychotherapists have reported being victimized by cult groups or being part of a group that has victimized children or other adults. Very few of these cases have been verified.

THE NOTION OF EVIL

Levin and Fox (1985) refer to multiple murderers as evil people (p. 210). In the "hard sciences" such as chemistry and physics, exactness and quantification are necessary requirements; however, the notion of evil is intangible and unmeasurable, and it is often used as a misnomer for inappropriate behavior. In Western culture the closest we come to quantifying good or evil is by observing that someone is a really good person or a really bad person. We have a tendency to judge people in terms of their goodness or badness, but seldom do we refer to others as being evil. Instead, *evil* is a label we reserve for those worse than bad.

"Badness" we expect to find in many people, but evil relegates individuals to a special classification that suggests some form of satanic affiliation. Interestingly, both bad and evil persons may engage in similar types of undesirable behaviors yet be categorized with different labels. Part of the problem in assigning such labels is determining exactly what constitutes good or evil. Some people believe that gambling is "of the devil," whereas others see it more as a benign form of entertainment or recreation. The same can be said of drinking alcohol, committing fornication, or illegal use of drugs.

But homicide is another matter. Killing for recreation is not only unacceptable, it elicits some of our deepest anxieties about being alone and meeting strangers. We can understand to some degree the typical domestic homicide—a husband and wife, or other family members, find themselves in altercations that end in someone being killed. One can even understand why a person with a grudge may finally lash out at his or her tormentor or why a friend or a family member may kill an individual dying of an incurable disease to halt his or her suffering. We may not agree in any way with the act of killing—most people believe that killing another human being is wrong. We do, however, understand to some degree the reason for killing and are able to place such homicides in context with everyday life. We consider them to be domestic "crimes of passion" or situational killings that can be explained away as marital problems, family disputes, or acts of mercy. These types of crimes are illegal and wrong in the eyes of society. However, we know that most of these offenders will not kill again. They have freed themselves from their intimate entanglements and most then want, at some point, to get on with their lives. Domestic homicides, however, are in stark contrast to serial murder.

Multiple-homicide offenders, especially serial murderers, are incomprehensible to society. If someone has murdered children because he enjoys killing, that raises serious questions about the offender's rationality. Surely no one in his or her "right" mind could rape and murder a dozen children simply for recreation. We find it disgusting to imagine such crimes and disturbing to hear words such as "enjoyment" and "recreation" associated with the taking of human life. For many, *evil* then becomes the appropriate label for those who apparently enjoy controlling and destroying human life. What greater crime exists than to deny another person his or her free agency, the right of self-determination?

The quest for power and control over the lives of others is exemplified by the case of Josef Mengele (see Profile 2.2), a physician and geneticist recruited into the Nazi ranks to direct the processing of concentration camp prisoners at Birkenau and Auschwitz during World War II. While Hitler stepped up his campaign for his "Final Solution," Mengele also promoted his own bizarre agenda for thousands of camp victims. Posner and Ware (1986), in their book *Mengele*, examine the depths to which one person is willing and able to descend, once given unbridled control over the lives of others.

Mengele was an intelligent, articulate individual who appeared dedicated to his work. Married, with a family, he managed to compartmentalize his life in and out of the camps. Under the guise of science he masqueraded as a medical researcher, but his rationalizations could not hide the truth. But do all people

PROFILE 2.2 Josef Mengele, 1943–1945

One of Adolph Hitler's most insidious goals was his Final Solution: genocide, the killing of all Jews in Europe and inevitably throughout the world. Genocide involves people killing large numbers of victims while at the same time remaining emotionally detached from the operation. Special techniques were routinely used to neutralize any guilt associated with the wholesale slaughter of humans. Large rations of alcohol were distributed regularly to many of the executioners; they were also provided with better food and housing than their peers. To professionalize the killing, special terminology, such as *human material* and *subjects*, was used to identify intended victims.

Physicians usually supervised the incoming trains at the death camps such as Auschwitz and Treblinka. Their job was to identify which prisoners would or would not be immediately sent to the gas chambers. For some of the doctors this was a very stressful task that evoked severe anxiety. This was not true of Dr. Josef Mengele; indeed, he regularly volunteered for selection duty. At 32 Dr. Mengele was an aspiring geneticist who held a passion for fame and notoriety. Disturbed by the lack of warmth between him and his parents, Mengele was determined to raise himself up in their eyes through a successful career in medicine. He easily accepted the Nazi philosophy that it was possible through selection, refinement, and genetic engineering to create the ultimate "pure" race. At the camps he had an endless supply of human material on which to experiment. Those who were not deemed fit for experimentation were usually gassed and cremated shortly after their arrival, except those prisoners who were forced to labor.

Mengele set himself apart from the other physicians and soon became known as the most feared man in Auschwitz. His "experiments" turned out to be ruthless, diabolical acts of torture that nearly always ended in death. Unlike many who simply followed orders, Mengele undertook his work with a passion. Witnesses reported having seen tables and walls in his laboratory lined with pairs of eyes from his experiments on dozens of victims. His obsession was to conduct comparative research on children, especially twins. He was constantly in search of identical twins. He often performed surgery on the children without anesthetics. In one case he took two children, one of them a hunchback, and surgically sewed them back to back.

Mengele never tired of his work and killed hundreds of children simply to dissect them. In one instance he had a hunchback father and his 15-year-old son, who had a deformed foot, executed, then had all the flesh boiled off their frames. After bleaching their skeletons, Mengele displayed the victims' bones for his colleagues to see. He also ordered several adult female prisoners to be shot and their breasts and muscles from their thighs extracted to be used as "cultivating material" for future experiments. According to the West German indictment, Mengele was reported to have jumped on pregnant women's stomachs until the fetuses were expelled and even dissected a one-year-old child while it was still alive.

His indifference to suffering was immense. He was charged with having three hundred children, most under the age of five years, burned alive. Witnesses recount the night when several dump trucks arrived and parked near a large pit fire that had been started earlier by soldiers. One by one the trucks backed up and emptied their load of screaming children into the roaring fire. Some of the burning children managed to crawl up to the top of the inferno. Under the direct supervision of Mengele, soldiers with sticks pushed the little girls and boys back into the pit.

Mengele went to great lengths to care for children who developed various diseases. Once they were cured, he sent them to be gassed. His goal was not to relieve misery but to succeed at his task. One survivor reported how sometimes he would calm frightened children whom he had ordered killed by making their last walk into a game he called "on the way to the chimney."

have such propensities? What, if anything, keeps most of humanity from such diabolical practices? Martin Buber, a noted Jewish theologian, examined the myths and notions of evil and found that some people are in a process of moving toward evil whereas others have been consumed by it. This may be analogous to a continuum along which we are constantly moving toward increasing degrees of goodness or increasing degrees of badness or, ultimately, evil. Some religions, such as Christianity, refer to the temptations people must endure and overcome in order to achieve a state of goodness; those who succumb become slaves to their own vices and passions. The ultimate notion of evil may be defined by those individuals who appear to have progressed past worldly temptations and have become devils unto themselves, completely without guilt, remorse, or compassion for their victims.

Erich Fromm (1973) refers to human evil as a process that includes the principle of agency or choice.

> Our capacity to choose changes constantly with our practice of life. The longer we continue to make the wrong decisions, the more our heart hardens; the more often we make the right decision, the more our heart softens—or better perhaps, comes alive.... Each step in life which increases my self-confidence, my integrity, my courage, my conviction also increases my capacity to choose the desirable alternative, until eventually it becomes more difficult for me to choose the undesirable rather than the desirable action. On the other hand, each act of surrender and cowardice weakens me, opens the path for more acts of surrender, and eventually freedom is lost. Between the extreme when I can no longer do a wrong act and the extreme when I have lost my freedom to right action, there are innumerable degrees of freedom of choice. In the practice of life the degree of freedom to choose is different at any given moment. If the degree of freedom to choose the good is great, it needs less effort to choose the good. If it is small, it takes a great effort, help from others, and favorable circumstances (pp. 173–178).

Dr. M. Scott Peck (1983) refers to evil people as the "people of the lie": They are constantly engaged in self-deception and the deception of others. He goes on to say that "the lie is designed not so much to deceive others as to deceive themselves. They cannot or will not tolerate the pain of self-reproach. The decorum with which they lead their lives is maintained as a mirror in which they can see themselves reflected righteously" (Peck, pp. 66–75). Peck observed that although it might be difficult to define evil people by the illegality of their actions, we can define them by the "consistency of their sins" (p. 71).

The notion of evil may best be understood if one perceives evil to be both a characteristic of an individual and a behavior. Men and women who commit evil acts are often perceived to possess evil characteristics. Thus serial killers not only *do* evil, but they also possess various developmental characteristics that may contribute to the evil. This differentiation between behavior and characteristics may depend on the type of serial killer. For example, some serial murderers possess highly developed narcissistic, or self-centered, qualities.

Fromm (1973), discussing the pathology of narcissism, refers to people who exhibit "malignant narcissism." Many of these offenders display an unrelenting will to promote their own wants and needs over everyone else's. As Peck (1983) observes, "they are men and women of obviously strong will, determined to have their own way. There is remarkable power in the manner in which they attempt to control others" (p. 78). The epitome of narcissism may well be the total domination of others (see Profile 2.3).

A good case example involves an offender who is believed to have murdered 12 to 20 victims during a series of robberies on the West Coast. He usually stalked and attacked dark-haired, attractive women working in stores and other places of business. After robbing his victims he would bind them with tape and force them to engage in sexual acts. This entailed the victim assuming a kneeling position and being forced to perform fellatio on her attacker. During these encounters he held a gun to the victim's head. Sometimes he forced the woman to look him in the eyes until he climaxed, at which point he fired a bullet into her brain. Usually those whom he executed were victims who became hysterical, cried, and begged for mercy. Those who survived had complied with his demands but remained calm, some even joking with their assailant. The killer sought total domination and submission over his victims before pulling the trigger. The victim's death symbolized the attacker's signature on a completed act of total control over another human being.*

When Evil Embraces Good

The notion of evil becomes complicated by the generally accepted belief that those who commit sins can repent and virtually turn their lives around. The Christian Bible is replete with exhortations to repent. Whether or not we accept the Christian principle of repentance, the fact remains that people can and do stop committing sins and crimes. This "change of heart" may precipitate in some a desire to correct the wrong they have done and to become productive rather than destructive members of society. Prisons seem to breed religious conversions, which sometimes do appear to effect a change in attitude and behavior.

Is it possible for convicted and incarcerated serial killers to experience this "change of heart," experience remorse for their crimes, and never engage in them again? The scope of this research does not provide concrete answers to this question, but a few brief observations can be made.

Frequently in the processing of offenders a judge is influenced in sentencing by the display of remorse. The general public is incensed when a convicted criminal displays no remorse for his or her crimes. Many people do not or cannot fathom homicide beyond the realm of television and expect those who commit such crimes to have some degree of remorse. We tend to equate remorse with the recognition that a terrible wrong has been committed and that the offender, recognizing his or her wrong, feels sorrow.

---

*Identity unknown; killed 12–20 victims between September 1983 and May 1987. Offender believed to be black and to have enjoyed mutilating his young female victims.

PROFILE 2.3 Gerard Schaefer Jr., Evil for Evil's Sake, 1972–1973

Gerard Schaefer Jr. graduated from Florida Atlantic University in Boca Raton at 22 with a degree in geography. He worked as a security guard, fishing guide, and deputy sheriff. He was refused a position as a police officer because he failed the psychological examination but later became a police officer at a small police department until he was fired six months later for not having "common sense." A few days after being hired as a police officer he abducted two 18-year-old girls and took them, gagged and blindfolded, to a secluded area in the woods and told them he was about to hang them from the trees. The girls managed to escape and Schaefer was arrested and served six months in jail for assault. By then he had already disposed of two other teenage girls and two women in their 20s. In 1973 Schaefer was convicted of two murders and received two concurrent life sentences at Florida State Prison. Investigators linked him to 11 other murders of women and girls. He will be eligible for parole in 2016. The following is from one of several stories written by the killer and found in his trunk after his arrest for the murders:

> I walk into the bar and look around. There is something special that I am looking for, or should I say, someone special. A woman with that look about her, that look of wildness, uncaring, a willingness to do anything for a price, a whore or someone like one. I have to be sure she is the right one because one blunder could be the end for me. When I find the one that I am looking for, I have to be sure through conversation. I'll make sure that no one notices me and then I'll make my offer. And if she accepts she has signed her death warrant. Everything has been arranged long before in preparation of this event. I take her for a ride. I am cordial enough and make no threatening motions. I give her no reason to become alarmed. I drive out to the place that I am going to leave my car, a place I have left it many times before, so as not to draw suspicion.

Recognizing words such as *sorrow* and *remorse* as qualitative terms and difficult to quantify, we are faced with the task of determining sincerity. Many serial murderers, some who have killed dozens of victims and are now in prison, profess a sincere conversion and deep commitment to God and/or Christian principles.

In one case an offender killed at least 12 victims. Some of those murdered were children whom he tortured and sexually attacked for hours before finally taking their lives. He recalled during an interview that on one occasion a young woman he attacked died too quickly. He was outraged that she had not lived longer for him to torture. In his anger he hung her from a ceiling and for several minutes bludgeoned and kicked the corpse. Later that day he found another young woman, who died much more slowly. This killer is now a converted Christian who is confident that God has forgiven him for his crimes and that he eventually will be set free.

Another offender killed 11 children over a period of one and a half years in the early 1980s. Seven of the 11 boys and girls were raped or sodomized. Some he bludgeoned to death with a hammer, others he strangled or stabbed

I could be an ordinary traveler out of gas or taking a nap on the side of the road. Nobody would think differently, not even the police. That is important.

I pull over and casually say that we are here, and for her to get out. This is the place I seek. I have been there many times before, only those times it was in rehearsal and there was no victim, only the fantasy of it all. But I do know what will be done and how to do it step by step.

The woman is by this time very frightened. This is good because the more frightened she is, the greater the thrill for me. I tell her to strip, but I let her leave her underwear on. I tie her to a branch and gag her if she is too noisy while I go about the business at hand. I bring over the white sheet and pillowcase to go over her head. I explain that I am going to hang her and she might as well accept the fact and cooperate. The gun is persuasive and there is always hope, so she cooperates. The limbs are arranged perfectly for the deed, all the right height and distance apart. It has taken a long time to find the right tree and the right person, but I finally did it. I arrange the rope and noose and I dress the woman in a white shroud, place the pillowcase over her head, and then if I feel like it, sit down and entertain her with a bit of my conversation. Terrorize her. Give her my ideas on what she will look like while she is hanging there, fighting the rope that is slowly choking the life out of her. Make it as real as possible for her, so that she is petrified with fear. Make her know that she is going to die.

The noose is arranged so that she will strangle slowly. I will leave and then return so it will be unbelievable to myself that I did the deed. I will not be able to remember doing it. Funny isn't it? Then I will dispose of the body, and it will soon rot away in the tropical heat, with the help of the bugs and vermin, the rats and raccoons that abound here. This is what I intend to do, but I do not know why (King, 1996).

to death. Apprehended for only the last missing child, he made a deal with the authorities. In return for money he would be willing to take authorities to the gravesites of other missing children, but without the money there would be no bodies. The parents of the missing children in the area naturally wanted to know if it was their son or daughter killed by this mass murderer or whether their child was still alive somewhere. The authorities, without public knowledge, agreed to the exchange, and the killer began locating the dead children. Each time a body was recovered, $10,000 was placed in an account bearing the offender's wife's name. After 10 bodies had been exchanged, the offender terminated the deal. He now resides in an isolation unit in a maximum-security facility, and as a result of public outrage, his wife was forced to return the $100,000.

He states that he understands what he has done is wrong, meaning legally wrong, but now claims no remorse for his deeds. When asked about his victims, he responded, "I have put this whole matter behind me now. They are my brothers and sisters in Christ. All the children are with our Lord Jesus Christ now, and some day I shall be there with them." Claiming to have always been a Christian, the offender enrolled at a divinity college, where he pursued coursework in religious studies. He has written essays condemning abortion and capital punishment (a reversal of his previous stance) and supporting the power and importance of prayer. In 2008 while incarcerated in a maximum-security prison he managed to join MySpace, where he began making new outside contacts.

A third offender sodomized and murdered five young boys over the course of several months. Once caught and sentenced to die, he expressed great remorse for his actions. He desperately wanted the families of his victims to forgive him. He sought forgiveness from God. He wrote letters to the victims' families. He cried bitterly over his crimes and to prove his remorse he stopped his appeals process. He stated that he deserved to die for what he had done. However, he also stated that despite his deep remorse, he knew that if he was ever again returned to society that he would start killing again because he had been consumed by powerful urges to destroy children.

These are only three of many cases of serial killers who ardently embrace God. Whether the embracing of God and/or Christianity will inevitably lead to productive rather than destructive lives remains to be seen.

When Good Embraces Evil

The more perversely and obscenely some murderers tend to behave or are depicted by the media to have acted, the greater the interest by the general public. Most persons are simply fascinated and shocked with the innovative destructiveness of multiple murderers. Most serial killers, especially those males viewed as attractive and charming, quickly draw a following of women, mostly young. These women attend the trial, write letters, and send photographs of themselves hoping to receive some attention from the killer. Some wish to help the offender recover from his aberrant behavior or are simply interested in having contact with someone so dangerous, but from a safe distance. We have yet to adequately explore the impact of media and public attention on serial killers and future offenders. We do know serial murders elicit an immediate response from some people who otherwise would in all probability never have contact with the offender. The relationship between the public and the offender is shaped to some degree by the amount of publicity, the types of victims, and the personality of the offender.

Inevitably some people are drawn to the offender because they have a desire to befriend and understand the person. Almost every known serial killer, incarcerated or not, has a group of followers. They are, themselves, a most fascinating group of people. They come from a variety of backgrounds, but most are female. In one instance a woman met an offender after he had been convicted and sentenced to prison for killing children. She came to believe that it was God's will that she devote herself to the betterment of this man's life and has every intention of remaining faithful to him. She understands the nature and the extent of his crimes but is convinced that the offender is salvageable. After 15 years of devotion, she married the offender, who is never expected to be released. This type of involvement by a convicted killer with morally "straight" members of the community raises several questions. What influence, if any, do such offenders have over members of the community? What factors create attraction between someone who has ritualistically killed children and another person who abhors violence? Is there an attraction between people who strive to do good and those who commit acts of evil? It is easy to ascribe naiveté to those who align themselves with offenders, but we fall short in understanding the dynamics of such relationships.

Psychopathology and Biogenics of Serial Murderers

LEARNING OBJECTIVES

- To explore biological and genetic foundations of violent behavior
- To examine insanity and mental illness as they relate to violent behavior
- To understand the *Diagnostic and Statistical Manual* spectrum of personality disorders as they relate to violent behavior
- To debunk myths surrounding the label psychopath and evaluate psychopathy as a spectrum of development
- To be able to differentiate female and male psychopathy
- To know the Factors in the Hare PCL-R and be able to distinguish the tools from the deficits
- To examine cases of serial murder committed by legally insane psychotic offenders
- To examine cases of serial murder involving offenders with mental illness, personality disorders, and psychopathy

The early schools of thought addressing biogenic explanations for homicide included the notion of "inheritance," or the belief that criminality is an inherited trait. For example, early research by Goddard (1912) included the case study of the offspring of Martin Kallikak and Ada Jukes. Among 2,000 descendants, researchers identified 450 paupers, 258 criminals, 428 prostitutes, and a variety of other socially unacceptable types (Dugdale, 1910; Estabrook, 1916, pp. 60–61). Most researchers today discount the inheritance school of thought, because it is impossible to determine if the criminal behavior is a product of inherited or acquired traits. Clearly, the propensity for homicide cannot be explained away by simply knowing the identity of a killer's parents.

PSYCHOBIOLOGY AND BIOCHEMICAL THEORIES OF VIOLENT BEHAVIOR

The earliest biocriminologists studied the shape of the head and the body, including facial features and bumps on the skull. *Phrenologists* were believed at the time to be able to detect criminal predisposition by examining bumps and abnormalities on the surface of the skull. Cesare Lombroso (1835–1909), often referred to as the "father of criminology," studied physical characteristics of criminals. He believed that people born with traits that lead them to commit crimes have particular atavistic anomalies—that is, physical characteristics typical of distant ancestors. These anomalies, or crimogenic physical traits, were believed to be inherited from degenerate family types and sometimes tempered by environmental factors. Lombroso believed born criminals (those biologically predisposed) were cold and cruel, showed no remorse, retained no close friends, and were prone to sell out their accomplices. The notion of born criminals provided the impetus for the eugenics movement of the early 1930s. Based on the belief that many criminal traits and mental illnesses were inherited, 27 states allowed the forced sterilization of the "feeble-minded," chronic offenders, and the insane. However, the work of Lombroso and those supporting "body-build theories" has yet to be proven as valuable in understanding criminal behavior. What is important rests in more scientifically sound research.

Today, efforts are being made to study the naturally occurring "lumps" on heads, but from a different vantage point. Scientists are very concerned about the role of brain injury in subsequent violent behavior. Considering that abuse is a common theme in the childhoods of serial killers, we must also be concerned with those who received head trauma. Although head trauma may not directly cause violent behavior, the persistent correlation must not be ignored. Many soldiers returning from Iraq and Afghanistan have incurred serious head injuries resulting from IEDs (improvised explosive devices, also referred to as roadside bombs). Other soldiers have returned with serious emotional problems related to posttraumatic stress disorder. Rates of suicide among soldiers have increased significantly as well as occurrences of violent behavior including several homicides at Ft. Bragg, North Carolina. Soldiers who were having marital or financial problems prior to deployment may find on their return that such stressors are more than they can handle.

Modern research now supports a variety of biochemical factors involved in criminal behavior, such as allergies, environmental conditions, and diet. Meta-analysis of five studies found that elimination diets (consuming polyunsaturated fatty acids) notably reduced hyperactivity-related symptoms and decreased violence. Other studies report vitamin/mineral supplementation in reducing antisocial behavior (Benton, 2007, pp. 752–774). Psychotropic medications continue to be used to control certain violent individuals. Also, vitamin deficiency and use of vitamin supplements continue to receive attention as factors in violent, aggressive behavior, but because of limited testing and methodological problems in sampling, little credible evidence of the connection currently exists

(Gray, 1986). Hypoglycemia, a state of low blood sugar that affects the functioning of the brain, has been connected to antisocial behavior, including homicide and habitual violence (Hill and Sargent, 1943; Podolsky, 1964; Virkkunen, 1986). Other research has begun to focus on contaminants in our ecosystem—including metals such as copper and lead, food additives such as artificial dyes and colors, and radiation from artificial lighting, television sets, and computer screens—that may negatively influence behavior (Ott, 1984).

Considerable attention has also been given to chromosome studies attempting to link an abnormal number of Y chromosomes (XYY) in men to violent behavior, but findings always remain tenuous (Mednick and Volavka, 1980). Even as late as the 1960s, screening was being performed to identify babies with an extra Y chromosome because research had indicated that the condition was conducive to criminal behavior. Other research involving adopted twins has been more concrete, but much more evidence is needed to establish a relationship among heredity, environment, and criminality (Mednick, William, and Hutchings, 1983; Rowe, 1986). In reviewing biogenic literature we must proceed with extreme caution to avoid confusing factors that may correlate with violent behavior and those that address causality. The argument that biological factors determine aggressive behavior remains premature, with little substantiating data. When Charles Whitman fired on dozens of students from the bell tower at the University of Texas, speculation arose that his violent behavior may have occurred as a result of a brain tumor later discovered during his autopsy.

However, studies continue in the area of hormones and their relationship to violent behavior. Hormone research has ineffectively attempted to link the principal male sex hormone, testosterone, to aggressive and violent behavior (Rada, 1983; Rada, Laws, and Kellner, 1976; Rubin, 1987). Review of premenstrual syndrome (PMS) research by Horney (1978) found little support connecting increased amounts of estrogen and progesterone with aggressive behavior in females. Indeed, Johns Hopkins University provides sex offenders estrogen and progesterone therapy to lower their testosterone levels. Some states, such as Texas, Michigan, and California, are recommending the use of hormones to perform chemical castration on convicted rapists. The movement toward biological definitions for explaining violent behavior carries with it political, religious, and economic ramifications. In Indiana, a bill was introduced in the legislature in 1989 to allow sex offenders the opportunity to be surgically castrated in exchange for reduced time in prison. The bill was defeated.

By 1995 increasing focus came to bear on psychiatrists, neurologists, biochemists, and geneticists to identify criminality and to forge links between brain chemistry, hormones, heredity, physiology, and violent behavior. Biological factors do not appear to explain single-handedly criminal causation but increasingly provide greater insights. Hall et al. (2007) found that the brains of persons who are characterized as aggressive, prone to substance abuse, displaying disinhibited personality, or exhibiting antisocial behavior reveal a deficit in the process of identifying errors in behavior, which in turn signals the brain for more executive control. In physically aggressive males the sex hormone testosterone can be found in higher levels. Exactly how that makes someone more likely to be aggressive is unclear. Everyone with higher testosterone levels does not become violent, but those who do must also be studied for social risk factors such as child abuse, divorce, and drug abuse. Van Honk and Schutter (2007) found that by increasing testosterone levels, a person's predisposition to antisocial behavior is increased by reducing his or her sensitivity to conscious facial threats. Indeed, Klinesmith et al. (2006) found that handling a gun significantly increased testosterone and aggression levels in comparison to those who simply handled a toy. Other research has examined pulse, pupil dilation, vocal tension, and blood levels of norepinephrine, a neurotransmitter, and of cortisol, a stress-regulating hormone, and their relationship to temperament. Reiss and Roth (1993), in their research on inhibition, suggest that inhibited children are less prone to aggressiveness and violence, whereas uninhibited children are more prone to violence. Children who face acute peer rejection and alienation are far more likely to aggressively lash out than accepted youth. Indeed, the most aggressive children were those who had not only been rejected but also were found to have experienced the highest levels of alienation (Reijntjes et. al. 2010). Still, temperament must also be measured with other social and psychological factors in forging strong correlates to criminal behavior. Consider the case of Arthur Shawcross, a typical serial lust killer (see Profile 3.1). What links can be made, if any, between Shawcross's biological composition and his violent behavior?

The role of neurobiology in violent crime is of growing importance in understanding the dynamics of the interactions among the forces of biology, psychological factors, and our environment. Some of the most recent research centers on the role of serotonin, a chemical that inhibits the secretion of stomach acid and stimulates smooth muscle and acts as a neurotransmitter in brain functioning. Connections between serotonin and aggression in animals have been studied for several years. The effect of serotonin on the central nervous system may well assist in studying violent behavior. Serotonin binds itself to various neural receptors, which in turn affect brain functioning. Jeffery (1993) suggests that an increase in serotonin reduces the drive toward violent behavior. Increasing the level of serotonin may then reduce violent behavior. Volavka, Martell, and Convit (1991) suggest that serotonergic transmission may be impaired in some violent offenders, a defect that may serve to reduce impulse control. Virkkunen, Nuutila, Goodwin, and Linnoila (1987) and Linnoila et al. (1983) examined both Finnish homicide offenders and arsonists. The subjects were classified according to their impulsivity in committing the crime. Where there was little or no provocation, the victim was unknown to the offender, or the attack was not motivated by money or property, those who murdered were classified as impulsive. Conversely, the non-impulsive classification was given to offenders who attempted robbery, knew the victim, or otherwise premeditated the crime. The researchers found that the impulsive group reported lower levels of CSF 5-HIAA (5-hydroxyindoleacetic acid, a principal serotonin metabolite) than the non-impulsive group. Lower levels were also found in the recidivist group or those reporting a history of suicide attempts. Those who set fires were all considered to be impulsive and all had lower CSF 5-HIAA levels than either the violent offender or non-offender control groups. However, more research using larger

PROFILE 3.1 Arthur John Shawcross, 1972–1990

Arthur Shawcross, born in 1945 in Maine, was arrested in the state of New York, January 3, 1990, and confessed to the murders of 11 women. He eventually died in prison for those murders. Shawcross, like some other serial killers, felt a need to return to the crime scene to relive the killing moments. He had sexually assaulted and mutilated most of his victims. He had cannibalized some of his later victims; he had retrieved body parts of others as trophies of his fantasies. He returned to the crime scene of one victim three days after killing her in order to eviscerate and consume her genitals. He had already served nearly 15 years for raping and murdering an 8-year-old girl and confessed to sexually assaulting and murdering a 10-year-old boy. He blamed his compulsion to kill on childhood trauma and post-traumatic stress disorder from serving in the Vietnam War. Nothing in Shawcross's military papers indicates he did anything more than process papers in a support company office.

His physical conditions and childhood experiences, however, may well have predisposed Shawcross to kill. He possessed an extra male chromosome, sometimes found in persons inclined to violent behavior. His IQ tests indicate below-average intelligence. Shawcross also suffered from kryptopyrroluria, a disorder that allows high levels of bile or uric acid to accumulate in the bloodstream. The disorder can affect short-term memory, temperament, and tolerance for stress. The indications are that Shawcross had 10 times the normal bile/uric level. Shawcross also suffered head injuries both as a child and as an adult. As a child he was knocked unconscious when struck by a rock and again as an adult when he fell off a ladder and struck his head. As a child he was once diagnosed with inflammation of the brain.

Childhood events must also be considered in connection with his physical condition. Shawcross claimed he experienced a very unhappy life as a child. His dysfunctional family life included frequent parental conflicts, beatings, and sexual abuse. By age 11 he had his first homosexual experience as well as sexual relations with animals. His youth was marked by bouts of stealing, vandalism, assaults on peers, and enuresis (chronic bedwetting). He was given the moniker of "Oddie" by his peers because he had a difficult time fitting in anywhere.

pools of subjects with stricter methodologies will be needed to address the affects of serotonin. Also, serotonin can fluctuate within the brain, depending on location and time sequence. Administering Prozac, a serotonin booster and antidepressant to control mood and behavior, may be at the expense of ignoring environmental factors that can exacerbate already predisposing genetic influences (Gibbs, 1995, pp. 101–107).

Hans Eysenck (1977), from a biosocial perspective, argued that criminal behavior, including homicide, stems from both interactions of environmental conditions and inherited personality traits. In addition, he concluded that the combinations of interactions of biological, environmental, and personality factors determine different types of crimes. Unlike those who believe in the born criminal, who is genetically programmed for criminal activity, Eysenck

Arthur Shawcross's Victims

Date	Name	Age	Occupation	Method*	Sexual Abuse or Mutilation
Apr. 1972	Jack Blake	10	Student	Bludgeoned	Yes
Sep. 1972	Karen Hill	8	Student	Suffocated	Yes
Mar. 1988	Dorothy Blackburn	27	Prostitute	Strangled	Yes
Jul. 1989	Anna Steffen	27	Prostitute	Strangled	Probable
Jul. 1989	Dorothy Keeler	59	Bag lady	Unknown	Yes
Oct. 1989	Patricia Ives	25	Prostitute	Strangled	Probable
Oct. 1989	June Stott	30	Prostitute	Unknown	Yes
Nov. 1989	Frances Brown	22	Prostitute	Unknown	Probable
Nov. 1989	Maria Welch	22	Prostitute	Unknown	Probable
Nov. 1989	Elizabeth Gibson	?	Unknown	Strangled	Probable
Dec. 1989	Darlene Trippi	32	Prostitute	Unknown	Probable
Dec. 1989	June Cicero	34	Prostitute	Unknown	Yes
Dec. 1989	Felicia Stephens	19	Prostitute	Strangled	Probable

*Mode of death was difficult to determine in some cases as a result of decomposition. Shawcross's typical pattern as a serial murderer was death by strangulation/suffocation followed by postmortem mutilation. He seldom varied in his methods but did appear to be escalating in degree of mutilation.

His impulsiveness contributed to a series of failed relationships. He was constantly dissatisfied with his marriages and other relationships because his growing deviant sexual fantasies were demanding more and more of him. In tandem with his fantasies were his variety of property and violent crimes. As a young adult his frequent setting of fires eventually placed him in prison for five years, where he claimed to have been gang raped. By the time he was released and married again for the second time, Shawcross, now 27 years old, had murdered his first victim.

attributed criminality to persons born with nervous system characteristics that are distinct from "normal" people. In turn, these characteristics interfere with their ability to conform to the rules, values, and laws of society. He contends that most people are not criminals because as children they were classically conditioned to obey the rules and laws of society—much like the dogs in Pavlov's experiments. According to Eysenck, most people avoid antisocial behavior because they have been trained to recognize the negative consequences.

In addition, Eysenck (1977) believes that *extroverts* are more likely than *introverts*, because of the biological differences in their nervous systems, to be involved in antisocial behavior. Serial killers are often viewed as charismatic, thrill-seeking types of individuals (Ted Bundy, Randy Woodfield, Clifford

Olson), although cases exist in which serial murderers are found to be quiet, introverted types (Richard Angelo, Donald Harvey). Certainly, this is one perspective that has yet to receive much attention by researchers.

Occasionally, when examined, serial killers and other violent offenders display abnormalities in their genetic composition. Such findings should stimulate further research rather than hasty conclusions of causality. Certainly, biological research holds great merit, and, in future explanations for homicide, particularly multiple-homicide offenders, new findings may well prove fruitful. However, given the current state of biogenic research, it is unlikely that in the foreseeable future biological factors will be established as the sole link between humans and violent behavior.

INSANITY: PSYCHO-LEGAL ISSUES

As far as the criminal courts are concerned, *insanity is a legal term*, not a psychiatric distinction. Most people's immediate response on learning that someone has murdered several people is that he or she must be crazy. This is especially common when an individual enters a schoolyard, a shopping mall, or a restaurant and begins shooting randomly. Many such killers are found to have a history of mental problems, drug usage, and encounters with the law. For example, in Stockton, California, in January 1989, an intruder entered the Cleveland Elementary School yard and began firing rounds from a Russian-made AK-47 assault rifle. Five children were killed and at least 30 other children wounded, many seriously, from the 110 expended rounds. The attacker then fired a bullet into his own head, killing himself instantly. Police and psychologists who investigated the case believed that something "snapped" in him and he reacted violently. The man's history indicated a life of drug abuse, arrests, and isolation. In this particular case the attacker appeared unable to cope any longer with an intolerable existence. He could not accept the fact that others around him were becoming successful. The feelings of inadequacy, loss of self-esteem, perceived rejection by others, and failure to achieve can become too much for some individuals to bear. They finally respond by lashing back at society. In this case the killer may have been exacting the greatest possible revenge on society by killing children.

Confronted with such cases, we sometimes employ terms that may blur the distinction between legal and medical definitions of mental disorders. Souza (2002), in her study of psychopathology and mass murder, found that most mass murderers, unlike serial killers, have a history of mental illness. The most likely diagnoses of mass murderers prior to their killings were schizophrenia (paranoid type), bipolar, and/or severe depression. She found that although mass murderers will most likely have a history of both childhood trauma and violent behavior, most do not have any significant history of institutionalization. However, most mass murderers were found to have had several major life events that precipitated the murders (Souza, pp. 36–37). Once an offender is charged with multiple murders, the "not guilty by reason of insanity" defense (NGRI) may be used as the defense strategy.

The courts usually determine the state of mind of the accused before a trial commences. During the trial the courts must then determine if the offender was insane at the time of the crime and to what extent he or she is responsible for the crime. Thus the legal system uses the term *insanity* to define the state of mind of an offender *at the time of the offense;* offenders may be deemed insane at the moment of the crime and *only* for that period of time. Insanity pleas have been commonly used by offenders charged with serious crimes such as homicide, especially when the defense team sees little hope of acquitting their client by any other means. Most legal jurisdictions ensure that NGRI offenders are automatically placed in psychiatric facilities, regardless of their present state of mind. In *Jones v. United States* (1983) the Supreme Court ruled that insanity may continue after the criminal act, and therefore the offender could be placed in a psychiatric facility until such time when he or she is determined to have recovered from his or her afflictions. For some offenders confinement in a mental institution is tantamount to a life sentence because they must be clinically evaluated and deemed no longer to be a threat to society before they can be released.

Less than 1% of all criminal cases use the insanity defense, and most of those are unsuccessful. Those who do plead insanity generally are nonviolent offenders. Contrary to popular opinion, most serial killers do not use the insanity plea, although one might expect such a defense. Legal determination of insanity usually stems from specific tests for criminal responsibility. American courts usually apply rules patterned after British law. In the United States, courts generally follow the M'Naughten Rule, the Brawner Rule, or the Durham Rule.

The M'Naughten Rule

The M'Naughten Rule is often used to define insanity because of its simplicity:

> To establish a defense on the ground of insanity, it must be proved that at the time of the committing of the act the party accused was laboring under such a defect of reason from disease of the mind as not to know the nature and quality of the act he was doing; or, if he did know, that he did not know he was doing what was wrong. (M'Naughten, 1843, p. 718)

The M'Naughten Rule is used in about 16 states to determine if the offender was unable to distinguish between right and wrong as a result of mental disability. Critics of the rule feel it fails to include situations in which offenders can distinguish between right and wrong but are simply unable to control their behavior. Some states used to supplement the M'Naughten Rule with the Irresistible Impulse Test, which allows an insanity defense when it can be determined that the offender understands the difference between right and wrong yet succumbs to uncontrollable impulses (Kadish and Paulsen, 1981). The defense then had to prove only that the offender could not control himself or herself during commission of the crime.

The Brawner Rule

Today the Brawner Rule, or Substantial Capacity Test, is commonly used in the United States to test for insanity because it combines the intents of the M'Naughten Rule and the Irresistible Impulse Test. It states in part:

> A person is not responsible for criminal conduct if at the time of such conduct as a result of mental disease or defect he lacks substantial capacity either to appreciate the criminality (wrongfulness) of his conduct or to conform his conduct to the requirement of the law. (*United States v. Brawner*, 1972)

Under this test, or rule, the accused need only show a lack of substantial capacity instead of total impairment. This partial incapacity, however, excludes repeated criminal behavior, such as acts committed by sociopaths or acts determined to have been committed by people with antisocial personality disorders.

The Durham Rule

Finally, the Durham Rule, known also as the Products Test, held in *Durham v. United States* (1954) that "an accused is not criminally responsible if his unlawful act was the product of mental disease or defect." Controversy arose over establishing "mental disease" or "defect" and defining the term *product.* Essentially, in such cases the jury has no standards to follow but instead must rely heavily on psychiatrists' decisions about defendants' mental faculties. Consequently, nearly all states have discontinued use of the Durham Rule.

Incompetency

Another important issue from a legal perspective is that some defendants are incompetent to stand trial. This has nothing to do with the court's determination of criminal responsibility, because anyone determined to be incompetent does not stand trial and thus has not been found guilty of a crime. The defendant's state of mind at the time of the crime may differ greatly from his or her state of mind later in court. If a person is found incompetent, he or she is usually placed in a mental institution until such time as he or she is considered competent by medical experts, after which the person must stand trial. Few serial murderers are found to be incompetent.

In recent years considerable public pressure has swayed some states to change their use of the insanity defense. For example, Alaska, Delaware, Georgia, Illinois, Indiana, Michigan, and New Mexico have created a "guilty but insane" defense. Under this plea, offenders are confined to psychiatric facilities until their mental states improve. They are then transferred to prisons to finish out their sentences. Another reason for some states to revise their rules for determining insanity is the federal government's 1984 revision of the criminal code, which abolished the Irresistible Impulse Test.

Public pressure does affect the judicial system. The extremely high visibility of serial murderers, although they are relatively few in number, draws increasing attention to offenders who to some extent have "beaten the system"—for example, by going to a psychiatric institution instead of to prison. The public is becoming frustrated with lengthy appeals, insanity defenses, and competency hearings and is anxious to see the application of swift and certain punishment. However, in our haste for reform we must not remove adequate protection under the law for those who were legally insane when they committed the offense.

Mental Illnesses and Personality Disorders

We are inclined to believe that persons capable of random homicides must indeed be mentally ill or sick. In many cases the term *mental illness* is a misnomer and is better stated as *mental disorder.* The differentiation is more than semantic. Illness implies some form of degenerative state that may possibly be cured given the appropriate psychotropic medications, electroconvulsive therapy, or, in some cases, psychosurgery. Mental disorders, on the other hand, often are states of mind that are neither degenerative nor curable. Instead, they may remain constant or simply controlled by medication. Much of the treatment is directly related to the severity of the disorder. The *DSM-IV* (2000) provides descriptions of diagnostic categories to assist clinicians in diagnosing, treating, and studying mental disorders.

As a society, we have long harbored feelings of fear and loathing toward those who appear to be mentally unbalanced. Defining states of mind according to behavior, our society has long felt a need to protect itself from mentally deranged individuals by confining them in a variety of institutions. Those who were particularly violent found themselves in institutions for the criminally insane and referred to as homicidal maniacs, a label still used by the general public. The following discussion of mental disorders identifies the most relevant states of mind as we explore the thought processes and behaviors of violent offenders.

Psychosis Attaining a clinical consensus on an exact description of psychotic behavior is often difficult. Psychosis has generally been viewed as a severe form of mental disease in which the individual suffers from a severe break with reality and may exhibit dangerous behavior. However, movies such as *Halloween,* depicting escaped mental patients slaughtering unsuspecting victims, create an unwarranted distortion of people suffering from psychosis. According to the *DSM-IV* (2000), psychotic disorders include one or more of the following symptoms: delusions, hallucinations, disorganized speech, or grossly disorganized or catatonic behavior. Some psychotic episodes are brief whereas others may linger. They can be induced by physiological malfunctioning, environmental stressors, or substance abuse. Most of the psychotic patients this author has encountered generally were not violent. Those who became dangerously violent were usually at a much greater risk of hurting themselves than anyone else. In one instance a young woman who was believed to be in a psychotic state was admitted to a hospital. The day after her arrival she sat quietly by herself, staring off into space. Suddenly she jabbed an index finger in behind her right eyeball, partially tearing it from the eye socket. She proceeded to nearly sever two fingers with her teeth before attendants were able to stop her. The woman appeared to have

PROFILE 3.2 Joseph Kallinger, the Shoemaker, 1974–1976

Born Joseph Lee Brenner III in Philadelphia in 1935, his biological father abandoned the family less than two years later. His mother, not able to care for Joseph, placed him in foster care. At age four he was adopted by Stephen and Anna Kallinger. Stephen was a shoemaker who controlled his family with both physical and psychological violence. Joseph was locked in closets, deprived of food, isolated from other children, whipped with belts, forced to kneel on jagged rocks, burned with irons, and forced to eat feces and engage in self-harm. Anna did not protect Joseph and sometimes engaged in the abuse. Stephen owned a leather-cutting tool that he showed to Joseph and told him to be good or he would have to cut off his "birdie," referring to his penis. At age 6 Joseph suffered a hernia from the abuse and was hospitalized. Upon awakening from the surgery he was in much pain. His father explained that because he had been a bad boy they had to cut off his "birdie." When he was 9 he was raped by a group of neighborhood boys. By his teen years Joseph had become defiant and rebelled against both his parents and school teachers. Any aspirations of normalcy, including a desire to become a playwright, dissipated during his teen years. At 15 he was sexually involved with a girl whom he married despite protests from his parents. Although they had two children, his wife Hilda filed for divorce due to extreme physical and emotional abuse.

Joseph found himself hospitalized in a psychiatric facility for treatment. At age 23 and upon his release from the hospital he married his second wife, with whom he fathered five children. Like his adoptive father he became a shoemaker and during the next several years spiraled deeper and deeper into insanity. He attempted suicide, was hospitalized in psychiatric facilities several times, and on three occasions set his house on fire. His descent into insanity brought voices and hallucinations. One, he would later speak of, was Charlie, a head with many tentacles floating in the air telling him to do bad things. His family endured much abuse including many of the same psychological and physical abuses that he had experienced at the hands of his foster parents. In 1972 three of his children had Joseph arrested for child abuse. While incarcerated he was diagnosed as a paranoid schizophrenic, but his children

experienced no pain during the self-mutilation and probably would have chewed off all her fingers had there been no intervention.

In another case a female patient in moments of psychosis would seek out the edge of a door casing on which to split open her skull. The poor woman would thrust her forehead against the casing until the front of her head began to split open. In such a state she also appeared to have no feeling of pain.

It is exactly these types of images of mental disease that are held and perpetuated by our communities. It becomes easy to believe that "psychotic" people are prone to kill others. However, empirically based research literature discounts notions that psychotics are particularly dangerous people. Henn, Herjanic, and Vanderpearl (1976) examined the psychiatric assessments of nearly 2,000 persons arrested for homicide between 1964 and 1973 and noted that only 1% were considered to be psychotic. Similar results were also reported in other studies (Hafner and Boker, 1973; Zitrin, Hardesty, Burdock, and Drossman, 1975).

Until recently, persons determined to be psychotic were routinely transferred into institutions for the criminally insane without ever having committed a criminal act—even though, as mentioned earlier, psychotics are more likely to recanted their accusations of abuse and Joseph was allowed to return home. The voice of Charlie grew louder and demanded that he kill millions of people and cut up their genitals. He began taking Michael, 13, and Joseph Jr., 11, into underground sewers and other dark places, where he began his plans to carry out Charlie's demands. Michael was to become his assistant, and Joseph Jr. would be the first to die. Killing Joseph while Michael was present bonded them to carry out more required murders. Joseph and Michael abducted an 8-year-old boy and took him to an abandoned building where the father cut off the boy's penis with the leather-cutting tool that had belonged to his father. The boy died from his injuries. In 1974 the father and son, pretending to be salesmen, rode buses and trains into several towns in Pennsylvania, Maryland, and New Jersey and randomly assaulted and sexually abused four families, killing three victims. In 1975 they entered a home in Pennsylvania, tied up three residents, and as more arrived also bound them with cords. The last person to be bound, thinking that this was about robbery, rebuked Joseph for his behavior. He responded by cutting her throat and killing her.

Joseph and Michael were eventually arrested for this home invasion and murder and later charged with the other murders as well. Joseph pleaded insanity but was deemed sane and sent to prison, where he attempted suicide several times including by setting himself on fire. He was sent to a psychiatric hospital in Trenton, New Jersey, in 1979, where he remained until his death in 1996 from an epileptic seizure. Michael was incarcerated until he was 21 then released because he was deemed to have been under his father's control at the time of the crimes. During an interview he gave while at the hospital, Joseph was asked if he still had a desire to kill people and mutilate their genitals. He responded by saying that yes, he did still have those thoughts, and that he would do it again but for the fact that they (staff) were always watching him. Indeed, the last 11 years of his life he was on suicide watch. (For more insights to Joseph Kallinger's life and crimes, read *The Shoemaker: The Anatomy of a Psychotic* by Flora R. Schreiber, also author of *Sybil*).

hurt themselves than others. Psychotics are perceived by the public as dangerous to others. By contrast, people who are called "criminally insane" often display few, if any, overt signs of mental illness. "Criminal insanity" is more of a contradiction in terms, an oxymoron of sorts. Most people who commit crimes are sane, whereas those who truly are insane commit few crimes. Serial killers are rarely found to be suffering from psychotic states. Joseph Kallinger, who now resides in a psychiatric institution, is clearly psychotic (see Profile 3.2).

Suffering from delusions and hallucinations, Kallinger managed to murder his own son and others in his community. He claims that a large, floating head with tentacles, which he refers to as "Charlie," instructed him to kill millions of people and cut up their genitals. The fact that he began carrying out those orders prior to his incarceration and still has strong urges to kill again will likely require his permanent hospitalization. The U.S. Supreme Court ruled in *Vitek v. Jones* (1980) that administrative hearings are mandatory prior to transferring psychotic individuals to institutions for the criminally insane (see Profile 3.3). Given the deplorable and limited facilities for the severely mentally disordered, it is unlikely that this ruling will significantly alter the flow of psychotic patients to such institutions.

PROFILE 3.3 Edward Theodore "Ed" Gein, American Psycho

No American serial killer has inspired more fictional murder movie characters than Ed Gein, including insane killers in *Psycho, The Texas Chainsaw Massacre*, and *Silence of the Lambs.* Ed Gein, born in Wisconsin, 1906, had one older brother, Henry George Gein. They were raised by a very religiously strict mother, Augusta, who read to them daily from the Bible, extolling the wages of sin such as drinking alcohol and immorality. She taught her boys that women, herself included, were nothing more than prostitutes and instruments of the devil. Augusta, a devoted Christian, was very unhappily married to George, a tanner and carpenter by trade but a chronic alcoholic. Unwilling to deter from her biblical teachings that condemned divorce, Augusta resigned herself to staying in the marriage and keeping her boys under her control. She feared that her boys would grow up to be like their father for whom she bore no respect. She eventually opened a small store and purchased a farm outside Plainsfield, Wisconsin. Augusta worried about outside influences on her children and rigidly monitored her two boys' activities. Life for Ed was either attending school or being at home, tending to the farm. Socially awkward, reclusive, and effeminate, Ed was forbidden by his mother to have friends or to socialize after school and was punished for any infractions. While Ed loved his mother, he was keenly aware that he often displeased her. Ed, confused with his own sexuality, desired to have a sex change operation and become a woman. He even tried more than once to castrate himself.

Within the next five years Ed would find himself completely alone. His father died in 1940 when Ed was 34 years old, and from that point on the two brothers worked as handymen to support their mother and the farm. However, Henry George became increasing unhappy with his mother's extreme views and often complained to Ed about her. He also noticed that Ed seemed to have an unusual sense of attachment to his mother. In 1944, under very suspicious circumstances, Henry was killed in a grass fire that he and Ed were containing while they burned off some of their marshland. Although he died of asphyxiation, George also had several bruises on his forehead. Accepting Ed's story, no charges were filed and the case was ruled an accident. A year later his mother died after suffering a stroke, leaving Ed at 39 to live alone. Ed was devastated by her death. He closed off most of the house and boarded up his mother's room.

During the early 1950s Ed, by his own account, made dozens of visits to three local graveyards and exhumed at least 10 graves of women, including his own mother. He began collecting body parts and fashioning them into household items such as bowls from skulls and lampshades and dresses from skin that he had tanned. From the corpses he made keepsakes such as a "nipple belt," a "mammary vest," suits, and masks, and sometimes wore these items while dancing in his yard under a full moon. Beginning in 1954 and ending in 1957, Ed progressed from mere grave robbing to killing female store owners and bringing them home for dissection. Ed would later be linked to several other murders of missing persons. His last victim was found decapitated, hanging upside down in Ed's barn, nearly split in half, her entrails and other organs removed. In his home investigators found several skulls, organs in the refrigerator, several masks, seat covers and a lampshade fashioned from human skin, human heads including a couple on bed posts, noses, vulvas, bones, and a pair of lips on a window shade drawstring.

Ed confessed to the murders, but denied ever being sexually involved with the corpses. He was found to be incompetent to stand trial and sent to a mental institution. In 1968 he was tried again and convicted but found to be legally insane. Ed was returned to a psychiatric hospital where he spent the rest of his life as a compliant patient. He died in 1984.

Neurosis *Neurotic* behavior generally has been defined as a variety of forms of mental disorders of less violent nature than occur in cases of psychotic behavior. As with psychosis, the term *neurosis* has remained vague and nebulous, including persons afflicted with high anxieties and compulsive and obsessive behaviors, to name but a few disorders.

The latest revision of the *DSM* has provided much clarification and reordering of the categories of disorders. For example, anxiety disorders include panic attacks, agoraphobia (fear of being in a crowd, being outside the home alone, or traveling on public transportation), obsessive-compulsive disorders, posttraumatic stress disorder, acute stress, and substance-abuse disorders.

Research efforts have failed to substantiate claims that what was formerly referred to as neurotic behavior is common among criminals. Brodsky (1973), in his review of nine studies of prisoner populations, found only 1% to 2% psychotic types and only 4% to 6% neurotic types among the inmates. Monahan and Steadman (1984), in their exhaustive review on the relationship between mental disorder and crime, found little evidence that the mentally disordered are more inclined to criminal activity than anyone else. By contrast, many inmates are diagnosed as having a variety of personality disorders. Currently some research points toward offenders reporting dissociative disorders and their influence on criminal behavior.

Dissociative Disorders

Researchers have recently begun to explore dissociative disorders and their relationships to serial killers. Such disorders include abrupt, temporary changes in consciousness, identity, and motor activity. Gallagher (1987) identifies different forms of dissociation, including dissociative identity disorder, formerly known as multiple personality disorder, the most widely known dissociative disorder. He noted that only a few hundred cases have been reported, and by 1978 approximately 100 cases were being treated in the United States (Gallagher, pp. 117–119). By 1996, dissociative identity disorder had become more common as a diagnosis but continues to be a rare disorder.

Dissociative Identity Disorder The 2000 *DSM-IV* defines dissociative identity disorder (DID) as "the presence of two or more distinct identities or personality states" (APA, 2000, p. 526). More commonly known as multiple personality disorder (MPD) and sometimes referred to as the "UFO of psychiatry" because of the debate as to its actual existence, little evidence has been produced to support multiple personalities as a true disorder (Ondrovik and Hamilton, 1991). Some argue that in most cases the disorder is actually *iatrogenic*, meaning that practitioners and clinicians are responsible for its occurrence.

In effect, we find what we want to find. Multiple symptoms can easily be interpreted as more than one disorder as well as the result of the power of suggestion to patients during hypnosis (Orne, Dinges, and Orne, 1984). Hale (1983) found fewer than 300 documented cases of multiple personality, whereas Sizemore (1982), herself a case of multiple personality, believes there are no more than 100 to 200 cases of true multiple personalities. However, by 1989 the number of cases of dissociative identity rose from 300 to over 6,000 primarily as a result of the APA officially classifying "multiple personality" as a disorder. To date the disorder has yet to have much impact as a defense in criminal trials (Slovenko, 1989).

Prince (1908) documented the classical case of Christine Beauchamp, a Radcliffe student who appeared to have three distinct personalities. Thigpen and Cleckley (1957), in their book *Three Faces of Eve*, observed that their patient Eve White experienced at least 22 completely different personalities. Chris Sizemore, who eventually revealed herself publicly as Eve, is not sure of the origins of her personalities but observed that "it was a defense and a unique coping mechanism which created satellite persons to cope with conflicts that were unbearable" (Suinn, 1984, p. 180).

Having more than one personality may be an attempt to suppress or deny severe traumatizations as a child. Gallagher (1987) describes the highly acclaimed multiple personality case of Sybil, who was initially believed to be controlled by three personalities—thirteen others became manifest during treatment. Sybil appeared to have begun developing these personalities at age three and a half. An only child born to a mother determined by psychiatrists to be paranoid schizophrenic, Sybil was forced to watch her parents engage in sexual activities and became the target of her mother's bizarre fantasies. Each morning Sybil was strapped to the kitchen table and, following a prescribed ritual, objects including knife handles, flashlights, a buttonhook, and bottles were inserted into her vagina. Frequently her mother administered enemas and forced Sybil to retain the contents while the mother played melodies on the piano. If the child soiled herself, she immediately received a vicious beating. There were times when Sybil was burned, had bones broken, was locked in trunks and other confined spaces, and hung upside down.

Sybil's psychoanalyst would later explain that Sybil's personality had split or divided into several selves as a mode of self-preservation from the nightmares to which she was subjected. The "new" personalities denied the existence of Sybil's mother as their mother, thus allowing Sybil to cope with the immeasurable amount of stress and pain placed on her (Schreibner, 1973, pp. 118–199). Schreiber suggested that Sybil was traumatized by her mother's attitude toward being a woman. When Sybil first menstruated, her mother jabbed her in the abdomen and remarked, "It's simply awful. The curse of women. It hurts you here, doesn't it" (p. 118).

Multiple personality as a dissociative disorder may be one way in which some people avoid or escape stressful or painful experiences. Much more common among females, those with dissociative identity are particularly impressionable, highly suggestible, and can be readily hypnotized. One plausible explanation for dissociative identity is that we all possess sub-personalities that reflect our moods and attitudes. Thus, a change in personality is little more than a shift in moods (Bartol, 1995, p. 167). Wilbur (1978), in her studies of multiple personality disorder, argues that all personalities diagnosed as dissociative had been battered as children. Stress that fuels anxieties may trigger a dissociative response to adapt to intolerable situations. Without such a defense mechanism the individual may be subject to a psychotic break with reality that inevitably could become self-destructive.

Using dissociative identity disorder (multiple personality disorder) to explain serial-murder behavior is a rare but usually highly publicized event. In the case of the Hillside Strangler, one of the killers, Kenneth Bianchi, while under hypnosis, suddenly revealed another personality whom he called Steve Walker. Initially, the explanation of MPD was eagerly embraced by many observers. Although on the one hand there was Ken, the kind, loving father and responsible individual, on the other hand there was Steve, the other personality, the cold, vicious killer. Psychiatrists postulated that Ken had deeply resented his mother and had repressed these feelings only to have them surface in the form of Steve Walker. Dr. Ralph Allison, an expert on multiple personalities, interviewed "Steve Walker" under hypnosis.

> "I fuckin' killed those broads ... those two fuckin' cunts, that blond haired cunt and the brunette cunt...."
>
> "Why?"
>
> "'Cause I hate fuckin' cunts." (Schwarz, 1981)

Bianchi explained to Allison during the hypnosis that he had met Steve while being abused by his mother. Allison recommended to the court that Bianchi was incompetent to stand trial as a result of his dual personality. Dr. Martin Orne of the Department of Psychiatry of the University of Pennsylvania Medical School was brought in to examine Bianchi to see if perhaps he could be faking the multiple personalities. Just before placing Bianchi under hypnosis, Orne mentioned to him that it was rare to find a case of MPD with only two personalities. Within moments after being hypnotized, "Billy" emerged as a third personality. Several people questioned Bianchi's disorder, including the police and the detectives involved in the case. Further investigation uncovered an academic transcript from Los Angeles Valley College that Bianchi had stolen from another student and then altered. The original owner of the transcript was Thomas Steven Walker. Bianchi, always the manipulator, had successfully deceived at least two experts. Before his capture he had easily conned a North Hollywood psychologist into allowing him to use some of his office space while he launched his counseling practice. Producing a phony master's degree in psychology from Columbia University, he deftly talked his way into a professional career, albeit short-lived. Bianchi, now under attack for faking MPD, dropped his plea of insanity and admitted guilt for the murders of several young women.

There do not appear to be any well-documented cases of MPD in serial killing. Even in single homicides, MPD is more likely to be used as a decoy defense than to be valid. Coons (1988), in his review of eight one-time murderers who used MPD as an insanity defense, noted that five were found guilty, one not guilty by reason of insanity (NGRI), and two people's guilt was never mentioned. In none of these cases in which MPD was claimed was the defendant ever described properly enough to substantiate an unequivocal diagnosis of MPD.

Dissociative Amnesia Although MPD has yet to be empirically proved in cases of serial murder, other forms of dissociative disorders that may play a role are only now beginning to receive attention. Dissociative amnesia, formerly referred to as psychogenic amnesia, is a loss of memory due to psychological reasons rather than organic problems. It is considered to be rare and can be triggered by highly stressful events such as war and natural disasters (Frederick, 1981; Hirst, 1982). Frequently, those afflicted display anterograde amnesia, or loss of memory after a traumatic experience (Golden, Moses, Caffman, Miller, and Strider, 1983).

Dissociative Fugue Another dissociative disorder, dissociative fugue, formerly known as psychogenic fugue, is described by the *DSM-IV* as sudden, unexpected travel away from home or one's customary place of work, with inability to recall one's past (APA, 2000, pp. 523–526). Those afflicted may engage in partial or complete identity change triggered by their loss of self-identity or confusion about their identity. Fugues are still considered rare among dissociative disorders. Kirshner (1973) noted that only 7 out of 1,795 cases of admissions to a medical facility were diagnosed as fugue states.

Depersonalization Disorder This dissociative disorder involves a person feeling detached from his or her mental processes or physical body. Sometimes referred to as an out-of-body experience, these experiences also cause significant impairment in social or occupational functioning (APA, 2000, p. 530). In one case, a man claimed that while having such an experience he got out of bed in the middle of the night, drove 30 miles to his father-in-law's home, and shot him to death. What we are beginning to learn from studies of dissociative disorders is that memories can be terrifyingly painful for some individuals. Porter and Peace (2007) found that a person's memories of traumatic experiences including those of violence were far more vivid than memories of positive events. Splitting off, blocking out, or not remembering anything may all serve as vehicles to thwart undesirable memories. Indeed, we all to some degree repress certain memories that cause discomfort. Memories of failure, divorce, death(s), rejection, even of always being the last child chosen for a ball team, all can cause that psychological "wincing" that most people prefer not to discuss in detail. Suinn (1984) found that individuals report poor memory of uncompleted tasks that imply a sense of failure. He suggested that memory can be very selective when dealing with threatening information, even in the mildest forms (Suinn, p. 175).

Psychoanalytic Factors

The notion of repression of feelings and thoughts was promoted by Sigmund Freud in linking abnormal behavior to mental problems induced by early childhood trauma. According to Freud, the mind is constantly engaged in balancing the three-part personality structure of id, ego, and superego. The id represents the primal component of a person's mental state, the driving force for the necessities to sustain life, including food, water, and sex. The ego develops from birth and serves to guide an individual's behavior to conform to rules, laws, and community standards. It is the pragmatic component of the mental state. The superego is the composite of moral standards and values learned within the family and community, which to some degree have been internalized. The superego sits in judgment of a person's behavior. The id and the superego generally oppose each other: the id seeks pure pleasure and the superego strives for morality and acceptable ethics. The ego, the arbitrator of the personality triad, constantly seeks to mediate between these two forces and generally provides a compromise. To illustrate the psychoanalytic concept, imagine someone being taunted by racial slurs. His immediate feelings (id) might be to strike the offending party in retaliation, but the superego senses that such behavior would be not only an overreaction but inherently dangerous behavior. Torn between the two forces, the ego guides the individual to a compromise. The individual may discount the event as meaningless and choose to ignore the situation or perhaps file harassment charges against the offender.

From the psychoanalytic perspective, violent persons appear to give little attention to morality, ethics, or standards when their id functions have been aroused. For example, Henry Lucas, a confessed serial killer of dozens of victims throughout the southern states, described himself as sometimes quick-tempered. On one occasion the 42-year-old Lucas became involved in a dispute with his 15-year-old lover and confidante. In anger the girl reached over and slapped Lucas, who responded by stabbing her repeatedly until she was dead.

Gallagher (1987), in describing the conflict between the id and the superego, concludes that abnormal behavior is the product of a conflict between innate human needs and societal norms (p. 47). Such conflicts usually stem from traumatic experiences during childhood that place tremendous stress on an individual. Most often the stress is generated by a conflicted parent-child relationship; the personality of the individual may become fixated or halted as a result of the unresolved conflict.

Such psychological scarring can be devastating to a young person. For instance, Edmund Kemper experienced significant childhood conflict with his mother, which left him with intense feelings of love and hate for her. At age 15 he killed both his grandparents because he was angry and wanted to know what it would be like to kill someone. After a few years of treatment Kemper was released into the care of his mother, which only escalated his feelings of rage toward her. He quietly went on a wild and terrifying homicidal rampage. Picking up female hitchhikers from the University of California at Santa Cruz campus where his mother worked, he sexually attacked and then butchered his victims. During this time Kemper was also fulfilling the terms of his parole and regularly attended sessions with his psychiatrist. During one of Kemper's visits the psychiatrist told Kemper how much better he appeared to be functioning and that he was pleased with his progress. During that particular visit, even as they spoke with each other, the head of one of Ed's latest victims lay in the trunk of his car. In this case, as in the cases of many serial killers, appearances were not only deceiving, but costly. Kemper eventually murdered several young female students before finally killing his mother and decapitating her. Kemper believed that once he had "resolved" the conflict with his mother his rages would subside, and he would not feel compelled to kill more victims. This seems contradicted by the fact that a couple of days after eviscerating his mother, Kemper invited her best friend over for dinner. On her arrival, Kemper murdered her and violated the corpse. Kemper was arrested again and is now eligible for parole. He feels he no longer is a threat to society.

According to psychoanalytic theory, there are several paths to fixation besides harsh treatment of a child and anxiety-producing infantile experiences. Various forms of sexual assault on a child, including parental abuse, exposure of a child to sexual activities, and acts of incest by older siblings, can also contribute to early childhood traumatizations (Nunberg, 1955). The efficacy of the emphasis on disrupted sexual development of the child is not the focus of this research, but the fact that some serial killers demonstrate symptoms of psychosexual dysfunctioning should be a point for future investigation.

August Aichorn (1934), a psychoanalyst associated with Freudian analysis, studied delinquent youths and concluded that societal stress alone could not explain a life of crime. He noted that a predisposition was also prerequisite for a youth to engage in antisocial behavior. *Latent delinquency*, a term he coined to describe a state in which a youth constantly seeks immediate gratification while neglecting the feelings or needs of others, centers on a lack of remorse or sense of guilt in satisfying instinctive urges.

Indeed, there now exists considerable literature that lends support to the belief that most seriously violent offenders (excluding serial killers) suffer from various forms of personality disturbances. Lewis and colleagues (1985) studied a group of nine youths who had been examined prior to their homicidal attacks. They found that all nine had manifested "extreme violence" as children and as adolescents. They also noted that factors that were associated with the violence clustered around neuropsychiatric and family factors. The boys were found to be the offspring of psychotic households filled with violent behavior and physical abuse. Most of the boys were found to have suffered neurological damage as a result of head injuries or seizure disorders.

Smith (1965), based on his studies of eight adolescent murderers, reported that each boy had experienced various forms of deprivation in his life that interrupted his ego development and facilitated violent aggression. Similarly, McCarthy (1978) found a tendency for homicidal behavior among young men who had experienced early deprivation and, in a study of 10 killers, noted complex feelings of low self-esteem and deep-seated anger. Sendi and Blomgren (1975) found that sexual abuse of a child by a parent was associated with homicidal behavior. Corder and associates (1976) found psychosis, chronic alcoholism, and criminal behavior among the parents of adolescent murderers. Malmquist (1971), commenting on the function of homicide, asserted that it "can serve the illusory function of saving one's self and ego from destruction by displacing onto someone else the focus of aggressive discharge" (p. 462). Pfeffer (1980) concluded that young men who victimize and murder others do so in an effort to neutralize early childhood traumatization. Dutton and Hart (1992, pp. 129–137) examined the institutional files of 604 federal inmates to determine the impact of childhood abuse and neglect on violent behavior as adults. Men abused as children were three times more likely than non-abused men to act out violently as adults. In addition, men who were physically abused were also the most likely to be violent, whereas those sexually abused were most likely to be sexually violent. Dutton and Hart note that their results are consistent with the cycle-of-violence hypothesis: abused children are more likely as adults to abuse others or even other children. Consider the true story of Eric Smith (see Profile 3.4).

PROFILE 3.4 Eric Smith, 1993

Eric Smith, age 13, appeared to be a very well-adjusted boy who was loved and cared for by his family. He was not an aggressive child and seemed to be outwardly happy. Unfortunately, outward signs can be misleading. One day while riding his bike in a local park he noticed Derrick, a blond-haired, 4-year-old boy, walking alone. Approaching the boy, Eric offered to show him a shortcut through a wooded area leading to his destination. Leaving his bike, Eric escorted Derrick a short distance into the woods. Without saying a word, Eric stepped up behind Derrick and strangled him. A short struggle ensued, followed by Eric smashing the little boy's head with large rocks until he was dead. Opening the child's lunch pail, he poured Kool-Aid onto the corpse, making special effort to put the liquid into the wounds. He then pulled the child's pants down and sodomized him with pieces of a tree branch.

A few days after the body was found, Eric admitted seeing Derrick in the park the day he was killed. He claimed never having seen the boy before. After several conflicting stories, Eric confessed to his family that he had killed Derrick. He stated that he did not know why he had killed the child.

What was it that made Eric kill? Perhaps he possessed some genetic makeup that predisposed or influenced him. Perhaps he was driven by some conscious or subconscious urge to destroy brought on by his environment. Let us now consider some additional information that may help the reader form some tentative ideas as to the etiology of Eric's violence.

Biologically, Eric was considered normal in most areas. He did possess deformed ears, an early childhood speech impediment, wore thick glasses, and had very bright red hair. Although none of these has any connection to violent behavior, each did provide a source of frequent embarrassment at school when other children would tease him. Eric was also diagnosed as having attention-deficit/hyperactivity disorder (ADHD), which appears to have affected his academic success. Environmentally, Eric experienced many problems. His poor school performance had necessitated keeping him back two grades. He had difficulty fitting in with children two years his junior. On one occasion he remarked: "My life is junk, kids treat me like trash." His grandmother, whom he loved dearly, had recently passed away. He had also lost a friend killed in a car accident. His family life was disturbing. He had lived much of his life with his grandparents because of his parents' divorce. His stepfather was very authoritarian and controlling. His 16-year-old sister Amy moved out under claims that the stepfather had sexually molested her. There were claims, but never substantiated, that Eric had been sexually abused. Perhaps this was the explanation for Eric's sexual assault on the child he killed.

Psychologically, Eric was a very angry youth. His self-esteem was nonexistent. He deeply resented the ridicule of his peers. When Eric confessed to authorities about the murder, he found himself really enjoying their attention. He joked and smiled as if oblivious to his situation. Eventually, Eric admitted that he had seen Derrick before. The little boy received lots of attention from his parents. Eric could tell that Derrick was very cute and very popular.

So, why did Eric kill? Do we have enough information to determine causation? Probably not, but we can talk about the correlation of predisposition, family dysfunctioning, abuse, low self-esteem, anger, fantasy, frustration, and rejection. Did he kill Derrick because of envy, because Derrick symbolized everything Eric was not going to be? Did he internally suffer from the effects of his parents' divorce and the continual feelings of failure at school? Was he influenced by the nightmare of childhood sexual abuse, his feelings of shame, disgust, and helplessness becoming fuel for violence? These become pieces of the puzzle. Perhaps there are more pieces to make the puzzle complete. What do you think?

David Abrahamsen (1973), in *The Murdering Mind*, found one common characteristic among people who murder. He observed that all murderers are intensely tormented and are constantly beset by inner conflict:

> The prime marks of the murderer are a sense of helplessness, impotence, and nagging revenge carried over from early childhood. Intertwined with this core of emotions which color and distort his view of life and all his actions are his irrational hatred for others, his suspiciousness, and his hypersensitivity to injustices or rejection. Hand in hand with these go his self-centeredness and his inability to withstand frustration. Overpowered by frequent uncontrollable emotional outbursts, he has a need to retaliate, to destroy, to tear down by killing. (p. 13)

Abrahamsen, as well as several others who subscribe to the Freudian perspective of psychoanalytic theory, places a considerable emphasis on psychosexual factors. Indeed, many childhood trauma experiences are sexual in nature. It is these sexual traumatizations that may later surface as aggressive, sometimes homicidal, behavior. Abrahamsen (1973) also noted an intimate connection between the offender and the victim as the "intertwining of our murderous and self-murderous impulses.... Every homicide is unconsciously a suicide and every suicide is, in a sense, a psychological homicide. Typically, the killer is afraid of killing himself, afraid of dying, and therefore he murders someone else" (p. 38). This effort to assert himself, to show that he is indeed capable and not a weakling, is an attempt to restore his "narcissistic" masculine self-esteem. Violence is an ego defense mechanism against intense inner pain and loss of self-esteem. Asserts Abrahamsen, "Frustration is the wet nurse of violence" (pp. 42–43). Konrath, Bushman, and Campbell (2006) found that not having a relationship with another person significantly contributes to narcissistic aggression. Participants measuring low in narcissism—meaning a continuous trait, not a personality disorder, whereby persons entertain grandiose and vulnerable self-views simultaneously (Thomaes et.al., 2009)—increased slightly in aggression when a shared relationship was presented. Researchers conclude that this may be due to a proneness for being self-serving when persons feel mistreated by someone they know.

For most, if not all, serial killers, frustration appears as a common theme from one homicide to the next. For many, the homicidal act is preceded by sexual torture. In one case, a serial killer in Michigan ritualistically rammed broken branches from trees and bushes into his victims' vagina. Sex as a vehicle to vent the killer's frustration, anger, hate, and fear becomes a powerful destructive tool. By contrast, there are various cases of serial killers who derive sexual gratification from watching their victims suffer and die without sexually assaulting them or overtly using sex in any way to harm or degrade them. One offender reported how he would administer poison to prostitutes and immediately leave, even before the chemical began taking effect. As he walked home he would revel in and fantasize about the agony his victim was now going through.

One might argue, however, that even in the last case the offender may have been vicariously experiencing sexual pleasure. Although some cases of serial murder appear to involve absolutely no sexual motivations, one may argue that latent sexual motivations exist unknown even to the offender. Psychoanalytic literature is replete with examples of defense mechanisms that serve to reduce anxiety states. Freud identified several, including denial, the conscious refusal to admit a factual event; repression, an unconscious exclusion from consciousness of anxiety-producing material or events; suppression, the conscious exclusion of anxiety-producing material; projection, the initial repression of a trait and subsequent attachment of it to others; displacement, the venting of unacceptable impulse(s) toward a substitute target; and sublimation, directing unacceptable impulse(s) into socially acceptable channels (Suinn, 1984). Each of these mechanisms appears at one time or another in the personality profiles of various serial killers. Persons in the general population who experience social anxiety have problems in generating positive experiences or developing meaningful relationships in efforts to avoid anxiety-producing events and anxious feelings (Kashdan, 2007). In lieu of dealing positively with such stressors, risk-prone behaviors are adapted to regulate anxiety. These include substance abuse, preemptive aggression, and pleasure seeking. Persons who are impulsive and lack self-control, however, tend to be less rational in their decision making, often walk away from demanding tasks, are less satisfied and committed in relationships, and are more likely to stereotype and show prejudice (Kashdan and McKnight, 2010). Serial offenders, as they develop, use much energy to mask personal deficits. A tendency does exist for serial offenders to engage in a process of blocking out past experiences too painful or stressful to accommodate. The magnitude of the role these and other psychoanalytic factors play in the mind of the serial murderer is only now beginning to be explored.

Personality Disorders

The *DSM-IV* (2000) indicates that personality disorders have an "enduring pattern of inner experience and behavior that deviates markedly from the expectations of the individual's culture" (p. 685). Patterns are generally manifested in two or more of the following ways:

1. Cognition (perception and interpretation of self, other people, and events)
2. Affectivity (range, intensity, and appropriateness of emotional response)
3. Interpersonal functioning
4. Impulse control

The *DSM-IV* (2000) notes that the enduring pattern is inflexible and pervasive across a wide range of personal and social situations and that this pattern leads to significant distress or impairment in social and occupational settings. This pattern can be traced back to adolescence or early childhood and is not a result of medications, substance abuse, head trauma, or some general medical condition.

The types and characteristics of the various personality disorders include the following: *paranoid*—a pervasive distrust and suspiciousness of others; *schizoid*—a pervasive pattern of detachment from relationships, including limited expression of emotions; *schizotypal*—social and interpersonal deficits, eccentric behaviors that inhibit the development of close relationships; *antisocial*—extreme disregard and violation of the rights of others; *borderline*—instability in interpersonal relationships and self-image, and extreme impulsivity; *histrionic*—excessive emotionality and attention seeking; *narcissistic*—grandiosity, need for praise, lack of empathy; *avoidant*—social inhibition, feelings of inadequacy, hypersensitive to criticism; *dependent*—need to be cared for, fear of abandonment, submissive and clinging behavior; *obsessive-compulsive*—preoccupation with orderliness, perfectionism, mental and interpersonal control, inflexible and inefficient behaviors (APA, 2000, pp. 685–729).

Personality disorders appear to be the most resistant to change. Their pervasive nature allows for the commingling of symptoms, which creates problems in identifying dominant disorders. Antisocial personality disorder (ASPD), common among violent offenders, includes a history of antisocial behavior beginning no later than age 15 for males, and for females anytime during the teen years. Antisocial behaviors may include one or more of the following: incorrigibility, theft, fighting during childhood, deceitfulness, excessive alcohol/drug use, reckless regard for the safety of self or others, impulsivity, and aggressive behavior during adolescence. As adults, antisocial persons have particular difficulty in developing and sustaining relationships. Indeed, this is also evidence in the noted *trolley problem* (Foote, 1967) that explored a set of moral dilemmas involving five persons about to be killed by a runaway trolley. By pushing a large man off a bridge into the trolley's path, the man will die but the five others will be spared. Most persons would not push a man onto the tracks to save others but in a related study would be willing to flip a switch to divert the train to save the five even if it meant sacrificing one man (Green et al., 2009). Psychopaths, because they lack attachments to groups or individuals, would be far more inclined to push the large man off the bridge or flip the switch. Persons with strong group attachments, however, would be willing to jump to their deaths to save human life (Swann et al., 2010). No doubt that psychopaths would certainly support them in that choice. Antisocial persons tend to demonstrate poor work habits and lack of responsibility; view the world in negative, hostile terms; and frequently show lack of insight into their problems and future plans.

Serial killers have often been portrayed as antisocial personality types manifesting aggressive, hostile behavior and a tendency to avoid developing close relationships. However, some serial murderers appear to be well-adjusted people leading rather normal lives; their closest friends and family members have been surprised and shocked by their confessions of multiple homicides. The point is: Offenders do not always come from the same mold. Each killer has evolved through different life events and has responded to those experiences differently. Although it may be argued that serial killers possess "fatal flaws," it remains indefensible to say that such flaws are overtly manifested. In short, some offenders may never reveal enough of themselves in daily life to allow the identification of particular personality disorders. In hindsight we are always able to identify fatal personality flaws once we know what the offender has done, but accurate prediction of homicidal behavior, particularly serial killing, continues to evade researchers and clinicians alike. Understanding the psychopathology of these

Jekyll-and-Hyde-like personalities appears increasingly complex as we explore the minds of serial murderers.

What we are seeing in the psychopathology of serial killers is that all serial killers exhibit antisocial qualities, but not all in the same manner. One way in which to conceptualize the personalities of serial killers is that they all share some common characteristics but also differ significantly. Serial killers share antisocial qualities, but much of what they reveal about themselves appears to be linked to intelligence and skill levels.

Asperger's Disorder and the *DSM-IV*

Theodore Kaczynski (a.k.a. The Unabomber; see profile in Chapter 13), who bombed dozens of American victims, was ultimately found to be guilty but was diagnosed as a paranoid schizophrenic. It is of interest to note that although several experts considered Kaczynski to be a paranoid schizophrenic, their findings were tentative and speculative. In retrospect there were few *DSM* criteria employed to diagnose Kaczynski. Indeed, there may have been more emphasis placed on societal expectations in explaining the etiological underpinnings of Kaczynski's behavior than in rigorous application of the *DSM* criteria. He appeared to exhibit a paranoid personality disorder but not the behavior and cognition of a paranoid schizophrenic. Silva, Ferrari, and Leong (2003) concurred and offered a compelling argument that Kaczynski was not only sane but likely suffered from Asperger's disorder. According to Silva et al. in their Neuropsychiatric Development Model of Serial Killing Behavior, Kaczynski suffered from prominent autism spectrum psychopathology rather than schizoid personality psychopathology. According to Silva et al.:

> Autism spectrum disorders coincide with autism, the *DSM-IV* category of pervasive developmental disorders that includes a milder variant of autism known as Asperger's disorder. The disorder is characterized by a tendency for isolation from others, repetitive thinking and behaviors and a pattern of actively rejecting other people's worldviews even when the others make themselves available for potential social interaction. (p. 17)

Silva et al. used the *DSM-IV* (2000) criteria to examine the mindset of Kaczynski, utilizing all well-known diagnostic systems for Asperger's disorder. They note that current research supports the belief that Asperger's disorder continues throughout the life cycle. They propose that serial killers, or at least some of them, can best be understood from a neuropsychiatric developmental approach. In the case of Kaczynski, there exists a dearth of psychological evidence supported by the *DSM-IV* to adequately substantiate that he was, indeed, a paranoid schizophrenic. Silva argues that much overlap exists between schizoid disorder and Asperger's disorder. Another problem cited by Silva et al. in serial-murder research is that criminologists often view serial murderers as fantasy-driven, with little attention given to psychobiological factors that may facilitate fantasy development. Indeed, much more research needs to focus on Asperger's disorder and other autistic spectrum disorders from a biological basis. Silva et al. tactfully call into question how much we actually know and understand about the psychopathology of behavior and its origins and offer an innovative yet sound approach to this field of research.

CONSTRUCTING THE PSYCHOPATH

The term *psychopath* was introduced by J. L. A. Koch in his 1891 monograph *Die Psychopathischen Minderwertigkeiten* in his description of "psychopathic inferiorities." In 1939 Henderson described psychopaths in his book *Psychopathic States* as those afflicted with an illness:

> The term psychopathic state is the name we apply to those individuals who conform to a certain intellectual standard, sometimes high, sometimes approaching the realm of defect but yet not amounting to it, who throughout their lives, or from a comparatively early age, have exhibited disorders of conduct of an antisocial or asocial nature, usually of a recurrent or episodic type, who, in many instances, have proved difficult to influence by methods of social, penal, and medical care and treatment and for whom we have no adequate provision of a preventive or curative nature. The inadequacy or deviation or failure to adjust to ordinary social life is not a mere willfulness or badness which can be threatened or thrashed out of the individual so involved, but constitutes a true illness for which we have no specific explanation. (p. 19)

Cleckley (1976) in *The Mask of Sanity* outlined 16 characteristics of psychopaths:

1. Intelligent
2. Rational
3. Calm
4. Unreliable
5. Insincere
6. Without shame or remorse
7. Having poor judgment
8. Without capacity for love
9. Unemotional
10. Poor insight
11. Indifferent to the trust or kindness of others
12. Overreactive to alcohol
13. Suicidal
14. Impersonal sex life
15. Lacking long-term goals
16. Inadequately motivated antisocial behavior

Thompson (1953) in *The Psychopathic Delinquent and Criminal* viewed such persons as those who seek momentary gratification, lack discretion, and fail to profit from experience, which leads to repeated failures.

The term *psychopath* is a non-diagnostic label used to describe a potpourri of individuals determined by societal standards to possess characteristics at variance with general community standards and practices. The term *psychopath* is used interchangeably with the term *sociopath*, both of which are no longer used in the *DSM* as diagnostic tools but still find utility as labels in describing psychosocial characteristics. These terms were eventually replaced in the *DSM* with *antisocial*, a term considered by many practitioners as vague, nebulous, and confounding. Consequently the terms *sociopath* and *psychopath* have been popularized by the public and used indiscriminately to describe many criminals who do not warrant such labels. People often confuse the popular label *psycho* with *psychopath* when actually the terms carry different meanings for practitioners. Most commonly the public makes the erroneous assumption that someone who is a serial killer must be "psycho" or crazy, out of his mind. Indeed, the behavior may be crazy or bizarre but the killer is usually anything but crazy. Far more appropriate is applying the term *psychopath*, or from the *DSM* perspective, the killer is antisocial. Indeed, most common criminals are neither "psychos" nor psychopaths, but these are labels easily and often erroneously applied to criminal behavior, especially when they may exhibit one or more characteristics associated with these labels. For example, even in professional settings the terms *psychopath* and *sociopath* are well-entrenched common verbiage. Staff assigned to a sex-offender unit learn quickly that most of these individuals were also regarded by the professional staff as persons with psychopathic behavior. In another section of the hospital where the habitual criminals are housed, patients often are called psychopaths or sociopaths. Even on the unit designated for persons on civil commitment, "psychopaths" were in abundance (author's files).

Psychopaths are generally viewed as aggressive, insensitive, charismatic, irresponsible, intelligent, dangerous, hedonistic, narcissistic, and antisocial. These are persons who can masterfully explain another person's problems and what must be done to overcome them, but who appear to have little or no insight into their own lives or how to correct their own problems. Those psychopaths who can articulate solutions for their personal problems usually fail to follow through. Psychopaths are perceived as exceptional manipulators capable of feigning emotions in order to carry out their personal agendas. Without remorse for the plight of their victims, they are adept at rationalization, projection, and other psychological defense mechanisms. The veneer of stability, friendliness, and normality belies a deeply disturbed personality. Outwardly there appears to be nothing abnormal about their personalities, even their behavior. They are careful to maintain social distance and share intimacy only with those whom they can psychologically control. They are noted for their inability to maintain long-term commitments to people or programs. We will learn from this discussion that although most serial killers are psychopaths or at least exhibit psychopathic characteristics, the majority of criminal psychopaths are nonviolent persons. Indeed, the majority of criminal psychopaths operate as white-collar criminals.

Dr. Robert Hare and Psychopaths

In 1980 Dr. Robert Hare, author of *Without Conscience: The Disturbing World of Psychopaths Among Us* (1993) and the most acclaimed pioneer in understanding the world of psychopaths, created a diagnostic tool referred to as the "Psychopathy Checklist." This tool was a system to measure levels of psychopathy on a 40-point scale. Known as "the Hare," the list was revised five years later and labeled the "Psychopathy Checklist Revised" or the PCL-R. One of the most important discoveries by Hare was that most psychopaths are nonviolent even though they are social predators. Psychopaths commonly engage in risky behaviors because winning the game is everything. Driven by narcissism and the need for cortical stimulation, psychopaths are oblivious or indifferent to the suffering they cause others. Hare refers to them as "sub-clinical psychopaths" who are drawn to positions of power and control and noted that many white-collar criminals are psychopaths.

Hare also found that psychopaths cannot relate to language that is emotionally laden. Feelings for others require mimicking emotions that they do not feel: sorrow, guilt, remorse, sadness, shame, and pain. Madoff's victims lost all of their investments, and although he can certainly understand the seriousness of this disaster, he is incapable of relating emotionally to their losses any more than he can understand how they must feel. Indeed, he will find his victims' responses curious and interesting, but nothing more. Hare estimates that about 1% of the population can be classified as psychopaths or that we have about three million psychopaths in the United States. Psychopaths are found on Wall Street, in government leadership, and in homes of chronic wife-beaters. Because they have no conscience they are naturally drawn toward controlling others, whether it be in the boardroom, the governor's office, or in the privacy of their homes.

Hare believes that the brains of psychopaths are most likely wired differently than the rest of the population. The brain of a psychopath appears to be understimulated compared to that of a normal person. Does this mean that psychopaths are genetic constructions or does it mean that portions of the brains of psychopaths atrophy from lack of use and nurturing? His fundamental assertion, if true, means that psychopaths could come from a variety of homes, including those that by societal standards are considered normal. Trauma-free psychopaths might be a difficult concept for those clinicians who assert that criminality is borne in dysfunctional homes rife with violence, abuse, and trauma. Con men and scam artists are prime examples of persons who do not understand or have empathy for the suffering of their victims. Don Lapre, known across America as the Infomercial King, was indicted in June 2011 for conning 226,000 victims out of 52 million dollars by selling fake vitamins. He was likeable, charming, believable, and had gullible victims clamoring to buy his phony products. Con artists like Lapre love the game and the thrill and highs they get from risk-taking and seeing how far they can go. When it all crashes down there is no place left to go and some commit suicide, as did Don Lapre in October 2011 while awaiting trial in a Colorado federal prison. The fact that such men lack empathy and are thrill seekers, liars, and masterful at manipulation does not necessarily mean they are true psychopaths, but certainly they are persons who would most likely rate much higher on psychopathy scales than a control group of non-con subjects.

Consider celebrity ministers like Ted Haggard, Jim Baker, Eddie Long, and Jimmy Swaggart, all men who headed mega Christian churches and ultimately faced mega scandals. Such scandals are often born from *reaction-formation*, or the double life some people live in response to unresolved personal conflicts. Driven by guilt, shame, fear, and anxiety, some persons build, often unconsciously, incredible personas to counter their personal deficits. These are individuals who develop social skills and incorporate some characteristics of psychopaths without actually being psychopaths. The task for psychologists and other professionals is to understand the similarities and differences between persons who are developing a constellation of personality disorders and behaviors common to the psychopath and persons without the disorders who develop some of the characteristics of psychopathy.

Differentiating the Sociopath, Psychopath, and Primary Psychopath

A helpful framework in which to examine sociopaths, psychopaths, and primary psychopaths recognizes the tremendous contributions Dr. Robert Hare has made in his examination of psychopathy and the distinctions made among these terms. To further illustrate some of these distinctions, let us first consider these three typologies in terms of intelligence and social skill levels.

The *sociopath* is antisocial. This individual possesses the demeanor of one familiar with the insides of jails and correctional facilities, and also has a history of criminal behavior. In addition, this person has acquired certain attributes that facilitate criminal activity: callousness, anger, indifference, and revenge fantasies. Average to below-average intelligence is commonly found in sociopaths throughout our state prison systems.

The *psychopath* usually does not have the lengthy history of criminal behavior. That is not to say that this person is never arrested but is more careful in avoiding arrest. The psychopath possesses all the attributes as described by Hare (1991) in the *Psychopathy Checklist Revised* or PCL-R used to measure psychopathic traits. This individual tends to have average to above-average intelligence and is less obvious to the investigator and therapist because psychopaths are less prone to show their antisocial attitudes. Psychopaths differentiate themselves from sociopaths in that psychopaths tend to display a higher level of skill in their criminal trade. Thus, they tend not to be arrested as often as sociopaths. Better adapted to his or her own deeply seated issues than sociopaths, the psychopath is less obvious as a predator. The psychopath often does not physically harm a victim. Remember, the core of psychopathy is power and control over the victim through whatever means necessary to maintain or improve his or her status.

The *primary psychopath* also is antisocial, but the untrained eye will never see the true nature of the offender. The victim may even defend his or her predator, believing wholeheartedly in the innocence of this person. Never underestimate the power of denial. Primary psychopaths are social chameleons who can blend into any environment. They range in intelligence from above average to highly intelligent and have developed skill levels far superior to other criminal types. They become consummate predators. They can lie so well that their words carry complete credibility. The primary psychopath personifies the PCL-R and can outmaneuver law enforcement personnel for lengthy time periods.

Sometimes the distinctions can become blurred. The salient factor for the investigator is the level of control exhibited by a person. Emotionally healthy people do not need to control others because they are already in control of themselves. Support for this differentiation between primary psychopaths, psychopaths, and sociopaths is noted in other research that suggests that psychopaths can be subdivided into primary and secondary categories. Lee and Salekin (2010), in studying a non-institutionalized sample of psychopaths, noted that those identified as primary psychopaths exhibited fearlessness and increased stress immunity. The secondary psychopath, however, was found to be more susceptible to stressful experiences, especially trait anxiety. Hicks et al. (2004) also found that the primary psychopath tends to be inoculated from negative events. These studies lend support to the notion that psychopaths can be better understood on a continuum of development rather than presented as a dichotomy of either being a psychopath or not being a psychopath. Other research examines correlations between psychopathy and posttraumatic stress. Harris (2011) in his exploration of psychopathic immunity to PTSD symptomology notes that these findings still do not adequately explore the full spectrum of interactions of psychopathy and PTSD. He notes the scarcity of data available to study such correlations that limits more definitive answers to this area of research.

Female Psychopaths

Cleckley (1976), in his text *The Mask of Sanity*, describes psychopaths as irresponsible, unpredictable, pathological liars who display a flagrant disregard for truth. He concluded that psychopaths are of above-average intelligence but are self-destructive in that they frequently involve themselves in high-risk ventures, generally blame others for their failures, and have no long-range goals. They are able to mimic the behavior of others but carry no actual burden of remorse for their crimes. Does this list of characteristics, which focuses upon male psychopathy, resonate with female psychopaths as well?

Although more research is being conducted on female psychopathy, there is a dearth of information regarding the core characteristics of female personality disorder. In fact, most of what we know about female psychopaths comes from applying male criteria to females, thereby tainting the diagnoses of psychopathy. Even then, are practitioners utilizing the same criteria to measure and diagnose psychopathy in women? Are the types of behavioral expressions of key traits gender consistent? Surprisingly little information exists that delves into the interpersonal, affective, behavioral, and etiological characteristics of psychopathy in women. This is problematic when trying to distinguish psychopathy from other personality disorders presenting similar core traits (Forouzan and Cooke, 2005). Female psychopaths do appear to lean toward histrionics rather than the narcissism found commonly in male psychopaths. All psychopaths seek others to gratify their personal needs, but female psychopaths with hysterical traits actively solicit the attention, support, and admiration of others around them. This extreme reliance on others serves as a buffer from the otherwise chronic dissatisfaction, looming depression, and negative feelings toward self. Furthermore, female psychopaths have trouble with self-perception, poor self-regard, poor interpersonal relatedness, limited understanding of the motivations of others, lack of empathy, and poor reality testing (Cunliffe and Gacono, 2005).

A partial explanation as to why there are relatively few female psychopaths compared to males who prey upon others is because female psychopaths exhibit a great need for attention and are so dependent upon others for approval. This need is based on wanting to be the center of attention rather than a desire for intimacy. They also appear to be less grandiose and show more superficial interest in and less violence towards others than male psychopaths. However, both male and female psychopaths display similar levels of conning and manipulation, pathological lying, and antisocial and criminal activity. The female psychopath increases her risk of offending against her own family, friends, and acquaintances due to her accentuated level of personal dependency, lack of understanding of others, and limited introspection. She may not seek the dominance or humiliation of others as often witnessed in male psychopaths, but her lack of empathy and her disregard for the well-being of others, despite her appearance of caring for others, are specific deficits (pp. 530–543). Some of these traits of adult female psychopathy can be traced to childhood and adolescence. In several studies of female juvenile offenders the girls experienced high rates of victimization, especially sexual abuse. It is their personal victimizations that may be key to understanding their later aggression: how persons may learn from or react to abusive interpersonal experiences (Odgers et al., 2005). Hicks et al. (2010) found that among incarcerated female adult offenders, primary psychopaths in comparison to secondary psychopaths have less PTSD symptomology and appear to have a predisposition to "psychological resiliency."

Female serial murderers appear to exhibit some traits similar to those of male serial murderers in terms of psychopathology. For example, the women tend to be insincere, amoral, impulsive, prone to exercise manipulative charisma and superficial charm, without conscience, and with little insight because they failed to learn from their mistakes. Guze (1976) concluded from a 15-year longitudinal study of female felons in prison that psychopathology was the most frequent personality diagnosis for these offenders.

It is unlikely that every psychopath, male or female, possesses all of these characteristics or that he or she constantly exhibits any of these traits. Instead, psychopathic behavior may be cyclical, like the Jekyll-and-Hyde syndrome. Although fewer in number, female serial killers may exhibit psychopathic characteristics similar to their male counterparts and can be just as lethal as the male offenders. Jane Toppan, from the witness stand at her trial for murder, stated: "This is my ambition—to have killed more people—more helpless people—than any man or woman has ever killed." Female serial killers are viewed as predominantly stay-at-home killers who operate carefully and inconspicuously and who may avoid detection for several years. In the 2004 study we see more female offenders mimicking their male counterparts in becoming more localized in their efforts to find and kill their victims. Does gender play a role in determining victim selection, or is finding victims a product of cultural filters, economic demands, and opportunities? One hopes that future research will focus more attention on exploring the psychopathology of female offenders. We have only begun to explore their motivational dynamics.

Current research in psychopathy involves a variety of noted scientists who are challenging some of the ways in which we think about psychopaths, stereotypes, the influence of biology and genetics, and environmental factors. Dr. Chris Patrick, professor of psychology at Florida State University is one of the more prolific researchers on the subject of psychopathy. He collaborates with a cadre of like-minded scholars to help bring clarity and validation to what we know and still need to know about psychopaths and the study of psychopathy (See Focus on Psychopathy).

Measuring Criminal Psychopathy

Currently, the best methodology in measuring criminal psychopathy is Hare's (1991) *Psychopathy Checklist Revised* (PCL-R). Based on Cleckley's (1976) observations of psychopathy, this instrument is used for the assessment of male offenders incarcerated in prisons or psychiatric institutions. Hare found that on the 40-point scale where normal persons rate about a 5, the typical male incarcerated offender in North America rates about a 23. Bona fide psychopaths, he believes, are rated at 30 points and higher. The reliability of this scale, which also requires the accompanying PCL-R scoring manual for accurate measurement as well as a licensed practitioner to do the evaluation, is quite remarkable. Persons with high PCL-R scores are three to four times more likely to recidivate than persons with low scores.

Revised Psychopathy Checklist

Factor 1: Measures a selfish, callous, and remorseless use of others and contains most of the personality characteristics considered central to the traditional clinical conception of the disorder. These traits are inferred, as opposed to explicit.

- Glibness/superficial charm
- Grandiose sense of self-worth/narcissism
- Pathological lying
- Conning, manipulative behavior
- Lack of remorse or guilt
- Shallow affect
- Callousness/lack of empathy
- Failure to accept responsibility for actions

Factor 2: Measures social deviance, as manifested in a chronically unstable and antisocial lifestyle. These traits are more explicit than those in the Factor 1 group.

- Need for stimulation/proneness to boredom
- Parasitic lifestyle
- Poor behavioral controls
- Early behavioral problems
- Lack of realistic, long-term goals
- Impulsivity
- Irresponsibility
- Juvenile delinquency
- Revocation of conditional release

Other factors:

- Promiscuous sexual behavior
- Many short-term marital relationships
- Criminal versatility

These factors appear to vary with the age, social class, cognitive abilities, alcohol and drug abuse or dependence, violent behavior, and recidivism of the psychopath.

Many of the Hare characteristics listed in the Factor 1 of the PCL-R individually and collectively represent a very significant framework of operating for the psychopath. In essence they are *tools* utilized by the psychopath to achieve his main purpose: control. Some of the characteristics are harbingers of psychopathy, meaning that being irresponsible and impulsive with poor behavioral control and a parasitic lifestyle are areas to be concealed from the vantage point of the observer. A charming person who deftly manipulates others through well-placed, believable lies and half-truths, uses emotional responses of others to control and manipulate them, replaces self-confidence with narcissism, can mimic remorse and guilt when necessary but feels none, preys upon others to fulfill his needs, rationalizes and justifies his actions, and is undeterred by the suffering of others, this is a dangerous person. Psychopaths, because their ultimate goal is to have control over others, are often not convicted criminals. Of course, many have not been caught for their actions because the victims fear them and want no further contact, even in court. Psychopaths develop their tools over time, through criminal and noncriminal experiences and developing social skills as tools of their trade. They know us far better than we know them, unless you have been married to one long enough to see past his veneer of perfection. Factor 2 contains more *deficits* of the psychopath, things that his tools will conceal through lies and manipulations, such as being irresponsible and impulsive, exhibiting a lack of planning, and living parasitic lifestyle.

There is, however, one tool missing from the PCL-R Factor list that is a signature or master tool of a psychopath. Each of the psychopath's tools is used differentially to gain control over others, whether it be financial, sexual, emotional, physical, etc. These tools can be used for long-term control of others or for more immediate, short-term control and gratification, depending upon the needs of the psychopath. The psychopath, above all else, does not want you to see past his facade, and to that end he uses *distraction* to remain hiding in plain sight. The psychopath engaging in a Ponzi scheme invites you onto his yacht, shows you fake reports of incredible returns for his investors, gives you gifts, and speaks of other respected investors with whom he does business. It is all a sham to keep you looking in directions other than the psychopath, and you feel good doing it (see Profile 3.5). For a child sexual predator who rates high on the

PROFILE 3.5 Bernard Madoff, 1980–2009

Bernard Madoff, the cunning and charming Wall Street investment broker who, for over 30 years, dealt in hedge funds, created the world's largest Ponzi scheme, which cost investors over 60 billion dollars. He owned several yachts and luxury homes around the world and held the trust and investments of many wealthy persons and others who sought fortune. The worldwide financial meltdown meant that Madoff could no longer keep up with the demands of investors who wanted their money. After 30 years of duping investors, the game simply came to an end. In March 2009 he pled guilty to 11 federal felonies that eventually earned him 150 years in Federal prison.

But, is he a psychopath? Charming, intelligent, and very helpful to others, Madoff chose a career in business rather than finish law school. Madoff was no small-time hustler. He saw opportunity on Wall Street and people willing to look the other way. He played on investors' greed, naiveté, and trust. He used investors to find him more wealthy investors, or persons wanting to be wealthy. People believed him and believed in him because everyone else did, or so it seemed. Yet there were some who were suspicious and tried to raise the alarm. Major derivative firms would not trade with him because they privately felt that his numbers did not make sense. Six times Madoff was "investigated" by the SEC, but due to incompetence or lack of caring or just being too busy with other more important concerns, nothing ever came of those investigations. Of course, many people made a lot of money, including Chase Bank, where he deposited his scam investments and about half of his investors. Madoff had access to Washington lawmakers and regulators through his business connections that kept him in the mix. He belonged to a long list of important business organizations including time as chairman of the board of the Securities Industry Association. These political and business connections and his prodigious networking were all to enhance his flourishing Ponzi scheme. He was a generous philanthropist (of course, he was giving away other people's money), which kept him on the lips of the elite.

Madoff was the man to go to for investing and help. He was like a fox in the henhouse. Everyone became a pawn in his scheme, including his family. Indeed, they were complicit, but Madoff was the mastermind, and he relished in the power and affluence it afforded him. When arrested, Madoff expressed amazement that he had not been caught earlier, pled guilty to all charges, and refused to cooperate with investigators who knew that Madoff had used others as well to help him front his Ponzi scheme. As Madoff saw the scheme beginning to unravel as he could no longer meet the payment demands of his investors by stealing from some to pay others, he withdrew millions for himself and tried to hide the money. His entire career was in the pursuit of using others for his personal gain. The extent of damage he did is enormous. Many charities had to close, and businesses and individual investors went bankrupt. His family faces multiple lawsuits. Some of them have changed their last names, others gone into hiding, some resigned from their places of employment. Three persons, two of whom were investors, have committed suicide as a direct result of the Madoff scandal, including his own son, Mark.

As an inmate, Madoff occupies himself by overseeing the prison landscaping budget. For more insights into corporate psychopaths read *Snakes in Suits* by Robert Hare and Paul Babiak.

PCL-R, he knows that parents raise their children not to go with strangers, but the child will go with a predator in search of a lost kitten or puppy. The child is no longer with a stranger but looking for a lost animal. Recent studies of three-year-old children have shown that they were misled more often by the presence of an experimenter than those who could only hear the experimenter. The research indicates that children are willing to believe what they are told rather than simply believing in other people (Jaswal et al., 2010). Thus the child is prone to believe that what he or she is being told is true. The adult victim is occupied with looking at how the charming man next to her presents himself and fails to see who he really is before it is too late. Distraction is such a powerful tool that actual violence is used only by certain types of psychopaths for specific purposes.

The perception of research on psychopaths indicates that most criminal psychopaths are not violent, but they are more dangerous than most other people. Although many psychopaths are not physically violent, they appear to be more prone to violent behavior than other people. Perhaps another way of viewing psychopaths is that they are all dangerous because that is their nature. It is their nature to be in control. Jacobson (2002), in his review of antisocial abusers (men who lack the capacity to empathize, use violence as a means of control, and have histories of criminal behavior), demonstrated a different physiological response to conflict than other men in similar circumstances. Jacobson referred to such men as *vagal reactors* because their heart rates decline during heated arguments that involve emotionally aggressive confrontations. (In the autonomic nervous system of some persons, the vagus nerve, when exposed to excitation, suppresses arousal.) He found that the most seriously belligerent offenders reported the greatest decrease in heart rate. The decrease in heart rate is a result of being in control of another person, common to psychopaths who seek control (Dutton, 2007). Healthy, normal people want to be in control of themselves, while the hallmark of psychopaths is the need to control or have power over others. Every psychopath wants control over his or her surroundings. A normal person who is having a bad day at the office decides to go to the gym and work out his frustrations. A violent psychopath will find someone to kill. It is this quest for control that makes them psychologically, if not physically, dangerous. They are dangerous in that they constantly seek control over others. If the notion is correct that psychopaths seek to control their environment, then what happens when they are unable to maintain that control? Meloy (1993), in his impressive text *Violent Attachments*, states:

> The nature of the psychopath's violent behavior is also consistent with his callous, remorseless, and unempathetic attitude toward his victims. I theorize that the psychopath was psycho-biologically predisposed to predatory violence, a mode of aggression which is planned, purposeful, and emotionless. (pp. 72–73)

Hare and Jutai (1959–1983) note that criminal psychopaths do not "peak" in their careers as do other criminals but instead are able to maintain a consistency in their criminal behavior. Criminal psychopaths are commonly found in institutions and constitute approximately 20% to 30% of prison populations.

A common trait of psychopaths is their constant need to be in control of their social and physical environment. When this control is challenged, the psychopath can be moved to violent behavior. One example from my experience is David, an intelligent man who was charming and engaging and who possessed tremendous skills for deceiving others. Transient, he moved from one locale to another, seeking out those whom he could use. He had married several times, often before the divorce from his previous spouse had been finalized. He carefully and systematically siphoned off, diverted, and used the financial resources of each new spouse. He embezzled money from his stepchildren by forging their names on government bonds. Constantly he borrowed money from others with no plans for repayment. Fastidious in his dress, versed in etiquette, and articulate in speech, he impressed everyone who had never been victimized by him as a responsible, gentle, and kind person. David also had a passion for organization. He constantly reviewed everything about his life, his daily plans, and his goals. He always knew where he had been and what he did on any given day, week, month, or year. Indeed, he spent so much time planning and creating checklists he never really accomplished anything. When confronted, he deftly sidestepped the issues, carefully staying out of the focus. He rarely allowed himself to be in situations in which he might not have control. On occasion he would engage in an athletic contest, such as basketball. A personality transformation inevitably occurred if his team was losing or if he did not give a stellar performance. Seething with anger and frustration, he would resort to vulgar language, extreme physical aggressiveness, and shouting at other players. The moment he was confronted about his behavior he switched back to his former, kind self, until he returned to the game. He was a true Jekyll and Hyde. Although he had never been in prison, it was only because of his manipulative abilities that he remained free (author's files).

There are problems with the label *psychopath*. It is a widely distorted and misused term, and researchers and clinicians alike have yet to arrive at a consensus as to the proper definition of the term. The layperson often cannot differentiate between psychopathy and psychosis (mental illness) even though these two constructs lie at either end of a psychosocial continuum. While mental illness can and should be treated, the opposite can be said for psychopaths. Criminal psychopaths, in one experiment, were given anger management and social skills training. They reported an 82% recidivism rate compared to 59% for psychopaths who were not given the treatment. Psychopaths are not amenable to treatment because they do not believe they need it, and if subjected to treatment, they will simply add that information to their arsenal of psychological tools they can later use to control others. Hare suggests that if we are to ever be able to effectively treat psychopaths we must be prepared to appeal to their self-interests, not emotionality. A potential problem with such a behavioral modification approach is that psychopaths do not fear pain or consequences. Fear, of course, is distinguished from anxiety both in clinical and behavioral neuroscience. The fact that psychopaths are believed to measure low in fear arousal does not preclude them from experiencing anxiety that can in turn differentially affect outcomes in Factor 1 and Factor 2 of the PCL-R (Fowles and Dindo, 2009). Telling a psychopath that he will go to prison if he acts out only means that he understands the rules of the game, and games are meant to be won, not lost. How can a psychopath lose if he does not feel the loss?

Constructing a framework for the sociopathic personality type is still in the early stages. The etiology of personality disorders has given rise to a plethora of literature describing various forms of dysfunctional personalities. What is very important to understand is that personality disorders are now being viewed in the research as being dynamic, not static. This means that the composition of traits, some of which are severely maladaptive, can show change in both stable and unstable environments (Clark, 2009). Possessing a personality disorder may be better understood as part of a *continuum of formation* rather than a simple label. Indeed, recent studies of aging research have concluded that personality traits continue to transform throughout adulthood, at any age. Moreover, people present unique patterns of transformation related to specific life events pertaining to an individual's stage of life (Roberts and Mroczek, 2009).

Thus, for the serial killer, the term *psychopath* seems to apply well if we can view the label as active as on a continuum of formation, meaning that psychopaths developmentally change over time. Heretofore, killers could, by societal standards, be labeled through generally accepted standards of stereotyping. Gradually, however, the media introduced the public to the "nicest-guy-in-the-world" killers, and the public discovered that psychopaths had no apparent overt characteristics to enable stereotyping. The catch-all label of *psychopath* serves adequately to describe serial killers mainly because there appears to be a variety of types of serial offenders. This variety, however, may be more of style than substance. The underlying pathology of serial killers typically is frustration, anger, hostility, feelings of inadequacy, and low self-esteem. These feelings may be manifested in many ways, but the source or underlying pathology appears as a common denominator. Meloy (1993, pp. 78–80) notes that psychopaths live in a "presocialized emotional world" in which feelings are experienced only in relation to self and never to others. Psychopaths are more narcissistic and self-absorbed than non-psychopaths and express themselves through self-aggrandizement and omnipotent control of others. This control is possible to achieve, as psychopaths are significantly detached individuals possessing little capacity to form emotional bonds with others. An insightful development into the personalities of psychopaths was discovered by Campbell et al. (2007) that questions the blanket statement that psychopaths are mired in low self-esteem that fuels inflated self-esteem. They conclude that psychopaths are more likely to harbor both negative and positive self-views. This seems to suggest that psychopaths engage in conflicting self-image struggles. For criminal psychopaths those struggles would be far less likely to exist as the offender embraces his persona as a criminal.

The continuum of psychopathic personalities includes representatives of many groups, including adolescents, sexual deviants, intellectual types, hardcore criminals, recluses, and extroverts, to name but a few. Many people at one time or another may play "mind games" with others in order to gain the upper hand in a relationship. This does not make one a psychopath. Psychopaths become adept at this psychological game playing and ultimately become proficient at controlling their environment. With cognition intact, psychopaths demonstrate a profound lack of morality and behavioral controls. They habitually violate

PROFILE 3.6 Mr. Carter, a Psychopath Exposed

Carter's behavior and writings indicate a man who is a prisoner of his own obsessive ambivalence. The journal clearly and repeatedly documents Carter's fears, anger, and frustrations with himself and others. He presents himself as a person controlled by his obsessions and compulsions. Although he attempts to portray himself to others as a successful and productive individual, his journal tells a very different story. Carter, reflecting on his unhappy state, writes:

> My inheritance has afforded me the luxury of not having to do anything with myself. Because of this, I have had a hard time joining society. My self-esteem has suffered as a result. I latch on to a girl and want to be consumed by the relationship. I smother them, and this causes them to tend to reject me. I lose myself too quickly and easily in the girl. I "set myself up" to be alone. It's almost like I set myself up for hard times.

By his own account he places blame on his family, especially his parents, as the source of much of his inner conflict. Carter chronicles in his journal his deep resentments toward his parents for the many perceived and actual pains they caused him.

Things Mom and Dad did:

1. Dad held me under the water in pool when I was 5—made me afraid of the water. Later I conquered it windsurfing.
2. Left me at boarding school
3. Mom went crazy and killed herself
4. Dad used to beat me for no reason
5. Broke bass guitar
6. Kicked me for selling colt pistol
7. Gave vacuform for straight "A" 2nd grade (instead of love)
8. Mom called me a sociopath
9. Dad built my tree house
10. Knocking my head with the ring
11. Knocking my head against the wall
12. Pulled me out of the house by my hair with Pat watching
13. Cut me off ($) when I left GA Tech
14. Left us at grandparents for three months, repeatedly
15. Forced me to stay in library every day during spring break
16. Threw out all my toys when house we grew up in was cleaned out
17. Didn't want to see me when I moved to GA Tech to be close to him
18. Wrote will such that his wife got to dispense with everything

The death of his parents and his unhappy childhood set the stage for his need to project his self-loathing and insecurities onto others while at the same time appearing to be a congenial, understanding, and tolerant person. For example, Carter accepted invitations to visit his sisters and stayed in their homes, while at the same time he vividly described his negative personal feelings about them in his journal. Regarding Stacy, he writes:

> Well—Stacy is really a spoiled child. I am really done with her this time. I don't give a shit if she does kill herself. At least then we would be done hearing her whine about how she is all bummed out about whatever the excuse of the week is. Think of the money I am going to save by not traveling to her house ever again. Frankly, I hope I live long enough to see her die. She will get hers. It is just a matter of time. She is such a bitch. Such a self-important, self-righteous bitch. Remember: I am better than they are. They have more security now, but it

> ain't over YET. When Al has a heart attack and dies, I won't be around to do anything for them. FUCK THEM!!

Of particular importance in these excerpts are the several references made by Carter regarding his death wishes for his sister Nancy, his desire to see Nancy "get hers," and his matter-of-fact indifference to the possibility that his other sister Stacy might take her own life. His systemic anger that frames his thoughts about his family and his desire to see them suffer for treating him poorly is a recurring theme in his journal. Carter demonstrates these same attitudes toward his friends and ultimately his victims. The following statements from Carter's journal highlight his pent-up anger toward others who have intentionally or inadvertently angered him. Note the forms of punishment Carter has selected for each person.

1. Pat C. had affair with dad, ended up with all his property. Make it look like an accident.
2. Carol I.... Trash her car. "Father" Tom. Meddling mother fucker... He will get what he deserves! I will see to it!
3. Nancy C. ... (Crusader Yacht Sales)—deserves something special: vandalize boats w/crusader signs on them!!!
4. Lisa (M sister) child/husband
5. Michael D. Wind surfing vacations—kill.
6. Steve H., lawyer—kill.
7. Norbert C.—find, kill.
8. Eric Z.—find, kill.
9. Don't get mad get even. Revenge is best served cold. Light bulb filament in gas tank—powered by car elec. system—when car is started: BOOM.
10. Scott W.—Fuck with car.

His inability to adequately resolve his personal inner conflicts is a core issue to his conviction for stalking activity. Unable to bring resolution regarding his conflicts with his deceased parents, Carter focuses his fantasies, frustrations, insecurities, and anger into developing relationships where he can be in control. These relationships are specific in that he is attracted to women who are assertive, goal-oriented, and self-confident: everything that he, according to his own account, is lacking. An example of his need to control is noted in his journal regarding his destructive relationship with his former girlfriend, Jane C.

> The things I did to her: Never let her have any time with friends. Never let her have any time alone. Couldn't talk to any guy without interrogation following. Physical violence. Being cruel when I knew that she couldn't get away or I wouldn't let her get away. Destroying things she gave me. Destroying her things. Threatening with violence. Saying mean things. Can't control myself.

Mary, another victim, would often attempt to break off the relationship. In his journal Carter expresses his rage toward her by threatening to kill her.

> She was not happy with this, and used her old threat of saying "goodbye then." I really don't think she has any idea what she is dealing with. I will kill her if she fucks with me this time.

Her friends stopped calling because they were uncomfortable speaking to or being around Carter. Often following one of his jealous tirades, Carter showed displays of

(continued)

PROFILE 3.6 (Continued)

affection and kindness in an effort to convince her that life would be better now, that all the ugliness was behind them. This tactic inevitably was followed by more acts of rage. Eventually his anger intensified and he punched her on the arm and threw her against a window. She moved out and tried to hide. In retaliation, Carter cut up her clothing and other personal property and erased her computer hard drive that contained important data she used for her business. On one occasion he was so angry that he again wiped out her computer hard drive and filled her coffeemaker with detergent. His aggression toward his victim was manifested in other ways, including killing her cat by crushing its head with a flashlight. Carter refers to the killing:

> Did kill the cat. After it bit me, it deserved as much. (Bashed its head with her roommate's flashlight.)

During the attack Carter was bitten severely on one of his fingers. After killing the animal, Carter returned to the residence and explained to Mary that, as he was leaving her residence, he tried to pet the cat when it suddenly turned and attacked him. Sympathetic, Mary bandaged his wound and then she and Carter spent an hour looking for her cat, which she believed had run away. It was not until weeks later that Carter informed her by telephone of the actual demise of her cat.

He would then call and harass her, followed by expressions of contriteness and apologies. His behavior follows the same pattern seen in domestic violence cases: the escalation of rage, the blowup, and finally the placating apologies, which become the hallmark of an abuser before the next cycle of acting out.

These incidents were punctuated over time with a series of telephone threats, several of them suggesting either physical or psychological harm to Mary:

1. "And I'll tell you something else cold-blooded bitch. I know where you are and the fun has just begun."
2. "Hmm, remember the nightmares you used to have? Aaah, they're nothing compared to what reality could be."

social contracts (fraud, cheating) and engage in chronic risk-taking. This may be explained, at least in part, by the fact that psychopaths show significant impairment on social contract rules, suggesting that they possess deficits in their reasoning processes (Ermer and Kiehl, 2010). For a psychopath, it is very much a learning and adaptation process that may favor honing social skills rather than their reasoning processes. Profile 3.6 examines the developing mind-set of a psychopathic offender arrested for stalking. Much of the information was obtained from hundreds of diary entries found in the offender's computer on his arrest.

Ressler and his colleagues (1988) argue that psychological motives for homicide do not find their roots in traumatization or stimulation; rather, offenders murder as a result of their thinking (p. 34). Thought processes, however, are influenced by life experiences that ultimately can affect the types of fantasies developed by individuals. Thus, negative experiences give rise to negative thoughts and fantasies, and positive experiences lay the foundation for positive thoughts and constructive fantasies. Wertham (1937) referred to persons experiencing *catathymic crisis*. This involves a person with underlying emotionally charged conflicts developing a fixed idea that he must kill his future victim. After a protracted period of rumination, the person in crisis carries out the murder. Catathymic crisis can be in

3. "You've wasted my time. The bill will come due. Rest assured the bill will come due."
4. Kissing sounds, music. "Nowhere to run, nowhere to hide."
5. "By the way you bitch, I enjoyed killing your little cat. Purr, purr, purr, till I crush your skull."
6. "I went out tonight and I found the dog. It was an annoying dog and I fed it Drano mixed in with hamburger and I watched it die. And I thought about various things."

All of these behaviors are clear manifestations of Carter's desire to control and/or harm his victims. In the beginning, his relationships appear to be positive. In the case of Mary, both parties seemed quite enamored with each other. Over time, Mary began to see and hear behavior that she found disturbing. As the relationship deteriorated and she tried to break off with him, Carter began to employ a variety of maladaptive behaviors in order to maintain control of the relationship. Moving from harassing phone calls to threatening phone calls, from minor vandalism to serious property destruction, from knocking a victim down to showing up at her home with a gun, from killing animals to dousing the victim's planter box and front porch with gasoline—each scenario denotes escalation toward increasingly violent behavior. The etiology of violent attachments is grounded in an internal drive for control. Carter can maintain the pretense of respectability and detachment from others, but internally he is drawn to women with whom he can develop an obsessive love/hate relationship. At an individual level, dysfunctional relationships created by Carter culminate in the forced termination of the relationship. Carter then retreats for a period of time to rethink his relationships. He re-emerges to seek another relationship, only to have it also destroyed. The pathological cycle appears endless, as do his levels of frustration and aggression. Carter may appear rehabilitated while under the scrutiny of the courts, but the prognosis is not good for future, unsuspecting victims. Carter served three and a half years in federal prison for stalking (author's files).

one of two forms, chronic or acute. The "crisis" involves the superficially integrated person who struggles with inadequacy, specifically sexual inadequacy. Ultimately the person in crisis resorts to violence when potential victims challenge his sense of integrity, adequacy, or sexual competence.

Compulsive homicides may also be sudden acts of violence induced by underlying conflicts. In comparison to catathymic homicides, compulsive homicides lie at the extreme end of the motivational spectrum, determined entirely by internal psychogenic sources with little environmental influence. Compulsive homicides, which can be opportunistic or methodically planned, also have strong potential for repetition, and the urge to act is powerful. The ritualistic acts are sexually motivated, and the act of aggression itself is eroticized (Schlesinger, 2004).

It is unlikely to find individuals who fantasize about helping others and then go out and kill other human beings. People who feel good about themselves do not kill others. The better a person's self-concept, the higher an individual's self-esteem, the less need he or she has to control and dominate others. One may wonder why so many people subscribe to magazines or prefer entertainment established and operated on the premise of violence. Perhaps those who have carefully controlled lives allow others to stand proxy for them in acting out

FOCUS ON PSYCHOPATHY

Christopher J. Patrick
Professor of Psychology, Florida State University

Dr. Patrick has been conducting research on the topic of psychopathic personality for over 25 years, dating back to his PhD study at the University of British Columbia, entitled "The validity of lie detection with criminal psychopaths." His mentor for this project was Dr. William Iacono, who completed his doctorate under the supervision of renowned psychologist Dr. David Lykken. Lykken's own dissertation, described in his classic 1957 paper "A Study of Anxiety in the Sociopathic Personality," served as the foundation for experimental studies of psychopathy conducted by many others since. In preparation for his dissertation, Patrick took a seminar at UBC taught by leading psychopathy expert Dr. Robert Hare, in which he learned about the Psychopathy Checklist (PCL/PCL-R; Hare, 1980/2003), a new interview-based inventory for diagnosing the disorder in prison inmates. Patrick used this inventory to identify psychopathic and nonpsychopathic prisoners for his study, which entailed testing of participants of each type by professional polygraph examiners to determine whether they had perpetrated a simulated theft within the prison (for details, see Patrick & Iacono, 1989). Patrick's experiences conducting this initial study raised a number of compelling questions that have guided his work ever since: Do distinct types of psychopaths exist with differing clinical presentations? Why do some psychopathic individuals appear physiologically under-responsive whereas others appear normally reactive or even hyperreactive? Can reactivity due to excitement be distinguished experimentally from reactivity due to fear? In what ways do psychopathic individuals who skirt serious trouble and attain success in society (e.g., as soldiers, lawyers, or corporate executives) differ from criminally-disposed psychopaths who end up repeatedly in prison?

After completing his doctorate, Patrick went on to investigate emotional reactivity deficits in psychopaths using a new methodology termed *fear-potentiated startle*. He found that prisoners diagnosed as psychopathic do not show enhanced blink startle reactivity to sudden noises occurring during viewing of frightful images (e.g., aimed guns, mutilated corpses), despite showing autonomic arousal—indicating excitement to such images rather than normal fear (Patrick, Bradley, & Lang, 1993). This finding has been replicated repeatedly (cf. Patrick & Bernat, 2009) and served as inspiration for many subsequent studies examining affective deficits in psychopathy—including recent brain imaging studies (for a review, see Patrick, Venables, & Skeem, 2012). Patrick's work on this topic also helped to clarify why only some high-psychopathic individuals show blunted emotional reactivity. He found that weak emotional response is tied specifically to the classic *interpersonal-affective* features of psychopathy (charm, grandiosity, manipulativeness, shallow affect, lack of remorse or empathy); individuals exhibiting mainly antisocial deviance features (impulsiveness, aggressiveness, persistent criminality) show normal or enhanced reactivity to

their fantasies of hostility and aggression. The boxer smashing his opponent's face, splattering blood; the matador who is gored by the horns of an enraged bull; the hockey player who slashes his opponent with his stick—each brings the fans to their feet, eager for more.

But most people do not kill; they just enjoy watching others do it on television and at the movies, or reading about it in books. Murderers take their fantasies further. Perhaps some of us have fantasies that resemble those of the murderer, yet we maintain control. Edmund Kemper (see Profile 4.3) spoke of the rage inside emotional stimuli (Patrick, 1994; Verona et al., 2004; Vaidyanathan et al., 2011). Patrick was recognized for his contributions to scientific understanding in these areas by Distinguished Early Career Awards from the Society for Psychophysiological Research in 1993 and the American Psychological Association in 1995.

In turn, his work on psychopathy and emotion led Patrick and his collaborators to undertake studies directed at identifying subtypes of psychopaths by using statistical methods to classify their personality test profiles. This work demonstrated that criminals diagnosed as psychopaths using Hare's PCL-R comprise at least two distinct subtypes—an *emotionally-stable* subtype low in anxiety and high in social dominance, and an *aggressive* subtype high in impulsiveness and disposed toward anger and violent acts (Blagov et al., 2011; Hicks et al., 2004, 2010). Yet another line of research by Patrick and colleagues over the past decade (e.g., Benning et al., 2003, 2005a,b; Ross et al., 2009; Sellbom et al., 2005) has focused on psychopathic tendencies in community samples, as assessed by two self-report based measures: the Psychopathic Personality Inventory (PPI/PPI-R; Lilienfeld & Andrews, 1996; Lilienfeld & Widows, 2005), and the Externalizing Spectrum Inventory (ESI; Krueger et al., 2007; Venables & Patrick, in press). This research has demonstrated distinct physiological correlates of interpersonal-affective and antisocial-externalizing components of psychopathy in nonoffenders paralleling those observed in prisoners (Benning et al., 2005c; Hall et al., 2007; Nelson et al., 2010) and shown evidence of a strong heritable basis to each (Blonigen et al., 2005; Kramer et al., in press; Krueger et al., 2002).

Patrick's extensive work along these complementary lines, in conjunction with that of others, has culminated in two theoretic models intended to serve as integrative frameworks for ongoing research on psychopathy. One of these, the *Triarchic Model* (Patrick, 2010; Patrick, Fowles, & Krueger, 2009; see also Skeem et al., 2011), conceptualizes observable ('phenotypic') symptoms of psychopathy in terms of three distinguishable constructs: *boldness*, entailing social dominance, emotional stability and venturesomeness; *disinhibition*, entailing weak behavioral restraint and impaired affect regulation; and *meanness*, reflecting impaired affiliative capacity and callous disregard for others. The other, the *Two-Process Model* (Patrick, 2007; Patrick & Bernat, 2009; see also Fowles & Dindo, 2009), posits at least two distinct causal mechanisms contributing to the symptomatic features of psychopathy and to subtypes of the disorder: *dispositional fearlessness*, reflecting weak reactivity of the brain's defensive motivational system (Kramer et al., in press; Vaidyanathan et al., 2009), and *externalizing proneness*, reflecting impairments in frontal brain systems that operate to guide and control behavior (Hicks et al., 2004, 2007; Krueger et al., 2002; Nelson et al., 2010; Patrick, 2008; Patrick et al., 2005, 2006, 2007). The first of these models was the subject of Patrick's presidential address to the Society for Scientific Study of Psychopathy in 2009. The second will form part of his upcoming (Fall 2012) address to the Society for Psychophysiological Research, for which he currently serves as President.

him that would not subside. He also discussed his fantasy of performing his next murder. By the time Kemper shoved a gun in the face of his first college coed, he had already mentally rehearsed the scenario "hundreds of times." Once he pulled out the gun, he knew there was no turning back (HBO, 1984). How often and how close do the fantasies of nonoffenders take them to the brink of killing?

Another approach in exploring the phenomenon of serial murder focuses on sociological explanations. Chapter 4 explores the various structural and social process theories that seek to elucidate the dynamics of serial killing.

Social Construction of Serial Murder

LEARNING OBJECTIVES

- To evaluate sociological theories as they pertain to violent behavior
- To understand the role of family and maladaptive childhood behaviors that may portend adult criminality, especially violence
- To examine the incidence of school shootings by juveniles compared to adults
- To examine the Myers and Kirby typologies of juvenile serial killers
- To explore the etiology of serial murder as it relates to Hickey's Trauma-Control Model
- To review the case studies as they relate to the process of becoming a serial murderer
- To understand the facilitators that influence the construction of serial murderers

UNDERSTANDING MURDER

In addition to the potential for genetic predisposition to violent behavior for some people, we must look into the mirror for additional understanding of why some become involved in criminal activities and others do not. Indeed, most persons have committed crimes for which they could have been arrested but went undetected or at least not officially sanctioned. Cheating on taxes, taking items from stores, borrowing things without permission, fraud, embezzlement, solicitation for sexual purposes, etc. are but a few of the many criminal events in which common citizens engage without perceiving themselves as being criminals. These *criminal distractions* may be infrequent, usually nonviolent, and often easily rationalized. Do you think that Randy "Duke" Cunningham, former U.S. congressman, or former Illinois governor Rod Blagojevich, both convicted of corruption, consider themselves to be criminals? In Illinois, the

"Land of Lincoln" where four out of the last five governors have landed in prison for corruption, former governor Rod Blagojevich was charged with attempting to sell President Barack Obama's former senate seat and a litany of other acts of corruption to which he believed as a powerbroker he was legally impervious. In sports, Marion Jones was publicly outraged at accusations that she had used illegal substances to enhance her athletic performances. Of course, she was guilty and had to forfeit her five gold medals. Even the former great O. J. Simpson, now serving a 9- to 33-year prison sentence in Nevada, was perplexed and frustrated at his conviction for robbery and kidnapping when he insisted that he was simply taking back what was "rightfully" his to begin with. Former New York governor Eliot Spitzer and Colorado evangelist Ted Haggard both solicited prostitutes while serving in their high-profile positions but certainly did not consider themselves to be criminals. Even former U.S. senator Larry Craig, renowned for his public bathroom shoe tapping solicitations, continues to reject the notion that he has done anything wrong, even though he pled guilty. The same can be said of former congressman William Jefferson, caught on tape taking bribes and storing the cash in his home freezer, who refused to resign from the elected office that he had disgraced.

So, then, who are the real criminals? Our society identifies them as habitual offenders, including individuals who commit atrocious acts such as murder or child molestation. Yet even many of these highly recidivistic offenders do not perceive themselves as criminals. Justification and rationalization are common tools for most persons, regardless of socioeconomic status, gender, race, religion, or culture. Does a person who habitually commits criminal acts have a criminal personality? How would such a personality be formed? Are criminals much different than noncriminals in personality, or is it a function of access to resources, opportunities, and socialization?

Those involved in criminological research often find themselves drawing on various sociological theories to understand crime and criminals. Some aspects of serial murder research remain the purview of exploration and speculation due to the many myths and preconceived notions that surround the phenomenon. Critical to sorting out fact from fiction is the importance of laying a theoretical framework that can account for sociological factors. Two relevant theories are social structure theory and social process theory.

Social Structure Theory

Social structure theories focus on individuals' socioeconomic standing, suggesting that poor people commit more crimes because they are stifled in their quest for financial or social success. Specifically, offenders, as a result of their racial, ethnic, or subcultural standing, are blocked in various ways from achieving the "American Dream" through legitimate means. Consequently, they seek success through deviant methods. Structural theories offer cogent explanations for many types of crimes, except for serial murder. Generally, serial killers do not belong to a racial or ethnic minority and do not appear to be particularly motivated, although there are a few exceptions, by social or financial gain. Certainly, serial offenders exist who rob their victims, but even then the financial reward is peripheral to the attraction of killing another human being. The few exceptions to this often are found among female serial killers, who constitute a small portion of the total number of serial murderers (see Chapter 9). Occasionally, as in the case of Belle Gunness of Indiana, who advertised in newspapers for suitors then promptly killed them once she gained access to their money, women will kill their husbands, fiancés, or lovers in order to improve or maintain their lifestyle. Over a 14-year period, one offender is believed to have murdered seven of her eight children for insurance purposes. Each time she needed money, another child would suddenly pass away. Even in these cases, however, we cannot be sure that money was actually the primary motive.

One structural theory that may at some point provide greater insight into serial murder is the perspective of urbanism. Murder rates tend to be highest in densely populated cities such as Gary, Indiana; Detroit; Miami; Birmingham, Alabama; New York City; and Washington, D.C. Urban homicide rates tend to be associated with social disorder, alienation, drugs, fear, disassociation, poverty, and broken homes (Messner and Tardiff, 1986). High-density populations increase the probability of victimization because of impersonalization and frequent encounters with strangers (Sampson, 1987).

Serial killers have been located in and around most major U.S. cities, although they also appear in some of the most isolated areas in America. Where the offenders commit their crimes, of course, depends on what type of serial killers they are and what kinds of victims they are after. High-density populations are attractive to those wishing to "melt" into their environment. Several of the most "effective" serial killers have operated in some of the more populated areas of the country. Whether serial murderers are attracted to such locales or they already live in the area is not exactly clear. We do know that California—followed by Florida, New York, Texas, Illinois, Georgia, and Ohio—reports the highest frequencies of serial killing in the United States. However, Rossmo (1995) correctly notes that those states with the highest *per capita rates* of serial murder, or states with more than twice the overall rate for the United States, are Alaska, Idaho, Wyoming, Utah, North and South Dakota, Kansas, Delaware, Vermont, and Rhode Island. For the serial offender who is specifically looking for women or children, the larger cities obviously offer an ample supply of unsuspecting victims. Ted Bundy was particularly at ease when working the crowds of people in shopping malls. Christopher Wilder specifically went to shopping malls to lure his victims by posing as a photographer. Yet, for some of these offenders, it is not the crowds they seek but the potential victims who walk, work, or play alone. Jeffrey Dahmer frequented gay bars, looking for attractive young males whom he could cull out of the crowd and lure to his apartment. Although areas with dense populations would seem likely places for serial offenders to find victims, further research is warranted on the connection between population density and occurrence of serial murders. DeFronzo et al. (2007), in their examination of male serial killer rates in two different states, where one was the state in which they received their primary socialization and the other where they killed their largest number of victims, found that cultural aspects and social structure accounted for much of the male serial killer variation among states. Indeed, serial killers appear to live and kill their victims in areas conducive to their cultural and social expectations.

Social Class Theory*

Leyton (1986a), in his pivotal work *Hunting Humans: The Rise of the Modern Multiple Murderer,* examines the status aspirations of serial murderers. He notes that a serial killer is "most often on the margins of the upper-working or lower middle classes who comes to feel excluded from the class he [sic] so devoutly wishes to join. In an extended campaign of vengeance, he murders people unknown to him, but who represent to him (in their behavior, appearance and their location) the class that has rejected him" (p. 23). Leyton points out that the killer's perceived social status of the victims becomes a catalyst for murder. Ritzer (1992) notes that some feminists are of the opinion that "the theme of violence as overt physical cruelty lies at the heart of radical feminism's linking of patriarchy to violence: rape, sexual abuse ... enforced prostitution ... sadism in pornography are all linked to the historic and cross-cultural practices of witch burning, the stoning to death of adulteresses ... and the savage practices of clitorectomy" (p. 336). Once patriarchy was established, Ritzer states, other power resources including economic, legal, emotional, and ideological were used to support it.

Caputi (1989) examines power and serial murder and suggests that females are usually selected as victims by male serial killers because of female powerlessness. She argues that we glorify serial killers in American society and that, as hierarchy dictates, such murders carry sexually political importance. These are murders rooted in a system of male dominance in a manner similar to the way the lynching of blacks was based on white supremacy. Caputi states that serial murder is the "ultimate expression of sexuality that defines sex as a form of dominant power; it, like rape, is a form of terror that constructs and maintains male supremacy" (1990, p. 2). Egger (1984) observed that the majority of victims are women who share common characteristics and are considered to be without power and prestige—women in lower economic groups including prostitutes, runaways, homeless, minorities, the poor, and the elderly. Gunn (2000), in her exceptional examination of social class and serial murder, found a connection between violence and social class. She noted that homicide patterns tend to be prevalent among the lower classes. Serial killers in her study came primarily from the working and/or underclass and chose victims at the same social standing or lower. She concluded that serial killers chose male victims based on their lower social class and female victims based on gender. Gunn

---

*The author strongly encourages those interested in the issue of social class and serial murder to read Lynn Gunn's (2000) study.

supports other researchers who contend a distinctive linkage between serial murder and social class.

Social Process Theory

Social process theories contend that criminal behavior is a function of a socialization process. This includes a host of sociopsychological interactions by the offender with institutions and social organizations. Offenders may turn to crime as a result of peer-group pressure, family problems, poor school performance, legal entanglements, and other situations that gradually steer them to criminal behavior. Process theories recognize that anyone, regardless of race or socioeconomic status, has the potential for criminal behavior. Central to the social process theory, as to some aspects of psychoanalytic theory, is the effect of the family on youths who engage in delinquent or violent behavior. Research studies continue to suggest that parents who divorce have children with higher levels of externalizing behaviors and internalizing problems, a decline in academic achievement, and greater problems in maintaining healthy relationships than those with parents who do not divorce. These effects, however, do appear to mitigate over time and for many youth, do not have long-term consequences. A generalized view that divorce will automatically have long-term negative consequences on children fails to take into account that the effects of divorce are influenced by many contextual factors between child and parent that are present both prior to and following the divorce (Lansford, 2009).

Theories of aggression vary extensively, but for understanding the etiology of serial murder, Albert Bandura's book *Aggression* (1973) provides valuable insights. According to social learning theory, a component of social process theory, one might explain the aggressive behavior of the serial murderer by examining the offender's past (see Chapter 3). Special attention by researchers should be given to childhood experiences for evidence of victimization or the witnessing of violent behavior. In earlier studies, Bandura and Walters (1963) noted that particularly aggressive boys were also hostile and antagonistic and that they experienced feelings of rejection from their fathers.

Brown (1984), in an application of social learning theory, found that emotional neglect and abuse were correlated with all forms of reported delinquency. However, he also noted a lack of correlation between physical abuse and any form of delinquency. This may suggest to those who study the psychodynamics of the serial killer that evidence of the social learning of aggression may be subtle.

Children who witness family violence are, according to ratings by their mothers, likely to demonstrate diminished social competence and behavioral problems (Wolfe, Jaffe, Wilson, and Zak, 1985). This "exposure to violence may have an indirect, yet significant, effect on children" (Wolfe et al., p. 663). The social learning of violence, therefore, need not be the result of one's having been a victim but simply a result of viewing violence. Wolfe and his colleagues add: "It is suspected by some researchers and clinicians that girls from violent families may not express signs of maladjustment in childhood, yet they may suffer higher rates of mental health and family problems in adulthood than many girls from nonviolent homes" (p. 663). Again, this suggests that the evidence of learned social aggression may not manifest itself in some cases for several years. The direct and indirect influence of family violence on future adjustment difficulties of boys was examined by Jaffe, Wolfe, Wilson, and Zak (1986), who found similar patterns of adjustment problems for those who had been abused by parents and those who had witnessed violence between their parents. Both of these groups differed from a control group in that they exhibited more aggressive behaviors toward others.

Ruth Inglis, in her book *Sins of Fathers* (1978), notes a strong relationship between abused children and subsequent violent behavior. In comparing abusive and non-abusive families, Webster-Stratton (1985) found that, in addition to low family income, "family history of parent abuse as a child was highly correlated with more negative and controlling interactions with children, which was correlated with the abusive family. This finding seems to support the social learning model that parents learn abusive parenting techniques from their own parents and then carry them out with their children, thus continuing the 'coercive cycle' across generations" (p. 67).

In another study, Dean, Malik, Richards, and Strinzer (1986) asked maltreated and non-maltreated children to tell stories about kind or unkind behavior initiated by a child toward a child, by an adult toward a child, or by a child toward an adult, and then asked the children to explain what the recipient would do next. In contrast to their non-maltreated counterparts, maltreated children between the ages of six and eight told more stories in which children reciprocated the kind acts of adults and fewer stories in which adults or peers reciprocated the kind acts of children. A second finding was that maltreated children of all ages justified their parents' unkind acts on the basis of their own bad behavior (Dean et al., pp. 617–626). This finding is echoed in many of the statements and accounts of serial killers.

Alice Miller in *For Your Own Good* (1984), an examination of child rearing and the roots of violence, provides a subjective, qualitative study of child abuse in which she explores the private hells of children who later become offenders. She discusses "soul murder" or the extraordinary beatings and sexual abuses perpetrated on young children by parents and relatives. She argues that "the earlier this soul murder [takes] place, the more difficult it will be for the affected person to grasp and the less it can be validated by memories and words. If he wants to communicate, his only recourse is acting out" (Miller, p. 231). Put another way, children may forget or repress what you say or do to them, but children never forget how you make them feel. It is these feelings that fuel the flames of anger and violence. Having interviewed several serial killers, I find considerable validation for this perspective. Of considerable importance is the continuation of exposure to violent environments. As children at risk become adolescents, some of them will find themselves engaged in what Erving Goffman referred to as "Total Institutions" or places where routine degradation processes are the norm for stripping away individualism in order for conformity, compliance, and altruism to flourish. Jails, prisons, juvenile boot camps, military boot camps, and state psychiatric hospitals all insist on cooperation. Castle and Hensley (2002) researched serial killers and possible links to military experience. They noted in applying social learning theory how serial killers learn to reinforce hostility, aggression, and murder in military boot camps. This does not mean that such institutions create killers, but for emotionally unhealthy persons the rigor of being in a locked facility can be devastating. Other theoretical frameworks also warrant examination.

Neutralization Theory

Sykes and Matza (1957) and Matza (1964) view the process of delinquent youths becoming criminals as a matter of neutralizing their personal values and attitudes as they drift between conventional behavior and illegitimate behavior. Matza points out that people are not criminals all the time. Often criminals participate in the normal functions of everyday life. Occasionally they drift toward illegal behavior just as they sometimes drift toward conventional behavior. In order for them to rationalize their drift toward illegal behavior they must use learned techniques of neutralization. These techniques include denial of responsibility, denial of injury, denial of the victim, condemnation of the condemners, and the appeal to higher loyalties—in other words, "it was not my fault," "no harm was done," "they had it coming," "society is to blame," and "I did it for them, not me." Denying the victim is a technique commonly used to shift blame and accompanying guilt. It also serves to lessen the value of the life destroyed. Bandura (1974) describes methods by which offenders can make inhuman behavior legitimate:

> Attribution of blame to the victim is still another exonerative expedient. Victims are faulted for bringing maltreatment on themselves, or extraordinary circumstances are invoked as justification for questionable conduct. One need not engage in self-reproof for committing acts prescribed by circumstances. A further means of weakening self-punishment is to dehumanize the victim. Inflicting harm upon people who are regarded as subhuman or debased is less likely to arouse self-reproof than if they are looked upon as human beings with sensitivities. (pp. 861–862)

Current research into the behavior of serial killers suggests they frequently dehumanize their victims before taking their lives. It appears to expedite the murder when, psychologically, instead of attacking another human being, they attack something without name, feelings, or identity. Henry Lucas, who confessed and recanted confessions to dozens of murders, once stated that when he had found a victim he would never ask her name and if she gave it he would forget it immediately because he did not want to know his victims' names or anything about them. Charny (1980), in explaining the process of dehumanization of others, notes that the process is actually much more subtle and commonplace than we would expect:

> Dehumanization is a process of ridding the other of the benefit of his humanity. The process extends along a continuum, leading to the ultimate step of removing the other person's opportunity to live. The "little" everyday dehumanizations we practice on one another are stations on a way toward the ultimate act whereby one person takes away another's very life. Thus, it is not simply the insult that we inflict upon another that is at stake in everyday dehumanizations. The fact is that we are learning to practice a devastating process, rehearsing it, achieving gratification from it, and perhaps preparing ourselves to participate one day in the removal of other people's actual lives. (p. 100)

One might argue that serial murderers drift between conventional and nonconventional behavior. Several serial killers have been known to be gainfully employed, married with families, active in civic organizations, and educated, and they were considered part of mainstream society.

Complete denial of injury to victims by offenders is a common ploy used by many serial killers. Others not only deny any involvement but readily name another person as the guilty party. One serial killer was found guilty in 1983 of murdering several women and presently awaits execution on San Quentin's death row. His female accomplice received two lengthy prison sentences. In December 1988 the male offender, in a letter to me, reaffirmed his complete innocence with regard to any of the killings.

> The sum total would prove beyond doubt to you that [she] was following a script for murder, and that she was and at times is ... wife of Theodore Robert Bundy.... It is utterly easy to show that [she] selected her own internalized victim/motivation and externalized it into the script of a book about a man she idolized.
>
> She lived one of the most bizarre lives from that point forward of any serial killer to date. She became a practicing lesbian. She engaged in degradation-sex, and S/M. She leapt the gender line with such frequency in her life, even marrying a flagrant homosexual, that her roles in sex and S/M became so blurred she would often be involved in utterly contradictory encounters with gender-blended persons, groups or persons, and in such a role-blended way with her sadomasochism she wanted to torture her deceased victims as she wished she dared be so tortured.
>
> You won't find a cesspool as vile as this case. But god damn it, I can prove I am a mere "substitute" for her partner ... whom she murdered. She could not testify against a dead man, so the next best deal shown to her was to testify and accuse against some living person. I was a man who stayed in her apartments, renting a room and bathroom, and on three occasions, dumb enough to let her talk me into sex with her. She had a man, proximate to vehicles, weapons, and herself. It was all

> the police wanted. In the aftermath of the terror of the Hillside Strangler case in Los Angeles, the authority-attitude was, solve this damned case fast.
>
> Within the first 18 days, August 11, 1980, to August 29, 1980, they committed themselves trustingly to her stories.
>
> That sealed it.
>
> The Ted Bundy legacy is still going on. If you don't have the sense and energy to see that everything I've said, and tons more, proves truly that [she] is the strangest of them all, then live on in the mediocrity of assuming those who are on death row MUST be guilty.... (author's files, November 30, 1988)

John Wayne Gacy, killer of 33 young males in Chicago, denied any involvement in the murders and suggested that someone else must have placed those 27 bodies in the crawlspace of his home while he was at work.

Other serial killers have admitted murdering women, especially prostitutes, but insist there have been no real victims because they were, in the offenders' eyes, scum of the earth. Thomas N. Cream argued that he had aided society and ended the suffering of scores of prostitutes. In 1995, an offender who murdered five homosexuals in Los Angeles stated to me that his victims "deserved what they got" and that "they were asking for it because they kept trying to pick me up." Another offender, Robert Carr, explained that those who died by his hands "grew" a great deal during their brief stay with the killer. Others killed because they believed it was God's will or because of allegiance to their partners or to assist the survival of society.

The problem with neutralization theory as an explanation for serial murder is its verifiability. One would have to be able to demonstrate that an offender first neutralized his moral beliefs before drifting into violent behavior. As it appears now, serial murderers who rationalize their behavior are believed to construct explanations *ex post facto,* or after the homicides have occurred. Given the current understanding of serial-murderer behavior, empirical evidence of neutralization will not likely appear in the foreseeable future.

Social Control Theory

Classical control theorists would argue that people do not commit crimes such as murder because of their fear of punishment. Punishment, they believe, can serve as a deterrent to committing crimes. However, for homicides in general, capital punishment or long prison terms usually do not deter people, because many homicides are "crimes of passion" in which the offender kills his or her victim as a result of an altercation. Briar and Piliavin (1965) have pointed out that fear of punishment alone is not sufficient for everyone to refrain from criminal behavior. They believe that a sense of commitment to society, family, and education serves as a deterrent to crime. Reckless (1967) has argued that youth can become isolated or insulated from criminal influences through what he terms "containments," including a positive self-image; ego strength; high frustration tolerance; goal orientation; a sense of belongingness; consistent moral front; reinforcement of norms, goals, and values; effective supervision; discipline; and a meaningful social role.

Hirschi (1969) expanded social control theory and introduced four elements of the social bond that apply to all social classes. These four elements—attachment, commitment, involvement, and belief—are bonds that individuals strengthen or weaken in relationship to the society in which they live. He noted that attachment to peers, schools, various social institutions, and especially family is critical if the individual is to develop a sense of conscious concern for others and a general acceptance of the social norms. Hirschi also believed that having a commitment to personal property, conventional goals, reputation, education, and so on will make people less likely to commit crimes and risk losing what they have worked to establish. Similarly, involvement in conventional endeavors allows little time for criminal behavior. Finally, if one shares a set of common beliefs with others, there exists a greater likelihood of conformity to societal expectations.

Hirschi found that youths who appeared to be closely attached to their parents were less likely to commit crimes. In comparison, most serial killers do not appear to have close relationships with their families. The majority appear to have experienced gradual or traumatic breaks with one or both parents while in their youth. The lack of commitment to conventional values is noted in the histories of other serial murderers who became heavily involved in drugs, alcohol, and other "marginal" behaviors. In addition, serial killers usually do not have meaningful, close relationships with peers but remain distant and isolated.

The application of Hirschi's social control theory may eventually provide additional insight into serial killers. These offenders do not appear to have the requisite ties to family, peers, and community that Hirschi found among those who tended not to engage in criminal behavior. The theory, however, was developed for measuring delinquent youths, not adults. Although serial offenders report weakened social ties, we have yet to examine youths who later become serial offenders in order to determine whether they had experienced weakened social bonds before their acts of homicide. Certainly there are case histories of offenders that reveal weakened social bonds, but such reports are usually developed after the homicides. In short, we find what we want to find: instead of a weak social bond causing one to become violent, becoming violent to the point of killing may cause the offender to weaken his or her social bonds.

Labeling Theory

Erving Goffman (1961), in his classical treatise on institutions, noted the stigma attached to persons who have spent time in an institution such as a prison or a psychiatric facility. This stigma is the result of having attracted the attention of society through abnormal or unacceptable behavior. Labeling theorists Lemert (1951) and Schur (1972) viewed negative labels such as "former mental patient," "ex-convict," "delinquent," "stupid," and "slut" as inflicting psychological damage on those to whom the labels are attached.

Labeling theory views abnormal behavior as a process by which a person graduates from primary deviance to secondary deviance (Lemert, 1951). According to labeling theorists the original deviant act, of which the origins vary significantly, is called *primary deviance.* In turn, by being labeled a deviant, the offender is carried along in a societal process of negative social sanctions that inevitably engender hostility and resentment in the offender. Then the offender reacts negatively to the label by acting against society and so concludes the process by affirming the negative label or deviant status.

It takes a certain amount of time for the offender to absorb the labels and for those labels, in turn, to affect the offender's self-concept. The negative feelings created by the labeling process multiply into feelings of inadequacy, low self-esteem, and anger. Clifford Olson, killer of 11 children in British Columbia, Canada, during the early 1980s, explained to me that society played a major role in his homicidal behavior. The courts had kept him in prison for nearly 30 years and then allowed him to go free. He was already a habitual criminal and a perceived threat to society. As Olson ruefully noted, "They never should have let me go." He claimed that the effects of prison made him much more dangerous. Combined with alcohol, he said, they triggered his murderous rampages (author's files).

The types of labels, their visibility, and the manner in which they are applied, including their intensity, duration, and frequency—as well as the individual's ability to cope with the process of labeling—may all help to determine an offender's commitment to a criminal career. The more an individual succumbs to the labels of failure and imperfection, as well as to remarks critical of his or her behavior, the more he or she discounts positive feedback.

The labeling process is expedited by the selective application of those labels. For example, Becker (1963) has described people who create rules as moral entrepreneurs: "Social groups create deviance by making rules whose infractions constitute deviance and by applying those rules to particular people and labeling them as outsiders. From this point of view, deviance is not a quality of the act a person commits, but rather a consequence of the application by others of rules and sanctions to an 'offender.' The deviant is one to whom the label has successfully been applied; deviant behavior is behavior that people so label" (p. 9).

Labels, by the nature of their construction, are inconsistently applied. The poor, racial minorities, and the socially disadvantaged are more likely to be labeled. The fact that most serial killers are white and many appear to maintain at least middle-class socioeconomic standing does not disprove labeling theory. It is plausible that some serial offenders have been affected by negative labels created to differentiate between the rich and the poor, white and nonwhite, the powerful and the powerless. In essence, labeling can create psychological disparities between individuals regardless of their race or socioeconomic standing. Wayne Williams, who is believed to have been involved in the murders of 22 to 28 young black men and boys in the Atlanta, Georgia, area, was described as one who hated his own race and preferred white people and who killed blacks because they reminded him of his own standing.

It is unlikely, however, that all serial killers destroy human life because of their socioeconomic status or race or because the law is applied to favor the powerful people in society. Individuals who have experienced a traumatic event or process of events involving extreme criticism, or those who are forced to feel the pain of failure when their egos allow only perfection, may eventually respond negatively. Inevitably their feelings of low self-esteem and worthlessness become their internalized "master status," constantly reminding them of their weaknesses. Psychologically, the stress and anxiety of labeling may be viewed as *cognitive dissonance,* which feeds a need to right the wrongs and restore balance. Labeling theory, then, is not concerned with the origins of serial killers' behavior but with the formation of the killers' perceived status as the result of experiencing traumatic events during their formative years.

JUVENILE MASS MURDERERS AND SERIAL KILLERS

Less than 10% of all homicides in the United States are committed by juveniles. The U.S. Department of Justice (2007) reports that cases of homicides committed by young people are more likely to involve multiple offenders than juveniles acting solo. Busch et al. (1990) compared juveniles who kill to delinquents who do not kill and found that those who kill have criminally violent family members, have histories of gang involvement, abuse alcohol, and perform poorly in school due to intellectual and perceptual deficits. Some cases of juvenile homicide include youth who attempt to escape extreme forms of environmental stress including family psychopathology (Rowley, et al. 1987; Darby, 1998). Research supports the salient factors of juveniles who kill: they frequently come from abusive family backgrounds where they often witnessed acts of violence or were the recipients of abuse (Heide, 1997; Darby, 1998; Bailey, 2000).

School Shooters

Schools, not surprisingly, become venues for juvenile violence and, in some cases, homicide. The actual average number of deaths per all types of school shooting incidents in the United States is 2.5 since 1966 (see Table 4.1). However, most *mass* murders in grammar schools, junior high and high schools, as well as colleges are perpetrated by adults. Indeed, there are numerous cases of youth making death threats, bringing weapons to school, and sometimes killing classmates and/or teachers but seldom on the *mass* scale of deaths played out at Columbine High School (see Profile 4.1), where the killers are young. Generally the youth who commit school shootings often intend to kill many but due to lack of preparation and sophistication often fall short of their objectives. In some cases, like the Virginia Tech mass murder of 32 students and faculty, there was evidence of careful planning and execution. This suggests that some

TABLE 4.1 School Shootings in the United States, 1966–2011

School Type	No. of Schools with Shootings	Total No. of Dead	No. of Schools with No Fatalities	Ave. No. of Dead per School with Fatalities
College	29	102	4	4.0
High School	50	80	9	1.9
Middle School	22	25	5	1.5
Elementary	8	14	2	2.3
TOTAL	109	221	20	2.5

SOURCE: © Cengage Learning, 2013.

who plan attacks on schools are more deliberate and methodical in order to generate a higher body count. According to the National School Safety and Security Services (2009), killings at schools in the United States have been generally declining for the past several years. Ewing (1990) refers to one type of school violence as *senseless killing*, involving juveniles acting on impulse or being influenced by other juveniles as a result of their seeking revenge for real or imagined wrongs experienced at school. Other influences may be related to socioeconomic status of the offender and location of the school.

One theme that often arises with juvenile school shooters is their experiences with rejection, social marginalization, public humiliation, being designated by peers as an outcast, developing a sense of personal victimization such as bullying and being demeaned by fellow students (Leary et al., 2003). A later study conducted by Fox and Harding (2005) noted that school administrators were usually oblivious to the personal issues of these students who ultimately used violence as a means of final resolution. Larkin (2007) in his analysis of the Columbine murders found that bullying and taunting was common in the school and several students carried weapons for protection. The climate of fear and intimidation appears to facilitate violent reactions by a few students. Students do not "snap" suddenly and start killing people. Lieberman (2006) in his expansive study of school shooters found that most of the incidents were premeditated. Brown et al. (2009) in their research on school violence examined the *culture of honor hypothesis*, where states that place high regard on social status and strength in regards to one's property, reputation, and family will have higher rates of violence and aggression than states classified as non-culture-of-honor states. In states classified as culture-of-honor states students were more likely to carry weapons to school and rates of school shootings were higher than in non-culture-of-violence states. Their research supports the notion that sociocultural variables play a role in school violence.

In some cases students who become school shooters carry out bifurcated attacks by first killing a parent(s) at home followed by an attack at school. In 1998 Kip Kinkel, 15, shot and killed his parents. This was followed by a school shooting where two students were also killed and twenty-five others wounded. Kip claimed that he killed his parents to spare them embarrassment after the school shootings.

Juvenile Serial Killers

Even less common are serial killers who begin their murderous careers while still juveniles. This is partly explained by the fact that most juveniles who kill are apprehended, incarcerated, and upon release do not kill again. The exceptions such as Ed Kemper (see Profile 4.3) have gone on to commit many acts of serial murder as adults. In some instances, such as in the case of Craig Price (see Profile 4.2), the juvenile becomes a serial killer prior to becoming an adult at age 18. Most serial murderers begin killing people in their 20s and early 30s. Indeed, there are many accounts of youth who commit murders in their teens, but few of them go on to become serial killers.

The Myers Studies

Myers (2002), in his study of 16 juvenile killers who committed sexual homicides, identified four types:

1. *Explosive:* Offenders release repressed feelings of sexual aggression with a desire to dominate and destroy females. The poorly planned attacks are likely to be spontaneous against victims in close proximity to the juvenile. PCL-R scores were medium to high ranges.
2. *Predatory:* Juveniles who hunt and stalk their prey, usually strangers, and are sexually aroused in anticipation of the murders. PCL-R scores were in high range.
3. *Revenge:* Juveniles who kill out of anger toward non-strangers who have in some way wronged them. Such murders usually involve detailed planning. PCL-R scores were all in high range.
4. *Displaced matricide:* A rare type of juvenile murder. The killers lived near the victims and the attacks had evidence of control and rage. PCL-R scores were lowest of all four types. Myers also noted that in comparison to non-sexual juvenile killers that *DSM* diagnoses were similar, and that both groups usually kill in response to developmental or environmental influences and not as a result of psychotic states.

Myers (2004) examined six juvenile serial killers with sadistic impulses, ranging in age from 10 to 16. Five of the six offenders had killed at least one male victim and 50% of their victims were strangers. Each case involved a sexual component and most often the offender used stabbing, cutting, or asphyxiation methods to kill his victims. The majority (80%) tortured their victims, while half of them masturbated at the crime scene and/or mutilated their victims. The duration of killing ranged from one month to slightly more than one year. At least half were arrested for other crimes that did not involve murder.

PROFILE 4.1 Columbine High School Massacre, 1999

"Good wombs hath borne bad
sons."—Shakespeare

"They're going to be put through hell once we do this," Eric Harris said of his parents. Indeed, it was hell and immeasurable, unbearable sorrow, untold grief, and devastating repercussions that affected not only his parents, family, and friends but the United States as a nation, and will do so for many years to come.

On April 20, 1999 (or "Judgment Day" as the killers called it), Eric Harris and Dylan Klebold, dressed in black trench coats and draped with 95 explosive devices and ammunition, walked through their high school in Littleton, Colorado, and gunned down 12 of their fellow students and a teacher. Their goal was to kill hundreds, but the bombs, left earlier throughout the school, failed them. Driven by revenge and hatred, the boys had plotted for a year to kill and injure as many as they could. Klebold said, "niggers, spics, Jews, gays, fucking whites, I hope we kill 250 of you." Five secret videotapes the boys made prior to the massacre reveal the depths of their scorn and their plans to punish those who had dispossessed them—the athletes and socialites. The social climate at Columbine, like so many schools, can foster a culture that is cruel, elitist, and relentless in its deprecation of those who don't fit into the "jock culture." As one athlete confirmed: "Columbine is a clean, good place except for those rejects. Most kids didn't want them there. They were into witchcraft. They were into voodoo dolls. Sure, we teased them. But what do you expect with kids who come to school with weird hairdos and horns on their hats? It's not just jocks; the whole school's disgusted with them. They're a bunch of homos, grabbing each other's private parts. If you want to get rid of someone, usually you tease 'em. So the whole school would call them homos, and when they did something sick, we'd tell them, 'You're sick and that's wrong.' "

Harris and Klebold, rejected and alone, found each other and became friends. Their synergism became their catalyst for violence. Harris said, "People constantly make fun of my face, my hair, my shirts." One parent whose son was killed said, "Jocks could get away with anything. If they wanted to punch a kid in the mouth and walk away, they could. Had I known this, my son wouldn't have been there." About the school he said, "They did nothing to protect students from each other." But others viewed the boys simply as "bad seeds," angry and fueled by a thirst for notoriety, not loners who acted desperately to seek reprieve from their persecutors. If that were the case, then they might have taken their guns and pipe bombs to the locker room and aimed at anything wearing a sports uniform (*TIME*, 1999, p. 42). Both Harris and Klebold were involved in school events and activities like other students, including attending the prom and participating in sports. But they did suffer humiliation and found support in each other. Their anger became generalized, and with distorted motives they sought not only retribution but also celebrity status and infamy. They even contemplated which movie producer would be suitable to carry

The Kirby Study

Kirby (2009) in her descriptive examination of 27 juvenile serial killers, 26 of whom were male, classified offenders into three categories:

Primary juvenile offenders: Fourteen were defined as murdering one victim at any given time, with the minimum of two victims prior to the age of 18.

their torch, to immortalize their revolution: Steven Spielberg or Quentin Tarantino. Klebold said, "Directors will be fighting over this story."

Surely there were "red flags," harbingers of volatility, evidence of deep and abiding resentment, signs of callous and truncated emotion. The purpose of the secret tapes was to have the "last word" with their oppressors, their parents, and those paid to theorize causation. On one tape Klebold blamed his extended family. He said, "You made me what I am. You added to the rage." Blaming day care and the snobs attending school, he said, "Being shy didn't help. I'm going to kill you all. You've been giving us shit for years." *TIME* (1999) reported, "Klebold and Harris were completely soaked in violence: movies like *Reservoir Dogs* and gory video games they tailored to their imaginations. Harris liked to call himself 'Reb,' short for rebel. Klebold's nickname was VoDKa (his favorite liquor, with the capital DK for his initials). On pipe bombs used in the massacre he wrote 'VoDKa Vengeance.' "

Klebold anticipated his parents' thoughts, "If only we could have reached them sooner or found this tape." Harris added, "If only we would have searched their room. If only we would have asked the right questions." The boys left journals and websites and secret tapes, all which could have been found by parents desperate to reconnect to their child. As clever as the boys wanted everyone to believe they were, they were not undetectable. At one point, Harris recalls how his mother watched him walk out of the house with a gun sticking out of his gym bag. She assumed it was his BB gun and asked no questions. Mr. Harris allegedly found a pipe bomb Harris had made and with him took it outside to detonate it. What's more, a clerk from Green Mountain Guns had called the Harris home to say the clips that had been ordered had arrived. Mr. Harris said he didn't order any clips and hung up. No questions asked. Harris said of this conversation, "If either one had asked just one question, we would've been fucked." Klebold said, "We wouldn't be able to do what we're going to do." But what of the emotions and attitudes attending such virulent aspirations? It is difficult to fathom that a healthy relationship between child and parent could thrive under such concealment. Indeed, it does not.

Investigators insist that the parents were fooled like everyone else. Of the Klebolds they said, "They were not absentee parents. They are normal people who seem to care for their children and were involved in their life" (*TIME*, 1999, p. 50). The Klebolds now realize they never knew their son. They search every interaction for clues to their son's unhappiness. In one videotape Klebold thanked his parents for teaching him "self-awareness, self-reliance ... I always appreciated that." He said, "I'm sorry I have so much rage."

Later, a parent of one of the victims committed suicide, and two more teenagers from Columbine High School were shot and killed. The identity of the killer(s) remains unknown. The couple was found dead in the local sandwich shop where one of them worked. The sadness and weeping for their lost friends and continuing tragedy has turned to despair that the pain will never stop, that they are cursed—with no hope, no future, and destined to suffer. Over 10 years have passed since the killings. What are the lessons we can learn from such a tragedy?

Primary offenders killed between two and seven victims, ranged in age between 10 and 17 at their first kill, 11 and 17 for their second kill, and 15 and 17 for their third kill. Kirby notes that only one juvenile serial killer murdered a fourth victim while he was only 15 years of age. Half of the offenders were Caucasian, 43% were raised by both parents, and 29% had experienced some form of

PROFILE 4.2 Craig Price, the Warwick Slasher, 1987–1989

On July 27, 1987, Craig Price, a middle-class African American youth, broke into a Warwick, Rhode Island, home only two houses away from his own home and, taking a knife from the kitchen, stabbed 27-year-old Rebecca Spencer 58 times. He was 13 years old. Over two years later Price, now 15 and a high school football player, broke into another neighbor's home while using marijuana and LSD and butchered three more victims. Joan Heaton, 39, was stabbed 11 times, her daughter Jennifer, 10, was stabbed 62 times, and her other daughter, Melissa, 8, died from having her skull crushed. His only other documented crime was that of petty theft. An accidental, self-inflicted knife wound led to his arrest, and he confessed to all four murders. He expressed no remorse. As a convicted minor, Price could only be incarcerated until his 21st birthday and then released. He talked about how he was going to make a name for himself upon his release. A community action group calling themselves *Citizens Opposed to the Release of Craig Price* lobbied to find ways to keep him in prison. When Price was ordered to undergo a psychiatric evaluation, he refused for fear that it would be used against him. The judge found him in contempt of a court order for refusing to submit to the evaluation, extortion for threatening correctional officers, and fighting with other inmates. For his efforts he was given an additional 10 to 25 years and is now eligible for parole in 2020.

childhood trauma. Over 85% were found to have histories of violence and 42% had been arrested prior to their first killing. At least half of the primary offenders were known to have committed a variety of violent crimes including assault and robberies. Their murder victims ranged in age between 3 and 83. Primary offenders, 54%, were known to exhibit a sexual component in their murders. Almost 61% of the victims were killed in a private location, the victim's residence or that of the offender.

Maturing juvenile offenders: Five were defined as murdering one victim at any given time, with the first victim prior to age 18 and the remaining victims prior to age 21. All were Caucasian, male, and averaged two to three victims per killer. They ranged in age from 14 to 17 at their first kill, 15 to 20 for their second kill, and 18 to 20 for their third kill. Approximately 40% of this group experienced multiple forms of childhood trauma, 80% had a history of violence, and only 20% were arrested prior to their first kill. Approximately 40% of this group had also abused illegal drugs. Fifty-three percent of their victims were female, ranging in age between 2 and 52. About one in four victims were killed at night, nearly half in their homes or the home of their killer, and one in four crime scenes were staged. The primary murder motive for this group was sexual, and over 60% of victims were strangers. None of these offenders were incarcerated between their murders.

Secondary juvenile offenders: Eight were defined as murdering one victim at any given time, with the first victim prior to age 18 and the remaining victims after age 21. All were male, 50% were Caucasian, and each killed between two and three victims on average. Although the majority of killings were not sexually motivated, nearly one in five victims were genitally mutilated. Their age range at the time of their first kill was between 14 and 16, their second kill, 23 to 51, and only one secondary offender killed a third victim and he was 24 at the time of the murder. Compared to the other two groups, secondary offenders experienced less childhood trauma, were far more likely to have been raised by both parents, and had less history of violence or having been arrested prior to their first kill. Over 70% of the victims were killed in public locations.

Overall about one-fourth of the 27 offenders experienced psychological disorders, 70% had histories of violent behavior, and 40% had committed multiple crimes. Of the 63 murders committed by these 27 offenders, one-fourth involved sadistic behavior. These studies provide more insight into persons who begin their careers as serial killers while they are juveniles. Consider the case of Craig Price (see Profile 4.2), who began and ended his serial murders while still a minor. What do you think may have motivated him to kill, and with such incredible brutality? Edmund Kemper (see Profile 4.3) killed his grandparents when he was 15, was incarcerated for six years, then went on to become one of the most horrific serial killers in the history of the United States. What motivated Kemper to kill not only his grandparents but several college students, his mother, and her best friend?

THE MACDONALD TRIAD

The childhoods of serial killers are varied and complex. Some serial killers as children were much more sociopathic than other children; they were more aggressive and more manipulative, expressed less remorse, and experienced fewer feelings of guilt. Yet similar characteristics can be observed in children who never grow up to become violent offenders. In truth, each child processes experiences differently. Children also react differently to stress. It is my contention that stress is the generic predisposer to many maladaptive behaviors in childhood. Because children do not possess the same coping skills to deal with life's stressors, some children are at greater risk of developing inappropriate behaviors. Psychopathology during childhood can be manifested in a variety of behaviors, some of which are more noticeable or detectable than others. Serial killers have been linked to childhood maladaptive behaviors such as torturing animals; enuresis, or chronic bed-wetting; and fire-setting. Any of these three behaviors, termed the *MacDonald Triad,* is not a good predictor of later adult violent behavior nor is the triad itself a valid instrument to measure future violence. Even a youth displaying all three behaviors is not guaranteed a life of violence during adulthood. However, there does exist a correlation between youth with such behaviors, and they do appear more often among the serial-killer population than among non-offenders.

Family Dynamics and the MacDonald Triad

Psychological profiles of those who commit homicide reveal portraits of frustration and intrapersonal conflict stemming from childhood. Justice, Justice, and

PROFILE 4.3 Edmund Emil Kemper III, 1964–1973

"I just wondered how it would feel to shoot grandma," Kemper, a boy of only 15 years of age, explained to police. His confession was calm and very matter-of-fact. He walked up behind his grandmother and shot her in the back of the head, shot her two more times in the back, and repeatedly stabbed her. Then he waited for grandpa to come home and shot him to death on the porch. Thus began Ed Kemper's career as one of the most notorious serial killers in American history.

Born in 1948, Ed was raised by Clarnell, his domineering mother who frequently berated him in public. His parents were divorced when he was nine. When he was eight, his mother had forced him to sleep in the cellar of the house for nearly eight months, his only exit through a trap door that usually had the kitchen table on it. Ed would later claim a deep love-hate relationship with his mother, which for him was a constant source of frustration. His mother married several times while Kemper was young, preventing him from ever drawing close to male role models.

As a child Ed sometimes acted out his own death through mock executions. His younger sister would act as the executioner, and Ed would role-play a person in his death throes in the gas chamber. He later admitted to fantasizing about killing his family, especially his older sister, who he believed received more love and attention. His sister remembered receiving a doll for Christmas only to find it a few days later with the head and hands cut off. Kemper's fantasies became more violent, and he killed the family cat by burying it alive and then decapitating it. He placed the head on a spindle and prayed over it. One day his sister teased him about the fact that he liked his schoolteacher and wanted to kiss her—to which he replied, "If I kissed her I'd have to kill her first." Years later this statement proved to be extremely insightful.

At 13, Ed ran away to see his father but was then quickly sent to live with his grandparents. Ed's mother warned her ex-husband that sending Ed to his grandparents could be very dangerous. A year and a half later, Ed killed them. Kemper turned himself in and was subsequently placed in the Atascadero State Psychiatric Hospital. During his incarceration he behaved as a model patient and impressed one psychiatrist so much that he allowed Kemper to administer psychological tests to other patients. He gained access to evaluation test questions and committed them to memory. Kemper learned the requisite psychological jargon and therapeutic skills

Kraft (1974) note that although the MacDonald Triad may indicate a troubled child, it is not certain that that child will grow up to commit violence. Hellman and Blackman (1966) suggest:

> The triad is proposed as a pathognomic sign, as an alert to both the parents and the community that the child is seriously troubled; that if this readiness to project and elicit fear or pain, to be violent and destructive, is not alleviated nor remedies found for it, this pattern of hostile behavior may well lead to adult aggressive antisocial behavior. (p. 1434)

These authors also suggest that a relationship exists between parental loss or rejection and the development of mental illness or personality disorders. "This loss or rejection of a parent causes not only primary separation anxiety but also aggression, the function of which is to achieve reunion. The aggressive outbursts of adults who murder are associated with a history of maternal or paternal deprivation" (Hellman and Blackman, p. 1431). The child who suffers consistently under to convince a parole board, against the advice of psychiatrists, to release him after only six years. Kemper returned to live with his mother and soon became embroiled in their usual fighting. However, Ed was now fully grown—280 pounds and 6 feet 9 inches tall. His IQ had been measured at 136, but he could only manage holding a job as a flagman for a construction company. At this point, his outward interests appeared normal for a young man, yet inwardly his violent rages and fantasies continued to grow.

In 1970–1971, Kemper began picking up young female hitchhikers, psychologically preparing himself for his mission. At the age of 23, Ed started killing again, a task that would last nearly a year and entail eight more victims. He shot, stabbed, and strangled them. All were strangers to him, and all were hitchhikers. He cannibalized at least two of his victims, slicing off parts of their legs and cooking the flesh in a macaroni casserole. He decapitated all of his victims and dissected most of them, saving body parts for sexual pleasure, sometimes storing heads in the refrigerator. Ed collected "keepsakes," including teeth, skin, and hair from the victims. After killing a victim, he often engaged in sex with the corpse, even after it had been decapitated.

On one occasion Kemper visited at length with psychiatrists, who stated at the conclusion of the interview that Ed was now safe and would not harm another person. They agreed at the meeting to have Kemper's juvenile record sealed to allow him to lead a normal life. Only Ed knew that, at that very moment, the head of one of his victims was in the trunk of his car in the parking lot. Kemper recalls an incident in which he was returning to his apartment with the head of a college coed he had just murdered. As he mounted the staircase carrying the bowling bag with the head, he encountered a young couple descending the stairs, apparently going on a date. Ironically, he mused that they were going on a date and so was he, but those realities were so very far apart. Kemper finally decided to kill his mother; early one morning on Easter weekend, he entered her bedroom carrying a hammer and a large hunting knife (which he called "General"). After smashing her in the head, he slashed her throat, cut out the larynx, and placed it in the garbage disposal. Severing her head, he had sex with the corpse.

these circumstances develops defense mechanisms including withdrawal and denial of stress. If, however, the child chooses to revolt, he begins to act out his feelings of rejection and resentment, exacting aggression and violence on society.

Kathleen Heide (1995), in her study on why children kill parents, noted that emotional neglect is damaging to a child's healthy development. "Parents who do not give their children clear messages that they are loved, whether by words or appropriate displays of affection, such as being held, cuddled, hugged, kissed, having hands shaken, and being patted on the back, are not meeting their sons' and daughters' emotional needs" (Heide, p. 30). Cummings and Davies (1994) write that child neglect when begun early interrupts all areas of emotional development, including bonding, cognition, play, and social skills. Children who continue to suffer this deprivation act out in vengeance and sometimes kill the parent responsible. By the age of 14, Ed Kemper had suffered much cruelty and rejection by his caustic mother. She berated and belittled him for not living up to her social expectations. Being sent away to live with his grandparents (whom he

PROFILE 4.3 (Continued)

Ed would later explain that he was killing his mother all along, and once she was dead he could stop the murder spree. Perhaps as a final insult to his mother, he invited her best friend over for Sunday dinner. When she arrived, Kemper strangled her and severed her head. Leaving a note for the police, Ed drove east to Pueblo, Colorado, where he had thoughts of climbing up a hill near the highway and shooting travelers as they drove by. Instead he called the police and, after being told to call back several times, convinced them he was the "Coed Killer," so named by the news media. Hours later, while Kemper was still waiting at the pay phone, police arrived and placed him under arrest.

In his confession Kemper stated five different reasons for his crimes. His themes centered on sexual urges, wanting to possess his victims, trophy hunting, a hatred for his mother, and revenge against an unjust society (Leyton, 1986a, p. 70).

Elliott Leyton insightfully integrated Kemper's often bizarre reasoning into one theory for his murderous behavior:

> As he slipped into the social niche of celebrated multiple murderer, he cured society's indifference to him and did so while exacting his fearful revenge and indulging all his repressed sexuality.... He had come to terms with that "total frustration," which all our multiple murderers remedy in their crusades.... This should not be any surprise, for he has confronted all the major issues in his life and resolved them. Kemper has, in his own terms, rewritten his personal history and, in the lunacy of destruction, created himself. (1986a, p. 72)

Edmund Kemper was sentenced to life imprisonment. He was denied parole at his first hearing in 1980 and at this writing remains incarcerated in a California prison.

killed at age 15) was further evidence of her contempt for him. Studies support the findings that children as young as one or two years of age may be hurt by the rejection or criticism of others (Leibman, 1989). Leibman also suggests that

> resentment brought about as a result of such rejection is frequently repressed by those who later commit murder. Repression often becomes a pattern of behavior leaving little need for release of anger. Upon reaching adulthood, the individual who thus far has adequately repressed rage since childhood may find himself in situations where he is unable to suppress hostile feelings. (p. 41)

It was not until Kemper's killing career had claimed several lives that he found he could no longer repress the hatred he felt for his mother, and killed her savagely.

The MacDonald Triad also reveals that the psychopathology of violent adult offenders often stems from the prevalence of such etiologic factors as paternal neglect, abuse, and rejection suffered in childhood. In a homicide study of four men who killed with extreme violence, authors Rosen, Satten, Mayman, and Menninger (1960) found that all of the men had extensive histories of losing control over aggressive impulses. Each case involved a history of extreme parental violence and emotional deprivation during childhood.

Edmund Kemper's Victims

Date of Murder	Name	Age	Relationship	Method	Sexual Assault	Corpse Mutilation
8/24/64	Maude Kemper	66	Grandmother	Shooting/ stabbing	No	No
8/24/64	Ed Kemper I	72	Grandfather	Shooting	No	No
5/7/72	Mary A. Pesce	18	Stranger	Stabbing	Body parts	Decapitated, dissected
5/7/72	Anita Luchessa	18	Stranger	Stabbing	Body parts	Decapitated, dissected
9/14/72	Aiko Koo	15	Stranger	Suffocation/ strangulation	Necrophilia	Decapitated, dissected, severed hands
1/8/73	Cindy Schall	19	Stranger	Shooting	Necrophilia	Decapitated, dissected
2/5/73	Rosalind Thorpe	23	Stranger	Shooting	Possible	Decapitated
2/5/73	Alice Liu	21	Stranger	Shooting	Necrophilia	Decapitated, severed hands
4/20/73	Clarnell Kemper	40s	Mother	Hammer/cut throat	Necrophilia	Decapitated, dissected
4/20/73	Sara Hallet	40s	Mother's friend	Strangled	No	Decapitated

From a young age, children raised in dysfunctional and abusive homes develop coping skills to deal with the inherent stress. Heide (1995) writes,

> Persons in dysfunctional families characteristically do not *feel* because they learned from a young age that not feeling is necessary for psychic survival. Family members generally learn it is too painful to feel the hurt or to experience the fear that comes from feelings of rage, abandonment, moments of terror, and memories of horror. (p. 48)

Some parents cannot distinguish between punishment and discipline. Anyone can punish a child and many parents do it out of frustration. Discipline requires time, patience, and love and may include some punishment. To punish children without discipline usually involves a parent who is frustrated and has turned to anger. Most Americans believe that spanking, for example, is an appropriate way to punish children despite compelling evidence to the contrary. Although some children do not connect the spanking with rejection, some most certainly do. If parents would not spank when they are angry, they would seldom spank at all. As one 11-year-old insightfully penned in his journal after being spanked by his father for not cleaning his room, "Yesterday Dad spanked me again. Why is it that Dad's pain is always my pain too?" Parenting by instinct does not always work well.

The pathology and psychological disturbance that can develop in children who have suffered the trauma of severely poor parenting is indicated by behaviors outlined in the MacDonald Triad and the *DSM-IV*. Conduct disorders (demonstrated by children who have behavioral problems, are rebellious, or are defiant to authority) can develop in preschool years but are not fully apparent until later childhood. These individuals often display low impulse control and failure to observe social norms through rebelliousness against authority. Emotionally truncated, they lack empathy and aggress arbitrarily with little apparent provocation. The psychopathology of animal cruelty, enuresis, and fire-setting can surface in some children concomitantly. Unfortunately, all too often parents and authorities are quick to punish without recognizing these behaviors as "red flags" that the child is suffering and needs help.

Animal Cruelty

> … the custom of children tormenting and killing beasts, will, by degrees, harden their minds even towards men, and they who delight in the suffering and destruction of inferior creatures, will not be apt to be very compassionate, or benign to those of their own kind. (Locke, 1705)

Even though some serial killers have displayed delight in harming animals, more appear to have enjoyed the vivisection and exploration of dead animals. The morbid curiosity of cutting into dead animals may facilitate the development of deviant sexual fantasies. To understand the role that animal cruelty plays in later homicidal aggression, we must first examine the etiology of animal abuse.

In America, a pet can be the object of affection or the target of displaced scorn. Many violent offenders report incidents of childhood cruelty toward animals. According to the Humane Society, animal cruelty "encompasses a range of behaviors harmful to animals, from neglect to malicious killing. Intentional cruelty, or abuse, is knowingly depriving an animal of food, water, shelter, socialization, or veterinary care or maliciously torturing, maiming, mutilating, or killing an animal." Felthous and Kellert (1985), in their study of 102 men serving time in federal penitentiaries, found that cruelty to animals during childhood occurred much more often among aggressive criminals than among nonaggressive criminals or noncriminals. In their study, they identified nine motivations for the childhood maltreatment of animals:

1. To control the animal
2. To retaliate against the animal
3. To satisfy a prejudice against a specific species or breed
4. To express aggression through an animal
5. To enhance one's own aggressiveness
6. To shock people for amusement
7. To retaliate against another person
8. Displacement of hostility from a person to an animal
9. Nonspecific sadism

Of pathognomic importance, Margaret Mead (1964) suggests that torturing or killing animals by children could be a harbinger of increasingly violent acts into adulthood. Elana Gill (1994), a family therapist, notes how children who are physically or sexually abused seem to mimic their mistreatment on their companion animals. Gill says that children learn the lessons of abuse: that people who love them hurt them, and that power and dominance are preferable to the victim's plight of helplessness. In some cases Gill observed that animal cruelty may signify a child's preoccupation with death and that abusers may be rehearsing their own suicides. Of the case of Miriam, a severely abused child, Gill writes,

> I learned this from Miriam, a six-year-old who had been abused sexually. When I asked her to make a picture of herself, she drew a bleeding dog and herself in heaven. Miriam's drawing revealed the depth of her despair. Her mother later informed me that Miriam had recently begun slapping and choking her dog and had injured him with scissors.

According to Patterson, DeBaryshe, and Ramsey (1989), there are two approaches to understanding risk factors that signal development of aggression and antisocial behavior in children: *coercive family interaction patterns* and *children's attributional biases.* The first factor is found in modeling theory, in which children emulate the parents' behaviors. Patterson et al. found that "ineffective parenting styles, relying heavily on punitive or aversive control, present children with models of coercion such that family members become enmeshed in a cycle where parent and child use aversive techniques to terminate each others' behavior" (pp. 329–335). The implications of this approach suggest that a cycle of violence develops in which children subjected to harsh and abusive treatment will view their abuse as normal and emulate this behavior in their interpersonal relationships. The second approach, according to Price and Dodge (1989), suggests that boys who show atypical aggression have deficits in *intention-cue detection.* These boys display attributional bias by interpreting ambiguous or neutral peer actions (e.g., being accidentally bumped in a lunch line) as being hostile and aggressive. This bias leads them to act aggressively, often causing strong peer retaliation. The parallel to animal abuse is apparent. The fact that a peer's intention cues can be ambiguous to a rejected child suggests that intention cues by animals, both companion and noncompanion, may also be misinterpreted. In one case a young boy brutalized, sexually assaulted, and eventually killed a stray dog. The boy stated that when he heard the dog barking at him, he interpreted the dog's demeanor as personally directed aggression, something he was not going to allow.

Animal abuse has been included in the *DSM-IV* diagnoses of conduct disorder since 1987. According to the Humane Society of the United States (2008), 43 states had felony provisions within their animal cruelty codes. This is in sharp contrast to only 18 states reporting felony-level provisions in 1997. Margaret Mead (1964) notes, "One of the most dangerous things that can happen to a child is to kill or torture an animal and not be held responsible" (pp. 11–22). Repeated acts of violence toward animals are a harbinger of adult violence. Lockwood and Hodge (1986), in *The Tangled Web of Animal Abuse: The Links between Cruelty to Animals and Human Violence,* note the importance of preventing animal cruelty by disciplining all such acts, even minor ones. Without proper intervention, children may graduate to more serious abuses including violence against people.

Enuresis

The trauma some children experience as the result of physical, sexual, or emotional abuse can trigger frequent bed-wetting. Like those who practice animal torture or experimentation, chronic bed-wetters appear to cease the maladaptive behavior as they approach adulthood. Defined as unintentional bed-wetting during sleep, persistent after the age of five, enuresis evokes emotional and social distress for the child sufferer. It is embarrassing as well as frustrating for the child, and parents find it annoying because it means persistent interrupted sleep. For approximately 80% of children who suffer enuresis, the causes have biological roots and heredity is a major contributing factor. According to Houts, Berman, and Abramson (1994), enuresis is, most often, caused by a failure of muscular responses that inhibit urination or by a hormonal imbalance that permits too much urine to accumulate during the night. A prescription of antidepressant drugs, which reduce the amount of urine produced, usually eliminates the problem. In some cases, children simply outgrow the problem. However, for about 20% of children with enuresis it is an indicator, a red flag, of something more serious.

Enuresis, in some cases, is considered to be an overt manifestation of internal turmoil usually caused by disturbance in the home. In one study conducted by Hellman and Blackman (1966), it was found that enuresis was tied to aggression and fantasies of destruction. Of the 84 prisoners who served as subjects, 31 were charged with aggressive crimes against the person and 53 were charged with misdemeanors and minor felonies. Thirty-six were found to have enuresis. Of the 36, 33 had enuresis past the age of eight years and in 70% this trait persisted into their teens. Though relatively insignificant by itself and not as visible as other traits in the MacDonald Triad, it is no less important a red flag in identifying maladaptive development in a child. However, unlike animal cruelty and fire-setting, enuresis is not listed as a diagnostic criterion for conduct disorder in the *DSM-IV*. Enuresis is an unconscious, involuntary, and nonviolent act, and therefore linking it to violent crime is more problematic than doing so with animal cruelty or fire-setting.

Fire-Setting

> He who lights a fire during the day will wet his bed that night. (German and Mexican-Spanish proverb)

The term *fire-setting* is generally used to describe the actions of juveniles, whereas *arson* describes adult behavior. Frequently the distinction is not clearly understood and the terms are used interchangeably. Some children display an abnormal fascination with or interest in fire. They engage in excessive fire watching, fire play, or compulsive collecting of fire paraphernalia. They are also more prone to trigger false fire alarms (Fineman, 1995, p. 32). California has experienced a significantly large number of fires set by juveniles. Nationally, juveniles set about 50% to 60% of all arson fires. Males are responsible for over 90% of all of these fires. Fresno, California, reporting the fifth-highest per capita rates of arson fires in the United States in 2007, had over 70% of its fires set by juveniles.

Fire-setting is best understood as part of a process, not merely an act. Singer and Hensley (2004), applying social learning theory to the childhood and adolescent backgrounds of serial killers, examined the linkage of three case studies of offenders with their involvement in fire-setting and committing serial murder as adults. Recent research of 1,200 juvenile fire-setters in Fresno found a disturbing pattern of psychopathology within the families of fire-setters. Noted family dysfunctions included low marital satisfaction, little or no display of affection, ineffectual role modeling, and excessive physical force in disciplining children (Hickey, 1996). Children frequently reported deep feelings of maternal or paternal rejection or neglect. The absence of a father is thought to contribute to aggressiveness and fire-setting in boys. Felthouse (1980) notes that deprivation by the father due to such dysfunctions as alcoholism frequently results in rejection of the boy. Other factors including divorce and separation from the father due to incarceration contributed to boys' fire-setting behavior.

Juvenile fire-setters commonly report anxiety, depression, and resentment when feelings of abandonment surface about their relationships with parents or significant others. In turn, the perceived rejection affects self-esteem and fosters feelings of anger, hatred, and revenge fantasies. Similar to profiles in psychopathy, fire-setters have less capacity for internalization, are less able to tolerate anxiety, and are less empathetic and able to form attachments to others. They are often diagnosed as having a conduct disorder and display antisocial personality characteristics. Incapable of feeling adequate remorse or guilt, juvenile fire-setters are more prone to be in conflict with authority figures. The most common psychological and behavioral problems observed in the Fresno group of juvenile fire-setters were the following:

- Learning problems
- Poor school behavior
- Poor concentration
- Lying
- Excessive anger
- Fighting with siblings
- Disobedience
- Being influenced by peers
- Attention seeking
- Impulsiveness
- Impatience

- Preoccupation with fire
- Unhappiness in dysfunctioning family
- Pronounced need for security and affection

These 14 characteristics parallel many of those noted in Fineman's (1995) profile of fire-setters. These children display distinct personality pathology, and fire play is but one of many maladaptive behaviors. Among the types of fire-setters identified by Fineman that fit the profile of certain types of serial killers were those who *cry for help*. The offenders consciously or subconsciously bring attention to themselves as a result of interpersonal dysfunctioning. Offenders are those with a hero fantasy, who "discover" a fire and may even help extinguish the flames. Sometimes a firefighter will be caught setting fires in order to draw attention to himself and be recognized for his heroics. Similarly, some of the most prolific serial killers on record have entered the profession of care providers to gain themselves easy access to extremely vulnerable victims. A second typology, the *delinquent or antisocial* fire-setter, generally displays little empathy or remorse for his crimes or victims. Much of his psychopathology has roots within his family dynamics (see Profile 4.4).

In the Fresno study, in which about half of the offending children were eight years old or younger, parental absenteeism was high. Parents consistently indicated being "present" about 80% of the time, even though the child's perception was considerably less. The main point is that *perception* is the key factor. It does not really matter what the parents say they are doing as much as it matters what the child perceives parents are doing or not doing. Young children perceive their surroundings differently than adults. In addition, fire-setters are more frequently spanked or isolated from others on a weekly or sometimes daily basis over periods of time. These children report "bad" experiences in homes often facing financial problems, family restructuring, or relocation.

But fire-setting appears to be a transitory method of pathological self-expression. Fineman (1995) points out that adult fire-setters usually have a history of setting fires as children but that most child fire-setters do not set fires as adults. Does this mean that children who are chronic fire-setters resolve their personal conflicts or mature out of the maladaptive behaviors? In all probability, many children do resolve the conflicts or mature out of the behavior. For other children, adolescence provides a transitory period during which the youth begins to find more personal, more deviant methods to express himself or herself.

The presence of the MacDonald Triad indicates a pattern of creating hurt because of hurt: the victim becomes the victimizer. Other behaviors also indicate pathology in children, including temper tantrums, excessive fighting, and truancy. Some experts feel that the MacDonald Triad is not a sufficient diagnostic tool. Justice et al. (1974) suggest that these other symptoms may be more predictive of the violence-prone individual. When correlated with the MacDonald Triad they become even more useful as childhood predictors of violence. However, the predictive value of all three traits found in the MacDonald Triad, persistent in childhood, is found in many studies of violent adults. As Hellman and Blackman (1966) illustrate:

PROFILE 4.4 Portrait of a Serial Arsonist and Pyromaniac

Richard A. spent several years in prison for serial arson. The tall, thin, Hispanic male, 37, who is gay, has, by his own admission, set hundreds of fires. He was instrumental in making Fresno the arson capital of California until his arrest and incarceration. He set his first fire at age 7 but did not begin setting fires in earnest until age 12. The fire and the men who fight the flames sexually motivated him. He liked to visit fire stations, meet the firemen, and learn all he could about the fire equipment and the fire district. Richard memorized the physical boundaries of each fire district in Fresno. He would often set two fires in a district to cause more personal excitement. He stared at the fire while his fantasies directed the firefighters in their work. Richard collected a box full of "souvenirs" from his 23 major fires and buried them. He often drove by the area thinking about digging up his collection. He has a long history of other crimes including prostitution at 15, theft of a police car, fraud, sexual assault, burglary, impersonation of a police officer, and assault. Richard set fires over an 11-year period. His first intentional fire-setting was at age 12, beginning with trash fires and escalating to burning down businesses at night. He never killed anyone, although several persons needed to be evacuated from an apartment complex when a fire he set spread out of control.

He is a friendly, talkative person who masks anger and frustration at being marginalized by a distrusting society. His father abandoned the family when Richard was very young. At age five a neighbor sexually molested him, and the molestations continued for several years. The man manipulated Richard into compliance by threatening to harm the dog that lived with the man. The man also inserted a barrel of a gun into Richard's rectum and pulled the trigger. For many years he harbored anger toward his mother for not protecting him from the neighbor and for not meeting his childhood emotional needs. (Since his release from prison he now reports that he and his mother have drawn much closer.) At age 14 he was raped by a 24-year-old male he met while making prank phone calls. Richard's mother discovered the two having sex and he fled with the man for three days before returning home.

Once diagnosed as a paranoid schizophrenic, Richard successfully completed three years of parole and is now off his medication and living alone. He has frequently relocated and has great difficulty finding suitable employment because most employers will not risk having an arsonist in the building. Ironically, Richard never sets fires to places he is affiliated with such as school, home, and work. Once he does find employment he seldom stays more than a few months. Boredom, a penchant for deviance, and lack of social skills lead Richard to quit or be terminated from jobs. Richard has not been caught in any criminal activity since his release in 2000. However, he continues to harbor pathological attitudes and behaviors and still maintains his interest and fantasies in fire but manages to keep them at bay. He likes to collect fire memorabilia and admits to having urges to start another fire, especially when he becomes stressed. He sometimes calls me just to talk or when he becomes anxious and starts fantasizing about starting fires. Indeed, there are no acceptable excuses for Richard's criminal behavior, but the pathology clearly points to his childhood victimization, poor socialization, and inability to form meaningful attachments. He hopes one day to earn a certificate of rehabilitation in order to have his felony record expunged. Richard also wants to prove that my negative prognosis for his success is wrong. I sincerely hope he does it. As of this writing he is unemployed and living with his mother.

> Albert was a 15-year-old male charged with murder and assault with intent to rob with malice. He was the second of three children. Enuresis occurred until age 8 and persisted as occasional bed-wetting into adolescence. As a child he frequently made small fires in ashtrays, wastebaskets, and played with matches. At the age of 12 he obtained a rifle and enjoyed shooting birds, dogs, cats, and other animals. Since the age of 8 or 9 he liked to stick pins and needles in his sisters' dolls.
>
> The boy's father was a chronic offender who had served time in prison, was twice dishonorably discharged from the Army, and had committed acts of oral sodomy on both of his daughters. The patient repeatedly gave instances where his mother had shown marked favoritism towards his two sisters. She often told him he would grow up to be a thief, a bum, and a sexual pervert like his father. (p. 1433)

ETIOLOGY OF SERIAL KILLING

So far we have briefly examined a number of psychological and social theories of deviant behavior. But how can we then explain the phenomenon of serial murder in a manner that will include all varieties of serial murderers and satisfy the psychologist, the psychiatrist, the criminologist, the geneticist, the sociologist, the biologist, the phenomenologist, and other scientists and researchers who investigate homicidal behavior? Because research into serial murder is in its infancy, the haste to draw quick conclusions about its etiology is not only speculative but also dangerous.

Some data and literature, however, allow researchers leeway in formulating tentative models to explain the construction of serial murder. We do know that alcohol and drugs are often cited as contributing factors to serial murder; some offenders even suggest it as a primary causal factor. Ted Bundy's declaration that pornography led him to his career in killing caused considerable debate regarding the degree of influence such material has on people who become murderers. Many people believe that pornography and/or alcohol cause people to kill. Yet millions of people in the United States frequently consume alcohol and indulge in pornography and never physically harm anyone.

The current belief in pornography and alcohol as causal factors in serial murder belies a much more complex set of variables. If our society were to ban pornography, should one expect the incidence of serial murder to decrease? If we restrict or ban the use of alcohol, would that affect serial murderers' behavior? Such a Band-Aid approach to a cure for serial killing ignores a host of more obscure factors. Also, by joining the bandwagon of "pornography makes murderers," we continue to avoid issues of responsibility that point in some way to non-offending citizens.

As long as we continue to seek quick answers without first constructing a framework for the discussion of serial murderers' behavior, we will continue to treat the symptoms of the illness rather than the illness itself. For example, we continue saying that anyone who kills, especially serial killers, must be insane.

No one would argue that what these offenders *do* is insane by society's standards, but the vast majority of serial killers not only are judged sane by legal standards but are indistinguishable from non-offenders as they move within our communities. However, there exists a degree of security for us in believing that such crimes occur as a result of insanity or violent pornography. Such cause-and-effect thinking creates a dichotomy of "them" and "us." "Normal" people are not considered to be at high risk for insanity, nor do they generally indulge in violent pornography. Therefore, criminal behavior is completely out of our control, and in no way must we bear any responsibility for such actions.

Ultimately, the common belief that pornography, drugs, alcohol, or insanity directly causes serial homicides is not only simplistic but fallacious. Certainly such factors *can* contribute to serial murder, but only as appendages to an etiological process.

TRAUMA-CONTROL MODEL OF THE SERIAL KILLER

We are beginning to learn that serial offenders are influenced by a multitude of factors that inevitably lead them to kill. It is unlikely that any one factor is directly responsible for homicidal behavior. People are no more likely to be born to kill than offenders are to acquire homicidal inclination from watching violence on television. However, this general truth does not preclude the existence of a predisposition for violent behavior or the fact that we may be influenced by what we see.

In addition, no one factor has been useful thus far in predicting who may be prone to serial murder. Social scientists have long engaged in creating models for predicting criminal behavior. Unfortunately, in serial-murder research, everyone wants to be the first to predict causation. Whether the explanation is excessive television viewing, head traumas, biogenics, childhood victimization, or a host of other "causes," it has been offered too quickly, without the support of sufficient and valid data.

Among serial killers there may exist one or more predispositional factors that influence their behavior. As mentioned in Chapter 3, some violent offenders have been known to possess an extra Y chromosome, but some men who possess an extra chromosome never become violent offenders. Similarly, there are many who drink heavily and indulge in pornography—even violent pornography—and never become serial killers. Thus, even for those influenced by predispositional factors, whether they be biological, sociological, psychological, or a combination thereof, an event or series of events, or traumas, seem to be required that gradually influence a person to kill. Figure 4.1 shows a proposed trauma-control model for understanding the process by which individuals become involved in serial murder.

In discussing the trauma-control model, the destabilizing event(s) that occur in the lives of serial offenders will be referred to as *traumatizations*. These include

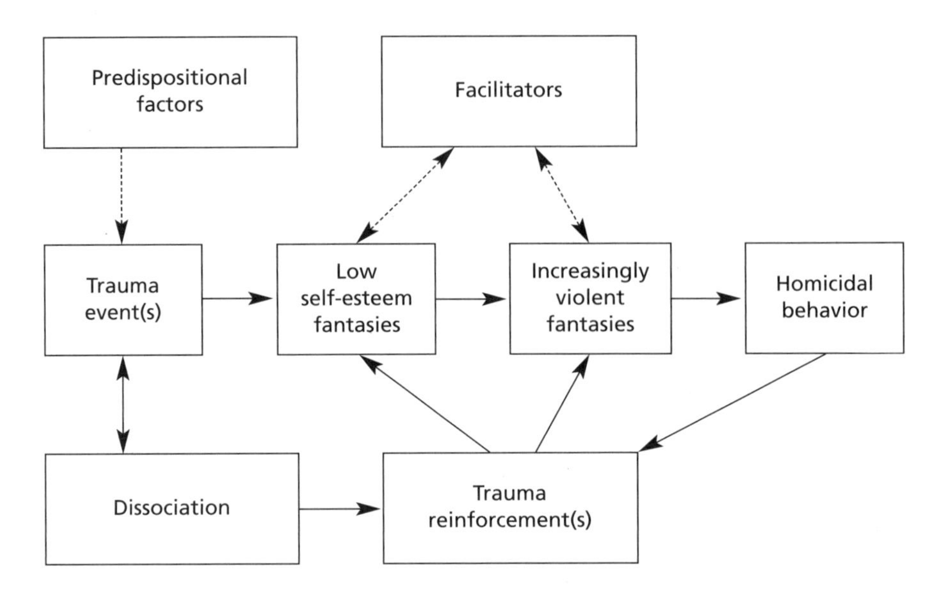

FIGURE 4.1 Trauma-Control Model for Serial Murder (Predispositional factors and facilitators may or may not influence the serial killing process.)
SOURCE: © Cengage Learning, 2013.

unstable home life, death of parents, divorce, corporal punishments, sexual abuse, and other negative events that occur during the formative years of the offender's life. Literally millions of U.S. citizens experience one or more of these traumatizations in their lives and never become offenders of any sort. Also, it is possible that individuals who have some predilection for criminal behavior and who experience some form of traumatization do not become violent offenders. However, Lange and DeWitt (1990), in their worldwide research of 165 "motiveless" murderers from 1600 to the present, state that many serial killers have had some form of head injury or organic brain pathology. They point out that neurological malfunctioning as a result of head injuries, epilepsy, or deep temporal-lobe spiking can generate interictal or postictal seizures that may lead to compulsive autonomic behavior. Thus, serial murderers act out during periods when they are experiencing uncontrollable brainwave activity. Although head trauma may well be correlated with serial murder, I suggest that the trauma is most likely exacerbated by social and environmental issues. Many people with similar head trauma do not become violent or antisocial.

Childhood trauma for serial murderers may serve as a triggering mechanism, resulting in an individual's inability to cope with the stress of certain events, whether they are physical, psychological, or a combination of traumatizations. For serial murderers the most common effect of childhood traumatization manifested is rejection, including rejection by relatives and parent(s). It must be emphasized that an unstable, abusive home has been reported as one of the major forms of rejection. The child or teen feels a deep sense of anxiety, mistrust, and confusion when psychologically or physically abused by an adult. Eth and Pynoos (1985) note some of the effects of traumatization on children who have witnessed murder, rape, or suicidal behavior. These effects include images of violence involving mutilations; destabilization of impulse control; and revenge fantasies. However, instability in the home environment may not be sufficient to trigger homicidal behavior. Other factors may be involved that in combination create a synergistic response, or enhanced reaction.

The combined effect of various traumatizations is greater than any single trauma. In other words, the combined effects should be viewed exponentially rather than arithmetically. As Nettler (1982) observes, "In synergistic situations, a particular effect may be 'more than caused.' It is not merely a metaphor to speak of 'causal overkill' " (p. 77). Other possible contributing forms of rejection include failure, ostracism in school, and exclusion from a group. Most individuals appear to cope constructively with rejection or at least to deal with the stress of rejection from a "self-centered" perspective. In other words, the individual deals with his or her feelings without the involvement of others, resorting to physical exercise, hobbies, travel, and so on. Others may become self-destructive through, for example, excessive eating, anorexia nervosa, bulimia, and other types of eating disorders. In more severe cases, rejection may prompt individuals to take their own lives rather than live with such uncomfortable feelings. Rejection as a stressor may contribute to a number of psychosomatic illnesses. For some people, confronting rejection may necessitate seeking out others who are able to provide emotional support to restore their psychological equilibrium.

Some individuals deal with rejection within a more destructive framework—perhaps by beating the family dog, breaking objects, or assaulting a spouse, a friend, or a relative. Each person deals with rejection differently depending on its perceived degree, frequency, and intensity. Similarly, children cope with various childhood traumatizations in numerous ways. In the case of children who later become serial killers, many have experienced some form of childhood trauma that was not or could not be effectively countered by therapeutic strategies. In some cases there appeared to be a series of traumatizations that psychologically affected these offenders. Cleary and Luxenburg (1993), in their study of 62 serial killers, found common characteristics of abuse and dysfunctional families. At this juncture in our research we can only speculate as to the number or strength of predispositions or predilections offenders may have had toward violent behavior. However, we do know that most of them have a history of childhood traumatizations. Hazelwood and Warren (1989) reported in their study of 41 serial rapists that 76% had been sexually abused as children. Considering that some serial killers in this study were rapists before they graduated to murder, we must not ignore the implication that sexual victimization during childhood may readily manifest itself in a negative manner during adulthood.

Traumatization experienced by the offender as a child may nurture within him or her feelings of low self-esteem. A common characteristic of most, if not all, serial offenders is feelings of inadequacy, self-doubt, and worthlessness. They do not cope constructively with the early trauma(s) and subsequently perceive themselves and their surroundings in a distorted manner. It is during this time of childhood development that a process of dissociation may occur. In an effort to regain the psychological equilibrium taken from them by people in authority, serial offenders appear to construct masks, facades, or a veneer of self-confidence and self-control. The label of *psychopath* given to most serial killers may actually describe a process of maintaining control of oneself, of others, and of one's surroundings. Indeed, a psychopath must become adept at perfecting rationalization and developing unconscious pretense, or the illusion that he or she is in perfect control of himself or herself. The truth is just the opposite—the psychopath, internally, is a social and moral cripple. He must devote his life to maintaining and living his image. For the psychopath, it becomes both his best defense and best offense against conflicts he cannot resolve.

The offender may suppress traumatic event(s) to the point where he or she cannot consciously recall the experience(s). This can be referred to as splitting off, or blocking out, the experience. Tanay (1976), in describing this state of dissociation, noted that the murderer appears to carry out the act in an altered state of consciousness. Such an ego-dystonic homicide, whereby the individual is faced with a psychologically unresolvable conflict, results in part of the psychic structure splitting off from the rest of the personality. Danto (1982) noted that dissociative reactions are types of anxiety states in which the mind is "overwhelmed or flooded by anxiety" (p. 6). For some children, certain traumatizations can generate extremely high anxieties. To defend oneself against a psychologically painful experience a person may block it from recall or, instead, not consciously suppress the fact the trauma occurred but suppress the hurt, fear, anger, and other feelings caused by the event(s). However, the pain of a traumatic event will eventually surface in some way. For the offender, a cycle of trauma and quest for regaining control can be generated at a very early age. Vetter (1990) suggests that serial killers resemble those with *Mephisto Syndrome,* or those who exhibit a combination of dissociation and psychopathy.

OBSERVATIONS OF A MALE SERIAL MURDERER

I was basically living a double life. I was one thing to this person and another thing to that person, all lies. And the reason for that is just a low self-image. You're not happy with who you are. You're not comfortable with who you are. You don't have any self-confidence. I wasn't out committing crimes all the time. One day I'd be fine, and the next time I'd be out, I'd have this compulsion to go out and kill somebody, and so I started looking back at each instance, what was I thinking, and this is what I came up with, and it's kind of a higher-stage process. The first stage is what I call distorted thinking. It's a distorted thought line, and I found that I was God's gift to Earth, I'm the center of the universe. I'm perfect. I'm the smartest guy that ever lived. Nobody's as perceptive as I am. So long as nothing came against that self-image, I was fine. But the problem with that was that it, as I mentioned earlier, was all lies.

Everything was a lie, and you know a lot of times the money that I had was my father's credit cards and it was a lie. I'd go on a date, and be living it up like this was mine. So long as I was living it out, I was all pumped up. I felt very important, just this immense personality, and that couldn't last because it was always based on lies. There was always going to be some challenge to this grandiose self-image. Sometimes it would be a lot of little things, sometimes it would just be the stress of having to live these little lies, having to always be looking over your back, and other times it would be a very definite event, a girlfriend leaves you or something like that. Whenever that happened, then there would be a fall. I was always way up here, and I think that's true of most serial types, serial offenders like I was, arrogant, maybe not outwardly, but at least internally. We're arrogant people, perceiving ourselves as almost godlike beings. All of a sudden we have this fall, psychological fall, and it's very debilitating, very disorienting, confusing, harrowing. It's a very scary feeling. I'm used to being perfect.

I'm not about to put up with anything that tarnishes my own sense of perfection, so that would lead to internal negative response, and that's what I was saying to myself. I'm not gonna have this, and instead of being scared, frightened, knocked off balance, I wheeled into a retaliatory mode. I'm gonna fight this. I'm gonna stand up for my self-importance. The way to deal with that was simply to prove it. You're going to be a somebody, and my means of being a somebody was violence. To me violence had already been reinforced through time as a means of being the star, center stage in this drama. Up to this point I've had a fall, and I felt like I'm not in control. I'm not top dog.

Violence to me had been reinforced as a means of taking control, as a means of getting even, getting even with the world. It's reaffirming that I was all those things, and the actual deed, the victimizing, the brutalizing of another human being, was my proof, a seal, a seal of approval, self-approval, my evidence that I'm really a somebody, and the result of that would be a triumph, a restoration, I'm restored. I'm doing not what other people will, but what I will, and that would restore all those feelings of largeness, power, self-importance that strengthened the overloaded ego that I had in the first stage, and I'd be fine. The act done, it wasn't done so much for fun as it was for restorative gain. As long as I was back in that first stage, there really wasn't any desire to go out and kill. It wasn't like I had an ongoing insatiable lust for murder, and it really wasn't a lust for murder.

It was a lust for self-importance at the expense of others, and that's basically the cycle. Sometimes it wouldn't take very much at all. I had a friend who owned a body shop, and I was working for him, and had no car and I get on a bus and I'm just filthy. I was just as filthy as can be, and I'm in distorted thinking. This gal gets on the bus, dressed up real nice and the seat next to me is the only one empty and she comes over and she looks at that seat and then she looks at me—all covered with dust and smelly—and she just turns her nose up in the air, spins around, and walks up and grabs a bar. How can you sit there?

Q: What kind of victims did you select?

A: It was people like kids, usually attractive, just like the ones I was in high school with, and I had felt rejected [by].

Q: Your victims, you say, were primarily white female teenagers.

A: Yes. I like kids. I always did. Back then it was perhaps self-serving. I used to take kids out to the ballpark. I got the praise and adulation of the parents. I enjoyed it, and here I killed two kids because I was in a frenzy—at that time I was in a fall and had been there for long enough and had failed to find somebody that fit the model. And there were these two victims of opportunity, like a wolf stalking.

Q: Hunting humans?

A: Yes.

Q: You say you killed approximately 12 victims. Did they progressively get closer together?

A: It was erratic. I mean, I just killed somebody and I'm infuriated because I didn't get done what I had to do, couldn't act out this ritual that accidentally killed this body, and within a matter of hours I had someone else. With this second victim it involved brutalizing, rape, and then killing. Actually rape ended the episode, killing was just getting rid of the witness. The first killing was not done that way. The first killing, the victim died before I had acted out even.... I did have a pattern and most serial killers do.

Q: There was a sexual component to most of the killings?

A: Yes. Sex was sort of a vehicle. So when that was done, climax was reached. You've already terrorized this person. You've already hurt them, beat them, whatever. But there would be a feeling of letdown. You're excited, and then all of a sudden you come down. Kind of like a ball game. All this had been acted out for years and in particular, it always involved stripping the victim, forcing them to strip themselves, cutting them, making them believe that they were going to be set free if they cooperated, tying them down and then the real viciousness started. The victim's terror and the fact I could cause it to rise at will ... their pain didn't register. All I could relate to was the ritual and the sounds. All this was proof to me that, I'm in control, I am playing the star role here, this person is nothing but a prop. I'm growing and they're becoming smaller. Once both the violence and the sexual aspect were completed, then that was it. That was the end of an episode.

Facilitators

At some point in the trauma-control process the offender may begin to immerse himself or herself in facilitators. Facilitators may include alcohol and other drugs, pornography, and books on the occult. Alcohol appears to decrease inhibitions and to inhibit moral conscience and propriety, whereas pornography fuels growing fantasies of violence. During the Reagan administration, the Meese Commission found that violent pornography was linked to violent sexual behavior. Cusator (2009), in his examination of sexual predators and sexual serial killers, noted a propensity for these offenders to facilitate their paraphilic behaviors and murders with the use of alcohol, drugs, and pornography. Bartholow and Heinz (2006) concur that alcohol is known to elicit aggressive thinking and behavior.

They also noted that simply being in the presence of alcohol can elicit aggressive cognitions and behavior. The study revealed that alcohol-related images also increased aggressive interpretations of others' behavior as well as aggressive responses to those interpretations. However, the connection made between pornography and violence can be misleading, because saying the two are "linked" can be interpreted in several ways. In any case, the fact that certain serial murderers have insisted that pornography was a major factor in their killing young women and children should not be ignored. In February 1989, Richard Daniel Starrett was arrested and charged in the murder of a 15-year-old girl in South Carolina. He was also believed to have participated in the abduction and sexual assault and murders of several other young women and girls. Starrett claimed that pornography had influenced his violent behavior. As police searched a rented mini warehouse, they seized 935 books and magazines belonging to Starrett that displayed nudity and sexual violence. Also found were 116 posters depicting bondage, violence, or sex; 18 calendars depicting sex or violence; and books on sex crimes, as well as dozens of hardcore videos.

Murray Straus and Larry Baron (1983) found that states with the highest readership of pornographic magazines, such as *Playboy* and *Hustler,* also had the highest rape rates. Dr. Victor Cline (1990) of the University of Utah outlined a four-factor syndrome that appears similar to the process experienced by serial killers who are reported to have used pornography extensively. The offender first experiences "addiction" similar to the physiological/psychological addiction to drugs, which then generates stress in his or her everyday activities. The person then enters a stage of "escalation," in which the appetite for more deviant, bizarre, and explicit sexual material is fostered. Third, the person gradually becomes "desensitized" to that which was once revolting and taboo-breaking. Finally the person begins to "act out" the things that he or she has seen. Wasserman (2000), in her study of adolescent sexual offenders, found that their motivation stemmed from sexual ignorance and sexual repression during puberty. Some youth, due to poor parenting skills, were forced to seek sexual information from pornographic sources that distorted reality and confused them. Puberty is a critical time for male youths, when some learn to masturbate to pornography.

We must remember, however, that not all serial murderers use pornography. Given the current state of limited research on serial homicide, it is dangerously premature to suggest facilitators as *causal* factors. What we can say is that a tendency to use pornography, alcohol, and texts on the occult has been noted frequently in serial offenders. But, we must recognize that pornography is produced in many different forms, both qualitatively and quantitatively. There exists not only difficulty in defining the parameters of pornography but also in discerning the effects it may or may not have on any particular person. In a recent study conducted by the FBI, it was found that 36% of serial rapists collected pornography (Hazelwood and Warren, 1989). Does this mean they all read *Playboy, Penthouse,* and *Hustler,* or perhaps the many publications that include hardcore acts of sadomasochism, bestiality, and other forms of sexual degradation? Can we give the same weight to all forms of pornography, including acts of violent sexual conduct?

PROFILE 4.5 Jeffrey Dahmer, 1978–1991

On July 22, 1991, Jeffrey Dahmer, age 31, was arrested in Milwaukee, Wisconsin, and entered the annals of America's most notorious serial killers.

When examining all the broken pieces, sometimes it is impossible to see exactly which piece broke first. What we do know is that his first murder, committed while a teenager, was only the beginning of a tortuous descent into multiple murder, sexual depravity, and cannibalism. Jeffrey Dahmer was raised in a family in which his father was oblivious to the inner struggles of his son. At age eight Jeffrey is believed to have been sexually abused by a neighbor boy. His father recalls that Jeffrey was a loner and a poor student. He was unaware of his adolescent son's use of alcohol, his more than scientific interest in dissecting road kills, and his penchant for young men. Only three weeks after his senior high school prom, at age 18, Jeffrey would kill and dismember his first victim, a 17-year-old male—a deed kept secret from everyone.

After several years of apparent family turmoil, Jeffrey's parents divorced. His mother took the youngest son to live with her while Jeffrey remained with his father. Jeffrey joined the military but was discharged for abuse of alcohol. He began working a night shift at the Ambrosia Chocolate Company in Milwaukee. In 1986 he received a year's probation for exposing himself to young boys. He struggled with his sexual orientation and felt that being gay was wrong. His inner struggles found him frequently contemplating suicide, but he was also developing aberrant sexual fantasies. His capacity for killing was being enhanced by these increasingly deviant sexual fantasies. He struggled against the urge to harm other human beings but was torn by sexual fantasies and driven by his need to control his life by controlling others. After the first homicide, Dahmer is believed by some to have visited graveyards in hopes of retrieving a corpse rather than killing another person. Unsuccessful, Jeffrey Dahmer finally yielded to his growing fantasies. Succumbing to their ever-tightening grip, Jeffrey continued to suffer a string of failures in his work and education.

To most of his victims he seemed like a very average person wanting to be sociable. A resident of Milwaukee's West Side, Dahmer lived alone in an apartment. He frequented bars, some of them gay, looking for contacts. Initially he used his grandmother's basement to have sex with drugged men and act out some of his deviant fantasies. He often rented cheap rooms at bathhouses, where he gave alcohol laced with drugs such as Halcion (a sleeping pill) to his victims. He had gotten the routine down very well. Potential victims, many of them African American or Asian, were then brought to his apartment. Others he brought directly to his apartment, had sex with them, and then offered them tainted alcohol. Dahmer then handcuffed his victims, who were unaware that the alcohol had been laced with drugs, and led them into the bedroom. This was his killing room, where he kept and disposed of his victims. Most of his victims he strangled to death. One 14-year-old boy, a Native American, was sexually assaulted, drugged, strangled, dismembered, and his corpse pulverized with a sledgehammer. While some of his victims lay unconscious, Dahmer would drill holes into their skulls in an attempt to make zombies out of them. In this state he either hoped or fantasized they would become his sex slaves and never leave him. Dahmer also cannibalized several of his victims. The goal of all this carnage was, in fact, pitiful. Dahmer had a fantasy: by consuming his victims, they would become part of him and make him more powerful. He fantasized having his two favorite victims, fully skeletonized, standing on either side of him. He, Dahmer, would be sitting in a large black chair like the one used by the antagonist in the movie *Star Wars.* Directly behind him on a shelf and between the two skeletons would rest the shrunken skulls of several of his victims. This scene was a powerful one for Dahmer. In his mind he would achieve the ultimate. Surrounded by his victims who now had become part of him, Dahmer fantasized a sense of power and control unlike any he had ever felt before.

The last victim he attempted to lure into the killing chamber managed to escape and alert two police officers on patrol. (Over the years four other potential victims had also escaped and told their stories to police and friends, but still Dahmer had remained free.) Responding to the man's complaint that Dahmer had tried to handcuff him and that his bedroom contained photographs of dead men, the police went to the apartment. Dahmer greeted them at the door and appeared very cooperative. Stepping into the apartment, the officers noticed a severe stench, like that of rotting carcasses. One of the officers asked for the key to the handcuffs still attached to the arm of the man. Dahmer insisted on retrieving it himself from the bedroom. Concerned for their own safety, one of the officers moved past him and entered the bedroom.

What he found would soon become international headlines. A blue barrel containing human body parts stood in one corner and two skulls lay unconcealed in a box. Restraining Dahmer, the officers looked around the apartment and counted at least 11 skulls (7 of them carefully boiled and cleaned) and a collection of bones, decomposed hands, and genitals. Three of the cleaned skulls had been spray-painted black and silver. These were to be part of the shrine fantasized by Dahmer. A complete skeleton suspended from a shower spigot and three skulls with holes drilled into them were found throughout the apartment. Dahmer had attempted to lobotomize some of his victims by pouring muriatic acid through the drilled holes and into their brain tissue. Chemicals, including muriatic acid, ethyl alcohol, chloroform, and formaldehyde, were also discovered, along with several Polaroid photographs of recently dismembered young men. A complete human head sat in the refrigerator.

The next day, Dahmer confessed to murdering and dismembering 15 to 17 young men and boys. He blamed no one or no thing for his crimes, including his parents, society, or pornography. Jeffrey Dahmer was sentenced to 15 consecutive life sentences (957 years) and incarcerated at the Columbia Correctional Facility in Portage, Wisconsin. There he was the recipient of much fan mail and letters from curiosity seekers. Several writers, some from as far away as South Africa and Europe, sent him money. In contrast, the families of the victims obtained judgments against Dahmer totaling more than 80 million dollars. Dahmer admitted that he should never be allowed freedom again because he still felt the compulsion to kill. Nor did he wish to remain in prison. On November 28, 1994, Dahmer was beaten to death by Christopher J. Scarver, another inmate serving time for murder. His remains were cremated, although efforts were made by his mother to have her son's brain donated to science.

How do we explain Dahmer's criminal behavior? Like other serial killers, there is no single causal factor. His biological father, Lionel Dahmer, outlines several possibilities that in combination may have triggered his son's urge to kill. Mr. Dahmer (1994) points out that Jeffrey's mother, Joyce, frequently used medications such as phenobarbital and morphine during her pregnancy with Jeffrey to deal with both psychological and physiological problems. Could these medications have affected Jeffrey's fetal development, or did he inherit mental illness from his mother or antisocial personality traits from his father? From a neuropsychological perspective, was there some genetic predisposition to violence inherited by Jeffrey? Mr. Dahmer does mention his own obsession with fire and a fascination with bombs and making explosives. Another possible factor was the constant family discord that seemed to alienate Jeffrey and led to divorce and further family disruption. Eventually, Jeffrey turned to alcohol to assuage his pain of abandonment, his feelings of low self-esteem, and his perceived pattern of failure in life. How do you explain Dahmer's diminished conscience, lack of empathy, and cold-blooded attitude as he hunted, selected, and killed each victim?

Also, can we exclude the possibility that pornography, like alcohol, may affect those people who harbor a predisposition for such stimulation more than others? In addition, pornography may actually serve as a retardant to serial offenders. If we are to believe, regardless of the presence or absence of pornography, that serial killers will commit acts of murder, then it is possible that some people may find sufficient gratification in and catharsis through various forms of pornography to avoid violence. As a release valve, the pornography lessens the demand for victims. We might argue that some serial offenders might have been motivated to kill earlier if pornography had not been available through which they could exercise their fantasies of control.

Proper scientific verification of these and other implications of pornography are needed in the construction of serial-murder etiology. We must be cautious in suggesting that there exists anything more than a tendency for pornography to affect those offenders involved in serial killing, regardless of how any of us may feel about pornography. If an argument is to be made that pornography (hard-core) is a primary causal agent for serial murder, then how are we to explain the behavior of serial killers who lived before the media explosion of the 20th century? Serial murderers have existed for several hundreds of years, if not longer. Before technology permitted society to produce violent and sexually graphic material, serial killers were at work in America.

However, one could also argue that the emergence of large numbers of serial killers beginning in the 1960s was a direct result of the recent media explosion. Alcohol and pornography are not mandatory elements in the construction of a serial killer, but they tend to provide vehicles the offender uses to express the growing rages within. In most instances these facilitators tend to be present to some degree in the profile of a serial killer. It is my contention, however, that without alcohol or pornography the offender in all likelihood would kill anyway. The circumstances of the acts may be altered, but the murders would inevitably occur. The offender still must gain control of inner feelings, anxieties, anger, rage, and pain. Using alcohol or pornography or other such types of graphic literature may be useful in expediting the offender's urge to kill (see Profile 4.5). Research on the usage of video games has yielded some additional insights into aggressive behavior. Carnagey and Anderson (2005) found that hostile emotions and aggressive thinking and behavior increased after participants in their study participated in video games that rewarded violent behavior. In video games where violence was punished, only hostile emotions increased but not aggressive behavior. Thus, being rewarded for violent behavior via video games is a catalyst for hostility and aggression. Sheese and Graziano (2005) found that participating in violent video games appears to increase antisocial and self-serving motives. Participants playing the violent video games were also more likely to engage in competitive versus cooperative social behavior. Contrary to popular belief, video games are not cathartic in releasing pent-up emotions but rather increase aggression (Anderson, 2010). Indeed, such false beliefs influence angry people to play violent games (Bushman and Whitaker, 2010). Bushman et al. (2007) also found that participants exposed to media violence and who identified with violent characters were more prone to participate in aggressive behavior prior to exposure to violence.

Frequently, serial offenders escalate their hunt for prey as they seek to fulfill deviant sexual fantasies of control. By the end of Jeffrey Dahmer's killing career, he was hunting another victim even before completely disposing of his most recent victim's corpse (see Profile 4.5).

As a postscript to Jeffrey Dahmer's case, I ask the reader to consider the perspective of the offender's family—a view seldom recognized or appreciated. I came to know personally some of Jeffrey Dahmer's family. Since the murders, I spent time with both Jeffrey's brother, David, and his mother, Joyce. If Jeffrey was angry or unhappy with his mother, these emotions were well concealed after his arrest. Both his mother, now deceased, and his brother were two of the kindest people a person could ever hope to meet. They have suffered immensely and struggle to understand how and why Jeff, a brother and son, could act so violently. Their lives, too, have been changed forever.

CYCLICAL NATURE OF SERIAL KILLING

The trauma-control model of violent behavior describes, in effect, the cyclical experience of serial offenders. Fantasies, possibly fueled by pornography or alcohol, reinforced by "routine" traumatizations of day-to-day living, keep the serial killer caught up in a self-perpetuating cycle of fantasies, stalking, and violence. Contrary to some claims, serial killers do not all wish to be caught, although some do and eventually allow themselves to be apprehended. Others subconsciously place themselves on pathways to exposure. One may argue that serial killers allow themselves to be caught because their narcissism and need for recognition overwhelms their desire to remain hidden. Others may briefly experience a moment of clarity in considering their deeds and decide to end the killing. Although this has happened, such offender behavior appears to be rare. Ed Kemper, after murdering several women in California, drove to Colorado, called the police, and told them he was the killer they were searching for. Kemper was accommodating enough to wait by the pay phone until the police arrived and arrested him. Some serial killers such as Ted Kaczynski, the Unabomer (Chapter 12), and Dennis Rader, the BTK Strangler (Chapter 7), can go on for many years and never allow their fantasies to become so consuming that they lose control of their surroundings and their ability to remain obscure. (Even these two serial killers eventually gave in to their need for recognition and to be heard.) For the killer, the cycle becomes a never-ending pursuit of control over one's own life through the total domination and destruction of others' lives.

Sexual Predators, Paraphilia, and Murder

LEARNING OBJECTIVES

- To explore the differences between sex offenders and sexual predators
- To examine the spectrum of criminal paraphilia that can contribute to escalation in sex crimes
- To be able to distinguish between non-violent and violent paraphilia
- To understand the role of Relational Paraphilic Attachment in sexual fantasy development and specific types of sex crimes
- To evaluate the current research on female sex offenders and public perception of women who commit sex offenses
- To objectively consider the current research, myths, and facts on clergy who abuse children
- To evaluate the cases of sexual predators presented in this chapter as examples of progressive sex crimes. Which cases have paraphilic themes?

Several types of profiling have been developed in the past 30 years, including crime scene, psychological, criminal, victim, and others that are discussed in Chapter 12. Enough research and profiling of offenders, victims, and crime scenes has been done to warrant a new type of profiling that focuses on the dynamics of sex offending. *Paraphilia profiling* (Hickey, 2006a) examines the role of paraphilia in the etiology of sex crimes, fantasy development, and the creation of sexual predators. This chapter examines the intersection of fantasy, paraphilia, and the development of sexual predators who become murderers.

DIFFERENTIATING BETWEEN SEX OFFENDERS AND SEXUAL PREDATORS

Problematic to investigating sex crimes, interrogating suspects, understanding victimization, and punishing and treating those who commit sex crimes is being able to differentiate between sex offenders and sexual predators. Ward and Beech (2007) note that comprehensive etiological theories underscore that sexual offending has multiple trajectories (p. 33), suggesting the complexity of understanding such offenders. To the general public, persons who commit sex crimes, regardless of what they do, are usually perceived as dangerous to the community and in need of incarceration. Indeed, many offenders are dangerous because of the types of crimes they commit. In California about two-thirds of the nearly 120,000 registered sex offenders have committed crimes against children. This fact alone is enough to create fear in any community.

Sex offending depends on many variables, including fantasy development of the offender, types of victims selected, opportunity to commit sex crimes, level of psychopathy, and development of paraphilic behaviors. Once offenders are caught and placed in the criminal justice system, each state must determine their suitability for probation and parole. Almost all persons who commit sex crimes will eventually be released back into the community. Almost all persons who commit sex crimes pose some level of risk of recidivism, but those levels will vary widely depending on their criminal histories and amenability to treatment. Some offenders will never commit another sex crime, while others will re-offend almost immediately. Sorting out which ones are the most dangerous is never an easy task, but there are some factors to keep in mind when determining dangerousness. On one end of a continuum, *sex offenders* often only commit one crime, usually have only one victim, often prey on a family member, tend to be non-progressive in sexually acting out, do not pose a threat to the general community, are non-psychopathic and capable of forming healthy emotional attachments, are non-paraphilic, and are amenable to treatment and control. On the other end of the continuum, *sexual predators* commit multiple sex crimes, prey on multiple victims or multiple counts on a victim over time, frequently have both stranger and/or familial victims, are progressively sexually exploitative, pose a threat to the general community, usually exhibit psychopathic traits, frequently have multiple paraphilia, and seldom are amenable to treatment. Somewhere between these two extremes exist offenders who are evolving in their fantasies, behaviors, and psychopathy. Although serial murderers who engage in sexual predation are more prone to be sexual predators, they do not all fall into that classification.

For some investigators, the sexual nature of the crime may be viewed as a subtype of one or more general taxonomies. In certain serial killings for the offender, the sexual attack is an integral part of the murder, both psychologically and physiologically. For other offenders the sexual attack may represent the best way to degrade, subjugate, and ultimately destroy their victim, but has little connection to the actual motive(s) for the killing (see Profile 5.1).

PROFILE 5.1 Charles Albright, the Eyeball Serial Killer, 1990–1991

Consider the case of Charles Albright, a serial killer in Texas, who between 1990 and 1991 murdered several female prostitutes. Charles was a white, 57-year-old, married male with children, with a history of juvenile delinquency, property crimes, and prior incarcerations. As a child he experienced mental and emotional abuse as well as rejection by his parents. A product of an unstable home, Charles developed an intense hatred for women. He derived great satisfaction in bludgeoning and shooting his victims.

Charles was no ordinary man. Very intelligent, he was fluent in Latin, Spanish, and French, or at least he promoted himself in that light. He became a biology teacher and a skilled taxidermist. Charles was a skillful painter and musician and was adored by women. He had a great sense of humor and was portrayed as the class clown in college. He was a ladies' man and enjoyed impressing them with his varied artistic talents. He was athletic and enjoyed coaching football and later playing slow-pitch softball. He was affable and mingled well in groups.

Yet there was a disturbing side to him that seldom could be seen. He could not hold a job more than a few months. Charles portrayed himself as a faithful family man, but he frequented prostitutes. He developed some masochistic attitudes. He carefully concealed his history of thefts. He forged his college transcripts, making it appear that he had graduated. He once referred to his biological mother as a prostitute, although there was no proof of his accusation.

He raped a 13-year-old girl when he was 51 years old but managed to minimize the incident. He became increasingly sexually aggressive with women. He was a consummate liar and con man, a true Jekyll-and-Hyde personality. Along the path of adolescence Charles also developed a fascination and obsession for eyes. He was always trying to paint perfect eyes. He would paint portraits without eyes because he felt he could not do the eyes justice. When the autopsies were performed on his victims, the staff discovered that the eyeballs of each victim had been surgically removed without damaging the eyelids. The eyeballs were never recovered. Now incarcerated in a state prison, Charles continues his obsession with eyes. He subscribes to a magazine devoted to iridology and has the first issue of *Omni* magazine (October 1978), which displays on the cover an eyeball, as if it is floating in the air (Hollandsworth, 1993; Matthews, 1996).

SEXUAL HOMICIDES AND PARAPHILIA

Most serial killers known widely to the public have usually been involved sexually with their victims. This may include rape, sodomy, and an array of sexual tortures and deviations. Indeed it is a shared belief among most law enforcement officials and many clinicians that most serial murders are sexual in nature (Lunde, 1976; Ressler, 1985, 1988; Revitch, 1965). There have been serial killings that appear to have no sexual connotations; however, not all sex murders *overtly* express sexual needs. In other words, some serial killing that may appear to be motivated by factors such as financial gain or cult-related goals may actually have sexual motives. In one instance a multiple murderer who had been killing patients for financial gain later admitted she also became aroused watching her victims die. This possibility cannot be accurately measured. Serial murder now has multiple categories that include both *expressive* homicides such as sexual killings or hate crimes and *instrumental* homicides or those more likely carried out for financial

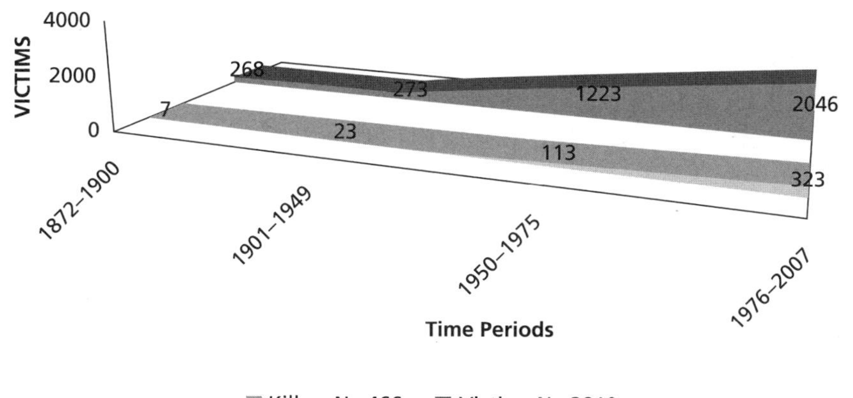

CHART 5.1 Sexual Serial Killers and Their Victims 1872–2007 in the United States
SOURCE: © Cengage Learning, 2013.

gain, which provides a much broader framework in which to study serial killing. This chapter focuses on sexual serial murder, meaning that the offender(s) demonstrated in some manner a sexual motivation for the murders. These types of serial killers have been documented for over 200 years (see Chart 5.1).

Some researchers differentiate sex murderers from lust murderers. The sex murderer kills often out of fear and a desire to silence his victim, whereas the lust murderer appears to harbor deep-seated fantasies. This certainly does not exclude the possibility that some rapists may also premeditate their killings and experience deep-seated fantasies. For killers such as Albert DeSalvo, the Boston Strangler, rapes are only a continuation of progressive sexual fantasies and behaviors that finally lead to murder. Revitch and Schlesinger (1981) noted that women, although less frequently than men, also are capable of developing homicidal fantasies and becoming involved in sadistic murders and mass killings (see Chart 5.2).

In recent years researchers have continued to note differences between rape murders and lust killings (Prentky, Burgess, and Carter, 1986; Ressler, 1985; Scully and Marolla, 1985). Special agents from the FBI examined a sample of 36 sexual murderers, 29 of whom were convicted of killing several victims. Specifically they were interested in the general characteristics of sexual murderers across the United States. They explored the dynamics of offenders' sexual fantasies, sadistic behaviors, and rape and mutilation murders. These investigators noted several deviant sexual behaviors practiced before, during, or after the victim has been killed. The act of rape, whether it be the actual physical act or a symbolic rape during which an object is inserted into the vagina, was found to be common among serial killers in this study. For some offenders the act of rape served as only one form of sexual assault; they engaged in a variety of mutilations, sexual perversions, and desecrations of the victim's corpse (Ressler et al., 1988, pp. 33–44).

Of course, sexual deviations have influenced our perceptions and definitions of those who kill. "Sex maniac" becomes the layperson's term for anyone capable of performing acts of sexual perversion on his or her victims. Each of the categories

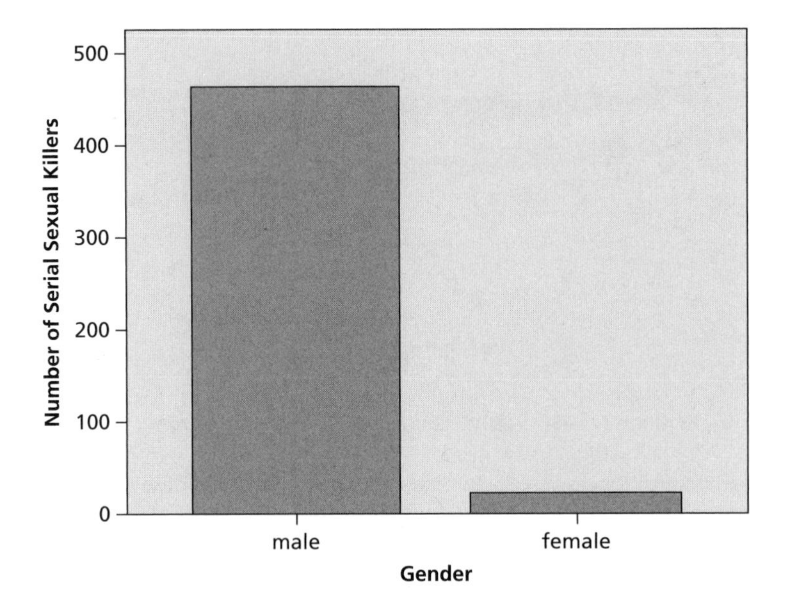

CHART 5.2 Gender and Serial Sexual Murder 1872–2008
SOURCE: © Cengage Learning, 2013.

listed in the next section describes a type of sexual behavior engaged in by one or more serial killers in this study, behavior that was believed to be in some way linked to the killings. In some cases the offenders as children were subjected to one or more of these sexual activities. In each case the sexual abuse was deeply traumatizing. The list is not exhaustive nor does it imply cause and effect. What is important to understand is how these categories of sexual behavior influence the typecasting of offenders.

A SPECTRUM OF PARAPHILIA

According to the *Diagnostic and Statistical Manual of Mental Disorders,* fourth edition (*DSM-IV*), published by the American Psychiatric Association (1994), many of the terms listed describe various forms of *paraphilia.* The *DSM-IV* describes three general classifications of paraphilia:

1. Preference for the use of a non-human object for sexual arousal
2. Repetitive sexual activity with humans that involves real or simulated suffering or humiliation
3. Repetitive sexual activity with nonconsenting partners

According to Money and Werlas (1982) a paraphilia is an erotosexual condition involving an obsessive dependence on an unusual stimulus, physical or fantasy, in order to achieve or maintain sexual arousal and/or orgasm. The *DSM-IV* also adds that such a condition covers a time frame of at least six months. A spectrum of paraphilia emerges as they range from those relatively benign to those extremely harmful to oneself or others. A number of deaths have been attributed to autoerotic asphyxia where persons experimenting for the first time or through miscalculation have accidentally killed themselves by hanging. Conversely, the desire to dress up in costumes or the urge to use pornography while having sexual relations does not physically harm anyone. Yet, the preference to secretly watch people undress, bathe, or engage in sex crosses lines of criminality. Many convicted rapists have histories of other sexual offenses (Hudson and Ward, 1997, p. 338).

Money (1990) noted that the term *paraphilia* comes from the Greek *para,* beyond, amiss, or altered, and *philia,* love (p. 27). Common almost exclusively to males, paraphilia involves sexual arousal through deviant or bizarre images or activities. For example, bestiality, or sex with animals, has been documented since the 1400s. In England, where bestiality is known as buggery, death sentences were common during the 1600s for persons having sex with animals. In early American history such behavior was considered a crime against nature and harsh punishments were meted out to offenders. In Utah during the 1800s, a soldier was caught having sex with his horse. The man was banished from the state while his horse was shot. In 1992 a man was sentenced to two years in prison for killing and having sex with his Rottweiler. He had previously sexually assaulted chickens and tried to have sex with geese. Currently 29 states have criminal sanctions for bestiality.

Paraphilia are considered by the *DSM-IV* to be sexual impulse disorders characterized by intensely arousing, recurrent sexual fantasies, urges, and behaviors (of at least six months' duration) that are considered deviant with respect to cultural norms and that produce clinically significant distress or impairment in social, occupational, or other important areas of psychosocial functioning. Many paraphilia involve various forms of *fetishes,* which are defined by the *DSM-IV* as recurrent, intense, sexually arousing fantasies, sexual urges, or behaviors involving the use of nonliving objects, occurring over a period of at least six months. Kafka and Hennen (2002) identified several paraphilia-related disorders in males including compulsive masturbation, promiscuity, pornography addiction, a strong desire for telephone sex, and severe incompatibility in their sexual urges (p. 350). For example, Kenworthy and Litton (2006) noted that fetishists commonly become sexually aroused by specific objects such as shoes and feet. Weinberg, Williams, and Calhan (1995) found that 45% of those who reported such sexual attractions had pleasurable memories of events in developing a foot fetish, noting that about one-third reported masturbating to feet or shoes during adolescence. Multiple paraphilia are also commonly found in one person, but usually one paraphilia becomes dominant until replaced by another. For example, a pedophile, or someone who is sexually attracted to children, may also succumb to fetishes, such as being aroused by a child's hair, rubber gloves, or self-administered enemas. Most psychosexual disorders are a result of an aberrant fantasy system fueled by traumatic childhood and adolescent experiences.

Occasional paraphilic fantasies are common. Crepault and Couture (1980) in their study of men's fantasies reported that 62% had fantasized having sex with a young girl, 33% raping a woman, 12% being humiliated during sex, 5% having

TABLE 5.1 Sexual Practices Considered to Be Very Appealing

	Men	Women
Activity	%	%
Vaginal intercourse	83	78
Watching partner undress	50	30
Receiving oral sex	50	33
Giving oral sex	37	19
Group sex	14	1
Anus stimulated by partner's fingers	6	4
Using dildos or vibrators	5	3
Watching others engage in sexual activities	6	2
Having a same-gender sex partner	4	3
Having sex with a stranger	5	1

SOURCE: © Cengage Learning, 2013.

sex with an animal, and 3% fantasized engaging in sex with a young boy. Other sexual activities are also common (see Table 5.1).

In a later study of male undergraduate students by Briere and Runtz (1989), 21% reported sexual attraction to children, 9% fantasized of having sex with children, 5% masturbated to thoughts of sex with children, and 7% admitted that they would act out their sexual fantasies with children if they could do so with impunity. Most of these men would not be diagnosed with paraphilias because such fantasies and behaviors were not their primary focus for sexual stimulation nor did they attempt to act out those fantasies (Nolen-Hoeksema, 2004).

FACTORS IN PARAPHILIA

According to the *DSM-IV*, for a person to be diagnosed with paraphilia, their fantasies, urges, and behaviors are examined for intensity, frequency, and duration. The paraphilia must be manifest for at least six months for there to be a clinical classification. The diagnostic category of paraphilias includes nine disorders, but there are many documented paraphilia, some more common than others. These include fetishes, voyeurism, exhibitionism, frotteurism, sadomasochism, and pedophilia. In addition, there are dozens of lesser-known paraphilia that may only have a few persons with the particular disorder. The Internet provides a venue for paraphiliacs to document real and imagined atypical sexual behaviors. Some paraphilia are legally tolerated (certain fetishes), while others involve criminal activities. Between these two spectrums lies a gray area of defining sexual activity as either criminal or noncriminal. Such definitions frequently require an examination of the legal conception of sexual crimes that usually involves issues of consent and aggressiveness (Smallbone and Wortley, 2004, p. 176). Some of the explanations for paraphilia include (1) *psychodynamic*—paraphilic behavior as a manifestation of unresolved conflicts during psychosexual development; (2) *behavioral*—paraphilia is developed through conditioning, modeling, reinforcement, punishment, and rewards, the same process that normal sexual activity is learned; (3) *cognitive*—paraphilia become substitutes for appropriate social and sexual functioning or the inability to develop satisfying marital relationships; (4) *biological*—heredity, prenatal hormone environment, and factors contributing to gender identity can facilitate paraphilic interests. (5) *interactional*—that development of paraphilia is a process that results from psychodynamic, behavioral, cognitive, and biological factors. Other explanations are linked to brain malfunctioning and chromosomal abnormalities. (Sarason and Sarason, 2004).

An interest in sexual excesses or improper sexual activities is classified by the *DSM-IV* into three categories: *Paraphilia, Impulse Control Disorder,* and *Sexual Disorder.* Some researchers consider many compulsive sexual behaviors to be impulse control–oriented because systemically it is the failure to resist temptations, urges, and impulses to sexually act out, with the knowledge that such behaviors are harmful to the perpetrator and to others. These impulses are of the same origin as those criteria related to pathological gambling or substance addiction. Milner and Dopke (1997) suggest that paraphilia may actually be related to the obsessive-compulsive spectrum of disorders that are affected by selective serotonin reuptake inhibitors (SSRIs) that affect abnormal hormone levels. Sexual disorders may also be correlated with addictive sexual activities such as anonymous sex or trading and paying for sex (Carnes, 2001). *Bipolar affective disorder* is often characterized by excesses of sexuality in the manic phase where the person exhibits "indiscriminate enthusiasm for interpersonal, sexual, or occupational interactions.... Increased sexual drives, fantasies and behavior are often present" (*DSM-IV*, 2000, pp. 328–329). Consider the case of the "Doctor Rapist" who used rape by fraud to have sex with dozens of female victims (see Profile 5.2).

The *DSM-IV* offers other possible explanations for paraphilic interests and behaviors, including *cyclothymic disorder*, which is similar to bipolar persons who present chronic, fluctuating mood disturbances including hypomanic symptoms that may feature hypersexuality. Another *DSM-IV* diagnosis is *substance-induced* mood changes due to the high correlation of drug addictions and evidence of addictive sexual behaviors.

Many of the offenders in this study fit into the extreme end of the paraphilic continuum because they engage in *erotophonophilia,* or lust/sexual murder. This involves the acting out of sadistic behaviors in the course of brutally torturing and murdering their victims. The following discussion of sexual behaviors is not intended to be exhaustive but rather specific to serial offenders in this research. Fantasy is a key component in facilitating these behaviors.

1. **Animal Torture**—stabbing or chopping animals to death, especially cats, and dissecting them. One offender admitted killing several puppies in order to relive the experience of killing his first child victim. Persons who become multiple-homicide offenders have often reported being cruel to animals when they were children. Certainly there are serial killers who do not harm animals or express a morbid interest in animal viscera. In children, such

PROFILE 5.2 The Doctor Rapist

John Huntington Story was a well-respected family doctor in the small town of Lovell, Wyoming. Many women visited his office for medical advice but left completely unaware that they had been raped. By the 1980s and after 25 years of practicing medicine, Dr. Story had given hundreds of pelvic examinations, even when the complaint was for a headache or ear infection. The procedure would often last two hours or more. His nurse was conveniently not present during these examinations. Pretending to examine the women, he made them into rape victims without their knowledge. Eventually, after accumulating over 100 victims, one of them reported her unusual visit to Dr. Story. Many women came forward with the same tale and Dr. Story was arrested, convicted, and sent to prison at Rawlins, Wyoming. He completed his time and was released in 2001.

Upon reading this case, most people find it difficult to believe that so many women could be raped by a doctor and not be aware of what was happening. He did not use drugs or anesthetics of any kind, but simply his powers of deception. Does this doctor exhibit any psychopathic characteristics? What would drive a person who has spent many years in college and medical school and who has built a trusted relationship for many years in a small town to risk having it all crumble if found out? Dr. Story did not pick a small town by accident but because the population was almost entirely of the same religion and he knew that he could manipulate and control trusting, naive minds, even his own wife. Although his medical license was revoked, Story, while in prison, had his wife retrieve the examination table he used to rape his victims. A souvenir or plans for future victims? The late Jack Olson covered this story in his true crime book, *Doc.* This is an incredible story from the victims' perspective as well as the psychopathology of this narcissistic sexual predator.

behavior may be explained as part of a *DSM-IV* conduct disorder that involves repetitive, persistent patterns of violating societal norms or the basic rights of others. Several serial killers as children had exhibited conduct disorders, manifest in animal torture or evisceration of dead or dying animals. These offenders were also found to exhibit aggression toward other people, destruction of property (fire-setting, vandalism), or theft.

2. **Anthropophagy**—eating the victim's flesh or slicing off parts of flesh from the body. Several of the offenders included in the present study practiced this form of cannibalism. Some are known to have eaten the breasts of victims, one cooked portions of his victim's thighs in casseroles, another delighted in a main diet of children and another, after cooking and eating his partners genitals while he was still alive, then killed him and dined for several months on his body parts (see Profile 5.3).
3. **Autoeroticism**—sexual arousal and gratification through self-stimulation. The most common form involves masturbation to pornography, fantasies, or images. Other forms of autoeroticism include erotic and aqua-erotic asphyxiation. Erotic asphyxiation or "scarfing" involves using devices or material such as scarves, ropes, and plastic bags to cut off one's oxygen supply to the brain in order to enhance sexual gratification. Several hundred

PROFILE 5.3 Armin Meiwes, the German Cannibal, 2001

In 2003, Armin Meiwes, 42, a homosexual German computer expert living in a historic manor house in Rotenburg, Germany, was charged with killing and eating the flesh of another homosexual man he met through an Internet chat room. Meiwes claimed that the victim, Bernd Juergen Brandes, 43, a microchip engineer from Berlin, had, in 2001, volunteered to participate—fully aware that he would ultimately be killed and eaten. Meiwes had posted a message: "seeking well-built man, 18-30 years old, for slaughter." A few months later, Brandes replied: "I offer myself to you and will let you dine from my live body. Not butchery, dining!!" When Meiwes's home was searched about 15 pounds of human flesh was found shrink-wrapped in his refrigerator. The rest he had barbecued in his garden over a nine-month period in 2001. Meiwes admitted that before Brandes was killed the two cannibals cut off Brandes's testicles and penis, then cooked and ate them. Meiwes then stabbed his willing victim to death.

On his website, Meiwes acknowledged his fantasy in seeking young men for "slaughter and consumption" and received over 400 responses to his request. On one occasion a man visited Meiwes and allowed himself to be wrapped naked in cellophane. Meiwes then marked off certain parts of his body to be butchered and frozen for later consumption. When the man realized that the paraphilic fantasy was about to become a reality, he begged Meiwes to let him go. Frustrated, Meiwes freed the man and returned to the Internet in search of more serious participants. Three other homosexual men were also permitted to leave, and one man was rejected outright because he was "too fatty." At his trial Meiwes reveled as he explained his fantasies and said that he looked forward to doing it again because he wanted someone to become part of him. He explained that he had fantasies of cannibalism often between the ages of 8 and 12. These fantasies involved eating his schoolmates and were enhanced by watching horror movies. He argued that his fantasies were never sexual where cannibalism was concerned. Meiwes is charged with murder "for sexual satisfaction" and "disturbing the peace of the dead" by carving up the corpse, and could receive up to 15 years for the killing. The defense hopes to prove a lesser charge of "killing on demand," which carries a maximum five-year jail sentence. There are no laws against cannibalism in Germany.

deaths each year can be attributed to erotic hanging. Often the person cross-dresses, uses pornography, and masturbates to his fantasies while slowly hanging himself. Generally the same elements apply to aqua-erotic asphyxiation except that the paraphilic uses partial drowning to induce increased sexual excitation. A few serial offenders have reported engaging in a variety of autoerotic activities. Consider Profile 5.4.

4. **Coprophilia**—an interest in feces whereby the offender may receive some sexual gratification from touching or eating excrement and/or urine. Although rare among serial killers, at least one is known to have eaten his own excrement.
5. **Exhibitionism**—deliberate exposing of one's genitals (usually male) to an unsuspecting stranger. According to the *DSM-IV*, such behavior must be recurring over at least a six-month period to be considered paraphilia. The exposure, followed by masturbation, serves to reinforce the behavior and in turn the behavior is repeated. Exhibitionism provides the offender with

PROFILE 5.4 An Auto-Erotic Death

Lewis, a 28-year-old Gulf War veteran, married and father of two children, told his wife that he would be back in time for supper and that he was going out to run some errands. When he failed to return by late evening, police were summoned and a search ensued for Lewis, who was not prone to simply disappear. After three days of searching, an officer happened to wander into the backyard and noticed a small utility shed several yards from the house. When the officer found the door to be locked from inside, he forced it open to discover Lewis in the center of the room hanging from a rope, quite dead. One might consider this to be a suicide except for a few telltale signs that it was something other than intentional death.

Dressed in a T-shirt and undershorts, Lewis was wearing women's panty hose on his right leg with his right foot strapped in a woman's high-heeled shoe. His right leg was bent with the high-heeled shoe resting on a box behind him. Most of Lewis's weight was on his left leg that was bare and his left foot on the floor. Blood had begun to pool in his extremities. He was leaning forward but kept in place by the rope that was connected to a pulley on the ceiling beam. A towel had been wrapped around the rope to avoid rope burns or neck discomfort. The pulley device had obviously jammed as Lewis leaned forward in an autoerotic asphyxic state. Directly in front of Lewis about a foot from his face was a shelf with a small light illuminating his pornography: the children's clothing section of a Sears store catalogue. Lewis had been masturbating to the images of children wearing summer clothing while he carefully asphyxiated himself. As he slipped into unconsciousness he relied on the device to release him as his weight pulled down on the rope. Unfortunately for Lewis, the rope jammed and he strangled himself.

How many paraphilic behaviors was Lewis involved with in his shed? What life events can you think of that may have influenced Lewis to develop such sexual interests? What questions, as an investigator, would you want to ask of his family, friends, and coworkers? Do you think, given the variety of paraphilic behaviors and the fantasies that Lewis engaged in, that he might have progressed to criminal activities?

a momentary sense of power and control. Exhibitionists who are caught often express sincere embarrassment and remorse for their crimes but on release quickly recidivate. Exhibitionists generally are not considered to be dangerous offenders only because we do not realize that many exhibitionists also engage in other forms of paraphilic behavior and that some of these paraphiliacs have escalated to more serious crimes, including rape and homicide.

6. **Fetishisms**—finding sexual gratification by substituting objects for the sexual partner. In one case a person (although not a serial killer) had been breaking into several homes in a city in Georgia. A voyeur, this person also enjoyed collecting women's underwear, and on his arrest police discovered over 400 pairs of women's underwear in his possession. In October of 1988 in Riverside, California, a man known as the "panty bandit" was arrested after a series of robberies. During the course of his robberies this man would often order the female clerks to remove their underwear and then would engage in sexual acts in front of his captive audience.

Serial killers have also been known to engage in a variety of fetishes. Some offenders have been known to remove the breasts of their victims for later use; another saved sex organs by placing them in containers; and yet another removed the skin of his victims, out of which he fashioned articles of clothing, ornaments, and even purses. Others have saved victims' teeth or hair as part of their "souvenir fetish." In one case the offender enjoyed decapitating his victims. Later, after shampooing their hair and applying makeup, including lipstick, he would have sex with the heads, sometimes while showering. A final example is the offender who cut off the foot of at least one of his victims. He kept the foot in his refrigerator so he could dress it up in red spiked heels for his personal gratification.

7. **Gerontophilia**—seeking out elderly persons of the opposite sex for sexual purposes. Those serial killers who seek out elderly persons are often believed to harbor hatred toward them. Some of these offenders reported sexual gratification from raping elderly women, some of whom have been in their 80s and 90s. One offender raped and killed several elderly tenants of an apartment complex, whereas another, referred to as the Boston Strangler, sought out elderly widows who lived alone.
8. **Klismaphilia**—sexual arousal through the administration of enemas. A klismaphiliac will substitute enemas for genital intercourse. While some enjoy receiving the enemas, others prefer to administer enemas to others. Sometimes children become the unsuspecting victims of klismaphiliacs who use enemas as a form of sexual abuse.
9. **Infibulation**—self-torture. Involves piercing one's own nipples, labia, clitoris, scrotum, or penis with sharp objects such as needles, pins, and rings. Albert Fish, a man who murdered children, cannibalized them, and wrote letters to victims' families telling them how much he enjoyed eating their children, was an infibulator who derived sexual gratification by jabbing sewing needles into his scrotum and penis. After his execution an autopsy revealed nearly two dozen needles in his genitals.
10. **Lust Murder or Erotophonophilia**—murdering sadistically and brutally, including the mutilation of body parts, especially the genitalia. One offender who chopped off the penis of a young boy with a pair of wire cutters still expresses a strong desire to mutilate sexual organs. Another would sometimes shoot his victims in the head while they performed oral sex, and another enjoyed crushing his victims' nipples with pliers and mutilating their breasts. Others have torn off the nipples of their victims with their teeth. On several occasions offenders have completely dismembered their victims' bodies, and then tossed the parts onto highways or into wooded areas, shallow graves, or sometimes left them for animals to consume. One offender was discovered with several pounds of body parts stashed in his refrigerator. A few offenders drank the blood of their victims. Sex murderers may perform similar acts but often are more spontaneous and react more out of fear of detection than lust murderers do.
11. **Necrophilia**—having sexual relations with dead bodies. This form of deviation is common among offenders who are involved sexually with

their victims. Generally, necrophilia is thought to be practiced only by males, but Gallagher (1987) notes that in 1983, a California woman confessed to having sex with dead people. This woman, a mortuary employee, said she would often climb into coffins to have sex with the corpse or drive corpses in a hearse up to the mountains where her "love making" would not be disturbed. Apparently she had been sexually "involved" with at least 40 corpses. In another case of serial killing, the offender had sex with the corpse of a child, and then placed her body under his bed so that he could repeat the experience. Several occurrences of necrophilia have been recorded among serial killers. As mentioned, one offender decapitated his victims and, while showering, had sex with the heads. Another offender robbed graves to have sex with the corpses and, as he noted, to have someone for company. In some cases the necrophile wants not only to have sex with a corpse but also to keep them nearby, such as in a closet or under the bed.

Necrofetishism is having a fetish for dead bodies. Some offenders actually enjoy keeping cadavers in their homes. In one case police found six decomposing corpses in the bedroom of one offender. Another offender liked to share his bed with various corpses, some of which had been decapitated. Jeffrey Dahmer was one of the most prolific necrophiles in the modern U.S. annals of crime.

Necrophilia can be described as typologies or as a process, depending on interpretation. Some necrophiles use fantasy to experience sex with a corpse. Some prostitutes cater to paraphiliacs and for the right price will ice themselves down, dust on white powder, and lay motionless with eyes closed in a casket, while her "john" acts out his fantasies. Other necrophiles seek out real corpses from funeral parlors, cemeteries, morgues, and hospitals. Serial killers such as Dennis Nilsen and Ed Gein both fulfilled some of their fantasies by grave robbing. Similar to these forms of behavior is *pygmalionism,* or the sexual involvement of a person with dolls or mannequins. Both pygmalionists and necrophiles avoid rejection by having sex with inanimate objects (dolls) or corpses. In both forms of behavior the paraphiliac exercises total control over his environment. The paraphiliac can do whatever he or she wants with the object or body and then dispose of it. Finally, a few necrophiles will kill people in order to use their corpse for sexual gratification. These three types of necrophilia may also be viewed as escalation in fantasy fulfillment. Both Nilsen and Gein eventually went on to kill people in order to sexually abuse the corpses. The act of necrophilia is having sexual relations with a corpse (Hickey, 2006b, p. 25). Most people imagine necrophilia as having sexual intercourse with a corpse, but other necrophilic behaviors may include touching or stroking a corpse, masturbating on or in the vicinity of a corpse, or rubbing one's body parts including genitalia on the corpse. Rosman and Resnick (1989) in their examination of 122 necrophile cases identified two forms of necrophiliacs:

1. *Genuine necrophiles:* These are persons who have persistent urges to have sex with corpses. They tend to be of one of the following subtypes:
    - *Necrophilic fantasies* or those who only fantasize about having sex with a corpse but make no contact. Usually they have living partners who

sometimes will accommodate the fantasy by taking cold showers, covering herself in white powder, and lying motionless while her partner has sex with her. Some prostitutes specialize in necrophilia by icing themselves, climbing into caskets surrounded by flowers, and remaining completely motionless with eyes shut while the customer performs his sexual acts (Masters, 1963). The Internet is another medium in which a person can engage in *virtual* necrophilia by linking to websites with photos of partially dressed women who appear to be dead.

- *Regular necrophilia* includes persons who use corpses for their personal sexual gratification. The majority of offenders work in morgues or mortuaries or as hospital orderlies, emergency medical technicians, or gravediggers. In some states having sex with a corpse is not a crime, and because of the stigma associated with such behavior, discoveries of persons engaging in such acts are frequently handled discreetly out of the public eye.
- *Necrophile homicide* involves persons killing others in order to obtain their bodies for sexual purposes. Such offenders usually become serial killers, including Edmund Kemper, Jeffrey Dahmer, Ed Gein, Dennis Nilsen, Gerald Brudos, and Andre Chikatilo. These necrosadistic murderers will have often engaged in other paraphilias related to necrophilia, including *partialism*, or the desire to collect specific body parts that the offender finds sexually arousing—this may include feet, hands, hair, and heads, among others; *somophilia*, or the desire to have sex with persons who are asleep or feigning sleep; *pygmalionism,* a term used for those who enjoy sex with mannequins; *vampirism,* offenders who enjoy drinking the blood of their victims; and *cannibalism,* the sometimes sexualized experience of devouring a victim in order that the victim will always be a part of the offender.

2. *Pseudo-necrophilia:* In most cases sex acts with corpses occur during violent assaults on a living person. During a frenzied attack where the victim is often killed brutally with a knife, hammer, axe, club, or strangulation, a sex act with the corpse may ensue. This sex act, however, usually is not the result of prior sexual fantasy or a primary motive for killing (Franzini and Grossberg, 1995).

Nobus (2002, p. 179) noted that necrophiles exhibit pervasive personality dysfunctioning that includes narcissism, sadism, and a need to destroy. In the Rosman and Resnick study, necrophiles were found to be generally intelligent with only 17% suffering from severe mental illness. About half were diagnosed with personality disorders. The vast majority of necrophiles reported having had non-necrophilic sex with many consenting partners. About 80% of pseudo-necrophiles and 44% of genuine necrophiles reported drinking prior to the assaults. Dimock and Smith (1997) found that necrophilia is associated with dissociative states (specifically fugue states), impotency or hypersexuality, voyeurism, and a variety of fetishes. Most offenders explained their necrophilic acts as a need to be with and possess a compliant, accepting partner without fear of any rejection (Franzini and Grossberg, 1995). Holmes (1991) noted that many necrophiles are insensitive people who harbor deep-seated hate toward females. Killing and degrading the corpse reduces the worth of that person, even in death, and all this is accomplished without rejection.

12. **Pedophilia**—having a sexual preference for children. A 16-year-old boy who had been arrested for sexual assault on children admitted that his favorite places to pick up children were the toy centers in department stores. Knowing that some parents are willing to leave their small children to look at toys while they go shopping for a few minutes, he easily found victims. He would simply select the youngest or most vulnerable-looking children and take them to the washrooms, where he would molest them. Females are far less likely to become sexual predators of children, but developing liaisons with a specific child is not uncommon. Frequently the female offender is a schoolteacher who preys on a minor (see Profile 5.5).

PROFILE 5.5 Mary Kay Letourneau, Child Sex Offender

Mary Kay Letourneau, 35, a married mother of four and Seattle, Washington, elementary school teacher, shocked her community in 1997 when she publicly admitted that she was having a sexual affair with a 13-year-old student. She told the court following her arrest that she was pregnant and was very much in love with the boy, Vili Fualaau. Letourneau gave birth to a baby girl and publicly stated that she was proud that Fualaau was the father. Fualaau's mother was given custody of the baby. Letourneau received a six-month jail sentence for rape and was ordered to undergo three years of counseling in a community-based program for sex offenders. Letourneau, six months later, acknowledged to the court, "I did something that I had no right to do, morally or legally. It was wrong and I am sorry.... It will not happen again.... Please help me ... help us all." She was court ordered to stay away from the 14-year-old boy and reminded that a 7½-year child-rape prison sentence awaited her if she violated the order. One month later, police found Letourneau and the boy having sex in her car. She was sent to prison and a few months after her arrival gave birth to her second child by Fualaau. In the summer of 2004, Letourneau was released and soon married her victim.

Letourneau appeared to have everything with her education, career, and family, but appearances can be deceiving. Her marriage was not a happy one, and her husband was having an affair. Could this have triggered her acting out on a child? Unlikely, but she was raised in a strict family where her father, a public figure, eventually admitted to having an affair with the babysitter. The parents divorced and Letourneau blamed her mother for her father's demise. His career in ruins, her father became ill with cancer and died after a long battle. Could the hidden reality be that her unhappy marriage was a replay of her parents, and this influenced her to act out in a manner that would attract public scrutiny, a mimic of her father? Female sex offenders usually have histories of traumatic events that drive them to act out. She is not the first teacher to become sexually involved with underage students. What is the best way to classify female sex offenders who target children that will help society better identify, apprehend, punish, and treat them as we do with males?

Female Sex Offenders

Over the past 50 years social scientists have examined a variety of male sex offenders in attempts to understand their psychosocial and behavioral characteristics. Many typologies and sub-typologies were identified and modified over time (Cohen et al., 1969; Groth, 1978; Quinsey, 1986). Holmes and Holmes (2002) expanded on some of these typologies to gain more understanding of the motivations of child molesters and victim compliance. These studies, of course, brought more attention to emerging cases of female sex offending. A few researchers over the past 30 years have examined cases of female sex offending and created typologies of these offenders. Sarrel and Masters (1982) identified four typologies of female sex offenders: *forced assault*, *baby sitter abuse, incestuous abuse*, and *dominant woman abuse*. Mathews et al. (1989) identified five types of female offenders: *Teacher-lovers* (see Profile 5.5) are women who feel no shame or remorse, feel that they are doing no harm and that they actually are helping the student; *predisposed child molesters* are women with histories of personal abuse and substance addictions who act alone in efforts to find emotional intimacy. These offenders initiate the sexual encounters without coercion. The third typology, *male-coerced sexual offenders*, is women with histories of abuse who assist men in preying upon minors, including their own children. In some cases the female offender, once exposed to abusing by the male, would initiate the abuse herself. *Experimenter-exploiter* offenders tend to be 16 years of age or younger and most often select a young male under the age of six years, and the *psychologically disturbed* category is where the offender is afflicted with uncontrollable libidinal impulses. Lawson (1993) identified four subtypes of female offenders: the *subtle abuse mother molester*, the *seductive abuse mother molester,* the *humiliation offender*, and the *overt sexual abuse offender*. Vandiver and Kercher (2004) identified six subtypes of female offenders—*heterosexual nurturers*, *noncriminal homosexual offenders*, *female sexual predators*, *young adult child exploiters*, *homosexual criminals*, and *aggressive homosexual offenders*—by examining offender characteristics, their offenses, and their victims. In 2005, Ferguson and Meehan, using similar types of data collection, created three more categories of female sex offenders. In more recent years several women have been arrested for engaging in teacher-lover crimes where the offender will have sexual relations with a minor. Typically these involve women seducing adolescent boys 13 to 17 years of age. Other female offenders who are not teachers have done similar crimes as well as crimes against younger children. In Roe-Sepowitz and Krysik's (2008) study of 117 female sex offenders, no stranger victims were reported, and Johansson-Love and Fremouw (2009) found that nearly 60% of their female offenders were biologically related to their victims. All of these studies contribute to the developing baseline date on female sex offenders, but we may be a bit premature in attempting to create labels.

Perhaps some of the confusion about female sex offenders is that we actually know very little about them in comparison to male offenders and in turn fewer females are apprehended (Bjorklund, 2008). Most of our perceptions about female offenders are framed in how we view male sex offenders. This alone may affect our accurately measuring incidence or prevalence of female sex offenders due to underreporting of such crimes. This may be a result of our culture that tends to view women as not fitting the role of sex offender or sexual predator, which is historically the purview of males. Denov (2004) noted that many people, including professionals such as police and mental health practitioners, are skeptical about females being sex offenders as we see in some males. She noted that police were more likely to view reports of female sex offending as unfounded. Carlson (2010) found in her research that a significant difference exists in peoples' opinions regarding male and female sex offenders. Indeed, stereotypes influenced by culture, religion, nationality, gender, race, age, education and socio-economic status all contribute to a persons perception of male and female sex offenders. Lawson (2008) found that women sex offenders display little or no interest in the plight of their victims and expressed little regret for any harm done. Their abilitiy to express intimacy, understanding and empathy were limited.

One of the main problems with creating typologies is being able to replicate them in other studies (Miller et al., 2009). Turner et al. (2008) used latent profile analysis in examining potential typologies of 79 female sex offenders, focusing on personality characteristics using the Personality Assessment Inventory (PAI), and identified three groups of offenders with low, moderate, or extensive levels of psychopathology and substance abuse. The study is useful due to its implications for treatment of female offenders with substance abuse and prior victimization. Terrell et al. (2009) note that all adult females involved in sex crimes against minors should receive a psychiatric evaluation due to the many psychological problems exhibited by these women. Miller et al. (2009), building upon the Turner study, examined the largest group of female sex offenders to date: 128 female cases compared with 162 cases of male sex offenders treated at the Hilltop Unit, Gatesville, Texas, where female sex offenders have been treated since 2001. Their crimes were considered to be more violent, such as assault or aggravated assault rather than child molestation, pornography, or prostitution. The study validates previous smaller studies of female sex offenders. Substance abuse was noted as a primary area needing treatment. For some others, extensive treatment may be required for their elevated levels of psychopathology (personality disorder, depression, and anxiety). Another area of research examines the relationships within offending. Wijkman et al. (2010) found in their study of 111 female sex offenders in the Netherlands who committed their offenses between 1995 and 2005 that nearly 77% had abused children and two-thirds of them had co-offended with a male co-offender, nearly 60% exhibited mental problems, and almost one-third had been sexually abused themselves.

It was not uncommon for the 16-year-old boy to find three or four victims in one evening. Although most pedophiles have no intention of violence toward their victims, some serial killers destroy their victims as a way of destroying the evidence against them. One serial killer who sexually assaulted several young boys admitted he killed them to cover up his sexual misconduct. Some serial killers have themselves as children been victimized by pedophiles and later, as adults, act out on children in the same manner in which they were abused. Pedophiles range in aggressiveness from very passive to extremely violent, depending on their fantasy development and orientation. One distinction must be noted in developing typologies of pedophiles. All offenders who have sexual attraction to children come under the *DSM* classification of pedophilia. However, some offenders can be distinguished as *child molesters*. Pedophiles usually seek relationships with children. They prefer their company and are socially, emotionally, and sexually attracted to them. Many do not think of themselves as predators but as people with a different sexual orientation over which they have no choice because they were born that way. Many of them, due to their pervasive denial and chronic fantasies, believe that children can and do give their consent for sexual contact with adults. Pedophiles seldom marry, are not sexually attracted to other adults, and in their own twisted perspective do not harm children because they care about them. When they do marry it is often to gain access to the spouse's children. They invest time into *grooming* their young victims and their families, winning their trust and support. Contact with certain victims can last several years. Pedophiles are often drawn to careers that afford them access to children, becoming teachers, priests, pastors, coaches, and youth group leaders (see Profile 5.6). While rape of children can occur by pedophiles, many are more likely to be molested by them.

Much confusion arises in discussions of pedophilia because society, including many professionals, views all pedophiles under the same lens. Pedophiles vary in degree of emotional and sexual attachment to their victims. On one end of the spectrum are those who enjoy the company of children and have emotional attachments and sexual attraction to children. Harming a child is not their goal (even though harm inevitably is done). They are more comfortable in the presence of children than adults and through distorted thinking believe that children are attracted to them and that sexual contact is mutually desirable. They spend time, energy, and money in grooming their child victims. Indeed, they do not see themselves as victimizers but rather persons who love and want to be with children emotionally and sexually. Child molesters also are drawn to children but differ behaviorally, cognitively, and emotionally from typical pedophiles. Child molesters often marry, have sexual relations with their spouse, and produce offspring. Sometimes they will molest their own children and sometimes they will cross over and molest other children. They do not usually seek out relationships (intimacy) with children nor do they appear as often to be drawn to professions that give them access to children. Instead they are opportunistic, are not in denial about their actions, and understand that they are sexually exploiting children. Indeed, there are predators, if an opportunity arises, who will sexually assault infants as well as children.

Rather than groom victims, child molesters are opportunistic and will molest children both in private and in public places, even when unsuspecting parents are close by. In extreme cases child molesters will abduct, rape, and kill child victims. Each year in the United States about 150 children are abducted, sexually assaulted, and killed by sexual predators. Commonly, these child molesters report hundreds of victims, and some molest both boys and girls. In one case a predator who admitted to over 400 instances of sexually touching children was offended when asked if he was a pedophile. He responded that he was "not one of those sickos" but that he was a child molester. He did not develop long-term relationships with any child and his sexual encounters were brief and opportunistic. He

PROFILE 5.6 Predator Priests: Myths and Realities

In a major study, *"The Causes and Context of Sexual Abuse of Minors by Catholic Priests in the United States, 1950–2010,"* by John Jay College of Criminal Justice (2011), nearly 14,000 cases were reported. The researchers found that homosexual priests were no more likely to abuse minors that heterosexual priests. A more compelling explanation for the abuse centered on the ease of access some priests had to male minors. Indeed, only 5% of abusing priests were sexually involved with prepubescent children. Approximately 70% of priests reported for sexual misconduct with minors also had sexual relations with adults. Abusing priests were also men who commonly had been sexually abused themselves as children, although the study did note that there was no one specific profile that emerged. This may suggest that priest-abusers come from more than one point on the spectrum of pedophilia and child molesters. Plante (2003) found that abuser priests represent only 2% of priests serving in the ministry, they tend to be more *ephebophiles* (men who sexually prefer adolescents in the age range of 15–19 rather than pedophiles who prefer prepubescent children usually in the 9–13 age group), and many of the offenders are heterosexual.

Falkenhain et al. (1999) identified four types of priests who abuse children: *sexually and emotionally underdeveloped*—these are clergy without apparent psychopathology but who exhibit social immaturity and fearfulness in navigating relationships; *undefended characterological*—these are men with noted personality disorders and possess the capacity to grasp that reality; *defended characterological*—these priests also possess personality disorders but refuse to admit or have the capacity to recognize their personal deficits; and last, the *significantly psychiatrically disturbed*—these persons are clearly emotionally disturbed individuals but represent a very small number of Catholic clergy. Songy (2003) noted that clergy who commit sexual abuse of minors possess a variety of deficits including lacking interpersonal skills, sexual immaturity or confusion about sex, confusion pertaining to their own sexual identity, immaturity, passivity, dependence, personality disorders, and sexual deviance. The costs of sexual abuse perpetrated by this group of priests on their victims, communities, and church are enormous and far reaching (see Chapter 10). Today, reports of actively abusing priests are relatively rare, although public perception is that many abuses continue to go unreported or are minimized or ignored. For more information on this subject, the many insightful and articulate works of Andrew M. Greeley, a noted theologian and scholar, are highly recommended.

insisted that I meet his wife to confirm his assertions. He insisted that he was normal in the sense that could engage in sexual intercourse with a woman but that he also liked to sexually touch children whenever the opportunity arose. These distinctions are simply to help in clarifying psychosocial characteristics and are not meant as diagnostic tools.

Today, pedophile organizations flourish on the Internet, including the most prominent of all, the *North American Man/Boy Love Association* (NAMBLA), a group with thousands of members primarily comprised of homosexuals who prefer sex with young boys. They are well organized, with offices in several major cities such as New York City (headquarters). They argue that accounts of child molesters and abductors are aberrations and that pedophiles hold responsible jobs and are law-abiding contributing members of society. Another organization, the Rene Guyon Society, is also nationally organized—their motto is "Sex Before

PROFILE 5.7 North American Man/Boy Love Association (NAMBLA)

The North American Man/Boy Love Association publishes the *NAMBLA Bulletin* as part of their efforts to educate people about sexual relations between men and boys. Other NAMBLA publications include *The Survival Manual: The Man's Guide to Staying Safe in Man/Boy Sexual Relationships* and *Rape and Escape*, a guide to help pedophiles lure children and avoid prosecution. These publications were allegedly found in the possession of Christopher Jaynes, 25, and his homosexual lover, Salvatore Sicari, who, in 1997, lured Jeffrey Curley of East Cambridge, Massachusetts, into a van. When the child resisted the attempted rape, they smothered him to death with a gasoline-soaked rag and raped his corpse. Jaynes was convicted of second-degree murder and kidnapping and will be eligible for parole in 15 years.

Sicari received a life sentence for first-degree murder, with no possibility for parole. Jaynes allegedly had visited the NAMBLA website shortly before the murder. The boy's family has filed a $200-million federal lawsuit against NAMBLA, alleging that the organization incites members to "rape male children" and "serves as a conduit for an underground network of pedophiles in the U.S." The *NAMBLA Bulletin* was mentioned in a diary kept by Christopher Jaynes, who noted that the *Bulletin* "was a turning point in discovery of myself. NAMBLA's Bulletin helped me to become aware of my own sexuality and acceptance of it." The *Bulletin* stated, as quoted in the lawsuit, "Call it love, call it lust, call it whatever you want. We desire sex with boys, and boys, whether society is willing to admit it, desire sex with us." NAMBLA is being defended by the American Civil Liberties Union.

Free speech is a First Amendment right that Americans cherish, but is it possible to go too far, especially in advocating sexual contact with children? Those who belong to NAMBLA do not think so, nor is it a crime or violation to belong to NAMBLA. However, if a direct link is made between the *NAMBLA Bulletin* and the murder of any child, does that affect their freedom of speech? What do you think?

Eight or Else It's Too Late." These groups provide support for members as well as promoting legislation to provide their organizations with greater freedoms (see Profile 5.7).

13. **Pederasty**—adults having anal intercourse with children (anal intercourse in general is called sodomy). This is a common act among serial killers who target children as victims. In some cases various "instruments" have been used to sodomize the child, including baseball bats shaped in the form of a penis.
14. **Pornography and Obscene Material**—using sexually explicit literature and photographs. Even among serial killers pornography tends to be used only by certain types of offenders. However, trying to determine how much and to what degree pornography affects an offender is nearly impossible. Some offenders admit to occasional or frequent use of pornography, sometimes violent material involving bondage and the torture of women and children. The advent of our computer era and the Internet has provided fertile ground for the production and distribution of pornography and obscene material such as "kiddie porn" or pictures sexually exploiting children. Downloading sexually explicit images of children is a felony and as of 2009 in some states even sending sexually explicit animated pictures of children is a crime.

15. **Pyromania**—intentional setting of fires on more than one occasion by a person experiencing tension or affective arousal. These persons often report a fascination with or curiosity about fire-setting. Offenders express feelings of gratification or relief when watching fires in progress and the individual or community response fires often command. Some adult offenders find the sound of emergency response vehicles coming to the scene of the fire to be exhilarating. Occasionally, pyromaniacs report sexual gratification (e.g., masturbation) in setting or watching fire scenes, but the role of sexuality in fire-setting does not appear as the primary reason for such behavior. In children, pyromania is often explained as a *DSM-IV* conduct disorder, which also requires other criteria, such as aggression toward people or animals and deceitfulness or theft. Fire-setting by children may be a response to severe stressors in the family, such as child abuse, drug and alcohol abuse, and family violence. Children sometimes report fires as being magical or that they feel better when they set fires. Children who are chronic fire-setters often report that such behavior provides a sense of control. Some serial murderers as children were fire-setters. However, as they age, serial offenders tend to cease fire-setting behaviors in favor of more controlling, focused acts of violence.
16. **Rape**—having forced sexual intercourse with another person. This appears to be the most common of all sexual behaviors among serial killers in this study. Often the rapes involve beatings and torture. One offender enjoyed taking his victims out into the desert, where he would lash them to the front of his car, tear off their clothing, rape them, and then strangle them to death. Some serial killers are paraphilic rapists who are driven more by specific fantasies of rape and domination than the terror experienced by the victim. For example, the offender may desire the victim to wear specific clothing or repeat certain words while being attacked.

DYNAMICS OF RAPE AND SEXUAL ASSAULT

Dussich (2001) cites three general explanations for rape: (1) *psychopathology of rapists* that places responsibility at the feet of mentally disturbed individuals but that their disorders are ultimately the cause of their behavior; (2) *feminist theory,* where rape is a product of our culture that teaches men to be aggressive and dominant, and women passive and submissive—in Japan, for example, rape is often viewed by young men as normal and socially acceptable and women are viewed as sexual objects; (3) *victim precipitation,* where victims are considered, to a degree, culpable for the sexual assault. In American society, victim blaming has long been utilized as a defense in alleged rapes and sexual assaults. Rozee (1993) noted in a study of 35 non-industrialized societies that some forms of rape are socially acceptable, including *marital rape* or undesired sexual intercourse; *exchange rape,* where sex is used to demonstrate solidarity or as a bargaining tool; *punitive rape,* which involves genitals used for disciplinary or punitive measures; *theft rape,* or the abduction of women for the sole purpose of use as a sexual or reproductive object; *ceremonial rape*, which includes defloration rituals, virginity tests, or where sexual intercourse is a required part of a ceremony; and *status rape*, which occurs when rank differences exist between persons and one is forced to submit. These are socially acceptable and encouraged behaviors in the societies in which they occur and are not considered rape in those societies.

Criminal law at one time considered sex crimes to be either rape (forced heterosexual penetration) or sodomy. Today, sex crimes have expanded to include an array of offenses that range from nonviolent touching of a person to forced sexual intercourse. The Uniform Crime Report provides several definitions for rape. *Forcible rape* is "the carnal knowledge of a female, forcibly and against her will" that includes assaults, threat of rape, and attempted forcible rape (FBI, 2000, p. 24). Many agencies adopt their own definitions, some more thorough than others, in defining rape, while others separate attempted and forcible rapes. *Statutory rape* involves the carnal knowledge of a female under statutory age, with or without her consent. Statutory age will vary state to state, with most states using either 16 or 18 as their limit. *Rape by fraud* is using fraudulent conditions to have consenting sexual relations. For example, in some states a psychiatrist who has consensual sexual relations with a patient could later be charged with rape (if the patient were to report the affair) for using his or her license to seduce the patient, even though the act was consensual. Such is the case with other licensed professionals including psychologists, medical doctors, clergy, and lawyers. Other forms of rape by fraud include direct deception whereby the professional sexually exploits the patient without her knowledge. Cases involving medical doctors, hypnotherapists, and psychiatrists have been documented in the United States. Rape and attempted rape account for approximately 4% of the six million criminal victimizations that occur each year (NCVS, 2003). Tjaden and Thoennes (2000) in a 16,000-interview study of men and women found that 18% of female respondents and 3% of male respondents reported having been raped at least once. The researchers estimated from the study that 1 in 6 women and 1 in 33 men will become a rape victim at some point in their lives. Almost 98% of all rape/sexual assaults involve a lone victim, and 92% of cases involve a lone perpetrator (NCVS, 2003). The good news is that according to the UCR (2010) forcible rape and attempted rape have decreased significantly over the past 20 years. Forcible rape in 1990 was 80.5 per 100,000 females in the United States. In 2000 the rate had dropped to 62.7 and continued to drop to 52.3 per 100,000 females by the end of 2009. Total forcible and attempted rapes decreased approximately 21% between 1990 and 2009 (Uniform Crime Report, 2010).

RAPISTS TYPOLOGIES

As a whole, rapists are prone to have histories of other criminal activities including burglary and petty theft. In a 2000 DNA study of Virginia men convicted of rape, about 40% began their criminal careers involved with property crimes of burglary and petty theft. This finding is consistent with other U.S. research as well as a British study that reported about 75% of convicted rapists having histories of burglary. These are considered to be excellent *gateway* or *predictor crimes* that are highly correlated with sexual assault and rape (Freeman, 2007). In contrast to child molesters, rapists demonstrate a much higher level of psychopathy. Porter et al. (2000) found that psychopathy differs in various sex offender groups and that rapists and mixed rapists/molesters all scored higher on the PCL-R than sex offenders who had targeted children exclusively. Of particular note was their finding that offenders who had targeted both children and adults ranged between 2 and 10 times as likely as other offenders to be psychopaths. Considering the paraphilic interests of some rapists, it is not surprising that the most common crime associated with fetishes is burglary. For those caught up in sexual fantasies, collecting souvenirs from victim's homes can be either the primary or secondary motivation for the burglary. In a Georgia case a burglar was caught stealing underwear from victims' homes. In searching his apartment over 400 pairs of women's underwear were found hidden in his bedroom. Sometimes these types of intruders become rapists. However, compared to other offenders with violent histories, convicted rapists have shorter criminal histories, lower rates of violence, and lower recidivism rates (Greenfeld, 1997). What becomes confusing is generalizing rapists as a group when each type of rapist has some distinctive characteristics. Nicholas Groth, a prison psychologist, is one of the pioneers in classifying rapists. Roy Hazelwood and Ann Burgess, building on Groth's work, created a four-type classification that has been used extensively by researchers. They organize their typologies based on issues of power and anger (see Figure 5.1).

Of specific interest in the Groth classifications is the fact that the least violent rapist (power reassurance) engages extensively in paraphilic behavior. The same is true of the least common and most violent stranger rapist (anger excitation), that they also engage in paraphilic behaviors. What is also notable is that while the reassurance rapist is attempting to have intimate, consensual, sexual relationships without harming the victim, the excitation rapist is aroused by the fear and suffering of his victim and will frequently kill his victim in order to sense her fear and feel her dying. The power assertive typology applies to men who wish to

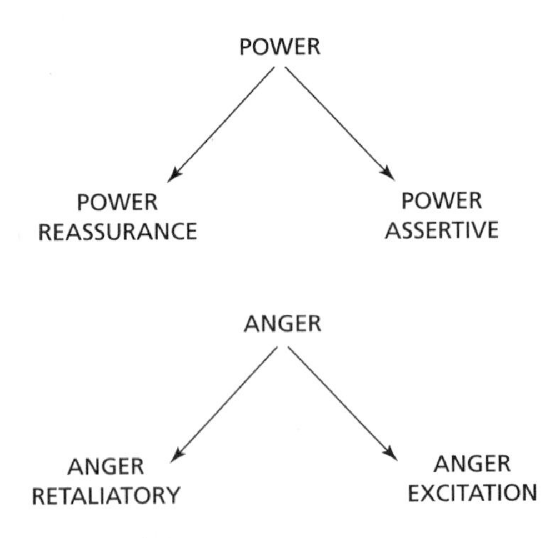

FIGURE 5.1 Groth Typologies of Stranger Serial Rapists
SOURCE: © Cengage Learning, 2013.

exert their prerogative to rape women when they so desire. They use moderate to excessive force and engage in sexual degradation of the victim. The anger retaliatory rapist is paying back women for real or imaginary wrongs they have committed against him. They will use excessive, brutal force and are even more likely to sexually degrade their victims.

While not all rapists fit conveniently into a specific category, these typologies have been utilized by law enforcement, criminologists, and psychologists in studying offenders. But typologies are subject to scrutiny and revision as we learn more about the etiology of rapists and their victims. A power/anger framework for categorizing rapists has been very helpful in understanding rapists from an *emotional* perspective. Another approach is examining rapists by their *relationship* to their victims. Four types of relational rapes are (1) *marital,* where the rapist is the spouse of the victim; (2) *courtship,* where an offender in pursuit of a relationship with someone he knows forces the victim into a sexual relationship; (3) *confidence or blitz* rapes, where offenders win the trust of a victim in order to carry out a sexual assault; and (4) *stranger* rape, which involves an attack on a victim who is a complete stranger to the rapist. By examining relationships (see "Relational Paraphilic Attachment") rapists can be better understood in their interactions with victims. Rather than viewing the victim as merely part of the crime scene, researchers can examine the dynamics of the relationships between victims and offenders. Juries have been prone to insert their personal biases regarding issues of victim facilitation, precipitation, and culpability when determining issues of guilt in rape cases. Examining victim-offender relationships in cases of rape helps the understanding of issues of power and control sought by the offender and victim responses in those relationships (see Profile 5.8). The Massachusetts Treatment Center (MTC) also identified four major categories of rapists:

- *Displaced aggression rapists* (a.k.a. anger-retaliatory or displaced anger) are usually violent and aggressive in their assaults, with little or no display of sexual feeling. Rape is a vehicle to injure, humiliate, and degrade females and a way to vent extreme anger. The victim is usually a complete stranger. She is brutalized by biting, slashing, and tearing. As the assault itself is not sexually gratifying for the offender, he often demands oral sex or masturbation in order to achieve an erection. Resistance to the assault invites even more violence. Often married, they attack women who display independence and assertiveness. The offenders tend to have stable, blue-collar jobs such as truck drivers, carpenters, or construction workers. The attack is often precipitated by an incident involving women, but the victim usually has no connection to the incident. Such offenders usually defend the attack as being a result of "uncontrollable impulses." Their childhoods are replete with neglect, unstable and chaotic homes, and single-parent families. Many were adopted or raised in foster homes.
- *Compensatory rapists* are sexually stimulated by their environment (a.k.a. power-reassurance, ego dystonic, or true rapist). These are passive, introverted, non-assertive men who have no desire to use violence against the victim but to

PROFILE 5.8 John Jamelske, Serial Abductor and Rapist

He viewed himself as unorthodox and a Casanova who had an eye for beautiful women. Prior to the abductions Jamelske had a 16-year-old girl move into his home with whom he had a sexual relationship. When he was found out he denied the affair and the girl moved out. In 1988, John Jamelske decided to act out his narcissistic, sexual fantasies. He would later claim that his wife, due to medical problems, could no longer have sex with him. He constructed an underground, concrete bunker where he would keep sex slaves to provide him with "monogamous, disease-free" sex.

For nearly 16 years he hunted for young women, married or single, to abduct and manacle in his secret dungeon, where they spent months or years locked away. He promised them, he says, financial compensation when they were released, but until then they had to remain in the bunker and be subjected to rape and other sexual abuse on a near daily basis. The room was equipped with a makeshift bed, a bucket for a toilet, and a garden hose for showering. Five women became his victims as he took them blindfolded to his home at night or when his wife was away. His wife remained unaware of his bunker and victims until her death in 1999. The women, once they had fulfilled his fantasies, were released as they had been abducted. It was not until his last 16-year-old victim got access to a telephone and called for help that Jamelske was stopped.

After his arrest he claimed that he had done nothing seriously wrong and that he expected no more than maybe 30 hours of community service for the unlawful imprisonments. He claimed that the women wanted to be there because he was paying them for the sex and that he never used force. He claimed that the women were not victims but his "buddies" who became close to him. His victims, however, had horrific stories of sexual assault and threats of death if they tried to escape. In 2003 he received 18 years to life for his crimes.

From a relational typology, Jamelske best fits the courtship classification of rapist. In his mind he was having relationships with females that he wanted to be consensual, yet he used coercion to have sex with his victims. But Jamelske also had developed paraphilic fantasies about keeping young women as sex slaves and acted on those fantasies. What other possible rapist typologies fit John Jamelske?

demonstrate prowess and sexual adequacy. They tend to be lonely, submissive, and reserved men viewed by others as nice people. Once considered to be men of little education and career success, evidence now suggests that they can be very well educated and successful in a career (see Profile 5.9). The rapists' fantasy world becomes a retreat for them. They are men who frequent porn shops and live in a world of fantasy that involves sexual intimacy and feelings that they are desired by women. This rapist does not cope with rejection well and seeks out women he senses would never want to be with him. His fantasies change everything. In his mind the sexual assault is more of a "date" than it is rape. He would enjoy seeing his victim again for an encore of intimacy. In truth, the offender is sexually naive and has little experience with normal sexual relations. He is a stalker and plans out his attack. If the victim can resist enough the offender will desist and flee, his fantasies unfulfilled.

- *Sexually aggressive rapist* (a.k.a. sadistic rapist) holds fundamental beliefs that what women really want is to be dominated, controlled, sexually assaulted,

PROFILE 5.9 Melvin Carter, the College Terrace Rapist (Compensatory Rapist)

In the 1970s a series of rapes brought fear to San Jose, California. A predator was breaking into homes of single women late at night and, at knifepoint, raping them. Victims remembered how he seemed concerned for their well-being and how he apologized for any disruption. His name was Melvin Carter and he was to become one of the most prolific serial rapists ever known to Californians. Born in Colorado, his father abandoned the family and he was raised by a very domineering mother. He was kept isolated from his peers and not allowed to visit other homes or have people to his home. He had his one and only birthday party when he was 12, but no one showed up. The painful truth for Melvin was that he was an intellectually gifted child who had limited social and emotional skills. At 16, his mother took him to his high school senior prom and made him dance with a girl, then promptly took him home. He was accepted into the School of Mines, a prestigious school of engineering, where he excelled. His sexual fantasies fueled his desire for female contact, and Melvin began engaging in voyeurism and trolling in public parks. He stalked women who were alone and at an opportune moment would quickly come up to them from behind and touch their breasts. As his fantasies developed so did his desire for further female contact. He purchased a German Shepard dog and, using ether on a handkerchief, practiced rendering the dog unconscious. He surmised that women were not much heavier. Returning to the parks, Melvin attacked several women over the next few months. Once they were unconscious, he would fondle and grope them and run away. He eluded police traps but was caught for voyeurism. His overnight in jail cost him his first-place finish in his college standings because he missed a final exam.

After graduation, Melvin, wanting to distance himself from Colorado, eventually moved to California, where he secured a job as a computer engineer in the Bay Area. His stalking and voyeuristic urges found him following women to their homes. When he was sure they were living alone, Melvin used burglar tools to let himself in while the victim was at work. After spending time in the residence so that he felt comfortable and knew the layout so he could walk around in the dark, Melvin left, leaving a window unlocked. Later that night, while the victim was asleep, Melvin returned to have his "date." Returning home Melvin remembered his sexual encounters as happy and fulfilling. He noted that her cries were cries of joy, as were her tears. Police sometimes found blood on the bed sheets of the victim and it was always Melvin's. Later they would discover that Melvin's M.O. was to use a knife to force compliance. However, in his fantasies of the encounters there was never a weapon, only two consenting adults finding intimacy together. He would never harm anyone (in his distorted thinking) and as a result he always had the blade of the knife against his thumb to ensure that he did not accidentally cut his date.

On one occasion after stalking his latest victim, Melvin returned to visit his "date" that night. She had come home early and rearranged the furniture and placed a large radio in front of the window by which he would enter. Melvin, in order to gain access, pulled the radio onto the access fire escape and entered the apartment. While walking down the corridor to have his date he suddenly realized that someone might see the radio and steal it. He went outside, retrieved the radio, and took it to his car for safekeeping. He then returned, had his "date," and headed home. As he reflected on the enjoyable evening he suddenly remembered the radio and instantly felt terrible because she would think him to be a thief. He immediately returned to her apartment, only to find that the police were there. Unable to return the radio, Melvin stated that he could not sleep for three nights knowing that he had her radio. He finally donated it to the Salvation Army. Melvin was eventually arrested, went to prison for several years, and now lives with a relative near San Francisco.

and raped. His sexual arousal stems from mixing violence and pain in the process of raping a woman. He revels in his sadism and may ultimately kill his victim in order to achieve the greatest possible sexual gratification. They are often married men with histories of many infidelities, divorces, and/or separations. Products of childhood neglect and abuse, these men have extensive histories of childhood conduct disorder, do not handle stress and frustration well, and have committed many misdemeanors and crimes as adolescents.

- *Impulsive rapist* (a.k.a. exploitative rapist) rapes spontaneously when an opportunity presents itself, such as when an offender is committing another crime where he has access to victims: bank robberies, burglaries. The offender has a long history of nonsexual crimes, and rape is a secondary crime. Thus violence is limited in the absence of sexual arousal.

While the MTC original four typologies of rapists are utilized for differentiating rapists, some refinements have been necessary to accommodate emerging typologies (Knight, 2010). Researchers added four motivations for rape—*opportunistic, pervasively angry, sexual,* and *vindictive*—to develop the MTC:R3. Each motivation appears to be a salient factor in effectively explaining why men rape. This classification of rapists is now the most widely used by researchers today. Using MTC:R3 criteria, researchers subtyped about 250 rapists currently or previously incarcerated at the treatment center and measured the concurrent and predictive ability of the new system. This typology includes nine subtypes of rapists that are classified according to dimensions that are important in differentiating rapists such as generalized, misogynistic, or eroticized anger, impulsivity, antisocial personality, degree of preoccupation with gratification of sexual needs, and social competence. The nine subtypes in this system include (1) opportunistic offender with low social competence, (2) opportunistic offender with high social competence, (3) pervasively angry offender, (4) overt sadistic offender, (5) muted sadistic offender, (6) sexualized, nonsadistic offender with high social competence, (7) sexualized, nonsadistic offender with low social competence, (8) vindictive offender with low social competence, and (9) vindictive offender with moderate social competence.

Such refinements underscore a continuing effort on the part of researchers to better understand rapists and their victims. A pervasive theme among rapists is the underlying anger/rage that is differentially manifested. For example, while compensatory rapists appear to be trying to establish relationships with their victims there is a pervasive, underlying frustrated and aggressive attitude held by these offenders. This attitude of aggressiveness becomes clearer when offenders are examined from a power/anger framework. Indeed, rapists harbor an intense need for control in relationships, and yet offenders exhibit severe dysfunction in their abilities to maintain healthy interactions with females. The opportunistic motivation includes impulsive, predatory offenders not driven by sexual fantasy or explicit anger but rather by opportunities for sexual assaults. The fact that relationships become eroticized by offenders is not surprising, but the depth of sexualized aggression to which some rapists operate in order to achieve that quest for power and control can be devastating. Sadistic rapists, for example, demonstrate incredibly violent acts of sexual aggression that go far beyond an exhibition of control by including acts of sexual mutilation and degradation. The power of physical and psychological force is sexualized into ritualized acts that have been constructed through violent fantasies. The violent acts themselves are deliberate, calculated, and sexualized, including bondage, torture, mutilation, and other paraphilic behaviors. Neuwirth and Eher (2003) in their study of anal and vaginal rapists found that those who raped anally were more aggressive and sexualized in their behavior than rapists who raped vaginally.

Classifying rapists and child predators exposes a common problem in the quest for improved descriptions of offenders: The closer we scrutinize the offenders, the more prone researchers are to create more typologies and subcategories in order to ensure that some offenders are not excluded in the profiles. As illustrated by the MTC, creation of so many subcategories that may well lead to further subcategorization ultimately creates confusion in profiling offenders. In turn, this can affect how we conduct criminal investigations and present expert testimony in court. Fisher and Mair (1998) recognize the MTC work on child molesters and rapists as being sophisticated but are concerned also that the research is based on a small and possibly unrepresentative sample. Despite these concerns, the MTC classification systems for child molesters and rapists are the most widely accepted among current researchers. There is much more to be done in this area as we delve ever more deeply into the minds and behaviors of sex offenders.

17. **Sadism and Masochism**—inflicting mental/physical pain on others (sadism) or oneself (masochism). Although masochism is not particularly common among serial killers, one offender over the years had inserted dozens of needles into his genital area, occasionally burned himself, and eagerly anticipated the experience of his own execution. Influenced by the 18th-century Marquis de Sade, the term *sadism* was first termed by Krafft-Ebing, one of the first academicians to examine sexual deviance. *Masochism* was named after Leopold von Sacher-Masoch, who was born in Lemberg, Germany. Freud is believed to have combined the two terms into one: *sadomasochism* (Drzazga, 1960). Sadism is considered a sexual disorder as it involves persons aroused by inflicting physical or psychological pain or suffering on another person. This is a complex paraphilia that is manifested in a variety of sexually violent offenders. Grubin (1994) defines sadism as

> the experience of sexual pleasure sensations (including orgasm) produced by acts of cruelty, bodily punishment inflicted on one's person or when witnessed in others, be they animals or human beings. It may also consist of an innate desire to humiliate, hurt, wound or even destroy others in order thereby to create sexual pleasure in one's self. (p. 5)

However, a key issue involving sadomasochism is consent. A cottage industry of persons who engage in S/M (sadomasochism) do so consensually and believe in their right to do so. Green (2001) observed salient features in consensual sadomasochistic encounters that include dominance and submission, role-playing, consensuality, sexual context, and mutual definition of the activities. In the context of sex crimes, S/M involves offenders and victims where consent is not given unless under duress. Offenders with sadistic tendencies developed such fantasies in childhood and act them out on animals or people when opportunities arise. Some children, when subjected to punishments such as spanking or physical abuse, may inadvertently eroticize their suffering in order to internalize the discipline of the parent. As an adult, the participant seeks sadomasochistic encounters for sexual gratification as well as to internalize his or her parent and punish the adult for bad behavior (Donnelly and Fraser, 1998). Cruelty toward a child, neglect, and other forms of child abuse can facilitate paraphilic development such as sadomasochism as well as other paraphilia (Drzazga, 1960). Karpman (1954) in his examination of sadomasochism suggested that sadism and masochism are bipolar manifestations of the same paraphilia.

According to the *DSM-IV*, sadism, as a disorder, must occur over a period of at least six months involving recurrent, intense sexually arousing fantasies. These sexual urges or behaviors involve real acts with a nonconsenting person in which the psychological or physical suffering (including humiliation) of the victim is sexually arousing to the offender. Such fantasies may also cause severe distress or interpersonal difficulty. Criminal sadists can find sexual gratification in various acts of violence including cutting, burning, stabbing, mutilation, strangulation, beating, rape, and murder. Masochism as a disorder must also occur for at least six months, include intense sexual fantasies and behaviors involving real acts of being humiliated, beaten, bound, or otherwise made to suffer. These fantasies, sexual urges, or behaviors cause clinically significant distress or impairment in social or occupational functioning (American Psychiatric Association, 2000). Such activities may include whippings, beatings, electrical shocks, piercing, and cutting.

Park Dietz, a renown forensic psychiatrist, describes the psychology of sadadism as one essential impulse: *to have complete mastery over another person,* to make him/her a helpless object of our will, to become the absolute ruler over her, to become her God, to do with her as one pleases. To humiliate her, to enslave her, *are means to this end,* and the most important radical aim is to make her *suffer* since *there is no greater power over another person than that of inflicting pain on her* to force her to undergo suffering without her being able to defend herself. The pleasure in the complete domination over another person is the very essence of the sadistic drive (italics in original). (Dietz et al., 1990, p. 165)

18. **Scatologia**—sexual gratification through the making of obscene phone calls. While callers seem to vary in their levels of sexual references, tone of voice, and desire to shock or frighten, the offender is often conditioning himself through masturbation to fantasies of control over his victims. Offenders calling the same victims repeatedly are engaging in stalking behavior, which has, in a few cases, led to violent confrontations (see Profile 5.10).
19. **Scopophilia (Voyeurism)**—receiving sexual gratification by peeping through windows and so forth to watch people. Several offenders in this study had at one time or another peeped through windows. One offender explained how he first began as a voyeur, then graduated to raping women,

PROFILE 5.10 The Night Caller

Married with children, Craig liked to self-stimulate by calling women, randomly, late at night as he worked his way through the telephone directory. There was a voice Craig looked for that made him press harder to the receiver. When Craig found that fantasy voice he began his series of questions, escalating in sexual content and threats. He loved to hear their responses of surprise, anger, and fear. Craig liked to masturbate as he talked softly and slowly to his victims. His compulsion to call was so great that he recorded every call for future sexual gratification. Craig made sure not to stay on the line too long and seldom called the same victim twice. Eventually technology caught up with him and he was identified as the obscene caller. He had over a hundred tapes when the police arrested him.

Does apprehension stop the paraphilic caller? Why would a married man with children want to make obscene phone calls? What other paraphilic interests or behaviors might Craig be involved with? Craig never sees his victims but instead has a fantasy about their voices. His sexual gratification is dependent on the response of the victim. Recipients of obscene phone calls should always report them to law enforcement. Very likely the offender has several other victims, and the more who report, the greater the probability of his apprehension.

and finally practiced necrophilia. The connection between voyeurism and homicide is not automatic. Most "Peeping Toms" never progress past this deviant stage, whereas some may later attempt rape or other violent sexual behaviors (see Profile 5.11).

One subcategory of voyeurism is *mixoscopia* or *troilism,* or the sexual arousal from seeing oneself in sexual scenes. This includes taking photographs of nude victims, which sometimes include the offender. A few sexual predators whose crimes have escalated to serial murder have utilized equipment such as ceiling mirrors, video cameras, and cameras. Troilism can also involve sexual gratification by sharing a sexual partner with another person, allowing the troilist to become the observer. Sometimes serial killers who work in groups have engaged in troilistic behaviors. One offender took snapshots of his nude victims, then enlarged the photographs and mounted them on his bedroom walls. Another offender took photographs of victims performing oral sex on his partner. Still other offenders used tape recorders to reproduce the screams and terror of dying victims as they were sexually mutilated. Offenders (both male and female) have admitted to watching while another offender raped or sodomized a victim. One female offender voluntarily watched while her male counterpart raped a child.

20. **Somnophilia:** Sexual arousal while watching a person sleep. Certain types of burglars who commit "hot" burglaries are aroused by the sensation of watching a sleeping victim. Such activities are often a precursor to sexual assault and rape (see Profile 5.11).

Paraphilia are common to those who commit sex crimes. Bogaerts et al. (2008), in examining persons who commit sex crimes, note that they have

PROFILE 5.11 The Stroker

In a California city, a man was seen peeping through windows and watching sorority students from a distance. This he did for hours on a weekly basis. He frequently called the sorority houses near the university campus and made obscene remarks while masturbating. The offender had been making calls for over 12 years without an arrest. The sororities dubbed him "The Stroker" and because they felt safe in their sorority house, some engaged him in phone conversations, laughed at him, and called him names. They failed to realize that was exactly what he wanted. For the predator there were so many pretty female voices and so many to fantasize about. The Stroker was known to engage in voyeurism around the sorority houses and liked to call girls after they have just arrived at the house to tell them that he was close by, what they were wearing, and that he was watching them. Angered by one girl's response, the Stroker called to announce that he was going to "get them soon," but physical contact was never made. After 12 years of phone calls, they finally stopped. Is this offender "dangerous" in regards to physically harming anyone? What other paraphilia might he be engaging in along with voyeurism and scatologia? Why does he choose sorority houses? Some of the girls unwittingly encouraged his fantasies and behavior by laughing at him or engaging him in conversation. The very fact that they talked to him was exactly what fueled his fantasies. In this case the best course of action was to report the calls to the police, keep a phone log, and/or screen all calls before answering. Harassment calls are punishable in all states.

between one and several paraphilia at any given time depending on their sexual fantasies and explorations. However, many acts associated with paraphilia are not illegal, nor do they lead to criminal behavior. It is important to note also that sex offenders, even those with paraphilia, commit a wide range of crimes, many of which are not sex related. However, some of those crimes may well mask a sexual motive, for example, an offender is convicted of burglary but had entered a residence with the expectation or fantasy of also committing a rape (see Profile 5.12). But as Smallbone and Wortley (2004) observed in their study, although some sex offenders are highly specialized in the types of sex crimes they commit, many are diverse in their criminal activities that include both sexual and nonsexual crimes. In fact, they suggest that paraphilia and sexual offending may be completely independent constructs, meaning that one does not affect the other. Rather than paraphilia being caused by sexual pathology, they may be better understood as one of many forms of general social deviance (p. 185). For the male serial killer, the paraphilia engaged in usually has escalated from softer forms to those that are considered not only criminal but violent as well. They range from unusual to incredibly bizarre and disgusting. As paraphilia develop, men affected by them often engage in several over a period of time. Most men who engage in paraphilia often exhibit three or four different forms, some of them simultaneously. For those with violent tendencies, *soft* paraphilia can quickly lead to experimentation with hardcore paraphilia that often involves the harming of others in sexual ways. For example, some paraphilic offenders prefer to stalk and sexually assault their victims in stores and other public places without getting caught. The thrill of

PROFILE 5.12 The Burglar and His Sexual Fantasies

Steve is a 17-year-old white male, physically attractive, with a high IQ, who maintains a 4.0 GPA in his senior year in high school. He is considered by his friends to be considerate, polite, and self-confident. His home life, however, reveals a torturous relationship with his stepfather, a successful physician, who has verbally rejected him since he married Steve's mother over nine years earlier. His mother, who clearly loved Steve, was not emotionally strong enough to protect Steve from the emotional abuse any more than protect herself from the beatings. On several occasions Steve watched his stepfather physically assault his mother, pin her down on the floor, and punch her repeatedly. Steve was 14 before he was able to rescue his mother from a particularly vicious beating. That was the last beating, but the verbal abuse continued. His sister, 10 years his junior, was adored by the father because she was his biological daughter. The rejection by the stepfather and earlier separation of his natural father affected Steve's self-perception. By the time Steve was 17 he was burglarizing homes of the affluent. By age 18, and now the mastermind behind the crimes, he specifically entered homes where people were present and asleep. He reported how powerful and in control he felt when standing in a bedroom of his victims while they slept. Eventually Steve was caught and sentenced to prison for his crimes. He will be released in less than three years. Does the reader note any potential for the development of paraphilic fantasies and behavior? Do you perceive any psychopathic characteristics present in Steve's psychological makeup? What type of prognosis would you consider for Steve? Is Steve a potentially violent person? Why? What other information would you want to make a better prognosis? Should Steve's sentence be mitigated as a result of his childhood trauma?

hunting an unsuspecting victim contributes to sexually arousing the offender (see Profile 5.13).

The Internet is replete with examples of paraphilia, many of which have little documentation or import. Of most concern is that readers view the sexual assaults as a process of sexual fantasy development culminating in lust murder. The following types of violent paraphilia, referred to as *attack paraphilia* (sexual violence involving others, including children), sharply contrast with *preparatory paraphilia,* or paraphilia that have been found as part of the lust killer's sexual fantasies and activities. This does not mean that having a preparatory paraphilia makes one a serial killer. The preparatory paraphilia listed here are those believed to be common to this group of serial killers. The process of sexual fantasy development may include stealing items from victims. Burglary, although generally considered to be a property crime, also is sometimes a property crime for sexual purposes. Stealing underwear, toiletries, hair clippings, photographs, and other personal items provides the offender with souvenirs for him to fantasize over. One offender noted how he would climax each time he entered a victim's home through a window. The thought of being alone with people sleeping in the house had become deeply eroticized. Another offender likes to break into homes and watch victims sleep. He eventually will touch the victim and will only leave when she begins to scream. He "began" his sexual acting out as a voyeur. This *paraphilic process* was also examined by Purcell and Arrigo (2001),

PROFILE 5.13 Preying in Public

In 2003 a young married woman was shopping in a popular grocery store. She was in need of a card for her husband and walked over to the aisle with birthday cards. As she pondered the cards a man watched her carefully from another aisle. He had been watching her since her arrival. The unsuspecting victim leaned down to pick out a card when she happened to look to her right and noticed the man now standing several feet away in the middle of the card aisle. She was unaware that now the aisle was clear of people except for the man. She went back to reading the card, trying to find the perfect one. As she read suddenly she felt someone walk behind her with a feeling that they may have slightly brushed against her as they quickly went by. The victim continued to look for a card, made her selection, and headed for the checkout line. Not until she reached back for her purse did she realize that her purse and sweater were covered in semen. The victim had been stalked and sexually assaulted without her knowledge. All of this was caught on store security tape, but the images were of such poor quality as to render them useless in identifying the perpetrator. What types of paraphilia were involved in this incident? Unlike many sex offenders who act out in privacy, this offender enjoys the excitement of committing a sexual assault in public without being apprehended. Is this offender likely to act out again? How dangerous is the offender's behavior? What can women do to protect themselves from such predators? Remember that sexual assaults can occur against women and children in seemingly safe, public places such as stores and parks. In this case the predator knew that the woman would be distracted as she searched for the right card and timed his sexual assault with her being alone in the card aisle.

who note that the process consists of mutually interactive elements: paraphilic stimuli and fantasy; orgasmic conditioning process; and facilitators (drugs, alcohol, and pornography). The probability of the offender harming a victim is extremely high given the progressive nature of his sexual fantasies.

PARAPHILIA CLASSIFICATIONS

Preparatory Paraphilia

- **Agonophilia**—person is aroused by partner pretending to struggle
- **Altocalciphilia**—high-heel shoe fetish
- **Autonecrophilia**—imaging oneself as a corpse or becoming sexually aroused by simulated corpses
- **Erotomania**—person develops an unreasonable love of a stranger or person not interested in them
- **Exhibitionism**—exposing body to inappropriate and non-consenting people for arousal
- **Frottage**—rubbing body against partner or object for arousal
- **Gerontophilia**—attraction to a partner whose age is that of a different generation

- **Hebephilia**—persons aroused by teens
- **Hyphephilia**—arousal from touching skin, hair, leather, fur, or fabric
- **Kleptolagnia**—arousal from stealing
- **Mastofact**—breast fetish
- **Mixoscopia**—orgasm dependent on watching others having sex
- **Retifism**—shoe fetish
- **Scatologia**—arousal by making phone calls, using vulgar language, or trying to elicit a reaction from the other party
- **Scopophilia (Voyeurism)**—arousal by watching others without their consent
- **Somnophilia**—fondling strangers in their sleep

Attack Paraphilia

- **Amokoscisia**—arousal or sexual frenzy with desire to slash or mutilate women
- **Anophelorastia**—arousal from defiling or ravaging a partner
- **Anthropophagolagnia**—rape with cannibalism
- **Biastophilia**—those preferring to violently rape their victims; also called raptophilia
- **Dippoldism**—sexual arousal from abusing children
- **Necrophilia**—sex acts with corpses
- **Pedophilia**—sexual involvement with minors usually via manipulation and grooming
- **Pyromania**—arousal from deliberate and purposeful fire-setting
- **Sadism**—empowerment and arousal derived from injuring others; often associated with other attack paraphilia

RELATIONAL PARAPHILIC ATTACHMENT (RPA)

Much can be said of the progressive nature of sex crimes for some sex offenders, whereas we do not find such progression in others. To understand this variation we must examine the framework of paraphilic relationships that develop between perpetrators of sex crimes and their victims. Healey (2006) observed that a child's psychosexual foundations are critical for healthy maturation and growth. Early childhood trauma such as sexual abuse has been linked to the development of paraphilic behaviors (Burgess et al., 1986; Hickey, 2006a; Purcell and Arrigo, 2001). Exposure to incestuous behavior, whether as a victim or as a witness, affects the psychosexual development of individuals (Beauregard, Lussier, and Proulx, 2004). In a study of 95 sexually violent predators, Stinson, Becker, and Sales (2008) found that antisocial behaviors were correlated with both paraphilia and substance abuse. Seto (2008) also noted that emotional dysregulation in children can affect their peer relationships and set the stage for them as men to seek out children to cope with their emotional stressors. Grant (2005) also found that severe depression in adult males is highly correlated to paraphilic behaviors and impulse control. Burgess et al. (1986) noted in their Motivational Model that three salient factors are correlated to those who become sexual predators: traumatic events, developmental failure, and interpersonal breakdown. Howitt (2004) concluded that many researchers have noted significant correlations between deviant sexual fantasies and incidents of childhood abuse. In turn these emotionally damaged males develop both normal sexual fantasies as well as sadomasochistic fantasies (Smith et al., 2005). Indeed, young men who engage in compulsive paraphilic behaviors will also engage in deviant sexual fantasies (Hazelwood and Warren, 2004; Schlesinger, 2004).

Money (1984) and Freund and Watson (1990) refer to *courtship disorders* that sex offenders develop with their victims. These disorders, such as voyeurism, frotteurism, exhibitionism, and somnophilia, are attempts to develop fantasized relationships with other persons. Cusator (2009) concurs that paraphilia are behaviors intended to fulfill fantasies of intimate connections by persons bereft of self-esteem and social acceptance. Indeed, offenders develop sexually deviant relationships with their victims in a similar fashion to healthy persons who meet and develop relationships. For example, a normal person sees another person to whom he is attracted. The voyeur also sees and fantasizes about the person to whom he is attracted. The normal person is seen by the person to whom he is attracted. The exhibitionist also wants to be seen, and exposes himself to his victims. The normal person, in developing a healthy relationship, touches the person to whom he is attracted. The frotteur, in like manner, also reaches out and touches another person, but without his or her consent. In a parallel sexually deviant fantasy world, men with paraphilia develop sexual relationships with their victims who have been fantasized about and then victimized. Much like a normal person who seeks intimacy, the paraphilic seeks connection with others. These nonconsensual sexual relationships or *relational paraphilic attachments* (RPA) are borne in fantasy and explored in sexually deviant behaviors (see Profile 5.14). This is in stark contrast to consensual sexual relationships that are borne of healthy, normal sexual fantasies and are socially acceptable. These attachments are developed through fantasy and acted out in paraphilic behaviors.

The fact that men with criminal paraphilia usually have more than one form of sexually deviant behavior can be a bit confusing as to which one(s) is their preference. Most likely a specific paraphilia dominates the sexual fantasies and criminal activities of the offender. Terry (2007) refers to noncontact and minimal-contact paraphilia compared to high-contact paraphilia. These may also be framed as *primary* and *secondary paraphilia*. For example, pedophilia may be viewed as the dominant or secondary paraphilic behavior of an offender. However, the pedophile may have also engaged in a variety of primary sexually deviant behaviors such as voyeurism, scatologia, or exhibitionism in his development of intimate relationships. These are paraphilia of exploration into the development of deviant sexual relationships. While the need to control is always present in primary paraphilia, it is not manifested in violence.

The offender, as a fully invested pedophile, has used these courtship disorders or primary paraphilia to develop sexual relationships with the victims that are fantasized as being consensual. In brief, the offender has used paraphilic behaviors to create relational attachments to his victims (see Chart 5.3). Note in the list of preparatory paraphilia that most of these behaviors do not place the victim in danger of physical harm, at least in the fantasy world of the paraphile. The offender is not attempting to harm his victims but rather develop intimacy for which he is woefully inept.

As these constellations of paraphilic behaviors coalesce into a secondary paraphilia there is usually physical harm to the victims (see Profile 5.15). This may well be a result of some offenders, such as certain types of rapists, developing or exhibiting sadistic behaviors that have been nurtured in fantasy. Of course, not all paraphiles become sexually violent offenders, but such offenders do not transition from normal sexual behavior to violent sexual behavior without requisite deviant sexual explorations. There also appears to be higher levels of psychopathy in those with attack paraphilia due to the fact that sadism is a salient factor for those who rape and sexually harm children and adults.

It is not surprising that rapists, aggressive pedophiles, child molesters, and other violent paraphiliacs are not usually amenable to treatment compared to those who do not exhibit sadistic traits. For example, in 1985 in Wisconsin, dozens of women received telephone calls from an individual described as an "emotional rapist." His goal was to psychologically gain control over his victims' emotions by persuasively convincing them that they were dying of cancer or a rare blood disease. The only cure for their acute disease, he insisted, was to inflict extreme embarrassment on themselves. Some were ordered to walk down city streets with their breasts exposed, and two others pierced their nipples and walked mutilated among the public. His ability to manipulate his victims amazed everyone, especially those who obediently followed his commands (*Newsweek*, 1985, p. 3a). The purpose of his ruse was to inflict as much pain, degradation, and humiliation on his victims as possible.

LUST KILLERS

Malmquist (1996) states that *sexual homicide* is a broad term that includes different types of sexual killing including rape killings, sexual lust killings, and killings after a sexual act in order to destroy evidence. Sexual serial killers tend to either kill after a rape or be involved in lust murders. These sexual killers are more inclined to seek out strangers for victims than other solo male offenders. Generally the women are prostitutes, hitchhikers, or students. For example:

> In late 2000, Robert L. Yates pled guilty to the murders of 13 mostly prostitutes in the Spokane County, and Tacoma, Washington, areas. The female victims were raped, shot in the head, and buried. He killed

PROFILE 5.14 The Banana Man*

In 2002, a man called a home in Shawnee, Kansas, asking to speak with a nine-year-old female at the house, stating he was with her dance studio. He said he wanted to tell her that class had been canceled due to a snowstorm. The mother of the child was suspicious, having never received a personal call from the studio in the past, and knowing the owner of the studio was a female. The call was later traced to a pay phone just outside of the Shawnee city limits. Five days later, the same mother received three calls from a male stranger saying he was with a (nonexistent) area newspaper and wanted to interview her nine-year-old child about her experiences at her dance studio. Since the child was not home at the time of the first two calls, he was told to call back. However, on the third call, the mother handed the phone to her daughter for the interview. The caller first gained the child's trust by asking some preliminary questions about her name, age, and how long she had been dancing at the studio. About two minutes into the questioning, his tone changed. He calmly asked who she thought was prettier, her or another girl in her class. He then asked her, "Would it hurt more if I put my hand in your vagina or your butt?" The mother, realizing her daughter had a shocked look, grabbed the phone in time to hear the caller make another lewd comment before hanging up.

The mother noticed that there had been two additional calls made to her house (noted on a Caller ID box) from the same pay phone number used by the offender on the earlier calls. She notified police. Not having reached his intended target, the man called a different house, home to two sisters ages 10 and 12. Both girls attended the same studio. He asked to speak to the 10-year-old but she was not home, so he settled for speaking with the 12-year-old. He carefully lured her into a conversation that included suggestions of very graphic sexual activity. The man referred to his penis as a "banana," asking the girl, "Do you know how big a banana is? Because that's how big I am ... and this is what I am going to do with it...." as a transitional phrase from originally gaining her trust. His conversations inevitably became sexual and threatening with his other victims as well.

Later, another 10-year-old gymnast in a nearby city received a terrorizing call from the same man using that same pay phone bank. Her parents immediately reported it to the local police department. Ten days later, a seven-year-old gymnast at the same gymnastics center received a hang-up call from the same pay phone. The man continued to call and contacted a new victim whom he called by her nickname and mentioned the name of her coach. A police report was made regarding the call. A Shawnee police detective traveled to the pay phone bank location, noting it to be attached to a very busy convenience store and gas station, across the street from a middle school and adjacent to several single-family homes. While at that location, a white male in a white pickup truck pulled up in front of the pay phones, turned off his vehicle, and smoked a cigarette while staring at the bank of phones. After several minutes, the man backed up his truck and pulled into a driveway of one of the adjacent homes. Suspicious, the detective copied the vehicle and tag information and noted the address at which the truck was now parked. Later that night, detectives returned to this house and collected the trash the resident had placed at the curb for pickup. In the first bag of trash was located information on several victims, including photos of young females in two-piece swimsuits, names, addresses, and phone numbers of several area gymnastics and dance clubs.

The next day, a search warrant was obtained for the house. When confronted, the man made several unsolicited, excited utterances in front of the police officers. This included: "I've fought disgusting impulses my whole life," "I had a penile implant surgery done four weeks ago with the idea that would increase my ability to fight disgusting impulses ... even though I can't afford it, there's nothing more disgusting in my life than the way I think sometimes," "I haven't always been this way. I think it started in summer camps. I used to only have dark thoughts about people my age, then 16, 15, 14 ... the girls in bikinis—they're beautiful!" "I need help! I'm disgusted and ashamed of myself," and "There are periods in my life when I do nothing wrong, then all of the sudden ... I don't know what happened."

The man had been attending gymnastic meets and dance recitals, collecting the "programs" distributed at the events, and videotaping and photographing young, prepubescent girls while they performed. All were fully clothed during the events. Nothing found in the investigation indicated he had ever physically touched a single victim. The man was locating his victims' home phone numbers by selecting young girls off the event program with very unique last names that could easily be found in the telephone book. He was able to call the victims by their nicknames and provide information on their coaches using information found in the event programs.

The man's claims to have had a penile enlargement were confirmed, as were his claims to have attempted suicide previously and to have sought help on several occasions. While in custody, the man stated, "I need help. Please help me," and mentioned that he often thought about killing himself to stop his sick fantasies. He thought that if he was ever in a situation where he was ready to physically act out his fantasy, he would kill himself. The man, 45, and white, was employed as a substitute teacher for grades 5–8 in a local school district. Originally from New York, he had moved to Kansas only six months prior to his arrest and was living with his married brother. Found guilty of criminal threats he was sentenced to probation. The next day he returned and advised the court that he felt he could never "make it" on probation and asked to be sent to jail. The judge complied with the request and sentenced him to six months in jail. Prior to his release from jail he was required to undergo a sexual offender evaluation and was ultimately determined to be a sexual predator. Through civil proceedings the man was confined indefinitely to maximum security in a state mental hospital. He appealed this ruling and a trial resulted in a hung jury. At that time, he was the only person ever in the state of Kansas to be deemed a sexual predator without having ever touched a child. Two years later, the civil case was dismissed and he was released. He now resides in a Kansas jurisdiction bordering Shawnee.

How do we classify this offender? Is he a true predator without ever having touched a child? Should stalking statutes be used to keep him incarcerated if he persists in calling the girls? What types of paraphilia does this man exhibit? Should such offenders be required to undergo sex offender treatment? What do you think?

---

*A special thanks to Susan C. Smith, Crime Analyst, Shawnee (KS) Police Department, for contributing this case for the sixth edition.

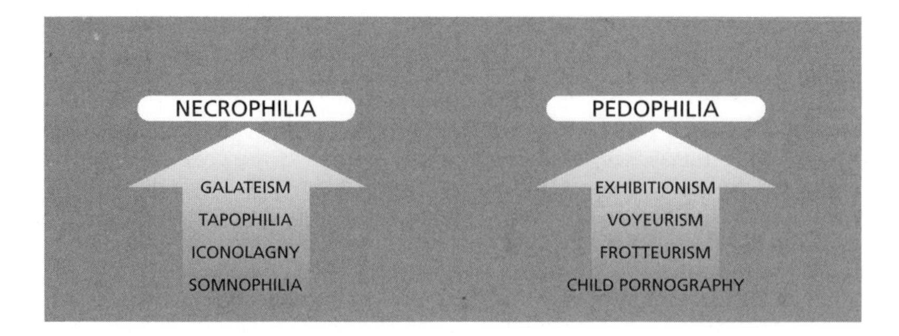

CHART 5.3 Paraphilic Processes in Developing Secondary Paraphilia

SOURCE: © Cengage Learning, 2013.

PROFILE 5.15 Westley Allan Dodd, Sadistic Child Killer, 1989

Westley Allan Dodd began sexually abusing children in 1974 when he was 13 years old. The abuse started when he began exposing himself to young girls and boys around his neighborhood. Dodd claims that he was driven to act out as a child because his parents fought constantly and that they did not provide him with emotional support. When his parents divorced, Dodd's behaviors escalated and he began molesting children. He sought out children whom he knew and were close to him. At the age of 14 he molested his cousins who were 8 and 6 years old. Dodd sought out situations where he would have access to children such as babysitting neighborhood kids and serving as a camp counselor. By the age of 18 he was seeking out children he did not know to molest. Dodd eventually joined the Navy and was stationed in Bangor, Washington, and preyed on children who lived on the base. He made trips to Seattle where he approached children in movie theater restrooms. Dodd started using money to lure children to secluded places where he would order them to take down their pants. Dodd was eventually arrested and discharged from the Navy and again arrested after accosting a young boy. Dodd served 19 days in jail. Throughout the next few years Dodd continued to act out on children and was arrested but spent little time in jail. By 1986, Dodd had sexually assaulted at least 30 children. Despite court-ordered counseling, he made no attempt to control his behavior and was indulging in fantasies of murdering children.

In 1987, Dodd attempted to murder his first victim, an eight-year-old boy whom he had met while working as a security guard, when he asked the child to help him find a "lost boy." The boy, sensing danger, told Dodd that he was going home and would be right back. The boy's mother called the police and Dodd was jailed for 118 days. He moved to Vancouver in 1989 and began stalking victims in David Douglas Park. On September 4, Dodd accosted two brothers, molested and stabbed them to death. He found he now felt more gratification in killing than molesting. On October 29, 1989, Dodd lured a child away from a schoolyard and took him to his apartment, where he bound the boy, molested him, and later strangled him while he was sleeping. After the murder, he hung the child in a closet and took pictures of him. The boy's body was found by Vancouver Lake.

Shortly after his third murder, Dodd was arrested after trying to abduct another boy from a movie theater restroom. Dodd finally confessed to the three murders and was charged with first-degree murder and attempted kidnapping of the boy in the theater restroom. He pled guilty to all charges, was sentenced to death, and was hanged on January 5, 1993 (King, 1993).

his first prostitute in 1988. However, in 1975 and only 23, Yates was working as a correctional officer. While target shooting he came upon two college graduates who were on a picnic. On a whim he killed them both. Yates continued to fantasize more and more about raping and killing women and now will spend the rest of his life in prison. (author's files)

Sometimes nurses, models, or waitresses were targeted. Although a few offenders randomly selected women who were at home alone, most victims succumbed to the ruses and con games played by offenders in both public and private areas. One offender, who now resides at the Florida State Prison in Starke, Florida, was able to talk his way into anyone's trust. Charismatic, irresponsible, unfaithful to his wife and family, he always blamed others for his problems. He felt completely invincible as he stalked his prey. After talking an attractive 38-year-old real estate agent into showing him some very expensive property, he led her into a wooded area in the backyard, where he beat and stabbed her to death.

Compared with other male offenders who acted alone, this subgroup similarly often targeted women who placed themselves at risk, including those who hitchhiked, worked as prostitutes, or walked alone at night. The majority of these offenders, however, sought out women who generally did not perceive themselves to be at risk. Swimming at a crowded beach, shopping in a mall, and walking home are not activities one generally considers to be risky, yet there are potential dangers in practically all public and many private activities. For serial killers like Ted Bundy (see Profile 5.16), the challenge is to exploit situations in which the risk of danger appears so remote that the victim never feels a need to be on guard.

It is especially this subgroup of killers that reinforces the belief that sex is the primary driving motive behind the murders. Because of these offenders' sexual abuse of their victims, the public believes that serial killers are motivated by particularly bizarre and perverted sexual urges. Certainly they experience a degree of sexual arousal and gratification in what they do, but this does not mean that sexual gratification is the primary motive for killing. When we begin to evaluate sexual acts as vehicles to gain control, maintain power, and degrade and inflict pain on the victim, we inevitably are making headway toward understanding the mind of the serial killer. Most offenders in this subgroup can be described as "lust killers" because sexual acts and associations are both overtly and subtly interwoven into their assaults. The *DSM-IV* terms lust killing as *erotophonophilia* or *dacnolagnomania*, which is sexually sadistic murder involving sexual arousal and gratification as part of the killing. The need for control was never more manifest than in this particular group of male offenders. Postmortem acts of mutilation and desecration were common, as were repeated and prolonged acts of sexual sadism and torture. Necrophilia also was very common. The fear of rejection appeared to be so powerful that some offenders would have sex with the victim only after she had died. In the perception of the offender, a corpse permits him to be intimate without risk of rejection.

Deviant sexual acts usually are part of the killing process, not the actual reasons for killing. News accounts of these lust killers portray them as sex fiends

PROFILE 5.16 Theodore Robert Bundy, "Ted," 1973–1978

In the end, society gave Ted what he so eagerly sought throughout his life: infamy, notoriety, and the attention of millions of people. Even though the lives of 30 to 40 young women, including several teenagers and a 12-year-old girl, were sacrificed, the final price Ted would pay was never a real issue for him. Like some other serial killers, Ted Bundy found his fortune in the recognition and celebrity status he acquired through his involvement with the judicial system of the United States.

Ted was born out of wedlock in Burlington, Vermont, in 1946, to Louise Cowell. During the next few years, Ted and his mother lived with Louise's parents. Some relatives believe it was during this period of time that Ted was deeply traumatized by his violent grandfather.

At age four, Ted and his mother Louise relocated to Tacoma, Washington. In a short time his mother married an army cook, Johnnie Bundy. Ted was forced to live a meager lifestyle and grew up deeply resenting not having money or respectable social-class affiliations. He nurtured feelings of inadequacy, of being unable to compete with others who possessed upper-middle-class standing. Michaud and Aynesworth (1983), who later interviewed Bundy, also discovered that he was deeply class conscious. As Leyton (1986b) explained in his profile of Bundy, "The status anxiety seemed particularly intense in his relationships with women" (p. 98). He dated infrequently while in high school and, as Leyton points out, "he ultimately captured and killed sorority girls, or their idealized models, for it was an obvious way in which his class-scarred soul could conceive of the possession" (p. 99).

His quest for identity served as a catalyst for constantly presenting himself, especially in physical disguises, to be somebody else. One person he truly did not want to be was Ted Bundy, the Nobody. Yet Ted seemed to lack the ability to comprehend the dynamics of social life, of being able to fit in, and admitted to his interviewers: "I didn't know what made people want to be friends. I didn't know what made people attractive to one another. I didn't know what underlay social interactions" (Michaud and Aynesworth, 1983, p. 68). Consequently Ted created a series of social fronts and disguises to help him blend into the "right groups." In truth, Bundy became the "mirror image" of himself. He lived to portray an image that he so desperately wanted to be but could never attain.

His decision to begin killing, however, was spurred only in part by his social-class paranoia. Ted later explained, using the third person, that he was eventually overcome by an internal force or an "entity" that constituted a "purely destructive power." In essence, Ted began to delve deeper into a world of sexual fantasy that became increasingly violent in nature. He consumed quantities of pornographic material depicting sexually violent acts. Bundy explained pornography "as a vicarious way of experiencing what his peers were experiencing in reality. Then he got sucked into the more sinister doctrines that are implicit in pornography—the use, abuse, the possession of women as objects" (Winn and Merrill, 1980, pp. 116–117).

He fed his sexual fantasies through voyeurism. For years he peeped through windows to watch women undress. Combined with his increasing appetite for alcohol, Ted was gradually preparing himself to begin his killing career. During this time he established what appeared to be an impressive record. He had been in the Boy Scouts, worked as an assistant programs director at the Seattle Crime Commission, and wrote, ironically enough, a booklet for women on rape prevention. He was even accepted to the University of Utah Law School, but attended only a few classes. This was all part of the image, the illusion he maintained in order to move freely about in fulfilling his growing deviant sexual fantasies.

His efforts to "fit in" vanished as he dealt with the sting of rejection. Each setback was perceived as devastating, regardless of its true magnitude. Like some other serial killers, Bundy began to act out his fantasies by first stalking his women and then attacking them. As Leyton (1986b) observed, "He decided to commit himself to another career ... having failed at social mobility" (p. 106). Like Ed Kemper, Bundy had already picked out some dumping sites for his victims. It is unlikely we will ever know exactly how many victims Bundy accrued, but there exists sufficient evidence to link him to at least 30 homicides, though many people believe he killed nearly 40.

The victims were all young, attractive females who appeared to come from middle- or upper-middle-class families, and many were students. He killed victims in at least five different states between 1973 and 1978, usually leaving the bodies in secluded wooded areas.

Several bodies were not found until all that remained were a few bones scattered by animals. Some victims were never recovered. Robert Keppel, a former detective who investigated eight Bundy killings in the Seattle area, believes he may have murdered over 100 victims. Ted was usually able to lure the intended victims to his car by asking them for assistance. He was always polite and friendly and sometimes wore his arm in a sling to appear as a harmless, well-bred young man simply in need of help. At other times he was known to lurk in dark shadows and attack women who were alone. An early victim was abducted from her basement apartment where she was sleeping.

Ted usually attacked his victims with a blunt instrument, such as a tire iron or a wooden club, and rendered them unconscious. Some of them died quickly from having their skulls crushed, whereas others would linger for hours or days until Ted strangled them. Once Ted had maneuvered his victim into a position that allowed him to be in control, the woman's fate was inevitable. Only one victim managed to escape death after he had placed her under his control. He raped most, if not all, of his victims; several were subjected to sodomy and sexual mutilations. Some of the victims had vaginal lacerations caused by foreign objects. In the Chi Omega sorority house killings in Tallahassee, Florida, Bundy left teeth marks on the breast and buttocks of at least one victim. In some instances Bundy would keep the body for days and is believed by some investigators to have shampooed the hair of and applied makeup to more than one victim.

Ted also liked to match wits with law enforcement personnel, and on two occasions he was able to escape from a jail and a courthouse in Colorado. Ted was able to avoid apprehension because of his degree of mobility. Moving from state to state, he drew in dozens of police agencies, all wanting to capture him.

In the end, Ted's own psychopathology appeared to have caused his downfall. Before his last kill, Bundy drank heavily and resorted to frequent thefts of wallets and sprees of shoplifting. In his last few days of freedom he was overcome with desperation, paranoia, and the inability to make and act on decisions that would allow him to remain free. His frequent and excessive use of stolen credit cards and his impulsive purchases of clothing, especially socks, were not the actions of the "old" Ted who had been in control. Fueled by his paranoia, fetishes, and constant intake of alcohol, perhaps he foresaw or even wished his inevitable capture. Bundy's final victim, Kimberly Leach, whom he randomly selected from a grammar school, was only 12 years of age. A few days after murdering her, Ted was pulled over by a suspicious patrol officer, and eventually police discovered that he had been placed on the FBI's Ten Most Wanted list.

(continued)

PROFILE 5.16 (Continued)

Bundy was convicted of three murders and sentenced to die in Florida's electric chair. Reveling in the notoriety, he defended himself in court and used his trial to bask in the light of national TV and newspaper coverage. He finally gained the prominence and self-validation he so desperately sought. In an interview with Dr. Ron Holmes of the University of Louisville, Bundy discussed the classic characteristics of serial killers but could not recognize those traits in his own personality (author's files). He continued to the very end to employ legal maneuverings to avoid the electric chair. His trial and appeals cost approximately nine million dollars. Bundy's court record was one of the longest in Florida's history, more than 28,000 pages, or about the size of the *Encyclopedia Britannica.* For Ted that was also a way to satisfy his desire for revenge on a society he believed had maligned him. For Ted there was no guilt, and as he declared on one occasion, "I don't feel guilty for anything ... I feel sorry for people who feel guilt" (Winn and Merrill, 1980, p. 313). As his interviewers, Michaud and Aynesworth, came to realize, Ted did not act under some irresponsible uncontrollable urge; rather, he consciously used his free will, his agency, to create the killer within himself. Bundy's fame attracted many young female followers who continued to send him letters of love and support. During his incarceration in Florida, Ted married and even managed to father a child. He had absolutely no remorse for his crimes. As Ted so aptly observed, "I'm the coldest mother-fucker you'll ever put your eyes on. I don't give a shit about those other people" (author's files).

But in the end Ted decided to confess his crimes, possibly to buy additional time for himself. The consummate psychopath lived out his image until the very end when he allowed a well-intentioned minister to interview him. The meeting was vintage Bundy. The minister wanted Bundy to explore the role of pornography in his life and its influence on him in committing the murders. Like a master craftsman, Bundy controlled and molded the interview. In the end Bundy gave the minister what he wanted without ever scratching the veneer of his own image. Finally, his confessions, his efforts to show he was insane, that he did not receive a fair trial, that he could take authorities to more burial sites, all faltered.

As Bundy's execution hour drew near, the nation watched with increasing interest. Talk shows, newscasters, and newspaper editors all began exploring the life of Ted Bundy and the phenomenon of serial murder in general. Some individuals and groups eagerly awaited his last moments. T-shirts with slogans such as "Fry-Day" and bumper stickers that read "I'll buckle up when Bundy buckles up" were common in Florida and other states where the killer had murdered young women. Radio stations played a song parody, "On Top of Old Sparky," and an Indianapolis station fried bacon on the air and held a "Bundy countdown" an hour before his execution. Dances and cookouts called "Bundy-Ques" were held in several locations. The execution in many respects took on the atmosphere of a circus. Even those strongly opposed to capital punishment were few in number at the Florida State Prison in Starke as dozens of people anxious to see him die cheered, set off firecrackers, and chanted "Burn, Bundy, Burn" as the appointed hour approached. Indeed, it was a disgusting end to a disgusting life. On January 24, 1989, at 7:00 A.M., Theodore Robert Bundy died in the electric chair. His last words before a black hood was placed over his head were "Give my love to my family and friends." The following statements by Bundy attempt to add a rational note to his murderous career.

- "Sitting there in a cell, I could convince myself that I was not guilty of anything."
- [Regarding confession] "Walking right up to the edge is a thrill, but I can't do it. I haven't allowed myself to choke."
- "They [society] will condemn Ted Bundy while walking past a magazine rack that contains the very things [pornography] that send kids down the road to being Ted Bundys."

Ted Bundy's Victims

Date of Murder or Disappearance	Name	Age	Occupation	Location	Method
1/31/74	Lynda Ann Healey	21	Student	Wash.	Clubbing
3/12/74	Donna Gail Manson	19	Student	Wash.	?
4/17/74	Susan Rancourt	18	Student	Wash.	Clubbing
5/6/74	Roberta K. Parks	22	Student	Ore.	Bludgeoning
6/1/74	Brenda C. Ball	22	Unemployed	Wash.	Clubbing/strangulation
6/11/74	Georgeann Hawkins	18	Student	Wash.	?
7/14/74	Janice Ott	23	Probation officer	Wash.	Bludgeoning
7/14/74	Denise M. Naslund	19	Secretary/student	Wash.	Bludgeoning
8/2/74	Carol Valenzuela	20	—	Wash.	Strangulation/clubbing
8/2/74	Unidentified victim	17–23	—	Wash.	?
10/2/74	Nancy Wilcox	16	Student	Utah	?
10/18/74	Melissa Smith	17	Student	Utah	Strangulation/fractured skull
10/31/74	Laurie Amie	17	Student	Utah	Strangulation/fractured skull
11/8/74	Debbie Kent	17	Student	Utah	?
1/12/75	Caryn Campbell	23	Nurse	Colo.	Fractured skull
3/15/75	Julie Cunningham	26	Ski instructor	Colo.	Fractured skull
4/6/75	Denise Oliverson	25	—	Colo.	—
1/15/78	Lisa Levy	20	Student	Fla.	Fractured skull
1/15/78	Margaret Bowman	21	Student	Fla.	Clubbing/strangulation
2/9/78	Kimberly Leach	12	Student	Fla.	Strangulation/slashed throat

Bundy also confessed, or is believed by investigators, to have also murdered: 1973 Rita Lorraine Jolly, 17, Clackamas County, Oregon; 1973 Vicki Lynn Hollar, 24, Eugene, Oregon; 1973 Katherine Merry Devine, 14, Seattle, Washington; 1974 Brenda Joy Baker, 14, Seattle, Washington; 1975 Nancy Baird, 21, Farmington, Utah; 1974–1975 Sandra Weaver, 17, Utah; 1974–1975 Sue Curtis, 17, Utah; 1974–1975 Debbie Smith, 17, Utah; 1975 Melanie Suzanne Cooley, 18, Nederland, Colorado; 1975 Shelly K. Robertson, 24, Denver, Colorado.

PROFILE 5.17 John Edward Robinson, the "Slavemaster," 1984–2000

The 56-year-old predator with a criminal history dating back to the 1960s met several of his young female victims in sadomasochistic Internet chat rooms. His Internet moniker was "Slavemaster." He pretended to own two international businesses to impress potential victims. At least five women were lured to his Kansas home with promises of work or kinky sex. After torturing and beating them to death, Robinson sealed each victim in a steel drum and placed some of them in a storage locker over the Missouri state line. Robinson was caught after two other intended victims managed to escape during their sadomasochistic encounters. They realized just in time that the rough sex was only going to get worse. The other victims all died from blunt head trauma. He was also charged with stealing over $900 of sex toys from one of his victims. Robinson depicted himself as a businessman and philanthropist who lived with his wife in a mobile home park that she managed. One associate of Slavemaster claimed that Robinson was involved in a sex cult in which rape, bondage, and torture were practiced. Robinson enjoyed the sexual degradation of women and the Internet became a useful tool in procuring his victims.

when in reality sex is another tool they use to appease sexual fantasies and express total domination over victims. The primary motive is control; such offenders must control others in order to feel that they themselves are in control of their own lives. The vehicle to achieve control is through sexual acts. Other male killers may use different methods, such as guns, to achieve a similar sense of control. In our study, offenders in this subgroup frequently carried out acts of rape and were also likely to express enjoyment or pleasure about the murders. Offenders often cited personal reasons for the murders such as an "urge to kill." Efforts to gain control are also influenced by technology. Some serial killers are now using the Internet to lure victims to their deaths (see Profile 5.17). Note the varieties of methods employed by these sexual serial killers to destroy their victims (see Chart 5.4). Strangulation/asphyxiation is by far the preferred method of killing, followed by shooting, then slashing, stabbing, or killing with an axe. Strangulation is common because it affords the killer direct manual contact with the victim whereby he can be in complete control of the victim's death, can sexualize the fear of the victim (if part of his violent sexual fantasy), can sexually assault the victim (if part of his sexual fantasy), and can leave his signature as a serial sexual predator who kills.

Another important characteristic of these lust killers was the "perversion factor." This subgroup was often prone to carry out bizarre sexual acts. These acts most commonly included necrophilia and trophy collection. Jerry Brudos (see Profile 5.18) severed the breasts of some of his victims and made epoxy molds. Brudos, like others, also photographed his victims in various poses, dressed and disrobed. The photos served as trophies and a stimulus to act out again. Other lust killers engage in cannibalism, including Albert Fish, Richard Chase, Ed Kemper, Jeffrey Dahmer, Otis Toole, Ed Gein, and Robin Gecht. There also tends to be a high correlation between men who cannibalize and Satan worship. Gary Heidnik in Philadelphia kept sex slaves, and when two died he dismembered them and cooked them for meals.

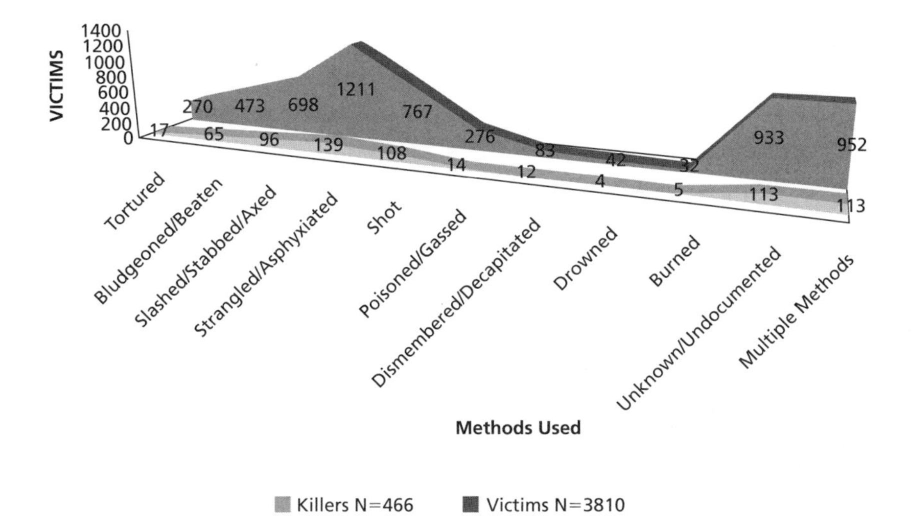

CHART 5.4 Methods of Sexual Serial Murder, 1872–2007, in the United States
SOURCE: © Cengage Learning, 2013.

The lust killers in this study frequently had histories of sex-related crimes and time in prison or mental institutions. Again, offenders in the subgroup were likely to have had more than one previous social or psychological problem. This may suggest that lust killers are influenced to commit violence as a result of such problems. Another explanation, and probably more accurate at this point in the development of serial-murder research, is simply that lust killers receive more attention from both law enforcement officials and researchers. Consequently, we are probably going to find more information on the sensational cases, especially if research is based primarily on the more gruesome statistics and facts and pays less attention to other details.

Regardless of the subgrouping of male serial killers who act alone, a recurrent problem noted in most of them is feelings of low self-esteem and worthlessness. These feelings, according to offenders, appear to stem from periods of rejection or denial by loved ones, especially parents, or by society in general.

PARAPHILIC FANTASY

Fantasies can be reinforced by powerful sex drives that, in turn, facilitate some unusual behaviors. During World War II, England was decimated by repeated German bombing attacks. Always lingering was the fear of poison-gas attack. Today, one has only to read the personal advertisements in British newspapers to see some of the long-term results—gas-mask fetishes are common. People seek partners interested in sexual activity using gas masks and rubberized raincoats (Dietz, 1994). Purcell (2000), in her insightful research on paraphilia, examined the etiology and development of paraphilic behavior through case study analysis.

The most critical factor common to serial killers is violent fantasy. Prentky and colleagues (1986), who studied repetitive sexual homicides, found that

PROFILE 5.18 Jerry Brudos, the Trophy Collector, 1968–1969

At an early age, Jerry Brudos developed a particular interest in women's shoes, especially black, spike-heeled shoes. As he matured, his shoe fetish increasingly provided sexual arousal. At 17, he used a knife to assault a girl and force her to disrobe while he took pictures of her. For his crime he was incarcerated in a mental hospital for nine months. His therapy uncovered his sexual fantasy for revenge against women, fantasies that included placing kidnapped girls into freezers so he could later arrange their stiff bodies in sexually explicit poses. He was evaluated as possessing a personality disorder but was not considered to be psychotic.

Jerry completed high school, served in the military, and then became an electronics technician. His sexual fixations carried into marriage; he insisted that his wife, Ralphene, stay nude while in the house. He would take pictures of her naked, and, according to his wife, he occasionally dressed in her panties and bra. He continued to collect women's undergarments and shoes. Prior to his first murder, he had already assaulted four women and raped one of them. At age 28, Jerry was ready to start killing. His first victim came to his home quite by accident, looking for another address. On January 26, 1968, Linda Slawson, 19, working in book sales, knocked on Jerry Brudos's door when he was home alone. He took her to his garage, where he smashed her skull with a two-by-four. Before disposing of the body in a nearby river, he severed her left foot and placed it in his freezer. He often would amuse himself by dressing the foot in a spiked-heel shoe.

His fantasy for greater sexual pleasure led him, on November 26, 1968, to strangle Jan Whitney, 23, with a postal strap. After killing her, he had sexual intercourse with the corpse, then cut off the right breast and made an epoxy mold of the organ. Before dumping her body in the river, he took pictures of the corpse. Unable to satisfy his sexual fantasies and still in the grasp of violent urges, he found his third victim, Karen Sprinker, 19, on March 27, 1969. After sexually assaulting Karen, he strangled her in his garage, amputated both breasts, again took pictures, and tossed her body into the river. Four weeks later, on April 23, 1969, he abducted his last victim, Linda Salee, 22, from a shopping mall. He sexually assaulted Linda, and, after strangling her in his garage, he shocked her torso with electric charges and watched her body jerk with spasms. Investigators also found needle marks on her body.

All of Brudos's victims were young, white, female strangers, whom he methodically killed in his garage under the special mirrors he had installed to help feed his fantasies. He later confessed that he enjoyed the killing, especially how his victims looked once they were dead. Brudos was sent to Oregon State Prison for the murders.

Twenty years later, Brudos is now granted a parole hearing every other year under Oregon's old parole system. He has adjusted to prison life and has turned his energies to his personal computer and printer, which make life in a cell much more meaningful. It is unlikely he will ever be paroled, but Brudos has not given up hope.

daydreams of causing bodily harm through sadism and other methods of sexual violence were common among offenders. The researchers concluded that the offender then attempts to replicate his or her fantasies. Because the offender can never be actually in total control of his or her victim's responses, the outcome of the fantasy will never measure up to his or her expectations. In any case, each new murder provides new fantasies that can fuel future homicides. Ressler and his colleagues (1988) concluded that "sexual murder is based on fantasy" (p. 33). Fantasy becomes a critical component in the psychological development of a serial killer. Although fantasies are generally associated with sexual homicides, they are likely to be found in the minds of most, if not all, serial killers.

The following case of a young man arrested for attempted rape and murder illustrates how consuming and powerful fantasies can become:

> Visiting a young woman in whom he was interested, Carl suddenly attacked and tried to rape her. During the course of the attack the girl's mother returned home. Enraged, Carl killed the mother and fled the home. Carl was adjudicated to be insane at the time of the attack and was confined to a mental institution until he could be considered safe to return to the community. After seven years and extensive therapy in a sex offender program, Carl was permitted to begin a community reintegration program. Working as an electrician's helper, Carl worked during the day and stayed at the hospital at night. He was also allowed certain weekend privileges, provided he followed the specific rules of his therapy program.
>
> One of Carl's problems had been his propensity for fantasy. When he was younger, he loved to set fires so he could view the flashing lights of the police and fire trucks. Over time he had graduated into some extremely violent fantasies that were believed by psychiatrists to have contributed to his homicidal behavior. During his years in the sex offender program Carl appeared to learn how to control his fantasies. On weekends he attended dances, movies, and other recreational activities. He was not permitted, however, to attend movies that contained any explicit sexual violence for fear he could still become caught up in his own fantasies of violence. One evening he violated his weekend pass by attending the movie *Dressed to Kill,* featuring Angie Dickinson. Later, he would report how he had attempted to "pick up a girl" during the movie but was rejected. Even before the violence in the movie had ended, Carl was also ready to kill. Going to his car engulfed in raging fantasies of violence, Carl located his electrician's knife and waited in the shadows while four unsuspecting female college students exited from the theater. His fantasy was to enter their car and cut each girl's throat. Walking quickly to the rear door of the vehicle, Carl reached for the handle. Just as he was about to open the door, the driver, unaware of his presence, stepped on the accelerator and drove off.
>
> Frustrated and in the grips of his violent fantasies, Carl later explained how he had then gone to the local park, hunting for a lone female jogger. He had decided to cut her into pieces. Waiting in some bushes for several minutes, Carl saw a woman jogging toward him. It was 11:30 P.M., and the park was deserted. Fortunately for his intended victim, a male jogger emerged from another direction at about the same time. Thwarted in his bid to kill and in fear of detection, Carl returned to his car. After driving around for a while and unable to locate any more suitable victims, Carl calmed down and returned to the hospital, where he explained to hospital staff his evening's experiences. It was decided that Carl was still in need of closer supervision, and his passes were revoked (author's files).

Most people's fantasies generally are perceived as harmless and often therapeutic. Fantasies can involve a continuum of benign to aggressive thoughts that usually generate little or no action on the part of the fantasizer. For serial offenders, however, fantasies appear to involve violence, often sexual in nature, whereby the victim is controlled totally by the offender. The purpose of the fantasy is not the immediate destruction of another human being but total control over that person. The element of control is so intense in the serial killer that in some cases the actual death of the victim is anticlimactic to the fantasized total control over the victim. In a case mentioned in an earlier chapter, an offender who is believed to have killed 14 young women used to place his revolver on the forehead of his victim and order her to perform fellatio. Those victims who cried and begged for mercy would invariably receive a bullet in their heads during the sexual assault. Those victims who cooperated with the killer but remained calm and did not show fear were spared. During an interview with one of the victims who survived the assault, the victim told how she had been ordered to kneel on the floor. In this instance the offender had placed tape over his victim's mouth. After he had taped her mouth, the killer proceeded to rub his penis against her face and insisted she look him in the eyes while he performed his sexual assault. The victim later recalled how she managed to remain calm and did exactly as he ordered her to do even though her attacker held a gun to her head. After a few moments the killer realized his victim was not responding the way he expected (and according to his fantasies), and so he abruptly fled the store (author's files).

The control fantasy becomes the highlight of the attack. The sexual assault is one vehicle by which the offender can attempt to gain total control of a victim. Sexual torture becomes a tool to degrade, humiliate, and subjugate the victim. It is a method to take away from the victim all that is perceived to be personal, private, or sacred. The offender physically and mentally dominates his or her victims to a point where he or she has fantasized achieving ultimate control over another human being. Once that sense of control has been reached, the victim loses his or her purpose to the offender and is then killed. One serial killer noted in a personal interview that he had developed a ritual for torturing his victims and that he seldom varied from those methods.

It is during the sexual assault, torture, and degradation that fantasies of the original childhood trauma may manifest themselves in acts of violence. In some cases, 10 or 20 years may have lapsed since the traumatic event(s) occurred; in others, only a short period of time may have passed. During the time elapsed between the traumatic event(s) and the homicides, the offender may have completely disassociated from the traumatic experience (which had split off from his or her consciousness) and may have protected himself or herself further by assuming a life of control and confidence. Psychologically the offender has been experiencing less and less self-control but desperately seeks to retain control of his or her inner self. Often the victims selected by the killers stand as proxies for the traumatic event(s) experienced by the offenders. In one instance an offender had received electroshock treatments as corrective therapy for his involvement in a gang rape while he was a teenager. In 1984, 22 years after his electroshocks, the offender tortured some of his victims by wiring their toes to electrical outlets and then turning the power on and off. In yet another case, an offender had been sexually abused, beaten, bound with heavy cords, and left in terrifyingly dark closets. Several years later he began torturing boys by beating them, tying them with heavy cords, and holding them captive in dark places. His attempts to replicate his childhood traumas were nearly successful except that the sense of control he sought remained elusive. Each victim experienced more extensive tortures and depravities than the previous victim until he died, at which time the killer butchered the corpse. His last victim was slowly dismembered and disemboweled while still alive (author's files).

Fantasies may be fueled by pornography and facilitated by alcohol. The anger that has continued to grow over the years is allowed to be expressed in images of violence and death. Once the total domination and destruction of the victim has occurred, the killer momentarily regains the sense of equilibrium lost years before. One offender described this moment as the "restoration stage," which allows the killer to "feel good" again. He explained that for many serial killers, the frequency of victimization is a direct function of the degree of completion of the restoration. In other words, if the offender is stymied or frustrated in some way in the act of ritualistically killing a victim, he or she may be prompted to quickly seek out another. Once the killer is able to complete the ritual of killing and feels that sense of control restored, he or she may not need to kill again for some time.

But fantasies can never be completely fulfilled or the anger removed or the missing self-esteem restored. For some, the experience of killing may generate new fantasies of violence. Exactly what does occur in the killer's mind between murders? It is possible for some offenders to become so consumed by their attempts at fantasy fulfillment that killing becomes a frequent experience. Yet there are many serial killers who wait long periods of time, months or even years, before they seek out their next victim. According to one offender, he felt good about himself and more in control of his life directly following a murder. Eventually he would experience another failure in his life, such as criticism of job performance or rejection by a girlfriend. He believed that such events should not have bothered him, but they seemed to act as catalysts for depression and low self-esteem. The sense of failure or rejection never failed to put him into a spiral of self-pity, anger, loss of confidence, and increased fantasies. Sometimes it would be months, but inevitably he would go hunting for young women to torture and kill (author's files).

Sex offenders use sex as a vehicle to gain control over their victims by inflicting pain and suffering. It is believed that the sexual involvement of many serial killers is a result of childhood experiences. Ressler and his colleagues (1988), in their study of 36 sexual murderers, explain fantasy as a process rather than merely an experience. Fantasies may begin at a very early age and appear to escalate over time. They report several cases in which offenders were involved in early construction of aggressive fantasies, including "sexualized rituals" or the repetition of sexual acts. They challenge the notion that murderers involved sexually with their victims make the decision to kill as adults: "The power of life and death and the realization that one decides whether to control, injure, or kill is a very early experience for these men" (Ressler et al., 1988, p. 38). Given that many serial killers report histories of traumatization, including sexual abuse, it might be useful for researchers to note exactly when these offenders remember wanting to kill. Alexander et al. (2005) noted that persons suffering from symptoms of posttraumatic stress disorder were able to accurately recall the memories of those emotional and trauma-related incidents. According to Gebhard (1965), "It appears that fewer sexual psychopaths than other offenders were able to make good adjustments with their parents and their peers throughout their childhood" (p. 856). De Young (1982) notes that "the sadist sees the child victim as a representation of everything he hates about himself as well as the dreaded memories of his own childhood" (p. 125). Karpman (1954) notes similar characteristics of masochists: "Aggressive sexual crime symbolizes the inferiority feelings of the masochist and expresses his hostility toward the objects of his lust; these tendencies are integrated in the personality of the sexual psychopath as a result of longstanding emotional conflicts and stresses" (p. 72). The offender, through violent acts, attempts to gain the control he or she has sought since his or her childhood experiences. As Stoller (1975) observes, "Many childhood defeats and frustrations feed into the dynamics of risk, revenge, and triumph" (p. 128).

The *sexual psychopath* is often referred to in serial-murder cases as a "lust killer" or one who practices erotophonophilia. The notion of lust suggests one who possesses a particular urge, not only to kill, but to ravage the victim. Even among lust killers, methods of killing vary widely, as do the types of mutilations that may occur before or after the victim has died. In one case an offender described his feelings about killing, focusing on the urge to mutilate and destroy his victims before he could find temporary relief:

Uncensored Exotics*

Vainly I crouch at the fireside,
For the flames on the hearth cannot warm me.
Vainly I put on coats
Against the cold of the star winds,
Blowing from Outer Gulfs in the darkness beyond Time.
Thick walls and roofs, you are useless
Against the breath of the star winds.
Red logs, why do you crackle,
Since you are mocked by the star winds?
And my bones are chilled within me
And my blood is become as water.
And now from the void behind me
Comes the piping of the piper,
That senseless, complaining piping,

*From J. Paul de River, *The Sexual Criminal*, 1949, pp. 210–211. Charles C. Thomas, Publisher, Springfield, Illinois. Reprinted by permission of the author's estate.

That tuneless, high, thin piping.
Swiftly I turn to assail him
But he keeps ever behind me,
So that I catch but a glimpse of him,
Piping behind the shadows.
Faceless, with malformed hands
Holding a flute of silver,
Blowing his senseless music.
Piping his high, thin piping.
During an age does his playing
Beat to my brain through my eardrums,
Covered by helpless fingers.
Then, with a shout, I surrender,
And leap to do the bidding.
From the wall I snatch my weapons
And rush from the house to the forest.
Where the road winds down the mountain,
Panting I lie in ambush,
Waiting for some poor traveler
Who shall bring me my release.
When he comes with laggard footsteps,
Sudden and fierce is my onslaught.
Like a beast I overcome him
And utterly destroy him.
And I cut out his heart and eat it,
And I guzzle his blood like nectar,
And I cut off his head and scalp him,
And hang his scalp at my belt.
Homeward I walk through the snowdrifts,
And my heart is warm within me,
And my blood and bones are new again,
And the star winds cease to chill me,
And the piping of the piper
Will be heard no more for a season.

Such an urge to kill is fueled by well-developed fantasies that allow the offender to vicariously gain control of others. Fantasy for the lust killer is much more than an escape; it becomes the focal behavior. Even though the killer is able to maintain contact with reality, the world of fantasy becomes as addictive as an escape into drugs.

SIGNATURES OF SEXUAL PREDATORS

Cases of serial killing share commonalities and characteristics. Anger, low self-esteem, fantasy, facilitation, and objectification of victims all are common denominators in understanding the general etiological roots of serial murder. Some cases, however, have distinctive behaviors that make the crime and the offender(s) unique. These are referred to as the *signature,* or personal marking, of the offender. Signatures include verbal and physical acts. For example, most cases of serial murder are described in terms of patterns of murder customized to

PROFILE 5.19 Cary Stayner, the Yosemite Park Signature Killer, 1999

Cary Stayner could have easily been a model gracing the pages of *GQ* magazine. Tall, dark, and striking, he rated high on "attractiveness" by many women. Due to his artistic giftedness, Cary was voted "most creative" by his graduating class and was expected to become a famous cartoonist. I had the opportunity to examine several drawings done by Mr. Stayner around 1995. These drawings depicted scenes of death and destruction, with heads of victims on the ground. The backdrop was Yosemite National Park. Those who know him describe him as amiable, easy going, and quiet. He is described as a naturalist, with a penchant for nudity, frequenting secluded lake areas to sunbathe unencumbered. His acquaintances were shocked at his confessions of multiple murder and even more so by the macabre means by which he killed.

First born of five children, Cary was eldest brother to Steven Stayner, who in 1972 was kidnapped and held prisoner by a child molester for almost eight years. He escaped, bringing with him a five-year-old child who had also been abducted. Making national headlines, Steven became the hero, his notoriety pushing his sibling into obscurity. Disgusted by the book written about his brother and the made-for-TV movie, Cary's resentment grew.

At Merced High School, Cary was considered a good student and was thought of positively. But his home life was deteriorating with the separation of his parents. He moved in with his uncle, Jesse Stayner, until 1990, when tragedy struck and an intruder shot Jesse to death. Cary was never considered a suspect and was believed to have been at work. His employers considered him a diligent worker and a proven employee, always showing up on time and never the object of customer complaints.

Between 1996 and 1997, Cary moved to El Portal in Yosemite National Park, where he worked as a handyman at several hotels. Those who knew him described him as likeable, a loner who never dated and was not inclined to close friendships. Though he occasionally smoked marijuana, he was not disposed to drinking, even when generous tourists at the hotel offered to indulge everyone with a "round." But such benign behavior only masked the brooding predator within. Rarely does evil not masquerade. For many years, Cary Stayner had fantasized about killing women.

In the winter of 1999, Eureka, California, resident Carol Sund, 42, her daughter Julie Sund, 16, and an Argentine friend, Silvina Pelosso, 16, were visitors to Yosemite National Park in California. On February 14, they checked in at Cedar Lodge, where fit the special needs and fantasies of each killer. The signatures are also referred to as "calling cards" or "trademarks" and can be used by repeat violent offenders who are not serial killers. A serial rapist may demand the victim to beg for mercy or tell him how much she is enjoying his sexual attentions to her. This pattern is not part of the modus operandi and sets the case apart from other murder cases. The "method of operating" (or MO) is separate from motive and signature. MO includes techniques to commit the crimes that may evolve as the offender becomes more skillful and confident in his crimes. Signatures are actions of the serial offender usually unnecessary to completing the murders. There are exceptions, however, as in the case of Cary Stayner, who enjoyed decapitating his female victims. Such signatures, or *paraphilic footprints*, are extensions of paraphilic fantasies and can facilitate the offender in actualizing his fantasies (see Profile 5.19).

Stayner worked and lived. They were last seen alive February 15. One month later, Carol and Silvina's charred bodies were found in the trunk of their burned-out rental car. On March 25, Julie's decomposed body was found several miles away. Her throat was cut so severely she was almost decapitated. Stayner was not considered a suspect. Almost five months later, after she was reported missing by her friends, Yosemite naturalist Joie Armstrong's body was found in a creek near her home. She was decapitated. A similar vehicle to Stayner's had been seen in the vicinity of Armstrong's home. Three hours after the body was found, Stayner told authorities he had nothing to do with her death. When he didn't show up for work the next day, authorities began searching for him and found him at a nudist colony in Wilton. He has confessed to all four slayings. The FBI had originally arrested other suspects and kept reassuring the public they had the right people in custody, only to suddenly retract those statements when Stayner gave them specific incriminating information that was privy only to law enforcement officials. Stayner has since pled guilty to the Joie Armstrong murder. He was convicted for the other murders and given the death penalty.

One of the most important clues linking these murders was the manner in which the victims died. Decapitation or nearly severing a person's head is not just about murder but is also about sexual fantasy and gratification. The offender becomes sexually gratified by the fantasy of cutting into a victim's throat. The sense of sexual power overwhelms the offender. Stayner had been fantasizing and drawing his fantasies of decapitation for several years. The method of killing became his sexual signature that could link him to other similar murders. While awaiting trial at the Fresno County Jail, Stayner enjoyed drawing pictures on the walls of his cell of decapitated heads of females. He also tried and failed to sell autographed photos of himself to the public. In one of his public statements he said, "I would like to say how deeply sorry I am for all the pain and sorrow I've brought upon so many people. Not only the Sunds, Pellossos [sic], Carringtons and the Armstrongs, but my fellow employees at Cedar Lodge, the community of El Portal, the people of Argentina, and all those across the nation who felt the sorrow of my victims' families. I am truly sorry." He then requested that a movie be made about his murders and sought an interview with NBC's Jane Pauley.

Sometimes postmortem mutilation becomes the signature of a particular killer. Others collect souvenirs such as body parts, pieces of clothing, or newspaper clippings. Harvey Glatman liked to abduct women and take photographs of them before and after the sexual assaults and murders. Dr. Robert D. Keppel, an expert in serial-murder cases, explains the significance of Glatman's desire to take photographs as his personal signature for murder:

> His photos were more than souvenirs, because in Glatman's mind, they actually carried the power of his need for bondage and control. They showed the women in various poses: sitting up or lying down, hands always bound behind their backs, innocent looks on their faces, but with eyes wide with terror because they had guessed what was to come. (p. 37)

Another offender liked to remove the eyeballs from his victims. One killer cannibalized the sexual organs of his young victims, whereas still another skinned his victims and made lampshades, eating utensils, and clothing. Bronswick (2001, pp. 85–89), a former psychotherapist for death row inmates, provides the following list of signature behaviors frequently found in serial-murder investigations:

- Aberrant sex
- Attacks at the face
- Body disposal
- Cannibalism
- Decapitation
- Dismemberment
- Mutilation
- Necrophilia
- Penile/object penetration
- Picquerism (sexual arousal from repeated stabbing of a victim)
- Restraints
- Souvenirs (photos, clothing, jewelry, newspaper clippings)
- Torture
- Trophies (victim body parts used for sexual arousal)
- Weapons

Signatures are helpful in profiling criminal behaviors and can link offenders to crimes. Signatures also can help determine the level of progression and sophistication of the predator. This usually means that a first-time offender will not demonstrate the savoir-faire found among veteran predators. A predator will sometimes change his MO in order to elude police, but it is far more difficult for him to alter his signature because it is fantasy based.

Healthcare Killers

LEARNING OBJECTIVES

- To understand the role of healthcare providers in committing serial murder
- To explore serial murder in the healthcare industry from a global perspective
- To examine the types of offenders in the healthcare professions who use their occupations to access and murder victims
- To explore gender within healthcare as a factor in offending and victim selection
- To examine cases of healthcare-related serial murder and factors facilitating those deaths

With some regularity we hear of persons who provide care in nursing homes and hospitals sexually exploiting their hapless victims. John Riems (see Profile 6.1) is a typical sexual predator who seeks out nursing homes to prey on defenseless victims. In another case Wayne Bleyle, 54, a respiratory therapist, worked in a convalescent center for children for over 25 years. There he selected the most brain damaged, sexually assaulted them, and took pornographic pictures that he placed on the Internet. When asked in a 2006 interview to identify the number of children that he had assaulted, he responded, "How many snowflakes are out there?" We seldom hear, however, of nurses and doctors killing their patients. When such cases occur we often associate such deaths with authentic euthanasia, where a medical provider is trying to ease the suffering of a patient and believes that letting him or her die or assisting him or her in dying is demonstrating mercy for the patient (which is still a crime in most states).

Every year in the United States approximately 80,000 persons die in hospitals unrelated to the reasons for which they entered hospital care. Some may succumb to one of many bacterial infections found in healthcare centers. Sponges and scissors are left inside patients after surgeries, incorrect dosages of medications are administered, or patients receive medications meant for another patient.

PROFILE 6.1 John Riems, Sexual Predator, 1985–2008

Riems, 49, began his career as a licensed nurse in 1985 and worked in at least 10 nursing homes in Ohio, where he sexually abused and assaulted over 100 patients. Arrested in 2008 for raping a partially paralyzed 55-year-old male resident at the Concord Care and Rehabilitation Home, Riems confessed to dozens of sexual attacks on elderly and infirm patients. He was known as a very reclusive individual who seldom spoke to his neighbors. He and his wife would leave Christmas cards on the neighbor's car windshield but avoid direct contact. His coworkers knew him as a man with a quick temper who sometimes threw medical charts and slammed his fist on counters or walls when summoned by patients for assistance. Patients were known to refuse medications because of their aversion to Riems, who often spent an hour or more alone with them. When asked by coworkers why he spent so much time with certain patients, he informed them that it was none of their business. Many complaints had been submitted by staff, but nothing was ever done to discipline Riems, not even a letter placed in his personnel file. Some patients refused their meds just to keep him out of their rooms. Others would insist to other staff that he was never to touch them again. Riems was tried for 15 counts of rape, sexual battery, and felonious sexual penetration, among other charges, of elderly male patients.

Sometimes charts are misread or misplaced, resulting in a healthy limb being amputated or the wrong patient being operated on because patient charts were mishandled. Indeed, persons under medical care of doctors, nurses, and other practitioners can easily become victims due to negligence, incompetence, or intentional malfeasance. This chapter examines cases where persons, including doctors, nurses, orderlies, nursing assistants, and certified home health workers, have murdered unsuspecting victims.

FOREIGN HEALTHCARE PROVIDERS WHO KILL

Worldwide there have been several notable cases of healthcare providers killing their patients. In some cases the skill and deception of the killer was sufficient to allow the murders to go on for many years. Such was the case of Harold Shipman, a quiet but deliberate man. Dr. Shipman (see Profile 6.2) was a British medical doctor who is now considered to be the most prolific documented serial killer ever in all of Europe. Note the victims he killed, his methods, his motivations, and his general characteristics, which all helped him elude typical criminal profiles.

Consider also that in some societies serial murder may have strong political or economic overtones that little resemble anything in our criminal profiles and yet are distinct characteristics of serial-murder cases. When social climates exist that promote the taking of life, persons who may never have killed otherwise find themselves embracing behaviors contrary to the very notion of civil life. How do professionals go from normal, civil life to the torture and destruction of children? Consider Dr. Heinrich Gross (see Profile 6.3), known as Dr. Vomit to many of his young patients. Did the German government convince him that he was needed for such a cause, or was it already in his nature to do so?

Such horrific cases of doctors and nurses who kill their vulnerable patients have drawn attention of researchers interested in understanding the phenomenon, its incidence and prevalence. Two of the most scholarly and reliable studies were done by Beatrice Yorker et al. (2006) and John Fields (2007).

THE YORKER AND FIELDS STUDIES

Yorker et al. (2006) examined 90 cases of serial murder from a global perspective in their article "Serial Murder by Healthcare Professionals." They, and other researchers, identify some common facts in serial murder of patients by healthcare providers such as an investigation often begins when a cluster of cardiopulmonary arrests and/or death occurs in a particular patient population. In some cases, suspicions are aroused because patients suffer multiple cardiopulmonary arrests and the resuscitation rate is unusually high. The typical scenario in the cases in the literature involves presence of a common injectable substance in post mortem, or postevent toxicology screens, deaths that cluster on the evening night shift, and the epidemiologic studies linking presence of a specific care provider to increased likelihood of death. (Yorker, 2006; Forrest, 1995; Beine, 2003; Stark, 1994, 1997)

One of the most important contributions of the Yorker et al. (2006) survey is their attention to defining their subjects so as not to confound their variables. They differentiated between authentic euthanasia and cases that were made to appear to be mercy killings yet the care provider was found to have ulterior motives. They excluded cases of extraordinary circumstances such as Hurricane Katrina, instances of assisted suicide, single murders of patients, murder outside the healthcare setting, and murders committed by healthcare providers outside the caregiver/patient relationship such as date rape and domestic violence. Half of these 90 worldwide cases were convicted of serial murder, with 24 more being indicted for serial murder, 4 convicted of attempted murder, 5 pled guilty to lesser charges, and another 8 were charged with serial murder but there was insufficient evidence to convict.

They found that 86% of their cases involved nursing personnel and that women were involved in 55% of the cases prosecuted. They also found that the majority of murders occurred in hospital settings and that victims were most likely to be critically ill, very young, very old, or with apparent vulnerabilities. Injections were the most common way to kill, but it was not uncommon for multiple methods to be employed. In the United States licensed nurses who used injections administered medications such as insulin, epinephrine, or potassium chloride into intravenous lines. Nurses in Europe were more likely to use morphine. Nurse's aides were more likely to suffocate, use poisons, or administer

PROFILE 6.2 Dr. Harold F. Shipman, "The Jekyll of Hyde," 1976–1998

Harold Frederick Shipman came from a blue-collar background. His father was a lorry driver, and the family lived in a small house in Nottingham. At 17 his mother passed away from cancer. Harold had been very close to his mother and often watched while doctors would inject her with morphine to ease her suffering. One day, while sitting in her armchair, she died. Harold developed an interest in medicine and eventually graduated in 1970 from Leeds University. Along the course of studies he also became addicted to pethidine, an opiate, and wrote illegal prescriptions for himself. He was caught and was removed from his position. In 1977 he returned to work in a Hyde medical practice, telling the agency that he was rehabilitated from his addiction. After 15 years of employment he left and began his own family practice, a one-doctor show. He was what one expects in a good doctor: caring, concerned, competent, and available. His popularity gained him over 3,000 patients. He worked alone and without regulation. No one was there to notice that Shipman's death rates and prescription rates were extremely high. During the course of his 24-year career, Dr. Death, as the media refers to him, killed regularly using the painkiller diamorphine, better known as heroin. His patients were all females between the ages of 49 and 81. Most were over 65. He would visit them and treat his patients as if he were an old friend. He often patted their hands as he injected them with large doses of heroin, telling them that their pain would soon be over. Many of his victims were left sitting in their armchairs while Dr. Death went back to his office to falsify their death certificates. During the latter part of his career over half of his patients died within an hour of his home visit. In the end he signed the financial assets of a wealthy victim over to himself and was caught when the daughter, an attorney, examined her mother's estate. Dr. Shipman denied everything but was convicted in January 1999 of murdering 15 women. He is linked to 23 other deaths and is believed to have killed between 200 and 300. One of the problems faced by investigators was that several victims had been cremated, making death certification impossible. Dr. Shipman was housed in England's highest-security-level prison in Durham, in northern England, until his suicide in 2004.

What about motivation? Was Dr. Shipman merely trying to ease the suffering of the elderly as doctors had done for his own mother? Did he simply get a bit greedy

oral medications. The research also found that healthcare providers who kill their patients are often diagnosed with Munchausen syndrome. Several offenders had injected themselves to draw attention or gave falsified reports of being sexually assaulted or threats of bodily harm to themselves prior to murdering their patients. Others, the survey revealed, were sadistic and enjoyed the power over life and death, while a few financially profited from the murders.

Fields (2007), in his rigorous and most insightful doctoral research *Caring to Death: A Discursive Analysis of Nurses Who Murder Patients*, noted the value of qualitative examination in studying social phenomena: "This discursive study is the very beginnings of a rambling (discursive) journey to surface the meanings surrounding nurses who murder their patients, all the while recognizing that the bodies of text constitute sets of beliefs that are and never will become fixed ideas." His scholarly examination of nurses who kill provides a foundation upon which to enhance discourse surrounding the phenomenon of healthcare providers when he had the opportunity to cash in on a wealthy victim? There is little evidence to indicate that he was killing for money, except his last victim. One plausible explanation is that Dr. Shipman enjoyed the control and being able to play God. He enjoyed controlling when a person would die and how they were to die. He is not the first British doctor to feed poison to his victims and then leave while they died. In the United States, Donald Harvey, a hospital orderly, also killed dozens of patients for no material gain. What then would drive a doctor, who vows to care for the ill, to kill patients methodically? Certainly the issue of control must be considered as part of the puzzle, but there is more. Consider the possibility of abandonment. Harold was his mother's favorite child. He knew that she was dying and knew that she could go at any time. There was absolutely nothing he could do to alter that inevitability. When she was gone, Harold, now Dr. Shipman, knew that no one he cared for would ever leave him again without his permission. By killing his female patients he controlled the when and how, two issues that he had no control over when his mother died. Remember that several died just as his mother did, sitting in their armchairs. None of them suffered from the injection, just like his mother, because he used large doses of heroin. He never had to wonder when one of his female patients might suddenly die, because he was in control, always.

Another issue centers on the fact that Dr. Shipman did not fit typical serial-killer profiles. As one investigator said, "He is the dullest serial killer I have ever met." He was not sealing up his victims in the walls of his home, taking body parts as souvenirs, nor was he a necrophile or some psychotic killer using a hammer and screwdriver to dispatch his victims as Britain had seen in other serial-murder cases. He was benign in appearance and affable in demeanor, although this did belie pervasive narcissism. He certainly did not fit general operational profiles created by the FBI. His killings were dutiful, regular, and methodical. These are the trademarks of place-specific killers. Those who work in the healthcare industry seldom are lust killers. Their motivations may systemically have similar origins, but how those motivations are expressed are a result of various filters including gender (many place-specific killers are female), age, intelligence, employment, location, and so on.

who murder patients. In short, the Yorker et al. and Fields research are tangible building blocks in understanding the etiological, social, and psychological implications of persons who murder in the medical profession and healthcare delivery.

This 2009 study also provides analysis to further the discourse on those who commit medical murders. This research focuses on American healthcare providers who murder patients. Building upon the Yorker (2006) and Fields (2007) research, I included healthcare providers for the analysis if they had been charged with killing or attempting to kill patients in the United States. This framework included multiple homicide offenders, persons with only one victim, and those suspected of murder. Authentic euthanasia cases were not included in this research, nor was the controversial case of Dr. Kervorkian. Each offender had to be engaged in some aspect of providing care for patients (see Table 6.1).

PROFILE 6.3 Dr. Heinrich Gross, Am Spiegelgrund Klinik, Lebensunwertes Leben, 1940–1945

The Steinhof psychiatric hospital in Vienna, Austria, more commonly referred to as Spiegelgrund hospital, was one of 31 centers established by the Nazis for euthanasia. Unlike the death camps designed by Hitler for his Final Solution, these centers were primarily for Germans considered disabled or defective. German children who were considered physically or mentally defective were sent to these hospitals under the guise of rehabilitation. During the time of operation of these centers, approximately 200,000 Germans, including 6,000 children, were euthanized. The death toll of children at Spiegelgrund was estimated at over 1,000, making it one of the top killing hospitals. The Third Reich viewed these children as an insult to the Aryan race because they possessed defective genes and were "useless eaters." The children, referred to as *Lebensunwertes Leben,* or "life unworthy of life," were housed in one of four pavilions, depending on whether they were deaf, blind, retarded, or disabled. Most of the children were in pavilion 15, where the majority of deaths occurred. Antisocial children were housed in pavilion 18 and the mentally disturbed in pavilion 17. Most of the wartime staff were Nazi party members who enthusiastically supported the concept of a pure race. Parents, encouraged by the Third Reich, brought their children to Spiegelgrund believing they would receive special care for their offspring. The hospital was peaceful and well kept and had a staff who offered assurances that the children would be well cared for by qualified doctors. The care they received was monstrous.

Staff selected children with harelips, children with eyes too far apart, or children who stuttered. Lethal injections or sleeping pills quickly euthanized selected children. Others were not so fortunate and were starved to death or placed outdoors to freeze as part of the experiments in testing human endurance. Some children, including babies, were dipped in ice water and then placed on balconies completely naked in the middle of winter. The children were timed to see how long before pneumonia developed and killed the child. Still others died from beatings or disease. Children who were considered antisocial were beaten into submission until they willingly conformed to the Nazi's scheme, or they were euthanized. There were daily torturings and denunciations of children by staff. The children, many of whom were seven to eight years of age, were starved and regularly told how useless they were to their country. They were beaten and had their heads placed in toilets.

One doctor is well remembered by survivors of Spiegelgrund. Dr. Heinrich Gross, whom the children referred to as Doktor Speiberl or Doctor Vomit, was known for his administrations of poisons. He was also known as Dr. Scythe because he wore polished boots and a Nazi colonel's uniform while he selected children to be euthanized. After the war some of the staff were hanged or given prison sentences for their part in euthanizing the children. Dr. Gross managed to avoid punishment and was even awarded prestigious honors for his research into the minds of defective children. Gross's interest in hereditary biology made him perfect for working at Spiegelgrund, where he had access to the brains of hundreds of children. He became an expert on the pathology of mental illness and, after the war, lectured and became an expert court witness in thousands of criminal cases. He was one of the highest-paid forensic experts in all of Austria. Dr. Gross's downfall was the discovery of hundreds of jars of formaldehyde containing the brains of children whom Dr. Gross used for his experiments. He had kept the jars hidden in a vault at the same hospital where the children were euthanized. Dr. Gross had also taken photographs of the children he treated. Of the 772 children known to have died in the clinic, Dr. Gross signed the death certificates of 238. Investigators found, through examination of the brains, that Luminal, a powerful sleep-inducing drug, had been administered to many of the children. The death certificates signed by Dr. Gross listed pneumonia as the cause of death. Even with such compelling evidence Dr. Gross eluded conviction (Silvers and Hagler, 1997). In 2000, at age 84 and while standing trial for Nazi war crimes, the judge declared Gross unfit to stand trial due to the onset of dementia.

TABLE 6.1 American Healthcare Providers Charged with Killing or Attempting to Kill Patients, 1970–2004 (n = 41)

Name	State	Work	Place	Years	Charge	Sentence
Joseph M. Swango	Mult.	Physician	Hospital	1970–2000	Murder	2 Life
*Filipina Narciso	MI	Nurse	Hospital	1975	Murder/Assault	Set Aside
*Leonora Perez	MI	Nurse	Hospital	1975	Murder/Assault	Set Aside
Mary Robaczynski	MD	Nurse	Hospital	1977–78	Pulled Plugs	Surrendered License
Genene Jones	TX	Nurse	Hospital	1981–84	Murder/Attempt	159 yrs.
David Richard Diaz	CA	Nurse	Hospital	1981	Murder	Death Penalty
Bobbie Sue Terrell	Mult.	Nurse	Nursing Home	1984–85	Murder	65 yrs.
Hal S. Rachman	CA	Nurse	Hospital	1986	Murder/Attempt	9 yrs.
Otha H. Hart	OR	Nurse	Hospital	1984	Murder	80 yrs.
Randy Powers	CA	Aide	Hospital	1984	Murder	Prison
Terri Rachals	GA	Nurse	Hospital	1985–86	Murder/Assault	Served 17 yrs.
*Gwen G. Graham	MI	Aide	Nursing Home	1986–88	Murder	Life
*Catherine M. Wood	MI	Aide	Nursing Home	1986–88	Murder	Life
Donald Harvey	OH	Aide	Hospital	1987	Murder	3 Life
Richard Angelo	NY	Nurse	Hospital	1987–89	Murder/Attempt	50 yrs.
Charles Cullen	PA	Nurse	Hospital	1987–2003	Murder/Attempt	11 Life
Michael Beckelic	AL	Med. Tech.	AFB	1988	Suspect/Attempt	Civil
Efren Saldivar	CA	Resp. Therapist	Hospital	1989, 1998	Murder/Attempt	6 Life+15
Milos Klvana	CA	Physician	Hospital	1989	Murder	53 yrs.
Jeffrey Feltner	FL	Aide	Nursing Home	1990	Murder	Life
Brian K. Rosenfeld	FL	Nurse	Nursing Home	1991–92	Murder	Life

(continued)

TABLE 6.1 Continued

Name	State	Work	Place	Years	Charge	Sentence
Joseph Dewey Akin	AL	Nurse	Hospital	1992–97	Murder/Attempt	Life
Richard Williams	MO	Nurse	Hospital	1992–2003	Murder—10 Counts	Charges Dropped
Orville L. Majors	IN	Nurse	Hospital	1993–99	Murder	Life
Aleata Beach	OK	Nurse	Hospital	1994	Murder	Surrendered License
Kristen Gilbert	NY	Nurse	Hospital	1995–96	Murder/Attempt	2 Life
Robert A. Weitzel	TX	Psychiatrist	Hospital	1995–96	Murder	15 yrs.—Overturned
Susan Hey	TX	Nurse	Hospital	1997	Murder	50 yrs. × 2
Michael Coons	OR	Nurse	Nursing Home	1998	Murder	Psy. Ill—Not Indicted
Cheryl May	IN	Nurse	Nursing Home	1999	Reckless Homicide	Prison
Jeanine H. Miata	TX	Aide	Home Care	2000–05	Murder/Injury	99 yrs.
Vickie D. Jackson	TX	Voc. Nurse	Hospital	2000–01	Murder	Life
Rhea R. Henson	VA	Nurse	Hospital	2000	Murder	2 yrs. & License Surrendered
James Mullins	FL	Nurse	Hospital	2000	Invol. Homicide	Prison
Heide Tenzer	PA	Aide	Nursing Home	2000	3rd Homicide	30 yrs.
John W. Bardgett	NH	Nurse	Nursing Home	2001–03	Manslaughter	Prison
Peggy S. Couse	IN	Nurse	Nursing Home	2002–04	Attempt Murder	20 yrs.
Coleen Thompson	MD	Nurse	Hospital	2003	Criminal Neglect	Prison and Fine
*Shermike Rainey	AK	Aide	Nursing Home	2003	Murder	30 yrs.
*Gayla Ann Wilson	AK	Aide	Nursing Home	2003	Murder	Life
Christine Ackley	CO	HC Nurse	Home Care	2004	Murder	Life+36 yrs.

*Team killers.

SOURCE: © Cengage Learning, 2013.

Compared to cases of non-healthcare serial murder, those healthcare providers who engage in murdering patients are quite rare. Over the 35-year period in this survey, approximately 10% appeared in the 1970s, 34% during the 1980s, 10% in the 1990s, and 27% between 2000 and 2004. In addition to the 32 American cases identified in the Yorker (2006) study, another 9 healthcare workers who fit definitional parameters were included in this 2009 survey. Of the 41 (38 cases) American healthcare providers identified, three conspired or were suspected of conspiring with another healthcare provider to kill patients. In terms of gender, 46% (19 offenders) were male, 54% female. Most of these offenders were nurses (66%) or nurse's aides (22%), and 12% were either medical doctors or other licensed medical care providers. Similar to non-healthcare providers these offenders came from a variety of states, the largest number appearing in heavily populated California, Texas, Michigan, and Florida. Nearly 60% of the cases occurred in hospitals, followed by 27% in nursing homes, accounting for 93% of all offenders in this survey. Over 85% of these offenders were charged, convicted, or suspected of killing multiple victims, while 15% were caught after killing their first victim. Prosecuting these healthcare providers is costly and embarrassing for the hospital or nursing home. In some cases proving the culpability of those charged is no easy task. Of those convicted 21 (51%) received life sentences or enough years (50+) that in effect they were life sentences. Approximately 17% received a specific number of years but less than 50. Almost 20% had a variety of outcomes, including four offenders having their sentences set aside or having the charges dropped.

CARE PROVIDERS AND SERIAL MURDER

No longer can we exclude healthcare providers who kill their patients from being classified as serial killers. Indeed, as we have seen thus far, serial killers come from a variety of backgrounds, kill a variety of victims, and kill in a variety of ways. The "angels of death" who work in hospitals and kill patients, or nursing home staff who kill the elderly, or the "black widows" who kill their family and relatives, also meet the general criteria for serial killing except for the stereotypic element of violence. These men and women do not slash and torture their victims nor generally do they sexually attack them; they are the quiet killers. They are also the kinds of people who could be married, hold steady jobs, or simply be the nice man or woman who lives next door. They are rare among serial killers, just as serial murders are rare compared with other types of homicide.

MALE "ANGELS OF DEATH"

One area that geographic profiling is not designed to address is murder I have described as *place-specific.* These are the stay-at-home or at-work killers who have no dumpsites for bodies. Surprisingly, nearly half are male offenders. In

New Jersey in 2003, nurse Charles Cullen confessed to the murders of at least 40 patients in nine different hospitals spanning a period of 16 years. Using the heart medication digoxin, Cullen claimed he was simply acting as an "angel of mercy" to suffering patients. Dr. Harold Shipman (see Profile 6.2), whose victims died in their homes, fit no particular geographic pattern. Donald Harvey (see Profile 6.5), another "angel of death," killed primarily in hospitals, again leaving no geographic pattern. Unfortunately, even utilizing psychological profiling fails to identify these types of serial killers until the body counts are often very high (see Profile 6.4).

As discussed earlier, there does appear to be an increase in the number of people being killed in nursing homes and hospitals. Sophisticated drugs such as digoxin, Pavulon, and potassium chloride are either difficult to detect or the procedures for testing for such drugs are not well established or too costly to check for routinely. At the Toronto Hospital for Sick Children in Ontario, Canada, dozens of infants were believed to have been killed with overdoses of the heart drug digoxin between 1980 and 1981. Authorities were never told until it was too late. By then evidence had been discarded, exhibits misplaced, bodies cremated, and files "cleaned up." One nurse, arrested for the crimes, was released because of lack of evidence. To date that case has yet to be resolved. Murders are increasing in nursing homes and hospitals because of the following reasons:

1. Victims are accessible and vulnerable.
2. An offender can easily operate without detection because no one expects such crimes would or could ever occur in such a setting.
3. An offender has access to a variety of murder weapons that are then easily disposed of without detection.

PROFILE 6.4 Efren Saldivar, "Angel of Death," 1988–1998

In 1998 Efren Saldivar, 28, a respiratory therapist for nine years at Glendale Adventist Medical Center in California, confessed to killing dozens of terminally ill patients over a 10-year period. He claimed to be an "angel of death" who had killed as many as 200 victims from several hospitals where he had worked part-time. Because there was no independent corroborating evidence police released Saldivar, who later recanted his confession, stating that he was depressed and wanted to be executed. An investigation continued into the possibility that Saldivar was telling the truth, but it was not until three years after his confession that he was arrested and charged with six murders. Saldivar admitted injecting fatal doses of Pavulon, a muscle relaxant that suppresses natural breathing, and succinylcholine chloride, a drug that also stops natural breathing, into 40 to 50 victims. Later, investigators realized that Saldivar probably had murdered closer to 200. Typically in such cases, hospitals terminate employees who may have been suspicious, but seldom report the suspect. In the case of Saldivar, five respiratory therapists were fired in 1998 following an internal investigation.

4. Often autopsies are not performed when a death occurs under the care of an attending physician. People routinely die in hospitals, especially in critical care units. Consequently, there is rarely a need to be suspicious. Doctors can misdiagnose the actual cause of death. Congestive heart failure, for example, may be induced through a variety of causes.
5. Supervisors or administrators sometimes minimize reports that somebody is acting suspiciously or could be harming patients. Scandals of purported murders inevitably can adversely affect admission rates. Negative publicity, in the minds of some administrators, is to be avoided at all costs.
6. Finally, prosecuting those who are believed to be involved in the deaths of patients can be very difficult as a result of lost evidence, sensationalism, and legal procedures. For example, in August 1975, FBI agents were called to the Ann Arbor Veterans Hospital to investigate 50 breathing failures spanning a six-week period. On June 16, 1976, a Detroit grand jury indicted nurses Filipina Narciso and Leonora Perez with mass poisoning. In July 1977, the two women were found guilty of injecting five patients with Pavulon, a drug that freezes the muscles necessary for breathing. A federal judge granted the pair another trial, citing misconduct by federal prosecutors that had denied the women a fair trial. Federal prosecutors then dropped the charges. (Wilcox, 1977)

Investigators need to realize that, with an aging population, the elderly are extremely vulnerable to serial murderers. Although other crimes against the elderly and other people requiring healthcare have remained fairly constant over the past 25 years, there has been a significant increase in serial murders involving the elderly.

Certainly these offenders who kill in hospitals and nursing homes do not fit the stereotype of the typical lust murderers who stalk and viciously attack young women, nor are they usually killing for profit. They are the quiet killers who go about dutifully performing their assigned tasks and, when the urge or opportunity arises, silently and dispassionately take the life of some unsuspecting, trusting patient. These offenders are usually not "Jack the Ripper" types nor do they attract media attention as do traveling serial killers. Instead, these are murders by people who enjoy, at some psychological level, the power of controlling life and death. Such people are difficult to identify because they can be so friendly and outwardly compassionate. Unlike typical serial killers, place-specific murderers, especially those providing care for the elderly and infirm, have access to potentially lethal weapons (medications) as part of their work routine. Hospital personnel in general are ill prepared to cope with their suspicions and the consequences of homicides. Sometimes, as in the case of Donald Harvey (see Profile 6.5) or Jane Toppan, the offender is simply asked to resign when suspicions surface, and the police are not involved.

In turn, such offenders inevitably find other hospitals or nursing homes in which to work and kill again. Hospital workers are in demand, especially anyone with some skills or experience. References are seldom checked, and even then

PROFILE 6.5 Donald Harvey, 1970–1987

Donald Harvey, "The Angel of Death," started killing when he turned 18 and began working as a nurse's aide at Mary Mount Hospital in Laurel County, Kentucky. He first killed an aunt, then committed what he referred to as "accidental homicides," followed by 10 more patient deaths—a total of 13 dead in 10 months. Some were suffocated, others had their oxygen supply shut off, and one victim died when Harvey shoved a wire coat hanger up his catheter tube, tearing his bladder.

Harvey then joined the Air Force, where he attempted suicide on two occasions. Unable to cope, he was discharged after only nine months of service, but he continued to receive psychiatric care. In 1975 he joined the nursing staff at the Veterans Administration Hospital in Cincinnati, Ohio. During a two-year period he is believed to have murdered another 17 patients. His remaining eight years at the hospital were spent working as an autopsy assistant in the morgue. Being exposed to death and corpses seemed to satisfy Harvey, and apparently he killed no one during this time. In 1985 he was asked to resign when a gun, books on the occult, syringes, and slides of human tissue were discovered in his hospital locker.

He then joined the staff at Drake Hospital, also in Cincinnati, without anyone ever checking his references. Most of the patients at Drake were the elderly and the terminally ill. Using cyanide, arsenic, and sometimes injections of cleaning fluids, Harvey was able to kill at least 21 victims in a two-year period. When he had no poison for their food or IVs, Harvey suffocated his victims. Harvey later referred to his actions as mercy killings. He had become the angel of death and held the power over who would live and who must die. He finally confessed when investigators discovered large amounts of cyanide in the stomach of a victim. This final victim brought Harvey's total number of homicides to between 54 and 58. Almost all of his victims were male; among his possessions police discovered a list of victims yet to be killed by Harvey. One of his female coworkers had serum hepatitis poured into her coffee by Harvey but miraculously survived her ordeal. Harvey also slowly poisoned his roommate, only to nurse him back to health.

During his confession, Harvey explained that during a 13-year period, starting when he was five years old, he had been subjected to sexual molestation by an uncle and a male neighbor. He did not believe that this frequent molestation had anything to do with the fact that almost all his victims were helpless males, older than himself; nor did he feel it had anything to do with the fact that he was a homosexual. He claimed to be a compassionate, caring person, which seemed to be validated by his fellow workers. They found Harvey to be dedicated, polite, and a good colleague. The courts found Harvey to be sane under law and competent to stand trial.

Harvey gave his confession only after being allowed to plea-bargain and thereby escape the death penalty. Dozens of bodies were exhumed, and the victims were found to have died as Harvey described. Never showing remorse or guilt, Harvey received three consecutive life sentences and will not be eligible for parole until he has served at least 60 years. He was also fined $270,000 and received a life sentence for the murders in Kentucky. After several years in prison Harvey has changed his mind about what influenced him to kill. He now states that the sexual abuse he experienced as a child was indeed a major contributing factor fueling his urges.

there generally is no formal documentation of the reasons for which a person left his or her previous employment. In the future, more attention will be needed in exploring these types of offenders if we are going to develop effective tools for profiling and apprehension.

FEMALE CARE PROVIDERS WHO KILL

Consider the case of Kristen Gilbert (see Profile 6.6). Given this information, does Gilbert fit any type of female serial-killer profile? Could the prosecution simply be overreacting to a coincidence? What psychological factors exist to support or contest the prosecution's charges? What questions should be asked about this case in order to develop a more complete picture?

We are now more likely to hear of killers, especially nurses and other healthcare providers, using potassium chloride, which is difficult to detect once the body has been prepared for burial (see Profile 6.7). Succinylcholine, another relatively undetectable drug, is used as an anesthetic to relax muscles during surgery. An excessive dose inhibits the chest muscles from functioning, and the victim simply stops breathing (Helpern and Knight, 1977, p. 26). This drug was used by Genene Jones (see Profile 6.8).

Serial killers usually seek out those less powerful than themselves. The healthcare industry is by and large populated with people who really do care for their patients. Indeed, there are regular cases of abuse, but cases of murder are quite rare. The offenders will need to be studied more closely to better understand their motivations and possible warning signs of their murderous intentions.

PROFILE 6.6 Kristen Gilbert, 2000

Charged with the murders of four patients at a Veterans Affairs Medical Center in Setauket, New York, nurse Kristen Gilbert, 33, may be yet another example of how women who kill serially target their victims. Her prosecutors say that she liked the thrill of medical emergencies and wanted to impress her boyfriend. She is believed to have injected her patients with large doses of adrenaline, causing their hearts to beat rapidly and uncontrollably. The defense argues that the patients all suffered from serious illnesses, which ultimately caused their deaths. They insist that Gilbert's coworkers turned her in because they sided with Gilbert's husband when the couple divorced. The prosecution argues that she initiated medical emergencies so that she could respond and receive attention from her coworkers and boyfriend, who worked as a security guard at the hospital. They noted that each victim had a healthy heart on entering the hospital intensive care unit where Gilbert worked, and each died following a visit from the defendant. For so many patients with healthy hearts to suddenly die for no apparent reason so close together in the same unit was believed by the prosecution to be practically impossible. The prosecution compared it to the probability of lightning striking the same location many times. Gilbert is also accused of trying to kill three other patients. The prosecution also alleges that Gilbert falsified medical reports and confessed to the murders, saying, "I did it! I did it! You want to know? I killed all those guys by injection," to her boyfriend and ex-husband.

PROFILE 6.7 Terri Rachals, 1985–1986

In March 1986, registered nurse Terri Rachals was indicted on six counts of murder and twenty counts of aggravated assault stemming from alleged poisonings of patients at Phoebe Putney Hospital in Albany, Georgia. The grand jury accused 24-year-old Rachals of injecting 11 patients in the hospital's surgical intensive care unit with potassium chloride, causing the deaths of six of them. (Potassium chloride is a colorless chemical used in small, diluted amounts in the treatment of nearly all surgery patients. It is used in large doses by states that perform executions by injection.) Her alleged victims ranged in age from 3 to 89 years, including both males and females. All died between October 17, 1985, and February 11, 1986. The 20 incidents of aggravated assault involved nine patients (many of them received more than one injection). Most of the patients injected by Rachals did not die because they were able to receive immediate attention.

Nine patients died of cardiac arrest in November 1985; the usual number was three to four deaths per month. The potassium levels in the bodies of several of the victims were found to be abnormally high. An investigation concluded that the only way the high potassium content in the IV line could be accounted for was through human intervention.

Nurse Rachals had worked at the hospital since 1981 and was described as an excellent, reliable surgical intensive care nurse. There had never been any serious problems with Rachals at the hospital nor did she have any police record. Very active in her church, she sang in the choir and regularly attended Sunday school with her husband, Roger, who suffered from cerebral palsy and was a printer at an Albany supply company. The couple resided with their two-year-old son, Chad, in a middle-class suburban Albany neighborhood. Neighbors refused to believe she could be capable of such atrocious acts. "If you believe your mother could do it, then you'd believe that she could do it. She's not a murderer. That's the craziest thing I've ever heard," stated one neighbor. Another friend said that "Ms. Rachals would be the last person one would suspect of harming anyone. They were just so nice, so average."

One month after the last victim died, Rachals confessed to the Georgia Bureau of Investigation that she had injected five of the patients, three of whom died. Later she recanted her confession, stating that she was confused at the time of her statement. Before her trial Rachals spent several months undergoing intensive psychiatric evaluation but was found competent to stand trial. The defense worked very hard to build its case around a woman who had been molested as a child by her adoptive father and subsequently experienced blackouts. The father denied the molestation charges. At age 16, after five years of his alleged sexual advances, Terri moved out. The defense stressed that there were periods when she could not account for her actions because she suffered from a mental illness that caused her to do unusual things she could not remember. She reacted to stressful events by entering fugue states in which she experienced personality changes and could not recall where she had been or what she had done, said Dr. Kuglar, the superintendent of the Georgia Regional Hospital in Augusta.

Dr. Omer L. Wagoner, a licensed psychologist appointed by the court to examine Rachals, agreed she suffered personality disorders but not a "dissociative order" and said he believed she "thoroughly knew the difference between right and wrong." Rachals, he stated, "believed she was relieving them (the patients) of their pain and misery" by causing their hearts to stop with potassium injections.

Because of the weight of circumstantial evidence and testimony that questioned Rachals's state of mind at the time of the killings, she was convicted of giving an 89-year-old patient a heart-stopping chemical. She was given 17 years for her conviction, but under the State of Georgia Board of Pardons and Parole guidelines, Rachals was eligible for parole after serving 24 months. Although she was found to be guilty and mentally ill, state psychiatrists decided she could be adequately served on an outpatient basis and was confined at the Women's Correctional Institution near Milledgeville, Georgia.

PROFILE 6.8 Genene Jones, 1978–1982

In February 1984, nurse Genene Jones was sentenced to a maximum term of 99 years for the murder of 15-month-old Chelsea McClellan. Testimony showed the little girl had died after injections of succinylcholine, a hard-to-detect drug that paralyzes. An expert witness stated at her trial that the drug has long been a favorite for killing because it is difficult to trace. Under Texas law, a 99-year term is equivalent to a life sentence. Jones will be eligible for parole in 2017.

Jones was also charged with using the drug to harm six other children at a physician's office where she had worked for three weeks. It is believed her motive was a need to prove there were enough sick children to justify construction of a pediatric intensive care unit in Kerrville, Texas. However, the scope of her criminal behavior also extended to a hospital in San Antonio, Texas, where she was charged with injuring at least one child. Investigators believe that as many as 46 babies and children were murdered at the San Antonio hospital during the time Jones worked there. It is believed that the children were given injections that stopped their hearts. A team of experts from the Centers for Disease Control in Atlanta, Georgia, found that seven children had been killed by a deliberate overdose of the heart drug digoxin. Digoxin was not ruled out in at least 21 other deaths. Jones was never tried for these homicides.

The Male Serial Murderer

LEARNING OBJECTIVES

- To understand the impact of male serial killers in American society
- To explore the "invisible" rise of African American serial killers, their behavioral characteristics, victims, and myths and facts surrounding these offenders
- To examine the role and types of stalking in predatory crimes that can lead to homicide and serial murder
- To evaluate the dark side of long-haul trucking and its contribution to the emergence of highway serial murderers
- To review several cases of male serial killers, their profiles, mobility, and techniques used to lure their victims
- To examine the latest research on male serial killers in the United States

Although not nearly as common as men who batter and kill their spouses, male serial killers in the United States appear with amazing regularity. They are found in local bars, working blue-collar jobs, or may be hitchhikers and transients. They are also men working in hospitals, independent business owners, and, most recently, predators "surfing the Net" hunting for just the right person. Between 2004 and 2011 several persons became homicide statistics to killers using the Internet and social media to attract victims. Victims of serial killers continue to be found throughout the United States. Some are found in boarding houses, homes for the elderly, hospitals, and private homes. Other victims will be found in wooded areas, ravines, and other isolated areas—victims of male serial killers. Usually these victims die much more violently than other homicide victims. In 1999, Gerald Parker, known as the "Bedroom Basher," was convicted of murdering five women and a full-term fetus in their homes. DNA evidence finally caught up with Parker. The personalized violence inflicted on helpless victims has no boundaries or limitations to which offenders subscribe.

For example, during 1990, a supposed male serial killer in San Diego, California, murdered at least five young women. One of the victims, a 20-year-old San Diego university student, was stabbed more than 50 times. That same year five students were stabbed to death in Gainesville, Florida, with a surgical instrument. One of the women was decapitated. Male serial killers wage personal wars against humanity, indifferent to the lives of others in their constant quest for control. Charles Starkweather, after his killing spree, casually observed, "shooting people was, I guess, a kind of a thrill. It brought out something" (Reinhardt, 1960, p. 78). Edmund Kemper, reminiscing about the start of his killing career, remarked, "I just wondered how it would be to shoot grandma."

Male serial killers represent the darkest, most sinister side of human existence, yet we are fascinated to read about them, to watch them portrayed in movies, and to learn of their obscenities. Drukteinis (1992) reminds us that serial murder is "at the extremes of conduct" defined in human interaction. These killers are especially dangerous because we understand so little about their actual motivations, their lives, and their personalities. Pollock (1995), in reviewing clinical and theoretical motivations for serial murder, concluded that most offenders exhibit malignant narcissism, an extreme form of narcissistic personality disorder manifesting as "pathologically grandiose, lacking in conscience and behavioral regulation with characteristic demonstrations of joyful cruelty and sadism." These summary descriptors of serial killers assist researchers in restructuring definitions of serial murder. From Cormier, Angliker, Boyer, and Mersereau's (1972) coining of the term *multicide* to Keeny and Heide's (1994, 1995) concise and logical redefining of serial murder as being premeditated, requiring three or more civilian victims over time, in separate cases, our understanding of this phenomenon has significantly accelerated. Our search for "commonality" helps us to create descriptive parameters and taxonomies, yet the horror generated by these offenders distorts their profiles, actual body counts, and inevitably our perception of them. In March 2000, Tommy Lynn Sells confessed to killing 13 people in seven different states. He killed men, women, children, and babies by using guns, knives, a bat, a shovel, an ice pick, and his bare hands. That same year Darrell Rich, a California serial killer, was executed for the brutal murders of four female victims. Most of his victims were young or teenage girls he sexually assaulted, then shot, beat to death, or crushed their skulls. His last victim, 11-year-old Annette Selix, was thrown off a train bridge. Contrast that form of rage serial killing to a person who quietly lived with the knowledge that 25 decomposing bodies lay under the floorboards of his house. Masters (1986) chronicled the life of Dennis Nilsen, a British serial killer and necrophile, and described how involved the murderer became with his victims after death. They were a source of company for him. In one instance, Nilsen stored the body of a young male under his floor and frequently would retrieve him for an evening's entertainment. This included propping the boy in a chair next to Nilsen, who carried on conversations with the corpse, bathing him, watching television "together," and performing sexual acts on the decomposing child.

Other serial killers have sex with their victims just before or immediately after death. Some are known for their habits of collecting trophies or souvenirs. For example, when the police arrived, Gary Heidnik was found to have several pounds of human flesh stored in his freezer while other body parts were simmering in a stew pot. Others have collected lingerie, shoes, hats, and other apparel. Some serial killers do not have any apparent sexual involvement with the victims, but their method of killing is so bizarre one can only speculate about their actual motivations. What we can say with absolute certainty about serial killers is that we cannot fit them into one single behavioral profile. The more we learn about them the more we realize that they have many ways of hunting and killing their victims. Some offenders want their victims to suffer horribly, while others want them to die quickly. Some offenders are necrophiles and others sadistic rapists, while others want to steal money from their victims. Only 7% have military or law enforcement experience (Castle, 2002). Some travel across the United States, while others kill all their victims in one place or in a localized area. Some prefer to kill with their hands, others with guns, some with ligatures, poisons, etc. Some are highly psychopathic and others rate relatively low on the scales of psychopathy and/or intelligence. A very small number (2%–4%) are legally insane. Some offenders may even be genetically predisposed to violent behavior, while others appear to be victims themselves of traumatic experiences. What we can safely acknowledge is that serial murderers are predatory and their disposition toward serial murder is developed through a learning process (Castle and Hensley, 2002). Indeed, we are learning more and more about the interactions of biological predispositions and nurturing styles. Does our society influence the development of serial killers by glorifying and sensationalizing them and their hideous crimes? Read on.

EMERGENCE OF MALE SERIAL MURDERERS

Intrigue and horror have generated several peculiar and chilling monikers for male killers since the mid-1800s. The following names (Table 7.1) are a sampling of monikers given to male offenders who acted alone.

TABLE 7.1 Monikers Given to Male Serial Killers in the United States

Year	Name	Monikers
1846–1871	Edward H. Rulloff	The Educated Murderer
1874–1909	James P. Miller	"Deacon" Jim
1879	Stephen Lee Richards	Nebraska Fiend
1890–1905	Johann Otto Hoch	Stockyard Bluebeard
1892–1896	Harry Howard Holmes	The Torture Doctor
1895	William H. T. Durrant	Demon of the Belfry

TABLE 7.1 Continued

Year	Name	Monikers
1910–1920	James P. Watson	Bluebeard
1910–1934	Albert Fish	The Cannibal
		The Moon Maniac
1911–1919	Joseph Mumfre	New Orleans Axeman
1921–1931	Harry Powers	American Bluebeard
	(aka Herman Drenth)	
1926–1927	Earle L. Nelson	The Gorilla Murderer
1933–1935	Major Raymond Lisemba	Rattlesnake Lisemba
1942–1947	Jake Bird	Tacoma Axe Killer
1945–1946	William George Heirens	The Lipstick Murderer
1949	Harvey Louis Carignan	The Want-Ad Killer
1957–1960	Melvin David Rees	Sex Beast
1958–1983	Richard F. Biegenwald	The Thrill Killer
1962–1964	Albert Henry DeSalvo	The Measuring Man
		The Green Man
		The Boston Strangler
1964–1965	Charles H. Schmid	Pied Piper of Tucson
1964–1973	Edmund Emil Kemper	Coed Killer
1965	Posteal Laskey	Cincinnati Strangler
1965	John Floyd Thomas	West Side Rapist
1967–1969	John N. Collins	Coed Murderer
1970	Richard Macek	The Mad Biter
1970–1987	Donald Harvey	Angel of Death
1970–1987	Jerry Marcus	Tuskegee Strangler
1970–2000	Tommy Lynn Sells	Coast to Coast
1972–1978	John Wayne Gacy	Killer Clown
1974–1975	Vaughn Greenwood	Skid Row Slasher
1974–1978	Theodore Robert Bundy	Ted
1974–1991	Dennis Lynn Rader	BTK Strangler
1974–1994	Ricardo Caputo	The Lady Killer
1975–1998	Robert Lee Yates Jr.	The Spokane Serial Killer
1976–1977	David R. Berkowitz	Son of Sam
		.44-Caliber Killer
1977–1978	Carlton Gary	Stocking Strangler
1977–1980	Richard Cottingham	The Ripper Jekyll/Hyde
1978	Richard T. Chase	Vampire Killer

(continued)

TABLE 7.1 Continued

Year	Name	Monikers
1978–1979	Gerald Parker	Bedroom Basher
1978–1996	Theodore Kaczynski	The Unabomber
1979–1980	William Bonin	Freeway Killer
1980s	Roger Kibbe	1-5 Strangler
1980s	Paul M. Stephanie	Weepy Voiced Killer
1980s	Craig Price	Slasher of Warwick
1980s	Randy Kraft	Scorecard Killer
1980–1981	David Carpenter	Trailside Killer
1980–1982	Randall Woodfield	The I-5 Killer
1981	Marion A. Pruett	Mad Dog Killer
1981–1982	Coral Eugene Watts	Sunday Morning Slasher
1982–1998	Gary Leon Ridgway	The Green River Killer
1984	Cleo Green	Red Demon
1984–2000	John Edward Robinson	Slavemaster
1985	Richard Ramirez	Night Stalker
1985–2007	Lonnie Franklin Jr.	Grim Sleeper
1986–2007	Walter Ellis	Milwaukee North Side Strangler
1987	Richard Angelo	Angel of Death
1989–1990	Danny Rolling	Campus Killer
		Gainesville Ripper
1990–1991	Cleophus Prince	Clairemont Killer
1990–1995	Keith Jesperson	Happy Face Killer
1992	David L. Wood	Desert Killer
1992	Thomas Huskey	Zoo Man
1993–1995	Glenn Rogers	Cross Country Killer
1993–1997	Michael Swango	Dr. Death
1994–1995	Roy Enrique Conde	Tamiami Strangler
1994–1996	Anthony Balaam	Trenton Strangler
1995–1996	Daniel Conahan	The Hog Trail Murderer
1997–1999	Angel Maturino Resendez	Railroad Killer
1998–2004	Derrick Todd Lee	Baton Rouge Killer
2001	Marc Sappington	The Kansas City Vampire
2002	John Muhammad and John Malvo	D.C. Snipers
2007–2009	Anthony Sowell	Cleveland Strangler
2010	Elias Abuelazam	Serial Stabber

SOURCE: © Cengage Learning, 2013.

It is these bizarre killings that have contributed to the often distorted caricatures of serial offenders during the past hundred years. Many of the males since 1800 in the present study earned some type of moniker. Unlike the monikers for female serial killers, most names for males were designed to create an aura of mystery and fascination. Some male serial killers, because of extended killing careers or notoriety, earned more than one name.

Male serial killers have murdered men, women, children, the elderly, prostitutes, hitchhikers, transients, and patients. Each case brings with it unique situations, methods, weapons, and motivations. Following World War II, an increase in serial murders began that sharply accelerated during the late 1960s and 1970s. This rather dramatic "emergence" began to attract national attention in the mid- to late 1970s. During the 1980s, serial murder became an increasing concern for law enforcement professionals and an important research area for social scientists. By the 1990s, several law enforcement agencies had begun addressing multiple homicide during in-service training and seminars, and colleges and universities began offering special-topics courses in serial crime and multicide. Between 1800 and 2004, approximately 96% (340) of serial killers began their killings after the year 1900 (see Chart 7.1). More specifically, between 1900 and 1924, 5% of offenders appeared; 7% between 1925 and 1949; 34% between 1950 and 1974; and 50% between 1975 and 2004. More offenders were identified in the 25-year time frame between 1975 and 2000 than during any previous 25-year span. Between 2000 and 2011 serial killers have emerged more slowly and quietly. In fact, over the past 15 years there has been a dearth of headline-grabbing killers like the Dahmers, Gacys, Kempers, Raders, and Bundys of the 20th century. However, there has been a gradual redefining and understanding of serial murder that now has a much broader scope than in previous years. Many serial killers have emerged in recent years who receive little media attention. *Part of the reason is that most of the new cases do not carry the social drama, social class, or high body counts to be of serious public interest.* Between 1975 and 2000 approximately 150+ serial killers were apprehended or left their calling cards. Between 2000 and 2011 over 150 serial-killer cases (male solos, female, and team killers) have appeared on the American landscape. We have more cases of serial killers in 11 years than we did in the previous 25. This is a mystery that can be explained. The following section provides an update of all male solo serial killers in the United States who were apprehended between 2004 and 2011. (Updates on female offenders and team killers are found in their respective chapters.) This seven-year period provides a long enough timeline to identify changing patterns and trends. Can you identify any significant differences from these current data to those previously reported? One of these important changes will be discussed later in this chapter.

Indeed, some of these changes in offender–victim data may be a reflection of a shift in offender–victim profiles. A dramatic decrease in homicides throughout the United States over the past several years is excellent news but belies the reality that serial murder is being redefined. We have become desensitized to such forms of killing, but certainly our fascination has not waned. Although the incidence of serial-killing cases is not as high as cases of mass murders (one every

Male Solo Serial Killers Update, 2004–2011

- Male solo killers ($N = 111$) account for 76% of all serial killers 2004–2011 ($N = 146$)
- Race of offender:
    - Caucasian: 38%
    - African American: 57%
    - Hispanic: 3%
    - Middle Eastern and East Indian: 2%
- Offender year of birth range: 1937–1992
- Average age of offender at first killing: 30
- Average age at apprehension: 38
- Average span of offender killing: 7 years
- Total number of victims: 482–618
- Average number of victims per offender: 4.3–5.5
- Span of offender killing: 1965–2011
- Offenders who killed all their victims in same year: 31%
- Offenders who killed in more than one year: 69%
    - 1–2 years: 12%
    - 2–3 years: 9%
    - 4–5 years: 9%
    - 6–9 years: 15%
    - 10+ years: 24%
- Method of killing:
    - Shoot only: 30%
    - Strangle only: 29%

10 days, including both public and domestic cases) in the United States, serial murders have become part of our culturally violent landscape—even though the United States homicide rate, as of 2010, is at a 40-year low. Indeed, 2011 saw a significant number of mass murders and attempted mass murders, including a case near Fort Worth, Texas, where a relative dressed up as Santa Claus shot and killed six relatives before killing himself on Christmas morning. Chart 7.2 identifies the proliferation of movies produced in the United States with serial-murder themes between 2000 and 2008. Note the increase in the number of movies with female killers and those with multiple offenders, especially in 2006.

Serial killers provide scripts for our slasher movies, sound bites for our newscasts, and fodder for crime novels. Table 7.2 lists a sample of films since 1995 with serial-murder themes. Many of the serial-killer movies spawned by the darkness of *Seven* and *Silence of the Lambs* go straight to video or experience a very brief theater running before appearing at video-rental outlets. Between 2000 and 2009 over 650 movies with serial-murder themes were produced by Hollywood and independent filmmakers! Over time a more criminally sophisticated audience has helped

- Stab only: 8%
- Beat/blunt force only: 7%
- Combination of strangling, beating, stabbing, and/or shooting: 26%

➤ In male solo cases:

➤ 38% involved shooting
➤ 43% involved strangling
➤ 21% involved stabbing
➤ 19% involved blunt force/beating
➤ 4% involved other forms of violence

➤ Victims of male solo killers:

- Adults only: 82%
- Elderly only: 7%
- Children only: 2%
- Adults and children: 7%
- Adults and elderly: 3%
- Offenders who targeted specific type of victim: 91%
- Average number of victims per offender: 4.3–5.5
- Strangers only: 93%
- Prostitutes: 23%
- Males only: 19%
- Females only: 53%
- Male and female victims: 29%.
- Involving more than one state: 22%

explain the decline of generic serial-killer movies making it to mainstream theaters. Television series such as *Dexter*, *CSI*, and *Cold Case Files* have attracted audiences wanting more depth to understanding murder as well as the requisite gore.

The sharp rise in serial homicides in the past 30 years, however, cannot be simply a product of the media. Other causal or influential factors may be (1) a belief in the emergence of a new breed of predatory criminal, (2) previous underreporting of such homicides, (3) self-fulfilling prophecy—you find what you expect to find by focusing specifically on serial killing, (4) inconsistency in defining the phenomenon, (5) the media's proliferation of "splatter" and "snuff" movies, (6) pornography depicting violence and other sado-erotic material, (7) a belief that changes in the economy are connected to surges of violent behavior, and (8) a feminist belief that serial killing is an extreme form of male domination of women based on patriarchy. Whatever the reasons for the apparent surge, we still must sort through and evaluate each case.

The proliferation of serial-murder cases has been experienced in varying degrees by most states. It is unlikely that there are any states that have not dealt

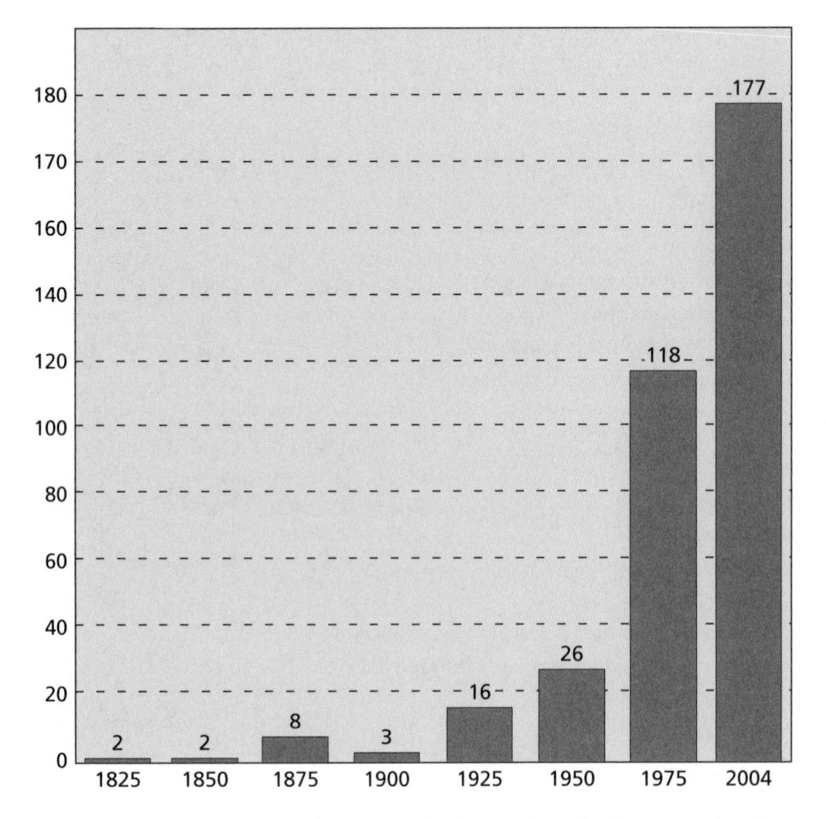

CHART 7.1 Frequency of Male Serial Killers in the United States, 1800–2004

N = 352 offenders

SOURCE: © Cengage Learning, 2013.

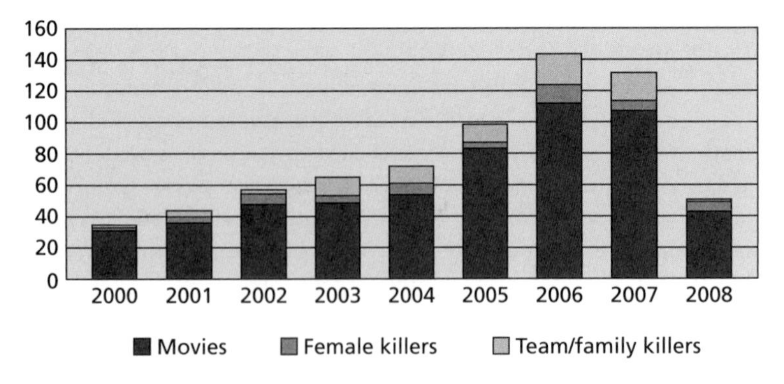

CHART 7.2 Serial Killers Movies Produced 2000–2008

SOURCE: © Cengage Learning, 2013.

with at least one or two cases in the past two decades. As far as the male offenders in the present study are concerned, every state reported having at least one case of serial murder since 1800 (Table 7.3). In all probability, cases have occurred in some states but have not been officially recorded because of lack of

TABLE 7.2 Sample of Films in the United States between 1995 and 2008 with Serial Murder Themes

Copycat; Seven

American Strays; Angel Dust; Bloody Friday; Closer and Closer; Countdown; Crimetime; Curdled; Cyberstalker; Deadly Sister; Dr. Ice; Freeway; The Glimmer Man; Jack Frost; The Limbic Region; Moonlight Murder; Paradise Lost; Quest; Ratchet; Revenge; Sailor Moon; Scream; Serial Bomber; Serial Numbers; Showgirls; Tails You Live, Heads You're Dead

8 Heads in a Duffel Bag; American Perfekt; Bloodmoon; Evil Obsession; Humanoids from the Deep; I Know What You Did Last Summer; Inspector Morse; Kiss the Girls; Kiss the Girls and Make Them Die; Labyrinth of Dreams; The Mask of Sanity; Papertrail; Profile for Murder; The Ripper; Rough Draft; Scream 2; Seaside Murder; Self Storage; Switchback; Turbulence; The Ugly; Wana

Bride of Chucky; Clay Pigeons; Fallen; Hypnotic Murders; I Still Know What You Did Last Summer; Lover; Nightwatch; Postmortem; Psycho; Serial; Sweetheart Murder

The Bone Collector; The Minus Man; Serial Killing 4 Dummys; Summer of Sam

American Psycho; The Cell; Eye of the Beholder; Scream 3; Superstar; The Watcher; Wedding Murder

Along Came a Spider; Ed Gein; From Hell; Hannibal; Killer Me

Red Dragon

Identity; Monster

The Grudge; Taking Lives; Twisted

2:13; Amusement; Aspiring Psychopath; Beyond Good & Evil; Bonding; Borderland; Buried Alive; By the Devil's Hands; The Capture of the Green River Killer; Changeling; Clay; The Cook; Craig; The Curse of Lizzie Borden II; Prom Night; The Devil's Chair; The Dungeon of Dr. Dreck; Fragments; Generator; The Horror Vault; Hush; Insanitarium; Intruder; Jack the Ripper; Juarez Mexico; Meet Market; The Midnight Meat Train; MR 73; My Kingdom for a Kiss; No Man's Land: The Rise of Reeker; No Place Like Home; Nobody Loves Alice; Pink Eye; Poison Sweethearts; Punk Rock Holocaust 2; Puppet Show; Reflections; Rest Stop: Don't Look Back; Return to Sleepaway Camp; Righteous Kill; Saw V; Silent but Deadly; Stoneman; Stump the Band; Subtle Seduction; Surveillance; Torture Toys; Trailer Park of Terror; Untraceable; Zombies/Blood Seekers/Blood Stalkers (3 films together)

SOURCE: © Cengage Learning, 2013.

evidence or, as Egger (1990) observed, linkage blindness, which prevents related cases of serial murder from being connected to each other.

California by far surpasses any other state in identified cases. This high number may be explained in part by the pattern of high mobility of people relocating to or exiting the state. Also, many serial killings occur in densely populated areas. Note that the second category of states includes some highly populated areas. As mentioned earlier, serial murders can occur anywhere, but anonymity is more likely among crowds of strangers, and the probability is greater for more randomized killings in large cities than in small ones. Even these explanations, however, do not fully explain the wide disparity between California and other states. Of course, these are absolute figures and are not related to population densities.

Rossmo (1995) segmented areas of the United States by comparing rates of serial-murder cases. Some states that are significantly less populated have higher

TABLE 7.3 Distribution of Cases Involving Male Offenders across the United States, 1800–2011

State	Number of Cases in Which One or More Victims Were Killed	State	Number of Cases in Which One or More Victims Were Killed
California	70	Alaska	
		Arkansas	
Florida		Colorado	
Georgia		Connecticut	
Illinois		Delaware	
New York	25–40	Hawaii	
Ohio		Idaho	
Pennsylvania		Iowa	
Texas		Kansas	
Alabama		Kentucky	
Arizona		Maine	
Indiana		Minnesota	
Louisiana		Mississippi	
Maryland		Montana	1–9
Massachusetts		Nebraska	
Michigan		New Hampshire	
Missouri	10–24	New Mexico	
Nevada		North Dakota	
New Jersey		Oklahoma	
North Carolina		Rhode Island	
Oregon		South Carolina	
Tennessee		South Dakota	
Washington		Utah	
Wisconsin		Vermont	
		Virginia	
		West Virginia	
		Wyoming	

SOURCE: © Cengage Learning, 2013.

rates of serial-murder cases per 100,000 population. In the present study, males were involved in over 90% (330 cases) of all serial-murder cases. In examining the age of offenders at the start of their killing careers, male offenders tended to be in their late 20s, with the average age at approximately 28.0 years.

AFRICAN AMERICAN SERIAL KILLERS

Even in the movies, unlike their white counterparts, African American serial killers have been practically nonexistent. In the early 1990s, however, a black serial killer was portrayed in the film *The Candyman,* in which the killer was driven by racially motivated revenge. Both Jenkins (1993) and I have found African Americans to be an important segment in serial-homicide research, considering that between 2000 and 2011 approximately 45% of all serial killers were identified as being black. Between 2004 and 2011 approximately 51% of all serial killers ($N = 146$) in the United States are African American. Since 2004, controlling for race and gender, 55% of all male serial killers in the United States ($N = 132$) are African American. Indeed, where solo male offenders are involved in serial murder ($N = 112$) African American males account for 56% of all the killers between 2004 and 2011. Society has failed to recognize poor blacks who kill poor blacks. This lack of recognition is rooted in minority status, socioeconomic status, and racism. Jenkins notes that black multiple homicides are usually discussed in the context of political motivation or terrorist activity, such as in the Zebra murders of the early 1970s. A group of African Americans known as "Death Angels" killed white victims in San Francisco, California. They were dubbed "Zebra" because investigators communicated on radio channel "Z." A plausible explanation for the lack of interest by media in black serial homicide is because the cases often involve poor blacks killing poor blacks. This does not sell newspapers nor earn high viewer ratings, as stories of whites killing whites or blacks killing whites do. There are exceptional cases such as Wayne Williams (Profile 7.1), believed to have killed 22 black children in Atlanta, and John Muhammad and John Malvo, the D.C. Snipers, which attracted national attention. In both cases investigators and the public initially believed the perpetrators to be white. Considering that there have been nearly 300 cases of black serial murder in the United States since the mid-1800s, little has been done to bring those cases to the public's attention.

Most persons can easily recite names of serial killers, all white, who have become household names—Gacy, Bundy, Kemper, DeSalvo, Dahmer, Rader—but few, if any, can recall even one name of a black serial killer. The disparity between the public attention given to white serial killers and their victims and those who are Black, is significant. Serial killers, regardless of race, must never be sensationalized or ignored. Too many lives are at risk. Jenkins (1993) explains that where black murders/murderers are concerned, the public perception is that they are all part of *urban homicide* or typical homicides that usually involve gang- and drug-related activities. Peterson (2005) in her study of serial killers between 1920 and 2004 also notes the disparity and lack of data collection involving African American serial killers. Vernon Geberth, (2012) a former NYPD homicide investigator and nationally recognized crime scene investigator, has also documented the surge of Black serial killers in the past several years. More attention to recognizing case linkage of Black serial murders inevitably

PROFILE 7.1 Wayne B. Williams, 1980–1981

For 22 months the residents of Atlanta lived in growing fear and outrage as a serial killer methodically hunted their children. The body count reached 30 victims before the killer was apprehended. They ranged in age from 7 to 28, and most were young males. Some were shot or strangled; others were stabbed, bludgeoned, or suffocated. All of the victims were black.

The deaths of so many young black people gave rise to a variety of theories and accusations, including belief in a plot by white supremacists to systematically kill all black children. Others began to think the children were being killed by Satan worshipers, blood cultists, or even copycat murderers.

The Ku Klux Klan came under close scrutiny, but no link could be made between its members and any of the murders. Atlanta became like a city under siege and inevitably attracted the attention of the entire country, including the resources of the federal government.

It appeared the murders would never stop until one night, as police staked out a bridge over the Chattahoochee River, they heard a car on the bridge come to a stop, followed by a distinct splash caused by something being dropped into the river. They pulled Wayne B. Williams, 23, over for questioning and finally arrested him as a suspect in the child murder cases.

Williams was found to be a bright, young, black man who lived with his retired parents and involved himself in photography. A media and police "groupie," Williams would often listen on his shortwave radio and respond to ambulance, fire, and police emergency calls. He would then sell his exclusive pictures to the local newspapers. At age 18, he was arrested for impersonating a police officer. He spent one year at Georgia State University but dropped out when he felt his "rising star" was moving too slowly.

Wayne's freelance work as a cameraman was never steady, and he began to focus his energies on music. As a self-employed talent scout, he eventually lured his victims into his control. He was known to distribute leaflets offering "private and free" interviews to blacks between the ages of 11 and 21 who sought a career in music. At his trial, Williams was depicted as a man who hated his own race and wanted to eliminate future generations. He was described as a homosexual or a bisexual who paid young boys to have sex with him. A boy, 15, claimed he had been molested by Williams, and several witnesses testified they had seen Williams with some of the victims.

Williams denied everything, and the prosecution had only elaborate forensics on which to base their case against him. The forensic evidence suggested a distinct link between Williams and at least 10 of the homicides and indicated a pattern surrounding the murders. The judge ruled the evidence admissible, and Williams was found guilty of murdering two of his older victims, Nathaniel Cater, 27, and Ray Payne, 21. Because of the nature of the circumstantial evidence, the judge sentenced Williams to two consecutive life sentences.

He was eventually named as being responsible for 24 of the Atlanta slayings, although some believe the child killings have not ended with Williams's arrest.

will save lives. Linda Lou Long conducted an intensive study of convicted serial killer Jerry Marcus, an African American who is believed to have, over a 17-year period, strangled seven young black women following allegedly consensual sexual encounters. Her book, *The Tuskegee Strangler* (2011), exposes us to a preview of how much there is to know and understand about offenders beyond their names and body counts. Revelations that Jake Bird, a black man, had actually stalked and killed many white women in the 1940s in multiple states or that a black man in Fresno, California, is now believed to have killed several white teenage females during the 1970s continue to challenge traditionally held profiles of serial killers. In 2009, police in Cleveland, Ohio, discovered 11 decomposing corpses in the living room, basement, crawl space, and backyard of the home of Anthony Sowell, 50, a decorated former Marine who lived alone. He became known as the Cleveland Strangler. He is now on death row, and police continue to search their cold case files for links to other possible murders by Sowell. Can you identify some of the several similarities that exist between Sowell and other well-documented white serial killers? Sowell, like so many other serial killers, had many victims long before he ever started killing.

While the existence of African American female serial killers is extremely rare (only one identified between 2004 and 2011), the opposite is true for black male offenders. Lorenzo Gilyard, a trash company supervisor in Kansas City, Missouri, is believed to have killed 13 prostitutes between 1977 and 1993. John Floyd Thomas, a sexual predator known as the West Side Rapist, killed several elderly white women over a 25-year period before being caught at age 72 in Los Angeles.

The rise in African American serial killers is also directly related to how the FBI now defines serial murder as constituting two or more killings where a pattern of murder has been established. This redefining of serial murder brings into question the notion that most people who murder, only murder once. There appear to be many cases of black homicide where the offender is convicted of one murder but has actually committed others or, upon release from prison, kills again. The challenge to researchers is to go beyond the stereotypes and focus upon sorting out fact from fiction.

Most of the cases involving black male offenders have been documented in recent years (see Table 7.4). In fact, between 1995 and 2004 approximately 44% of identified male serial killers have been African American. Even though blacks now represent at least one out of every two serial killers in the United States, the public perception is that serial killers are white. Stereotypes are very difficult to overcome.

For example, Chester D. Turner, one of the most prolific serial killers in Los Angeles between 1987 and 1998, received little public attention compared to white serial killers with similar numbers of victims (see Profile 7.2).

Chicago alone produced three black serial killers in 2000. Given the growing concentration of blacks in several major U.S. cities, coupled with the plight and blight of urbanization that has especially affected black people, we should not be surprised to see the "emergence" of the black serial killer. Some of the outward motivations for killing may appear different for blacks, including poverty and various forms of discrimination, but the final product will be the same. In truth, when blacks are killing blacks, especially when the victims are black

TABLE 7.4 A Sampling of African American Serial Killers

Offender	Location	Dates	Number of Victims*
Benjamin Atkins	MI	1991–1992	11
Jake Bird	WA	1947	44
Eugene Britt	IN	1995	11+
Debra Brown	OH/MI/IN/IL	1984	8
Jarvis Catoe	Washington, D.C./NY	1935–1941	9
Nathaniel R. Code	LA	1984–1987	8
Alton Coleman	OH/MI/IN/IL	1984	8
Andre Crawford	IL	1993–1994	10
Paul Durousseau	FL/GA	2001–2002	6
Walter Ellis	WI	1986–2007	7
Colin Ferguson	NY	1993	6
Kendall Francois	NY	1996–1998	8
Carlton Gary	GA	1970–1978	7+
Lorenzo J. Gilyard	MO	1977–1993	13
Harrison "Marty" Graham	PA	1987–1988	7+
Vaughn Greenwood	LA	1974–1975	11
Kevin Haley and Reginald Haley	CA	1979–1984	8
Clarence Hill	PA	1935–1941	6
Waneta Hoyt	NY	1965–1971	5
Calvin Jackson	NY	1973–1974	9+
Richard Jame white	NY/GA	1993–1994	15
Milton Johnson	IL	1983	5
Derrick T. Lee	LA	1992–2004	7
Devernon LeGrand	NY	1968–1975	Unknown
Michael Player	CA	1986	10
John Lee Malvo (accomplice: John Muhammad)	Washington, D.C./ VA	2002	15
Bobby Joe Maxwell	CA	1978–1979	10
Eddie Lee Mosley	FL	1979–2000	20+
John Allen Muhammad (accomplice: John Malvo)	Washington, D.C./ VA	2002	10+
Christopher Peterson	IN	Unknown	Unknown
James Pough	FL	1990	11
Craig Price	RI	1980s	3

TABLE 7.4 Continued

Offender	Location	Dates	Number of Victims*
Cleophus Prince Jr.	CA	1990	6
Robert Rozier	FL	1984	6
Anthony Sowell	OH	2007–2009	11
John Floyd Thomas	CA	1965–2009	25–30
Chester D. Turner	CA	1987–1998	10–13
Henry Louis Wallace	NC	1992–1994	9–20
Coral E. Watts	MI/TX	1979–1983	10+
Wayne Williams	GA	1979–1981	23–28

*Approximate number.

SOURCE: © Cengage Learning, 2013.

PROFILE 7.2 Chester D. Turner, 1978–1998

Born in Arkansas in 1966, Turner was raised by his mother after his parents divorced when he was five. The mother relocated to Los Angeles, where Turner attended public schools and worked as a cook and deliveryman for Domino's Pizza. When she decided to move to Utah, Turner stayed in Los Angeles, dropped out of high school, and frequented homeless shelters. He managed to be arrested six times for nonviolent offenses and once on an assault charge. Turner was concealing much more violence than anyone knew about, as he would eventually be DNA-linked to 13 murders of young women in the Los Angeles area. His pattern was almost always the same: victims were found partially nude, raped, strangled, and left in bushes, vacant buildings, and along roadways. Turner was arrested for the murders while serving an eight-year sentence for rape after Los Angeles Cold Case detectives were able to use DNA to link him to the string of murders. He was convicted of 10 of those killings as well as the killing of an unborn fetus. During the 11 years that Turner was committing his murders, another man, David Allen Jones, who was mentally handicapped and a part-time janitor, was arrested and convicted of some of these murders. Later police used DNA from the crime scenes and Jones was exonerated. Jones was released from prison in 2004 and awarded over $700,000 in compensation for the wrongful convictions.

prostitutes, national press coverage is usually very limited in comparison to white offenders killing white victims (see Profile 7.3).

Although serial murder is usually intraracial, cases such as the Stocking Strangler (see Profile 7.4) in Columbus, Georgia, or the black serial killer in Jackson, Mississippi, who murdered whites (see Profile 7.5), or John Floyd Thomas, killer of several elderly white women, suggest that racial boundaries may not be as significant as we previously thought. Rarely, however, do blacks and whites team up as accomplices in serial killing, as most develop their own preferences for victimization (see Profile 7.6).

PROFILE 7.3 Henry Louis Wallace, 1992–1994*

Henry Louis Wallace, an African American, was convicted of killing nine African American women over a 22-month period in an urban area of Charlotte, North Carolina. Wallace committed 60% of the murders within one mile of his residence. An additional 20% were committed within three miles of his home. He also worked within a half mile from his residence. Fifty percent of his victims worked within a mile from his home. Wallace began his murders of nine young, attractive, adult African American women on June 15, 1992, and killed the last one on March 12, 1994. The relationships between Wallace and his prey ranged from close friends to acquaintances. Some of his victims went to college, others worked in the fast-food industry, while others were employed as bank tellers, clothes merchants, and/or grocery store managers. These relationships made it easier for Wallace to gain physical access to them. One of his victims was the roommate of his girlfriend at the time, and another victim was close to the same friend.

Wallace befriended his victims by acting as a big brother, lending a listening ear and giving advice about boyfriend problems, helping with handyman duties, going out clubbing, giving them a ride, organizing barbeques, and/or just making them laugh. Once he had charmed them, they became his victims of murder, rape, robbery, burglary, car theft, and arson. The victims were killed inside of their homes. Wallace would oftentimes bring his tools of murder with him; other times, he used whatever was nearby. He often brought a pillowcase or a towel to the crime scene. His primary method of killing was his signature double-ligature strangulation. He enjoyed taking his victims in and out of consciousness while he sexually assaulted them. Wallace was also involved in necrophilia. Two of his victims were repeatedly stabbed and a 10-month-old baby was strangled, but survived.

Wallace demonstrated characteristics associated with both organized and disorganized serial killers. Initially, he made efforts to clean up crime scenes by wiping off fingerprints, washing dead bodies, and re-dressing and positioning them in bed beneath the covers. He would take pubic hair from a victim and plant it in the clothing of the victim's former boyfriend. In one case Wallace set fire to a victim's house in order to destroy physical evidence. Sometimes after he had cleaned up a crime scene he would return to see if the victim's body had been found. While there, he would search for more evidence to destroy, make phone calls, and smoke crack cocaine. Wallace stole items from his victims and sold them to feed his drug habit. He also gave pieces of the victims' jewelry to friends, including his girlfriend. As his drug habit worsened, he began getting careless and disorganized. He did not bathe or re-dress the later victims. He left fingerprints. Toward the end of his killing spree, Wallace's victims were physically almost double the size of his earlier victims. These larger women, according to Wallace, were more difficult to subdue. Toward the end, Wallace killed three of his victims within 72 hours. Two of these victims lived in the same apartment complex.

Wallace went to the funerals of some of his victims. He spoke with family members and feigned compassion to victims' families, even giving sympathy cards to a few. In his confession he described how he murdered the nine Charlotte women and two other earlier victims. He explained that although he robbed and stole from these women, sex, power, and domination were his primary motives. His girlfriend did not know that he was a murderer. Early in the investigation, the FBI informed Charlotte investigators that they did not appear to have a serial killer because the modus operandi was not typical of serial killers: the killer appeared to know his victims. Police were also accused of being less diligent about investigating the murders because the victims were African American and came from working-class areas of the city. Police denied these claims, citing a lack of financial and manpower resources (obsolete computers and only six homicide officers to handle 122 murders, the most ever in Charlotte in a year).

Detectives noted that Wallace's cleverness and meticulous attention to removing evidence made him hard to catch. Wallace was captured and arrested within 48 hours after he murdered his last victim.

The defense claimed that Wallace was mentally ill. Wallace, who was 180 lbs. and 6'1" at the time of his arrest, weighed over 300 lbs. by the time the trial started. His attorneys said that his weight gain was due to inactivity, antipsychotic drugs, and food. The trial took four months, with over 100 witnesses and 400 exhibits. Wallace, however, was found guilty in all of the nine murders. He was also found guilty of a myriad of other felonies including the attempted murder of a victim's 10-month-old son. Wallace was given 9 death sentences, 10 life sentences, and 322 years for the other felony convictions. Rebecca Torrijas, a nurse who worked with psychiatric patients, met Wallace at the jail and fell in love with him. Jail administrators soon terminated her employment, but she attended court daily and provided Wallace with money and clean clothes. On April 17, 1998, Torrijas, in her mid-50s, married Wallace, 32 years old, in a room next to the North Carolina death chamber.

Henry Louis Wallace was born November 4, 1965, in Barnwell, South Carolina. He was rejected by his mother because she hated men, especially Henry's father for abandoning the family. Wallace and his older sister were raised in poverty and often the object of ridicule in his family (Albarus, 1996). His mother humiliated him and he was often beaten as a toddler because he soiled himself and she wanted him trained so she could return to work. She berated him by saying that she wished that she was not his mother. Along with these abuses she exposed him to hardcore pornography. As a young boy he was molested by older children, but his need for affection was so great that he perceived sexual exploitation to be affection (Albarus, 1996). This abuse prepared him for his later rapes and killings. He described himself as an avenger for male abuse victims. Wallace was active in high school as a cheerleader (the only male on the team), a student council member, and a part-time deejay. He was a charmer who impressed his dates. Wallace was a philanderer. When arrested, he had a child from a previous marriage, was estranged from another wife, and was living with his girlfriend. Another woman was pregnant by him and he was having consensual sexual relations with about 10 other women.

In 1984, 10 years before his arrest for the murders, Wallace joined the navy and served as a weapons technician aboard the U.S.S. *Nimitz.* In 1987, he was suspected of stealing but was granted an honorable discharge. Wallace developed a penchant for burglaries and spent four months in prison. In 1990, he was arrested for the aggravated attempted rape of a 16-year-old female and was placed in a program for nonviolent offenders. After having moved to Charlotte in 1991, Wallace was caught shoplifting a rifle. During this time he worked as a cook and manager at various Charlotte fast-food restaurants. Increasingly, he was overcome with homicidal urges. His psychiatrists diagnosed Wallace as having sexual disorders, depression, and a personality disorder. Wallace confessed to his psychiatrist that he had committed between 35 and 100 rapes.

*Case contributed by Dr. Charisse T. M. Coston and Dr. Joseph B. Kulhns III (2003).

PROFILE 7.4 Carlton Gary, 1977–1978

Between September 16, 1977, and April 20, 1978, seven elderly white females were strangled to death in their homes in Columbus, Georgia. Two attempted murders of elderly women also occurred during this period of time. Eventually Carlton Gary, 34, "The Stocking Strangler," was arrested and charged with three of the homicides. Initially, Gary admitted he had been involved in all seven cases, but later he insisted that he was only present and did not participate in the murders. He was simply there to burglarize the residences, claimed Gary, but his history of crime seemed to suggest otherwise. His police record revealed a history of crimes involving robbing fast-food restaurants and steak houses in South Carolina, Georgia, and Florida. In 1970 he had been charged with the robbery, rape, and murder of an elderly woman in New York. He plea-bargained his way out by testifying against his partner.

Gary is described as a charmer, a ladies' man, very intelligent, and a "chronic talker." It was not until 1984 that police received a tip about a stolen gun that eventually linked Gary to the homicides. After his arrest he seemed to enjoy the notoriety he had gained so quickly. Eventually he attempted escape, and when that failed he tried to kill himself. As the trial date drew closer, Gary attempted to feign mental illness but was unable to convince anyone.

Raised in a home without a father and then sent to his grandmother's house when his mother left, Gary had little home life. He dropped out of school in 1966, married, and was soon arrested for auto burglary. He and his wife moved to New York and started raising two children while Gary worked as a janitor and played drums in a band. By 1970 Gary had deserted his wife and children. His former wife described Gary as "gentle, kind, and dangerous." Gary traveled around under several aliases until he became involved in the murder of 74-year-old Nellie Farmer in New York. Gary escaped from prison in New York one month before the stranglings began in Georgia, where he had moved to hide out. In 1979, after the killings in Georgia had ceased, he was arrested for a series of robberies in South Carolina and sent to prison for 21 years. Gary again escaped from prison in 1984, when he walked away from Goodman Correctional Institute in South Carolina, and headed to Florida to see his wife. Shortly afterward, Gary was arrested as the "Strangler." Gary was found guilty of three of the Stocking Strangler cases, although a definite pattern had been established in the other cases and some palm prints had been found. He was convicted of murder, rape, and burglary in all three cases and sentenced to death for the crimes.

Carlton Gary's Victims

Date	Name	Age	Marital Status	Method	Sexual Assault
9/16/77	Mary F. Jackson	59	Widow	Strangled	Possible
9/25/77	Jean Dimenstein	71	Single	Strangled	Yes
10/21/77	Florence Scheible*	89	Widow	Strangled	Yes
10/25/77	Martha Thurmond*	69	Widow	Strangled	Yes
12/28/77	Kathleen Woodruff*	74	Widow	Strangled	No
2/12/78	Mildred D. Borom	78	Widow	Strangled	Possible
4/20/78	Janet T. Cofer	61	Widow	Strangled	Possible

*Gary officially charged with the murder.

PROFILE 7.5 Calvin Jackson, 1973–1974

Calvin Jackson, 26, worked as a porter at the Park Plaza Hotel, a run-down building in New York City. Many elderly and those on fixed incomes lived there, trying to make ends meet. They did not realize that their porter was an ex-convict who had a long history of robberies and burglaries. He also was a regular drug user and had been involved in several assaults. On one occasion Jackson had plea-bargained a robbery charge and, instead of getting a 15-year sentence, he served 30 days. For years he moved from one dilapidated hotel to another. On his arrival at the Plaza, he decided to start burglarizing apartments there, except this time he would kill the occupant. He ransacked each victim's apartment and stole radios and television sets along with other items of small value. He attacked and killed at least nine women, most of them older. He usually strangled or suffocated his victims, although at least one was stabbed to death. All the victims were sexually assaulted, some after death, and, except for his final victim, they all lived in the Plaza Hotel.

Jackson was finally captured after he was seen carrying a TV set down a fire escape at 3:00 A.M. He confessed to all the pattern killings and was judged sane by the courts. His defense argued that Jackson would often make something to eat after he had killed his victim and sit and watch her, sometimes for an hour, to make sure she was really dead. The defense believed that only an insane person could do that. The courts did not agree and convicted Jackson on nine counts of homicide. He was given 18 concurrent life sentences, making him eligible for parole in the year 2030.

MOBILITY, STALKING, AND VICTIMIZATION

Since 1975 approximately 74% of all male offenders have been categorized as local serial killers—those who stay within a specific location, area of a city, or county but do not carry on their killing patterns in more than one state (see Table 7.5). Approximately one-quarter of all male offenders killed victims in more than one state, and approximately 10% used their own homes or places of employment as killing sites. These data refute the stereotype that serial killers are men who primarily travel across the country in search of victims. Based on cases examined here, most offenders never killed outside the state in which they began their killing careers. However, we often associate serial murder with offenders who travel (see Profile 7.7).

This may be in part due to rapid urbanization and a lessening need to travel in order to maintain anonymity. Finding, killing, and disposing of victims in and around cities appeals to offenders because they are familiar with the area and can usually avoid detection more readily.

Overall, the greatest percentage of victims were killed by local offenders. In recent years, two-thirds to three-fourths of all victims were murdered by offenders killing in only one state. A slight decrease was noted in the number of victims of traveling offenders, challenging the popular myth that this group inflicts the greatest number of victims. Proportionately, the mobility type of offenders responsible for the greatest percentage of victims are those who remain in one state.

PROFILE 7.6 Samuel Dixon, 2000–2001

Samuel Dixon, an African American ordained minister, committed four sexual homicides of men and women of various ethnicities over an 11-month period between 2000 and 2001. The murders occurred in Los Angeles and San Diego counties, areas where Dixon either lived or visited. Dixon, 59 at the time of the first murder, preyed upon a mentally disabled man, a homeless woman, and the sexually promiscuous—all easy targets for an aging offender. Three of the victims were casual acquaintances and all four victims engaged in consensual sexual activity with him while they were under the influence of drugs and alcohol. When his victims tried to end the sexual encounters, Dixon bound them and drugged them with amitriptyline. Two male victims were spared when the drug was not effective enough to give Dixon the control he needed. Dixon strangled and/or suffocated his victims and continued sexual relations with the corpse for up to two days after the victims had died.

This type of paraphilia is known as pseudo-necrophilia, which is a transient attraction to corpses rather than a preference for them. After the bodies' appearance and smell became unbearable, he poured lye and bleach on the bodies to dissolve evidence. After discovering that this disposal method was unsuccessful, he dumped the third victim in a local park. The fourth murder occurred in the victim's apartment. Dixon was caught when he revisited the crime scene with the intent to burglarize the residence, and eventually confessed the murders to a correctional counselor. Although his psychiatric history contained episodes of depression and mania, Dixon claims that no active symptoms were present during the murders.

A self-admitted con man, Dixon's long history of antisocial behavior began prior to adolescence. His adult arrest history began at age 22 and includes both property and violent crimes. Dixon's deviant sexual history includes a host of paraphilia—exhibitionism, fetishisms, frottage, necrophilia, and bestiality—as well as instances of adolescent male molestation, sexual contact with parishioners, and frequent use of prostitutes. Dixon spared several of his potential victims from death, including five males and three females, because the drug was ineffective or to prove to himself that he could resist the urge to rape and kill. These "almost kills" occurred between the murders of the second and fourth victims. Seven to fourteen days had elapsed between each of the first three murders, with the final murder occurring eleven months after the first. Dixon's crimes were planned, purposeful, and predatory and, if given the opportunity, he would very likely have murdered more people.

Dixon exhibits underlying feelings of inferiority and is a compensatory narcissist. He is humiliated and ashamed of his dependence on others for validation of his sense of worth. He feels entitled and overvalues his personal worth. Indeed, he is a very conflicted man. Dixon requires that others validate his own perception that he is supremely talented, superior, and special—the murders serve to reaffirm these beliefs. He admitted suffering from a grandiose delusion that he was God's instrument meant to signal the end of the world. Beyond this, Dixon has little insight into his own motivations, rationalizing his behaviors as the only way to obtain what he wanted. To him, the murders were a means to an end; a body was needed, dead or alive. Highly sensitive to rejection and susceptible to feelings of worthlessness and inadequacy, Dixon resentfully compares himself unfavorably to others and envies traits that he sees others possess. To escape these uncomfortable feelings he then seeks out others to control.

TABLE 7.5 Victims of Male Offenders in the United States, 1800–2011 One State vs. Multi-State Mobility

	1800–2011		1975–2011	
Mobility Classification of Killers	Percentage of Victims (*N* = 3,322–5,082)	Percentage of Offenders (*N* = 512)	Percentage of Victims (*N* = 1,782–2,672)	Percentage of Offenders (*N* = 331)
Total	100	100	100	100
Multi-State	31–32	32	26–33	26
One State	68–69	68	67–74	74

SOURCE: © Cengage Learning, 2013.

PROFILE 7.7 Bruce Mendenhall, 1992–2007

As a truck driver who traveled around the United States, Bruce Mendenhall, 56, had easy access to truck-stop prostitutes who live transient lifestyles and often associate with drugs. In 2007 he was convicted in the slaying of Sara Hulbert in Tennessee and has been charged with three other murders in which the victims were taken from truck stops in Alabama, Indiana, and Tennessee. In addition he is believed to have been involved in the abduction and murders of women in Texas, New Mexico, Georgia, Illinois, and Oklahoma. Many of the victims were shot, while others were stabbed and suffocated. Upon his arrest investigators discovered in his truck latex gloves, black tape, handcuffs, knives, a rifle, a nightstick, and sex toys. DNA from these items linked him to five women. While he was in prison his wife died leaving him insurance money. He attempted to hire inmates to carry out assassinations to lead investigators to believe that the killer was still at large. For the conspiracy to commit murder conviction, he received an additional 30 years. Due to his lack of cooperation, his actual total number of victims will likely never be known. Do you think Bruce Mendenhall started killing in his 50s? His modus operandi appears to be fairly typical of long-haul truck drivers who kill, and we can learn from these murders ways to reduce such abductions. Technology such as GPS, E-ZPass, and credit card payments as well as trucker logs can help investigators develop timelines linking abductions to times when specific suspects were in the area. But what are some of the ways we can protect persons from truck-stop serial killers?

Male offenders who roam the streets of U.S. cities and towns and remain relatively close to their killing sites appear to be the most common type of serial murderer in recent years as well (see Profile 7.8).

Place-specific cases often receive limited press coverage unless they involve high body counts and the victims died violently. This can be partially explained by the types of victims selected. Usually, place-specific killers quietly poison and/or suffocate their patients, family members, and other persons under their care, whereas Bundy brutally tortured and sexually mutilated young females.

PROFILE 7.8 Robert Joe Long, 1984

During an eight-month period in 1984, at least 10 young women ranging in age from 18 to 28 were abducted in the Tampa Bay, Florida, area. Each victim was bound, sexually assaulted, and then murdered. The victims, most of whom were prostitutes, were strangled, although one had her throat cut and another died from a gunshot. The perpetrator, Robert Long, 31, generally drove his car around an area frequented by prostitutes and then lured his victims into his vehicle. Long, who was on probation for assault, was divorced and unemployed. He experienced sadistic pleasure from fashioning a collar and leash from rope and using them on his victims. Shortly before his capture, Long abducted Lisa McVey from a doughnut shop in Tampa. He took her to an apartment and subjected her to 26 hours of sexual assault and then released her. The information she provided allowed police from three jurisdictions to "zero in" on Robert Joe Long. The impressive forensic work, involving the comparison of his clothing fibers, carpet fibers, semen, tire treads, ligature marks, and rope knots, influenced Long to make a full confession. Fiber evidence alone linked most of Long's victims to his vehicle. Long pled guilty in a plea-bargain arrangement to eight of the homicides and the abduction and rape of Lisa McVey. He received 26 life sentences, 7 requiring no parole for 25 years. Long then received two separate death sentences for the murders of Virginia Johnson and Michelle Simms. He now sits on death row in Florida (Terry and Malone, 1987).

Robert Long's Victims

Date Victim Missing	Date Victim Found	Name	Age	Occupation	Method	Mutilation
3/28/84	11/22/84	Artis Wick	18	Unknown	Unknown	Unknown
5/10/84	5/13/84	Long thi Nguyen	20	Exotic Dancer	Strangled	Bludgeoned
5/25/84	5/27/84	Michelle Simms	22	Prostitute	Cut throat	Head bludgeoned
6/8/84	6/24/84	Elizabeth Loundeback	22	Factory worker	Unknown	Unknown
9/7/84	11/16/84	Vicky Elliot	21	Waitress	Strangled	Unknown
9/30/84	10/31/84	Kimberly Hopps	20s	Prostitute	Unknown	Unknown
10/1/84	10/7/84	Chanel Williams	18	Prostitute	Gunshot to head	Neck puncture
10/13/84	10/14/84	Karen Dinsfriend	28	Prostitute	Strangled	Head bludgeoned
10/15/84	10/16/84	Virginia Johnson	18	Waitress/ prostitute	Strangled	Unknown
11/9/84	11/12/84	Kim Swann	21	Student/ nude dancer	Strangled	No

HIGHWAY SERIAL KILLERS

Although the majority of serial killers remain in a local area to hunt, kill, and dispose of their victims, there are some who prefer to travel to other cities, other states, other countries to seek victims. John E. Armstrong, 26, a Navy veteran of seven years, confessed in 2000 to murdering 11 victims, all prostitutes he found in Seattle, Hawaii, Hong Kong, Singapore, Bangkok, and Virginia. An amiable and professional petty officer, Armstrong had a dark side that harbored a deep hatred for prostitutes. He would pay for sex then afterward yell, "I hate whores," and strangle them. His last three victims were in the Detroit area. He was arrested once DNA evidence conclusively linked him to some of the earlier murders. Wayne A. Ford, 36, a long-haul truck driver, turned himself in to California police in November of 1998, claiming to have killed four female prostitutes or hitchhikers dating back to 1997. The victims had been killed in different counties in California. To prove that he was serious, Ford produced a bag from his jacket pocket containing a woman's breast. Ford said that he was angry with his ex-wife, who denied him visitation with their son. Ford started killing and dismembering the women as his frustrations and anger toward his ex-wife increased. The victims were strangled and beaten to death. One corpse he kept in a refrigerator but would not explain his motivations for doing so. Angel M. Resendez, 39, also known as Rafael Resendez-Ramirez, "The Railroad Killer," is believed to have killed between 8 and 13 victims in five states. All the killings occurred in homes near the railroad tracks. Resendez entered the United States illegally several times since 1976. He killed both men and women and then hopped freight trains to other areas of the state or country. Married with a young child, no one suspected this mild-mannered man to be someone who used over 30 aliases and raped, shot, and beat victims to death. Angel claims to have killed many, many more victims, and investigators are looking for connections between Angel and nearly 200 young women abducted and killed in northern Mexico.

Some of these offenders are individuals who live in one state but travel to others, while some simply wander from location to location and kill similar numbers of victims. This makes tracking such individuals very difficult for law enforcement. The FBI between 2009 and 2011 developed the Highway Serial Killing Initiative to identify victims of traveling serial killers in the United States. Over the past 30 years over 500 bodies of victims have been found alongside or near freeways and highways (see Chart 7.3). This information is gathered from the FBI's Violent Criminal Apprehension Program (ViCAP) and the National Center for the Analysis of Violent Crime. Since the inception of this FBI initiative 10 arrests have been made and over two dozen murders solved.

The FBI has amassed a database of over 275 suspects in the highway murders, and almost all of them are long-haul truck drivers. These are men who are nearly invisible to the public even though they are constantly on our highways. These are men with little or no supervision, who are extremely mobile and have easy access to a never-ending supply of victims. About half of the victims identified in the FBI initiative are prostitutes who usually loiter in

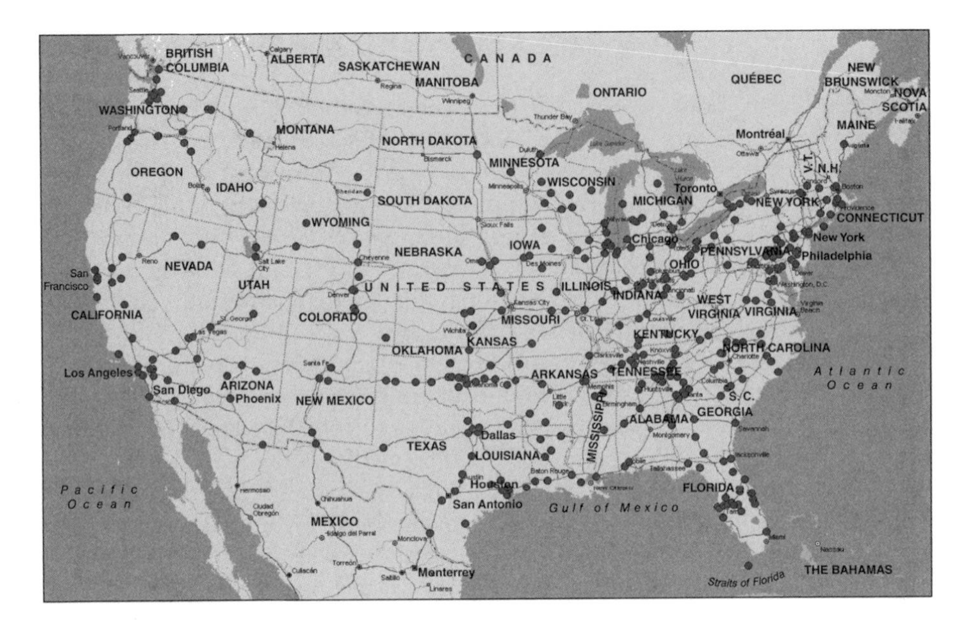

CHART 7.3 FBI Highway Serial Killings Initiative, 2009–2011

SOURCE: The FBI, Federal Bureau of Investigation. http://www.fbi.gov/news/stories/2009/april/highwayserial_040609

and around truck stops. Known by the drivers as *lot lizards*, these women are easy targets for traveling serial killers. They blend in with drug dealers, homeless persons, and hitchhikers and can be picked up at a truck stop and dumped in another state. These types of murders have not received much attention because of the prior difficulty in making connections of victims being killed by the same person. DNA and travel itineraries are now helping to point investigators in the right directions. The remaining half of the victims are stranded motorists, hitchhikers, and persons who inadvertently come into contact with these killers. Truck stops attract not only violent predators but also sophisticated criminals such as drug dealers and con artists, thieves, pickpockets, and an assortment of persons who loiter. All these persons add to the mix of potential threats toward travelers. Certainly the vast majority of long-haul drivers are not a threat to anyone, but for those who want anonymity and victims, being a long-haul driver can be very accommodating in facilitation of serial murder (see Profile 7.7).

STALKING

The role of stalking in male serial murder merits exploration because it can help to explain both cognitive and behavioral aspects of victim selection and subsequent murder. The act of *stalking* did not become a crime until 1990, when the state of California passed antistalking statutes to protect individuals or groups from harassment, intimidation, or violence. Since then, every state has implemented some form of antistalking legislation. Stalking generally requires three elements: a pattern of harassment over a period of time; implied or explicit threats; and intent to harm, intimidate, or create great emotional stress. We usually consider stalking in reference to celebrities such as tennis star Monica Seles, who in 1993 was stalked and stabbed during a tennis match. We are more likely to see stalking in cases of domestic problems in which the offender relentlessly pursues a former spouse, lover, or friend.

The Threat Management Unit of the Los Angeles Police Department has classified stalkers into four categories: *simple obsessional*, in which the offender knows his victim and stalks as a result of perceived mistreatment or separation; *love obsessional*, which involves stranger-to-stranger stalking in which the offender harasses the victim to draw attention to himself; *erotomania*, which typically involves a celebrity, who the offender believes is in love with her (most offenders are female); and the rare *false-victimization syndrome*, in which the offender falsely accuses another person, real or imaginary, of stalking him or her in order to assume the role of the victim. Most of these forms of stalking seldom end in actual violence to the victim. Oddie (2000) provides insight into the prediction of violence in stalking cases and notes that prediction is a most difficult process.

Hickey, Margulies, and Oddie (1999), in their study of 210 victims of stalking, revised the manner in which we view the process of stalking, the offenders, and the victims. Hickey et al. identify two general categories of offender-initiated stalking: *domestic* and *stranger*, each with its own types of stalkers. A third category involves victim-initiated stalking or *factitious* reporting (see Table 7.6).

All serial murderers utilize various forms of stalking in order to lure their victims and create attachments of control. Specific to our discussion of serial murder, most serial killers who are not strangers to their victims and stalk their victims are either power/anger or obsessional types. Serial killers who are strangers and stalk their victims are usually power/anger, obsessional, or sexual predators.

Domestic-power/anger stalkers harbor feelings of hatred, revenge, and domination over their victims. Sometimes offenders are so consumed by their anger that they are inappropriately designated as being obsessed. These offenders may exhibit antisocial characteristics, low self-esteem, lack of self-confidence, insecurity, and fear, but they are not obsessed in a clinical sense. Their inability to manage their personal or public life creates a state of perpetual frustration and

TABLE 7.6 Hickey Stalker Typologies

Domestic	Stranger	Factitious
Power/Anger	Power/Anger	False Victimization
Obsessional	Obsessional	Hero Fantasy
Nuisance	Nuisance	
	Sexual Predator	
	Erotomania	

SOURCE: © Cengage Learning, 2013.

anxiety. In turn, their frustrations and emotions lead them into increasingly violent acts. This is the most common type of domestic stalker and the most likely of this group to do physical harm to the victim. The victims are usually women caught up in dysfunctional relationships who leave their husbands, lovers, boyfriends, or even acquaintances because they fear for their own personal safety and/or the safety of their children. Enraged, the offender often begins a campaign of relentless pursuit by harassing, threatening, and assaulting and, in some cases, killing the victim. Melton (2007) found in her domestic violence research that stalking was more likely to occur where the victims were no longer in relationships with the abuser, the abusers had drug or alcohol problems, offenders were controlling in their behavior, and the victims had been stalked before by the abuser.

The *domestic-obsessional* stalkers usually have motivations less obvious than the power/anger stalker. Their victims are former friends or lovers, coworkers, acquaintances, and relatives. Often plagued by psychological disorders including schizophrenia, paranoia, and personality disorders, the offender becomes fixated on his or her victim and relentlessly pursues that person. What separates the obsessional from other types of stalkers is their often irrational and illogical behavior caused by psychological dysfunctioning. These offenders sometimes are persons who are gainfully employed and may appear to most others as quite normal. For the victim, however, contact with the obsessional offender becomes a series of frequent telephone calls, house calls, letters, gifts, followings, and harassments. Caught in obsessions, the offender will often make claims that the victim wants to be with the offender and that they are meant to be together.

In other instances the offender believes the victim to be an enemy who is plotting to do harm and must be stopped. The obsessional attachment is based in delusional beliefs that the victim is an enemy to the offender and the community in which he or she resides. The offender believes that no one else is truly capable of stopping this threat and feels he is on a mission to save everyone.

Stranger-power/anger stalkers are primarily men who look for random victims to control, intimidate, and harm. The Internet is quickly becoming a popular tool for such offenders. These men exhibit antisocial characteristics and, as a result of a lack of self-confidence and self-esteem, they hunt for proxy victims upon which to vent their anger. In times of economic hardship such men turn to others upon whom to place blame. Neo-Nazis, skinheads, right-wing extremists, men marginalized by society, and sexists all want to vent their rage and frustrations. The Internet is proving to be an excellent tool for harassing others and spreading the messages of hate toward minorities and women. Much of what appears in e-mail as threats tends to be cathartic and goes no further in stalking escalation. However, these offenders are not passive and are known for their boldness in striking out at random victims. The Internet is another way for those wanting to affiliate to band together. Other power/anger stalkers prefer anonymity and will send repeated messages of hate to public officials, minorities, and women. In most cases the messages tend to be cathartic and end quickly. Those who pursue sending threatening e-mails should be considered extremely dangerous.

Stranger-obsessional stalkers are individuals who suffer from a variety of psychological disorders including paranoid schizophrenia and bipolar and dissociative disorders. They generally should be considered dangerous because of their level of unpredictability. The object of their attachment is a stranger. Obsessionals attach because they have come to learn or believe something about another person or organization that may be completely false but that acts as a catalyst for the attachment. The Internet is attractive to obsessionals because it allows them unlimited access to their victims. Often, obsessionals will use additional means to reach their victims.

Stranger-sexual predator stalkers are some of the most dangerous offenders known to our criminal justice system. They include rapists, pedophiles, child molesters, and paraphiliacs, some of whom evolve into serial killers. They are always dangerous because the outcome is frequently the actual sexual assault of a victim or psychological sexual violence of a victim. The Internet is a perfect medium for sexual predators to solicit potential victims and do it with relative impunity. Offenders frequently have criminal histories, display various psychopathic characteristics, act alone, and become very adept at using tools such as the Internet to find victims.

Site and Nonsite Stalking

The level of personal and physical dangers to a victim can usually be measured by whether the offender is participating in *nonsite* or *site stalking*. Nonsite stalking refers to offenders who do not make personal, direct contact with the victim but instead engage in one or more of the following behaviors:

1. Telephone calls
2. E-mails, e-cards
3. Fax messages
4. Letters
5. Gifts
6. Voice mail and texting
7. Instant messaging
8. Video messaging and other forms of recorded messages

These offenders, although often creating tremendous psychological stress for their victims, do not pose a physical danger. Psychologically, however, this type of stalking behavior often makes the target feel as though the offender is physically present and could harm them. For the offender, nonsite stalking can be cathartic and provide a sense of control and power over their victim without actually having physical contact. Indeed, some types of nonsite stalkers would not feel comfortable nor in control were they to come face to face with their victims. Offenders who are married or have careers and reputations they do not want placed in jeopardy will employ nonsite tactics to harass, intimidate, and control their victims. In cases of domestic nonsite stalking, offenders are careful to avoid any acknowledgment of their stalking behaviors to their victims, who may also be their coworkers, acquaintances, or relatives. Other nonsite stalkers will escalate their activities into site stalking, in which the offender makes direct contact with the victim. Site stalking is preferred by some stalkers over nonsite stalking because they feel a greater sense of control and the direct contact fulfills physical and sexual fantasies. Site stalkers engage in one or more of the following behaviors:

1. Following
2. Workplace visits
3. Home visits
4. Signatures
5. Vandalism
6. Sending or leaving "gifts"
7. Displaying weapons

Some stalkers will only use nonsite stalking, whereas others will exclusively use site stalking and some will engage in both site and nonsite stalking. A critical factor for law enforcement personnel and victims is understanding that site stalking opens a Pandora's box of both physically and psychologically dangerous behaviors.

Cyberstalking

Cyberstalking may be best viewed as a *method* of stalking employed by either domestic or stranger stalkers. However, Freiberger (2008) in her study of cyberstalkers notes considerable differences in classifying generalized stalking in comparison to incidences of cyberstalking. She notes that many variations exist when examining motivations and victim–offender relationships between typical stalking cases and those involving cyberstalking. Typically, we find that most cyberstalking appears to be committed by strangers, given the vast number of sexual predator, celebrity, and nuisance stalkers currently using the Internet. The stalking landscape will continue to fluctuate as more individuals from all socioeconomic statuses, ethnic/racial backgrounds, political persuasions, and religious belief systems embrace the cyber-world. For example, the fastest-growing group of persons now gaining access to the Internet is that earning a wage of under $25,000 per year.

The greatest focus surrounding those who cyber-stalk and their victims involves sexual predators. Most commonly noted are pedophiles and child molesters. Differentiating between pedophiles and child molesters is not an easy task because they are not mutually exclusive in their fantasies and behaviors. Pedophiles prefer the company of children both socially and emotionally. Although many pedophiles work in adult settings, they always prefer the company of children. They usually are not married and live alone or with a relative. Their fantasies involve being emotionally attached and, if possible, physically involved with a child. They appear on a continuum from reclusive and self-gratified (where the pedophile does not actually seek out children but instead uses movies, props, photographs, etc., to fulfill fantasies and sexual desires) to the aggressive pedophile who seeks out children for sexual purposes, including murder. The child molester also prefers children but is more likely to be married and have a family. The key distinguishing factor is sexual contact with children. Once the pedophile begins to approach children, he is no longer in a benign status, engaged in only sexual fantasies involving children. Pedophiles and child molesters can be affiliated with NAMBLA (North American Man/Boy Love Association), Free Spirits, the Renee Guyon Society, and other organizations of similar ilk.

The Internet has become a labyrinth in which such predators lurk. Internet chat rooms, especially those designed for younger persons, have become virtual playgrounds for sexual predators. Pedophiles who may have kept their fantasies to themselves now have a forum to discuss their thoughts with other pedophiles as well as daily opportunities to visit chat rooms and begin relationships with unsuspecting victims. In California, a 60-year-old ophthalmologist contacted a 13-year-old girl and after a few e-mail exchanges began sending her sexually explicit photographs. Eventually the doctor asked to meet the girl and she agreed. The girl turned out to be a police officer working Internet sex crime cases. The doctor felt that law enforcement officials were overreacting, because there was no proof of intent to harm the child. In his words, "I only sent her a couple of photos and asked to meet her."

Internet and cell phone technologies now provide the predator with a plethora of tools and options to use in the process of stalking children. Photographs, texting, e-mail, Twitter, Facebook, GPS, spy ware software and keystroke logging hardware, chat rooms, Skype, caller ID, hidden video cameras, prepaid calling cards, online databases, and information brokers are some of the technologies now available that assist predators in connecting with their targets (Southworth et al., 2007). Potential rapists can use the same tools in hunting victims. From a criminal's perspective, bars have long been places of gathering for men seeking women to rape. The advent of the Internet now provides a forum for would-be rapists to stalk women. Unfortunately, people find themselves more willing to talk openly about personal topics on the Internet than if they were face-to-face with a stranger. The computer provides a false sense of anonymity and security that leads potential victims into sharing too much information.

In Detroit, December 2011, four young African American women were found dead in burned-out cars. Most of them had been linked to an Internet escort service known as Packages. In another case the predator used his computer to lure victims to his home for sexual activities or promises of employment. Thus far the bodies of eight of these women have been located after the predator had raped, tortured, and murdered them.

Stalking Fantasy

Stalkers have been psychologically categorized as having antisocial, borderline, or narcissistic personalities but also have been diagnosed with impulse-control, intermittent explosive, and substance abuse disorders. Some of the most noted celebrity stalkers, such as Ralph Nau, known as the Hollywood stalker who sent thousands of letters to over 40 celebrities, or Michael Perry, who escaped from a mental institution and managed to murder five people, including his parents, while stalking Olivia Newton-John, were found to be psychotic or paranoid schizophrenics.

For most sex offenders such as rapists, pedophiles, voyeurs, and exhibitionists, *stalking fantasies* are critical in the process of offending and relational paraphilic attachment (see Chapter 5). Consider the voyeur who goes about looking for opportunities to watch people undressing or engaging in sexual activities. Voyeurs derive a sense of personal control when they secretly watch unsuspecting victims. Thinking about and completing the act of voyeurism provide the offender with reinforced fantasies that will once again need to be satisfied. Like many sex offense acts, voyeurism causes the offender's fantasies to escalate and increases the risk of victim contact.

Indeed, serial killers also engage in psychological stalking prior to physically stalking their victims. This form of psychological foreplay is an essential component for many serial murderers. Ed Kemper (see Chapter 4) recounted how he would visualize female victims sitting beside him in his car while he pulled out a gun. Stalking fantasies prepare an offender for opportunities to physically stalk selected victims. In other cases, stalking is accomplished in fantasy only. Eventually, when the "right" victim appears, the offender is prepared to move quickly in isolating her. Indeed, the more focused the fantasies, the greater the danger to potential victims.

VICTIMS

As mentioned earlier, findings from the present study support the belief that serial murder involves primarily stranger-to-stranger violence. Overall, about 91% of all male offenders since 1975 killed at least one stranger (see Table 7.7). The killing of family and acquaintances by male serial killers all but disappeared in recent years. Although male offenders killed a large variety of strangers, they appeared to have their preferences. Table 7.7 provides a list of strangers, acquaintances, and family victims sought out by the offenders in this study.

Young females, especially if they were alone, ranked the highest in general preference of offenders. Of this category, prostitutes appeared to be the most

TABLE 7.7 Percentage of Male Offenders Murdering Family, Acquaintances, and Strangers in the United States, 1800–2011

	1800–2011	1975–2011
Relationship	Percentage of Offenders (N = 474)	Percentage of Offenders (N = 287)
Strangers	82	91
Acquaintances	9	7
Family/Friends	9	2

SOURCE: © Cengage Learning, 2013.

readily accessible victims who could also be easily disposed of. However, many women who never engaged in prostitution were also victimized. Hitchhikers, students walking alone, women living alone or seeking employment, and women engaged in certain professions and jobs (such as nurses, models, and waitresses) sometimes or frequently increased their risk factor by associating with total strangers. Females who had lifestyles or employment that tended to bring them into contact with strangers appeared to increase their chances of being victimized. (Prostitutes and hitchhikers were at the highest level of risk.) In some cases the community was aware that a serial killer was operating in the area. Yet some women would continue to take risks because, as Edmund Kemper, serial killer "extraordinaire," pointed out, "They [the victims] judged me not to be the one" (see Profile 4.3). This does not mean that female victims should bear culpability but that in most cases women are much more vulnerable to men than men are to women by nature of physical strength and perceived motivation to kill. Male serial killers also frequently target children as victims (category A2 in Table 7.8). Primarily, the majority of victims were the powerless being exploited by the more powerful. (As one researcher pointed out, you don't ever hear of these offenders going after bodybuilders.) The rest of the categories also include victims who were easily isolated and taken by surprise.

The next-largest group of target victims, after strangers, was acquaintances. Again, young women were the most frequent victims identified. Finally, in the category of family victims, wives were most likely to be killed, followed by in-laws and children. Although people are more likely to be spanked, whipped, beaten, and killed in their own homes by family members than anywhere else or by anyone else (Gelles and Cornell, 1990), serial murderers seldom are the perpetrators. Despite the fact that much of what they have become is rooted in family dysfunction and trauma, serial killers usually do not kill family members, except for mothers (fathers are not targets because almost always the father has left the home via divorce, prison, death, or abandonment of the family). According to an in-depth study by Underwood (2000), siblicide, or the killing of a sibling by another sibling, very often is initiated by alcohol and culminates in a shooting death. Serial killers are much more likely to direct their aggression outside the family. Although we often hear of serial killers who hated their mothers, mothers are rarely victims. A myth has been created and perpetrated about serial offenders killing their mothers because such cases tend to be frequently dramatized (Lucas and Kemper, for example). There exists a much greater likelihood that offenders wanting to kill their mothers inevitably find themselves killing someone else. These proxy killers continue to kill their mother's image repeatedly by seeking out unsuspecting females.

Patterns in victimization should also be examined for additional insight into the mind of the murderer. Forty-five percent of male offenders targeted females only, whereas just over one-fifth killed males exclusively (see Table 7.9). Only 35% of offenders killed both males and females. As expected, males were more likely to kill females than males. Almost four-fifths of offenders killed at least one female victim. Surprisingly, however, 55% of male offenders killed at least one male victim. Often the primary targets were female, but frequently males were killed, which suggests that a person's gender did not preclude victimization.

TABLE 7.8 Rank Order of Types of Victims Selected by Male Serial Killers

A. Strangers		
1. Young females alone	4. Young males alone	7. Patients
Prostitutes	Hitchhikers	Elderly
Hitchhikers	Skid-row derelicts	Infants
Students	Laborers	Others
Women at home selected randomly	Military	8. Police
Women seeking employment	5. Employers/business	9. Racial
Nurses, models, waitresses	Gas stations	targets:
2. Children alone	Fast-food outlets	Blacks
Boys	6. Elderly alone	Whites
Girls	Female	10. Citizens walking in
3. Travelers	Male	public
People in cars		Random
Campers		

B. Acquaintances	C. Family
Young women	Wives
People in community	In-laws
People in own group/ coworkers/employers	Children Mothers, brothers, grandparents
Neighbors	
Children	
Visitors, transients	
Schoolmates	
Patients	
Roommates	

SOURCE: © Cengage Learning, 2013.

Approximately 55% of all offenders killed only adults, whereas only small percentages of offenders specifically targeted children, teens, or the elderly. Whereas serial killers tend not to kill children and teens exclusively, about half of all male serial killers murdered at least one child or teenager, and nearly 9 out of 10 offenders killed at least one adult. In addition, one in six offenders murdered at least one or more elderly persons.

Female adults were victimized by over two-thirds of these offenders, whereas only about half reported killing at least one adult male victim. Slightly more than one-fourth of offenders were found to have killed both male and female adults. Often offenders killed both adults and teens, but they rarely killed both adults and children. In short, adult victims appeared to be the most frequent

TABLE 7.9 Percentage of Male Serial Killers Murdering People in Specific Victim Age and Gender Categories, 1800–2011

Age Only		Gender Only	
Children	3	Females	45
Teens	4	Males	21
Adults	55	Both	35
Elderly	4	**At Least One**	
At Least One		Female	78
Child or Teen	49	Male	55
Adult	87		
Elderly	15		

N = 491

SOURCE: © Cengage Learning, 2013.

TABLE 7.10 Degree of Victim Facilitation in Being Murdered by Male Offenders, 1800–2004

	1800–2004	1975–2004
Facilitation	Percentage of Offenders (*N* = 327)	Percentage of Offenders (*N* = 169)
Low	64	55
High	16	21
Both	20	24

SOURCE: © Cengage Learning, 2013.

targets sought out by male serial killers. Children were frequently victimized, but not as often as adults.

Table 7.10 gives the percentages of victim facilitation. Overall, most victims did not place themselves in particularly vulnerable positions at the time they were targeted, but this appears to have changed slightly in recent years. Since 1975 approximately one in five offenders attacked and killed victims who had facilitated their own deaths by placing themselves at risk. One-fourth of all offenders in recent years targeted victims in both high and low categories.

In cases of serial murder, seldom do we perceive victims as having precipitated their own deaths through acts of provocation. Most victims were unaware of the immediate danger when first they met their killers, especially in cases where males targeted females. In addition, not all offenders concerned themselves with the easiest target. In one case, the offender felt the urge to kill and tried to abduct a woman who was sitting in her car at a street intersection waiting for the light to change. Another just moved around neighborhoods, knocking on doors, until he found somebody at home.

The element of surprise is particularly operative in serial murder. Consequently, offenders take time to stalk a victim without giving warning signals.

Thus, a "selective" hitchhiker—one who is careful about getting in with "just anybody"—probably incurs the same risks as anyone else who hitchhikes. One investigator described serial killers as "charming" people; however, once they get you into their "comfort zone" it's too late to back out (see Profile 7.9).

OFFENDERS' BACKGROUNDS AND OCCUPATIONS

The male serial killers in this study came from a wide variety of backgrounds and occupations. Educational attainment was often only high school or less, some vocational training, or a year or two in college. Very few offenders held college

PROFILE 7.9 Albert Henry DeSalvo, 1962–1964

Perhaps he could have been stopped, but the signs were ignored or missed, and Albert DeSalvo—also known as "The Measuring Man," "The Green Man," and "The Boston Strangler"—murdered 13 innocent women. Born in Chelsea, Massachusetts, in 1931, DeSalvo was forced to live in extremely impoverished conditions. Often hungry and cold, he was subjected to cruel beatings at the hands of his alcoholic father. He was also forced to watch while his father abused and beat his mother. On one occasion he watched as his father broke each of his mother's fingers one after the other. On another occasion his father sold him and his sister into slavery to a farmer for several months. In 1944 Mrs. DeSalvo divorced her husband, taking her six children with her.

His love for his mother and his hatred for his father seemed to bring out the worst in Albert. He remembered later how much he enjoyed shooting cats with his bow and arrow, especially when the arrows protruded through their bellies. His father had trained him well in stealing from stores, and Albert became proficient at the task. He gradually developed a liking for breaking and entering homes, which he began to do frequently.

By the time he was 12, Albert had been arrested twice, once for larceny and once for breaking and entering. He was incarcerated at Lyman School for delinquent boys, where he learned a great deal more about burglary. After his release he began to apply himself full time to breaking and entering homes. Albert constantly seemed to try to bridge the gap between himself and those who had money and possessions. He was no more able to attain middle-class respectability than he was able to satisfy his apparently enormous sex drive. He became sexually active with both girls and homosexuals in the neighborhood and gained a reputation for his remarkable sexual capacity. At 17 he joined the military and served with the occupation forces in Germany. Before returning, he won the U.S. Army middleweight boxing championship and married his wife, Irmgard. In 1955, at age 23, Albert was charged with his first sex offense, involving the molestation of a 9-year-old girl. The charges were dropped when the parents refused to proceed with the case. In 1956, he was honorably discharged from the military.

In 1958 Albert's first child was born and he briefly ceased his breaking-and-entering activities. However, his wife refused to submit to his excessive sexual demands, and his financial status seemed to be worsening. In a short time Albert received two separate suspended sentences for breaking and entering. Before long, he earned the nickname "The Measuring Man" by conning his way into scores of apartments by explaining that he represented a modeling agency and was in search degrees. Offenders generally held blue-collar jobs, but a few managed to secure professional work as teachers, doctors, musicians, and ministers. Table 7.11 provides an overview of various types of employment held by male offenders before or during their killing careers. Some offenders held responsible positions that provided regular employment. Some used their employment to facilitate victim selection: for example, a building contractor lured boys in search of work; a nurse's aide killed patients; a bartender killed his female employees; a farmer killed his laborers; a hotel clerk killed tenants; a physician killed his patients; a few salesmen killed their customers. The BTK Strangler used his education, training, and work to locate suitable victims (see Profile 7.10). Other offenders

of talent. Producing a measuring tape, he would take occupants' personal measurements, touching them inappropriately whenever possible. He later would claim that most of his victims were quite willing to have their measurements taken, that few complained and a few even removed their clothing. He never attacked or harmed any of them but promised they would soon be hearing from his agency.

Eventually Albert was arrested once again for breaking and entering and was sentenced to two years' imprisonment. He earned his release in 11 months. According to police, at that time DeSalvo was still known only as a breaking-and-entering criminal. He returned home, only to be rejected by his wife again, until such time that he could prove he had mended his ways. Overwhelmed with frustration, Albert began changing from the harmless "Measuring Man" to an aggressive, violent personality. He began tying up some of his victims and raping them. He always wore green pants during these forays and was soon dubbed "The Green Man." Police estimate he attacked several women. Feelings of rejection, sexual frustration, and inferiority to others became intolerable by June of 1962, when he attempted his first murder of a woman in her apartment. Apparently, during the attack he saw himself in a mirror by the bed and it jolted his sensibilities, so he stopped. A week later he began killing in earnest.

Most of DeSalvo's victims were strangled and sexually assaulted. Over 60% were older women, although most of his last few victims were young women. He seemed to enjoy desecrating the corpse and then ransacking the apartment.

Although DeSalvo was unsure of his motives for killing, he was even less sure why he suddenly stopped in January 1964. Perhaps he felt he had given the supreme insult to society through the explicit humiliation of his last victims. DeSalvo continued to enter the homes of unsuspecting women as "The Green Man," tying them up and raping them, but he no longer killed his victims. Eventually, after a description had been given to the police by one of his victims, Albert was arrested as "The Green Man" and was linked to sexual assaults in Massachusetts, Connecticut, New Hampshire, and Rhode Island. He was sent to Bridgewater, a mental institution, for evaluation, but not until the spring of 1965 did he confess to being "The Boston Strangler." DeSalvo's confession, however, was given under special circumstances that protected him from prosecution for the murders. He never came to trial for the murders but instead was sent to prison for his many sexual assaults committed as "The Green Man." In 1967, he entered Walpole State Prison to serve a life sentence. Six years later Albert DeSalvo was stabbed to death by a fellow inmate.

(continued)

PROFILE 7.9 (Continued)

Albert DeSalvo's Victims

Date of Murder	Name	Age	Method	Sexual Assault	Corpse Desecration	Residence Searched by Killer
6/14/62	Anna Slesers	55	Blow to head/ strangulation	No	Bow under chin	No
6/28/62	Mary Mullen	85	Strangulation	No	No	No
6/30/62	Helen Blake	65	Strangulation	Yes	Bite marks; legs apart; bow under chin	Yes
6/30/62	Nina Nichols	68	Strangulation	Yes	Bottle in vagina; legs apart; bow under chin	Yes
8/19/62	Ida Irga	75	Strangulation	Yes	Legs apart and propped up on chairs; bite marks; twisted pillowcase around neck	Yes
8/20/62	Jane Sullivan	67	Strangulation	Yes	Body left in kneeling position, face down in bathtub; exposed	Yes
12/5/62	Sophie Clark	20	Strangulation	Yes	Legs apart; gag in mouth; bow under chin	Yes
12/30/62	Patricia Bissette	23	Strangulation	Yes	Bow under chin	Yes
3/9/63	Mary Brown	69	Fractured skull/stabbing/ strangulation	Yes	Table fork embedded in breast	Yes
5/6/63	Beverly Samans	23	Multiple stab wounds to throat and breast	Yes	Gagged; legs apart tied to bed posts; bow under chin	
9/8/63	Evelyn Corbin	58	Strangulation	Yes	Underpants stuffed in mouth; bow tied on ankle	Yes
11/23/63	Joann Graff	23	Strangulation	Yes	Bite marks on breast; bow under chin	Yes
1/4/64	Mary Sullivan	19	Strangulation	Yes	Legs apart; broom handle in vagina; bow under chin; Happy New Year card	

TABLE 7.11 Selected Occupations of Male Offenders before or during Their Career of Murder

Skilled	Semiskilled	Unskilled
Aircraft builder	Woodsman	Laborer
Shoemaker	Truck driver	Hotel porter
Car upholsterer	Warehouse employee	Gas attendant
Electrician/carpenter	Bartender	Garbage collector
TV repairman	Boiler operator	Kitchen worker
Plumber	Farmer	Handyman
Electronics technician	Nurse's aide	Criminal
Building contractor	House painter	Thief
Computer operator	Barber	Con artist
Mechanic	Factory worker	Pimp
Nurse	Construction worker	Burglar
Truck painter	Motel clerk	Robber
	Store clerk	

Government/professional	Other
Security, auxiliary police officer	Transient/drifter/vagrant
Military personnel	Cult follower
Minister	Student
Business owner: hotel, plantation, ranch, bakery	Former mental patient
Lecturer	
Physician	
Clerk	
Salesman	
Musician	
Social worker	
Postal worker	
Accountant	
Photographer	

SOURCE: © Cengage Learning, 2013.

did not connect their employment in any way to their victims, and still other offenders were transients, unemployed, or recently out of jail or prison.

Contrary to popular opinion, male serial killers in this study were not often highly educated nor did they commonly hold professional or even skilled careers. Occasionally an offender did appear to be extremely intelligent or had a prestigious occupation, but this type of offender tended to be the exception, not the rule. Because of the sensational nature of the serial-murder phenomenon, it is not surprising that we tend to seize on unsubstantiated evidence, especially if

PROFILE 7.10 Dennis Lynn Rader, "The BTK Strangler," 1974–1991

One of the Achilles heels of psychopaths is their narcissism. Dennis Rader had "successfully" murdered 10 people in the Wichita, Kansas, area over a 17-year period. His moniker was "BTK," meaning "bind, torture, and kill." Rader had served in the military for four years and then worked for ADT Security Services, where he gained knowledge of how to disarm home alarm systems. He killed mostly women whom he stalked, often waiting for them in their homes. He regularly sent taunting letters to police and media detailing his crimes. After his 10th victim, nearly 13 years passed and BTK had not been heard from nor had he killed again to the knowledge of the police. Rader was one of those few high-profile serial killers, much like the Zodiac Killer, who most likely would never be caught. But narcissism has a way of trumping concerns for capture and punishment and thus Rader, in 2004, began writing letters again to the police taking responsibility for another murder overlooked as belonging to him. However, DNA had become a wonder tool in linking persons to crimes and for Rader resulted in his inevitable capture in 2005. It was as if he wanted to be caught just so he could take public acknowledgment for his murders. He actually asked the police in a letter if it was possible to trace information from a floppy disk. The police said there was no way to know which computer had been used to format and record the floppy, when the opposite was true. Rader sent them a floppy disk with a message, and police immediately checked the metadata of the Microsoft Word document and found the name of Dennis and a link to a Lutheran church. An Internet search easily located Rader. Other serial killers such as Kemper, Kaczynski, and the D.C. Snipers also could not resist the temptation to keep the attention of investigators. In court Rader pleaded guilty to his 10 murders and reveled in giving explicitly graphic accounts of each of the killings. Kansas did not have the death penalty during the time of his murders, so he was given 10 consecutive life sentences, making him eligible for parole in 2180.

What made Dennis Rader a serial killer? Readers are encouraged to research Rader's childhood. Is there anything you can find that could explain his adult murderous behavior? Do you consider Rader a true criminal psychopath? How does Rader "fit" and not "fit" the serial killer profile?

such information tends to create further distortion of offender profiles. Indeed, offenders' ability to kill reportedly without detection appears to be more a function of cunning and deceit than intellectual abilities or academic attainments. Commonly, offenders have been profiled as the "law student," the "lecturer," or the "businessman" when in reality they have had very little exposure to those roles. This appears to happen most often in the more sensationalized cases. For example, Ted Bundy was portrayed as a law student, but he had never completed any coursework. "Law student" was merely a status symbol that Bundy used to infiltrate more easily the communities in which he roamed. In short, we have perpetuated a myth about male serial killers that is based on only a few sensational cases. Blue-collar work and unskilled labor have been found to be much more common among male offenders than higher-level employment.

Two of the most important factors in the construction of the stereotypic serial killer are found in the methods and motives of offenders. Table 7.12 provides a breakdown of methods used by offenders to kill their victims, based on police and autopsy reports, which specify the exact cause of death as well as

TABLE 7.12 Methods and Motives of Male Serial Murderers in the United States, 1800–2004

Methods (*N* = 367)		Motives (*N* = 367)	
Some firearms*	38%	Sex sometimes*	47%
Some strangulation/suffocation	35	Control sometimes	31
Some stabbed	32	Money sometimes	18
Some bludgeoning	25	Enjoyment sometimes	15
Firearms only	18	Sex only	8
Stabbed only	13	Racism	7
Strangulation/suffocation only	12	Money only	7
Bludgeoning only	9	Mental problems	6
Some poison	6	Cult-inspired sometimes	5
Poison only	5	Hatred	4
Some drowning	3	Urge sometimes	3
Other	2	Attention	3
Combination of the preceding methods	43	Enjoyment only	2
		Combination of the preceding motives	51

*"Some" or "sometimes" denotes that offenders killed one or more victims by a specific method or for a specific reason.

SOURCE: © Cengage Learning, 2013.

other contributing factors, including nonlethal injuries. In serial killing we are often faced with a process of murder rather than a brief act. Consequently, offenders were frequently found to have used a variety of nonlethal, potentially lethal, and lethal attacks on the victim. In contrast to typical homicides, domestic or otherwise, male serial offenders do not commonly use guns as their sole means of killing. In this study, firearms were used in approximately 38% of the cases, but not as the main mode of death.

The victims in this study may have actually died from strangulation, a bullet to the head, or a stab to the heart, but these often were the final acts committed after the victim had been successfully tortured, mutilated, and/or beaten by the offender. Conversely, a few offenders, such as necrophiles, would kill their victims as quickly as possible before they began their sexual assaults, mutilations, and trophy collecting. Other offenders engaged in physical assaults before, during, and after the death of the victim. In one case the offender tortured his victims for several days before finally killing them. The fact that such acts of torture, beatings, and mutilations often preceded the act of murder indicates they should be viewed as part of the methodology of serial killing. One offender stated in an interview with me, that "the response of the victim was everything." This meant that without torture, killing a victim was merely going through the motions (see Profile 7.11).

Another commonly held myth about male serial killers is that their primary motivations for murder are sexually rooted. Consequently, the typical stereotype of the offender is the "lust killer," who is driven to kill for sexual gratification. Most

PROFILE 7.11 Robert Hansen, 1973–1983

Robert Hansen, 44, admitted having a "severe inferiority complex with girls." To compensate, he began raping women and inevitably started torturing and murdering them. Hansen, considered to be Alaska's worst mass murderer in history, confessed to killing 17 prostitutes, nude dancers, and other women whom he resented. Hansen described to police how he—while working as a baker in Anchorage—abducted young women over a 10-year period. Hansen later worked as a respected businessman and was nationally known for his big-game hunting. He explained how he had abducted more than 50 women and taken them in his plane to his mountain retreat. If they gave him free sex, he would spare their lives, but any demand for money sealed their doom. Hansen would often strip his victim naked and then give her a head start to escape from him in the wilderness. He explained how much he enjoyed hunting victims down with his .223-caliber Ruger Mini-14 rifle, a weapon used by hunters. He usually kept his victims tied up in his cabin for several days of sadistic rape and torture before sending them naked into the woods to be hunted.

serial killings we hear and read about involve lust murders. Thus, it becomes that much easier to view sex as the primary motivating force behind the serial offender. Some serial killers, however, never become sexually involved in any way with their victims. Some experts may argue, however, that "enjoyment" is related to sexuality.

Sexual motivations were found to be the most common explanations of serial murder, but only 8% of offenders gave it as the sole reason for killing. Similarly, offenders frequently stated that they enjoyed killing but rarely killed for enjoyment only. Money was a factor for approximately one in five of the offenders, yet infrequently did they kill for money only. Even those who killed in order to engage in perverted sexual acts seldom committed the murders to carry out perverted acts only. As discussed in Chapter 5, sex may serve much more as a vehicle to degrade and destroy. Ultimately, by depriving a victim of things she or he holds sacred, such as dignity and self-respect, the offender achieves his most important goal, which is to have complete control over the victim. In short, many of the offenders' stated "motivations" may actually have been methods by which they achieved ultimate power and control over other human beings. One offender pointed out how good it made him feel to completely control another person's life. To have that control over life and death, he noted, gave him a special thrill.

Another area of research pertaining to the male offender is his prior history of violent, criminal, or abnormal behavior. We tend not to think of male serial killers as having criminal records but rather as embarking on a unique form of criminal activity. After careful examination of the lives of 211 male serial killers, I compiled data indicating that nearly two-thirds of them had had prior incarceration(s) in prison(s) or mental institutions (see Table 7.13). Over one-third were found to have histories of sex-related crimes, whereas nearly half (45%) had been convicted of thefts, burglaries, and robberies. Twelve percent reported prior homicide records, whereas 17% of male offenders were discovered to have had illegal drug involvement and 14% had been charged with animal abuse or fire-setting. Over two-thirds were found to have a history of a combination of

TABLE 7.13 Percentage of Male Offenders Reporting a History of Violent, Criminal, or Abnormal Behavior, 1800–2004

History	Percentage of Offenders ($N = 211$)
Prior incarceration in prison or mental institution	63
Property crimes	45
Sex-related crimes	38
Crimes against children	17
Illegal drugs	17
Fire-setting or animal abuse	14
Homicide	12
Assault	8
Combination of preceding behaviors	68

SOURCE: © Cengage Learning, 2013.

criminal activities. In short, most of the offenders examined were found to have some form of criminal history. Instead of being faced with a new breed of offender, the criminal justice system may have failed to adequately deal with the "old" criminal before his career of serial killing began (see Profile 7.12).

PROFILE 7.12 Paul John Knowles, 1974

Paul Knowles had a history of criminal behavior long before he started his killing spree. As a teenager and an adult, Knowles had spent time in jails for petty theft, car theft, and burglary. By the time he was released from prison, the 28-year-old Florida resident suffered from loneliness, rejection, and failure. Sandy Fawkes, a woman he met (but chose not to kill), described Knowles as a man who could be thoughtful and even protective. He also appeared to be confused as to his sexuality. Some of the rapes he confessed to were never completed because of his sexual inadequacies. One of his male victims appears to have been associated with homosexual behavior. Knowles met him in a gay bar and was invited to spend the night at his home but killed him following an argument. Knowles decided to make his mark on society and began a four-month killing rampage that would cover seven states and include at least 18 victims. He later claimed to have killed at least 35 people; the admissions were never confirmed.

Knowles's killings were generally random; he often murdered someone to conceal detection or to rob him or her. Some of his victims he simply killed for enjoyment. He murdered children, teenagers, adults, and elderly persons. Most of his victims died by strangulation, although at least five were shot to death. Most of them were female, but he raped or attempted to rape only a few. He managed to elude law enforcement through cunning and sheer luck as he drove thousands of miles, killing along the way.

Finally he abducted a police officer and another male traveler, handcuffed them to a tree, and shot both in the head, killing them instantly. After running a roadblock, he smashed his car into a tree and fled into the woods. He surrendered moments later when confronted by a local resident pointing a shotgun at him. After his arrest Knowles reveled in the notoriety and gave several interviews. He made a point of telling the press he was the "only successful member of his family." The next day Knowles was shot and killed as he attempted to escape from the police.

(continued)

PROFILE 7.12 (Continued)

Paul Knowles's Victims

Date of Murder	Name	Age Range	Gender	State	Method	Sexual Assault	Area of Killing or Where Body Found	Stolen Items
7/74	Alice Curtis	Elderly	F	FL	Suffocation	No	Home	Money/car
7/74	Mylette Anderson	Child	F	FL	Strangled	—	Swamp	—
7/74	Lillian Anderson	Child	F	FL	Strangled	—	Swamp	—
7/74	Marjorie Howe	Adult	F	FL	Strangled	—	Home	TV
8/74	Hitchhiker	Teen	F	FL	Strangled	Rape	Woods	—
8/74	Kathie Pierce	Adult	F	FL	Strangled	No	Home	—
9/74	William Bates	Adult	M	OH	Strangled	Possible	Woods	Car
9/74	Emmett Johnson	Elderly	M	NV	Shooting	No	Camper	Credit cards/car
9/74	Lois Johnson	Elderly	F	NV	Shooting	No	Camper	Credit cards/car
9/74	Unidentified	Adult	F	NV	Strangled	Rape	Car	—
9/74	Ann Dawson	Adult	F	AL	—	—	—	—
10/74	Dawn Wine	Teen	F	CT	Strangled	Rape	Home	Records/tape recorder
10/74	Karen Wine	Adult	F	CT	Strangled	Rape	Home	—
10/74	Doris Hovey	Adult	F	VA	Shooting	No	Home	—
11/74	Carswell Carr	Adult	M	GA	Stabbing	No	Home	—
11/74	Miss Carr	Teen	F	GA	Strangled	Attempt	Home	—
11/74	Officer Campbell	Adult	M	GA	Shooting	No	Woods	Car
11/74	James Meyer	Adult	M	GA	Shooting	No	Woods	Car

TABLE 7.14 Percentage of Male Offenders Who Experienced Forms of Traumatization as Children

Traumatization	Percentage of Offenders (*N* = 77)
Rejection	49
Unstable home	38
Mental/emotional abuse	32
Physical abuse	31
Divorce/absent father	20
Alcoholic parent	18
Sexual abuse	17
Parents deceased	12
Adopted	11
Illegitimate	11
Poverty	11
Prostitute mother	5

SOURCE: © Cengage Learning, 2013.

Another important area of background research is the killer's childhood history. In 77 cases of male offenders, various degrees and types of traumatization occurred while they were young (see Table 7.14). This does not preclude the possibility that other offenders also may have had similar experiences. Trauma, in this instance, was defined as rejection, including being abandoned by parent(s), being neglected by parent(s), and being rejected by significant others. Rejection was by far the most common theme surrounding the lives of these killers as children, which very likely originated from the experience of a dysfunctional family, sexual abuse, alcoholism, and so on. The feelings of rejection and anger appear to be residual effects of the traumatization. However, most people have experienced rejection to a lesser or greater degree than serial killers have, yet they do not become violent killers. Many people have lost their parents; experienced divorce, poverty, and unstable homes in which parents drink heavily; used drugs; or been involved in prostitution or sexual abuse. However, most people who have had such experiences do not turn to homicide. Serial killers may be different in that they were not prepared or able to cope with the stresses the trauma created (see Chapter 4). Such an explanation will require more extensive research but may eventually provide us with greater insight into causation. For the present, it appears that early childhood trauma can and will influence future behavior to the extent that some individuals will become violent offenders.

DISPOSITION OF SERIAL KILLERS

There has been considerable concern about the disposition of serial offenders. Given that some states* do not have capital punishment and that several serial

*As of 2012, 34 states, the federal government, and the U.S. military currently impose the death penalty.

TABLE 7.15 Disposition of Male Serial Killers after Apprehension

Disposition	Percentage of Offenders ($N = 366$)
Prison sentences	43
Death penalty sentences	29
Pending in courts	7
Suicide	3
Killed before trial	3
Confined to mental institution	3
Escaped	1
Now free	1

SOURCE: © Cengage Learning, 2013.

killers were removed from death row when capital punishment was struck down by the U.S. Supreme Court in 1972, many offenders are spending the rest of their lives in prison instead of waiting to be executed (see Table 7.15).

Of the 366 male offenders examined for sentencing, 29% have received death penalty sentences as of this writing. A few committed suicide or were killed before a trial could be held. In total, nearly 35% of all offenders are now dead or currently await execution. At least half of all male offenders spent or will spend the rest of their lives in prison or confined to psychiatric institutions. The chances of parole or early release for any of these offenders is extremely small, if not nonexistent. A California appellate court, in 2010, was unfortunately forced, due to insufficient evidence, to release convicted murderer Loren Herzog, a man linked to several murders. In 2012 Herzog committed suicide. He discovered that Wesley Shermantine, his partner in the murders who was on death row, made a deal with prosecutors to help locate the victims' bodies and implicate Herzog in those murders.

Team Killers

LEARNING OBJECTIVES

- To explore through case review the profiles and characteristics of serial murderers who operate in teams of two or more offenders
- To understand the synergistic dynamics of team serial killers in pursuit of their victims
- To examine the role of females as frequent participants in team serial murder
- To review the latest research on team serial killers

On February 23, 1996, William George Bonin, age 49, known as the "Freeway Killer," was executed by lethal injection in the state of California. Between 1978 and 1980, Bonin is believed to have sodomized, beaten, and murdered at least 21 young men and boys. He was convicted in 14 cases of murder in the Los Angeles and Orange County areas. A neglected and sexually abused child, Bonin matured into a young man with a keen interest in young boys. He spent five years incarcerated in a psychiatric hospital and then in prison for sexually assaulting five boys. He finished his sentence and within 16 months he was caught for raping yet another boy. From then on he left no witnesses. Most of his victims were in their teens and each had died a gruesome death by strangulation or stabbing. One victim was fed chlorohydrate and then had an ice pick jammed into his right ear and into his brain. Bonin knew no boundaries. He also enjoyed having accomplices who assisted him in his constant search for victims. This chapter focuses on serial killers who prefer to hunt in packs. Indeed, they are an oddly assorted group, ranging from the vicious savagery of Henry Lee Lucas and partner Ottis Toole to the quiet stealth of the D.C. Snipers, John Muhammad and John Malvo.

The primary catalyst for serial-murder victimization stems from a perceived need to acquire power and control over others. Of course, human nature, practically by definition, includes a drive for power of some type, in some degree. For some people, however, the road to power is strewn with human sacrifices. Power can be all consuming and justifies every means and method to obtain it.

In the drive for domination, the intensity, frequency, and subsequent interpretation of murder are more fulfilling for some killers than for others. The lust for power is the chameleon of vices and as such can be perceived and experienced in many different ways. For some multiple killers, murder must be simultaneously a participation and a spectator endeavor; power can be experienced by observing a fellow conspirator destroy human life, possibly as much as by performing the killing. The pathology of the relationship operates symbiotically. In other words, the offenders contribute to each other's personal inventory of power.

In the mid-1960s, Walter Kelbach and Myron Lance went on a killing spree for several days. In some of the murders, the killers would toss a coin to see which one would get to stab the victim to death. Alone, they may never have killed. What they could never become alone, they could aspire to collectively. Inhibitions and fears were dissipated by the interaction of the two men. History is replete with examples of the destructive forces of group behavior. In groups of people who kill, there are often a few who play subservient roles. They provide an immediate audience "privileged" to experience or witness the destructive power of the main actors. Serial-killing groups are frequently masterminded by one person—for example, Angelo Buono in the "Hillside Stranglings" in California; Douglas Clark in the "Sunset Strip" killings in Hollywood; Charles Manson and his "Family"; and Gary Heidnik, "The Fiend of Franklinville," in Philadelphia.

Like other subgroups of serial offenders, team killers, or those who kill with one or more accomplices, have been documented for many generations. They have generally been considered anomalies that occur infrequently; thus, little attention has been given to the nature of team killing.

IDENTIFYING TEAM KILLERS

By 2004, known cases of serial murder in the United States had declined sharply, including cases involving team killing. Unfortunately, serial murder is not a passing modern-day phenomenon and will, like other violent crimes, increase again. Forty-nine cases, comprising 114 offenders or 26% of all serial killers (431) in this study, constitute this subgroup. Female offenders participated in 17 of the 49 cases of team serial killing. Seventy-two percent of team killers were white, 27% African American, and 1% Asian. The majority of cases involved only two offenders, whereas the remaining cases had three or more offenders in each group. The largest group was identified as having five offenders. Several of the cases or offenders involved were labeled by the media, by the community, or by

TABLE 8.1 Relationship Groupings of Team Offenders, 1850–2004

A. Relatives	B. Nonrelatives
1. Husband/wife	7. Male-dominated teams
2. Father/son	8. Heterosexual lovers
3. Brothers	9. Gay lovers
4. Mother/son	10. Lesbian lovers
5. Father/mother/daughter/son	11. Female-dominated teams
6. Cousins	

SOURCE: © Cengage Learning, 2013.

themselves with creative monikers, such as the Zebra Killers, the Lonely Hearts Killers, and the .22-Caliber Killers.

Several of these cases attracted public attention and have inspired books and movies, including *The Hillside Strangler* and *Helter Skelter*, both of which were popular at the bookstore and the box office.

The emergence of team killers has mirrored the rise of solo offenders, and we will likely see more of them in the 21st century. Law enforcement personnel are becoming educated about serial killings and are now more likely to recognize patterns of serial murders that may involve more than one offender. In addition, law enforcement personnel now have much improved forensic technology and expertise with which to investigate serial crime. Also, fluctuations in the stability of the U.S. economy have a profound effect on the psychological well-being of some individuals. Another factor may be desensitization to the value of human life that continues as a result of violence portrayed in the media. Finally, the elderly are a fast-growing group of particularly accessible potential victims.

Only time will prove the accuracy of the gloomy predictions of an increase in serial murders. In the meantime, understanding some of the characteristics of team killing may assist in unraveling its etiology. As briefly discussed earlier, relationships between or among team killers can reveal a great deal about the offenders and the motivations for murder. Table 8.1 indicates that team offenders form dyads, triads, and even larger groupings; sometimes they are both legally and blood related; sometimes they are strangers and acquaintances (see Profile 8.1).

In the 2004 study, the relationships were widely distributed, including several sibling and parent-child combinations. Nonrelated team killers were subdivided into four groups, some of which included offenders who were intimately involved. Other groups had either males or females who provided leadership to the group. The following section provides an update of serial-murder activity amongst team offenders in the United States from 2004 to 2011. Do you see any changes between their current activity and what we already knew about them?

PROFILE 8.1 Kenneth Bianchi and Angelo Buono, 1977–1978

On October 18, 1977, the nude, strangled body of Yolanda Washington was discovered in Los Angeles. She had been a part-time waitress and prostitute who worked the streets of Hollywood. On October 31, the body of 15-year-old Judith L. Miller, a runaway, was found along a roadside, strangled and sexually abused. The child had been severely tortured. There would be at least eight more victims of Bianchi and Buono, "The Hillside Stranglers." Except for Yolanda Washington, who was killed in a car, all the victims were taken to Buono's house, where they were bound, gagged, raped, sodomized with instruments, beaten, and finally strangled to death. The corpses were dumped along the highways and hillsides of Los Angeles and Glendale, except for Cindy Hudspeth, who was found in the trunk of her car in a ravine.

Buono, age 44, and Bianchi, 26, were cousins who decided to kill someone just to see what it would feel like. Each killing, sexual attack, and torture session became easier for them, a game that they looked forward to with excitement. Lauren Wagner was burned with an electrical cord placed on her body. Kristina Weckler was injected with a cleaning solution so they could watch her convulse and then was gassed by having a bag placed over her head with a hose attached to a stove. The killers abducted not only prostitutes but schoolgirls, like 12-year-old Dolores Cepeda and 14-year-old Sonja Johnson. In a span of five months, at least 10 homicides had been linked to the Hillside Stranglers.

Bianchi relocated to Bellingham, Washington, and the murders ceased in Los Angeles. A year later, the bodies of Karen Mandic and Diane Wilder, college roommates, were found raped and strangled, and Bianchi, a prime suspect, was arrested. The similarities in the killings and other circumstantial evidence linked Bianchi to the Hillside killings. Bianchi first tried to convince authorities he suffered from multiple personalities and was not responsible for his actions. When that failed, he agreed to plea-bargain and testify against Buono in order to avoid the death penalty. Although they both had developed a taste for killing, Buono and Bianchi were quite different in personality. Bianchi was a bright, smooth-talking ladies' man, a con artist who had nearly mastered the art of lying. Buono, much less articulate, remained silent throughout his trial. He had been married three times and fathered at least seven children. With only a ninth-grade education, Buono had begun his own upholstery business and also pimped for prostitutes. He enjoyed sex with pain and had abused many women sexually. Bianchi, who was married at the time of some of the murders, had concealed his actions from his wife and newborn son, Sean.

It was California's longest criminal trial at the time and was very costly. Several witnesses spoke on behalf of the killers, especially Buono, but there were always those who knew of his dark side as well. In 1984, Buono received life in prison without parole, and Bianchi is required to spend 26 years and 8 months in prison before his first parole hearing can be scheduled. Judge George, who had remained impartial throughout the long trial, commented to the two sadistic killers, "I'm sure, Mr. Buono and Mr. Bianchi, that you will only get your thrills by reliving over and over the tortures and murders of your victims, being incapable, as I believe you to be, of ever feeling any remorse." In 1986, in a brief ceremony at Folsom Prison, Angelo Buono, then 52 years old, married Christine Kizuka, 35, a supervisor at the Los Angeles office of the State Employment Development Department. His conviction in nine murders apparently did not diminish his attractiveness to at least one woman (Levin & Fox, 1985, Chapter 11). In 2002 Buono died in prison of a heart attack.

Team Serial Killers Update, 2004–2011

- Team killers ($N = 29$) account for 20% of all serial killers 2004–2011 ($N = 146$)
- Gender of killers: males 76% and females 24%
- Average number of accomplices: 1
- Race of offender:
  - Caucasian: 55%
  - African American: 38%
  - Hispanic: 7%
- Offender year of birth range: 1931–1991
- Average age of offender at first killing: 30.6
- Average age at apprehension: 33.4
- Average span of offender killing: 3.1 years
- Total number of victims: 73–91
- Average number of victims per offender: 2.5–3.1
- Span of offender killing: 1994–2010
- Offenders who killed all their victims in same year: 41%
- Offenders who killed in more than one year: 59%
  - 1–2 years: 14%
  - 2–3 years: 17%
  - 4–5 years: 7%
  - 6–9 years: 7%
  - 10+ years: 14%
- Method of killing:
  - Shoot only: 40%
  - Strangle only: 13%
  - Beat/blunt force only: 13%
  - Combination of strangling, beating, stabbing, and/or shooting: 34%
- Victims of team killers:
  - Adults only: 100%
  - Offenders who targeted specific type of victim: 100%
  - Average number of victims per offender: 4.6–5.7
  - Strangers only: 100%
  - Prostitutes: 7%
  - Males only: 33%
  - Females only: 13%
  - Male and female victims: 53%
  - Involving more than one state: 20%

FEMALES AS MASTERMINDS IN SERIAL-MURDER RELATIONSHIPS

In the nonrelative category, males almost exclusively assumed leadership. Cases were extremely rare in which nonrelated females masterminded multiple homicides, but they do occur (see Profile 8.2). In other rare cases women dominate the male in the killing relationship, as was the case of Martha Beck and Raymond Fernandez (see Profile 8.3).

This also tended to be true for cases of male/female lovers. In short, although women frequently became involved in serial murder as a part of team killing, they generally were not the decision makers or main enforcers. Pearson (1995) suggests that such perceptions, in part, explain why the FBI Behavioral Science Unit, which develops psychological profiles of male serial killers, had, by 2004, only one category, "compliant victim," for female perpetrators. An FBI study of seven women offenders involved with male offenders who were their husbands or lovers described the relationship as "straightforward male coercion." The FBI concluded that females took part in the killings as a result of compliance, fear, or stupidity. Such findings are based on bias and lack of objectivity. Women do become the leaders in some murder cases, albeit rarely. There are other types of male-female team serial killers that do not fit traditional concepts of serial murder, yet they are serial killers by definition. Consider the case of the Tene Bimbo Gypsy clan (see Profile 8.4).

Indeed, female "Rippers" have yet to make their mark in the United States. Such perceptions do not, however, refute the fact that women can be as deadly as men, as witnessed in the case of Aileen Wuornos (see Chapter 9). Pearson (1995) argues that females who commit murder have the "best of both worlds" because the female offender is empowered during the killing and is able to fulfill her own fantasies, sexual or otherwise. Following the murder(s) the female offender can revert to a submissive, compliant role. The females described in this text who are part of the subgroup of male-female team killers tend to be, with a few exceptions, followers, not leaders. However, some of these followers quickly learned how to kill, became "equal partners in the killing," and participated directly in some of the bloodiest murder cases ever chronicled (see Profile 8.5).

MALES AS MASTERMINDS IN SERIAL-MURDER RELATIONSHIPS

Without exception, every group of offenders had one person who psychologically maintained control of the other members of the team. Some of these leaders were Charles Manson types who exerted an almost mystical control over their followers; others used forms of coercion, intimidation, and persuasive

PROFILE 8.2 Olga Rutterschmidt and Helen Golay, 1999–2005

In 2008 Olga Rutterschmidt, 75, and Helen Golay, 77, were convicted of first-degree murder and conspiracy to commit murder for financial gain. The two women had been luring homeless men from Hollywood Church in Los Angeles with promises of food and shelter. Each victim was moved into a comfortable apartment and given care for a two-year period. Each of the victims, aged 51 and 73, were also insured for over 5.7 million dollars by using multiple insurance agencies. Victims unwittingly signed policies, unaware they were signing their death warrants. At the end of two years, the time frame needed for the insurance policies to be incontestable, the hapless victims were drugged, taken to back alleys, and run over to make it appear that they had been killed in hit-and-run accidents. The women, who had spent approximately $64,000 to care for their victims, collected over 2.8 million dollars with their scheme.

The women were very methodical. Obviously grateful for his newfound fortune, one of the victims invited four or five other homeless men to share his living quarters. When Olga and Helen discovered these unwanted men they had them evicted and hired security to guard the apartment from other intrusions. The five-year time lapse between the first and second victims was intended to sufficiently separate the two killings so as not to draw attention. However, an investigator who had been looking into the most recent death fortuitously overheard another investigator discussing an earlier death that bore striking similarities. At the trial, a video was shown by the prosecution of the two killers sitting in a police interview room unaware they were being recorded, discussing which one of them was most responsible for the pair being apprehended. Both killers were given life sentences without the possibility of parole. Serial murder is a relatively rare form of violent crime. Just how rare do you think this particular case is in relation to other forms of serial murder in general? Among team killers? Among female serial killers? Among the various methods used to commit serial murder and compared to the general profile of serial killers?

techniques. In team murders, not all of the participants shared equally in the "thrill" of the kill. As one offender pointed out, real serial killers are people who make it their life's work. Certainly not all team offenders in this subgroup shared exactly the same motivations or abilities for killing. Given time, however, several became molded to the task.

Truman Capote, in his acclaimed *In Cold Blood* (1965), described the relationship between two killers, Dick Hickock and Perry Smith. In the aftermath of the vicious murders of the entire Clutter family, Perry begins to question the normality of people who could do such a thing. Dick's response reaffirms in his own mind his superiority over Perry: "'Deal me out, baby,' Dick said. 'I'm a normal.' And Dick meant what he said. He thought himself as balanced, as sane as anyone—maybe a bit smarter than the average fellow, that's all. But Perry—there *was*, in Dick's opinion, 'something wrong' with Little Perry. To say the least" (p. 108).

Such relationships tend to be built on deception, bravado, and intimidation. Often in the aftermath of apprehension by police and eventual

PROFILE 8.3 Martha Beck and Ray Fernandez

Martha was born in 1920 into poverty. Raped at 13 by her brother, she continued to gain weight, appeared emotionally unstable, and suffered from low self-esteem and self-worth. She would eventually marry and divorce three times. Authorities removed her two young children when she was declared an unfit mother. One of the children was illegitimate. When Martha pressed for marriage, the father elected suicide rather than marrying her. Martha completed high school and worked as a nurse until she was fired in 1947 from a city maternity hospital. She began sending letters to the "Lonely Hearts Club" only to meet her future murder accomplice.

Ray Fernandez was born in Spain in 1914. Considered a shy, introverted man, Ray was happily married until he received a head injury at age 31. His demeanor changed, as did his personality, and he began to believe that he possessed psychic powers that enabled him to get women to fall in love with him. For the next few years he was described as a "sleazy gigolo with a toupee and a gold tooth" who managed to swindle dozens of women out of their financial assets. He was caught in 1949.

Beck proposed that she and Fernandez become partners to continue the confidence games. She would pose as his sister. Although Fernandez found her unattractive, they became sexual partners as well, engaging in extremely "degenerate" practices. Martha eventually became jealous of the relationships Ray developed with their victims and began putting barbiturates into their food. Ray would then kill the unsuspecting victim. In one case Ray killed a woman and Martha assisted by drowning the woman's two-year-old child in the bathtub. She initiated the killing and appeared to enjoy watching the small child struggle for life as she held him in a death grip. In another case she killed by striking the victim repeatedly on the head. The duo were linked to approximately 20 murders when they were apprehended, convicted, and executed on March 8, 1951 (Seagrave, 1992).

PROFILE 8.4 Tene Bimbo Gypsy Clan, 1984–1994

Five elderly men, all in their 80s and 90s, died in San Francisco between 1984 and 1994. Their bodies were exhumed and each was found to have died from overdoses of the drug digitalis, a heart drug. Each man had been involved in a May–December romance, and each man's sweetheart was a female associated with Tene Bimbo, a Gypsy clan. Prosecutors believe that the women, in collusion with men in their clan, seduced the elderly men, swindled them, and then killed them with digitalis, a drug from the foxglove plant that is lethal in high doses and mimics natural death. The clan gained notoriety in Peter Maas's 1974 book *King of the Gypsies* and a film by the same name. In each case, younger women in their 20s and 30s from the clan sought out wealthy elderly men. In some cases the women actually married the men in order to gain access to their money. In one case investigators found that immediately following the death of the victim, $70,000 was drained from his estate and funneled to an Atlantic City casino (Cole, 1998).

PROFILE 8.5 Alton Coleman and Debra D. Brown, 1984

A man with an explosive temper and ready to fight, Alton Coleman had committed a long list of violent crimes and sex offenses by the age of 28. He was living with Debra Brown, whom he frequently beat and threatened. Alton was raised in the black slums of the Midwest, the son of a prostitute who died when Alton was a teenager. Having no father and being rejected by his mother while still an infant, Alton went to live with his grandmother. She apparently provided a good home for Alton, who nevertheless was characterized as an unhappy, bitter child, who was called "Pissy" by schoolmates because he wet his pants so often. As he grew older, he became more aggressive. He gambled frequently and began to hustle women, whom he usually abused through beatings and sexual assaults. He spent at least three years in prison, where he was known for his aggressive homosexual behavior. His brutality with women and his fascination for bondage, violent sex, and young women ended his first marriage after only six months. He is believed to have raped several women and young girls before his murder spree.

His first victim was nine-year-old Vernita Wheat, whom Coleman had abducted from an acquaintance. She was raped, strangled, and stuffed into a small closet. While police investigated her disappearance, Alton and Debra left the area. Three weeks later they attacked two girls, ages seven and nine. The younger, little Tamika, was kicked in the face and chest and strangled until she died. Alton then beat and raped the second child and left her unconscious. For the next several weeks, the couple traveled back and forth through five different states, including Ohio, Indiana, Illinois, and Michigan, where they murdered, raped, and robbed several more people, both black and white, young and elderly, male and female. A mother, Virginia Temple, and her 10-year-old daughter were beaten, raped, and strangled and left in a basement crawl space. Coleman possessed a real talent for gaining the trust of strangers and eluding the police, who placed him on the FBI's Most Wanted list. One psychiatrist, who was familiar with Coleman, described him as a "pansexual," a person who enjoys sex with anyone—man, woman, or child. His sexual enjoyment was surpassed only by his ability for sadism and viciousness.

Debra Brown was described as a high school dropout, from a family of 11, who was easily influenced and dominated. On meeting Coleman, she almost immediately broke off her engagement to another man. Her ability to kill seemed to come easily. In one instance Coleman and Brown attacked a husband and wife who lived in suburban Cincinnati using an array of devices, including a four-foot wooden candlestick, a crowbar, visegrip pliers, and a knife. The wife, Marlene Waters, died after being bludgeoned to death. Other victims were shot to death. After eight weeks, the two killers were captured without a struggle while watching an outdoor basketball game in Evanston, Illinois. Bond for Coleman was set at 25 million dollars, full cash, and 20 million dollars cash bond was set for Brown. They are believed to be guilty of at least eight murders in addition to a variety of abductions, beatings, robberies, thefts, and sexual assaults. Brown remained loyal to her lover; moments before his first sentencing they signed documents creating a common-law marriage. Perhaps in an effort to save Coleman from the death penalty, Brown stated in court regarding one of the victims, "I killed the bitch and I don't give a damn. I had fun out of it." When the courts finished with Coleman, he had received four separate death sentences and more than a hundred years in prison. Debra Brown, after receiving her second death sentence, life in prison, and dozens of additional years in prison, apologized for her part in the killing and wrote, "I'm a more kind and understandable and lovable person than people think I am" (Linedecker, 1987). Alton Coleman was executed in 2002, while Debra Brown resides in the Ohio Reformatory for Women and still faces the death penalty in Indiana.

incarceration, the leaders of some groups tend to go through a process of self-abdication and place culpability for the murders on the followers. In one case the group leader, denying absolutely any involvement in a series of horrific mutilation murders, contended that his ex-girlfriend had conceived and executed the murder plans. From his perspective, he was always just a bystander. The case involving Douglas Clark and Carol Bundy (see Profile 8.6) also illustrates this point.

Parents and children as well as husbands and wives have also been serial killers. Imagine the dynamics of a family whose mom, dad, son, and daughter systematically killed 14 victims! In one case, the wife had never been involved in any form of violent criminal behavior. By the end, she helped in luring victims to an automobile that she then drove while her husband raped, beat, and strangled them in the backseat.

At what point does a person acquiesce and agree to assist in murdering victims? What enables someone to convince others that murdering people is the direction to follow? It appears unlikely that some male and female offenders ever would have indulged in such crimes had they not been exposed to group dynamics and the power of persuasion and manipulation. Some of those who led groups of team offenders experienced a sense of power and gratification not only through the deaths of victims but also through getting others to do their bidding. Robin Gecht in Chicago surrounded himself with loyal followers who obediently killed with and for him. Charles Manson needed only to provide direction for his eager band of devotees. Dean Corll, involved in killing dozens of young males, used his charisma to entice delinquent youths into his gang of procurers. This does not negate in any way the culpability of team offenders. Indeed, many of them were quite anxious to become involved, but they became killers because of another's influence. For some of these followers, killing first became acceptable and then desirable. Others continued to kill solely as a result of their relationship with whoever held the reins of leadership. The next sections explore social data surrounding team offenders that may be helpful in further understanding group killers.

OCCUPATIONS OF TEAM SERIAL KILLERS

For the most part, team offenders who held jobs were employed in blue-collar work that required limited training. The occupations listed next reflect some types of employment held by team offenders. In contrast to the myth that serial killers often are financially successful, economically stable individuals, offenders in this subgroup were not from the professional occupations. Similarly, with only a few exceptions, most of these offenders did not receive college education, and only a few received postsecondary education, such as vocational training. In brief, they were generally ill prepared to achieve occupationally successful careers.

Occupations of Team Offenders Before or During Their Career of Murder

Skilled
Aircraft company employee
Shoemaker
Car upholsterer
Electrician
Carpenter
Nurse

Semiskilled
Woodsman
Truck driver
Warehouse employee
Bartender
Boiler operator
Farmer

Unskilled
Laborer
Waitress
Gas station attendant

Government
Security/auxiliary police
Military personnel
Minister

Criminal
Thief
Scam artist
Pimp
Burglar
Robber

Other
Transient
Cultist

TEAM KILLING AND MOBILITY

Team serial offenders (114 offenders) were responsible for 426–583 murders or 14% to 15% of all deaths in this study. Twenty-six percent of all offenders ($N =$ 429) were identified as team killers. This means, in general, that group offenders did not kill on the average as many victims as other serial-offender subgroups. Team offenders on the average were responsible for four to five killings per offender (see Table 8.2).

In general, it seems that solo serial killers caused greater destruction than team killers did. Certainly there were exceptions: Bianchi-Buono, Corll-Henley-Brooks, the Benders, and Lake-Ng all killed more than the average number of victims. But several teams managed to kill "only" three, four, or five victims. By dividing the number of cases into the number of victims, team killers averaged 9 to 12 victims per case, whereas solo killers averaged slightly more. In brief, having more than one offender involved in serial killing did not increase the number of victims per case. Solo offenders were a little more likely, on the average, to kill more victims. This discrepancy might result in part from the greater number of offenders involved in team killing, which may increase the possibility of discovery by law enforcement officials. When two or more offenders are involved in a case, the chances of somebody talking or leaving evidence at or near the crime scene increase.

PROFILE 8.6 Douglas D. Clark and Carol A. Bundy, 1980

Clark, son of a retired U.S. Navy admiral, liked to call himself "the King of the One-Night Stands." He enjoyed exploiting women emotionally, sexually, and financially. Since childhood, his sexual fantasies had been fueled by the wearing of women's undercloth-ing. He acted out perverted sexual fantasies with women who would care for his bizarre needs, regardless of their sometimes dowdy appearance. He met Carol Bundy, a nurse, while working as a boiler room engineer at a Burbank, California, soap factory. Carol had recently been jilted and was quickly attracted to the smooth-talking Clark. She felt that he might be the solution to her problems because she was lonely, had poor eye-sight, was diabetic, and was in need of comfort. Clark immediately moved in with Carol, but, much to her dismay, he insisted on regularly cruising Sunset Boulevard in Holly-wood, California, in search of young prostitutes. He told Carol of his fantasies to have sexual intercourse with the corpses of recently murdered girls. Carol, believing she really loved Clark, became a compliant assistant in his efforts to actualize his fantasies.

Carol began photographing Clark while willing teenage girls he had brought home performed oral sex on him. She even watched while he had sex with an 11-year-old girl who had been rollerskating in a nearby park. Clark next targeted two female hitchhikers, whom he shot to death and then had sex with: Gina Marano, 15, and Cynthia Chandler, 16, had run away from home to enjoy the excitement of living on Sunset Strip. To display his work, Clark later took Carol to the site where he had disposed of the bodies. Female corpses began appearing with regularity. The body of a female was found behind a res-taurant in Burbank. The same morning, a man discovered a headless woman lying in an alley. Three days later, the severed head appeared in a box at the entrance to another neighbor's driveway. The head had been cleaned, frozen, and made up with lipstick and other cosmetics. Both of these victims, Karen Jones and Exxie Wilson, had been young prostitutes. Clark, now dubbed the "Sunset Slayer" by the press, had developed a pattern of abducting and shooting young hookers and runaways in order to engage in necrophilia.

Carol later confessed how Clark kept the heads of some of the victims in the refriger-ator. On at least one occasion, she applied cosmetics to a victim's head that Clark then used sexually while in the shower. He claimed that he hated prostitutes and loved to watch them die. He frequently hired prostitutes for oral sex and, as he reached a climax, shot them in the head. Panties became another trophy Clark would save after he had sex with the corpse. He even carried a "killing bag" in his car that contained a knife, rubber gloves, and plastic sacks. One victim abducted from a shopping mall managed to pull free from her two captors, but only after she had been stabbed 27 times (Linedecker, 1987, Chapter 12).

TABLE 8.2 Victims of Team Killers in the United States by Mobility Classification, 1850–2004

Mobility Classification of Killers	Percentage of Victims (426–583)	Percentage of Cases (N = 49)	Percentage of Offenders (N = 114)	Average Number of Victims per Case	Average Number of Victims per Offender
Total	100	100	100	8–12	4–5
Traveling	35–36	39	34	8–11	4-5
Local	43–47	47	53	8–12	3–5
Place-specific	19–22	14	13	12–18	6–9

SOURCE: © Cengage Learning, 2013.

Although Carol was a willing participant in the murders, it was Clark who initiated the hunts for victims along the Strip. Clark allegedly told her on one occasion that if Carol ever told, he would kill her two young children. Later Carol would inadvertently disclose information about the killings to her former boyfriend. When he decided to tell the police, she lured him to a secluded spot where they had sex together. She then stabbed him to death, slashed open his buttocks, and decapitated him. The head was never found.

Eventually Carol decided she wanted no more of the killing and told her story to her coworkers. She became the star witness for the prosecution but still claimed to love Clark. While in jail awaiting trial, Clark began to exchange letters with a woman who was in custody for attempted murder. She had tried to establish a fake alibi for yet another serial killer, Kenneth Bianchi, one of the "Hillside Stranglers." They appeared to derive great pleasure in writing letters that made reference to necrophilia, murder, blood, torture, and mutilation. In 1983, Clark was found guilty of six counts of first-degree murder and sentenced to die in San Quentin's gas chamber. Carol, who admitted killing at least one prostitute and her former boyfriend, was given consecutive sentences of 25 years to life and 27 years to life in Central California Women's Facility in Chowchilla (Linedecker, 1987, Chapter 12). She died in 2003 at age 61.

Clark, on death row in San Quentin, California, at the time of this writing, vehemently denies any involvement in any murders. He claims that his accomplice, Carol A. Bundy, was the real mastermind and the person who carried out all the killings. Her actual partner, claims Clark, was John Murray, her former boyfriend, whom she murdered. After Murray was killed, Clark was left to "take the rap" because he had stayed in one of her rented apartments. Clark claims that Carol Bundy fantasized herself to be the wife of the now-deceased serial killer Ted Bundy and that she was merely mimicking his pattern of murders. Since Clark's arrival on death row, he has married a woman who champions his quest for freedom while he continues his appeals process. He expresses great bitterness toward law enforcement personnel and the criminal justice system, which he feels has used him as a scapegoat to cover up their own failure to prosecute the real offender.

On a prison visit, I spoke with Carol Bundy, frail and ill with diabetes. I asked her if she ever communicated with Clark. She responded, "Oh no, he is not allowed to send me mail anymore." As I was leaving her cell, she reflected on Clark and said, "You know, Dr. Hickey, Douglas Clark is a very disturbed man." Unfortunately, I did not have a mirror to give her.

Offender mobility data indicated that team killers were most likely to remain in local proximity to their killing sites and least likely to be classified as place-specific offenders. The greatest number of victims were killed by these local team offenders, in some contrast to those with greater mobility (see Profile 8.7).

Place-specific offenders had the fewest number of cases and were responsible for the smallest percentage of team victims, yet they averaged the highest number of victims per case. By contrast, local team killers represented double the number of place-specific cases but averaged significantly fewer victims per case. This may suggest that place-specific offenders, although few in number, were much more difficult to detect. Such offenders could carry on seemingly

PROFILE 8.7 Henry Lee Lucas and Ottis Elwood Toole, 1976–1982

"Joe Don ... I've done some bad things" was something of an understatement from Henry Lee Lucas to a jailer when he was incarcerated for illegal possession of a .22-caliber weapon. Within a few days Lucas had confessed to killing about 100 victims in several states. Within a few months the figure rose from 100 to 600 victims. He claimed to have killed in most of the 50 states and to have had at least a dozen victims in Canada.

Born in Blacksburg, Virginia, in 1936, to a woman who worked as a prostitute and suffered from alcoholism, Henry seemed to be doomed from the beginning of his life. Lucas experienced rejection from both within and outside his family. His IQ was considered to be slightly below normal. He dropped out of school in the fifth grade after his brother accidentally gouged out his right eye with a knife. By the time he was 13 he had already served time in Maryland for auto theft. At age 14 he killed a girl, also 14, in order to conceal a sex crime. He continued to accumulate a history of criminal behavior of burglaries and thefts. At age 23 he stabbed his mother to death during an argument. He was sent to prison in Michigan and was paroled in 1970, only to return quickly for another four years for attempted abduction. He was released in 1975, and a year later he teamed up with Ottis Toole, a tall, rough-looking character who served at times as Lucas's homosexual lover. Toole also had been involved in various criminal activities. He would later confess to having killed several homosexuals and to having started several fires simply because he found them exciting. Apparently Toole enjoyed killing his victims, then mutilating the corpses.

The pair traveled through many states, picking up hitchhikers to kill along the way. Most of the victims were female, although Lucas did confess to killing a few males, such as a police officer in Huntington, West Virginia. Many of the victims were sexually abused, and necrophilia and even cannibalism may have been involved. He also had another traveling companion and sexual partner, 15-year-old Freida "Becky" Lorraine Powell. Toole was her uncle and had managed to gain custody of the orphan girl from a state institution. While in Texas, the slightly retarded girl became involved in an argument with Lucas about leaving the state. Lucas later confessed how Becky reached over and slapped him, to which he immediately responded by stabbing her to death. According to Lucas, he then raped her, dismembered the body, stuffed the pieces into pillowcases, and left the remains in a field. Ironically, this young girl was the only person for whom Lucas claims to have had affection.

routine lives while they methodically killed and disposed of victims in their own homes or places of employment. In some cases of local team killing, offenders were easier to detect because bodies of victims were discovered quickly.

Team offenders in this subgroup appeared in several states, the majority surfacing in California. Table 8.3 indicates the distribution of team killings and the number of offenders by state. Except for California, the number of cases was relatively even and did not appear to be concentrated in any particular area of the country. However, along with California, a few states, including Illinois, Texas, and Pennsylvania, reported noticeably higher numbers of offenders per case than all other states.

Lucas claimed to have killed his victims in every imaginable fashion. He never wanted to know their names, and if a victim did give his or her name, Lucas would put it out of his mind. He claimed to have killed very young children and people 80 years of age. Lucas's first confession after he was jailed in 1983 solved the unexplained disappearance of 80-year-old Katherine Rich, who had been living in north Texas not far from Lucas. He chopped her into pieces and tried to incinerate the remains in his stove. Investigators would later find pieces of human bones in the trash of Lucas's home. Most of the Lucas/Toole victims were female hitchhikers who willingly got into their car. Lucas perceived that women who hitchhiked rides were like prostitutes, and he harbored a real hatred for them. Lucas remembers as a child having to watch his prostitute mother have sex with men, and how poorly he was treated by her.

Other victims were killed during robberies or while Toole was sexually attacking a male victim. When asked if he (Lucas) had any morals at all, he responded that he never stole from the victims; he never took their money or their jewelry. After Lucas started his confessions, he decided to help locate the bodies of the victims. He claimed that God helped him get over his hate, and it was time to change his life and start again. But did Lucas/Toole actually kill as many as 600 victims? One investigator was quoted as saying, "This is a man who will confess to anything you want." He is believed to have confessed to many of the murders because of the publicity he received (Peyton, 1984).

Lucas was convicted of 10 homicides, but in early 1985 he began to recant most of his confessions, claiming that law enforcement officers pressured him into confessing or tried to bribe him with special perks. He claimed that police were simply trying to clear cases and use him as a scapegoat. In early 1988, shortly after interviewing Lucas, one investigator stated that Lucas probably killed between 40 and 50 victims. He killed mainly because he enjoyed the experience; most of his killings were probably done in Florida, Texas, and Louisiana, although authorities in other states believe he was involved in additional homicides. Lucas's death sentence was commuted to life in prison in 1998 by then–Texas governor George W. Bush, and he died of natural causes in 2001. Toole later died of cirrhosis of the liver in a Florida prison. In December 2008 the state of Florida officially identified Toole to be the killer of five-year-old Adam Walsh, whose father would later create the television series *America's Most Wanted*.

VICTIM SELECTION

Team killers did not appear to be gender-specific, and equally selected both males and females as targets, especially those who were adults. About half of all team cases and offenders killed both males and females. Strangers were the most common type of victim, and there was a preference for adults over children. In one case offenders would cruise in their van along city streets looking for opportunities to drive up beside an intended victim and pull her in through the side door. The victim was then gagged, tied, and tortured to death. Overall, in 73% of the cases, at least one female was murdered.

TABLE 8.3 Distribution of Cases and Team Killers by State, 1850–2004

State	Number of Cases	Number of Offenders	State	Number of Cases	Number of Offenders
California	16	43	Montana	2	4
Florida	6	8	Utah	2	4
Illinois	5	19	Tennessee	1	2
Texas	5	13	Oklahoma	1	2
Ohio	4	4	Nevada	1	2
Washington	3	6	New Jersey	1	2
Pennsylvania	3	12	Iowa	1	2
Arizona	3	5	Minnesota	1	2
Indiana	3	6	South Carolina	1	2
Virginia	3	6	Vermont	1	2
Michigan	2	4	Georgia	1	2
Nebraska	2	4	Massachusetts	1	2
Oregon	2	4	Louisiana	1	2
New York	2	7	Alabama	1	2
Kansas	2	4	Maryland	1	2
Colorado	2	4			

SOURCE: © Cengage Learning, 2013.

As indicated in Table 8.4, very few cases or offenders that specifically targeted children or teenagers were identified. Nearly one-fifth of all cases included one or more male or female children. Females were also the most common targets among teenage victims. Overall, team offenders targeted female teens twice as often as male teens. In addition, when team offenders killed victims from more than one age category, adults and teenagers were the most likely targets. Conversely, team offenders, in all cases, were least likely to select both teenagers and children as victims.

The majority of cases involved stranger-to-stranger violence (see Tables 8.5 and 8.6). Two-thirds of female team offenders and three-fourths of male team offenders targeted strangers. Again, this reinforces the belief that strangers are preferred as victims by serial killers. Very few cases involved the killing of a family member or an acquaintance.

Stranger-to-stranger homicide facilitation was influenced by several circumstances, including time of attack or abduction, accessibility to victims, age and race of victims, and location of potential victims and offenders. Although research has yet to explore some of these factors, it would appear that not all strangers were equally at risk. Individual lifestyle appeared to be a critical factor in determining the types of strangers who fell prey to serial killers. Risk-takers such as prostitutes and hitchhikers appeared to be at greater risk than those who avoided such lifestyles.

TABLE 8.4 Percentage of Team Offenders Murdering Specific Victim Age and Gender Categories, 1850–2004

	Percentage of Cases (*N* = 49)	Percentage of Offenders (*N* = 114)
Gender		
1. Females only	28	24
Males only	26	28
Both	46	48
	100	100
2. At least one female	74	71
At least one male	72	74
Age Grouping		
Adults only	42	45
Teens only	8	9
Children only	2	2
Gender and Age Grouping		
1. Adults:		
One or more females	68	64
One or more males	60	64
Both males and females	40	40
2. Teens:		
One or more females	36	37
One or more males	18	23
Both males and females	6	12
3. Children:		
One or more females	16	14
One or more males	18	16
Both males and females	10	7
4. Age combinations:		
Adults and teens	22	24
Adults and children	8	6
Teens and children	2	3
All ages	14	14

SOURCE: © Cengage Learning, 2013.

Table 8.7 compares cases and offenders with the degree of facilitation provided by the victims. Did the victim walk alone at night? Did he or she hitchhike or pick up partners in bars? Perhaps the person was too trusting of strangers instead of exercising caution. In any case, recent team offender cases appeared to involve more frequency of facilitation by victims than in earlier years. For example, overall since 1800, 59% of these cases were reported to have one or more victims rating low in facilitation. Since

TABLE 8.5 Percentage of Team Offenders Murdering Family, Acquaintances, and Strangers in the United States, 1850–2004

Relationship	Percentage of Cases (*N* = 48)	Percentage of Female Offenders (*N* = 19)	Percentage of Male Offenders (*N* = 93)	Percentage of Total Number of Offenders (*N* = 112)
Strangers	75	68	81	79
Strangers/ acquaintances	11	5	7	6
Strangers/family	4	11	2	4
Acquaintances	4	11	4	6
Acquaintances/family	2	—	1	1
Family	4	5	3	4
All	4	—	2	1

SOURCE: © Cengage Learning, 2013.

1975, however, that number has dropped considerably. This in turn raises questions of whether victims are actually taking more risks, taking greater risks, or whether offenders are merely exploiting a pool of risk-takers they had earlier ignored. What has changed considerably from the first study is that several more offenders who target victims with both low and high facilitation ratings have been identified.

METHODS AND MOTIVES

Guns were commonly used by team offenders during the commission of their crimes (see Table 8.8). However, guns only were used in approximately one out of four cases as the sole method of killing. As in other serial murders, the purpose was usually not to dispose of victims quickly but to keep them alive so they could be subjected to tortures and mutilations. Consequently, more than half of team offenders used two or more methods to kill their victims. Mutilations, including stabbings, dissections, and other forms of cutting, were particularly common. Several offenders expressed enjoyment in being able to perform acts of sadism. The case of Dean Corll and followers graphically illustrates this point (see Profile 8.8).

Team killers were more likely than other offenders to kill for cult-related reasons. A few team offenders were involved in ritualistic torture of victims. Most of these offenders belonged to larger teams of killers and were not the planners and decision makers. As mentioned earlier, cult activities involved extensive torturing of victims and using human blood and body parts for altar offerings. Enjoyment of torture and killing was more frequently expressed by this group of team killers than by other serial offenders. This, in part, may be due to the bravado some of the group members may have felt was necessary for the public to hear and see once they were apprehended.

Almost identical to other serial offenders, team killers most likely had motives of a sexual nature (see Table 8.9). Rape, sodomy, fellatio, and so on were recurrent forms of sexual acting out. As discussed earlier, such "motives" appear to fall under the category of methods; the sexual assaults appeared to be methods of gaining

TABLE 8.6 Order of Types of Victims Selected by Team Killers

A. Strangers

1. Females: young females walking alone
   Hitchhikers
   Prostitutes
   College students
   Handicapped
   Respondents to newspaper ads
2. Travelers/campers
3. People at random in homes
4. People at random on street
5. Young boys
6. Employees/businesspeople
7. Children at play
8. Police officers

B. Acquaintances

9. Neighbor children
10. Females: people on street
    Waitresses
11. Males: group members
    Visitors
    People in authority

C. Family

12. Children
13. Wives/brothers/mothers

SOURCE: © Cengage Learning, 2013.

control over victims. Money was found to be commonly cited as a motive for murder, although it was much less likely noted as the sole reason for killing. Similar to all serial killers, team offenders could rarely be legally classified as insane. Regardless of how obscene some of the murders were, insanity could not be established.

OFFENDER HISTORY

Research data were sometimes limited regarding certain biographical information on team serial killers. In approximately half of team offender profiles, sufficient data existed to examine previous violent, criminal, or abnormal behaviors. Offenders having such histories were most likely to have been incarcerated in prison or a mental institution. Team offenders reported similar records of incarceration in comparison to their male solo counterparts (see Table 8.10). They were also likely to have criminal records for theft or sex-related crimes, or

PROFILE 8.8 Dean A. Corll, David O. Brooks, and Elmer Wayne Henley, 1970–1973

Born in Fort Wayne, Indiana, Dean Corll relocated to Houston, Texas, about the time his parents were divorced. A model student, he played trombone in the high school band and was never a disciplinary problem. He was often referred to as "good ol' Dean." He became active in his family's candy business and eventually became vice president. For a two-year period he left the Corll Candy Company to care for his widowed grandmother. He later served time in the military and received an honorable hardship discharge to return and help his mother with the family business. Corll's generosity and kindness became well known among the local children, and they came regularly for candy handouts. The candy company dissolved in 1968, and Corll entered an electricians' training program. He began to move frequently, and in 1969 he met David Brooks, who became attracted to Corll's personality.

Brooks's parents had divorced. He had a short history of theft before he was sent to live with his grandfather, then with his grandmother; finally he moved in with Corll. He always maintained to his friends that "nobody can figure me out." He continued to steal, shoplift, and burglarize while Corll helped him purchase a Corvette. The two became sexually involved, and Corll began giving money to Brooks for sexual favors. Elmer Wayne Henley, 17, also began associating with Corll. He too had come from a broken home, and helped support the family after his father left. As his grades dropped, Henley left school in the ninth grade. He had tried to enlist in the navy at 16 but was rejected. Life worsened for Henley, and he was arrested for breaking and entering and assault with a deadly weapon. He began drinking heavily and associating with Dean Corll, but unlike the bisexual Brooks, Henley, was not interested in any homosexual liaisons.

The two young men, however, were willing to procure young males for Corll to sexually abuse. They would later state in confessions that Corll agreed to pay them $200 for every boy they picked up. The two found male hitchhikers and brought them to Corll's apartment for glue-sniffing parties. When the boys passed out, Corll would

histories of psychiatric problems. Considering that 26% of all serial killers report a history of various psychiatric problems, team killers are only slightly higher (29%). However, team offenders (28%) were less likely to have criminal records for sex-related crimes than solo killers (38%).

Team offenders were likely to come in contact with one another as a result of prior incarcerations and criminal records. There appeared to be somewhat more interest in financial gain among team serial killers than solo offenders in considering past crimes. Indeed, some team killers grouped themselves together in almost businesslike ventures that culminated in murder. Such is the case of Leonard Lake and Charles Ng (see Profile 8.9).

TABLE 8.7 Degree of Victim Facilitation in Being Murdered by Team Offenders, 1850–2004

Facilitation	Percentage of Cases (*N* = 49)	Percentage of Offenders (*N* = 111)
Low	59	65
High	10	10
Both	31	25

SOURCE: © Cengage Learning, 2013.

molest them. Eventually Corll wanted more and began torturing and killing the boys. He would tie or handcuff them to a seven-by-three-foot board and then sodomize, strangle, and shoot the boys. Their deaths often were gruesome; Corll would sometimes chew off the victim's penis or assault the youth with a 17-inch double-headed dildo. Most of the victims came from the Heights area in Houston, and some were neighbors. The victims ranged in age from nine years to college age. Corll killed several of his victims in groups of two, and on at least two occasions he killed brothers. Henley seemed to enjoy the sadistic killing; on one occasion he fired a bullet up the nostril of one of the victims and then shot him again in the head. Brooks later testified that Henley "seemed to enjoy causing pain." The killing went on until Corll decided to kill Henley after they had disagreed. Henley managed to convince Corll not to kill him, and when Henley was freed, he grabbed a gun and shot Corll five times, killing him on the spot.

The story became public when Henley decided to call the police and tell the entire story. Police found 17 bodies of young white males under a boathouse near Pasadena, Texas. They had been placed in sheets of heavy plastic and covered with lime. Various smaller plastic containers held an assortment of body parts, primarily sex organs. Ten other bodies were exhumed at two additional sites under the guidance of Henley. Some observers believe police stopped searching for bodies once they had surpassed the existing number of homicide victims found in a single case at that time.

Elmer Wayne Henley eventually was found guilty of helping to murder six of the boys and sentenced to six sentences of 99 years each. A Texas appeals court in 1978 overturned his conviction as a result of pretrial publicity, but in a second trial, in June 1979, Henley was convicted and sentenced again. David Brooks was convicted of only one murder and sentenced to life in prison. Ironically, Dean A. Corll's coffin was covered in an American flag in keeping with the tradition that we honor those who have served their country honorably (Nash, 1981a).

TABLE 8.8 Methods Used by Team Offenders to Kill Their Victims, 1850–2004

Methods	Percentage of Cases ($N = 45$)	Percentage of Offenders ($N = 104$)
Firearms	64	62
Strangulation	36	34
Stabbing	32	35
Bludgeoning	29	32
Firearms only	27	27
Suffocation	9	7
Poison	7	9
Drowning	5	4
Combinations of methods	54	53

SOURCE: © Cengage Learning, 2013.

TABLE 8.9 Motives Reported by Team Offenders for Killing Their Victims, 1850–2004

Motives	Percentage of Cases (*N* = 49)	Percentage of Offenders (*N* = 101)
Sexual	49	43
Money	31	32
Control	33	27
Enjoyment	25	26
Cult expectations	12	18
Racism	9	19
Combination of motives	60	61

SOURCE: © Cengage Learning, 2013.

PROFILE 8.9 Leonard Lake and Charles Ng, 1983–1985

On June 2, 1985, a man arrested in San Francisco was detained and charged with illegal possession of a weapon with a silencer. A few moments later the man swallowed a cyanide capsule and collapsed; he died four days later, after being removed from life support systems. Fingerprints indicated his name was Leonard Lake, a 39-year-old Vietnam veteran who was described by neighbors as "quiet, strange, and somewhat arrogant."

He allegedly attended weekly Bible classes. It is also believed that he and an accomplice, Charles Ng, who fled to Canada, may have murdered 25 or more males and females in a specially constructed cinder-block bunker located near Sacramento in a mountain retreat that was used as a torture chamber. Some victims were lured to the house by a promise of work, whereas others answered classified ads. Apparently, some of the earliest victims were relatives, friends, and neighbors because they were easiest to lure to the bunker. The goal was to seek out sexually attractive females who would then be used as sex slaves, subjected to sexual torture, and often killed. Males were targets simply because they were companions of the women or because they had credit cards, cash, or desirable identification. It has been speculated that some of the men may have actually worked at the retreat prior to their deaths.

Some reports indicate that Lake was involved in clandestine cult meetings where human sacrifices were discussed. Some photographs show Lake wearing robes worn by modern-day witches and posing with a goat made up to look like a live unicorn. Police also discovered that Lake had skipped bail in 1982 after he was arrested on charges of possession of explosives and illegal automatic weapons. Shortly after this arrest, Lake's wife divorced him. Two years earlier Lake had been arrested for grand theft for stealing building materials from a low-income housing project. Ng, a 24-year-old who also had many encounters with the law, had been involved in several incidents of stealing and shoplifting as a youth. Following a hit-and-run accident, Ng joined the marines, where he was arrested for stealing a variety of weapons, including grenade launchers, machine guns, and handguns. Ng escaped from the marine detention, and, after seeing an ad placed by Lake in a magazine for mercenary soldiers, he joined forces with Lake in a spree of killing.

TABLE 8.10 Percentage of Team Offenders Reporting a History of Violent, Criminal, or Abnormal Behavior, 1850–2004

History	Percentage of Cases (*N* = 49)	Percentage of Offenders (*N* = 55)
Theft	43	49
Prior incarceration in prison or mental institution	43	43
Psychiatric problems	27	29
Sex-related crimes	27	28
Drug/alcohol-related crimes	12	20
Crimes as a juvenile	15	14

SOURCE: © Cengage Learning, 2013.

When investigators went to the secluded ranch where the bunker was located, they found a sign posted on a vehicle that read, "If you love something, set it free. If it doesn't come back, hunt it down and kill it." Entries found in one of Lake's diaries indicated that some of the men brought to the ranch may have been used as game animals to be hunted down and executed. Wrote Lake, "Death is in my pocket and fantasy my goal" and "the perfect woman is totally controlled; a woman who does exactly what she is told and nothing else. There is no sexual problem with a submissive woman. There are no frustrations, only pleasure and contentment."

The diaries revealed graphic illustrations of sexual abuse, torture, murder, kidnapping, and cremation. Lake believed he would be a survivor of the nuclear holocaust in his concrete bunker filled with sex slaves, weapons, and food. Police found several tapes and pictures of women being sexually abused and tortured. Some of the tapes showed Lake and Ng raping and sodomizing their victims. When the two had finished, they executed their victims by shooting or strangling them. It appears that victims then may have been cut up into pieces with power saws and tree trimmers found at the site and placed in metal drums for incineration. The remaining bones were then pulverized and buried. Police found 45 pounds of bone fragments, including many teeth. Some victims, including some campers, were buried around the ranch area. Lake had made a map of "buried treasure," which police thought meant gravesites. The exact number of the victims of Lake and Ng will never be known. Ng, while incarcerated in a Canadian prison, fought extradition to the United States but after several years was returned to stand trial in California. After nearly 14 years Ng was brought to trial, convicted, and sentenced to death. His conviction is currently on appeal. Lake was cremated but his brain was preserved for scientific research into the causation of homicidal behavior.

The seven-month trial of Charles Ng was so traumatic and emotionally draining for the jurors, after being forced to repeatedly watch video recordings of the grisly murders, that several had to seek professional counseling.

PROFILE 8.10 Gerald A. Gallego Jr. and Charlene Gallego, 1978–1980

When Gerald Gallego Jr. was born, his father, a 19-year-old convict, was doing time in San Quentin prison. Gerald Jr. was nine years old when, in 1955, his father was executed in Mississippi for having killed two correctional officers. His father, whom Gerald Jr. thought had died much earlier in a car accident, wrote a letter telling others, especially youth, to avoid breaking the law. But less than a year later Gerald Jr. began getting into trouble. At age 13, he was detained by the California Youth Authority for sexual involvement with a 6-year-old girl. From that point on his life gradually continued to self-destruct.

By the age of 32, Gerald Jr. had been married seven times, one wife having married him twice. He was known to have been married to more than one woman at the same time, and when he married Charlene he did not bother to divorce his previous wife. By this time, Gerald was developing a real penchant for violence and sadism. By the time of his final arrest, Gerald had compiled an amazing history of murder, deviant sexual conduct, a jail escape, an armed robbery, and several other crimes.

Unlike her husband, Charlene apparently grew up in a family that provided love and support and had the respect of neighbors and friends. Why she decided to attach herself to an ex-convict who referred to her as "Ding-a-Ling" is unknown, but she quickly accepted his lifestyle, including his bizarre and perverted sexual fantasies.

Gerald decided it was time to seek out young female virgins that he could keep in a secluded hideaway where he would be able to use them as his personal sex slaves. His first two victims, 17-year-old Rhonda Scheffler and 16-year-old Kippi Vaught, were abducted September 11, 1978, from a Sacramento shopping mall. Their bodies were later found badly beaten, both having been shot in the head with a .25-caliber handgun. Autopsies indicated both girls had been sexually abused. On June 24, 1979, in Reno, Nevada, two more girls, 15-year-old Brenda Judd and 14-year-old Sandra Kaye Colley, were abducted from a crowded fairground. Their bodies were never recovered. On April 24, 1980, 17-year-old Stacy Ann Redican and Karen Chipman-Twiggs disappeared from a Sacramento shopping mall. In July, picnickers

Another important area of biographical data concerned the degree to which team offenders had experienced traumatization while in their youth (see Table 8.11). In comparing male team killers to male solo killers, changes from the original study were found. For example, in the original study, team killers were twice as likely to come from unstable homes as solo killers. With a much larger data set of solo killers, it was found that little difference existed between the two groups. This included alcoholic parents, prostitution by mother, incarceration of parent(s) (see Profile 8.10), periodic separation from parents due to troubles at home, and psychiatric problems involving the parents. We do continue to see a gap between the two groups when reporting on rejection. Solo offenders were much more prone to report feelings of rejection than team serial offenders. Other areas were also higher for the solos, including remembering beatings as children (32%), being adopted (14%), and parents dying or the offender recalling his youth as an orphan (14%).

near Reno discovered the girls' bodies in shallow graves. They too had been beaten severely with a blunt metal object and sexually abused. On June 6, 1980, Linda Teresa Aguilar, age 21 and expecting her first child, was abducted while hitchhiking from Port Orford, Oregon, to Gold Beach. She too was later found in a shallow grave, tightly bound with her skull crushed in by blows from a metal object. The autopsy report indicated she had been buried while still alive. The next victim, 34-year-old Virginia Mochel, mother of two, was abducted while walking to her car from the bar and grill where she worked as a waitress. Three months later her body was discovered outside Sacramento. On November 1, 1980, Mary Beth Sowers and her fiancé, Craig Raymond Miller, were kidnapped from a parking lot. Gerald had no particular interest in Craig, and on arriving in a secluded area, shot him in the head three times. Later Gerald raped and sexually abused Mary Beth and also shot her in the head three times.

Police were finally able to apprehend Gerald and Charlene after a friend of the engaged couple witnessed the abduction and was able to memorize the license number of the car driven by Gerald. After a difficult manhunt that took authorities to several states, the Gallegos were captured. After their return to California, the couple pled innocent to charges of murder and kidnapping. Because Charlene was not legally married to Gerald, she eventually agreed to testify against him in exchange for a plea bargain. She explained how she would help lure the girls to the car where Gerald could overpower them. She admitted sitting in the front seat while Gerald would rape, beat, and sodomize his victims and force them to perform oral sex and sometimes kill them. Charlene also admitted holding a gun on two of the girls while Gerald raped them. She described in detail the 10 gruesome murders in her husband's quest for the perfect sex slave. She admitted watching while Gerald used a hammer to beat his victims to death. The Gallegos were convicted of murder, and Gerald was sentenced by the state of Nevada to die by lethal injection but died of cancer in 2002. Charlene is now serving two concurrent 16-year, 8-month sentences in Carson City, Nevada, for her part in the murders (Linedecker, 1987).

TABLE 8.11 Percentage of Male Team Offenders Who Experienced Forms of Traumatization as Children, Compared with Male Solo Offenders

Traumatizations	Male Team Killers (*N* = 23)	Male Solo Killers (*N* = 56)
Unstable home	47	43
Rejection	39	47
Beatings	23	32
Divorce of parents	9	22
Illegitimate	23	9
Sexual abuse	16	18
Parents died/orphaned	7	14
Poverty	16	11

SOURCE: © Cengage Learning, 2013.

TABLE 8.12 Disposition of Male and Female Team Offenders after Apprehension

Disposition	Percentage of Offenders ($N = 98$)
Prison sentence	67
Death row	24
Killed before trial	4
Suicide	3
Confined to psychiatric institution	2
	100

SOURCE: © Cengage Learning, 2013.

DISPOSITION OF OFFENDERS

Of this study's group of team killers, 24% have been executed or await execution on death row (see Table 8.12). Seven percent were either killed before a trial could be held or committed suicide. In total, 67% were incarcerated for life or sentenced to serve a specific number of years in prison. A few of these offenders are currently awaiting court dispositions. Occasionally an offender has been placed in a mental institution. Rarely has anyone convicted of such crimes escaped or been freed from prison. The problem, however, is not being able to keep these offenders incarcerated but rather freeing other convicted psychopathic felons every year who will go on to become some of America's most infamous serial murderers.

More than half of the serial killers in this study are destined to live out the rest of their lives in prison. What efforts, if any, are being made to study them or rehabilitate such offenders? What are the issues surrounding sentencing? Is capital punishment the best response to these offenders? Both physiological and psychological forensics must play a role in combating serial crime.

The Female Serial Murderer

LEARNING OBJECTIVES

- To understand the emergence, societal scope, and impact of female serial murderers
- To examine cases of female serial killers and their modus operandi and victim selection
- To explore the motives and psychopathology of female serial killers
- To review the latest research on female serial killers

The orientation of criminological research focuses primarily on male criminality, especially in the area of violent crimes such as homicide. However, during the 1970s, when the United States experienced a growth in the women's liberation movement, some scholars hastily observed "a tremendous increase of serious crimes by women" (Deming, 1977). In her book *Sisters in Crime,* Freda Adler (1975) predicted "a new breed of women criminals" who would be significantly involved in violent crimes (p. 7). Yet other research discounts such notions (Chapman, 1980; Schur, 1984; Steffensmeier & Cobb, 1981). Weisheit (1984b), in his review of women and crime perspectives, noted that "the factors leading to the current interest in female criminality—the perception that female crime was on the rise, the link between liberation and crime and the sexist nature of previous research on female criminality—have been challenged" (p. 197). In any case, the number of women who kill is still very low in comparison with the number of men who kill. Can women be as sadistic as men in committing violent acts? We do not think of women in roles of violent sexual predators, yet given the right circumstances women have proven to be as sadistic and detached as men. Consider Dr. Herta Oberheuser, who was a medical doctor in the Auschwitz death camps. She killed children with oil and Evipan solution, a surgical anesthetic used intravenously that lasted about 20 minutes. From the time of the injection until death was three to five minutes, during which time the child was fully conscious. While they watched she removed organs and limbs from her victims.

She was known for her sadistic medical experiments, inflicting deliberate wounds on her victims in order to simulate combat wounds of German soldiers. These wounds would then be rubbed and smashed with foreign objects such as rusty nails, broken glass, and dirt. For this Dr. Oberheuser received a 20-year sentence, but was released after serving only 7 years. Few people are even aware that female doctors such as Oberheuser worked in the death camps, as we historically focus on the more infamous male German doctors such as Mengele and Gross (see Chapter 6).

IDENTIFYING FEMALE SERIAL MURDERERS

Because of the constant focus on male criminality, women are seldom viewed by the public as killers. Certainly, our crime statistics support this view. Because those women who kill do so primarily in domestic conflicts, there is even less reason to suspect women to be multiple killers (Hickey, 1986; Kirby, 1998). Thibault and Rossier (1992) state:

> Although some women may kill in the home in self defense, female killers in the home also plan to kill and kill because they want to. We need to take a close look at the courts that are letting these women get away with murder. Has our sexist society, by defending these female murderers, made it open season for women to kill men, as long as the killing is in the home? (p. 126)

Consequently, those few females who are serial murderers may be even less likely to come under suspicion than their male counterparts or females who commit other types of murder. Of those women who commit multiple murders, rarely does one go on any kind of rampage like that of Richard Speck, who killed eight nurses in Chicago in 1966, or of James Huberty, who in 1984 during a 10-minute shooting spree killed 21 victims and wounded 19 others in a McDonald's restaurant in San Ysidro, California. Female serial killers, especially when they act alone, are almost invisible to public view and can kill over many years (see Profile 9.1).

Freiberger (1997), in her efforts to apply current serial-murderer typologies to female serial killers, concluded that such classifications were not adequate in understanding female offenders. These are the *quiet* killers. They are every bit as lethal as male serial murderers, but we are seldom aware one is in our midst because of the low visibility of their killing. Keeney and Heide (1994) conclude from their review of 11 studies of serial murder that only two address the notion of females as serial killers. They note that such offenders are easily overlooked:

> For female serial murderers who have killed their patients, for example, health care facilities appear to have been extremely reluctant to bring charges against an employee with the resultant probability of trial and media attention. One case in this sample was indicative of this type of administrative bungle. Genene Jones, a Texas nurse, was continually

PROFILE 9.1 Betty J. Neumar, "Killer Granny," 1952–2007

Born in 1931 in Ohio, Betty Neumar was good at many things in her life, but her forte, many believe, was marrying men and killing them or having them killed in order to collect the inheritance. Over a 55-year period Betty married at least five men and each died leaving her with some money. None of them were wealthy, which may have been the reason she kept remarrying. At least three of her husbands died of gunshot wounds and one from possible arsenic poisoning. Only one person, the brother of her fourth victim, was suspicious and persistent enough to attract the attention of law enforcement. His brother had been found with multiple gunshot wounds, leading investigators who reexamined the case to believe that a hit man was hired to do the killing. Other husbands were likely killed with poison, possibly arsenic. Betty had a penchant for living well that meant fine clothes and jewelry. While married in 2000 she and her husband at the time filed for bankruptcy, citing over $200,000 in debts on 43 credit cards while only receiving a combined income of $1,800 a month. With her debts resolved Betty was able to move on to another husband and new victim. She appeared as a typical white-haired senior citizen who could not have the capacity for such crimes, but she was believed by investigators to be involved in the deaths of all of her husbands from Ohio, Florida, North Carolina, and Georgia. Betty was released on bail bond in 2008 and died in 2011 in a Louisiana hospital before she could be brought to trial.

> employed in a hospital long after numerous complaints and charges that she was injuring the children in her ward. In addition, family and friends may be unwilling to confront female killers with their suspicion regarding murder. The husband of Mary Beth Tinning, the New York woman who murdered eight of her children, apparently did nothing to stop her behavior, suggest that she get therapy, or take steps to prevent further birth. (p. 394)

Controversy should no longer remain as to whether females who are multiple-homicide offenders fit the "true" definition of a serial killer. When Aileen Wuornos was linked to killing seven men with a gun, the FBI quickly labeled her the nation's first female serial killer. Investigators argued that she fit the profile of the *male* serial killer because she had many of the typical characteristics including past physical and sexual abuse, alcohol and drug abuse, abandonment by family, and possible organic brain damage from her extensive drug abuse. As a lesbian who had been brutalized by males, Wuornos harbored hatred for men. She was physically strong and could become very aggressive when provoked. She killed like a male, except for the fact that most of her victims were shot in the torso, which is more typical of female killers; males are more prone to shoot into the victim's head. We need to move beyond comparing women to men and compare women to women. Epstein (1995) notes that female serial killers are seldom portrayed to the public with accuracy:

> Actual murders by women who meet the definitional requirements of serial killing frequently involve the killing of children, the elderly, or

> the sick. This type of serial murder is not depicted in film. Rather, female serial killer characters are typically presented as avenging a gang rape, as reacting to a wrong, or as motivated by an evil supernatural force. (p. 69)

Heckert and Ferraiolo (1996) conducted a study of college students in which they examined perceptions of female serial killers. Most respondents did not have a conceptualization of a female serial killer. The few who did have an image visualized the female serial murderer in a variety of ways. No dominant image emerged except that she would be in her 30s and have a slovenly appearance. Most respondents imagined that she was without any prior criminal record, was not a brutal killer, did not use torture techniques, and used a gun to dispatch her victims. They perceived her to have experienced extreme childhood/family trauma and to be distinctly mentally ill and of high intelligence. Not surprisingly, such perceptions ultimately distort an accurate depiction of female serial killers.

To say that a woman cannot be a "true" serial killer unless she acts like a male is myopic. Women can be just as lethal as males, but they use different methods to achieve their goals. The real issue is method. If Wuornos had used poison to kill men she never would have received her distinction as the first female serial killer. In brief, the belief is that "real" killers use male methods to kill. This chapter challenges that assumption. Wuornos was not the first female serial killer, as the reader is about to discover, but rather an anomaly. Wuornos was an atypical female serial killer. We have almost no documentation of anyone similar to Wuornos, and there is nothing to suggest we will see many more like her in the foreseeable future. In truth, every serial killer, male or female, has certain distinguishing features that identify them as serial killers and make them unique even though they fit the serial-killer mold. Female serial killers are some of the most fascinating criminals within American society. We have much to learn from them.

This chapter focuses on the cases of 64 females (61 cases), approximately 15% of the total number of serial killers in this 2004 study. Some acted alone (69%), others with partners (31%), murdering altogether between 410 and 628 victims. Most of them are white (93%), and the remainder are African American (7%). Many of these killers, where identified, were predominantly unskilled, skilled, or professional in occupation. Several of them were "black widows," nurses, and other types of care providers. (Black widows are women who kill their husbands, children, or other relatives.) Frequently they had remarried several times in order to kill again and again. Those who made up the nurse and care-provider group victimized people over whom they had control. Elderly men and women, and especially babies, became their targets (see Chapter 6). Of course, some female offenders were unemployed or were in jobs unrelated to their accessing victims. The following is a summary update of female serial killer cases that have occurred in the United States between 2004 and 2011. What changes can you identify between this smaller more recent update and the larger studies discussed in this chapter?

Female Serial Killers Update, 2004–2011

- Female killers ($N = 14$) account for 10% of all serial killers 2004–2011 ($N = 146$)
- Percentage of offenders in team cases: 50%
- Race of offender:
  - Caucasian: 93%
  - African American: 7%
- Offender year of birth range: 1931–1975
- Average age of offender at first killing: 40.7
- Average age at apprehension: 47.4
- Average span of offender killing: 7.1 years
- Total number of victims: 39–55
- Span of offender killing: 1952–2008
- Offenders who killed all their victims in same year: 29%
- Offenders who killed in more than one year: 71%
  - Over 1 year: 14%
  - 2–3 years: 14%
  - 4–5 years: 7%
  - 6–9 years: 21%
  - 10+ years: 14%
- Method of killing:
  - Poison only: 21%
  - Strangle/smother only: 21%
  - Shoot only: 7%
  - Stab only: 7%
  - Blunt force only: 7%
  - Combination of poisoning, beating, strangling, stabbing, and/or shooting: 37%
- Victims of female killers:
  - Adults only: 93%
  - Children only: 7%
  - Average number of victims per offender: 3.1–4.2
  - Strangers only: 50%
  - Prostitutes: 7%
  - Elderly: 14%
  - Patients: 14%
  - Males only: 43%
  - Females only: 21%
  - Male and female victims: 36%.
  - Involving more than one state: 29%

We can speculate that the annual victim count produced by this group of females is very low. They appear to be atypical of female criminality. They tend to be viewed as anomalies, aberrations in female homicide patterns. They are ignored because there has not been an appropriate "pigeonhole" in which to place them and because of the belief that they represent a statistically small number of offenders. The public displays more amusement than concern about cases like that of Linda Sue Jones of Torrance, California. In September 1988, Jones admitted having tried to kill two previous husbands in order to collect insurance. The day after she was sentenced to 20 years in prison, Jones married again in a ceremony performed by the same judge who sentenced her. It is less troublesome simply to label such people "insane" and somehow less important, at least statistically, than other female offenders. The Ted Bundys, the John Gacys, and the Jeffrey Dahmers are also atypical of males who commit homicide, but yet they have attracted international attention and a host of researchers. However, important comparisons can be made between women who are serial killers and other women who commit homicide.

EMERGENCE OF FEMALE SERIAL MURDERERS

Of the 64 female serial killers identified in this research, approximately 10% started their killing between 1826 and 1899, whereas the remaining 90% appeared since 1900. Several of the females had accomplices when they murdered and therefore are included in Chapter 8, which deals with team killers. This analysis focuses on the behavior and, when possible, the personal lives of these women, who ranged in age from 15 to 69 at the time they first began to kill. They are responsible for the deaths of 410–628 men, women, and children, or 14% to 15% of all victims killed by offenders in this study (see Table 9.1a).

Approximately three-fourths of these females began their careers in killing since 1950. Like the statistics for male serial offenders, this number may be explained in part by improved police investigation and reporting procedures, population growth, and increased media attention. Although relatively few in number, female serial killers emerge periodically and thus merit our attention. Consider the number of victims believed to have been killed by these few offenders. The average number of victims per case and per female offender

TABLE 9.1a Number of Cases of Serial Murder Committed by Females in the United States, 1826–2004

Years	Total Number of Cases	Number of Cases per Year	Number of Offenders	Percentage of Offenders	Percentage of Offenders per Year
1826–2004	61	0.34	64	100	0.28 (178 yrs)
1826–1969	32	0.22	34	53	0.24 (144 yrs)
1970–2004	29	1.17	30	47	0.85 (35 yrs)

SOURCE: © Cengage Learning, 2013.

TABLE 9.1b Victim/Female Serial Murderer Comparisons in the United States, 1826–2004

Year	Number of Cases	Number of Cases per Year	Number of Victims	Number of Victims per Case	Number of Victims per Year
Total	61	0.34	427–612	7–10	2–3 (178 yrs)
1826–1849	1	0.04	2–5	2–5	0.1–0.2 (24 yrs)
1850–1874	1	0.04	11–30	11–30	1 (25 yrs)
1875–1899	4	0.16	63–125	16–31	3–5 (25 yrs)
1900–1924	8	0.38	45–46	6	2 (25 yrs)
1925–1949	7	0.28	64–100	9–14	3–4 (25 yrs)
1950–1974	13	0.52	62–67	5	2–3 (25 yrs)
1975–2004	27	0.9	180–239	7–9	6–8 (30 yrs)

SOURCE: © Cengage Learning, 2013.

ranged from 7 to 10 (see Table 9.1b). The number of victims per case has fluctuated modestly since 1900. There was also a noticeable rise in the total number of victims since 1975. The average age of the female offender was 31, slightly higher than that of their male counterparts. Most of these females went on killing for several years before they were finally apprehended. The killing period for this group of females ranged from a few months to over 34 years.

Many of the women were unemployed or listed no occupation. Some were drifters or held jobs infrequently. Some of the unemployed were homemakers who found opportunities for killing. Others were professionals such as nurses who became adept at killing patients. Very few of these women were found to have a criminal history, or a criminal "career" (see Chapter 6). Others hired out as housekeepers, worked as waitresses, or operated small businesses. Of those reporting, only 8% reported no particular employment status (see Table 9.2). Most of these offenders were transient or living with relatives.

TABLE 9.2 Reported Occupation of Female Offenders in the United States, 1826–2004 (N = 64)

Occupation	Percentage
Unemployed	8
Unskilled	10
Semiskilled	15
Skilled	5
Professional	11
Other	11
Unknown	40
	100

SOURCE: © Cengage Learning, 2013.

Weisheit (1984a), in his research on incarcerated female homicide offenders, found that between 1981 and 1984, 77% of offenders had been unemployed at the time of their offense. He reported that the median age during this time frame was 27 years, that 65% of the female offenders were black, and that 76% had children (p. 478). Although the percentage of female serial offenders having children is comparable to female homicide offenders in general, some interesting differences exist between the two groups. For example, the female serial offenders were older (median age of 31), and 95% were white. The contrasts diminish, however, when we examine the reasons for women committing homicide.

With regard to murders in general, Wolfgang (1967) noted a preponderance of killings among the lower socioeconomic classes, where interpersonal violence was more "acceptable":

> When homicide is committed by members of the middle and upper social classes, there appears to be a high likelihood of major psychopathology or of planned, more "rational" (or rationalized) behavior. The fact that they commit an act of willful murder, which is in diametric opposition to the set of values embraced by the dominant social class establishment of which they are part, often means that these persons are suffering severely from an emotional crisis of profound proportions. Or they have been able ... to meditate and mediate with their own internalized value system until they can conceive of the murder act without the consequence of an overburdening guilt and thereby justify their performing the deed. This self-justificatory behavior undoubtedly requires the actor considerable time and much introspective wrestling in order to remain within, yet contradict his supportive value system.... Our thesis contains principally the notion that the man from a culture value system that denounces the use of interpersonal violence will be restrained from using violence because of his positive perspective that conforms to his value system, not because of a negation of it.
>
> The absence of that kind of value system is hardly likely to be a vacuous neutrality regarding violence. Instead, it is replaced by a value system that views violence as tolerable, expected, or required. As we approach that part of the cultural continuum where violence is a requisite response, we also enter a subculture where physically aggressive action quickly and readily can bleed into aggressive crime. The man from this culture area is more likely to use violence, similarly because of a positive perspective that requires conforming to his value system. Restraint from using violence may be a frustrating, ego-deflating, even guilt-ridden experience. Questions of the risks of being apprehended and the distant, abstract notion of the threat of punishment are almost irrelevant to he who acts with quick, yet socially ingrained aggressivity, neither reasoning nor time for it are at his disposal. (pp. 6–7)

This notion of subcultural violence, Wolfgang noted, was based on a differentiation in value systems. He separated out middle- and upper-class people and explained homicide in those classes as a result of "major" psychopathology, or planned, rational behavior. This explanation may well fit the two-thirds of female serial offenders (author's data) who were classified within the various tiers of middle- and upper-class social hierarchies. Regardless of the social class, however, all but one of the offending women were white. Weisheit (1984a) found that, between 1981 and 1983, 42% of the female homicide offenders in his study killed for money, up from 18% between 1940 and 1966 (p. 486). Overall, 73% of female serial killers were motivated at least partially by money, and 26% murdered only for money. Weisheit also reported that women were less likely now to kill in response to abuse than in the past. By contrast, female serial murderers are more likely to kill in response to abuse of various forms, although this motive appears to be less apparent than greed and the desire for money. Several of the cases that I examined, especially those of recent years, report various forms of physical and psychological abuse at the hands of husbands, lovers, friends, and other family members. In addition, women, regardless of social class, may be motivated to kill in response to a list of unfulfilled needs. Sometimes the needs are economic, and other times they are emotional. For some, the needs for economic and psychological well-being are virtually the same.

In earlier decades of American history, spouse abuse was not considered a justification or an explanation for female homicide. Today, however, emphasis is placed on understanding the nature of domestic violence and its relationship to murder. Women may be more likely now (than they were before the emergence of the women's movement) to explain homicidal behavior as a result of physical and/or mental abuse. The fact that women who commit homicides in general are increasingly reporting their motives as economic does not negate the possible link between societal discrimination against women and domestic violence. In short, women who kill more than once may manifest their behavior differently according to social class, but the stimulation for their behavior may stem from parallel class-related motivations. Whether the stimulation is psychopathology or a tolerance for violence, both may be the product of abuse the offenders have endured. Further discussion of motivations for killing will be undertaken later in this chapter. Consider now the case of Aileen Wuornos, a woman who claims to have been victimized as a child and later achieved international attention as one of the most violent female serial killers of our era (see Profile 9.2).

VICTIM SELECTION

Regardless of gender, homicide usually involves an offender and a victim who are acquainted or related to each other. Weisheit (1984b) observed in studying victim-offender relationships in which the offender was female that "once again, the data fail to support the notion of a new breed of murderess" (p. 485). While this fact is true of homicides in general, such is not the case when females are involved in serial homicides. Instead, one-fourth of female serial killers reported having killed strangers only and nearly one-third had killed at least one stranger

PROFILE 9.2 Aileen Carol Wuornos, 1989–1990

On January 9, 1991, Aileen Wuornos, age 34, also known as Susan Lynn Blahovec, Lee Blahovec, Lori Kristine Grody, and Cammie Marsh Greene, was arrested near Daytona Beach, Florida, just outside the Last Resort Bar. This female drifter, who was living out of a suitcase and sleeping wherever possible, had been connected to the murders of seven men found along central Florida highways. Wuornos would eventually provide a three-hour videotape confessing to the murders and claim that the men were trying to hurt her and she was only acting in self-defense. Wuornos was erroneously dubbed by the FBI as the first true female serial killer.

Wuornos was born in Oakland County, Michigan, in 1956 to a 16-year-old girl and a 19-year-old handyman. The marriage lasted only a few months. Her father was later imprisoned for kidnapping, rape, and other crimes and eventually committed suicide while in jail.

Wuornos, at six months of age, was abandoned by her mother. Her grandparents in Troy, Michigan, adopted her and raised her as their own child. Wuornos at age 10 would learn from other children at school the truth about her real parents.

Wuornos claims to have been raped at 13 and became pregnant. Her grandparents did not believe her and sent her to a home for unwed mothers. After giving the baby up for adoption and moving back to her grandparents, she was told to leave by her grandfather. Shortly after, her grandmother died. Wuornos was only 15 when she began living on her own in an abandoned car. She earned money from prostitution and panhandling. Wuornos dropped out of school in the ninth grade after much trouble with her teachers as a result of coming to school stoned on acid, pot, or mescaline.

Wuornos became very adept at hustling men while hitchhiking but also remembers being raped and beaten between 10 and 12 times. Her life was an emotional roller coaster, and by the age of 22 Wuornos claims at least six suicide attempts. When Wuornos was 20 her grandfather committed suicide. She then married a 70-year-old man but left him after only a month because of her claim of physical abuse. He explained that she beat him to get the car keys. In one suicide attempt, Wuornos shot herself in the abdomen and was hospitalized for two weeks. At age 25, while under the influence of drugs and alcohol, Wuornos robbed a convenience store. She was arrested, convicted, and served 14 months of a 3-year sentence in prison for the robbery. While incarcerated Wuornos was disciplined six times for disruptive behavior. One year after her release she entered a short-lived lesbian relationship with a woman she had met while job hunting. One day Wuornos returned home to find her

(see Table 9.3). Overall, one-third of female offenders killed only family members, whereas about half of all these offenders murdered at least one member of their family. Female serial offenders murdered more family members than strangers, but since 1975 there has been an increase in killing strangers. Table 9.4 indicates the percentage of victims targeted by female offenders. Overall, victims were more likely to be strangers to their killers than an acquaintance or a family member.

Among the groupings of strangers, acquaintances, and family members, female offenders appeared to have preferences in the types of victims selected.

gone. A few months later Wuornos was arrested for check forgery but failed to appear for sentencing.

She had moved on to Daytona, where she met Tyria Moore and moved in with her. Eventually, fearing for her own safety, Moore returned home to her parents. By that time Wuornos had begun her killing career.

Aileen Wuornos's Victims

Date	Name	Age	Occupation	Method
Dec. 1989	Richard Mallory	51	Store owner	Shooting
May 1990	David Spears	43	Equipment operator	Shooting
June 1990	Charles Carskaddon	40	Rodeo worker	Shooting
July 1990	Peter Siems	65	Missionary	Shooting
Aug. 1990	Troy Buress	50	Truck driver	Shooting
Sept. 1990	Dick Humphreys	56	Child abuse investigator	Shooting
Nov. 1990	Walter Antonio	60	Police reserve	Shooting

Wuornos claims to have killed only men who attacked her while she plied her trade of prostitution. Several of her victims were found nude or partially clad. They were all robbed and shot several times, most of them in the torso. Wuornos might be viewed as fitting the profile of the typical serial killer because she sought out male strangers, killed them, and was very careful not to leave much evidence. Her victims were carefully selected because she deliberately sought out men with more expensive cars. Like male serial killers, Wuornos portrayed herself as dominant and aggressive. However, she also argues that she killed in self-defense—that she was handling many johns a day and only became violent when someone would become too physical or if she felt in danger of being raped, beaten, or killed. Prior to the trial, Wuornos was adopted by Arlene and Robert Pralle and became Aileen Carol Wuornos Pralle, again adding to her list of names. Convicted in 1992, Wuornos was executed in 2002 by lethal injection in Florida. In 2003 the movie *Monster* was released, depicting Wuornos's own victimization as the cause of her string of murders. For some she will always remain a battered woman who tried to escape the trauma of abuse. For others, Aileen Wuornos was a sadistic woman who enjoyed watching men die. In truth, she became both.

Table 9.5 shows the rank order of victims; when the victims were classified as strangers, both young boys and girls were the most likely targets. However, in the case of female serial killers who acted alone, patients in hospitals, nursing homes, and other care facilities were the preferred victims (see Chapter 6). Either way, where strangers were concerned, offenders went after the weak and the helpless. When family members were victims, husbands overwhelmingly became the primary target. Indeed, some female serial killers have given new meaning to the term *serial monogamy*. (For example, consider the case of Nancy (Nannie) Hazel Doss [1925–1954] described in Profile 9.3.)

TABLE 9.3 Percentage of Female Offenders Killing Family Members, Acquaintances, and/or Strangers in the United States, 1826–2004

Relationship	Percentage
Family only	35
At least one family member	48
Acquaintances only	18
At least one acquaintance	34
Strangers only	25
At least one stranger	31

N = 64

SOURCE: © Cengage Learning, 2013.

TABLE 9.4 Distribution of Victims by Their Relationship to Female Offenders, 1826–2004

Type of Victim	Number of Victims	Percentage of All Victims of Female Offenders
Family	107–135	22–25
Family and acquaintances	45–52	8–9
Acquaintances	47–88	11–14
Acquaintances and strangers	34–78	8–13
Strangers	132–166	27–31
Strangers and family	46–78	11–13
All	3	1

N = 427–612

SOURCE: © Cengage Learning, 2013.

TABLE 9.5 Rank Order of Types of Victims Selected by Female Serial Murderers, 1826–2004

A. Strangers

Children: young boys and girls

Patients: hospitals/nursing homes

People in stores, businesses, and on streets

People in homes

Travelers

Others: e.g., older women, police officers, prostitutes

B. Family

Husbands

Children

In-laws

TABLE 9.5 Continued

Mothers
Others: aunt, uncle, nephew, sister
C. Acquaintances
Friends/members of own group
Male suitors
Children
Older men and women
Others: landlord, neighbors, patients

SOURCE: © Cengage Learning, 2013.

In the case of child victims, some offenders took years to systematically kill each child. Of acquaintances, strangers, and family, acquaintances were least likely to be killed by offenders, but of those who were singled out, friends seemed to receive the most attention. Unsuspecting men wishing to marry the offenders did not fare much better.

Female offenders appear to have specific age groups of victims (see Table 9.6). Twenty percent killed children only, and nearly one-third targeted adults only. Female offenders also killed from a variety of age groups, except for teenagers. Nearly three-fifths murdered at least one adult, and 38% murdered at least one child. Over one-quarter of all female offenders killed at least one elderly person. Those offenders who selected their victims from more than one age group were most likely to have killed adults and children. Few offenders were prone to kill from all age groups.

Table 9.6 indicates that when the variables of age and gender are combined, female offenders were equally prone to kill female or male children. There was little difference between males and females when the victims were teenagers. Not surprisingly, female offenders were more likely to select at least one male adult victim, but also were involved (51% of offenders) in killing adult females. Conclusions based on these data must be considered tenuous at best, considering the small numbers of victims. However, we do know that males are more likely to be victimized than females when the female serial offender concentrates on killing adult members of only one gender. In the case of children, it is unlikely that any real gender preferences exist, considering the small difference between the numbers of male and female child victims and the motives for killing them.

Table 9.7 shows the mobility classification of female offenders. Traveling serial killers are almost exclusively males who move from city to city and across state lines, killing victims at random or seeking out a specific type of victim. Because of a lack of crime-data correlation, this type of offender has been recognized only in the past few years. Fourteen offenders, or 22% of all female offenders, were identified as traveling. Among serial killers who had at least one partner and traveled from state to state, again only a relatively small proportion involved female offenders. Twenty-eight offenders, or 44% of female killers, were classified as local killers, or serial offenders who sought out their victims

PROFILE 9.3 Nannie Doss, the "Giggling Grandma," 1925–1954

The media dubbed her the "Giggling Grandma" because Nannie laughed and smiled while admitting to police that she had killed four of her five husbands. In 1921, at age 15 and working in the Linen Thread factory, she met and married Charles Bragg. He would be the only husband to escape her murderous designs. In 1954, when Nannie was finally arrested, Bragg spoke with reporters and explained the very difficult eight years the two were together. Her constant infidelity finally forced Bragg to leave her, but most of their five children were not so fortunate. One died right after she was born. Two others died while they were still young, raising questions by some of the neighbors, who felt something was not quite right.

Charles Bragg told another reporter, "Back at that time, I didn't know about poison. The undertakers told me at the time they were poisoned. Some of my folks warned me about Nannie, and when she got mad I wouldn't eat anything she fixed or drink anything around the house. She was high-tempered and mean." Bragg felt the reason she did not murder him was the fact that he had no insurance.

Her second husband, Robert F. Harrelson, married her in 1929, and 16 years later, when she was 39 years old, Nannie murdered him by putting liquid rat poison with arsenic into his corn whiskey. She told police he was an "awful drunkard" and decided to teach him a lesson. At the time, the coroner listed the cause of death as acute alcoholism. He was buried near his two-year-old grandson, who, Nannie observed, "just might have gotten hold of some rat poison."

Two years later, Nannie married her third husband, Arlie J. Lanning, a factory worker, in North Carolina. Five years later she poisoned him because "he was running around with other women." One year later, Lanning's mother, Sarah E. Lanning, then 84 years of age, died while in Nannie's care. Nannie next married Richard C. Morton Sr., whom she met through a lonely hearts club. Four months after their wedding, she murdered him with arsenic because "he was fixing to run around with another woman." She collected on five insurance policies for a meager sum of $1,400.

Later, Nannie would smile and say she "didn't like to poison nobody, even if he wasn't no good." Yet the "feeling" that a husband was about to "pass on" seemed to provide her with morbid delight. She claimed to be a genuine romantic and was often seen perusing her favorite magazine, *True Romance.* Apprehended after poisoning her fifth husband, Samuel Doss, with her stewed prunes, Nannie finally confessed after questioning that she had killed several of her spouses. She insisted that she had killed for romance. "Yes, that's about it. I was searching for the perfect mate, the real romance of life," explained Doss. Some thought Nannie had killed for financial gain, but the amounts collected on each victim were small, and Nannie was offended when asked if her motive was money.

The truth was that Nannie liked to kill. Whenever she got the "urge," she would select a victim. At the age of 30 she started a killing spree that lasted over 20 years. She murdered four husbands, her mother, two sisters, two children, one grandson, and one nephew. She denied killing her mother, claiming she loved her mother more than life. Very likely there were others who also sampled Nannie's stewed prunes. Each of her victims died agonizing deaths after being fed large amounts of liquid rat poison laced with arsenic. She was arrested on October 6, 1954, in Tulsa, Oklahoma, where she was working as a babysitter and a housekeeper.

Nannie Doss was convicted and sentenced to life in prison, where she continued her obsessive reading of romance novels and wrote her memoirs for *Life* magazine. In 1965 she died of leukemia in prison at the age of 60.

TABLE 9.6 Percentage of Female Offenders Murdering Victims According to Specific Age and Gender Categories, 1826–2004

Age Only		**Gender and Age Only**	
Children	20	Females	10
Teens	0	Males	17
Adults	31	Both	67
Elderly	13	Unknown	6
At Least One		**At Least One**	
Child	38	Female child	31
Teen	8	Male child	31
Adult	57	Both	27
Elderly	28		
		At Least One	
Combinations		Female teen	6
Teens and children	6	Male teen	2
Adults and children	18	Both	0
Adults and teens	8	**At Least One**	
All age groups	3	Female adult	51
		Male adult	59
		Both	44

N = 64

SOURCE: © Cengage Learning, 2013.

within the boundaries of one state or city. Place-specific killers, common among female offenders, repeatedly murdered their victims in the same location. Some of the common locations were nursing homes, hospitals, and private homes. One-third of all female serial murderers were identified as place-specific.

Each mobility category was examined for the number of victims killed. Those females identified as place-specific were responsible for nearly half (43%–46%) of all murders committed by female offenders. Although offenders classified as traveling killed more victims per offender and per case than the local category (7–10 vs. 5–7), place-specific offenders murdered more victims per case and per offender.

Thirty-four percent of all female offenders were categorized as place-specific, whereas only 10% of all male offenders followed this same pattern. Since 1975, the number of place-specific female offenders has appeared to have dropped considerably, while their male counterparts have remained about the same (see Chapter 7).

One reason place-specific offenders killed more victims was because they went undetected for longer periods of time; because the murders occurred in one place, there was less likelihood of detection. In addition, one typically does not imagine a serial murderer as a mother, a grandmother, or the nice lady next

TABLE 9.7 Victims of Female Serial Murderers by Mobility Classification in the United States, 1826–2004

	Number of Victims	Percentage of Victims	Number of Cases	Number of Offenders	Percentage of Offenders	Average Number of Victims per Offender	Average Number of Victims per Case
Total	427–612	100	61	64	100	7–10	7–10
Traveling	99–134	22–23	14	14	22	7–10	7–10
Local	144–195	32–34	28	28	44	5–7	6–8
Place-specific	184–283	43–46	22	22	34	8–13	9–13

SOURCE: © Cengage Learning, 2013.

door. The rarity of such murders compared with other types of homicides may have influenced the length of time required to apprehend female serial offenders.

Homicides in general often have victims who place themselves in precarious positions, such as domestic disputes, or who provoke the attack by striking the first blow. As mentioned earlier, many victims play a prominent role in their own demise by facilitating the encounter with the offender (see Chapter 10). Generally, victims of serial murder played little or no part in their own deaths. Female offenders almost exclusively killed victims who were categorized as low-facilitation homicides (the victims played a small role, if any, in their own deaths).

METHODS AND MOTIVES

Female offenders, as indicated in Table 9.8, were most likely to use poisons at least some of the time to kill their victims (see Chapter 6). Some of the poisons administered to induce death quickly or gradually were large doses of potassium chloride, which attacks the heart, and strychnine or arsenic. Arsenic was popular for hundreds of years as a method of murder. In the 1800s arsenic could be purchased at any chemist's shop and was commonly used in small quantities by women to improve their facial complexions. Male customers often purchased arsenic to use in their gardens to kill rats and mice. As Gerald Sparrow noted in his book *Women Who Murder* (1970), "the poison eaters" regularly ingested arsenic to improve their attractiveness. The *Chambers Journal* and *Black Woods*

TABLE 9.8 Methods and Motives of Female Serial Murderers in the United States, 1826–2004

Method		Motive	
Some poison	45%	Money sometimes	47%
Poison only	34	Money only	26
Some shooting	19	Control sometimes	14
Some bludgeoning	16	Enjoyment sometimes	11
Some suffocation	17	Sex sometimes	10
Some stabbing	11	Enjoyment only	3
Suffocation only	11	Sex only	0
Shooting only	8	Combinations of the preceding motives	15
Some drowning	5		
Stabbing only	3	Other motives including (1) drug addiction, (2) cults, (3) to cover up other crimes, (4) children become a burden, feelings of being an inadequate parent, and so on	23
Combinations of the preceding methods	32		

$N = 64$

SOURCE: © Cengage Learning, 2013.

Magazine, published during the 1850s, carried a series of articles on the poison eaters.

> It is not generally known that eating poison is actually practiced in more countries than one. In some districts of Lower Austria and in Styria, as far as the borders of Hungary, the strange habit of eating arsenic is quite common. The peasantry in particular are given to it. They obtain it under the name of Hedri from the traveling hucksters and gatherers of herbs, who get it from the glass blowers, or purchase it from cow-doctors, quacks or mountebanks. The poison eaters have a two-fold aim in their dangerous enjoyment: one of which is to obtain a fresh healthy appearance, and also to acquire a degree of sexual desire. On this account gay village lads and lasses employ the dangerous agent, that they become more attractive to each other; and it is really astonishing with what favorable results their endeavors are attended, for it is just the youthful poison eaters that are, generally speaking, distinguished by a blooming complexion and an appearance of exuberant health. (Sparrow, 1970, p. 88)

Sparrow goes on to describe the "miraculous cosmetic properties" found in arsenic. Thus, we see that arsenic was readily available without suspicion to anyone wanting to use it to commit murder. Although arsenic does not mix well with cold water, it is nearly undetectable in hot food and drinks, especially coffee or cocoa. The length of time required to kill a person with arsenic varies, depending on such factors as the amount of poison administered and the general health of the intended victim. A large dose brings on death usually in a few hours, but death may be prolonged by using small amounts. In such cases the victim may live for several weeks or even months.

Arsenic poisoning is a particularly gruesome manner of death because it causes severe and frequent vomiting coupled with intense pain. Naturally, fever, vomiting, and pain may be indicative of several maladies, so arsenic poisoning was seldom raised as a diagnosis. Once a killer was discovered and the bodies were exhumed, arsenic could be easily detected because it acted as a strong preserving agent after death. Today, pure arsenic is no longer readily available, but it is often found in pesticides.

Poisoning was so common a method for killing that nearly half of the female offenders in this study used some poison to commit their murders. Most of these women were offenders who acted alone to kill their victims. Other female offenders resorted to more violent methods, such as shooting, bludgeoning, or stabbing. Not surprisingly, most female offenders who had an accomplice(s) used violent means to kill the majority of their victims (see Chapter 8). About one-third of the female offenders used a combination of methods in their killings.

Female serial killers differed noticeably from their male counterparts in methods and motives. Males were more mobile and attracted more attention than the women. Although both groups selected the powerless as victims, or at least those who were easily rendered powerless, their methods of killing usually differed. Males often selected more violent means of killing, including sexually attacking and frequently mutilating the corpse. Women in this study, with a few exceptions, generally were not sexually involved with their victims, nor did they kill them by particularly violent methods in comparison to their male counterparts. These comparisons lead us toward the inevitable question of why these women commit multiple murders.

We must begin our discussion of motives with the premise that the reality of female crime is largely unknown. Historically, female crime has been explained in terms of a biological framework. The likelihood of a woman committing a crime was believed (and many still subscribe to such interpretation) to be linked to hormonal changes, menstruation, maternity, and other physiological explanations. Only recently have theorists begun to consider social-structure influences on women and crime. Of these influences, money was found to be the most common motivator for murder. This seems to contradict motives stated for homicides in general, at least at the North Carolina Correctional Center for Women in Raleigh, where John T. Kirpatrick and John A. Humphrey conducted a study of 76 women who had killed. They noted that "in order for women to kill, it had to be perceived by them as a life-threatening situation affecting their physical or emotional well-being" ("Women Who Kill," 1987). But are women who kill under these circumstances really any different from women who are classified as serial killers? Although the list in Table 9.8 does show a ranking of motives, more involved explanations may exist that reflect social and cultural influences generally ignored in the epidemiology of homicide.

At the turn of the 19th century, researchers involved in the study of criminal behavior leaned heavily toward a biological explanation for crime. Lombroso and Ferrero (1916) insisted that biological factors were the keys in understanding criminal behavior in women:

> We have seen that the normal woman is naturally less sensitive to pain than a man.... We also saw that women have many traits in common with children; that their moral sense is deficient; that they are revengeful, jealous, inclined to vengeances of a refined cruelty.
>
> In ordinary cases these defects are neutralized by piety, maternity, want of passion, sexual coldness, by weakness and an underdeveloped intelligence. But when a morbid activity of the physical centers intensifies the bad qualities of women, and induces them to seek relief in evil deeds ... it is clear that the innocuous semi-criminal present in the normal woman must be transformed into a born criminal more terrible than any man.... The criminal woman is consequently a monster. (pp. 150–152)

Sigmund Freud's influence was felt as psychobiological explanations for female crime began to emerge. Pollak (1950) argued that women appeared less often in criminal statistics because of their innate ability to deceive others. This, according to Freud, was due to the fact that they are born sans penis (Strachey, 1961). Consequently:

> Man must achieve an erection in order to perform the sex act and will not be able to hide his failure ... and pretense of sexual response is impossible for him, if it is lacking. Woman's body, however, permits

> such pretense to a certain degree and lack of orgasm does not prevent her ability to participate in the sex act. It cannot be denied that this basic physiological difference may well have a great influence on the degree of confidence which the two sexes have in the possible success of concealment and thus on their character pattern in this respect. (p. 10)

Gradually, other studies involving professional researchers began to make tentative connections between female criminality and alcohol, women's liberation, menstruation cycles, and hormonal imbalances. These last connections appear to have found more credence among professional researchers.

Dr. Eva Ebin, professor of psychiatry at State University of New York, noted that some women experience a postpartum syndrome that can cause them to become psychotic. She observed a shift in a woman's personality that causes her to "break" under stress. Caring for a newborn may create stresses that the mother is not emotionally prepared to handle. In Pennsylvania in 1985 a woman killed her month-old son by tossing him into a mountain stream, and in 1986 a West Virginia mother wrapped her newborn child in a plastic bag and dropped her into the Shenandoah River. In 1995, Susan Smith placed her two young sons in the back seat of her car, released the brake, and walked away while the automobile rolled into a lake, drowning the boys. In all of these instances the mothers fabricated stories of their children being kidnapped. Dr. Ebin explains these concocted stories as "a trick of the mind. It's a dissociative reaction. It's wishful thinking that they hadn't done it. They need to believe it in order to go on" ("When Moms Kill Their Infants," 1988). Not all mothers who kill their children fabricate stories. Andrea Yates, after suffering years of deepening depression, the weight of more children to bear and care for, and the lack of familial support, filled her bathtub and drowned each of her five children. She then called her husband and told him that she had done something very bad.

Resnick (1970) reported that two-thirds of the mothers who commit filicide (the killing of a child over 24 hours old) suffer from various forms of psychosis, such as severe depression, and that they make frequent suicide attempts. Resnick also found that mothers who committed filicide were motivated by altruistic reasoning—that the children were better off dead. In addition, Rosenblatt and Greenland (1974) reported that before killing their children, over 40% of the mothers intimated their fear or intent of killing to friends, physicians, or social-service-agency personnel.

We have only recently begun to connect female crime to stress-related factors and to understand how stress affects behavior. It is believed by some experts that stress is the generic cause of many diseases, both physiological and psychological. Societal factors, such as the fact that women do not earn as much as men, could be facilitating variables in homicide. But these factors should not be considered the primary cause. More likely in the Kirpatrick-Humphrey study reported in "Women Who Kill," the cause is linked to the women's life histories and to the kinds and severity of the stress they encountered. Nearly all of the women in the study came from very violent upbringings and experienced high levels of domestic violence—seeing their mothers and fathers fighting, often with weapons ("Women Who Kill," 1987).

In addition to witnessing conflict, several offenders in the Kirpatrick-Humphrey study were beaten or sexually abused as children. Half of the women had lost a loved one either in childhood or adulthood. "Loss is an important source of stress because not only is it stressful in itself but it also precipitates other stress, as when they have to move in with grandparents or drop out of school due to the death of a parent.... These are women who feel at once overpowering aloneness and simmering resentment of others" ("Women Who Kill," 1987). Christine Falling, described in Profile 9.4, appeared to have experienced many of these stressors.

The available biographical data on female serial murderers also indicate several instances of broken homes, displaced children, and other emotionally traumatic experiences. However, we must again proceed with caution in suggesting that stress explains all such criminal behavior. Considering that the majority of American serial killers are psychopaths, Robert Hare reminds us that psychopaths may be genetically wired differently than the non-psychopathic population (see Chapter 3). Indeed, our society includes many victims of child abuse of all varieties, as well as children who are displaced or who experience other traumas or stresses, who do not become murderers or criminals of any type. Although there are exceptions, according to the available data, female multiple murderers generally do not appear to have experienced more traumas as children than other criminals or perhaps even noncriminals. A critical factor may be their inability as children or as adults, whether it is genetically or environmentally based, to deal constructively with their own sense of victimization. This inability may be fostered by significant others, strangers, and the various societal institutions that affect everyone to varying degrees. Simply because we ascertain that children who later become mass murderesses have been exposed to the same traumatizations that other children experience does not mean they are able to cope with those experiences in similar fashions.

If we are to accept the taxonomy of motives in Table 9.8, then women's motives for serial murder appear to center on financial security, control enjoyment, and sexual stimulation. Those who murdered children seemed to display little or no psychosis. Although data are limited regarding biographical information, several cases in the present study revealed histories of child abuse—including sexual molestation, prostitution, and neglect—extreme poverty, and unstable marital relationships.

DISPOSITION OF FEMALE OFFENDERS

To some extent our society has become increasingly desensitized to death. The media often provide a distortion of reality that is pervasive throughout much of our movie industry. The "splatter movies" with their endless sequels perpetuate bizarre images of those who kill. Some of these movies surpass our own worst nightmares. However, although male offenders have received media profiling that incites fear and paranoia in our communities, women fail to receive similar caricaturization. Even those few female killers who have received national

PROFILE 9.4 Christine Falling, 1980–1982

Nineteen-year-old Christine Falling was a high school dropout with the vocabulary of a sixth-grader. Obese, epileptic, and intellectually stifled, Falling lived in Perry, a town in southern Florida where poverty is a way of life. She had been born into an unstable family; her mother, Ann, was only 16 and already had two children, and her father, Tom, age 65, worked in the woods. Frequently her mother would leave for periods of time and Tom would have to care for the children. Eventually Falling and her sister were adopted by a couple named Falling. Conflict quickly generated between the couple and the two girls, resulting in frequent family fights. Finally at age nine, Falling and her sister were placed in a children's refuge near Orlando.

Falling's personality profile by age nine indicated some potentially serious problems. She had been known on more than one occasion to torture animals, such as cats, by throwing them high into the air or wringing their necks. She later explained this behavior by saying she was trying to find out if cats really had nine lives. Staff members at the refuge described her as a compulsive liar and thief, a child who would break rules to gain attention. She frequently was the brunt of her peers' jokes because of her obesity and dull-wittedness. After continuing problems with the Falling family, Christine, now 12, left in search of her mother near Blountstown, Florida. She found her mother and then married a man in his mid-20s. After six weeks of fighting, the marriage ended. A year later she began making frequent visits to the hospital, claiming an array of problems and illnesses. During this two-year period, the hospital recorded at least 50 visits from Falling.

Falling began babysitting and gained a reputation as one who loved children, especially babies, and was very good at caring for them. Unfortunately, no one knew what methods Falling used to quiet the infants. Two-year-old Cassidy "Muffin" Johnson became her first victim on February 25, 1980. One year later, four-year-old Jeffrey M. Davis succumbed to Falling's loving care. Three days later, while the funeral was being held for the boy, Falling was caring for two-year-old Joseph, a cousin to the victim. He also died while sleeping, his parents still at the funeral. In one year, three children died strange and unexpected deaths while in the care of the young babysitter. Always distraught at the tragic deaths, Falling appeared as baffled as everyone else about the causes of death. Physicians explored a variety of medical explanations, but no one was ever quite sure what had happened.

Falling decided to stay away from children for a while and became a housekeeper for 77-year-old William Swindle. The day she began caring for him, Swindle was found dead on his kitchen floor. No autopsy was performed, and it was assumed he had died of natural causes. Falling next babysat eight-month-old Jennifer Y. Daniels, the daughter of her stepsister. Mrs. Daniels had left Jennifer momentarily with Falling while she went into a store. On her return Falling announced the child had just stopped breathing. Cause of death was listed as sudden infant death syndrome.

In 1982, after moving back to Blountstown, Falling was asked to babysit 10-week-old Travis D. Coleman. He, too, died in his sleep. Five deaths and several near-death situations, all with small children, all in two and a half years, all in the care of the same person, finally caused people to start questioning Falling. To avoid the death penalty, she eventually confessed in a plea bargain to killing Muffin, Jennifer, and Travis. Falling described her method of killing as "smotheration" and stated in her confession: "I love young 'uns. I don't know why I done what I done.… The way I done it, I saw it done on TV shows. I had my own way, though. Simple and easy. No one would hear them scream."

Falling was given a life sentence and became eligible for parole in 2007. She is presently incarcerated in Florida's Broward Correctional Institution.

attention do not instill the fear that male killers do. Certainly, this is not unexpected, because males do most of the killing, are usually responsible for most of the sadistic and perverted acts committed against victims, and consequently end up in Hollywood horror movies. Our underestimation of the ability of women to commit murders as heinous as those that males commit may be a factor in the perceived differential treatment of women in the criminal justice system. Consider the monikers given by the media to female serial murderers (see Table 9.9).

Historically, female offenders in this study received monikers that were either neutral or trivializing in their relationship to the crimes committed. The "Beautiful Blonde Killer," the "Giggling Grandma," "Old Shoe Box Annie," and "Killer Granny" are stereotypic, patronizing, and sexist. Even more recent monikers for female offenders are gender based: Black Widow, Death Angel, and Damsel of Death. Conversely, males have received some of the most fear-inducing names imaginable, such as "The Strangler," "The Ripper," "The Night Stalker," "The Moon Maniac," and so on. The distinction appears to be based on the method of killing and the degree of violence and viciousness displayed by the killer. Even in those cases in which males were accomplices to females in serial murder, the moniker seemed to be influenced by gender, for instance, "The Bloody Benders" and "The Lonely Hearts Killer." Apparently, not only are we less likely to suspect female offenders but also less likely to accord them

TABLE 9.9 Monikers of Selected Female Offenders

Year Killing Began	Number of Victims	Name
1864	12–42	Queen Poisoner/Borgia of Connecticut
1872	14	The Bloody Benders/The Hell Benders
1881	8+	Borgia of Somerville
1901	27	Sister Amy
1901	16–20	Belle of Indiana/Lady Bluebeard
1913	3–5	Duchess of Death
1914	11+	Mrs. Bluebeard
1920	3+	Old Shoe Box Annie
1925	11–16	Giggling Grandma
1925	3	Borgia of America
1931	15	Beautiful Blonde Killer
1949	3–20	Lonely Hearts Killer
1964	5	Grandma
1975	2+	Black Widow
1984	9–12	Death Angel
1989	7–9	Damsel of Death
2008	4–5	Killer Granny

SOURCE: © Cengage Learning, 2013.

TABLE 9.10 Adjudication of Female Offenders in the United States, 1826–2004

Status	Percentage
Never apprehended	5
Killed before apprehension	4
Confined to psychiatric hospital	5
Given prison time (including life)	66
Death row	19
Pending	1
	100

N = 58
SOURCE: © Cengage Learning, 2013.

the same degree of dangerousness as we do males. In reality, some of these female offenders have killed several more victims than many of their male counterparts. Part of this disparity in treatment of offenders can be traced to the writings of Pollak (1950) and W. I. Thomas (1907, 1923). Women were observed to be accorded differential treatment because of the "chivalry" of a system dominated by men. Women were also treated more "humanely" because they were not considered dangerous. From these earlier writings, there appears to have been some confusion about the assignation of causes. Women were viewed as being deceptive, manipulative, and devoid of emotion. Stereotyping women in general with these qualities was overkill to say the least. What is closer to the truth is that these qualities can be attributed to some women and some men as psychopathic tendencies. Regardless of gender, those people who manifest psychopathic qualities are much more likely to inflict harm on society than are members of the general population.

The perception of violence may play an important role in our treatment of female offenders. Historically we are less willing to execute women than men. Table 9.10 indicates by percentage the adjudication of women in this study. Although 19% of female offenders were placed on death row, only two have ever been executed. Seventy-one percent received life in prison or shorter sentences or were sent to mental institutions. My intent here is not to point out a lack of punishment but to underscore the apparent preferential or discriminatory treatment experienced by female offenders.

SUMMARY

We have examined the cases of several females identified as serial killers. Although they appear to be increasing in absolute numbers, they still represent only a small portion of serial-murder cases. In America, this type of offender was noted even in the early 19th century and only seldom receives media attention. Several female serial killers acted alone. Those who had male partners were much more likely to use violence in killing their victims, whereas those who acted alone often used poisons. Females in this study appear to kill approximately the same number of victims on the average as their male counterparts (7–10 for females and 7–12 for males). Because of the relatively small number of female offenders, however, such findings are more likely to raise suspicions than encourage agreement. The women, on the average, tended to be slightly older than the male offenders. The most likely occupational categories for females were semi-skilled, unskilled, and professionals. Some of these, as well as some of the "homemakers," earned the dubious moniker of "black widow." Several offenders categorized as nurses or healthcare providers were found to be "angels of death" (see Chapter 6). Very few females were known to have criminal records and, with few exceptions, the majority were white.

Over the past few years, female offenders killed fewer family members while increasingly targeting strangers. Female offenders who acted alone were more likely to kill hospital and nursing home patients than female offenders with accomplices. Husbands were the primary target of offenders who targeted family members. Approximately one-third of these offenders killed at least one child and one fourth an elderly victim. A majority killed at least one adult. Regarding children, gender seemed to make little difference for female killers. Since 1975 female offenders have become more local in their areas for killing, a trend that increases their public visibility. Historically, poison has been the most commonly selected mode of killing for female offenders, who were less inclined to employ violent methods than male offenders were. In more recent years, women who killed with poisons were far more likely to select poisons that are difficult to detect. Most female offenders had experienced various forms of abuse as children, including sexual abuse and broken homes. Many appeared to be motivated to kill for financial gain, yet the literature suggests more complex explanations of psychopathology. Similar to their male counterparts, several of these females appeared to have developed socio-psychopathic personalities. Compared with male offenders, female serial killers in this study appeared to have been preferentially treated by the media and the criminal justice system.

Victims

LEARNING OBJECTIVES

- To understand the scope of serial-murder victimization in the United States
- To explore victim facilitation in serial murder
- To examine the demographics of vulnerable populations in the United States including children, gays, prostitutes, women, and the elderly
- To review case studies of men who prey upon other males
- To understand the role of the National Center for Missing and Exploited Children

By the end of 2010, crime rates continued to drop to levels not seen in 40 years. Why then all the concern about victimization? One reason is that criminologists and psychologists have recognized for some time the need to understand victims and their involvement with offenders. Hewitt (1988) reviewed the body of literature of victim–offender relationships in homicides based on data from a large heterogeneous population. He then examined demographic characteristics of victims and offenders in the often-publicized community of "Middletown, U.S.A." (Muncie, Indiana) and found the victim–offender relationships to be similar to those in larger cities. Studies in victimization assist in clarifying the victim side of the offender–victim relationship, measure in part the degree of vulnerability and culpability of certain victims, and often reveal the social dynamics of criminal acts. Case study analysis in serial murder has begun to provide researchers with insightful information, however tenuous. Elliott Leyton (1986a), for example, in his book *Hunting Humans,* provides an in-depth investigation into the lives and minds of a few contemporary serial killers and their relationships with their victims. The purpose of this chapter is to contribute to this body of knowledge by focusing on the victims of serial murderers and the demographic factors associated with their victimization. Such demographic data can assist in determining variations, if any, between the victims of homicides in general and the victims of multiple murderers. Also, from a historical perspective, we are able to challenge current notions pertaining to serial murderers and their victims by drawing on this extensive database of serial-murder victims.*

One of the most perplexing questions researchers are unable to answer is, "How many serial murderers have killed or are presently killing in the United States?" Agents from the FBI at one time estimated the number of offenders active in the United States at 35, but there may be as many as 100 or more. This does not mean that there are 35–100 *new* offenders each year but rather that 35–100 serial killers may be active in a given year. Of the 431 offenders in the 2004 study, more than half committed their murders over a period of at least one or more years. Some of these offenders were active for several years. When controls were made for gender, female offenders often reported operating years longer than their male counterparts, a time factor that may be a function of killing method or the types of victims selected. Of the 367 cases of serial murder, 43 (11%) were exclusively female. Several of the cases involved women who were care providers.

Quinet (2007) raises a very important question regarding measuring the extent of serial murder. There are 30 to 40 thousand estimated missing persons in the United States. These are documented or reported missing persons. There is another group that Quinet refers to as *"the missing missing,"* or missing persons who were never reported as missing and some of whom could easily be victims of serial murder. This possibility suggests, for example, that many more prostitutes could be victims of serial killers without that information ever being known. The Long Island murders of prostitutes were accidentally discovered, suggesting that other victims of serial killers, some reported missing as well as "the missing missing," may yet await discovery.

Between 1950 and 1975 the number of identified serial killers surged compared to previous years. By 1980 the rise had become even more dramatic (see Figure 10.1), but has tapered off in recent years. The decline of serial-murder cases mirrors the long-term decline of homicides in general. Homicide rates tend to be cyclical and we may see a resurgence of serial murder in years to come. Certainly media attention has been instrumental in creating public awareness of the serial murderer. It is unlikely, however, that media attention alone is responsible for the "emergence" of serial killing.

According to the time frame of the 2004 study, nearly 80% of the 367 cases (431 offenders) appeared since 1975. Although we recognize that the "dark figure," or the unknown killer, will always exist, the study's data may be viewed as indicating trends in serial murder. One of the trends indicated a tremendous increase in the number of cases between 1975 and 1995 in comparison to the previous 175 years. However, between 1995 and 2004 cases of serial murder sharply declined. By 2008 there have been a few cases of serial murder, but not

*Portions of this chapter are based on material from "Etiology of Victimization in Serial Murder," by E. W. Hickey, in S. A. Egger (ed.), *Serial Murder: An Elusive Phenomenon* (Praeger Publishers, New York, 1989), copyright 1989 by Steven A. Egger. Material also used from "Responding to Missing and Murdered Children in America," by E. W. Hickey, in Albert R. Roberts (ed.), *Helping Crime Victims*, 158–185, copyright 1990 by Sage Publications, Inc.

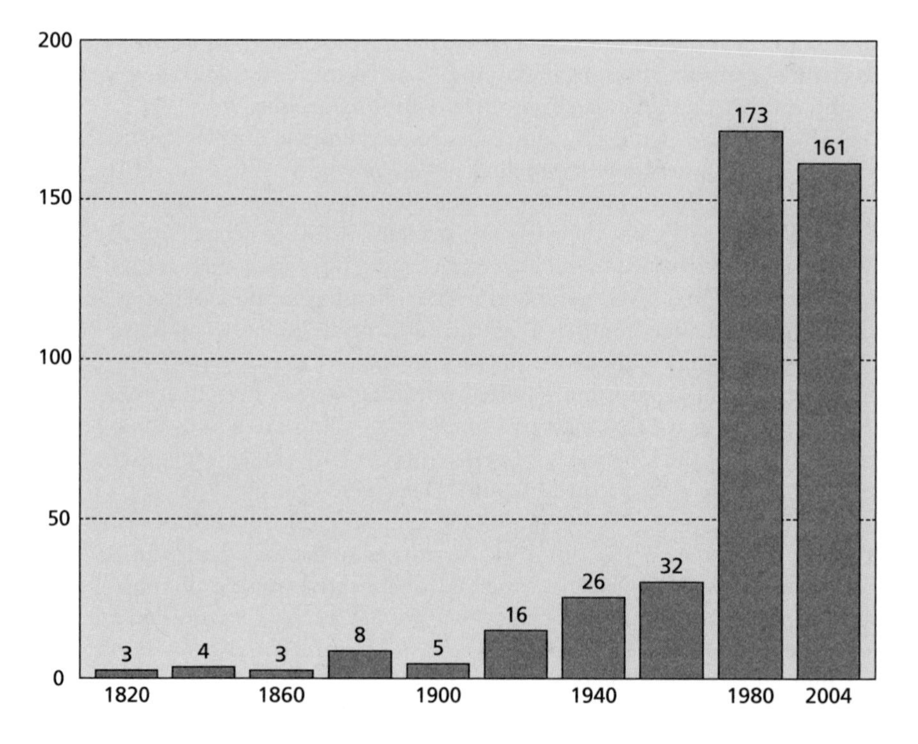

FIGURE 10.1 Number of Serial Killers in the United States by Decade, 1800–2004

N = 431 offenders

SOURCE: © Cengage Learning, 2013.

TABLE 10.1 Number of Serial-Murder Cases and Offenders in the United States, 1800–2004

Years	Total Number of Cases	Number of Cases per Year	Number of Offenders	Percentage of Offenders	Number of Offenders per Year
1800–2004	367	1.8	431	100	2.1 (204 yrs)
1800–1969	133	8.0	152	35	0.9 (169 yrs)
1970–2004	234	6.9	279	65	8.0 (34 yrs)

SOURCE: © Cengage Learning, 2013.

to the extent we saw up to the year 2000. While there may be a respite from serial killers, their crimes carry a tremendous impact (see Table 10.1). Understanding the dynamics of victimization will in all likelihood enable researchers to better understand the etiology of serial murder.

The following update provides a thumbnail sketch of serial-murder victimization in the United States between 2004 and 2011. Do you notice any changes in victimization during this short time frame compared to the 1800–2004 data?

Victim Data Update, 2004–2011

Estimated number of victims: 600–752

Total: 146 offenders; male 90% and female 10%

Victim Data:

- Offenders murdered:
  - Average # of victims per offender: 4.4–5.4
  - Male victims only: 22%
  - Female victims only: 46%
  - Male and female victims: 32%
  - At least one male victim: 54%
  - At least one female victim: 78%
  - Adult victims only: 91%
  - At least one adult victim: 98%
  - Child victims only: 9%
  - Adult and child victims: 7%
  - At least one elderly victim: 9%
  - One or more family members: 5%
  - Strangers as victims: 93%
  - Prostitutes as victims: 21%
  - Case involved victims from more than one state: 23%
- Method of killing:
  - Shoot only: 31%
  - Strangle only: 26%
  - Stab only: 8%
  - Beat/blunt force only: 7%
  - Poison only: 2%
  - Other: 1%
  - Combination of strangling, beating, stabbing, poisoning, and/or shooting: 25%
- Offender killed victims within: (*N* = 146 offenders)
  - Same year: 34%
  - 1–4 years: 29%
  - 5–9 years: 18%
  - 10–19 years: 8%
  - 20–29 years: 7%
  - 30+ years: 4%
- Average span of killing per offender: 6.8 years

DEMOGRAPHICS OF VICTIMIZATION IN SERIAL MURDER

As indicated in Table 10.2, the number of known victims of serial murder has risen markedly since 1950. For those who fall prey to these offenders, their plight is a deplorable one indeed, but the odds of becoming a victim are minuscule when one considers the size of the population as a whole. Of all types of crimes, homicide in general has one of the lowest victimization rates. Indeed, homicides were at 30-year record lows in many cities, but by 2008 had begun to rise in some larger cities. Murders represent less than 1% of all violent crimes in the United States. We run a greater risk of being a victim of domestic homicide and an even greater risk of being a victim of other violent crimes than we do of dying at the hands of a serial killer. In a 2004 study by Kraemer, Lord, and Heilbrun, a comparison was made between 157 serial-homicide offenders (608 victims) and a subsample of serial-homicide offenses to a control group of single-homicide offenders. They found that serial-homicide offenders target more women than men and kill more strangers than family or friends. Single-homicide offenders kill men and women with equal frequency but kill family and friends more often than strangers and are more likely to be motivated by anger. Serial murderers, they found, were much more likely to be sexually motivated when they killed. These findings support the premise that serial murderers usually have distinctive victim-selection criteria, motivations, and sexual interests that set them apart from other types of killers. Thus, many people, because of their routine activities, employment, socioeconomic status, education, where they live, and other social indices, will have varying probabilities of being targeted by serial murderers. In short, some of us are at much greater risk than others. This is

TABLE 10.2 Victims/Serial Murderer Comparisons in the United States, 1800–2004

Years	Total Number of Cases	Number of Cases per Year	Number of Victims	Number of Victims per Case	Number of Victims per Year
1800–2004	367	1.8	2,738–4,286	7–12	13–21 (204 yrs)
1800–1824	2	0.08	104	52	4 (25 yrs)
1825–1849	3	0.12	10–16	3–5	4–6 (25 yrs)
1850–1874	8	0.32	86–138	11–17	3–6 (25 yrs)
1875–1899	7	0.28	114–384	16–55	5–15 (25 yrs)
1900–1924	24	0.96	207–286	9–12	8–11 (25 yrs)
1925–1949	33	1.32	236–416	7–13	9–17 (25 yrs)
1950–1974	107	4.3	773–1,064	7–10	31–43 (25 yrs)
1975–2004	183	6.1	1,208–1,878	7–10	40–63 (30 yrs)

N = 367 Cases/431 Offenders

SOURCE: © Cengage Learning, 2013.

often true when examining population density. As noted in Table 10.2, the number of victims per case has remained fairly constant since 1900.

Several of the states reporting between one and five cases of serial murder have small populations (see Table 10.3). Generally, states with larger populations and large metropolitan areas are more likely to report cases of serial murder. Except for California, the most populous state, there does not appear to be regionality in serial killing. Instead, serial murder appears to be correlated with population density more than regional variations. Inevitably, we expect to find cases in every state. Except for New York, which reported the second highest number of cases of serial murder, California reported more than double the cases found in any other state between 1800 and 2004. Three other states, one northern and two southern, reported between 16 and 30 serial-homicide cases. In group three we again see representation both from the North and the South. In each succeeding group of states we see representation from each region of the United States. In contrast, homicide rates in general can vary dramatically from one geographic region to another in the United States. Per capita analysis, however, shows a somewhat different picture. Some less populated states, such as Alaska, have more serial killers than more populated states such as New York and Texas.

Gastil (1971) and, later, Doerner (1975), explaining the consistently higher murder rates in the southern states, concluded that a regional subculture of violence exists in this area. Blau and Blau (1982), controlling for income inequality, found, however, that poverty and southern location were not related to homicide rates, and the number of blacks in the community was a poor prediction of violence. This lack of consensus regarding a regional subculture of violence is pervasive among researchers. Unlike homicide cases in general, in which, according to police records, African Americans are responsible for over 50% of the deaths, black serial murderers constitute approximately 20% of the offenders in the 2004 study. Most persons thinking about serial killers are prone to stereotype them as white males, often unaware of the fact that some very prolific serial murderers are African American (see Chapter 7).

Serial murderers are often portrayed by the media as wanton killers who travel aimlessly across the United States in search of victims. As noted earlier, Hickey (1985, 1986) created a mobility classification for serial murderers and identified three distinct killer types (see Table 10.4). First are the place-specific offenders, or those who murder within their own homes, places of employment, institutions, or other specific sites. For example, John Wayne Gacy Jr. murdered 33 young males in his home over the course of nearly a seven-year period. Second are the local serial killers who remain within a certain state or urbanized area to seek out victims. In 1986 Michael D. Terry confessed to killing six male street prostitutes, all of whom were encountered within a 14-square-mile area of downtown Atlanta, Georgia. Third are the traveling serial murderers, distinguished by their acts of homicide while traveling through or relocating to other areas in the United States. Randall B. Woodfield, also known as "the I–5 Killer," is believed by many to have murdered as many as 13 victims while he traveled the 800-mile stretch of freeway through Washington, Oregon, and California.

TABLE 10.3 Distribution of Serial Murderers by State, 1800–2004

State	Number of Cases in Which One or More Victims Were Killed	State	Number of Cases in Which One or More Victims Were Killed
California	53+	Oregon	
		Utah	
New York	34	Colorado	
		Kansas	
Texas		Louisiana	
Florida	16–30	Tennessee	
Illinois		Idaho	
		Montana	
Ohio	11–15	North Dakota	
		Arizona	
Georgia		New Mexico	
Washington		Alaska	
Oklahoma		Wyoming	
Alabama		Nebraska	
Nevada		Minnesota	
Wisconsin		Missouri	1–5
North Carolina	6–10	Iowa	
New Jersey		Maine	
Connecticut		Kentucky	
Massachusetts		Virginia	
Pennsylvania		Arkansas	
Michigan		Maryland	
Indiana		Mississippi	
		South Carolina	
		West Virginia	
		Delaware	
		Vermont	
		Rhode Island	
		New Hampshire	
		Hawaii	
		South Dakota	

N = 367 cases

SOURCE: © Cengage Learning, 2013.

TABLE 10.4 Victims of Serial Murder in the United States, 1800–2004, by Mobility Classification

Mobility Classification of Killers	Percentage of Victims (N = 2,760–4,340)	Number of Cases (N = 367)	Percentage of Offenders (N = 431)	Average Number of Victims per Offender	Average Number of Victims per Case
Total	100	367	100	6–10	8–12
Traveling	34–39	124	34	6–12	8–14
Local	38–44	191	52	5–9	5–10
Place-specific	20–24	52	14	9–17	11–19

SOURCE: © Cengage Learning, 2013.

In using these typologies to analyze victim data, it was found that overall, 20% to 24% of victims were killed in specific places, whereas 38% to 44% were murdered by offenders identified as local killers. The traveling killers accounted for 34% to 39% of the victims. These data indicate that the majority of serial killers (66%) operated in a specific place or general urbanized area but did not travel into other states. In grouping these two mobility typologies, it was found that 58% to 68% of all the victims were killed by men and women who generally stayed close to home. The data indicate a shift in mobility since 1975, with those who travel out of state declining somewhat. Conversely, those offenders classified as local killers increased in frequency. One explanation for these changes may be related to the increase in urbanization. With nearly three-fourths of the U.S. population distributed among large urban areas such as Los Angeles, New York, and Chicago, offenders are able to maintain anonymity and also have access to a large pool of victims.

Also, the number of place-specific offenders has decreased, in part because of methods of killing. Poisons such as arsenic and cyanide, once commonly used by female killers to murder their families and friends, are now more easily detected. Consequently, between 1975 and 2004 the number of victims killed by place-specific offenders in this study declined significantly. The percentage of victims killed by local offenders between 1975 and 2004 increased noticeably. There was also a smaller decline in the number of victims killed by traveling offenders during this time.

Two major 20th-century homicide studies by Wolfgang (1958) and Pokorny (1965) found that the number of victims of homicides was divided almost equally between those killed in the home and those killed in areas outside the home. By the end of the 20th century, patterns in serial murder were well established. Victims were more likely to be killed away from their homes, suggesting that they may be vulnerable in areas of the community where their assailants have easy access.

According to the numbers for the three mobility groups in Table 10.4, place-specific cases were the least common and were responsible for the smallest percentage of homicides but represented the greatest average number of victims per case. These findings contradict the general belief that serial killers are primarily offenders who travel across the United States, murdering many victims as they go. According to these data, perhaps a greater area of concern should be focused on serial killing in hospitals, nursing homes, and private residences.

A commonly held notion about serial murder is that offenders have a tendency to operate in pairs or groups, making the abduction and/or killing of a victim an easier task. Of the 431 offenders surveyed, 27% had at least one partner in committing their homicides. Although the number of team offenders in this study is significant, the majority of offenders apprehended tended to commit their murders alone.

Another important issue concerns the types of victims serial killers single out. One of the most common beliefs concerning serial killing is that the offender often develops a pattern in his or her modus operandi. However, to a great extent the offender's behavior is directly related to the type of victim selected. For homicides in general, victimologists agree that sometimes the offender and the victim are "partners in crime"—or at least that the victim can precipitate his or her own demise. Many domestic disputes that lead to fatalities are initiated by the victim. Karmen (2004) refers to this notion of shared responsibility as victim blaming. Homicides in general often include this element, especially because of the prior relationship of the victim to the offender. In Wolfgang's (1958) study and Pokorny's (1965) Cleveland study, a replication of Wolfgang's work, the findings showed a similar pattern. In both studies, those directly involved in the homicide were usually family relatives or close friends. A common assumption, however, is that victims of serial murder are killed primarily by strangers. Using the three categories of family, acquaintances, and strangers as potential victims, Figure 10.2 indicates that stranger-to-stranger serial homicides increased

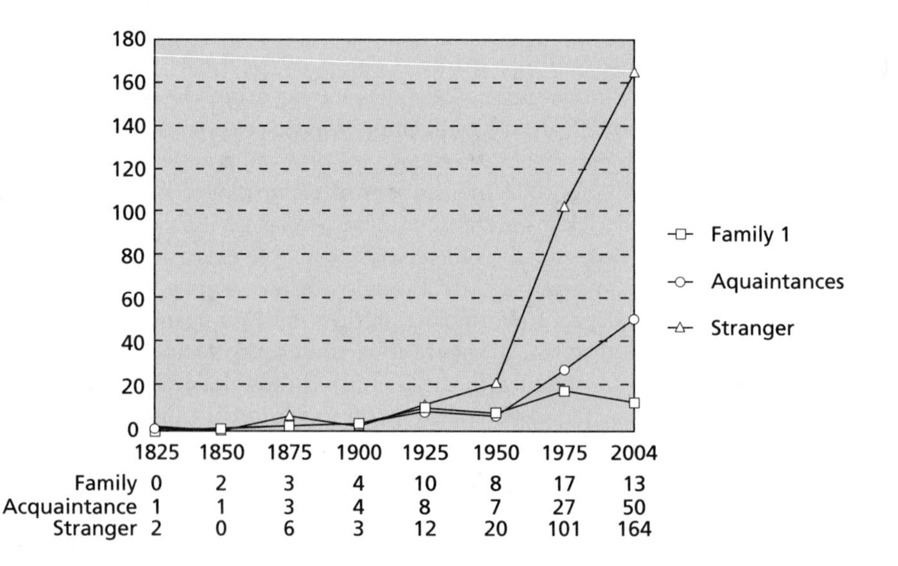

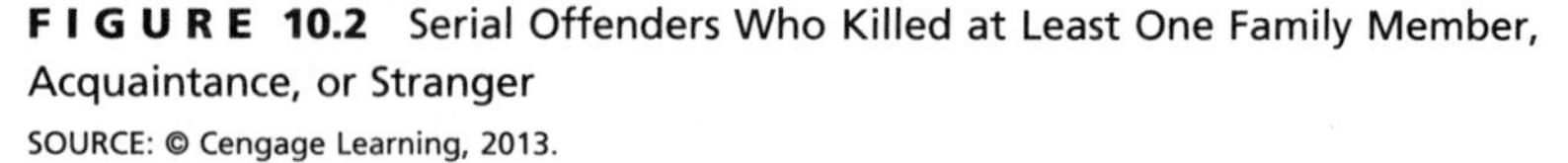

FIGURE 10.2 Serial Offenders Who Killed at Least One Family Member, Acquaintance, or Stranger

SOURCE: © Cengage Learning, 2013.

TABLE 10.5 Preferences of Offenders toward Murdering Family, Acquaintances, or Strangers as Victims in the United States, 1800–2004

	Percentage of Male Offenders (*N* = 356)	Percentage of Female Offenders (*N* = 64)	Percentage of Total (*N* = 420)
Family only	3	35	8
At least one family member	9	48	15
Acquaintance only	8	20	10
At least one acquaintance	25	34	26
Strangers only	70	23	61
At least one stranger	87	31	76

SOURCE: © Cengage Learning, 2013.

markedly between 1950 and 2004. According to these data, the number of offenders killing at least one stranger continued to increase until 2004.

To further illustrate this apparent rise in stranger-to-stranger serial murder, offenders were surveyed regarding preferences toward strangers, acquaintances, or family members as victims (see Table 10.5). Historically, 8% of offenders were found to murder family members only, with female offenders nearly 12 times more likely to do so. Only 10% of all offenders targeted acquaintances only, and these offenders were again more likely to be females. In contrast, 61% killed strangers only, with male offenders three times more likely to do so than female offenders. Gender differences in serial killing between female and male offenders have also attracted the attention of researchers. Keeney and Heide (1994) found gender variation in the method and means of serial killing, including damage and torture to the victim, weapon and method used in killing, stalking versus luring behaviors, crime scene organization, motive, history of substance abuse, and psychiatric diagnosis. Similarities were found in educational level, familial dysfunction, race, history of child abuse, and occupation. These differences underscore a need to focus research efforts on examining victim–offender relationships.

At least 26% of all offenders in this study killed one or more acquaintances, whereas 15% killed one or more family members. These figures have changed very little from the previous studies, suggesting that the target trend for victims continues to lean toward stranger-to-stranger homicides. Since 1975, very few offenders were found to have killed family members. By contrast, offenders murdering only strangers increased sharply. Overall, 76% of serial killers murdered at least one stranger.

Various reasons can be offered for such a dramatic trend. Killing strangers is probably perceived by most offenders as providing safety from detection. Also, the anonymity and thrill derived by seeking out unsuspecting strangers certainly must attract many killers (Leyton, 1986b). Perhaps even more important, offenders can much more easily view strangers as objects and thereby dehumanize their victims. On his capture, one offender confessed that he did not want to know his victims' names or anything about them, and if they did give a name, he would quickly forget it.

Another factor influencing victim selection is the degree of power and control the offender is able to exert. Serial killers rarely seek out those who are as physically or intellectually capable as themselves. Instead, by either randomly or carefully targeting victims, serial killers mentally and/or physically stalk their prey. Because strangers seem to be the primary target, offenders were also surveyed as to the specific type of stranger–victim they most commonly murdered (see Table 10.6).

Although many of the categories under the heading of "strangers" in Table 10.6 are not mutually exclusive, they do represent the actual types of strangers reported in this study. Thus, "young women alone" in category 1 may also fit into the category of "hitchhikers" or "people walking on streets." "Young women alone, including female college students and prostitutes" was the most commonly noted stranger–victim category. The second category of "children (boys and girls)" was also frequently noted as a desirable class of victims. Combined, these two categories accounted for most of the stranger–victim serial murders.

When offenders murdered acquaintances, friends and neighbors appeared to be the most common victims, although they were followed closely by "children (girls and boys)." With the addition of "women alone, including waitresses and prostitutes," these first three categories represent the majority of the acquaintance-victims. In the family grouping, offenders were most likely to kill their own children, husbands, or wives, although several other relatives were represented. The most salient factor among the groupings of strangers, acquaintances, and family members was that most of the victims were women and children. Whatever the specific motives of the killers were, they chose to act out their aggressions on those perceived to be weak, helpless, and without power or control. Males certainly were not exempt from victimization, but they were the minority. These figures differ from those for homicides in general; in 2003 about 75% of murder victims were males. In addition, the typical murder victim generally is a member of a racial or an ethnic minority. Nearly half of murder victims in the United States in 2003 were African Americans (Uniform Crime Report, 2004). The opposite is true of the victims surveyed in the present study, in which the majority of the victims (and offenders) were Caucasian.

Offenders in this study did not overwhelmingly target a specific age group (see Table 10.7). For example, only 6% of offenders murdered children only, and 5% specifically targeted teens. Young and middle-aged adults were the most likely targets (78%), but only 36% of all offenders killed only adults. Overall, 5% of offenders killed only elderly victims. Although we might expect a substantial percentage of offenders to kill at least one child or teenager, the number of offenders (16%) killing at least one elderly person was much higher than anticipated. Very few offenders killed victims in all age groups, and in respect to all combinations of victim relatedness, offenders were most likely to kill adults and teens.

TABLE 10.6 Order of Types of Victims Sought Out by Serial Murderers

A. Strangers

1. Young women alone, including female college students and prostitutes
2. Children (boys and girls)
3. Travelers, including hitchhikers
4. People at home, including entire families
5. Hospital patients, including the handicapped
6. Business people, including storeowners and landlords
7. People walking on streets/in stores
8. Older women alone
9. Police officers
10. Employees
11. Derelicts/transients
12. People responding to newspaper ads
13. Racial killings

B. Acquaintances

1. Friends and neighbors
2. Children (girls and boys)
3. Women alone, including waitresses, prostitutes
4. Adult males
5. People in authority, including landlords, employers, guards
6. Members of one's own group—e.g., gangs and inmates
7. Patients

C. Family

1. Own children
2. Husbands
3. Wives
4. In-laws
5. Other relatives—e.g., nephews, nieces, uncles
6. Mother of the offender
7. Siblings
8. Grandparents

SOURCE: © Cengage Learning, 2013.

Since 1975, the data indicate a shift in some of the trends, which may be a foreboding of things to come. By 2004 offenders were increasingly targeting the elderly. Also, the overall trend in cases of serial killing involving at least one or more elderly persons has risen significantly. This noticeable rise in the serial killing of the elderly may indicate a continued increase in such crimes as the

TABLE 10.7 Percentage of Offenders Murdering in Specific Victim-Age Categories, 1800–2004

Age Range of Victims	Percentage of Offenders
Only	
Children	6
Teens	5
Adults	36
Elderly	5
At Least One	
Child	23
Teen	37
Adult	78
Elderly	16
Combination* ***(N*** **= 124)**	
Teens and children	10
Adults and children	26
Adults and teens	59
All age groups	1

*Calculated on the number of offenders who killed only in combinations. *N* = 431

SOURCE: © Cengage Learning, 2013.

American population continues to get older. The increasing number of people in nursing homes and the rising demand for home care of the elderly may attract individuals wishing to fulfill an "angel of death" fantasy. This fantasy motivates offenders who for some reason nurture hatred for the elderly, believe in "mercy killing," derive pleasure from watching unsuspecting powerless individuals die, or simply wish to be recognized as someone of importance. In one instance, an orderly confessed to poisoning patients so that when they stopped breathing he could be the first one on the scene to save them. Unfortunately he noted that in his quest to be a hero, several patients died. In another case, Donald Harvey, who worked as a nurse's aide in Ohio, was arrested in 1987 and pled guilty to the deaths of 54–58 people, almost all hospital patients and many of them middle-aged and older.

In recent years the number of hospital patients and those in residential care who become prey to serial killers has been increasing. Orville Lynn Majors is linked to 110–130 murders of hospital patients between 1993 and 1995 in Vermillion, Indiana. A killer who loathed the elderly, Majors injected large doses of potassium chloride into his victims and watched them as their hearts stopped beating. In 2000, Michael Swango was linked to nearly 200 murders of hospital patients both in the United States and other countries. However, Swango, Donald Harvey, Orville Majors, Charles Cullen, and other hospital killers are seldom convicted for most of the deaths. Prosecutors usually attempt to obtain convictions in five or six cases to avoid lengthy, expensive trials. Majors was

TABLE 10.8 Percentage of Offenders Murdering in Specific Victim-Gender Categories, 1800–2004

Gender of Victims	Percentage of Offenders
Only	
Females	39
Males	21
Both	40
At Least One	
Female adult	66
Male adult	47
Both	32
At Least One	
Female teen	28
Male teen	13
Both	3
At Least One	
Female child	16
Male child	16
Both	8

N = 418

SOURCE: © Cengage Learning, 2013.

convicted in six deaths and received a 360-year sentence, and Swango received life in prison for killing four victims.

Offenders were described earlier as being more likely to target women and children than males. The data in Table 10.8 support the claim that, in general, serial killers have victimized female adults (66%) consistently more than male adults, but nearly half of all offenders surveyed had killed at least one male adult. Over one-fourth of offenders targeted at least one female teen. An equal number of offenders (16%) killed at least one female or one male child. This shift may in part be due to the increasing accessibility men have to women as they become more visible in the workplace and institutions of higher education.

VICTIM FACILITATION

A final consideration regarding the etiology and demographics of serial-murder victimization focuses on the concept of *facilitation*, or the degree to which victims make themselves accessible or vulnerable to attack. Wolfgang (1958), in his noted Philadelphia study, examined the notion of "victim-precipitated" homicide. He observed that some victims are catalysts in their fatal attack by rendering either the first blow or threatening gesture. Among Wolfgang's several conclusions, he found that the victim was often the spouse of the offender, had been drinking, and had a history of assaultive behavior. He concluded that the victim may be one of the critical precipitating causes of his or her own death (Wolfgang, pp. 245, 264). In addition, Reiss (1980) studied victim-prone individuals and found they were more likely to experience the same form of victimization than to be subject to two different criminal acts. McDonald (1970) observed that victim-prone people have acquired particular attitudes and lifestyles that increase their vulnerability. According to Doerner and Lab (1995), victim precipitation is a "major contributing factor" in serious violence. Wolfgang (1958) noted that in many instances the characteristics of homicide victims in general resembled those of their assailants. Who became the offender and who became the victim often was determined more by chance than any other factor. He noted that few women committed murder and that most women who did commit murder were responding to the violent behavior of males. The Philadelphia study also revealed that most murders were intraracial: blacks killing blacks and whites killing whites. As discussed earlier, the victims of serial murder appear increasingly to fall prey to strangers. Unlike homicides in general, in which the victim often knows the offender and provocation plays an important role in the killing, involvement of the victims of serial murder in their own victimization may be best determined by the degree of facilitation created by the victim, or the degree to which the victim placed himself or herself in a vulnerable situation (see Table 10.9). For example, picking up hitchhikers can place the driver or the passenger of a vehicle in a highly facilitative position for killing. Low facilitation was defined as sharing little or no responsibility for the victimization. For example, a child is abducted by a stranger while playing in his yard, a patient is poisoned to death during a hospital stay, or a woman is abducted from a shopping mall during daytime business hours. Usually these types of victims are completely unsuspecting of any imminent danger.

In the 2004 study, offenders were examined regarding the methods used to obtain victims, and, in turn, data on victims were examined as to their lifestyles, type of employment, and their location at the time of abduction and/or killing. The overall trend indicated that 13% to 15% of all victims in this research were

TABLE 10.9 Degree of Victim Facilitation in Serial-Murder Cases in the United States, 1800–2004

Facilitation	Number of Victims	Percentage of Victims	Percentage of Cases	Number of Victims per Case
High	391–530	13–15	14	9–12
Low	1,535–2,573	60–64	69	7–11
Combination	646–905	23–25	17	12–16
Total	2,572–4,008		100	

N = 329 cases

SOURCE: © Cengage Learning, 2013.

highly facilitative in their own deaths. Some were hitchhiking, others worked as prostitutes, and still others placed themselves in some way at the mercy of strangers. In over two-thirds of all cases victims were generally in the right place at the wrong time and became a homicide statistic.

Although some people argue that much of the preceding research substantiates the contention of those claiming that our society has experienced a dramatic emergence of serial killing, others may argue that such claims are the product of vague definitions, variations in reporting, the omnipresence of high-tech media, or a statistical artifact. However, of greater concern than the extent of serial murder is its reality. The pervasiveness of serial murder will never challenge that of domestic homicide. What does seem to be increasingly apparent is that we are confronted with a phenomenon for which we have little explanation and that we have little ability to deter. The risk of victimization in our general population appears to be extremely small, yet there are those who are at greater risk as a result of their age, gender, place of residence, or lifestyle.

The etiology of victimization is of concern to researchers wishing to expand their explanations of criminal behavior. Victim profiling can be an effective tool in understanding causation as well as providing direction for deterrence efforts. The victims in this study, except for those from California, exhibited little regionality. Increasingly they were targets of offenders who operated locally in areas with higher populations. Unlike homicide in general, in which the victim often knows his or her attacker, serial murder usually involves stranger-to-stranger situations. Young women and children are at greatest risk of victimization, especially those who are alone or can be isolated. Males, although not as frequently targeted, are also well represented as victims. In respect to age groups, offenders appear to kill young adults in greater proportion, yet in recent years the elderly have been frequently selected as victims. Most victims do not facilitate their deaths as a result of their lifestyle, although in recent years increasing numbers of victims have appeared to place themselves at risk.

In so many cases when a serial killer is caught, the neighbors will state that "he seemed like such a nice man" or "I knew something was up with him!" The truth is we seldom know the dangers that surround us. Our "gut instincts" often fail us because they are not trained to know about and react to a sexual predator or serial killer living next door. Indeed, many of us are blindsided by victimization. Mary Ellen O'Toole and Alisa Bowman (2011), in their book *Dangerous Instincts: How Gut Feelings Betray Us*, concur with this premise. O'Toole, a long-term FBI veteran who has investigated many cases of violence and deceit, agrees that so often we do not "see it coming." I highly recommend this book, as it offers self-tests throughout so that you can check your responses and reactions to specific risks. How do you know when you are being conned? Many, many astute people were conned by Bernie Madoff. How well can you deflect a psychopath's charming lures when he seems like such a nice guy? If you have read the first nine chapters of this book then you understand the importance of knowing and responding to potential dangers.

MISSING AND MURDERED CHILDREN

In 1979, six-year-old Etan Patz walked along a busy New York street to await his school bus. He had walked that one block to the bus before, but today was the first time his mother felt he was capable of going alone. Etan never arrived at the bus stop and has not been seen or heard from since his disappearance 25 years ago. He is believed to have been abducted by a known sexual predator in the area, taken into the sewers, and killed. In 1981, six-year-old Adam Walsh was abducted from a shopping mall when he was momentarily left unattended. His head was eventually recovered by investigators. In 2008 Florida officials announced that Ottis Toole, a now deceased serial killer, was the offender who abducted the boy.

These two cases attracted extensive media coverage and motivated the creation of the Adam Walsh Child Resource Center in Ft. Lauderdale, Florida. However, in many other instances the offender, not the victim(s), receives the national media attention. In 1981–1982, 11 children disappeared in the area of Vancouver, British Columbia. Eventually, Clifford Robert Olson was arrested in the murder of the 11th missing child. Although Olson was a suspect in the other disappearances, no one was sure what had become of the children and teenagers, ages 12–17. Olson, a man with an extensive history of criminal behavior, offered to take investigators to the graves of several victims in return for money. Without the money there would be no names or bodies returned, and the parents might never know if their child had been one of his victims or had disappeared for some other reason. If Olson had in fact killed their children, the families wanted to know and desperately wanted the bodies returned for a proper burial. After some deliberation the British Columbia government agreed to pay Olson $10,000 for each body returned to them. The killer responded by leading them to 10 gravesites. Olson's wife was given the $100,000* and has since divorced him and relocated with her son. Olson now resides in a Canadian prison where he must serve a minimum of 25 years before he will be eligible for a parole hearing (author's files; interview with offender).

These types of abductions, murders, and serial killings of children generally precipitate alarm and fear in any community. The true extent of the problem of missing and murdered children is often subject more to speculation than fact. In 1983 the U.S. Department of Health and Human Services stated that 1.5 million children were reported missing every year. The executive director of the National Center for Missing and Exploited Children (NCMEC), a nonprofit clearing house set up by the government in 1984, indicated that strangers were responsible for the abductions of 4,000 to 20,000 children each year. In addition, the NCMEC reported that 25,000 to 500,000 were victims of parental kidnapping ("How Many," 1985). Other organizations, such as the FBI, strongly disagree with such figures and report much smaller numbers of victims.

Sometimes children are abducted for sexual purposes. Dr. Wayne Lord, former director of the FBI's child abduction unit, found that about 62% of the

---

*After extensive public outcry the money was returned to the government.

3,200 to 4,600 annual occurrences of nonfamilial child abductions were committed by strangers. Among those are about 100–150 yearly abductions by predators who sexually assault and/or kill their child victims (Lord, Boudreau, and Lanning, 2001).

Part of the disagreement over current data can be traced to two sources: methodological issues in data collection and operational definitions of the categories of missing children. Only in recent years has national attention been focused on the plight of missing children. For example, AMBER Alert has been very helpful in alerting the general public when a child is abducted, and as a result some abducted children have been safely recovered. Sorely needed are more national surveys that can be compared to regional and statewide data. A need is also apparent for consistency in defining the types of missing children. Most missing children can be classified as runaways, many leaving home several times in one year. Each time they run away, however, they can be counted again as missing children. Most runaways eventually return home, whereas other cases can be classified as parental kidnappings (Abraham, 1984). Most abductions of children are by parents or relatives, often engaged in custody battles with their former spouse or relative. The following list expands and refines the various categories used until now to clarify missing and murdered children:

1. **Runaways**—children who voluntarily leave home without parental/guardian permission.
2. **Parental abductions**—children abducted by the noncustodial parent or the parent who does not have legal guardianship.
3. **Relative abductions**—children abducted by a relative, such as an uncle, aunt, or in-law who takes a child from the parent or legal guardian.
4. **Discarded children**—children who are forced to leave their homes by parents or guardians who reject them.
5. **Disposable children**—children who are murdered by their parent(s) or legal guardians.
6. **Stranger abductions**—children who are taken by persons who are strangers to the victim and the victim's family.
7. **Abbreviated abductions**—children who are abducted for a short period of time (minutes or hours) and then released. These children may never be recorded in police records.
8. **Aborted abductions**—children who manage to escape the attempted kidnapping.

In this study, runaways represented the greatest percentage of children found alive, whereas stranger abductions accounted for the greatest percentage of children found dead. Abraham (1984) found that only 3 out of every 10 children kidnapped by a parent will ever see the other parent again, and that physical and sexual abuse of the abducted child is common. Nearly one-fourth of the children that were abducted by a parent or a relative and were later found had been murdered. According to the NCMEC, parental and relative abductions accounted for nearly half of all missing children reported to the agency. In contrast to its earlier findings of several thousands of children being abducted by strangers each year, data indicated approximately 150 stranger abductions per year during the three-and-a-half-year study (FBI, 1988). By 2011 this number of stranger abductions had remained steady between 100–150 victims per year. Other important U.S. Department of Justice facts* regarding missing children include:

- 797,500 children (younger than 18) were reported missing in a one-year period of time studied, resulting in an average of 2,185 children being reported missing each day.
- 203,900 children were the victims of family abductions.
- 58,200 children were the victims of nonfamily abductions.
- 115 children were the victims of "stereotypical" kidnapping, where someone the child does not know or of slight acquaintance holds the child overnight or transports the child 50 miles or more, kills the child, demands ransom, or intends to keep the child permanently.

Finkelhor et al. (2005), in their study of online victimization of youth for the National Center for Missing and Exploited Children, found:

- Approximately one in seven youth online (10 to 17 years old) received a sexual solicitation or approach over the Internet.
- Four percent (4%) received an aggressive sexual solicitation such as a request to meet them somewhere, or were contacted by telephone or sent offline mail, money, or gifts.
- Thirty-four percent (34%) had an unwanted exposure to sexual material such as nudity or persons engaging in sex.
- Twenty-seven percent (27%) of the youth who encountered unwanted sexual material reported the experience to a parent or guardian. If the experience was viewed as distressing and evoked fear or made them feel very or extremely upset, only forty-two percent (42%) informed a parent or guardian.

Approximately 20% of all girls and 10% of all boys in the United States will be sexually victimized before reaching adulthood. Compared to other developed nations, the United States has one of the highest rates of child homicide: 8.0/100,000 for infants, 2.5/100,000 for preschool-age children (age 1–4 years), and 1.5/100,000 for school-age children (age 5–14 years). By comparison, Canada is half that rate. Researchers suggest that rates of child murder by parents are underestimated (Friedman et al., 2005). According to the Department of Justice, in 2008 there were 1,494 child (under age 18) homicides in the United States. Of those killed, 69% were male and 31% female.

---

*Andrea J. Sedlak, David Finkelhor, Heather Hammer, and Dana J. Schultz. U.S. Department of Justice. "National Estimates of Missing Children: An Overview" in *National Incidence Studies of Missing, Abducted, Runaway, and Thrownaway Children*. Washington, DC: Office of Juvenile Justice and Delinquency Prevention, Office of Justice Programs, U.S. Department of Justice, October 2002, p. 5.

Controlling for all age categories, male children are more than twice as likely to be murdered. When the 15–19 age group is excluded, the ratio nearly evens out between males and females. In other words, the percentages of male children being murdered in all age categories, with the exception of the 15–19 group, are similar to those of female children in respective age groupings. The dramatic difference between murders of males and females, age 15–19, may be explained in part as a result of drug- and gang-related violence. This figure, of course, includes children killed by their mothers or fathers, as well as abducted and murdered child victims. Most nonfamilial child abduction victims range in age between 4 and 11, and often the circumstances involve the child being snatched or lured from a street. Most runaways are not in immediate danger when they first run away, but nearly 75% of child abduction murder victims are killed within two to three hours of being abducted (Ragavan, Schaffer, Dotina, and Lobet, 2001).

The risk of a child being abducted and murdered by a stranger is much lower than previous estimates had determined (U.S. Department of Justice, 2002). Of all children missing in 1999, 99.8% were returned home alive or located. Of the 0.2% or approximately 2,500 not located or returned home, the vast majority were runaways from institutions. In 1999 there were approximately 58,200 child abductions by a nonfamily perpetrator, including 115 stereotypical kidnappings (Office of Juvenile Justice and Delinquency Prevention [OJJDP], October 2002). Where strangers are concerned, the preliminary data suggest that girls are at greater risk than boys; in addition, the rates for black children are three times higher than for white children. The fact remains, however, that some children do fall prey to strangers, some of whom are serial offenders. Based on the 2004 study, the following section explores factors in the murders of children who were victims of serial killers.

Children as Victims of Serial Murderers

If we are to protect children from adults who would kill them, we must be willing to look beyond the traditional notions of victim–offender relationships. Although researchers are still attempting to measure the extent of the serial-murder phenomenon, the evidence is clear that young women and children are the prime targets of such attacks. According to the case files of 420 known serial killers in the United States, 100 (24%) had killed at least one child. The child-killer group included males (74%) and females (26%); overall very few of the offenders were black (author's files). Most serial offenders are white and lower middle class or middle class, and their homicides tend to be intraracial. The fact that some major urban centers are now predominantly black and are politically controlled by black citizens may in part explain why increasing attention is being focused on the plight of missing and murdered black children. As mentioned earlier, in 1981 Wayne Williams, who is black, was arrested in the killings of 22–30 black youths in Atlanta, Georgia. The murders and their investigation attracted national media and government attention. In recent years a few blacks have also been involved in interracial serial killings and have received considerable publicity for their crimes. Indeed, African Americans are disproportionately represented in serial murder, but most kill adults, not children. In 1985 Alton Coleman and his

TABLE 10.10 Relationship of Serial Murderers in the United States to Their Child Victims

Relationship	Percentage of Male Offenders (*N* = 72)	Percentage of Female Offenders (*N* = 23)	Percentage of Total (*N* = 95)
Strangers	67	9	53
Strangers/acquaintances	14	0	12
Family	1	66	16
Family/acquaintances	4	17	7
Family/stranger	6	0	3
Acquaintances	5	8	7
All	3	0	2
Total	100	100	100

SOURCE: © Cengage Learning, 2013.

companion Debra Brown, both black, went on a killing spree in the Midwest, murdering several victims, including young children both black and white. As expected, female killers of children from this group were more likely to murder victims from their own families or other relatives, whereas males were more than seven times more likely to be total strangers to their victims (see Table 10.10). In addition, female offenders were more prone to use poisons to kill their victims; males who killed children frequently mutilated, strangled, shot, or bludgeoned their victims.

By using the mobility classifications to analyze the child homicide data, offenders were almost equally divided between killing locally and those traveling to various states (see Table 10.11). Only one in five stayed in one location such as a home or hospital to murder. Male offenders were more than twice as likely to travel and hunt for child victims as female offenders. Also, females who killed children were more likely to be classified as local than place-specific or traveling. Although several women were classified as place-specific, with the murders occurring in their own homes or places of work, some of the females teamed up with males. By contrast, the largest group of male offenders operated as traveling types, followed closely by local offenders. One implication derived from

TABLE 10.11 Mobility Classification of Serial Murderers in the United States Who Have Killed One or More Children

Mobility	Percentage of Male Offenders (*N* = 74)	Percentage of Female Offenders (*N* = 25)	Percentage of Total (*N* = 99)
Place-specific	12	36	19
Local	40	44	41
Traveling	48	20	40
Total	100	100	100

SOURCE: © Cengage Learning, 2013.

TABLE 10.12 Reported Motives of Serial Murderers in the United States Who Have Killed One or More Children

Motives	Percentage of Male Offenders (N = 75)	Percentage of Female Offenders (N = 25)	Percentage of Total (N = 100)
Sexual gratification	71	8	52
Control	41	16	35
Enjoyment	26	8	21
Monetary gain	14	40	21
Personal reasons*	12	0	9
Mental illness	8	4	7
Combination of motives	58	32	52

*Males generally reported an "urge to kill," whereas female offenders reported that "they were not good mothers," "children were a burden," or they were trying to hide other crimes. Sometimes the killings were reported to have been motivated by racism or hatred.

SOURCE: © Cengage Learning, 2013.

these data is that children, when targeted by a serial killer, can be at risk both in and out of the home. Although the likelihood of a child being murdered by a serial offender is remote compared to the much higher risk of being the victim of domestic homicide, the fact that any risk exists underscores the need for increased education regarding the etiology of serial murder.

For male offenders the primary motive reported for the killing of children was sexual gratification (see Table 10.12). In one case spanning several months, the offender lured several young boys into his control and then sexually molested them. He later confessed to killing the boys for fear that they would tell someone about the molestation.

The female offenders were much more likely (40%) to kill children for financial reasons. In several cases female offenders had murdered their own children, other relatives, or even neighbors in order to collect the insurance. In addition, both male and female offenders sometimes reported deriving enjoyment (21%) from the killing of children. Overall, males were much more inclined to report a combination of motives for killing (58%) compared to their female counterparts (32%). The desire to exert control over the child victim was also a primary motivation in killing, particularly in the case of male offenders (41%).

Another important key to understanding the serial killer of children is to dispel notions of lunacy, mental illness, or psychosis. As mentioned in Chapter 3, very few offenders—whether they kill children or adults—are found to be insane by legal definitions. Most serial killers who target children are psychopaths. For some offenders, killing children may represent an act of revenge on an unjust society or perhaps a desire to prevent others from experiencing the joy and happiness in life they themselves felt denied. Such reasons for murder make children prime targets for offenders. They are viewed as being more trusting, naive, and powerless than adults and are more easily abducted.

Certainly not all psychopaths are violent offenders, and possessing psychopathic characteristics does not always lead individuals to criminal behavior.

However, the majority of offenders in this study appear to possess many psychopathic personality defects. The ability and need for these offenders to control others is tremendous. Children become prime targets because they can be easily controlled and manipulated. Parents need to be just as concerned about where their children *go* in their unsupervised time as they are about teaching them not to "take candy from strangers." Robert Theodore Bundy was executed in the state of Florida for the murder of 12-year-old Kimberly Leach, whom he kidnapped from the grounds of her junior high school in 1978. Bundy also lured a 15-year-old girl into his car while she was attending a youth conference at Brigham Young University in Provo, Utah, in June 1975. Because of his charisma and his ability to persuade his victims to ignore taking precautions with a total stranger, he was able to abduct, sexually torture, and murder several dozen young women.

Luring Children

We have all heard horror stories about abducted children. Unfortunately, child abductors can be particularly creative in their methods of finding suitable victims. One 16-year-old offender being evaluated for a sex-offender program in a psychiatric facility in the western United States noted how simple it was for him to find child victims to molest. His favorite "hunting grounds" were shopping malls because he always found parents who were willing to leave their children, sometimes even young children, alone for a few minutes around the toy counters. The children whom he approached, escorted to the washroom, and molested inevitably seemed to trust him. Some of his victims were so young he was sure they would not understand what had occurred once he allowed them to leave. On a "good" night he claimed he could lure three to four children to the washrooms.

In another case a 15-year-old offender who had been arrested in Hawaii for sexual molestation of children was never prosecuted because his family relocated. A few months later the offender abducted a three-year-old child while she played inside her fenced front yard. After raping and strangling the infant, he left the body in a vacant building.

In 1977 Operation Police Lure was organized in Oakland County, Michigan, by a law enforcement task force in response to a series of seven unsolved child homicides. At the time some people believed that a serial killer was responsible for several of the abductions. In the area where the children were probably lured and abducted, a survey was administered to students in 54 elementary and junior high schools in grades four through nine in an effort to gather more data on child molestation and abduction. The children reported 782 incidents of attempted or actual cases of molestation that had never been reported to authorities. Police investigators also found that children aged 10–12 were the most likely targets and that males and females were victimized at about the same rates. Although victims were approached at different times of day, 3:00 to 6:00 P.M. was the time most frequently reported. Children profiled the offenders as white males, usually in their 20s or 30s, who often attempted to lure them by asking for help, such as looking for a lost puppy. When vehicles were used, the abductors and molesters also seemed to prefer two-door blue models (Wooden, 1984).

Child abductors, of course, do not come in only one mold and generally do not fit the stereotype of the peculiar-looking "dirty old man." Some very benign-looking individuals are arrested for child abductions and molestations. Creating a new typology of such offenders becomes problematic because it excludes many variations of the traditional stereotype. Some important aspects, however, can be noted about the nature of child abductions. Although coercion, bribery, and other such methods to lure victims are frequently employed, asking for help from a child is not only effective from an offender's perspective but also creates difficulty for parents in protecting their children. The thought of helping find a lost animal, such as a puppy or a kitten, can easily distract the child from paying attention to the person seeking the assistance. Similarly, the offenders may use a badge or a blue vehicle to appear as an authority figure to the intended victim. Most children are taught or have learned by experience a degree of respect for authority figures and will automatically respond to their commands.

Alexander (2011), in his study of sexual predators, offers some frameworks in which to understand offender behavior over time. He incorporates Routine Activities Theory (RAT) and Life-Course Theory (LCT). RAT is based on a rational choice perspective of an individual's motivation and opportunity, while LCT views sex offending as strongly influenced by structural position. While these two theories have different approaches, together they provide a unique framework for conditioned activities. Routine activities of sex offenders are altered by certain life events that serve as turning points, which can, in turn, influence persistence or cessation in offending. Alexander found that child victim recruitment varies across the life course. The desire and/or opportunity to recruit is linked to changes in the offender's social position and influenced by the process of aging. This study underscores the importance of understanding the psycho-social and behavioral characteristics of those who seek out children to exploit. Some offenders become extremely adept at luring children, skills that they have acquired over time, maturity, and seized opportunities.

Wooden (1984) outlines a variety of child lures used by offenders, including an appeal to a child's ego by telling the child that he or she is to be in a beauty contest or a television commercial. Some offenders tell the child that an emergency has occurred and they have come to escort the child home immediately. Wayne Williams was believed to have posted employment advertisements for young men throughout the area in which he resided. In the case of Ted Bundy and others like him, similar themes are used but in a more sophisticated manner. Wearing a cast to evoke sympathy or displaying fictitious business cards initially alleviates fears of dealing with a stranger. Offenders who have become adept at manipulating can exert complete control over others, especially children. The following tragic story illustrates how devastating the control some offenders have over their victims can be.

*A Child Killer's Story**

I remember it was late fall and I was living in T______, Arizona, on the run from the law in Montana. At 24 I had already committed several

*This story was edited from a taped interview I conducted with a multiple homicide offender December 5–6, 1988. By request of the offender his identity will remain anonymous.

violent crimes and was basically out of control. Deep into depression and frustrated, I found myself walking across a field about 4:00 P.M. one cold, dreary day. I thought I was alone when I noticed two girls also walking across the field. Immediately I knew I was going to kill them. Moving in their direction, I began to speak to them in a friendly voice. They said they were on their way to play badminton. Both were 11 years of age but one looked physically more mature than the other. It was really very easy, and I was so persuasive, the girls did not even hesitate when I suggested we go to a secluded area. They were such trusting children.

I pulled out my knife and told them to do as I said or I would hurt them. I could see the surprise and fear in their eyes as I ordered the smaller of the two to remain where she was while I moved the second child to another area. They were prevented from seeing one another. Each child was staked out on the ground "spread eagle" and their clothes torn off. They didn't dare scream, for each time they tried I beat them. I systematically tortured them, going back and forth, but spent more time with the smaller child. I had other plans for the prettier girl. The more they responded to the torture, the more I tried to hurt them. I burned them with cigarettes, I beat them repeatedly and hurt them sexually. After about two hours the first child was not responding very well, she was very cold, her eyes appeared glazed, and she appeared to be in shock. I took the handle of her racquet and strangled her to death.

I untied the other girl and told her to get dressed and that if she did as I said we would come back for her friend. I told her not to worry, that I would not hurt her anymore, but she must obey me. I gave her my coat, as her blouse had been cut away in the attack. As we left, I noticed it was after 6:00 P.M. I decided to take her to my home and kill her there. We walked quickly across the field, the child trying her best to keep up with me. As we started along the sidewalk, a police car came around the corner and pulled up beside us. They had their public address system on and were looking for the two missing girls. Apparently the mother of the child walking with me had gone out looking for her daughter when she realized her child had left for the courts without her coat. When neither of the girls could be located, the concerned parents had contacted the police.

Now I was walking less than five feet from the patrol car. The girl was behind me several feet and in a moment I expected the child to run to their car and give me away. I quickly walked down the street, anticipating the command to halt. After about 30 yards I suddenly heard the little girl yelling at me, "Mister, Mister, please slow down you're walking too fast!" I glanced over my shoulder and was amazed to see her still walking behind me. The police had seen us but there was nothing about our behavior that was suspicious and she was hurrying after me. I took her hand and we walked on. In a few moments we approached another street corner when suddenly she saw her father drive by in a car. "There goes my Daddy! He's looking for me," I remember her saying. She did not call out and her father drove on, oblivious to how close he had come to finding his missing child.

> She walked with me to my place without any struggle or protest. I again went through my ritual of removing her clothes and staking her out. She was all mine from about 7:00 P.M. till 3:00 the next morning. She never screamed because she knew I would not take her back to her friend if she failed to obey my every command. When I finished, I suffocated her to death. Later that day I borrowed a car and carried her body into the mountains. Searchers found the first child about an hour after we left the secluded area and the second child about a day after I dumped her body. They never would have caught me had I not left the sack in which I had wrapped the second child. It was an odd weave and had the child's blood on it. Police showed the sack on television and someone recognized it as mine. I was captured in another state a few days later.

The offender's initial charisma and his subsequent intimidating and brutal methods were used in succession to gain total control over the children. Even the offender admitted surprise in finding his second victim following him past the police car. In frustration we want to understand why a victim would not run from her attacker. This is reminiscent of the Stockholm syndrome, in which the victim begins to identify with his or her captor. The child, concerned for her friend and mentally numbed from her ordeal, was incapable of fleeing her assailant.

AGENCIES FOR MISSING, MURDERED, AND EXPLOITED CHILDREN

At the national level a multitude of agencies are now beginning to organize themselves to specifically address the issues of missing, exploited, and murdered children. Established in 1984 by the U.S. Department of Justice, the National Center for Missing and Exploited Children operates as a national clearing house for information about missing and murdered children and sexual exploitation, including child pornography and prostitution.

- Since 1984, the National Center for Missing and Exploited Children (NCMEC) has assisted law-enforcement with more than 182,000 missing-child cases, resulting in the recovery of more than 169,000 children.
- In the last quarter of 2011, the National Center for Missing and Exploited Children's hotline (1-800-THE-LOST®) handled an average of 558 service-related calls per day. Since its 1984 inception, the toll-free hotline has handled more than 3.4 million calls.
- Since 1997, the AMBER Alert program (America's Missing: Broadcast Emergency Response) has been credited with the safe recovery of 542 children. Dozens of children each year are recovered because of AMBER Alerts.
- The National Center for Missing and Exploited Children continues to expand its services to protect children. Their Child Victim Identification Program (CVIP) has information on more than 3,800 child victims (as of September, 2011) from around the world seen in sexually abusive images.

CVIP analysts reviewed child pornography collections from more than 29,000 investigations in the United States through the Child Recognition and Identification System (CRIS).

- CyberTipline, an agency mandated by the Congress in 1998 and an arm of the NCMEC, provides an avenue to report crimes against children and has received more than 1,226,000 reports of child exploitation since its inception. Reports to CyberTipline involve the possession, manufacture, and distribution of child pornography; online enticement of children for sex acts; child prostitution; child sex-tourism; child molestation (nonfamilial); unsolicited obscene material sent to a child; and misleading domain names. ***Reports can be made anytime at* www.cybertipline.com *or by calling 1-800-843-5678.***

National Center for Missing and Exploited Children
Charles B. Wang International Children's Building
699 Prince Street
Alexandria, VA 22314-3175
1-800-THE-LOST

This hotline (1-800-843-5678) is available to anyone with information about missing or exploited children. The Telecommunications Device for the Deaf (TDD) hotline is 1-800-826-7653. The U.S. Department of Justice publishes a variety of brochures that address parental kidnapping, child protection, runaways, and sexually abused or exploited children that list whom to contact if your child is missing and that examine a host of other topics regarding children. Anyone or any group interested in the safety and welfare of children would be well served to contact this agency.

The parent agency that directly coordinates the many federal agencies pertaining to children is the U.S. Department of Justice, Office of Juvenile Justice and Delinquency Prevention, Washington, D.C. 20531. The U.S. Department of Justice's Coordinating Council on Juvenile Justice and Delinquency Prevention includes representatives from the Department of Health and Human Services and the Department of Education. This council, working in conjunction with the Attorney General's Advisory Board on Missing Children, coordinates communications with the Federal Bureau of Investigation and the National Obscenity Enforcement Unit (both agencies of the Department of Justice), the U.S. Department of State, the U.S. Postal Service, the U.S. Customs Service, the Interstate "I SEARCH" Advisory Council on Missing and Exploited Children, and the National Center for Missing and Exploited Children. The U.S. Department of Justice is very active in collecting and disseminating information about missing and exploited children and publishes reports summarizing its progress.

In 1996, California opened its Registered Sex Offender Directory, which contains the names, addresses, and photographs of the state's worst repeat sex offenders. In 2008 California reported over 100,000 registered sex offenders, many thousands of whom are classified as serious and chronic offenders. There is also a Child Molester subdirectory that allows concerned citizens 18 years of age or older with identification to sign in and use the manual. This may well prove to be a useful tool for the public to keep track of sex offenders moving into their neighborhoods. Concerned citizens may, for a $10 fee, use California's Child Molester Identification Hotline by dialing 1-900-463-0400. This service has a list of over 50,000 registered, convicted child molesters. Governor Schwarzenegger passed a bill in 2005 that placed names, addresses, and photographs of all registered sex offenders in California on the Internet.

OTHER SPECIFIC VICTIMS OF MALE SERIAL MURDERERS

Women

Given the variations among the types of serial killing, the cases can also be subdivided into a number of taxonomies, subgroups, or categories. These subgroups may provide valuable information about the methods, motives, victim selection, or mobility patterns of particular serial killers. Examination of different subgroups may, in the final analysis, provide insight into the mind and behavior of serial killers, as well as generate new areas of research. This section focuses on male serial offenders who primarily killed young women. This subgroup was selected for a number of reasons: (1) the public tends to associate the phenomenon of serial murder with young women as victims; (2) young women are the most likely targets of serial killers; (3) these murderers generally receive more extended media coverage than some other groups of serial killers; and (4) these offenders display habits and traits that tend in some ways to set them apart from other serial offenders.

Myers et al. (2006) refer to the primary motivation to commit serial murder as the *traditional sexual motivation hypothesis* that stems from theoretical explanations for rape. The primary focus is to obtain sexual gratification (Kirby, 2009). These are the types of killers we so often hear or read about in the media. These are the rapists who enjoy killing and, often, indulging in acts of sadism and perversion. These are the men who have engaged in necrophilia, cannibalism, and the drinking of victims' blood. Some like to bite their victims; others enjoy trophy collecting—shoes, underwear, and body parts, such as hair clippings, feet, heads, fingers, breasts, and sexual organs. Offenders in this subgroup have earned monikers such as "Bluebeard," "The Torture Doctor," "Demon of the Belfry," "Sex Beast," "The Thrill Killer," "BTK Strangler," and "The Coed Killer," which are designed to evoke our disgust, horror, and fascination. While we do experience such monsters in American society, they are indeed an anomaly compared to other forms of sexual assault and homicide. McNamara and Morton (2004), in their 10-year study of the frequency of serial sexual homicide victimization in Virginia, found the frequency to be very low (0.05), similar to the findings of other researchers.

Compared with serial killers who pursued victims other than young women, these offenders tended to kill more victims. Perhaps males who target young women are more devious, more obsessed, and more intelligent than other males who kill solo. Or young women may simply be the easiest targets and more accessible. In this subgroup, most of the offenders killed young women. The majority of these women-killers were classified as local offenders. Other killers who are more mobile also have made a significant impact in the American landscape. These are the offenders who have been known to travel thousands of miles in a month, eluding police, in search of easy victims. However, like other types of information regarding serial murder, this has been subject to exaggeration. For example, Henry Lee Lucas, a self-confessed serial killer in Texas, said he had killed in nearly every state and claimed he sometimes drove his car 100,000 miles in a month. This means he would have averaged 3,225 miles per day, in a 31-day month, if he drove nonstop, maintaining a speed of 134 mph for the entire month. Obviously, such statements are ludicrous, but it is exactly this type of misinformation that helps to create stereotypes. Some serial killers do travel throughout the United States and Canada, and a few even travel overseas. They commit crimes in several different law enforcement jurisdictions, which they often use to their own advantage. In such situations, poor interagency communications, as well as limited cooperation among agencies, can keep a strong police response from ever developing. As you will see in Chapter 12, efforts are being made to deal with the particular problems created by the traveling serial killer.

The remaining serial killers in this subgroup maintained their territoriality by staying place-specific. Few of these types were strictly stay-at-home killers; some waited for victims to come to their homes, but they also roamed locally in search of prey. Jerry Brudos, about whom Ann Rule wrote *Lust Killer* (1983), would return to his home with his captured victims; however, he also victimized women who made the fatal mistake of knocking on his door.

Prostitutes

Quinet (2011), in her study of prostitutes as victims of serial crime homicide, examined trends and characteristics of their victimization between 1970 and 2009. She noted that prostitutes represented 32% of all victims of serial homicide. Since 2004 that number has dropped to 21% of all victims of serial murder in the United States. She also found that prostitute killers amass a greater number of victims than serial killers who target other types of victims, and they also appear to kill for longer periods of time than other serial offenders. This may be partially explained by the fact that prostitutes live on the fringes of society and their disappearance draws little attention from the community at large. Quinet (2011) also notes that serial murder in general has declined. Actually, it only appears to have declined but instead has become less *visible* because more minorities are now included in the scope of serial murder and its definition: two or more victims. The impact of redefining serial murder has triggered a seismic shift in how we need to view serial murder in the 21st century. Much research is needed to assist in understanding these important changes in serial murder. Have they always been there and we just did not notice, or has the redefining actually uncovered another layer of serial killers?

Serial murderers select victims who are easily dominated, because their systemic issue is power and control. There are some victims who are also selected due to fantasy or paraphilic appeal to the offender. Karmen (2004) points out that people who appear at the "right time" or "right place," or maintain certain lifestyles, expose themselves more than others to risk of victimization. Egger and Egger (2001) suggest that in some cases of serial murder the offender is selecting victims who reflect his general lifestyle. Indeed, offenders may even be relating the victim to the killer's *previous* lifestyle or *fantasized* lifestyle. Sometimes offenders are drawn to victims who represent what they consciously or subconsciously desire for themselves. The fact that the offender is driven by deep-seated feelings of inadequacy becomes manifest in his desire to destroy that which he ultimately cannot possess. If he cannot have these attributes, then his victims will not have them either. Serial-murder cases are replete with offenders who engage in *proxy* murders. Through proxy murders, they are killing someone who reminds them of or symbolizes that which they desperately want but will never have. These attributes, tangible or intangible, haunt the offender and serve as reminders of his own limitations. Ultimately he seeks to destroy persons of beauty, wealth, or assertiveness. Other offenders destroy those who symbolize what they fear or loathe, including gays, the homeless, prostitutes, the elderly, and the infirm.

The dehumanization of victims renders them as objects of hatred and lust. Killing the victim carries no greater moral impact than smashing a bottle or discarding old clothes. This may help in understanding the love-hate relationship between some serial killers and their mothers. Ed Kemper was deeply attached to his mother in that he loved her because she was his mom, yet he hated her for abandoning and rejecting him. After Kemper destroyed and cannibalized several college students from the University of California, Santa Cruz, where his mother was an employee, Ed butchered his mother, cut out her larynx, and used her decapitated head as a dartboard.

Egger and Egger (2001), in their insightful examination of victims of serial murder, note that society affords many offenders near-hero status, whereas the victims serve only to enhance the killer's persona. This is manifest in serial-killer portrayals in movies. Egger and Egger refer to victims as the "*less-dead* … devalued strata of humanity." According to Steve Egger, the "less-dead," in reference to victims of serial murder,

> comprise most of the victims of serial killers. They are referred to as the "less-dead" because they were "less-alive" before their violent demise and now become the "never-were." These victims are the devalued and marginalized groups of society or community. They are the vulnerable and the powerless. For example, prostitutes, migrant workers, the homeless, homosexuals, institutionalized persons, and the elderly who are frequently the victims of serial killers are considered "the less-dead." These groups lack prestige and in many instances are unable to alert others to their plight. They are powerless given their situation in time, place, or their immediate surroundings. (1992, p. 2)

By this reasoning, victims receive their "just desserts," because in American society victims of crime are often perceived as losers, not typical Americans. Thus, victims get what they deserve or what we think they deserve and the killer is admired for his intelligence, skill, and elusiveness. Egger and Egger (2001) observe:

> It is only when the "less-dead" are perceived as above the stature of prostitutes, homosexuals, street people, runaways, or the elderly that our own at-risk vulnerability becomes a stark reality. Even when we begin to take on an identity with the killer's prey, we shirk such feelings and intellectualize the precipitant behavior of victims and their lifestyles as the reason for their demise. (p. 2)

They go on to state that the majority of victims of serial murder are "less-dead." Such assertions are supported by the disdain Americans hold for those outside our societal mainstream. Kim Egger (1999) found in her study of serial killers between 1960 and 1995 that 78% of all victims were female prostitutes. Egger also noted that between 1991 and 1993 there was a total of 198 prostitutes murdered by serial killers, an average of 9 victims per case. Again, prostitutes were far more likely to be targets than any other group of victims (Egger and Egger, 2001, p. 8). These "less-dead" victims are easy prey and will not draw a serious public outcry. The Green River serial murders of prostitutes produced 48 verifiable victims and spanned 21 years before the suspect, Gary Leon Ridgway, was arrested and confessed. Consider the public reaction if the 48+ victims had been respectable, middle-class, tax-paying, law-abiding citizens. Egger and Egger (2001) note that when female drug addicts and prostitutes are being murdered, the residents of that community may recognize, before law enforcement, that a serial killer is in their midst. Such cases are rather common, but no two cases are exactly alike (see Profile 10.1).

Gay Men

Serial killers select a variety of victims contingent on their own perceived needs and abilities. Given the apparent reality that male offenders prefer to attack women, what types of men would elect to kill males? During the settlement and expansion of U.S. territories, men killing men was a common phenomenon, especially during the taming of the "Wild West." Gunslingers and other outlaws were a constant threat to those wishing to establish order and preserve the peace. By definition, gunslingers who roamed the country in America's early days met some of the criteria of what a serial killer is or is "supposed" to be.

However, given the fact that carrying guns was established as the rule of law for many years, it is not surprising that men frequently killed men. Most people carried weapons, especially guns, for protection. Others carried guns in order to commit property crimes, and some killed during the completion of such crimes.

The term *cold-blooded killer* was commonly affixed to outlaws such as the members of the Dalton gang, Jesse James, and other robbers because they often killed men who tried to interfere with their pursuit of criminal activity. But these men are not the types of offenders generally thought of as serial killers, even though they killed over time. Generally, they are excluded from the definition of serial

PROFILE 10.1 The Prostitute Murders, California, 2000–2001

In a small town in the western United States, prostitutes were being murdered. There were four victims thus far. Each victim was poor and a welfare recipient. All were prostitutes or "strawberries" (women who perform sexual acts for drugs), and all except one were mid- to late 20s; the other was a 15-year-old. All were known to be petty crime offenders, and except for the teenager, the drugs and exposure to street life had taken a toll on their physical appearance. They were all killed in the early morning hours. The killer appeared to easily lure his victims and overpower them. His attacks were brutal, utilizing several methods of subduing, torturing, and killing each victim. Most of the victims were beaten horribly, strangled, throats cut, and/or mutilated. The teenager, unlike the others, had her face severely mutilated, perhaps because the killer viewed all prostitutes as ugly. Using an ice pick, the killer also inflicted nearly 150 stab wounds around her genitalia. Now she fit his perception. Another victim had both her arms broken, probably with a tire iron. None of the victims had been raped. Each body was left in open view outside of town. The killer was patient and waited for an opportune time. He preferred to kill when the moon was full.

In this case the other prostitutes were very much aware of the disappearances of the victims even before the bodies were discovered. Although violence is viewed as an occupational hazard, prostitutes try to "size up" a john before going off with him. In this case they each had judged him not to be the killer. Law enforcement personnel kept the public from knowledge of the murders so as not to create "panic." Public reaction, once news of the killings was made known to the community, was typically loud and predictably short. In most cases of murdering prostitutes, the offender does not usually change his type of victim. Indeed, there are exceptions, but generally this tends to be part of the modus operandi of the serial killer. In recent years several men working in professions such as the military, transportation, and sales, which require extensive or frequent travel, have been arrested for the murders of prostitutes. We can expect that as global mobility increases so will the numbers of men who target prostitutes in other states or in overseas countries.

killers because their primary objective was to rob, not kill. However, the question could be asked: How do we know the exact intent of their criminal activity? Some outlaws who robbed may have also looked forward to killing innocent bystanders. The same question could be asked about organized crime figures, military personnel, or even police officers. As with other subgroups of serial killers, efforts were made in this study to identify offenders of earlier eras using the contemporary definition of serial murder. Even by omitting most outlaws, certain offenders who fit the intended definition of serial killers were identified. These men were identified as serialists because their primary objective was clearly to kill others. It was not until the 20th century that information about the sexual involvement of serial offenders who killed men began to surface. This may have been more a function of limited record keeping than a puritan spirit. Eventually, as record keeping became more complete and crimes of a sexual nature were more openly discussed, in the cases of men killing men an array of perversities began to be documented. Table 10.13 gives a list of homosexual serial killers in the United States.

TABLE 10.13 A Sampling of Homosexual Serial Killers in the United States, 1910–2001

Name	Decade	State	Moniker/Accomplice
Carl Panzram	1910s–1930s	Multiple	
Albert Fish	1930s	Multiple	
Dean Corll	1960s–1970s	Texas	
Elmer Wayne Henley	1960s–1970s	Texas	Corll (acc.)
David Owen Brooks	1960s–1970s	Texas	Corll (acc.)
Patrick W. Kearney	1960s–1970s	California	Trash Bag Killer
David Hill	1960s–1970s	California	Kearney (acc.)
John Wayne Gacy	1970s	Illinois	Killer Clown
Juan Corona	1970s	California	
Vaughn Greenwood	1970s	California	
Donald Harvey	1970s	Multiple	Angel of Death
Paul Bateson	1970s	New York	
Randy S. Kraft	1970s–1980s	Multiple	Scorecard Killer
Wayne Williams	1970s–1980s	Georgia	
William Bonin	1970s–1980s	California	
Vernon Butts	1970s–1980s	California	Bonin (acc.)
Henry Lee Lucas	1970s–1980s	Multiple	
Ottis Toole	1970s–1980s	Multiple	Lucas (acc.)
Jeffrey Dahmer	1970s–1990s	Multiple	
Larry Eyler	1980s	Multiple	
Alton Coleman	1980s	Multiple	
David Bullock	1980s	New York	
Michael Terry	1980s	Multiple	
Westley Allen Dodd	1980s	Multiple	
Robert Berdella	1980s	Kansas	
Orville Lynn Majors	1980s–1990s	Indiana	
Michael Swango	1980s–1990s	Multiple	Dr. Death
Herb Baumeister	1980–1996	Multiple	
David E. Maust	1981–2003	Multiple	
Arthur G. Bishop	1984	Utah	
Sean P. Flanagan	1989	Nevada	
Sean Hanify	1989–2004	Colorado	
Andrew Cunanan	1990s	Multiple	
Gary R. Bowles	1994	Multiple	
Ronald J. Dominique	1997–2006	Louisiana	
David P. Brown	2000	Montana	
Marc Sappington	2001	Kansas	Kansas City Vampire

SOURCE: © Cengage Learning, 2013.

PROFILE 10.2 Randy Kraft, the Southern California Strangler, 1972–1983

The California Supreme Court upheld Randy Kraft's death sentence in 2000 for the murders of several young men, many of them military personnel or hitchhikers. He is believed to have tortured and killed at least 16 victims in southern California, Oregon, and Michigan and is linked to as many as 45 deaths. A graduate of Claremont Men's College and considered highly intelligent, Kraft was stopped one day in 1983 for suspicion of drunk driving. The patrol officer found a dead marine in the passenger seat along with pictures of other victims and a death list with addresses of victims. Kraft became known by the media as the "Scorecard Killer" because he kept a detailed record of all his murders. Kraft developed his own "signatures" when he killed, yet was not concerned about changing "signatures" when it suited him. Victims frequently had a cigarette lighter burn on their left nipple, had their left testicle removed while still alive, and objects such as tree branches rectally inserted. When the torture was complete, victims were strangled slowly with their own belts. Most victims had been given Valium along with alcohol before they were bound and raped. Torture was a critical part of the slow killing process. One victim had his eyelids cut off so that he might witness all the horror being inflicted on him. Once victims were dead, they were often pushed out of a speeding vehicle. J. J. Maloney, once a reporter for the *Orange County Register* and assigned to investigate the numerous freeway killings in southern California, noted that many of the murders could have been averted had prosecutors done their job. In 1975 Kraft had been arrested in connection with one of the murders but prosecutors declined to pursue the case. Maloney also points out the confusion created when investigating serial-murder cases that have similar characteristics. Kraft was erroneously dubbed the "Freeway Killer" when in fact the title belonged to William Bonin, who murdered 21 men between 1979 and 1980. Bonin was executed in San Quentin in 1996. Kraft maintained his innocence and, like so many serial killers, attracted numerous "groupies" to champion his cause.

In this study, serial killers who murdered men came from a wide spectrum of educational levels and social classes, including transients and local politicians, farmers, and racists. The most common thread among this particular subgroup, which also sets them apart, appears to be that offenders were involved homosexually with their victims or killed as a result of homosexual liaisons. Most homosexual serial killers select young boys or gay men as their victims and will sexually assault them either before or after the killing. Rarely do heterosexual serial killers target gay men. A few do engage in sexually assaulting/killing females as well. Some offenders, like Jeffrey Dahmer, killed their victims after engaging in consensual sex, although such cases are also relatively rare (see Chapter 5, Profile 5.3, the case of Armin Meiwes, homosexual cannibal). There is fallacy in suggesting that homosexual serial murders are more bizarre than heterosexual serial killing. Serial murder is, by its very nature, obscene. The homosexual serial murders by Dahmer, Gacy, Baumeister, and Kraft are equally rivaled by the heterosexual savagery of Bundy, Kemper, Robinson, and DeSalvo (see Profiles 10.2 and 10.3).

PROFILE 10.3 John Wayne Gacy, 1972–1978

Few other serial killers have attracted as much attention as John Wayne Gacy, "the Killer Clown," one of the most prolific murderers of all time. Born on March 17, 1942, he appeared to have experienced a rather normal childhood, but there were a few dark sides. His father, Gacy Sr., was an alcoholic and frequently mistreated the family by beating his wife, abusing John, and terrorizing his daughters. John could never seem to gain the approval of his father regardless of the efforts he made. As a child, John was accidentally struck in the head by a swing. For five years he experienced blackouts until a blood clot was diagnosed and dissolved by medications. He dropped out of high school in his senior year and left home for a short time, working in a mortuary in Las Vegas. But Gacy had been strongly influenced by his mother since childhood, and, succumbing to that influence, he returned home to live. After finally graduating from a business college, he began selling shoes. His friends found him to be a braggart, because he frequently talked about his time in the military. However, Gacy had never served time in the military.

In 1964, Gacy, now 22, married and went to work for his father-in-law as a worker for, then manager of, a chain of Kentucky Fried Chicken establishments. Gacy joined the local Jaycees and became chaplain of the Waterloo, Iowa, chapter and chairman of the group's first citywide prayer breakfast. In 1967 he was named outstanding vice president and honored as the best Jaycee club chaplain in the state of Iowa. In the spring of 1968, Gacy started his downward spiral, a trip that would take 10 years before ending. A grand jury indicted Gacy for handcuffing an employee and trying to sodomize him and also for paying a youth to perform fellatio on him. He had also hired someone to beat up the youth after the youth testified against him. He pled guilty and was incarcerated at the Psychiatric Hospital, State University of Iowa. After being diagnosed as a bisexual with a personality that was "thrill-seeking or exploratory," Gacy was sent to prison. Because he was a model prisoner and an active community member, Gacy was paroled after serving only 18 months.

Gacy's first wife, who had had two children by John, divorced Gacy during his trial. On his release from prison, Gacy went back to Chicago to live with his mother again. For a while he worked as a cook and then told his mother he had decided to buy his own home. In 1971 he was arrested for picking up a teenager and attempting to force the youth to engage in sex. The case was dismissed when the youth failed to appear on the court date. Gacy was now living in Des Plaines, near Chicago, and had begun his own construction business. He married again, to Carol Hoff, who remembered how John started bringing home pictures of naked men. After four years the marriage ended because of a lack of sexual relations between the couple and because John would often stay out very late at night in his car. John's wife had also learned not to ask questions about personal items she found while cleaning. Gacy had become enraged when she asked him about her discovery of some wallets belonging to young men.

Gacy had begun to add onto his home, and part of the construction included building a large crawl space under the addition. He frequently had some of his young employees help in digging a trench in the crawl space. During this time Gacy was actively involved in the community. In 1970 he claimed to be a Democratic precinct captain and even had his picture taken with First Lady Rosalynn Carter shortly before his arrest in 1978. He became a local celebrity, dressing up as Pogo the Clown and performing at children's parties and at hospitals. He frequently held summer parties at his home, inviting local dignitaries and neighbors. Sometimes people would comment about the peculiar smell, but John simply explained that in the crawl space there was a lot of dampness that created the odor.

Only Gacy knew that the crawl space held his personal collection of bodies of young males whom he had sexually tortured to death. Some of his victims were males who had worked for Gacy; others were male prostitutes he had picked up late at night at "Bughouse Square," a well-known locale in Chicago frequented at night by homosexuals and male prostitutes. Gacy would lure the victim to his home, promising money or employment. When they arrived, he would talk his victim into participating in his "handcuff trick." Once he had the youth in handcuffs, he would chloroform the victim and then sodomize him. Next followed the "rope trick," usually when the victim was conscious. Gacy would tie a rope around the victim's neck and, after fashioning two knots, would insert a stick and proceed to twist it slowly like a tourniquet. The terrifying deaths sometimes were accompanied by Gacy reading passages from the Bible.

John managed to bury 29 victims in the crawl space and cement driveway. Four other victims, for want of space, were discarded in the Des Plaines River. The police were led to Gacy after one of his intended victims escaped and reported him. Investigators eventually demolished Gacy's house and dug up most of his yard in search of bodies. Gacy confessed at least five times, only to recant his statements later. He claimed other people must have put the bodies there. "Where the hell could I have found time? I was working 16 hours a day, and the rest of my time was devoted to the community, charity affairs, and helping you people." During the determination of Gacy's sanity, he was described as a veritable Jekyll-and-Hyde. His defense attorney, Mr. Amirante, cited passages from Robert Louis Stevenson's *The Strange Case of Dr. Jekyll and Mr. Hyde*, quoting Dr. Jekyll: "If I am the chief of sinners, I am the chief of sufferers, also. Both sides of me were in dead earnest." The prosecution, however, described Gacy as having an "antisocial personality," as "a psychopath, a person who commits crimes without remorse."

In 1980, John Wayne Gacy was found guilty of all counts of murder and sentenced to die in the electric chair at Menard Correctional Center in Chicago. Three years after his trial, Gacy stated he was opposed to capital punishment on religious grounds: "Let he who is free of sin cast the first stone." He believed a lengthy appeals process could save him from execution. While in prison Gacy claimed to be a quiet and kind person. He blamed some of the parents for the deaths of their own children because their sons were prostitutes. He said he was incapable of violence and allegedly received letters every day from "kind people," most of them women. "Ninety percent of the writers are women, and I have 41 people on my visiting list. I'm allowed three visits a month," explained Gacy. Although the prosecution portrayed Gacy as a skillful, competent torturer and killer who enjoyed the "God-like power" of life and death, Gacy said it was a lie: "How could I live on top of those bodies?" (Simons, 1983). Yet in a 1986 interview with author Tim Cahill, he remarked that if he could spend 15 minutes in a room with the parents of the people he killed, "they would understand."

Gacy spent much of his prison time painting pictures and having them sold to the public. He loved the attention. I received several letters from Gacy hopefully seeking assistance in his efforts to avoid the executioner. On May 10, 1994, John Wayne Gacy was put to death by lethal injection. Shortly after his death, several of his paintings were purchased at an auction for $20,000. The buyer, wanting to send a clear message to the public, burned Gacy's artwork.

PROFILE 10.4 Herb Baumeister, 1980–1996

On July 3, 1996, with police closing in, Herb Baumeister committed suicide while eluding police in a provincial park in Canada. He typified the Jekyll-and-Hyde personality cycles common to many serial killers. He was a very successful businessman who had built a chain of thrift stores in Indianapolis. He was known for being an entrepreneur and generous in his gifts to charities. Married and father to three children, he was respected by his family, peers, and community. The man appeared so normal, calm, and secure: exactly what every sexual psychopath practices, the art of pretense. Baumeister was very discreet in the timing and manner of luring young, gay men to his estate for sex, torture, and murder. His wife was unaware of his penchant for autoerotic asphyxia or his desire for gay men. For 20 years she believed that her husband was all good and was shocked to learn that he was actually one of Indiana's most prolific serial killers of gay men. In all, he probably killed 20 or more victims in Indiana and Ohio. Police linked him to 16 murders. Several of his victims' bones were found buried on the Baumeister estate. His 13-year-old son accidentally came upon the remains of one of the victims, thus opening the door for investigators to search the property.

Lust killers use sex as a vehicle to destroy their victims; often men who kill men use sex in a similar fashion. Some of the offenders in this subgroup committed their crimes while traveling; others searched for victims locally or used their own homes or places of employment for the killing sites. For the most part, these offenders were single, lower middle class or middle class, and had histories of deeply troubled lives. Other offenders were highly intelligent, educated, and successful in careers (see Profile 10.4).

The Elderly

In 2005 Raymont Hopewell, 35, pled guilty to murdering five Maryland senior citizens between 1999 and 2005. Four of the victims were women and had been raped as well. Those who prey upon the elderly are mainly male offenders, many with paraphilic tendencies. The most publicized case was that of the Boston Strangler. People tend to think of Albert DeSalvo as a man who raped and strangled young women; however, he attacked mostly older women: 8 of his 13 victims (62%) were 55 years of age or older. As mentioned earlier, rape is not necessarily motivated by sexual desire. The reality of these killings suggests that raping women has much more to do with power, control, and desecration than it does sexual desire. A 30-year-old man raping and sodomizing an 86-year-old woman is not only disgusting, vicious, and perverted but also forces us to reconsider our perceptions of exactly what motivates rapists.

Many of the cases in this subgroup involve men who killed older women. In these cases, most of the women had been sexually assaulted. The patterns in the killing of these elderly victims were just as distinct as the patterns in the murders of young women. The sexual assaults and tortures rivaled those inflicted on younger victims. Burgess and Morgenbesser (2005) investigated the incidence and prevalence of sexual violence on seniors between 1995 and 2004. They point out the crises and trauma that follow such assaults both for the victims and their families and the need for brief and crisis-oriented intervention.

The victims generally lived alone or were institutionalized. Either way, offenders could obtain relatively easy access to their intended victims. In addition, most older victims were completely powerless against these offenders. As America "grays," more elderly people become potential victims. Although young women are still the most frequent victims, cases of elderly serial murder have increased from 1975 to 2004. Future policies of the healthcare industry will undoubtedly focus on the aged. As of 2012, work has been done in some medical facilities to provide better security for the elderly. Elderly people who are alone and unprotected unknowingly provide accessible targets for serial offenders.

Families

Most serial killers are portrayed as offenders who seek out individual victims. Occasionally some killers elect to abduct two victims at the same time. However, few offenders attempt such abductions, because dealing with more than one victim tends to weaken their control. Serial killers in this study, especially the lust killers, often wanted "private" time alone with the victim. Team killers tend to be the exception (see Chapter 8).

A few offenders have killed several victims at once, including entire families. However, such occurrences appear to be rare in serial killing; also, these types of murders by male offenders occurred mostly before 1940. Some of these cases involved "Bluebeards," or men who killed one spouse after another (see Profile 10.5). Most of these cases did not include sexual attacks, and often money appeared to be a primary motivating factor in the killings. Guns and poisons were more likely to be used, with less emphasis on torture and strangling.

Both Men and Women

The final subgroup in this chapter includes offenders who kill both men and women. Some of the cases could be referred to as "spree serial killings" because they occurred within a relatively short time frame. Anger, revenge, greed, madness, sadism, and delusions of heroism were often associated with these killers' homicidal actions. This subgroup includes some well-publicized cases, including "Son of Sam" (see Profile 10.6), Charles Starkweather, and the "Night Stalker" case in California. In several of these cases, guns were used as the sole means of

PROFILE 10.5 James P. Watson, 1910–1920

Like many con artists, James P. Watson, "Bluebeard," went by several aliases. When asked by police for his real identity, he simply replied, "I don't know." His last official residence was in California, but Watson operated from Mexico to Canada. A very bright individual but not without his own peculiar sexual quirks, Watson was married to at least 18 women and possibly as many as 26, several of them at the same time. He frequently placed ads in newspapers luring women into marriage.

> Personal: Would like to meet lady of refinement and some social standing who desires to meet middle-aged gentleman of culture. Object matrimony. Gentleman has nice bank account, as well as a considerable roll of government bonds.
>
> H. L. Gorden
> Hotel Tacoma
> (Pearson, 1936, p. 132)

There were always several women who eagerly responded and happily accepted the fact that he worked for the secret service and would need to be on the road frequently. He was very careful to marry women of wealth, which he quickly maneuvered into his control. He began to act out his fantasies of killing women, because he believed they were the root of all evil. He murdered at least 7 and possibly as many as 15; the exact count was never established. Some of them he drowned; others he beat to death with a hammer. They died in Washington State, Idaho, California, and probably other states as well. His fantasies led him in at least one murder to sexually mutilate his victim. He would later confess to investigators:

> All I felt after killing seemed largely, in each instance, some kind of relief, yet unexplainable. The sensation experienced was a sensation of ease as if I had been relieved. Instead of remorse, I had passive satisfaction or passive pleasure. I had no sexual sensation at the time but maybe for a day or two afterwards feeling more that way than normal. The greater sexual desire shortly after was from a memory of the killing. Sometimes I have looked at the body in a way of satisfaction, a kind of pleasure. Yet there was no reason why I should do that because I had seen the same person in married relations. (Ellis and Gullo, 1971, p. 20)

Watson agreed to lead them to the body of one of his victims in return for a guarantee he would receive a life sentence and not death row. The courts agreed, and he went to San Quentin, where he eventually died.

killing the victims. Some of the killers were extremely violent in their attacks, whereas others quietly poisoned or suffocated their victims. In contrast to the lust killers, most offenders in this subgroup were not involved in sexual attacks or particularly perverted acts. This type of serial killer tended to resemble the profile of the mass murderer, who kills all his victims in a few minutes or hours. Although some of the offenders had developed a distinct pattern in their murders, several cases involved a high degree of randomness in victim selection. Except for the "Night Stalker" case, which was allegedly connected to some form of self-styled Satanism, most of the cases were less ritualistic and more impulsive and spontaneous.

PROFILE 10.6 David Richard Berkowitz, 1976–1977

For 13 months David Berkowitz, "the Son of Sam" or "the .44-Caliber Killer," was able to hold the attention of millions of people in New York City and across the country. During that time he shot 13 young men and women on eight different occasions. Six of his victims died, and seven others were severely injured after he fired on young women or couples parked in their cars at night. Investigators finally tracked him down through a parking ticket placed on his car while he was in the area looking for someone to kill. They expected to find "the .44-Caliber Killer" to be a monster but instead found a well-mannered, 24-year-old postal worker who lived alone. His apartment was filthy, littered with liquor bottles, and the walls scratched with graffiti. On one area of the wall he had scrawled: "In this hole lives the wicked king."

To those few who knew him, he lived a rather uneventful life. Born out of wedlock, he had been placed for adoption. He was an exceptional student who frequently was taunted by his classmates for being Jewish. He served three years in the U.S. Army, worked as a security guard, and once worked as an auxiliary New York police officer. His main character trait seemed to be that he was introverted and liked to roam the streets alone at night. On July 29, 1976, two young women, Donna Lauria, a medical technician, and Jody Valenti, sat talking in their car when David walked out of the shadows and fired five shots through the windshield. Donna died quickly; Jody was wounded in the thigh. In October, he fired on a young couple through their rear windshield, wounding the young man. In November, David walked up to two women sitting in their car in Queens and, as he asked for directions, pulled out his .44-caliber gun and fired at both women, paralyzing one of them. On January 30, 1977, a young couple were saying goodnight to each other when the windshield shattered with gunfire. Christine Freund died a few hours later of her injuries. On March 8, 1977, an Armenian student, Virginia Voserichian, was approaching her mother's house when David met her on the sidewalk and shot her directly in the face, killing her instantly. On April 17, 1977, in the same area as some of the other attacks, David shot to death Alexander Epaw and Valentina Swiani as they sat in their automobile. A note was found at the scene that read in part: "I love to hunt. Prowling the streets looking for fair game—tasty meat. The women of Queens are prettiest of all." The .44-Caliber Killer had identified himself as "Son of Sam" in letters he had sent to a New York columnist, James Breslin. By now the city was beginning to panic, but David still easily found victims. In June he shot out the windshield of another car but only wounded the two occupants.

In July David decided to relocate his killing to the Brooklyn area in order to throw off the police. At 1:30 A.M. he fired four shots through the windshield of a car, striking a young couple. Stacy Moskowitz died a few hours later, and her friend Robert Violante was blinded for life. It was here that David's car was ticketed and shortly thereafter linked to the killings. David was arrested exclaiming, "You finally got me!" But he had planted several clues during the long year's ordeal. David had sent threatening notes to his Yonkers neighbors. Sam Carr had made reports to police that David was out to get him because his dog barked too much. Carr's dog had been shot by David with his .44-caliber gun on April 27, shortly after David sent him the letters. David's capture proved to be providential for several young New Yorkers. He told police that he was planning a raid on a Hampton discotheque that night and that authorities "would be counting bodies all summer." Police found a

(continued)

PROFILE 10.6 (Continued)

submachine gun and a note to authorities lying on the seat of his car (Leyton, 1986a, Chapter 5).

At first Berkowitz claimed he committed the killings because demonically possessed dogs commanded him to do so. Years later, he would recant those claims publicly by saying that it was the need to justify those shootings in his own mind that caused him to fabricate the demon story. He said he simply wanted to pay back his neighbor, Sam Carr, for all the noise his dog made, so he created the story that Sam was telling him to kill by using the dogs as a medium. In a letter he sent to David Abrahamsen, a psychiatrist who determined Berkowitz to be competent for trial, he conceded:

> I will always fantasize those evil things which are part of my life. I will always remain a mental pervert by thinking sexual things, etc. However, almost everyone else is like me, for we commit numerous perverted sexual acts in our minds day after day. I will always think of violence, for only a monk, perhaps, could ever succeed in eliminating these desires and thoughts. But what I hope to do is mature to such a point in which I will develop a deeper respect for human life and an increased respect and appreciation for humanity. (Abrahamsen, 1985, p. 23)

David Berkowitz received six 25-to-life consecutive sentences for the murders to which he confessed, with a recommendation that he never be paroled. He is now serving his time at Sullivan Correctional Facility in Fallsburg, New York. New York passed a "Son of Sam" statute prohibiting criminals from profiting financially from their crimes, which has been challenged in the courts in recent years. Berkowitz converted to Christianity in 1987 after reading a Bible given to him by an inmate. In 1998, in a collaborative effort with evangelical pastors, Berkowitz helped produce two Christian videos, *Son of Sam/Son of Hope* and *The Choice Is Yours with David Berkowitz,* in efforts to persuade others to repent.

Serial Murder from a Global Perspective

LEARNING OBJECTIVES

- To understand the extent of global mass and serial murder
- To expose readers to cultural and racial diversity in serial murder
- To examine cases of serial and mass murder in Japan, South Africa, Germany, Canada, England, Russia, and Australia
- To compare methods, motives, and demographics of serial killers in several countries

Just like in America, mass murder is common globally. Serial murder tends to be overshadowed by accounts of mass murder that occur with amazing regularity (see Profiles 11.1 and 11.2). Offenders seem to bear common traits regardless of their race, ethnicity, or nationality. Most suffer from various forms of mental disorder or have experienced severe psychological stress and are unable to cope. Their capacity for violence is accelerated by fantasy, access to guns, and alienation. They finally arrive at a point where they are so disconnected from society, family, and friends that violence becomes a viable option.

BEYOND JACK THE RIPPER

Serial murder also finds its roots in stressors such as rejection, abandonment, loss, humiliation, and hatred. The offenders are rarely considered under law to be insane or deranged, as they often are in cases of mass murder. These observations, however, are from an American perspective, examining American serial killers using American criminal profiles. Most Americans have frequently heard of Jack the

PROFILE 11.1 Anders B. Breivik, 2011

Diagnosed as a paranoid schizophrenic by court-ordered psychiatrists, Anders Breivik was believed to be delusional when he bombed government office buildings in Oslo, Norway, killing 8, and then traveling several miles away to the island of Otoya, where he attacked a Labor Party youth summer camp, killing 69. Breivik, who had undergone plastic surgery to look more Aryan, advocated the expulsion of all Muslims from Norway and from Europe by 2083. He felt betrayed by his own countrymen for allowing them to invade his homeland. Deciding to send a loud and clear message, he carried out the largest bifurcated mass murder in Norwegian history by attacking government officials and children of parents who supported the government. His aspiration was to one day help govern Norway as a white Christian nation. In his far right militant text, *A European Declaration of Independence*, which he distributed the day of the attacks, he voiced his belief in ultra- and white nationalism, cultural conservatism, Islamophobia, and Zionism among others.

An antifeminist, Breivik was critical of his parents for their liberal views, especially his mother for her support of feminism and providing him a feminist upbringing without any real structure. His parents divorced and by his mid-teens Breivik had become rebellious. He hung out with a gang of "taggers" who sprayed graffiti on walls of public buildings. His father cut off contact with him when Breivik, then 16, was caught spray painting. His gang eventually turned their backs on him as well, adding more to his isolation. He was deemed unfit for mandatory military service even though he was physically fit. Two years later he underwent the cosmetic surgery.

Although he was considered a good worker and got along well with people, those of Asian or Middle Eastern descent he did not care for. At age 22 he began his nine-year mass murder plan. Although not a farmer, he set up a geofarm to produce vegetables. The farm provided him cover for his master plan. He purchased a Glock 34 pistol and a Ruger Mini-14 rifle, six tons of fertilizer, and some primer explosives. He practiced with the explosives on his farm to ensure success, and on July 22, 2011, he carried out his plans. When police finally arrived on the island nearly two hours later, Breivik surrendered without a fight. He was found by psychiatrists to be psychotic, and displaying no empathy for his victims or others. Breivik believes that he was meant to save his people and that he is the "knight Justiciar grand master" of the Knights Templar. This organization is often used in the rhetoric of extreme right-wing groups such as the English Defence League in England and the Nashi movement in Russia. Breivik also believed that he would oversee the selective breeding of white Norwegians in order to preserve the purity of their countrymen. Much like Theodore Kaczynski, who also wrote a manifesto, Breivik disagrees with the findings of the court. Without a finding of guilt, however, under Norweigian law, Breivik cannot be sent to prison but instead will be sent to a psychiatric hospital, where at some point he might be eligible for release. Undoubtedly this is a concern for all Norwegians.

- Readers should compare the profiles of Theodore Kaczynski and Anders Breivik.
- What do these two men have in common even though one is a serial killer and the other a mass murderer?
- Delusions alone do not mean a person is insane. Many people have strange delusions yet keep within societal boundaries. Do you think global economic hardship such as we currently experience could contribute to the rise of more such attacks? How do race, ethnicity, religion, and feminism contribute to such a mind-set?

PROFILE 11.2 Martin Bryant and the Port Arthur Massacre, 1996

Martin Bryant, a 28-year-old man carrying sports bags full of handguns and automatic rifles, entered a café in Port Arthur, Tasmania, on April 28, 1996, and, after having lunch, began shooting customers. As people fled the building he walked outside and shot several more tourists as they ran, hid under buses, or hid behind trees. Leaving the area in his car, with a surfboard on top, Martin came upon a woman walking alongside the road with her young daughter and carrying a baby. Martin exited the car and shot and killed all three. He got back in the car and proceeded to drive along the road, shooting at oncoming vehicles. After killing several more victims in their cars he took a hostage and barricaded himself in a cottage. He would eventually kill the hostage before setting fire to the building, nearly killing himself. Except for the owners of the burned cottage, whom he had killed several hours earlier in an effort to secure more guns, the massacre took just under nine minutes. The final count was 35 men, women, and children dead along with 18 others seriously wounded. Witnesses reported that Bryant was laughing during the shooting and seemed indifferent to the human suffering he was creating. Like many mass murderers, Martin was a loner who exhibited many antisocial characteristics. As a child he displayed cruelty toward animals as well as toward other children. He was indifferent to the suffering of others and was often inappropriate in his language when speaking to females. His father had committed suicide, and the woman Martin lived with—a wealthy, eccentric widow—had recently been killed in an auto accident. Martin had a low IQ and was emotionally void, antisocial, and completely disconnected from intimacy; life was for him a surrealistic experience. He carefully planned the attack by securing weapons and purchasing items that he would later use. He calmly executed his victims, very similarly to other mass murderers. Sometimes a person under incredible stress and unable to find manageable or acceptable solutions to his dilemma might decide to kill himself. Often, once that decision is made, the person becomes very calm as he prepares to carry out his plan. For the mass murderer, the attack is in many ways a form of suicide. He has thought through the attack many times in rage fantasy and now he finally creates the opportunity to carry out his death wish. For Martin, the actual killing may have been anticlimactic to the fantasy and preparation stages of his death plan. He currently is serving a life sentence, no parole, in Hobart, Tasmania. (Readers are encouraged to use the Internet to more closely examine the Port Arthur massacre and the mind-set of Martin Bryant.)

Ripper (see Profile 11.3) because he is considered by many to have ushered in the concept of serial murder, even though such a form of killing has been on the Earth for hundreds of years. The Ripper's twisted sense of humor and his brutal method of killing and dismemberment brought to bear the attention of the world. To this day visitors can go to Whitechapel and retrace the footsteps of Jack the Ripper.

GLOBAL ISSUES IN SERIAL MURDER

Three key issues surface as we explore serial murder from a global perspective: (1) serial murder is defined or viewed differently in other cultures; (2) cultural differences influence the methods and motives for serial murder; and (3) serial-murderer

PROFILE 11.3 Jack the Ripper, 1888

By comparison to other serial killers, Jack the Ripper was not prolific in his murders, but, like Ted Bundy, the Ripper has become a criminal icon and a name used to measure other serial killers. The Ripper killed at least 5 London prostitutes, and more likely his death toll was closer to 10 or 15. No one knows for sure, but the Ripper promised through missives to the British media that he would not stop until he had killed 20 victims. His interest in postmutilation of the corpse set him apart from others who, at the time, preyed on prostitutes. The Ripper was very adept at eviscerating the victim and removing her organs. His first victim was murdered on Easter Monday in London's Whitechapel. The Ripper clearly derived sexual gratification from her dismemberment. Once the victim was killed according to his sexual fantasy, the Ripper proceeded to examine body parts. If he was not pressed for time as in the case of Jeanette Kelly, the Ripper had at least two hours to thoroughly complete his task. She had her throat cut to the spinal column, nearly severing the head. Her ears had been removed, as was the nose, and placed on a severed breast in an effort to create a face. The other severed breast lay on the nightstand covered with her kidneys and heart. Close by was the right thigh, upon which rested the liver. Her sexual organs were never recovered. This practice was common among most of his victims. The Ripper seemed to take delight in excising the uterus. Jack enjoyed taunting police and newspapers and would send letters written in a victim's blood vowing death to all prostitutes. Jack even sent a victim's kidney to a citizen's vigilante committee formed to catch him. Jack the Ripper was never caught, and many theories currently abound as to the actual identity of the killer.

What many Americans do not know, however, is that since Jack's debut, there have been other "Rippers" in England. European countries have also had their share of multiple killers. For example, Harold Smith (1987) identified several noted serial killers in Europe, and Jenkins (1988) chronicled the activities of multiple killers in England between 1940 and 1985. Indeed, serial killings have appeared and been documented in most countries. Even Russia, which used to underreport crime, has reported cases (see Profiles 11.8 and 11.9). In one instance a Soviet newspaper, *Sovetsky Sport*, reported that the director of a teenage sports club murdered several children and photographed their hanging corpses. The offender, Slivko of Nevinnomyssk, was executed for his crimes. The paper also noted that the crimes had occurred over a span of several years. Another Soviet publication reported the execution of a locksmith in Byelorussia for the murders of 33 female victims. France has experienced "Bluebeards" and "Rippers"; England, "Vampire Killers" and "Rippers"; Germany, "the Monster of Dusseldorf" and "the Ruhr Hunter"; and Ecuador, "the Monster of the Andes."

profiles constructed in the United States are often contradicted by profiles created by law enforcement agencies in other countries. One of the contentions about serial killers in the United States as viewed by the FBI was that nearly all serial killers were lust killers, men who are sexually motivated to murder. Since the San Antonio Symposium on serial murder we now have some consensus that serial murder involves a variety of offenders. Indeed, many of these killers are sexual predators, but others do it for gain, power, etc. Some are women, some use poisons, and others are African American. The symposium has helped resolve many of the serial-murderer stereotypes exploited by the media and Hollywood. Is it possible that simple greed and not lust can motivate serial killers? We now know that women can kill serially and not be sexually motivated. Can the same be said of some male serial killers?

GERMAN SERIAL KILLERS

During the 1800s the notion of murders by vampires and werewolves (see Chapter 2) attributed to much folklore. This was especially apparent in European countries such as Germany, Austria, and France. Benezech et al. (1981) discuss the origins of vampirism and hematolagnia, or the sexual gratification from drinking blood (see Chapter 5 on paraphilia). Drinking blood in most countries is not a crime, but the activity is usually done in the presence of others. Most persons engaging in this form of paraphilia also have participated in or have co-occurring paraphilia often harmful to others. In addition, a "true hematolagniac" is a fantasy-driven psychopath and to be considered very dangerous. According to Noll (1992) such desires are founded in severe childhood abuse. The child may engage in auto-vampirism in tasting his own blood and during puberty. These acts are eventually sexualized and reinforced through masturbation. A progressive paraphilic stage during adolescence is the sexual arousal of eating animals and drinking their blood (zoophagia) while masturbating. The compulsive, fantasy-driven, sexual nature of this paraphilia creates a very dangerous adult. Consider the following two cases of German vampires (see Profile 11.4A and 11.4B).

Today we understand much more about serial killers and that there are differences between cultures and nationalities. Andreas Ulrich (2000) in his article *"Morderisches Mirakel" ("Murderous Miracle")* explains the behavioral attributes of German serial killers. Ulrich notes that in the case of Ulrich Schmidt, a German serial killer convicted of four murders and a suspect in others, Schmidt did not appear to have the same motive for each murder. German police also found that nearly 10% of all homicides resulting from robberies and sexual offenses are committed by serial killers. They examined all cases of serial murder between 1945 and 1995 in Germany that included three or more victims and found 54 male serial killers and 7 female serial killers. According to this study, sexual motives as

PROFILE 11.4A Fritz Haarmann, The Butcher of Hannover, 1919–1924

Haarmann endured a very dysfunctional childhood and loathed his father. Although as a homosexual he lived with another man, Haarmann's real sexual passion was for young males whom he found at railway stations. His psychopathic ability to manipulate others made the boys easy targets as he lured them to his apartment, where he tortured, sodomized, and killed them by biting through their throats. He was known to have engaged in necrophilia, cannibalism, vampirism, and ephebophilia. After killing and dismembering 24–27 victims Haarmann was apprehended, convicted, and sent to the guillotine in 1924 (Prins, 1985).

PROFILE 11.4B Peter Kurten, the Vampire of Dusseldorf, 1883–1931

Kurten was raised in a very physically and sexually abusive home where he witnessed his alcoholic father raping his mother and sisters. He also engaged in sexually abusing his sisters and eventually ran away from home. At age 9 he claimed to have drowned two other boys while swimming and became a thief and fire-setter. At age 11 he was taught by the local dogcatcher how to torture dogs and sheep while masturbating. He developed multiple paraphilia including vampirism, hematolagnia, necrophilia, erotophonophilia, and zoophagia and was known to drink directly from the severed jugular of his victims. He raped, tortured, and killed at least nine known victims, although he was believed to have murdered several others. He used hammers, knives, and scissors to kill both young girls and women and admitted that he was sexually aroused by the blood and violence. Some victims incurred many more stab wounds than others, and when asked about this variation he explained that with some victims his orgasm was achieved more quickly. Kurten was extremely adept at manipulating people, including his wife, who was unaware of his double life. Eventually he was apprehended and sent to the guillotine. Before his beheading he asked if he would be able to hear the blood gushing from his neck stump because "that would be the pleasure to end all pleasures" (Prin, 1985).

profiled by the FBI were not substantiated in the German cases. Homicides resulting from robberies were equally as frequent as those with sexual motivation. In the case of Gerhard Schroeder from Bremen, who murdered three prostitutes during the late 1980s, investigators sought a sexually motivated offender only to discover after his capture that the killer selected the victims primarily because he believed that they would have substantial money in their possession. This incorrect profile had police searching in the wrong areas, which afforded Schroeder more time to kill (Ulrich, 2000).

Investigators at the Bundeskriminalamt (BKA) are now utilizing the "ViCLAS" system (Violent Crime Linkage Analysis System) developed in Canada. Investigators use a questionnaire comprised of 168 checklist items focusing on evidence and offender characteristics. The investigators now look for killers based on patterns that often do not fit typical criminal profiles, especially in cases once thought to be sexually motivated. In Harbort's (2000) study of German serial killers, he found that the typical killer possessed minimal to average intelligence, was emotionally void, and had a history of criminal behavior. Similar to those in the United States, German serial killers report abusive childhoods marked by rejection, alcoholism, and violence. Many of the offenders were found with various brain abnormalities. The study also notes that German serial killers do not rearrange the crime scene, rarely leave behind signatures, and seldom take gruesome trophies. In support of Hickey's 1997 findings of American serial killers, German offenders do not travel widely to find victims. Most of the offenders found their victims within 30 kilometers of their residence. Sometimes the killers would rob the victims, as in the case of the "Choker of Ricklingen" (Wuerger von Ricklingen). Another offender suffocated five victims between 1986 and 1993, all in his own neighborhood in Hannover, Germany. In addition, they also found that the higher the intelligence level of the offender, the faster the arrest of the killer. High-IQ German serial killers averaged four and a half years until arrest following their first murder, whereas less intelligent offenders took twice as long to be apprehended. Harbort notes that the less intelligent offenders were harder to catch because they did not fit criminal profiles utilized by investigators. Joachim Georg Kroll, known as the "Laundry Room Killer" from Duisburg, with a 76 IQ, could barely add or subtract or carry on a conversation but was able to kill eight people over 20 years and is believed to have killed many more (Ulrich, 2000).

ASSESSING GLOBAL DATA ON SERIAL MURDER

The chronological lists in Tables 11.1 and 11.2 of non-U.S. serial killers are only partial listings of such offenders in other countries. They essentially comprise some of the more sensational and publicized cases. We are hampered by differential reporting patterns, definitional problems, and impediments to accessing pertinent data. Some general comparisons can be made between serial killers in the United States and in 22 other countries that I researched.

TABLE 11.1 A Sampling of Non-U.S. Male Serial Killers

Year(s)	Name	Number of Victims	Country
1430	Gilles de Rais	800+	France
1600	Sawney Beane	1,500+	Scotland
1785–1808	Andreas Bichel	50+	Bavaria
1790–1840	Thuggee Buhram	931	India
1820	William Burke	32	Scotland
1840	Billy Palmer	14	England
1861–1864	Joseph Phillipe	8–18	France
1865	Pierre Voirbo	11	France
1869	Jean Baptise Troppmann	8	France
1871–1872	Vincent Verzeni	12	Italy
1890	Alfred Deeming	20	Australia, England
1894–1897	Joseph Vacher	10–20	France
1898–1901	Ludwig Tessnow	30+	Germany
1901–1903	George Chapman	3+	England
1908–1936	Adolf Seefeld	12	Germany
1911–1915	George J. Smith	3	England
1913–1920	George Karl Grossman	50+	Germany
1913–1930	Peter Kurten	15+	Germany
1915–1922	Henri Desire Landru	11+	France
1918–1922	Fritz Haarmann	30–40	England

(continued)

TABLE 11.1 Continued

Year(s)	Name	Number of Victims	Country
1920–1923	Albert Edward Burrows	4	England
1924	Carl Denke	30+	Poland
1941–1946	Dr. Marcel Petiot	63	France
1942	Gordon F. Cummins	3	England
1942	Edward Joseph Leonski	?	Australia
1943	Bruno Ludke	85	Germany
1943–1953	John R. H. Christie	6+	England
1944–1949	John George Haigh	9	England
1945–1963	Teofilo Rojas	592+	Colombia
1946	Neville Heath	5+	England
1953–1963	Efrain Gonzales	117	Colombia
1958	Peter Manuel	9	Canada
1959	Wendell Lightborne	3+	England
1959–1976	Joachim Kroll	14+	W. Germany
1960–1961	Michael Copeland	3	Germany, England
1960–1964	Klaus Gossman	7	Germany
1961–1963	William MacDonald	?	Australia
1962	Lucian Staniak	20	Poland
1962–1966	Jurgen Bartsch	4	W. Germany
1962–1971	Graham Young	?	England
1963–1964	Ian Brady	3+	England
1964	Hans Van Zon	5	Holland
1965–1967	Raymond L. Morris	1+	England
1966–1976	Charles Sobhraj	10	England
1969–1984	Daniel Camargo Barbosa	71	Brazil
1971	Sjef Rijke	2+	Holland
1971	Fran Hooijaijers	5–250	Europe
1971–1983	Peter Sutcliffe	13	England
1973	Bruce Lee	26	England
1973–1975	Patrick David Mackay	5–7	England
1973–1981	Clifford Olson	11+	Canada
1974–1981	James Odo	3+	Canada
1976–1998	Dr. Harold Shipman	200–300	England
1977	Pedro Lopez	300+	Ecuador
1977	Al Marjek	3	Syria
1977–1980	Arn Finn Nesset	22–25	Norway
1977–1983	Dennis Nilsen	15–17	England

TABLE 11.1 Continued

Year(s)	Name	Number of Victims	Country
1978–1990	Andrei Chikatilo	53	Russia
1980–1981	Robert E. Brown	9	Canada
1982	Barry Peter Prudom	?	England
1983–2000	Robert Pickton	62	Canada
1984–1985	Pawel Alojzy Tuchlin	9+	Poland
1984–1986	Thierry Paulin	14	France
1985	Angel Piaz Balbin	8	Peru
1986	Sohrab Aslam Khan	13	Pakistan
1987	"Locksmith"	33	Russia
1990–1991	Scott Cox	20+	Canada
1991	Marcelo Costa de Andre	14	Brazil
1992–1999	Luis Alfredo Garavito	140+	Colombia
1992–2006	Alexander Pichushkin	49–63	Russia
1993–1995	Andonis Daglis	3	Greece
1993–1995	John Brown	5	South Africa
1993–1995	Samuel Coetzee	5	South Africa
1995–1996	Marc Dutroux	4	Belgium
1996	Andre Cassimiro	5	Brazil
1996	Giovanni Faggi	6	Italy
1996	Leszek Pekalski	12+	Poland
1997	Roman Burtsev	6+	Russia
1997	Gerd Wenzinger	12+	Brazil
2003–2004	You Young-chul	19–25	South Korea
2010	Russell Williams	2	Canada

SOURCE: © Cengage Learning, 2013.

1. Many countries appear to have a similar problem of certain cases being defined as "superkillers." This means that some offenders have claimed or have been accused of hundreds of murders. The problem with these numbers is that they are usually not verifiable. Many of the "superkillers" lived in earlier centuries when documentation was practically nonexistent. In all likelihood, the large numbers are a product of sensationalism and exaggeration. For example, in the United States during the 1800s, Charles Gibb, John Murrell, H. H. Holmes, and Jane Toppan allegedly murdered collectively more than 900 people. In other countries, dating back as early as the 1400s and as late as the 1970s, 11 offenders, including Thuggee Buhram of India; Susi Olah of Hungary; Gilles de Rais of France; Teofilo Rojas of Colombia; Pedro Lopez of Ecuador; Countess Elizabeth Bathory of Hungary; and

TABLE 11.2 A Sampling of Non-U.S. Female Serial Killers

Year(s)	Name	Number of Victims	Country
1610–1614	Countess Elizabeth Bathory	600	Hungary
c. 1660s	Catherine la Voisin	1500+	France
c. 1660s	Madame de Montespan	1400+	France
1676	Marie de Brinvilliers	100+	France
1809	Anna Marie Zwanziger	3+	Bavaria
1811	Anna Marie Schonleben	3+	Germany
1828	Gesina Gottfried	20+	Germany
1830–1850	Helena Jegado	60+	England
1852–1871	Mary Ann Cotton	14–21	England
1890	Greta Beier	4	Germany
1908	Jeanne Weber	9+	France
1909–1929	Susi Olah	100+	Hungary
1924–1926	Antoinette Scieri	6	France
1927–1947	Lily Young	100+	Canada
1936	Dorthea Waddingham	?	England
1953–1963	Maria de Jesus Gonzales	91+	Mexico
1953–1963	Delfina de Jesus Gonzales	91+	Mexico
1963–1964	Myra Hindley	3	England
1968	Mary Flora Bell	2	England
1971–1987	Rosemary West	12+	England
1977	Cecile Bombeek	3–30	Belgium
1977–1983	Dahlia Allam	4	Austria
1981	Phoolan Devi	20	India
1983	Maria Velten	5	W. Germany
1983–1989	Maria Gruber	49–300	Austria
	Irene Leidolf		
	Stephanija Mayer		
1990–1992	Karla Homolka	3–6+	Canada
1991	Anna Villeda	8	Mexico
1991–1997	Kathleen Atkinson	4+	England
1992	Beverly Allit	4	England
1992–1995	Elfriede "Sugar" Blauensteiner	5	Austria

SOURCE: © Cengage Learning, 2013.

Abbe Guibourg, Madame de Montespan, Catherine la Voisin, and Marie de Brinvilliers of France supposedly murdered over 6,400 victims!

2. Well-publicized cases in which females are the offenders appear to be much more common in foreign countries. Similar to female offenders in the United States, there does not appear to be a "Jack the Ripper" type of female offender in other countries. In cases where physical violence was used, women usually had at least one accomplice. Also, most female offenders who lived during earlier times resorted to poisons, as their female counterparts in the United States did.
3. Team killers, or those who killed with accomplices, appear to be much more common in the United States than in other countries. However, in-depth examination of cases in other countries may yet reveal many more team-killer cases. For the present, those designated as team killers in other countries appear to kill twice as many victims each as their U.S. counterparts.
4. Team killers and solo killers, regardless of whether they were American or foreign, murdered approximately the same percentages of all victims.
5. U.S. killers appear to be much more mobile and travel more than foreign offenders do; those in other countries are much more likely to be classified as "local" killers. This may in part be due to proximity to population centers, language barriers, cultural diversities, or availability of transportation.
6. In the majority of cases, both U.S. and foreign offenders were strangers to their victims. Foreign killers also appear to target acquaintances as victims.
7. Torture, strangling, and stabbing/chopping as modes of death seem to be used in similar percentages of cases. Americans sometimes use guns to kill or torture their victims; however, foreign offenders appear to rarely use firearms.

Empirical study of serial killers worldwide has been limited. Although many countries have recorded cases of serial killing, the majority of cases appear to come from industrialized nations. Philip Jenkins (1988) conducted his study of serial killers in England between 1940 and 1985. He also conducted a historical-comparative study of serial murder in relation to social issues occurring in England, Germany, and the United States between 1900 and 1940.

Canter, Missen, and Hodge (1997) identified 164 serial killers in the United Kingdom since 1860. They were able to conclude that Britain probably has about five active serial killers at any given time and that they account for more victims proportionately than American serial killers. I corresponded with serial-murder investigators from South Africa. Dr. Gérard Labuschagne, Brigadier of the Investigative Psychology Unit in Pretoria, whose sole job is to track serial killers in South Africa, indicated that most cases of serial murder in his country are relatively new and some do not conform to traditional profiling techniques used in the United States. In the past several years, white farmers have become the targets of blacks who wish to take over lands controlled by whites; there are also other cases in which the motivation is greed fueled by culture, not sex.

PROFILE 11.5 Clifford Robert Olson, 1980–1981

One of Canada's most prolific and horrendous serial killers of the 20th century, Clifford Olson killed 11 children and teenagers in British Columbia between 1980 and 1981. He lured victims he considered to be troubled youth into his comfort zone, and after raping and sodomizing many of them, he bludgeoned each with a hammer. During an interview with me, Olson explained that he killed the teens because he did not want them to suffer as he had suffered as a child. He contended that he only killed children who came from homes where they were not loved. According to Olson, these "mercy killings" would not have occurred had these children been raised in loving families. Not surprisingly, Olson was raised in an abusive and dysfunctional family.

When asked how he compared himself to other serial killers such as Ted Bundy, he retorted that Bundy was a pervert. When I reminded Olson that he had also sexually assaulted his victims, he emphatically pointed out that he had never been *convicted* of a sex crime, only murders. He sent me documentation that explained the charges against him but did not contain sex charges. His denial of the obvious was only exceeded by his pervasive lack of self-esteem and systemic rage against society.

An opportunistic sociopath, Olson was an impulsive, manipulative personality of limited intelligence. He selected victims who reminded him of his own pain. He sexually degraded them just as he was victimized, and he destroyed them in a rage. Each victim stood proxy for those who tormented him. Olson was housed in a maximum-security facility in Saskatchewan, Canada, for most of his incarceration and enjoyed the media attention, groupies, and anyone else willing to listen. In late 2011, Clifford Olson, 71, died of cancer.

CANADIAN SERIAL KILLERS

Canada also has had several serial killers. Three of the most notable cases include Clifford Olson, who murdered 11 children, Robert "Willy" Pickton, alleged killer of as many as 50–60 prostitutes (see Profiles 11.5 and 11.6), and Col. Russell Williams (see Profile 11.7). Pickton, after the murders, is believed to have fed his victims to his pigs. Olson, who reveled in his notoriety as Canada's most prolific serial killer, appears to have been replaced by Pickton. Williams was picked as the top newsmaker in Canada for 2010 as the utter depravity of his paraphilic crimes was exposed.

RUSSIAN SERIAL KILLERS

As Gorby (2000) notes, serial murder has been hidden from the public in some countries. Iran executed a man, now referred to as the Tehran Vampire, for raping and murdering nine women. For many years the Soviet Union would not allow information about serial killers to become public knowledge either. With

PROFILE 11.6 Robert "Willy" Pickton, Operator of the Piggy Palace Good Times Society, 1983–2002

On February 5, 2002, Robert "Willy" Pickton, a pig farmer in the community of Port Coquitlam, 22 miles outside Vancouver, British Columbia, Canada, was arrested and formally charged with 11 counts of first-degree murder. Several months later an additional four charges were added, bringing the total to 15. What the ensuing investigation unraveled closely resembled scenes from the serial-murder movie *Hannibal.* Pickton allegedly murdered his victims, dismembered them, and fed them to his pigs, which he frequently bought and sold at local auctions.

Known as somewhat of a loner, Pickton preyed on his victims in Vancouver's Downtown Eastside, an area known nationally as one of the seediest strips in the country. Frequented by heroin users, dealers, and prostitutes, it became an ideal trolling ground for Pickton. Over the course of nearly two decades, beginning in the early 1980s, there had been a total of 61 women reported missing. Rebecca Guno, who was last seen on June 22, 1983, would become the first of many missing women. This case paralleled the Green River Murders in the Seattle, Washington, area, where nearly 50 prostitutes had vanished.

Pickton and his farm were apparently well known to those who frequented the streets. Robert and his brother David Francis frequently hosted parties at their registered Canadian social society called the "Piggy Palace Good Times Society." According to neighbors, the parties went well into the evening and were often attended by prostitutes solicited from downtown Vancouver. However, many of the women avoided the farm, not only because of the distance involved in getting back to the city but also because in 1997 "Willy" was charged with attempted murder when one of his would-be victims escaped after receiving several stab wounds. Although the reason is unclear, Pickton was never convicted of this charge.

Over the course of several years and more disappearances, a pattern began to emerge. However, it wasn't until 1998, when a concerned social activist group demanded a formal investigation, that it was suggested that Vancouver might have a serial murderer on its hands. Whether this laxness on the part of the police is a reflection of an attitude viewing those who work the streets as being expendable, or indicative of the complexity of solving murder cases when there is little or no relationship to the victim, is purely speculative. What is clear is that there was a substantial amount of time where "Willy" hunted without detection.

Due to a media ban by the court, little is known about Robert Pickton or his farm activities. Over 50 anthropologists and many police officers painstakingly searched the farm for remains of more victims. Unfortunately, efforts to connect Pickton were complicated by the nature of the crimes. According to experts, pigs will devour human remains in an attempt to get to the bone marrow. This insatiable appetite of pigs coupled with the nature of pig farming (i.e., constant feeding, trading, and slaughtering) slowed the investigation. Given the circumstances in which Pickton allegedly carried out his crimes, we may never know how many actual victims he killed. Remains of 31 victims were identified. Robert Pickton is now recognized as the most prolific serial killer in Canadian history.

PROFILE 11.7 Colonel Russell Williams, 2007–2010

Canada has few serial killers, but those they do have are important to understand. Indeed, in some ways Col. Russell Williams defies most stereotypes of sexual predators and serial killers. He was the epitome of a military man. He commanded the largest air base in Canada at CFB Trenton, Ontario. He was married to a very professional woman, Mary Elizabeth Harriman. They had no children but owned a cat named Rosie. The couple had purchased a home together in Ottawa and owned a cottage in Tweed, Ontario. This highly distinguished and decorated Canadian Air Force colonel was a rising military star on track to be promoted to general. His security clearance allowed him to fly the prime minister of Canada, the queen of England, and other VIPs in military jets. He had been assigned to high security clearance locations around the world. Well respected and accomplished, Williams appeared to have everything: power, control, affluence, and influence. Yet, he became one of the most prolific sexual predators and murderers in Canadian history.

While Williams built his public life he also created a double life of sex crimes and murder. Williams began as a voyeur at night, sometimes stripping naked and masturbating outside his victim's homes while watching through their windows. He was neighbors with some of his victims. In fall of 2007 Williams began a series of break-ins (five), acting out his fetish for panties and lingerie. He stole and wore underwear of young girls. Some homes he picked locks, pushed in windows, or simply walked in through unlocked doors or windows. He targeted girls as young as nine and well as young adult women. The break-ins escalated in 2008 (36) and even more in 2009 (40), during which time he engaged in taking pictures of himself wearing the bras and panties of his victims. Some of the homes he broke into more than once. One home was hit nine times. Williams was very good at remaining invisible, as 61 of the 82 break-ins went undetected or unreported.

He liked going into bedrooms of women and girls, dressing in their panties and bras and masturbating while lying on their beds. He took thousands of pictures of his panty and bra souvenirs and stored them on his computer hard drive. He kept a massive collection of stolen underwear and admitted to burning some of them because he had no more room to store them all. He was believed to have worn some of these panties under his military uniform. He photographed himself in sexual acts with personal items belonging to his female victims that he did not steal, knowing they would use them again. Sometimes he spent hours in victims' homes going through personal items, masturbating, and photographing himself in their underwear.

Williams escalated from voyeur to fetish panty thief to "hot burglaries," or entering homes when the victim was present. He later admitted that he experienced excitement as he escalated his crimes. In one case he stripped naked and entered the bedroom of a woman who was showering. He stole her panties. Eventually Williams began sexually assaulting young women. He bound, beat, and took pictures of them, sometimes while they were blindfolded. He did all this while logging his crimes on his computer, tracking police reports, and even leaving taunting messages for some of his victims. He then videotaped himself beating, raping, and strangling Marie France Comeau, a flight attendant at his air force base. He made sex tapes of Jessica Elizabeth Lloyd after kidnapping her and taking her to his Tweed cottage where he raped and tortured her for nearly a day before killing her and dumping her body in a field.

Williams, in all likelihood, would have killed many more women had it not been for the keen observation of an officer at a security checkpoint that Williams had to pass through to get to work. An unusual tire track had been collected by crime scene investigators at one of the abduction sites. Williams always drove his BMW to work but on that day he drove his Pathfinder with the unusual tire tread. He was brought in for questioning and immediately confessed to everything. Canada does not have the death penalty, thus Williams received two life sentences. He was, of course, stripped of his military rank and immediately dishonorably discharged.

For the reader, this case is just beginning. We are learning about a man who began his paraphilic activities as a voyeur and stalker who progressed to a lingerie fetish and cross-dressing to committing hot burglaries to serial brutal rapes and ultimately to sadistic serial murder. Several important questions for you to consider are:

- Is Williams a psychopath? From research we know that psychopaths are all about control and power. Why, then, would he immediately confess and give up the control that he has held for so long? What do you think? Is it possible that he is not a true psychopath but only exhibits some psychopathic characteristics?
- The seeds of serial murder are believed to be sown in childhood. Search the Web and investigate what may have led Williams to progress to serial murder. What did you learn about his family?
- Serial killers generally start their murders during their 20s and 30s. What kept him from killing until he was 45?
- Paraphilia are usually developed at a younger age, especially courtship paraphilia. According to police reports, Williams began his stalking and voyeurism in 2007, when he was in his early 40s. Is it possible that Williams started his voyeurism at a much earlier age?
- Some serial killers in this book were married or in a "committed" relationship during the time of their killings. Once caught for the murders most of them made efforts to shield their significant others from prosecution and/or media exposure. Does this sound like the behavior of a true psychopath?
- If you research Williams in detail you will see that he was extremely calculating in his crimes. He also, through his writings and photographs of his crimes, exposes a very dark side of his thinking and personality. What did you find? Does it help us to understand his motivations, his paraphilia, or his personality?
- Why did Williams choose these two women to kill? Did they have something in common? Was it simply opportunity, or did he have some previous fantasies about them that led him to murder?
- What ways can we protect ourselves and families from such predators?

the dissolution of the Soviet empire and greater globalization, Russia has been much more forthcoming regarding their new cases of serial murder. Tragically, many victims have died because the public was not aware that predators were in their midst. The horrific case of Andrei Chikatilo is an excellent example of what can happen when the press and law enforcement officials are silent (see Profile 11.8). Chikatilo represents one of Europe's most prolific serial killers. He was a man consumed with the destruction of children and adolescents. He could have and should have been stopped very early on in his killing career, but like so many other serial murderers, he was able to evade law enforcement. If cultural filters play any role in serial murder, distinguishing the murders, the offender, or victims in certain characteristic ways, they do not seem to differentiate this Russian serial killer in any significant respect from those roaming the streets of the United States. Andrei Chikatilo was a man of low self-esteem and much anger and hatred who acted out his paraphilic fantasies on vulnerable youth. We would be naive to think this killer is an anomaly in the Russian social landscape any more than Alexander Pichushkin, the "Chessboard Killer of Moscow" (see Profile 11.9).

THE GORBY STUDY*

Much closer empirical examination of serial-homicide data in other countries was recently conducted by Gorby (2000). He compiled an impressive data set of 300 serial killers representing 241 cases of serial murder identified in 43 different countries, excluding the United States, between the years 1800 and 1995. About half of the cases were found in four nations: United Kingdom (20%), Germany (15%), South Africa (8%), and Australia (7%). European countries represented 57% of the cases, Asian countries 14%. North American (excluding the United States), African, and Oceanian countries each accounted for 8%, whereas only 6% were found in South America, Central America, and the Middle East combined. About 9% of cases were transnational where the offender killed in more than one country (Gorby, p. 54). Gorby explores the emergence of serial murder by comparing European and non-European countries. Table 11.3 indicates that since 1900, the percentage of European cases has decreased steadily while just the opposite is occurring in non-European countries.

He noted that the length of serial-murder cases ranged from less than 1 year to 37 years. About a third of all cases were 1 year or less, about 33% more than 5 years, and nearly one in five cases lasted over 10 years. Gorby also found that females comprised about 25% of his serial killers, whereas in the United

*The author wishes to express appreciation to Brad Gorby for his permission in using some of his findings from his 2000 study of foreign serial killers.

PROFILE 11.8 Andrei Chikatilo, 1978–1990

Also known as the "Russian Ripper" who brutally killed 14 young girls, 21 boys, and 18 women, Chikatilo continued his stalking, murdering, and cannibalizing for 12 years. Born in the Ukraine in 1936, Chikatilo was known as an intelligent man of modesty who enjoyed playing chess. His education from Rostov University included degrees in Russian language and literature, engineering, and Marxist-Leninism. During his career of killing, Chikatilo was married with two children, a boy and a girl, about the same ages as many of his victims. He was considered a steady wage earner and one who never was forceful or beat his children. By the time he was arrested for the "Forest Strip Murders" in the town of Novocherkassk, Chikatilo was a gray-haired grandfather living a reclusive lifestyle. Yet he was far from being a recluse.

Life had been hard for Chikatilo. His older brother Stepan had been abducted and cannibalized during the Ukrainian famine of the 1930s. He grew up fearful, insecure, and envious of a more successful career. Everything he did, including his military experience, he perceived as inconsequential. He harbored a hero fantasy to compensate for his sense of failure. A successful career had been thwarted in part by his father, who, after the war, had been sent to a prison camp for allowing himself to be taken prisoner by the Germans. Chikatilo had a disturbing employment record. He first worked as a dorm monitor at a local mining school. His history of peeping through keyholes and wandering into girls' bathrooms eventually expedited his termination.

His forced relocation to Shakhty in the south of Russia meant a reduction in job status and quality of life for his family. A man of low self-esteem and a pronounced sense of inferiority around groups of people, Chikatilo became a master at manipulating and molesting children of all ages. His increased attraction to children gradually stifled any desire he might have had for his wife. As a manifestation of his own self-hate, he admitted his "sexual weakness" to the police. He explained to them that his interest in children was something of his distant past. Now that he was married with children, Chikatilo reasoned, he had overcome such urges. To the police, the explanation seemed plausible enough. Unfortunately for dozens of children, Chikatilo's pedophilia would not be examined closely enough to see through his deception.

By this time he had murdered two children. His first victim in 1978 was nine-year-old Lena Zakotnova. He had lured her to a dilapidated shack he used for his private retreat. Lena was bound, choked, and stabbed three times in the abdomen and sustained vaginal injuries before she was tossed in a nearby river to die. He had tied a scarf around her eyes so she could not see him. Considering the amount of evidence Chikatilo left behind, his capture should have been inevitable. A bungled investigation and a desire by investigators to close the case led to the confession and conviction of another man.

His progressively violent fantasies fueled his next murder of 17-year-old Larisa Tkachenko. After strangling her into unconsciousness, he stuffed her mouth with dirt. She too sustained vaginal injuries. Chikatilo then, with his teeth, tore off her nipples and swallowed them.

Chikatilo was promoted to senior engineer in 1981. This promotion would require that he travel within the region. He relished the opportunity to meet young people traveling alone. Chikatilo hunted his victims in and around train and bus stations on his way to and from work. He kindly offered them candy, money, and comfort as an enticement to take a little walk with him over to the forest strips where they could be alone. He became adept at targeting naive, trusting victims who perceived him as a nice man.

(continued)

PROFILE 11.8 (Continued)

Chikatilo's escalation in brutality was incredible. Because of his sense of inferiority, he would not allow his victims to look at him during the attacks. The victim's stare, even in death, disturbed the killer's paraphilic fantasies. He soon resolved the problem. His third victim was a 12-year-old girl whom he had picked up at a bus stop and then escorted into some nearby bushes. He stabbed her 41 times, several of them into her eyes. Victims would look no more upon him during his rage. By July he had killed three more victims—two girls, ages 14 and 16, and a 9-year-old boy. After subduing the little boy, he had the child stick out his tongue. Chikatilo then, with his own teeth, ripped it off.

Sexually inadequate, Chikatilo could never use his own genitals to actually penetrate his victims. Methodically, after ejaculating externally onto his victims, he used a twig to place his sperm into their vagina or anus. His desire for viscera was increasing. In December 1982 he murdered 10-year-old Olya Stalmach by stabbing her in the eyes, torso, and vagina over 50 times. He then eviscerated her. His appetite for removing internal body parts earned him the name of "Ripper." For the next eight years Chikatilo killed in earnest. He hunted runaways, intellectually slower children, and young women who thought him to be just another man looking for a sexual encounter. He seldom varied from his established methods. He stabbed his victims between 30 and 50 times. One boy he stabbed over 70 times. He nearly always mutilated their eyes. Older girls had their breasts or nipples severed or chewed off and their uteruses removed. He found distinct pleasure in eating the uterus as he walked home after a kill. With boys, he would cut off their penises and/or remove their testicles. Victims were often still alive during the taking of his trophies. His monstrous acts never abated. He began removing the upper lip and nose of his victims and then placing them into the victim's stomach or mouth.

In 1984 he was faced with a criminal complaint for theft, was dismissed from his job, and lost his membership in the Communist Party. His anger and fantasies continued to escalate his attacks. One of Chikatilo's later victims, 11-year-old Yaroslav Makarov, was killed shortly before his capture in 1990. Chikatilo tore out his intestines and heart with his bare hands.

Initially, the murders were investigated by local police. With the frequency of new victims, the Russian attorney general's office took control of the investigation. The case had been bungled from the start and was rife with incompetence. Police had decided that they were looking for a dishonorably discharged police officer. Chikatilo was no police officer, but he did harbor a sincere interest in police work. By 1984 police had arrested, detained, and interrogated dozens of men who were known pedophiles, several mentally disordered youth, and hundreds of homosexuals. In 1985, Inspector Kostov joined the manhunt. Other law enforcement agencies, including the FBI, consulted with Kostov. The persistence of Kostov ultimately led to Chikatilo's capture and his confession to all the murders (Cullen, 1993; Lourie, 1993). In 1994 Andrei Chikatilo was executed with a bullet in the back of his. International interest in this case led to the making of the video *Citizen X* and the writing of at least three books.

States, Hickey (2006a) found only 15% of his offenders to be females. Gorby noted that offenders ranged in age between 13 and 60 at the onset of their killings, the average age being 30. By the time offenders finished their killing careers (last murder) the age range was 16–70 and the average age was 35 (see Table 11.4).

PROFILE 11.9 Alexander Pichushkin, the Chessboard Killer, 1992–2006

At age 33 Pichushkin was living with his mother in a southern Moscow apartment while working as a supermarket employee. He kept a chessboard on a table with names on most of the 64 squares. His plan was to fill all 64 squares with victims' names and surpass Andrei Chikatilo as Russia's most prolific serial killer (see Profile 11.8). Although when apprehended he claimed 62 murders, investigators had only enough evidence to convict him of 49 deaths. Pichushkin was a man with deep-seated anger and never forgot those who crossed him. In 1992 when he was 18 he killed the boyfriend of a girl he liked. His body was found years later in the park where he would later hunt for most of his victims. In 2006 he killed his landlord because he insulted Pichushkin about his dog. He found most of his elderly male victims between 2001 and 2005 (3 of the 49 were female, and one escaped) while trolling Bitsevsky Park in Moscow. As a child the park was his favorite place to wander and watch people. He would lure his victims with promises of vodka or beer, and once they were inebriated he hit them with a hammer or other blunt objects and tossed them into a sewage pit. At least 40 men died in this manner. He liked to ram sticks and broken Vodka bottles into the crushed skulls of some of his victims. He claimed the murders gave him orgasms. He told police, "I felt like the father of all these people, since it was I who opened the door for them to another world.... For me, a life without murder is like a life without food for you." He went on to say, "I never would have stopped, never. They save a lot of lives by catching me."

As with many other serial killers, psychologists examined his childhood in hopes of explaining Pichushkin's desire to kill. His mother thought trauma might have been caused to her son when he was four and hit on his head by a swing. As is the case with many of those who become prolific serial killers, his father had abandoned the family when he was young. His grandfather, with whom he had lived and was close, had died, creating more loss in his life (Attewill, 2007). From the many profiles in this book common themes of abandonment and rejection emerge as salient factors in serial murder. What do you think?

Similar to Hickey (2006a), Gorby (2000) found that about 33% of offenders had at least one accomplice compared to 26% found in the United States. Nearly 80% of the team killer cases consisted of only two offenders. One team had eight offenders. However, although a third of the cases were team killers, they only accounted for 13% of the total murders. About half the teams were comprised of both male and female offenders, whereas 38% were all-male teams and 10% were all-female teams. He also found that one-third of the teams were made up of family members.

Gorby (2000) also noted that offenders in his study killed an average of 12 victims per case, similar to the Hickey (2006a) study. Nearly 80% killed non-family members and 5% killed only family members. Females were also far more likely to murder an adult male, a child or an elderly person than their male counterparts (see Table 11.5). Gorby also examined the issue of mobility among his serial killers and found that 85% killed in a local area with only 15% traveling to other cities, states, or countries. As in the United

TABLE 11.3 Year of First Murder by Geography of Serial-Murder Case

Year	European	Non-European	Total
1800–1824	5 (100%)	0 (00.0%)	5 (2.1%)
1825–1849	5 (100)	0 (00.0)	5 (2.1)
1850–1874	7 (100)	0 (00.0)	7 (2.9)
1875–1899	10 (71.4)	4 (28.6)	14 (5.8)
1900–1924	22 (75.9)	7 (24.1)	29 (12.0)
1925–1949	19 (63.3)	11 (36.7)	30 (12.4)
1950–1974	27 (54.0)	23 (46.0)	50 (20.7)
1975–1995	42 (41.6)	59 (58.4)	101 (41.9)
Total	137 (56.8)	104 (43.2)	241 (100)

SOURCE: © Cengage Learning, 2013.

TABLE 11.4 Age of Offender at Time of First Murder by Gender of Offender

Age	Males	Females	Total
13–20	33 (18.9%)	11 (26.1%)	44 (21.7%)
21–25	35 (20.0)	6 (14.2)	41 (20.2)
26–30	33 (18.9.)	5 (11.9)	38 (18.7)
31–35	20 (11.4)	6 (14.2)	26 (12.8)
36–40	16 (9.1)	3 (7.1)	19 (9.4)
41–50	33 (18.9)	4 (9.5)	37 (18.2)
51+	5 (2.9)	7 (16.6)	12 (5.9)
Total	175 (100)	42 (100)	217 (100)

SOURCE: © Cengage Learning, 2013.

States, women were far more likely to kill at home or at work than male offenders. Rarely did they travel to other cities or countries to continue their killings (see Table 11.6).

Finally, Gorby (2000) examined methods of killing (see Table 11.7). Males overall preferred to strangle or asphyxiate their victims, as did 35% in the Hickey (2006a) study. As the only method of killing, the Gorby study found that 20% of males chose this method compared to just 12% in the Hickey study. American serial killers, not surprisingly, were twice as likely to use firearms (38%) sometimes to murder as compared to 21% in the Gorby study. Most females in the Gorby study used poisons or withheld medical assistance. A few others strangled their victims, but in only one case was a gun used or a victim bludgeoned to death.

TABLE 11.5 Age/Gender of Victim and by Gender of Primary Offender

Victims	Male Cases	Female Cases	Total
At least one female adult	132 (67.7%)	20 (43.5%)	152 (63.1%)
At least one male adult	85 (43.6)	29 (63.0)	114 (47.3)
At least one female child	61 (31.3)	20 (43.5)	81 (33.6)
At least one male child	49 (25.1)	21 (45.7)	70 (29.0)
Only female adults	44 (22.6)	0 (0.0)	44 (18.3)
At least one female elderly	26 (13.3)	17 (37.0)	43 (17.8)
At least one male elderly	16 (8.2)	16 (34.8)	32 (13.3)
Only male adults	19 (9.7)	3 (6.5)	22 (9.1)
Only female children	9 (4.6)	1 (2.2)	10 (4.1)
Only male children	10 (5.1)	0 (0.0)	10 (4.1)
Only female elderly	6 (3.1)	0 (0.0)	6 (2.5)
Only male elderly	0 (0.0)	1 (2.2)	1 (0.4)
Some victims unknown	19 (9.7)	12 (26.1)	31 (12.9)

N = 241

SOURCE: © Cengage Learning, 2013.

TABLE 11.6 Case Mobility by Gender of Offender

Mobility	Male Offenders	Female Offenders	Total
Place-Specific	7 (3.6%)	14 (30.4%)	21 (8.7%)
Local	154 (79.0)	29 (63.0)	183 (75.9)
Traveling	14 (7.2)	1 (2.2)	15 (6.2)
Transnational	20 (10.3)	2 (4.3)	22 (9.1)
Total	195 (100)	46 (100)	241 (100)

SOURCE: © Cengage Learning, 2013.

TABLE 11.7 Methods of Murder by Gender of Offender

Method	Male Cases	Female Cases	Total Cases
Some strangled/asphyxiated	96 (49.2%)	8 (17.4%)	104 (43.2%)
Only strangled/asphyxiated	38 (19.5)	4 (8.7)	42 (17.4)
Some stabbed/cut	72 (36.9)	0 (0.0)	72 (29.8)
Only stabbed/cut	24 (12.3)	0 (0.0)	24 (10.0)
Some poison/withheld medical treatment T_x	25 (12.8)	34 (73.9)	59 (24.4)
Only poison/withheld medical treatment T_x	17 (8.7)	28 (60.9)	45 (18.7)

(continued)

TABLE 11.7 Continued

Method	Male Cases	Female Cases	Total Cases
Some beat/bludgeoned	46 (23.6)	1 (2.2)	47 (19.5)
Only beat/bludgeoned	7 (3.6)	0 (0.0)	8 (3.3)
Some firearms	40 (20.5)	3 (6.5)	43 (17.8)
Only firearms	19 (9.7)	1 (2.2)	20 (8.3)
Some unknown methods	22 (11.3)	8 (17.4)	30 (12.4)
All unknown methods	4 (2.1)	3 (6.5)	7 (2.9)
Some burned/fire	6 (3.0)	0 (0.0)	6 (2.5)
Only burned/fire	1 (0.5)	0 (0.0)	1 (0.4)
Some other methods	3 (1.5)	3 (6.5)	6 (2.5)
Only other methods	1 (0.5)	2 (4.3)	3 (1.2)

SOURCE: © Cengage Learning, 2013.

SERIAL MURDER IN JAPAN: THE AKI STUDY*

While the Gorby (2000) study allows us to derive some very interesting comparisons of serial killers in the United States to those in other countries, we know very little about serial murder comparisons that account for racial, cultural, or ethnic differences. Most Asian countries including Japan report low crime rates. Research indicates that Japanese violent crime is at significantly lower levels than violent crime in the United States (Messner and Rosenfeld, 2001). In 1995 the official robbery rate in the United States was 220.9 per 100,000, but in Japan the rate was 1.8 per 100,000. Dussich, Friday, Okada, Yamagami, and Knudten (2001, p. 36) observe that personal danger as a crime victim is still viewed as relatively rare among the Japanese. In fact, the U.S. murder rate is approximately 16 times that of Japan. Messner and Rosenfeld found that U.S. homicide rates were 8.2 per 100,000 population between 1993 and 1995, whereas Japan reported a mere 0.5 per 100,000 population during the same period.

According to Messner and Rosenfeld (2001), one of the explanations for the high homicide rates in the United States in comparison to those in other industrialized nations is conspicuous consumption of material goods and a profound sense of individualism that undermines respect for cultural and social support. Kaori Aki (2003) notes that although Japanese also enjoy the pursuit of materialism, they are much more group-oriented rather than individual-centered. In turn, the drive for individualism places people in harm's way and facilitates aggression. Japan, as a society, maintains a homogeneity (95%) that fosters above all else a sense of honor. For example, the Japanese adhere strictly to *giri*, social obligation that emphasizes duties and

*The author wishes to express his deep appreciation to Kaori Aki for her permission in using some of her findings from her 2003 study of Japanese serial killers.

responsibilities. Japanese culture also encourages *wa*, harmony among its people, thus avoiding litigious disputes. According to Aki, crime in Japan is deterred more by shame and embarrassment to one's self, family, and friends than by legal punishments.

Even culture, however, cannot preclude the emergence of societal anomalies that can take root and defy community solidarity. Aki (2003) observes that Japan has no diagnosed antisocial personality disorders or *Han-Shakaisei Jinkaku Shougai*, while the United States reports many such offender profiles. Japanese clinicians can still use the diagnosis, but its proper translation from the English version of the *DSM-IV* to Japanese language remains controversial. The disorder is viewed with deep suspicion as the antithesis of Japanese social norms and mores. In truth, Japan has reported several cases of violent offenders who exhibit characteristics common to American descriptions of psychopaths. Aki found that the term *psychopath* or *Seishin Byoushitsu* was often used in Japan between 1955 and 1965 but gradually faded from usage in Japanese psychiatry. While controversy may exist in accepting and applying definitions and diagnoses of psychopathy, the fact remains that a small but steady number of serial killers continues to emerge even in Japanese culture. In the 1940s, shortly following World War II, Yoshio Kodaira raped and killed 10 women. Posing as someone who could help them locate rice for families without food, he was able to lure unsuspecting women to their deaths. During the early 1970s, when Japan was emerging into an economically strong nation, Kiyoshi Okubo, a sexual predator who portrayed himself as an artist or teacher and drove expensive cars, lured, raped, and killed at least eight women.

The fact that serial killers exist in Japanese society is now well documented (Aki, 2003; see Table 11.8), but explaining these cases from an American perspective becomes complicated. One of the most salient factors in serial-murder cases in the United States is that many of them are lust murders; many U.S. serial killers have used pornography to facilitate fantasies and violent behavior. Indeed, American culture has mainstreamed pornography to the extent that it permeates our daily lives. Violent pornography is considered to be a critical factor in sexual homicides. Modern Japan has also witnessed a tremendous increase in sexually explicit materials as well as sex-related industries or *fuuzoku*. Given this mainstreaming of sex-related industries in Japan, one might hypothesize that Japan, like the United States, would experience some increase in sex-related crimes. Aki (2003) found, however, that lust murder continues to be very rare in Japan and that sex crimes in general have been decreasing for decades. Diamond and Uchiyama (1999) suggest that one of the reasons sex crimes have been decreasing in Japan is actually due to the increase in pornography. The number of sex offenders, especially juveniles, decreased by 85% between 1972 and 1995. This apparent inverse relationship requires not only a deeper understanding of the impact of pornography but also an understanding of how it is integrated culturally. High homicide rates have long been noted in American culture. Even with U.S. crime rates at a 30-year low in 2003, homicide rates were the exception.

Though serial murder in Japan is relatively rare when compared to the United States, Japan has witnessed several notable cases. Kaori Aki (2003) examined 82 Japanese serial killers between 1880 and 2002. Similar to Gorby's (2000) study, the Aki study also excluded murder cases related to white-collar crimes,

TABLE 11.8 Japanese Serial Killers, 1880–2002

Case No.	Name	Japanese Name		Gender	Year(s)[1]
1.	Shimizu, Sadakichi	清水	定吉	male	1880–1886
2.	Okubo, Tokisaburo	大久保	時三郎	male	1905
3.	Ooyone, Ryuun	大米	龍雲	male	1913–1914
4.	Fukigami, Satarou	吹上	佐太郎	male	1923
5.	Onishi, Seijirou	大西	性次郎	male	1925
6.	Ogawa, Kiku	小川	きく	female	1928–1930
7.	Kawamata, Hatsutaro	川俣	初太郎	male	1933
8.	Nakamura, Seisaku	中村	誠策	male	1941–1942
9.	Ishikawa, Miyuki	石川	みゆき	female	1944–1948
	Ishikawa,[2] Takeru	石川	猛	male	1944–1948
10.	Kodaira, Yoshio	小平	義雄	male	1945–1946
11.	Harada, Chisato	原田	千里	male	1946–1947
12.	Unknown			male	1946–1947
13.	Kim, Nansho	金	南壽	male	1947–1948
14.	Kurita, Genzo	栗田	源蔵	male	1947–1952
15.	Unknown			male	1950
16.	Unknown			male	1951
17.	Kobayashi, Kau	小林	カウ	female	1952–1960
	Nakata,[2] Mataichiro	中田	又一郎	male	1952
	Oonuki,[2] Mitsuyoshi	大貫	光吉	male	1960
18.	Onishi, Katsumi	大西	克己	male	1955–1958
19.	Nakajima, Kazuo	中島	一夫	male	1957–1966
20.	Sugimura, Sadame	杉村	サダメ	female	1960
21.	Moriyoshi, Kouki	森吉	幸喜	male	1963
22.	Nishiguchi, Akira	西口	彰	male	1963–1964
23.	Furuya, Soukichi	古谷	惣吉	male	1965
24.	Tsukamoto, Ryuichi	塚本	隆一	male	1966–1967
25.	Takayama, Masahiko	高山	雅彦	male	1967–1968
26.	Watanabe, Kiyoshi	渡辺	清	male	1967–1975
27.	Nagayama, Norio	永山	則夫	male	1968–1969
28.	Sekiguchi, Masayasu	関口	政安	male	1970–1973
29.	Ookubo, Kiyoshi	大久保	清	male	1971
30.	Unknown			female	1971–1975
31.	Unknown			female	1971–1975
32.	Takada, Wasaburo	高田	和三郎	male	1972
33.	Haruyama, Hiromoto	晴山	広元	male	1972–1974
34.	Etou, Matsue	江藤	松枝	female	1972–1982

TABLE 11.8 Continued

Case No.	Name	Japanese Name		Gender	Year(s)
35.	Katsuta, Kiyoshi	勝田	清孝	male	1972–1982
36.	Kawaguchi, Tetsuo	川口	鉄夫	male	1975–1977
37.	Matsue, Teruhiko	松江	輝彦	male	1975–1989
38.	Takai, Kimie	高井	貴美枝	female	1976–1985
39.	Nagasaki, Masayasu	長崎	正恭	male	1977–1979
	Kotani,[2] Yoshiki	小谷	良樹	male	1977–1979
40.	Hamada, Takesige	浜田	武重	male	1978–1979
41.	Hukuoka, Michio	福岡	道雄	male	1978–1981
42.	Ida, Masamichi	井田	正道	male	1979–1983
	Hasegawa,[2] Toshihiko	長谷川	敏彦	male	1979–1983
	Unknown[2]			male	1983
43.	Unknown			male	1981
44.	Fujima, Shizunami	藤間	静波	male	1981–1982
45.	Higashino, Sayoko	東野	佐代子	female	1982–1985
46.	Kitagawa, Susumu	北川	晋	male	1983–1986
47.	Miyashita, Masahiro	宮下	政弘	male	1984–1991
48.	Kamata, Yasutoshi	鎌田	安利	male	1985–1994
49.	Fujioka, Mitsuo	藤岡	光雄	male	1986
50.	Miyazaki, Tsutomu	宮崎	勤	male	1988–1989
51.	Seko, Yasuhiro	迫	康裕	male	1986–1991
	Nagone,[2] Hidetoku	名郷根	秀徳	male	1986–1991
	Okazaki,[2] Sigeo	岡崎	茂男	male	1986–1989
52.	Nishikawa, Masakatsu	西川	正勝	male	1991–1992
53.	Ueda, Gihan	上田	宜範	male	1992–1993
54.	Simoyama, Nobukazu	下山	信一	male	1993
	Wong,[2] Isan	黄	奕善	male	1993
55.	Ueda, Masaru	上田	大	male	1993
56.	Sekiya, Gen	関谷	元	male	1993–1995
	Kazama,[2] Hiroko	風間	博子	female	1993–1995
57.	Unknown			male	1994
	Unknown[2]			male	1994
	Unknown[2]			male	1994
58.	Matsumoto, Akihiro	松本	昭弘	male	1994–1996
	Matsumoto,[2] Kazuhiro	松本	和弘	male	1994–1996
	Shimoura,[2] Eiichi	下浦	栄一	male	1994–1996
59.	Etou, Sachiko	江藤	幸子	female	1995

(continued)

TABLE 11.8 Continued

Case No.	Name	Japanese Name		Gender	Year(s)
60.	Yagi, Shigeru	八木	茂	male	1995–1999
	Take,[2] Mayumi	武	まゆみ	female	1995–1999
	Kawamura,[2] Anarie	カワムラ	アナリエ	female	1995–1999
	Morita,[2] Takako	森田	孝子	female	1995–1999
61.	Hidaka, Hiroaki	日高	広明	male	1996
62.	Matsunaga, Tai	松永	太	male	1996–2002
	Ogata,[2] Junko	緒方	純子	female	1996–2002
63.	Sakakibara, Seito	酒鬼薔薇	聖斗	male	1997
64.	Hoshino, Katsumi	星野	克美	male	1998–1999

$N = 82$

* There are 82 Japanese serial killers who constitute 64 cases.

1. Year(s) designates from the year offenders committed their first killing to the year a murder series ended.

2. Indicates accomplice (second offender).

SOURCE: © Cengage Learning, 2013.

war crimes, political/religious terrorists, organized crime groups, and street gang activities. Aki compared several variables including victims and duration, mobility, age and gender, team versus solo killing, methods and motives, and sexual activities.

Victims and Duration

Offenders in this study killed an average of 12 victims per case, similar to the Hickey (2006a) study. Nearly 80% killed nonfamily members and 5% killed only family members. Aki noted that the length of Japanese serial-murder cases ranged from less than 1 year to 37 years. About half of all cases were 1 year or less, about one-third were 2-5 years, and 13% lasted between 6 and 10 years (see Table 11.9).

Mobility

Aki (2003) also examined the issue of mobility among Japanese serial killers and found that 41% killed in a local area with exactly 50% traveling to other cities,

TABLE 11.9 Comparison of Duration of Japanese and American Serial-Murder Cases

No. of Years Duration	Percentage of Japanese Cases ($N = 82$)	Percentage of American Cases ($N = 365$)
1 or less	51.2	54.0
2–5	34.1	27.0
6–10	13.4	8.0
Over 10	1.2	11.0

SOURCE: © Cengage Learning, 2013.

TABLE 11.10 Mobility of Serial Killers

Mobility	Percentage of Japanese Offenders	Percentage of U.S. Offenders
Local	41.5	53.1
Traveling	50.0	33.2
Place-specific	8.5	13.7
Total	*N* = 82	*N* = 401

SOURCE: © Cengage Learning, 2013.

states, or countries. As in the United States, women were far more likely to kill at home or at work than male offenders (see Table 11.10).

Age and Gender

Aki (2003) also found that half of all Japanese serial offenders fell within the age range of 26–40. They ranged in age between 13 and 60 at the onset of their killings, the average age being 30. By the time offenders finished their killing careers (last murder) the age range was 16–70 and the average age was 35 (see Table 11.11). Aki also found that females comprised about 18% of Japanese serial killers, whereas in the United States, Hickey (2006a) found approximately 15% of his offenders to be female. Most females in the Aki study used poisons or withheld medical assistance. A few other females strangled their victims, but in only one female Japanese case was a gun used or a victim bludgeoned to death. As in the United States, a few Japanese women murdered children. In one case in 1986, a 41-year-old woman was arrested for suffocating her nine newborn babies over a 10-year period. A search of her apartment revealed nine mummified infants stored in plastic boxes. Aki noted that among the Japanese offenders, 8 of 64 cases involved females who committed filicide or infanticide.

Team Killers

Aki (2003) found that about 44% of offenders had at least one accomplice compared to only 26% found in the United States (see Table 11.12). In Japan, nearly

TABLE 11.11 Age and Gender of Japanese and American Serial Killers

Demographic	Percentage of Japanese Offenders	Percentage of American Offenders
Gender	*N* = 82	*N* = 402
Male	81.7	84.6
Female	18.3	15.4
Age at first murder	*N* = 78	*N* = 275
25 or younger	26.9	43.6
26–40	50.0	48.4
41 or older	23.1	8.0

SOURCE: © Cengage Learning, 2013.

TABLE 11.12 Team Characteristics of Serial Killers

Team	Percentage of Japanese Offenders	Percentage of U.S. Offenders
Solo or team	*N* = 82	*N* = 400
Solo	54.9	72.5
Team	43.9	26.3
Both	1.2	1.2
Team gender relations	*N* = 37	*N* = 109
All male	40.5	59.6
All female	0.0	1.8
Mixed	59.5	38.6

PROFILE 11.10 Kau Kobayashi, 1952–1960

In 1952 Kau Kobayashi, 22, conspired with her lover to poison her husband. In 1960 she conspired with her second lover to kill his wife in order to inherit her hotel business. She hired a homeless man with whom she also had an affair to do the killing. A month later, she conspired with her new lover (the homeless man) to kill her second lover. He was poisoned, stabbed, and strangled. Later, with a new accomplice, she conspired to kill her lover, the homeless man, but was finally caught and convicted. Kobayashi was hanged in 1970 for her three murders.

80% of the team-killer cases consisted of only two offenders. One Japanese team had ten offenders compared to one American case with 8 offenders. About 60% of the Japanese teams were comprised of both male and female offenders (see Profile 11.10), 41% were all male teams, but no teams were comprised of only female offenders. About one in four U.S. offenders had one or more partners in serial murder. Americans, however, were more likely to kill alone than the Japanese offenders. Aki noted that U.S. teams were most likely to be comprised of only male offenders, whereas the Japanese offenders were most likely to be a mix of both genders. In a few cases, both in the United States and Japan, women not only had an accomplice but were also the leaders in the murders.

Methods and Motives

Aki (2003) also examined methods and Gender motives in Japanese serial murder. Japanese male offenders overall (60%) preferred to strangle or asphyxiate their victims, compared to 35% of offenders in the Hickey (2006a) study. When strangulation or asphyxiation was the sole method of killing, Japanese and male offenders were more likely than their American male counterparts to murder using this method. American serial killers, not surprisingly, were at least five times more likely to use firearms (38%) to carry out serial murders as compared to 7% in the Aki study. Although the U.S. offenders did not use guns as their solo means of killing, shooting was still the most common method among the U.S. offenders.

This finding may correlate to gun ownership. Rates of gun ownership are much higher in the United States than in other industrial nations. According to a 1989 crime victimization survey of 14 developed countries, 29% of the U.S. households owned a handgun, while no other nation had a handgun-ownership rate higher than 7% (Dijk, Mayhew, and Killias, 1991). In contrast, Aki (2003) found that shooting was least likely to be the chosen killing method among Japanese serial offenders because of unavailability of guns (possession of firearms is illegal in Japan). Only five Japanese offenders used firearms as deadly weapons; these offenders obtained guns either by stealing from a police officer or from a U.S. military base. Japanese offenders were far more likely to kill for financial gain than their U.S. counterparts.

Sexual Activities

American serial killers were slightly more likely to be involved in postmortem activities including mutilation. American offenders were also nearly twice as likely to exhibit paraphilic interests and were much more likely to be ritualistic in their process of murder. For example, American serial killers were more likely to collect body parts and record or photograph their crimes. In a rare Japanese case, Tsutomu Miyazaki, a sexual predator, killed and mutilated four young girls for his sexual pleasure. During one of his murders he cooked and ate the hands of a child victim. However, lust murders were found to be relatively rare in Japan. Aki (2003) also found that in some cases of Japanese serial murder there were no records of prior offenses, especially for sex crimes. Without prior arrest records, law enforcement personnel have much more difficulty in conducting their investigations.

SERIAL MURDER IN SOUTH AFRICA

Murder and how it is differentially expressed is often rooted in culture. South Africa, for example, reports a variety of homicides that are similar to those in the United States, including domestic murders, sexual predator killings, and mass murders. South Africa has a murder rate over seven times that of the United States. In 2000 there were approximately 18,000 murders in the United States, a country of 260 million people. South Africa, with 47 million people, reports approximately 15,000 to 20,000 murders per year (for current statistics see the South African Police Service website at www.saps.gov.za) with the recent 2010/2011 figures being 15,940 murders for that time frame, which translates to 33.9 per 100,000. To sort out and investigate the more unique of these murders and other crimes, South Africa has formed, as in many countries, a special unit to assist with crimes that appear to have psychological motivation.

The Investigative Psychology Section of the Forensic Services Division of the South African Police Service

The Investigative Psychology Section (IPS), which was formed in 1996, is headed by Brigadier Gérard Labuschagne, who teaches Psychologically Motivated Crimes courses to homicide and sexual offenses investigators. The three-week course is required of all law enforcement personnel who will be involved in serial-murder investigations. To date over 400 investigators have finished the course. The South African Police Service (SAPS) is one of the few law enforcement agencies in the world that specifically offers investigative psychological services from within its structures. The IPS's roles are to provide investigative assistance, train detectives, and conduct research. All profiling is done through the IPS, including the investigation of serial-murder cases. Each province in South Africa has a monitor who coordinates the services of the IPS, and the IPS hopes to expand into each of the nine provinces with satellite units over the next few years. Brigadier Labuschagne has created a section that is scientifically based and as a result has had an astonishing success rate in clearing cases of serial murder (see Table 11.13).

TABLE 11.13 South African Serial Murders, 1936–2009

Series Name	Province	Suspect Name	Years of Operation	# of Murder Victims
Johannesburg	Gauteng	Cornelius Burger	1936–1937	5
Cape Town	Western Cape	Salie Lingevelt	1940	5
KwaZulu-Natal	KwaZulu-Natal	Elifasi Msomi	1953–1955	15
Pangaman	Gauteng	Elias Xitavhudzi	1960s	16
Athlone	Western Cape	Noor Ahmet	1968–1969	4
Atteridgeville	Gauteng	John Phukokgabi	1974–1978	16
Soweto	Gauteng	Joseph Mahlangu	1979	13
Pietermaritzburg	KwaZulu-Natal	Phillip Khehla Magoso	1983	5
Station Strangler	Western Cape	Unsolved	1986–1994	22
Northern Cape	Northern Cape	Tommy Williams	1987–2008	3
Klerksdorp	North West	David Motshekgwa	1988	12
Norwood	Gauteng	Cobus Geldenhuys	1989–1992	5
Port Elizabeth	Eastern Cape	Brydon Brandt	1989–1997	4
Boetie Boer	Eastern Cape	Stewart Wilken	1990–1997	7
Cape Town	Western Cape	Wessels & Havenga	1991	4
West Rand	Gauteng	Moses Mokgeti	1991–1993	7
Cape Prostitute	Western Cape	Unsolved	1992–1995	19
Eva Nosal	Gauteng	Christiaan de Wet	1993–1994	2

TABLE 11.13 Continued

Series Name	Province	Suspect Name	Years of Operation	# of Murder Victims
Witbank	Mpumalanga	Unsolved	1993–1994	3
Cross-dressing	Gauteng	Brown & Coetzee	1993–1995	5
NASREC	Gauteng	Mazankane & Motsegwa	1993–1998	17
Concordia	Western & Northern Cape	Robin Cloete	1993–2007	3
Cleveland Strangler	Gauteng	David Selepe	1994	14
Pinetown Strangler	KwaZulu-Natal	Unsolved	1994–1995	3
Atteridgeville Strangler	Gauteng	Moses Sithole	1994–1995	38
Donnybrook	KwaZulu-Natal	Christopher Zikode	1994–1995	8
Phoenix	KwaZulu-Natal	Sipho Twala	1994–1997	18
Louis Trichardt	Limpopo	Willem Grobler	1995	2
Mdantsane	Eastern Cape	Vuyani Mpezo	1995	2
Kranskop	KwaZulu-Natal	Bongani Mfeka	1995	4
Wemmerpan	Gauteng	Cedric Maake	1995–1997	32
Lenyenye	Limpopo	Unsolved	1996–1997	5
Eastern Cape	Eastern Cape	Nicolas Ncama	1996–1997	3
Carltonville	Gauteng	Unsolved	1996–1998	6
Thohoyandou	Limpopo	David Mbengwa	1996–1998	10
Roadside	North West	Francois Potgieter	1996–2000	16
Langlaagte	Gauteng	Unsolved	1996–2000	2
Pyromaniac	Gauteng	Norman Hobkirk	1997	3
Saloon Killer	Mpumalanga	V. Nglanamandla	1997–1998	16
Corn Field	Free State	Daniel Ramayisa	1997–1998	3
Upington	Northern Cape	JAC Nel	1997–1998	2
Peninsula Nightmare	Western Cape	Unsolved	1997	3
Barbed Wire	KwaZulu-Natal	Unsolved	1997–1998	16
Sleepy Hollow	KwaZulu-Natal	Unsolved	1997–1999	8
Capital Park	Gauteng	Samuel Sidyno	1998	7
Spider Valley	Gauteng	Michael Barnard	1998–1999	3
Juan Jordaan	KwaZulu-Natal	Juan Jordaan	1999	2
Barberton	Mpumalanga	Frank Ndebe	1999	4
Sewage Farm	Western Cape	Unsolved	1999–2000	9
Riverman	KwaZulu-Natal	Unsolved	1999–2001	13
Little Fountains	Gauteng	Unsolved	1999–2001	5

(continued)

TABLE 11.13 Continued

Series Name	Province	Suspect Name	Years of Operation	# of Murder Victims
RDP Strangler	Limpopo	Ephraim Legodi	2000	4
Kwa Dukuza	KwaZulu-Natal	Unsolved	2000–2001	4
Shallow Grave	Western Cape	Zola Jackson Mqombuyi	2001	5
Keiskammahoek	Eastern Cape	McPherson Nyonga	2001	2
PE Prostitute	Eastern Cape	Unsolved	2001	4
Randfontein	Gauteng	Unsolved	2001–2003	7
Stellenbosch Child Murderer	Western Cape	Unsolved	2001–2003	4
Siloam	Limpopo	Freddy Mulaudzi	2002–2006	12
Mapelo Hans	North West	Master Lucas Makgamatho	2002	4
Highwayman	Gauteng	Elias Chauke	2002	5
Newlands East	KwaZulu-Natal	Unsolved	2002–2003	13
Quarry	Gauteng	Richard Nyauza	2002–2007	16
Johannesburg Mine Dump	Gauteng	Sipho Dube	2003	7
Rustenburg Child Killer	North West	Awaiting Trial	2003	2
Barberton 2004	Mpumalanga	Mthethwa Nkosi	2004	5
Cape Town Child Murderer	Western Cape	Unsolved	2004	3
Newcastle	KwaZulu-Natal	Themba Anton Sukude	2004–2005	4
Modimolle Child Killer	Limpopo	David Randitshene	2004–2006	10
Boschkop N4 Killer	Gauteng	Unsolved	2005–2006	5
Philippi	Western Cape	Jimmy Maketta	2005	16
Railway Killer	Gauteng	Unsolved	2005	5
Mhluzi	Mpumalanga	Van Rooyen & Makhubela	2005	7
Knysna	Western Cape	Heinie Van Rooyen	2005	2
Kinross	Mpumalanga	Unsolved	2005	3
Tonga	Mpumalanga	Unsolved	2005–2006	5
Khalahari Express	North West	Minus Kubu	2005	7
Volksrust	Mpumalanga	Awaiting Trial	2006	3
Moffat Park	Gauteng	Gcunumuzi R Makwenkwe	2005–2006	5

TABLE 11.13 Continued

Series Name	Province	Suspect Name	Years of Operation	# of Murder Victims
Umbumbulu	KwaZulu-Natal	Unsolved	2006	5
Nest Inn Serial Murders	Gauteng	Unsolved	2005–2006	6
Umzinto Sugar Cane	KwaZulu-Natal	Tozamele Taki	2007	13
PE Prostitute 2007	Eastern Cape	Riaan Stander	2007	2
Witbank 2007	Mpumalanga	Unsolved	2007	4
N3 PMB 2007	KwaZulu-Natal	Unsolved	2007	4
PPS North West Butcher	North West	Patrick Lesejane	2007	5
SOWETO	Gauteng	Dumisane Jonathan Mthobeni	2007	4
Rustenburg Prostitute	North West	Unsolved	2007–2008	5
Amanzimtoti	KwaZulu-Natal	Awaiting Trial	2008	4
Engcobo	Eastern Cape	Awaiting Trial	2008	4
Vredendal	Western Cape	Awaiting Trial	2006–2009	2
Witsand/Atlantis	Western Cape	Unsolved	2008–2009	3
Delareyville	North West	Unsolved	2008–2009	3
Westonaria	Gauteng	Jack Mogale	2008	16
Orange Farms	Gauteng	David Nocela	2008	3
Randfontein-Potchefstroom	Gauteng- North West	Refiloe Ndlovu	2007–2008	4
Brighton Beach	KwaZulu-Natal	Awaiting Trial	2011	4

SOURCE: © Cengage Learning, 2013.

Since 1990 the IPS has handled over 100 murder series, with a solving rate of 70%. Of those cases that have gone to court, the SAPS has successfully prosecuted all of them. One of the reasons for this success is the level of education, experience, and training that is the hallmark of the IPS. Brigadier Labuschagne holds a doctorate in clinical psychology, and is also co-appointed as a Senior Research Fellow at the Department of Psychology of the University of Johannesburg, but also is a police investigator. Although the IPS has only five members, they have resolved all the major cases they have assisted on. Besides the brigadier, the IPS is staffed by Captain Elmarie Myburgh, who holds degrees in psychology and criminology; Captain Marina Genis, a clinical psychologist; Lieutenant Colonel Jan De Lange, a 22-year veteran detective; and Captain Suzette Knoetze, an 18-year veteran detective.

The combination of education and experience is also enhanced by the fact that the IPS operates throughout South Africa, the SAPS is a national police service and thereby jurisdictional issues are not as prevalent, and the IPS serves as a clearing house for all psychologically motivated crimes. Also, all law

PROFILE 11.11 Stewart Wilken, 1990–1997

Born in 1966 east of Johannesburg, South Africa, Stewart Wilken became a prime example of cases that do not fit traditional profiles of violent offenders. Wilken killed black, white, and colored* victims ranging in age from 8 to 42 years old. Using their clothing, he strangled both males and females who were strangers, acquaintances, and family. He engaged in cannibalism, necrophilia, and incest as he targeted black and colored female adult prostitutes as well as white and colored boys. He had pre- and postmortem sex with most of the victims but claimed that his stepdaughter was an exception. Wilken said that he enjoyed the way people's faces looked while they were being strangled. He referred to this as the "jelly bean effect." He was finally arrested for killing his last victim but police, at that point, were unaware of his links to other murders. During the course of interrogation Wilken confessed to his serial murders. He explained his homicidal behavior as a result of mixing marijuana and Mandrax (methaqualone). He blamed his wife by saying that she refused him sex and that she sometimes worked as a prostitute. He also felt that his frequenting prostitutes contributed to his opportunities to murder.

As a child Stewart was abandoned by his mother and had no recollection of his biological parents. He was raised by foster parents who physically and sexually exploited him. At age 10 he was sodomized by a member of his church. He failed in school and came to distrust everyone. Sent to reform school, he was sodomized again and began using marijuana. He would later observe of his childhood, "I began to feel like an object, not a person." Eventually he was drafted into the army but was discharged after only four months as a result of a suicide attempt.

He married a woman who was unfaithful to him and after nine years they divorced. Wilken was treated for psychiatric problems and another suicide attempt. In 1990 he entered his second marriage and in 1995 was arrested for sodomizing his stepchildren. He solicited prostitutes and eventually began strangling them during acts of sodomy. He also killed boys in the same manner. His first five victims were prostitutes and the last four were children age 13 and younger. Note the variation in victims but that his signature (strangulation) was constant. Unlike his adult victims, Wilken liked visiting the remains of his child victims. He engaged in postmortem sex with two of the child victims. He then covered their bodies with branches to ensure that their souls would go to heaven.

*The term "colored" is used differently in South Africa than in the United States. It is a recognized population group designation as per the South African government census consisting of the Khoi and San people who originally occupied the southern part of South Africa and people brought from Malaysia and other Far Eastern countries hundreds of years ago for labor purposes. They have a distinct culture and speak predominantly Afrikaans and English and refer to themselves as "colored."

enforcement officials use one DNA and fingerprint database. This organizational streamlining avoids the linkage blindness that is often a problem in the United States. The members of the IPS provide investigative services such as offender profiling, crime scene assessments, equivocal death assessments, interviewing of offenders and witnesses, investigative guidance, and expert evidence in the form of linkage evidence and sentencing evidence. Indeed, the IPS has become known as the forerunner in the use of linkage analysis as evidence in serial-murder trials. Besides serial-murder cases, the IPS assists in investigation of spree and mass murders, domestic murders, infant rapes, extortion cases, child murders, abductions, death threats, murders with bizarre circumstances,

Wilken's Victims

- Victim one was a black prostitute about 25 years old. They had consensual vaginal sex and then he raped her anally while strangling her with her clothing. He climaxed while strangling her.
- Victim two was a colored prostitute about 29 years old. When she demanded money before sex he strangled her with her clothing and then, after she was dead, had sex with her.
- Victim three was a black child prostitute about 14 years old. While sodomizing the teen he strangled him. Wilken said of the experience: "I continually orgasmed while strangling him."
- Victim four was also a black prostitute but an adult about 32 years old. Again, they had consensual sex before he raped her anally and strangled her with her clothing. With this victim he noted: "I enjoyed it while she struggled, it was so nice I came." After her death Wilken inserted a knife into her vagina and cut off her nipples and ate them.
- Victim five was a black prostitute about 26 years old. Wilken strangled her and had sex repeatedly with the corpse.
- Victim six was a black street child about 13 years old who performed masturbation for money. Wilken sodomized the young teen and strangled him with a belt.
- Victim seven was his own 10-year-old daughter. He took her to a forested area where he strangled her, removed her clothing, and placed it over the corpse. Wilken felt that his children were being abused and neglected and commented: "Why must my children go through what I went through?"
- Victim eight was a 12-year-old white boy who was the son of a neighbor. Wilken had been asked to escort the boy somewhere. Hidden in bushes, the child was molested, sodomized, and strangled, bringing Wilken to orgasm.
- Victim nine was a black boy about eight years old. He sodomized and strangled the child while climaxing. Wilken later analyzed the final murder by saying: "I took out everything that happened to me as a child."

ritual "muti" murders, and serial-rape investigations. In recent years the IPS has been placing more emphasis on training crime scene photographers because they often operate over large geographical areas and are extremely useful in facilitating the linkage of crimes and offenders. The IPS also provides training to prosecutors; forensic experts; organized crime, sexual offenses, and general investigation detectives; nongovernmental organizations; and various local and international universities.

Labuschagne and his IPS profilers have discovered several differences between serial murder in the United States and South Africa. Out of their past 50 cases, 22 South African offenders murdered interracially (see Profile 11.11).

Such murders do occur in the United States, but not nearly as often. Offenders (approximately 34%) may also kill both male and female victims rather than be gender specific. There also appears to be a wider age range of victims. Both your author and the IPS found a combination of methods of killing to be common in serial murder. In South Africa, the IPS noted that offenders tend to prefer strangulation, stabbing, and blunt force trauma as the means of murdering the victim, often a combination of these throughout the series. Despite the relative availability of firearms, firearms are rarely used in murder series. The IPS has provided assistance with serial-murder investigations to neighboring countries such as Swaziland and Namibia, and more distant countries such as England where they assisted Scotland Yard with a suspected ritual murder, and India with a serial-murder investigation. The investigative model provided by South Africa is indeed impressive. The IPS is not only faced with previously described crimes, but also murder cases that are rooted in culture and that have the appearance of other murders but under closer inspection do not fit traditional murder profiles.

Muti Murders in South Africa*

Rajs, Lundtrom, Broberg, Lidberg, and Linquist (1998) identify four types of criminal mutilation based upon motive: *defensive mutilation* (dismemberment) is intended to dispose of a body and/or to make identification difficult; *aggressive mutilation* is evoked through an act of rage killing—victims' faces and genitals are sometimes mutilated following death; *offensive mutilation* is typically seen in lust murders and necro-sadistic murders—offenders have either a necrophilic urge for postmortem sexual activity with the corpse that includes pre- or postmortem mutilation or a sadistic desire to inflict severe pain, humiliation, or death while engaged in sexual activity that also involves pre- or postmortem mutilation; and *necromanic mutilation,* which involves sexual contact with a corpse as seen in regular necrophilia but with the added desire to mutilate or use body parts as trophies or to fulfill fetishes.

For centuries *muti murder* has been a distinctive part of African cultural beliefs. These types of murders do not fit traditional Westernized criminal profiles of murderers and can cause considerable confusion when attempts are made to distinguish them from sadistic, serial, cult, and other types of killing where criminal mutilation may occur (Labuschagne, 2003). The word *muti* is a Zulu word that means medicine and when used in the context of murder implies the intentional gathering of body parts for use in traditional African medicine (Minaar, 2001). The etiology of muti murders is primarily greed that drives a person

*Special thanks to Dr. Gerard Labuschagne, Commander of the Investigative Psychology Section of the South African Police Service, for use of his article "Features and Investigative Implications of Muti Murder in South Africa" (2004) and for providing insightful information about the IPS and serial-murder case information. Dr. Labuschagne is one of the world's foremost experts in profiling psychologically motivated crimes. For further information about the Investigative Psychology Section please contact Dr. Gerard Labuschagne at psychinv@saps.org.za.

to want to gain more money, power, control, and prestige. It has also been noticed over recent years that more and more criminals are using muti to protect them during their crimes, or afterwards to prevent being arrested by the police. Traditional healers are often consulted before committing crimes such as heists of vehicles transporting money to and from banks, so-called Cash-in-Transit robberies.

Muti murders are not ritual murders per se in the sense of a sacrifice. Indeed, the muti murders are done in a proscribed manner, but they are not ritual or sacrificial acts. Ritual murder in South Africa may include the mythical sacrifice of Venda virgins thrown to the crocodiles or drowned as offerings to ancestral spirits. Such ritual killings are often not looked upon as murders because those doing the killings are submitting to cultural norms, not evil intentions, and are for the good of the greater community. In African traditional society, people believe they are bequeathed with a specific amount of luck. Those exhibiting more good fortune than others often are suspected of using the supernatural for self-promotion. One avenue in obtaining this luck is through strong muti or strong medicine. Often this will involve the need to collect human body parts to add to a potion to create strong muti. Human body parts removed from persons while still alive are considered to be exceptionally powerful for making strong muti, and according to beliefs, are more likely to be successful in helping the user achieve their aim.

There are usually four role players involved in muti murder: the client, the traditional healer or "witch," the murderer, and the victim. The *client* seeking personal gain such as money, power, or protection approaches a traditional healer/witch. The client may pay as much as $1,000 (a hefty sum in South African currency) to the traditional healer/witch. The client is not usually involved in the murder except to hire a traditional healer/witch and collect the muti once it has been prepared. The *traditional healers/witches* usually involved in muti murders are not considered by the community to be mainstream healers and are rejected by other healers. Most mainstream healers take offense when those who use human body parts are referred to as "traditional healers," and insist that such people should be referred to as "witches." Their reason for this is that a traditional healer is there to heal and help people, while a person practicing "black magic" does so to inflict harm and suffering upon another and is therefore regarded as a "witch." The traditional healer/witch, once contracted by the client, decides which herbs, roots, and body parts to use and hires another person to act as the *murderer.* He or she tells the murderer which body parts to collect and how they should be removed from the body. Once the murderer has delivered the body parts, the traditional healer/witch mixes the muti and instructs the client in how to use the potion for the greatest effect. The murderer is instructed that the body parts must be removed while the *victim* is still alive in order for the muti to be the strongest. The motive for the murderer is typically one of two options, either he is paid for his involvement or he himself is an apprentice of the traditional healer/witch. He must, however, make sure that the victim fits the desired qualities asked for by the healer.

Victims range from infants to adults, male and female, strangers to relatives. In some cases the intended murderer resorts to grave robbing or stealing body parts from hospitals or mortuaries in order to avoid having to kill someone and risk being caught. The elderly are generally not targeted because it is believed that their life essence is waning and therefore the body parts will not be as powerful. Labuschagne (2004) believes that when an individual plays the first three roles by himself, that person most likely is suffering from some form of mental illness. He also notes that in some muti-motivated attacks, the victim survives. This underscores a significant difference between ritual sacrificial murder and the goal of a muti attack, which is not necessarily to end the life of the victim. Another issue that can complicate investigation of these murders is that body parts may hold different meaning or symbolism depending upon which traditional healer/witch is being employed by the client. Dr. Labuschagne notes the following body parts and their uses:

- Breast: Considered "mother luck" and will attract women to a person's place of business. The fat in the breast is considered to be very lucky.
- Genitals: "Luck" is found in the genitals of both men and women. Enhances virility, and can be used to help someone who is infertile.
- Hands: Used to attract business because they beckon customers and receive money.
- Skull: Protects members from one tribe against another tribe. For example, an enemy's head is buried in the village to protect the village.
- Eyes: Provide far-sightedness.
- Adam's apple: Used to silence a witness intending to testify against a client in a court case.
- Tongue: Believed to smooth the way to a girl's heart.
- Fat, urine, and semen: Considered to bring good fortune.

Profilers and homicide investigators must be adept at differentiating muti murders from sadistic or serial killings where mutilation of the body may also be a feature. While the aim of the sadistic murderer is to inflict many wounds prior to death with the intention of causing much suffering to the victim, the muti murderer is functional and only inflicts wounds necessary to harvest the proscribed body parts. While the sadistic killer sexually degrades a victim through anal, oral, and vaginal rape, the muti murderer has no sexual theme. Also, unlike the sadistic killer needing to fulfill fantasy, the muti murderer is fulfilling a contract with specific instructions. Serial killers are also driven by fantasy and will often leave distinctive patterns of mutilation on more than one victim, especially where lust murder is involved. In serial murder body parts sometimes are removed and kept as souvenirs. For the muti murderer there is usually but one victim contracted, mutilation is specific to the body parts being removed, and those parts are always given to the traditional healer/witch. Key to an investigation where mutilation exists is determining whether the mutilation was part of the purpose for committing the crime or secondary and inflicted to delay identification or to hide the corpse (see Profile 11.12).

PROFILE 11.12 Muti Murder of a Family Member

On August 13, 2009, police were called to a murder scene in the Winterveld area near the capital city of Pretoria. The body of a 12-year-old girl had been found in the yard of her home. The body was completely naked and the victim had a long incised wound from her sternum down to the pubic region. She was lying on her stomach and some of her intestines were protruding. Her body had been discovered by her mother, a Sangoma (a practitioner of traditional African medicine and witchcraft who have the power to intervene or change the course of a person's life)), who had gone into the backyard in the morning after realizing that her daughter was not in the house.

Police at the scene searched the house and the yard for evidence. Outside in an empty oil drum an old blanket was found with possible human blood on it. Inside the mother's traditional healer practice three further items were found with possible blood, all of which were sent for forensic analysis. Once police had finished processing the crime scene, detectives decided to bring the mother in for questioning at the local police station, due to their suspicion that she, despite being the mother, could be the killer.

Shortly after the questioning of the mother began, she decided to confess. She said that since she had qualified as a traditional healer the year before, her practice had not been financially successful. She therefore decided to murder her daughter for body parts to make her practice flourish. In the early hours of the morning she had carried her daughter from her bed, taken her outside to the same location where the body was found, and stabbed her in the chest and neck. She then made the long incision with the intention of removing the necessary body parts, such as the gall. However, she became confused as to which body parts to take and ultimately did not remove anything. She also stated that she washed the body. The mother confirmed that the exhibits seized by the police were involved in the crime. She made a written confession before an independent officer of the South African Police Service who was not involved in the investigation, and also made a formal pointing out of the crime scene to another independent officer who was not involved in the investigation. During the pointing out she identified the weapon used, a kitchen knife, and another exhibit used during the commission of the crime that the police had not discovered during their initial processing of the crime scene.

This case illustrates that muti victims can include the very young, and even be family members of the offender. Also consistent with other muti cases was the fact that the body was left where the murder took place and not hidden. Water was also used by the offender to wash the body afterwards. What was different from most instances was the fact that the actual murderer was the traditional healer, as opposed to another person. Most likely the reason for this was that the offender's

(continued)

PROFILE 11.12 (Continued)

business was flagging therefore she could not afford to pay someone to commit the crime, the muti was intended for herself as opposed to a paying client, and she was too newly qualified to have her own apprentice. What was also different was the fact that the body was found completely naked. This was most likely due to the fact that the incised wound began at the sternum and ended just above the vaginal area, requiring the offender to remove all the clothing. What undoubtedly also contributed to the success of the investigation was the fact that specialized detectives and crime scene investigators, with knowledge of muti murder cases, were called to the crime scene to assist the local detective branch.

- Muti murders have appeared in other countries besides South Africa. See if you can find some of these cases and explain these unusual occurrences.
- Can you think of other groups of people who perform rituals to enhance their personal wealth or safety? See Chapter 2.

Responding to Serial Killers

LEARNING OBJECTIVES

- To explore the global scope and integration of forensic science
- To evaluate the utility of current types of profiling
- To understand the role of NCAVC and ViCAP in serial-murder investigations
- To examine the role of cold case units, cold case review teams, and specific cold case files
- To learn about problems and techniques in conducting interviews with serial killers
- To explore how the courts handle serial killers

Apprehending serial killers is often very difficult. Several factors set them apart from typical domestic killers and other violent criminals. Serial killers can be highly mobile and traverse many law enforcement jurisdictions while still remaining in a relatively small geographic area. Offenders generally prefer strangers as victims and are usually careful to minimize the amount of evidence left at the crime scene. Months can pass before a community realizes that prostitutes are disappearing. Consequently, much time may go by before there is sufficient inter-agency communication to recognize a common pattern of homicides. Coordination of information can be even more difficult when offenders cross several state lines, such as truck-stop predators, abducting and murdering along the way. Although there has been considerable criticism of law enforcement in tracking down serial killers, police have made concerted efforts in some cases to join forces and conduct multiagency investigations. In several cases task forces have been organized, including the Michigan murders of 1969 involving John Norman Collins, killer of seven young females; the Atlanta child murders ending in 1981 with the arrest Wayne B. Williams, believed to have killed at least 20 young black males; the Green River killings of over 100 prostitutes that ended in the arrest of Gary Ridgway in 2001; the Grim Sleeper case ending in 2002 with the arrest of Lonnie Franklin Jr., killer of at least 10 prostitutes; and the current 2012 Long Island, New York, serial murder case of several prostitutes. No one has been arrested in this latest case.

Public anxieties demand quick apprehension of a serial offender; however, conducting investigations requires an enormous amount of agency coordination and resources. Montgomery (1992, 1993) notes that nearly 20,000 suspect names were collected in the Green River Killer case at a cost to taxpayers of over $20 million. Police also examined data on 185,000 persons in England's Staffordshire case of serial murder (Canter, 1994), and in the Yorkshire Ripper case, 268,000 names of possible leads were collected using over five million man-hours of police work and $6–7 million in costs (Doney, 1990). Considering the increasing costs of task force investigations, the Unabomber case (see Profile 12.4), which spanned 18 years and three task forces, cost approximately $75 million including the costs of prosecution. Glover and Witham (1989) identified four issues in managing major cases:

1. **Media impact**—Long-term media coverage creates immense pressure on law enforcement efforts. Police must nevertheless establish an acceptable working relationship with the press.
2. **Management of departmental resources**—Who will take charge of the investigation and maintain a coordinated flow of command?
3. **Multiagency jurisdiction**—Coordinated investigations, reporting, and expenditure of resources need to be addressed.
4. **Unusual complexity of the case**—Numerous victims, locations, and modes of death can create problems in sorting out evidence, investigative leads, and so on (pp. 2–16).

Doney (1990, p. 102) adds to this list by noting that some serial killers improve in their ability to select and kill victims and thus avoid detection. Also, false confessions, copycat murders, and political pressures for an arrest to be made all contribute to the complexity of serial-murder investigations.

FORENSIC SCIENCE

Part of the aftermath of the 1995 O. J. Simpson trial was the reassessment of the role of forensics and forensic experts in criminal trials. Although some may feel that forensics now stands on weaker ground as a result of the 1993 Supreme Court decision changing the rules by which scientific information is to be used in courtrooms, others view it as a blessing. In *Frye v. United States* (1923) the courts followed a "general acceptance standard" that requires new information be examined by the court prior to presenting it to a jury. Under *Frye*, scientific evidence must be based on a technique accepted in a field to which it pertains. In *Daubert v. Merrill Dow* (1993) the courts gave more discretionary power to trial courts in determining the probative value of scientific evidence. The *Daubert* decision gave what appeared to be much more flexibility and power regarding admissibility of evidence. However, because *Daubert* was based on statutory grounds and not constitutional grounds, the courts are much more inclined to follow the more restrictive *Frye* standard (Wint, 1998). Physical evidence is critical to cases, and pressure is being applied to find the most qualified experts who can withstand courtroom scrutiny. But forensics means much more today than simply working with physical evidence, creating even more challenges to what actually constitutes acceptable scientific evidence and who can be considered as an expert. In 1998, I was asked to consult as an expert witness in a federal case of stalking. Psychiatrists for both the defense and prosecution were quickly accepted by the courts as experts in their fields. Although I am a recognized criminologist with considerable expertise in the area of stalking, I was forced to undergo nearly two hours of examination by a most adept defense attorney. The judge finally ruled that I qualified as an expert. This was not only an issue of having a new type of expert (in this case, a criminal psychologist) but an unlicensed expert asked to testify in a case that drew its experts primarily from licensed psychiatrists. (The offender did receive a three-and-a-half-year sentence.)

The term *forensics* means belonging to or used in courts of law. This has given rise to forensic medicine or the use of medical expertise in legal or criminal investigations. In turn, forensic psychology has begun to offer insights into criminal behavior and the criminal mind. Criminology and psychology join forces to create criminal profiling, or the creation of criminal portraits that assist those in law, law enforcement, mental health, or academics to better understand crime and criminals.

Increasingly, pressure is being placed on law enforcement personnel, social scientists, and biologically oriented researchers to identify which individuals will become involved with criminal behavior, who their victims will be, and which appropriate criminal justice measures should be used to deal with the offender. Predicting criminal behavior accurately has never been an exact science, but more than ever a demand for accuracy exists. The movement today is toward integrating sciences and technology into an interdisciplinary approach to criminality. This approach encompasses behavioral, psychological, and biological explorations of criminal behavior and their legal applications. This exploration must incorporate various academic and applied disciplines such as those related to the courts, corrections, law enforcement, and victimology. Disciplines such as criminology, criminal justice, psychology, psychiatry, sociology, law and jurisprudence, mathematics, statistics, geography, and behavioral medicine, to name but a few, need to be integrated into the field of forensic science. We might envision forensics as a hub of a wheel with the spokes representing the sciences. Eyewitness identification, known to produce specific biases, is now heading in some radical new directions to improve accuracy (Brewer and Wells, 2011). Lie detection is also developing some very innovative methods to separate truth tellers from liars (Vrij et al., 2011) that will aid in investigations, prosecutions of suspects, and avoiding false confessions (Gudjonsson and Pearse, 2011). The application of graphology in conducting handwriting analysis can offer important insights into ransom notes and other documents, as psycholinguistics can highlight the relationship between linguistic behavior and the psychological process of a suspect. Geography is now a tool used to address issues of crime and victimization.

PROFILE 12.1 The Frog Boys

On a quiet day, from a small town in South Korea in 1991, five young boys, ages 9–13, went on a hike on a nearby mountainside in search for frogs. They were never seen alive again. When the boys failed to return home, thousands of local townspeople, police, and military searched the mountainside, but to no avail. The mystery lasted about 10 years, when in 2002, following very heavy rains, a person walking along a trail about halfway up the mountainside came upon a small skull of a child that had washed out from the hillside. Investigators soon found a shallow grave containing the five boys, each carefully laid side by side with their shoes placed beside them. The killer(s) was never found and in 2011 a Korean documentary exploring the murders was released, titled *Children.*

Many questions have been asked about these murders: how such a horrible thing could happen to such little boys, why they were not found in the initial search, and who could ever kill five young boys. South Korea is not a country known for much violence by its citizens, at least not to this magnitude and complexity. Solving such a case requires expertise that ultimately brings applications of forensic crime scene analysis, forensic psychology, criminology, criminal justice, culture, geography, victimology, forensic anthropology, criminal profiling, weaponry analysis, task force management, politics, and, of course, media coverage. These investigations are very costly and time consuming, often requiring years of investigation.

As a cold case, the Frog Boys continues to perplex investigators. By now you may have some ideas about motive for the murders and/or even the type of person(s) who did these crimes. Now, to develop a working profile, please search online for additional information about the Frog Boys and review the following additional facts of this case. Are your opinions influenced by this information?

- Each of the boys had been struck in the head several times with a sharp object, most likely a pointed tool, such as a pick or chisel point rock hammer used by geologists, or a sharp stone. Each victim had scarring on his skull from the blows until finally the weapon broke through, leaving a hole.

This approach is referred to as *spatial mapping* or *environmental criminology* and is used to generate geographic profiles of offenders, victims, and crime scenes. Computers are now being used to identify crime locations in urban and suburban areas by plotting where they have occurred over time. This geo-mapping approach to crime prediction has tremendous implications for future urban development, police administration, and policy development. Spatial mapping can also be applied to understanding criminal victimization, victim profiling, and promotion of victim protection. Professor David Canter and Dr. Donna Youngs of the University of Huddersfield, England, direct the International Association for Investigative Psychology (IAIP). Dr. Canter, a prominent psychologist and one of the pioneers of offender profiling, has established a program in investigative psychology in which computer models are used to predict criminal offending. Much can be learned about the offenders, of course, from their victim selection. For example, in South Korea between 1986 and 1991 a serial killer attacked and killed 10 women, each of whom was wearing red clothing at the time of the assault. The linkage between offender, victim, and location in these types of cases requires an integrated forensic analysis approach.

- Although all the boys appeared to have been attacked in the same manner, one boy had also been strangled.
- All the boys had their clothes on except for the strangled boy, who had his shirt tied over his head, which prevented him from seeing, and his ankles appeared to have been tied with his pants.
- The shoes of the victims were not simply tossed into the grave but carefully placed alongside the bodies.
- According to reports, investigators do not believe this is a sexually motivated case.

What do you think?

- Was this the work of one offender? Why do you think so or not?
- If only one person was involved in the murders, how did he manage to control all five boys?
- What is the likelihood that this is the work of a serial killer?
- Is this most likely a sex crimes case? Why or why not?
- Was this a crime of opportunity or was it planned?
- Do you think the offender(s) harmed children prior to these murders? Why or why not?
- Would the offender(s) possibly kill again? Why or why not?
- What cultural influences should be considered in developing appropriate profiles and investigative strategies?
- What additional information would you want to have before completing an offender profile?

What suggestions or ideas do you have in resolving this case?

Consider the case of the Frog Boys of South Korea (see Profile 12.1) and the many applications of forensic science, forensic psychology, criminology, victimology, and criminal justice that have come to bear on this incredible case.

Criminalists work in crime labs conducting tests and analyses in ballistics, serology, toxicology, hair-fiber evidence, DNA, latent prints, and other areas relevant to determining the nature of collected physical evidence. Physical forensics is often critical to the outcome of criminal cases, thus the importance of expertise in areas of forensic anthropology, forensic sculpting, forensic pathology, evidence collection, recovery of human remains, crime scene contamination, and crime scene reconstruction. In addition, physical evidence frequently helps investigators explain the psychology of the crime and that of its perpetrator(s). Thus enlightened, criminal psychologists promote greater understanding of criminal personalities among researchers, the courts, and law enforcement agencies. Forensic psychology is also of practical value to correctional and law enforcement administrators interested in the classification of prisoners or in the provision of training for personnel who investigate and manage offenders and offender populations.

Academically based institutions are beginning to find their role in forensics and have begun implementing programs that are broadly based in the sciences. The California School of Forensic Studies at Alliant International University is home to the first and largest forensic studies program in the United States. It includes a spectrum of forensic studies such as forensic psychology, criminal psychology, police psychology, correctional psychology, and many other specializations related to the areas of cognitive and behavioral science (see http://ForensicStudies.alliant.edu). Forensic psychologists are also in great demand with the movement in health care toward managed care and due to the greater emphasis on classification of prisoners.

With the victims movement having become firmly entrenched in the American court system, the voices of victims are being heard at long last. California State University–Fresno was the first university to offer a four-year program in victimology and victim services as part of its general criminology program. The California School of Forensic Studies now offers a doctoral program in forensic psychology with an emphasis area in victimology. Victimology is an integral part of forensics as we learn more about victims' rights and victim–offender relationships. I am very fortunate to be part of this program, to teach criminal psychology, and to consult in various cases of homicide, sex crimes, arson, and other violent crimes. Several of my graduate students have embraced such topics as serial murder, mass murder, serial bombing, serial arson, serial rapists, criminal paraphilia, and stalking. Like me, they have come to share the passion for understanding—as Gwynn Nettler (1982), one of my instructors, often referred to—the many roads, the many whys, and the many contingencies of criminality. It is particularly enjoyable to work with students who have a desire to explore the changing parameters of forensic studies and to shape the role they will one day play in helping to harness the sciences into exact forensic tools.

PROFILING

Profiling draws upon many areas of forensics. For example, Owen (1998), noted author of *In the Mix*, developed inmate profiles by examining the lives and crimes of incarcerated women at Central California Women's Facility in Chowchilla, California. Her work has provided clarity and insight into life behind bars for female felons. Wallace (2001) in his domestic violence research profiled the types of criminals who target the elderly. Over the past 15–20 years profiling has increasingly become a tool used in criminal investigations. In 1996 Wilson and Soothill stated that profiling needed a framework that has some flexibility. This remains true in 2012. They propose that profiling can be for the following:

- Use as an investigative tool where leads are limited
- Providing direction to a lagging investigation
- Giving psychological insights in conducting interviews
- Offering psychological advice for witnesses or juries

- Developing systematic computer tracking of unsolved serial-murder cases
- Facilitating communication among jurisdictions dealing with serial offenses
- Offering critique of investigative procedures, forensic evidence collection, and sampling
- Providing insights for the application of theories used to explain crime and criminal behavior
- Evidence corroboration

Profiling is developing as a science but continues to receive mixed reviews. Some professionals, such as Canter (2000), Kocsis (2006), and Levin and Fox (1985), have been skeptical of the utility of profiling, particularly the psychologically based approach that has not received scientific scrutiny and validation. Some law enforcement in other countries even argue that profiling can be harmful to an investigation (Devery, 2010), while there appears to be more interest in profiling within the United States. Other researchers express varying degrees of support for the success of psychological profiling development, including Egger (1985), Geberth (1983), Holmes (1990), and Ressler and his colleagues (1988). Torres, Boccaccini, and Miller (2006), in their Internet exploratory study of the perceptions of criminal profiling among forensic psychologists and psychiatrists, measured their opinions and experiences with profiling and their perspectives on "criminal investigative analysis" as having any impact on their decisions as professionals. Only 10% of those surveyed had profiling experience, although 25% considered themselves informed and knowledgeable about profiling. Less than 25% believed that in general, profiling was scientifically reliable or valid, while 40% felt that criminal investigative analysis was scientific and reliable. Although most see a need for more scientific analysis of profiling, many of these professionals considered profiling as a useful tool for law enforcement and are supportive of profiling research.

Richard Kocsis (2006), one of the most prominent researchers in the world on profiling, takes a very scholarly approach in evaluating the efficacy of profiling in his seminal work, *Criminal Profiling*. His balanced and scientific approach to understanding and developing profiling will undoubtedly lay the foundation for future scholarly research. Another foundational scholarly work on profiling is Wayne Petherick's (2006) *Serial Crime*. Both of these Australian researchers are part of a growing number of academicians worldwide who see the relevancy of developing sound methodological approaches to profiling.

Indeed, psychological profiling has yet to function as a "magic wand" to solve serial killings, but it is still too early in its development to be considered a failure. Programs such as those developed around profiling often require several years of testing and refinement before we are able to evaluate them. For profiling to fulfill its potential, law enforcement personnel must be willing to collaborate with those in the academic and medical professions. For example, psychiatrists can be of particular value in profiling, provided law enforcement officials are willing to accept and use their profiles. The problem in dealing with lust killers, for example, is that as offenders they present a very complex set of behavioral and psychological characteristics. Psychologists Purcell and Arrigo (2001) illustrate the complexities of such killers by proposing an integrated model of lust killing and paraphilia. Liebert (1985), in evaluating the contributions of psychiatry to the investigation of serial murders, such as lust killings, stated:

> Acceptance that the Borderline or Narcissistic Personality Disorder, with severe sociopathic and sadistic trends, can commit murder as a substitute for normal erotic pleasure or even non-violent perversion is the foundation for exploration of motivation in serial murders. With a mutually respectful desire to learn about the bizarre world of the lust murderer, the investigator and psychiatric consultant can enhance their sense of "type" for a suspect. The investigator is less likely to make a mistake in judging the grandiosity of pathological narcissism and the manipulativeness of sociopathy with "normalcy." The lust murderer can present a facade of relationships and effective, perhaps even superior, performance. Not infrequently, he will be in the bright-superior intelligence range and, therefore, potentially a skilled impostor. (p. 197)

Of course, part of the stereotype is thinking that most serial killers are exceptionally intelligent. While there are a few who rate such a designation, most are average in intelligence but have developed superior social skills that, as Liebert noted, allow them to deceive their victims with impunity.

Using four *"crime phases"* of a murderer's behavior, investigators develop offender profiles and gain insight into their personalities (McCrary, 2004):

- **Antecedent**—Was the killer involved in fantasy about killing, simply planning to kill, or both? Was the act spontaneous or did the murderer have a plan, including a designated day and time laid out prior to the attack?
- **Method and manner**—What type of victim or victims did the murderer choose and what method was used to kill, such as poisoning, shooting, stabbing, beating, drowning, strangulation, or something else?
- **Body disposal**—Did the murder(s) and body disposal occur in the same location?
- **Post-offense behavior**—Is the killer using the media to insert himself into the investigation? Does the killer make contact with investigators?

Crime phases help investigators develop databases and benchmarks for serial crime. Over the past 30 years the intersect between law enforcement investigations and science has drawn the attention of psychologists, demographers, and criminologists in attempts to create and validate typologies and profiles of offenders, victims, crime scenes, and criminal activities.

Types of Profiling

The term *typology* has lent itself to the development of various forms of profiling that are now used as criminal investigative techniques from white-collar crimes to serial murder. The following forms of profiling will help to illustrate the emerging issues involved in criminal investigations. Geographical profiling and the scientific, empirically based offender profiling by David Canter and colleagues (2000) are both becoming leading approaches in criminal investigations. They can offer tremendous assistance to investigators in making profiling more scientific and precise. Investigative profiling today can be viewed from several perspectives:

1. **Offender Profiling**—Law enforcement agencies collect data, often using case studies or anecdotal information, which then are transformed into general descriptions of the types of persons most commonly associated with a certain type of criminal activity. This stereotyping is common in seeking out drug couriers and terrorists. This form of profiling can often be invasive and legally tenuous. Civil rights advocates quickly point out the flaws in using physical characteristics to profile criminals. Dodd (1998) also found that such profiling could be very misleading. For example, one might consider that people involved in fraudulent insurance claims usually are in need of money. The opposite was reported in Dodd's study of fraudulent insurance claimants. Of the 209 false claims, only 13% were in need of the money, whereas 57% earned a regular income. David Canter and S. Hodge along with Gabriella Salfati (1999) from England have made significant progress in elevating offender profiling from a street-level operation to a sophisticated approach to criminal investigation. Indeed, Canter (2000) takes umbrage with American profiling, stating that profiling was originally the purview of psychologists, not the FBI. He rejects the detective deductions of profiling as being anecdotal, "deductive, fictional hero" approaches to solving crimes through "gut-feeling" investigations (p. 26). Clinical observations alone are insufficient in making decisions about criminal behavior. Indeed, criminologists, psychologists, and psychiatrists have been ineffectual in accurately predicting criminal behavior. Our predictive capabilities are replete with *false positives*, or incorrectly predicting that someone will behave in a certain criminal manner. Canter (2000) believes that many profilers today operate under the guise of informed speculation. Like psychic detectives and astrologers, such profilers are shrouded in ambiguity and therefore can shift their explanations to fit the situation. In addition, Copson (1995) found that only 3% of profilers in his study of criminal cases actually helped to identify the offender.

   Canter (2000) and Farrington (1998) also remind us that psychology is germane to explaining a variety of crimes and that there are many differences *between* offenders and nonoffenders. Salfati and Canter (1999) established a scientific classification system of homicide crime scenes, offenders, and themes associated with those crime scenes. Canter promotes his *radex model* (Canter, 2011; Canter and Alison, 2000) as a powerful tool in differentiating criminals. Using his circle theory approach, Canter (2000) explains that mathematically, using a computer, criminal behavior can be examined and measured at a very general level (center of the circle) to more specific "styles of offending." As we move conceptually away from the circle center, we see more differentiation between offenders. The power of the radex model is that it identifies the salient aspects of a crime (Canter, Hughes, and Kirby, 1998). Kocsis, Cooksey, and Irwin (2002), in their study of offender characteristics in Australian sexual murders, examined 85 cases using the statistical tool of multidimensional scaling (MDS). The technique produced a five-cluster model of sexual-murder behavior. The central cluster represented typical behaviors to all patterns of sexual murder. Outlying patterns revealed "rape," "fury," "predator," and "perversion" zones, each with distinct offense styles. This empirical model of sexual murder underscores the complexity in understanding the dynamics in the relationship between sexual activity and violence. Approaching criminal profiling from a scientific, actuarial model is having a very impressive influence on proactive investigators. American law enforcement will benefit greatly by integrating profiling techniques with the computer modeling espoused by the Canter school.

Another prominent researcher in offender profiling is Dr. Gabrielle Salfati at John Jay College of Criminal Justice in New York City. In recent years Salfati has focused on research methods in offender profiling research (2011), psychological and methodological issues in measuring behavioral consistency in offenders (2008), and the Homicide Profiling Index (2006, 2007), a tool for measurements of crime scene behaviors. The Homicide Profiling Index (HPI) has both practical and theoretical applications. Salfati summarized three interlinked areas of profiling research: individual differentiation, behavioral consistency, and inferences about offender characteristics. *Individual differentiation* attempts to identify differences between the behavioral actions of offenders that can be used to identify subgroups of crime scene types. *Behavioral consistency* is used for understanding both the development of an offender's criminal career and an individual's consistency involving a crime series that can create linkages between crime scenes. *Drawing inferences about offender characteristics* applies consistency analysis to establish the links between subgroups of crime scene behaviors and subgroups of offender background characteristics. This can be used to make predictions about an offender based on the offender's criminal actions at the crime scene that in turn can assist police in narrowing their suspect pool.

2. **Victim Profiling**—Profilers identify the personality and behavioral characteristics of crime victims who tend to fall prey to certain types of offenders. Information can be gathered through personal records; interviews with witnesses, victims, family, and friends; crime scene examination; and autopsies. Investigators will enhance their effectiveness in murder investigations as victim–offender relationships are more closely scrutinized. Victims, even in death, are often storybooks about the offender and the circumstances of the crime.
3. **Equivocal Death Profiling**—Also referred to as *psychological autopsy*, investigators apply nonscientific information to explain the motivations of a person or group engaged in suicide pacts or difficult-to-explain deaths.
4. **DNA Profiling**—In recent years several cases of murder have been solved as a result of the advent of DNA profiling or genetic science. This includes

gathering DNA from crime scenes, victims, and offenders in efforts to match perpetrators to specific crimes. Between 1979 and 1986 a serial killer stalked, raped, and murdered at least six victims in Southern California. Newly found DNA evidence from rape kits found in archived cases conclusively linked these murders. Investigators then used other profiling techniques by examining the predator's stalking and killing habits to link the killer to four more murders.

5. **Crime Scene Profiling**—Also referred to as *criminal investigation analysis,* this form of profiling is based on the FBI model developed by its Behavioral Science Unit. Investigators focus on crime scene descriptions, photographs, offender behavior before and after the criminal act(s), traffic patterns, physical evidence, and victim information and place less credence on psychological data. Psychosocial data are compared to similar cases and investigators engage in an experiential-informational guessing technique to reconstruct the offender's personality. From the FBI's 1988 study of 36 serial sexual murderers, a dichotomy of offender characteristics was developed. The "organized" offender is methodical, premeditated, mature, resourceful, and usually involves sexual perversion in the offense. The "disorganized" type of killer was found to act much more randomly, opportunistically—opposite characteristics of the organized offender—and often with some form of mental disorder (Ressler et al., 1988). Their dichotomous profile includes the following characteristics:

Organized	*Disorganized*
Good intelligence	Average or low intelligence
Socially/sexually competent	Socially/sexually incompetent
Stable work history	Lack of stable work history
Controlled during crime	Anxious during crime
Living with someone	Living alone
Very mobile	Lives near crime scene
Follows investigation in media	Little interest in media
May leave town/change job	Little change in lifestyle
Uses alcohol prior to crime	Little alcohol use
Premeditated offense	Spontaneous offense
Victim a stranger	Victim or location unknown
Conversation with victim	Little conversation with victim
Demands submission	Sudden violence to victim
Uses restraints	Little use of restraints
Violent acts prior to death	Postmortem sexual acts
Body hidden	Body left in view
Weapon/evidence absent	Weapon/evidence often present
Transports body	Body left at scene

The problem with this dichotomous model is the lack of rigorous reliability and validity testing. Even though the model was used extensively by investigators, it did not have the utility previously thought. Kocsis, Irwin, and Hayes (1998) found that although there is some merit to the dichotomy, a more useful evaluation of criminal behaviors is necessary. Kocsis, Cooksey, and Irwin (2002) noted that

> this conceptual failing of the organized/disorganized dichotomy is more apparent when it is recognized that it makes no distinction between behaviors that commonly occur in all offenses and those that discriminate aspects of a specific offender. For example if an offender uses a knife in a sexual murder, this may not actually be a behavioral clue about the specific offender, but rather … simply a common behavior pattern observed in most sexual murders.… [S]ome incorrect offender characteristics could be concluded from the use of a knife when it truly just represents a common behavior amongst most sexual murders. This failing to empirically distinguish between common behaviors and those which are discriminatory of a specific individual is a flaw that prevails throughout much of the literature on profiling in general. (p. 5)

6. **Psychological Profiling**—Tracking the serial killer and the multitude of problems posed by such a task has led, in the past few years, to the development of psychological profiling, a tool used to prioritize a variety of homicides and other serious crimes. Psychological profiling, also known as criminal personality assessment, is applied to criminal behavior profiling, offender profiling, victim profiling, and crime scene profiling. It is used by law enforcement agencies in the United States, Canada, and Britain. Swanson, Chamelin, and Territo (1984) define the intent and purpose of this type of profiling:

> The purpose of the psychological assessment of a crime scene is to produce a profile, that is, to identify and interpret certain items of evidence at the crime scene that would be indicative of the personality type of the individual or individuals committing the crime. The goal of the profiler is to provide enough information to investigators to enable them to limit or better direct their investigations. (pp. 700–701)

Profilers match the personality characteristics of a certain type of offender with those of a suspect. Investigators use batteries of interviews and testing to establish their base of information. Experts are frequently called on to predict future behavior of offenders including pedophiles, child molesters, rapists, and other sexual deviants. The investigator usually has a particular offender that he or she is profiling. In efforts to improve the effectiveness and credibility of psychological, crime scene, and criminal profiling, organizations such as the Academy of Behavioral Profiling, founded by Brent Turvey, attract investigators and researchers interested in both the forensic and investigative criminal analysis.

7. **Geographical Profiling**—While investigators have been working to improve both crime scene profiling and psychological profiling, other researchers and investigators such as former detective Dr. Kim Rossmo from Canada have been actively developing a geographical approach to criminal investigations. Also referred to as spatial mapping, this technique combines geography and environmental criminology to connect crime scenes to offender habitats and hunting grounds. Such profiling is empirically based and has not placed much value on motivation or personality. It does help law enforcement personnel in deciding where to begin knocking on doors and setting up stakeouts. In the case of the "Railroad Killer," the offender had stayed near trains and therefore was likely a drifter or transient. The geographic similarities linked him to many killings and he was eventually identified, arrested, and sent to prison. A geographical profile includes the elements of *distance*, *mobility*, *mental maps*, and *locality demographics*. Offenders are profiled by the amount of distance covered by a serial offender. Some may travel because they have access to transportation, whereas others are limited in their access. This can create problems in profiling some serial offenders; for instance, Ted Kaczynski, the Unabomber, used buses to transport his bombs, or mailed them. *Mental maps* refer to an offender's cognitive images of his or her surroundings. As an offender becomes more comfortable with his tools and surroundings, the more likely he will be to expand those boundaries. Offender travel routes can be critical to a serial-murder investigation. Kim Rossmo (1999), one of the noted pioneers of geographic profiling, identifies four offender styles in hunting for victims:

    1. **Hunter**—identifies a specific victim in his home area.
    2. **Poacher**—prefers to travel away from home area for hunting victims.
    3. **Troller**—an opportunistic killer, he attacks victims while carrying out his regular activities.
    4. **Trapper**—a spider-and-fly scenario in which an offender enjoys laying a trap for a victim.

Rossmo (1995) conducted an impressive critical examination of serial-murder cases using data sets from the FBI and me. His eclectic approach to geographic profiling utilizes not only empirical data but also psychological information. A geographical profile includes a study of area maps, examination of crime scenes, interviews of witnesses and investigators, and knowledge of abduction and body dumpsites where serial murder is involved. Rossmo's Criminal Geographic Targeting, a computerized program, produces a topographical map based on crime scene information. The more crime scenes, the greater the predictive ability of the program. Using the 11 crime scenes of serial killer Clifford R. Olson, who raped, sodomized, and hammered boys and girls to death, Rossmo was able to pinpoint the killer's area of residence to within a four-block radius. In another case of serial rape, Rossmo used 79 crime scenes to pinpoint the actual basement of the offender's home as the location of the attacks. Scotland Yard, Dutch police, the FBI Behavioral Science Unit, and many other law enforcement agencies in need of better science to solve their cases frequently use Rossmo. Godwin (1999), in his work *Hunting Serial Predators*, prefers geographic profiling to the methods employed by the FBI because he feels that there is greater predictive value. Godwin, author of the computer program Predator, used for geographic profiling, believes that using both body dumpsites and locations of victim abductions or where they were last seen will provide the best results in locating the offender. Godwin refers to "landscape layouts" that include bars, nightclubs, red-light districts, economically depressed and poverty-ridden areas of a community, parking lots, jogging paths, rest stops, and college campuses as preying grounds for serial killers. The killer tends to hunt for victims in relation to where the offender works, lives, and carries out his routine daily activities. This geographic comfort zone becomes the hunting grounds for a serial offender. Geography is fast becoming a tool in offender profiling that law enforcement agencies can use with increasing accuracy.

Journey-to-Crime: Increasingly researchers are focusing on *environmental criminology* to better understand serial crime. Within this framework *journey-to-crime* research suggests that crimes are more likely to occur closer to an offender's domicile and that the farther away he or she travels from home base the fewer crimes he or she will commit. Serial predators prefer to operate within comfort zones, and experience a *distance decay function* as they leave that comfort zone. However, it is believed that serial predators usually create a buffer zone between their crimes and their residence. Hammond and Youngs (2011) note that it is unclear as to what form of decay function best characterizes this relationship. Different forms of decay functions are inevitable and imply a variety of psychological processes amongst offenders. Hammond and Youngs determined in their examination of decay functions and criminal spatial processes that while decay function has important theoretical relevance for understanding offender spatial behavior, variations of decay functions do not significantly impact the effectiveness of geographical profiling systems.

Routine Activity Theory (Cohen and Felson, 1979) expands this journey-to-crime approach, suggesting that crime occurs when an opportunity arises within noncriminal spatial activities including the normal areas an offender travels to and from work, recreation, school, and community activities. *Rational Choice Theory* suggests that offenders are more likely to act on their first opportunity in relation to their buffer zone. In short, the offender prefers to travel the least amount from home base to achieve the desired target all the while keeping attention away from his residence. *Crime Pattern Theory* (Brantingham and Brantingham, 1993) has expounded for many years that crime sites and opportunities to commit those crimes are not random. The theory focuses upon an offender's mental maps of his spatial surroundings and the availability of desired victims.

Conceptually these theories can be very useful in investigating serial crimes. One of the challenges, as more offender profiles are validated, is understanding these theories in relationship to the level of psychopathy of an offender. Do serial offenders who score high on the PCL-R also develop patterns of behavior similar to non-psychopathic offenders? Trojan and Salfati (2011), in their study of the linkages between criminal histories and crime scene behaviors in both single-victim and serial homicides, found that in only a small group of serial homicide offenders did they commit similarly themed prior offenses and homicide behaviors. They suggest this may raise questions about behavioral consistency underlying offender profiling. For a more complete review of all research that has been done evaluating the accuracy and usefulness of offender profiling, see Puniskis, M. J., and Gekoski, A. (2011) *Accuracy and usefulness of offender profiling: a review of the research.*

8. **Paraphilia Profiling**—As explained in Chapter 5, paraphilia profiling involves the identification of various forms of paraphilia engaged in by the sexual offender or sexual predator. Critical to the understanding of paraphilia is the role of relational paraphilic attachment (RPA) and how offenders explore their attachments through fantasy and behavior with their victims (see Chapter 5). Crime scenes are often replete with evidence of paraphilic behavior, ranging from those that appear to be rather innocuous to those that are extremely violent. Paraphilic behavior can be expressed in the use of specific language, behaviors, physical objects, sounds, smells, voices, and many others that are particular to the offender. This includes such things as the use of recording devices, ligatures, posing victims, photographs of victims, or specific weapons such as knives, hammers, scissors, etc. Also in the application of paraphilia profiling is the determination of the progression of the sex crime. Has the offender continued to use nonviolent courtship attachments such as voyeurism, frotteurism, and exhibitionism or has there been evidence of violent paraphilic attachments? This form of profiling needs much more research as it has great potential as a viable profiling technique.

   The following are two examples of profiling in action: In New York a police department submitted an unsolved case after months of intensive but futile investigation. A woman had been strangled and brutally beaten, her mutilated body left on the roof of the Bronx housing project where she had lived. FBI profilers suggested to police that they look for a white male, 25–35 years of age, who lived or worked in the area, a high school dropout, and living by himself or with one parent; very likely police had already interviewed him. A few months later police arrested a 32-year-old white male, a high school dropout, living with his father on the fourth floor of the victim's building. Police had interviewed the son but then removed him from their suspect list because he had been confined to a mental hospital at the time of the murder. Further investigation revealed that patients at the hospital were able to come and go as they wished (Barnes, 1986).

   In a second case, several young women had been killed in various states. As police began to gather data, agents noticed similarities in the modus operandi. Victims tended to be found along major interstate highways and trucking routes. Eventually a truck driver was arrested in the murders.

Problems in Profiling

Profiling can be very useful, but caution must be exercised to avoid constructing hasty or poorly grounded profiles that may lead investigators in wrong directions.

This inevitably places a strain on resources and, most importantly, additional lives may be lost. Errors in the information transmitted to NCAVC (National Center for the Analysis of Violent Crime), mistaken assessments by the evaluation team, and other potential glitches mean profiles can and do go wrong. In one case, for example, a profile on a criminal suspect told investigators the man they were looking for came from a broken home, was a high school dropout, held a marginal job, hung out in "honky tonk" bars, and lived far from the scene of the crime. When the attacker was finally caught, it was learned the psychological assessment was 100% wrong. He had not come from a broken home; he had a college degree, held an executive position with a respected financial institution, did not use alcohol, and lived near the scene of the crime. With this possibility for error, the bureau warns investigators not to become so dependent on the evaluation that they neglect other leads or become biased to the point where they blindly follow only the clues that match the scenario described in the profile's report (Goodroe, 1987, p. 31). In 1996, Richard Jewell, a security guard at the Olympic Games in Atlanta, Georgia, noticed an unattended knapsack. Concerned that it might contain a bomb, he immediately reported his findings to his superiors. While Olympic visitors were being evacuated, the sack exploded, killing one woman and injuring over 100 others. Jewell quickly became a suspect because he "fit" the profile of someone who would set a bomb and then become a hero for saving others. He seemed to be enjoying the sudden notoriety of the event and being recognized as a public hero. Investigators also noted that he had mentioned to the media how he hoped to land a permanent job with law enforcement after the games. Jewell became a prime suspect and quickly became subject to an intensive investigation. The media harassed him for several months before investigators were forced to admit that they had the wrong man. Indeed, not until November 2000 was Eric Robert Rudolph indicted, in absentia, for several bombings of abortion clinics and three Atlanta bombings, including the explosion at the Olympic Games. Sometimes profiling does not work simply because the offenders/crimes do not fit traditional profiles. Indeed, we cannot predict all behavior. In many mass murders the offender is often viewed by neighbors, friends, and coworkers as being such a "nice guy." Consider the case of Bruce Pardo, the Santa Claus Mass Murderer (see Profile 12.2). Was there anyone who could have predicted such an outcome?

Investigators must always be prepared for exceptions. For example, no one ever considered the possibility that the D.C. Sniper was really a team of two offenders and they were both African American. Even more unlikely was the fact that one of the killers was only in his teens (see Profile 12.3).

Sometimes investigators ignore or fail to understand offender profiles and are quick to rush to conclusions based on a piece of physical evidence. In the case of Cary Stayner, the Yosemite Park killer who had abducted and murdered a woman, her daughter, and her daughter's friend, four suspects were arrested. The suspects had some physical evidence that linked them to the murders. The FBI was adamant that the killers were behind bars. When interviewed by local media, I explained that the probability of these murders being committed by several people was very low. Given the facts of the case at that point, the profile,

PROFILE 12.2 Bruce Pardo, the Santa Claus Mass Murderer, 2008

Nine months before he would murder his ex-wife and eight of her family members, 45-year-old Bruce Pardo never let on to anyone his true feelings. He had lost his job at ITT Electronic Radar Systems in Van Nuys and his wife had begun divorce proceedings. She had discovered that Pardo had a son by another marriage but never disclosed it to her, nor the fact that due to his negligence, his son, who was a toddler at the time, had accidentally fallen into the family pool. Although Pardo rescued him, the son, now nine, sustained permanent brain damage and was confined to a wheelchair. Whatever Pardo was feeling he was careful not to reveal it to anyone. Instead, he carefully planned the Christmas Eve mass murder in Covina, California, six months in advance by purchasing hundreds of rounds of ammunition and building a device to spray highly flammable propellant throughout the home of his former in-laws. He had a Santa suit custom made extra large so he could conceal guns and ammunition. Months passed and on December 18 the divorce settlement was reached: he would get the house and cars and she would receive $10,000, along with her diamond wedding ring, and the family dog. By then Pardo had rented two getaway cars and booked a flight to Illinois. He had also planned on killing the divorce attorney and even Pardo's mother, who showed too much sympathy for his ex-wife. No threats were made, just calm half-smiles and much planning for the rampage.

That Christmas Eve Pardo arrived at 11:30 P.M. at his former in-laws' home wearing his Santa suit, carrying four guns and the fuel sprayer device. An eight-year-old girl opened the front door to greet Santa and was immediately shot in the face. Pardo calmly walked through the house shooting at the 25 people trying to escape. The nine people he killed were his ex-wife, her sister, her sister's 17-year-old son, both of her parents, and her two brothers and their spouses. Others were injured trying to escape. While spraying the house with propellant Pardo was also severely burned, yet he still managed to change clothes, shoot out the lights on the street, and drive to his brother's home 40 miles away. He wired the rental car with black powder that when ignited would set off hundreds of rounds of ammunition. Later the car exploded while a bomb squad was trying to dismantle the device. Knowing that he could not escape and probably in severe pain, Pardo killed himself in his brother's home with a single shot to the head. Police found $17,000 in cash strapped to his legs and waist along with his plane ticket to Illinois.

Loss is a stressor to all of us, but we differentially internalize it and respond to it. What do you think was the catalyst for Pardo's rampage? He had lost his job, his marriage, his dog, and money. More importantly, he was never going to escape the guilt and frustration of being responsible for his son's brain damage and the tremendous costs involved, both financially and emotionally. He faced the shame and guilt with his first family, and again, with his second wife and her family, he felt the scorn and ridicule, real or imagined. How can we profile someone like Pardo, who had no criminal record and no history of violence? It may be important to note that men are far more lethal than women when it comes to suicide. Men are three times more likely than women to commit suicide, and firearms are the weapon of choice. Some men, when they feel that they have lost everything that matters to them, feel empowered because they do not feel anything else can harm them more than what they have already experienced. It is a sense of trying to hang on just as long as humanly possible, and when playing by all the rules fails, there are no more rules, just decisions of who is going to die, when, and where. Death is no longer a deterrent; it is an embrace of finality and control. What do you think? Could Pardo have been stopped?

PROFILE 12.3 John Allen Muhammad and John Lee Malvo, the D.C. Snipers, 2002

Early in the morning on Wednesday, October 2, 2002, the first of many shots were fired that began a reign of terror transforming Washington, D.C., and the surrounding area into a killing field. Routine activities such as pumping gas, shopping, sitting on a bench, or waiting in a bus became matters of life and death. No one in public view was safe until the suspects were apprehended on October 24, 2002. These spree murders, however, did not begin in the D.C. Beltway area. Eight months earlier in Tacoma, Washington, Keenya Cook was home alone with her six-month-old daughter. She rose to answer the doorbell and was shot point blank in the face with a .45-caliber handgun. Her aunt had taken sides with Mildred, wife of John Allen Williams, during their separation/divorce proceedings, and was supposed to pay for that decision with her life. Instead, her niece Keenya died.

After the shooting, John Allen Williams, also known as John Allen Muhammad, left Tacoma with 17-year-old John Lee Malvo, his protégé and self-proclaimed stepson. On September 21, 2002, Kellie Adams was locking up the ABC Liquor Store in Montgomery, Alabama. She later recalled how she felt like she "had been hit by lightning" when a bullet entered her head. A moment later, Claudine Lee Parker, a coworker, was shot in the back and died almost instantly. Police, arriving at the scene, saw John Lee Malvo rummaging through a victim's purse. He escaped, leaving nothing behind except one fingerprint. Two days later, in Baton Rouge, Louisiana, Malvo and Muhammad were suspected of firing a single shot that killed Hong Im Ballenger as she left her job at the Beauty Depot. Malvo stole her purse and fled through the woods, evading bloodhounds and police. Ballistic examination linked the rifle used in the Louisiana shooting to the shooting in Alabama.

The South was no longer a safe haven for the two fugitives from Washington State. They began to move north and east, eventually ending up in the area surrounding the U.S. capital. At 5:20 P.M. on Wednesday, October 2, 2002, an unsuspecting shopper was walking in front of a craft store in Aspen Hill, Maryland. A shot rang out but it missed the shopper's head and shattered a plate glass window. After that attack there were no more misses. A few minutes later, in Silver Springs, Maryland, just two miles from the craft store, James D. Martin was killed in the parking lot of a grocery store where he had stopped to run an errand for his wife. He was a Vietnam veteran who was working as an analyst for the National Oceanic and Atmospheric Administration.

On October 3, 2002, at 7:41 A.M. in Rockville, Maryland, James Buchanan Jr. was mowing a client's lawn when he was shot once in the torso. He died a few minutes later. Three miles north and 31 minutes later, Premkumar Walekar was filling his cab with gasoline in preparation for his workday when he was shot and killed. A few minutes later and two miles north of the gas station where Walekar was shot, Sara Ramos was sitting on a bench in a small shopping center. She was shot once in the head and died at the scene. Five miles from the shopping center in Kensington, Maryland, at 9:58 A.M. Lori Ann Lewis-Rivera had stopped to vacuum out her minivan when a shot to the torso killed her. The snipers did not strike again until 9:15 P.M., when they killed an immigrant from Haiti, 72-year-old Pascal Charlot of Washington, D.C., while he walked his dog in his neighborhood.

One witness believed that he saw the suspects flee in a burgundy-colored Chevrolet Caprice. Another witness claimed that two men in a white van sped away after one of the shootings. In spite of looking at hundreds of white vans and meticulously investigating each of the victims, no usable information was discovered. Other than ballistics and location there appeared to be no common links. Schools were placed under emergency lockdown and children were kept away from windows; people left work early or remained home; nonessential appointments were canceled and customers stayed away from businesses.

The next day at 2:30 P.M. a rifle shot struck a woman while she was unloading packages into her minivan in a craft store parking lot. Despite being critically wounded, she survived. By this time ATF (Alcohol, Tobacco, and Firearms) agents had confirmed that the sniper had used a high-powered rifle using .223-caliber ammunition in at least four of the shootings. They concluded that the scarcity of witnesses could be explained only if the victims were shot from considerable distance. It was known that the weapon is considered accurate to up to 650 yards.

Except for the funerals, which began on Sunday, October 6, all was quiet in the Beltway area. The next day, a 13-year-old boy was being driven to school by his aunt. As she was driving away, she heard the report of a rifle and saw her nephew drop to the sidewalk. The media had recently reported that all the victims were adults and that children did not appear to be the target. The snipers immediately responded to the ill-fated public information. Investigators also discovered a tarot card with the message "Dear Policeman, I am God" written on it. Possibly the sniper was trying to establish a relationship with the police similar to the unsolved Zodiac case in San Francisco and the Son of Sam murders committed by David Berkowitz in New York.

Two days later on Wednesday, October 9, at 8:15 P.M., Dean Harold Meyers was filling his gas tank in Manassas, Virginia, when he was killed by a single shot. He was the seventh person to die and the ninth victim in the Beltway area. Despite an immediate response by law enforcement personnel, evidence was rare and witnesses unhelpful. The last three attacks had occurred near major highways and witnesses had repeatedly described a white van at the scene. Police responded by stopping dozens of white vans, but nothing was found. Two days later at 9:30 A.M., Kenneth Bridges was fatally shot while he stood filling his car with gasoline in Fredericksburg, Virginia. The attack occurred with a Virginia State Trooper parked within 50 yards of the station. The officer heard the shot but never saw the shooter. Once again, witnesses reported a white Chevy Astro Van leaving the scene. Authorities blocked all of the major arterial routes within minutes but failed to catch any suspects. By then law enforcement was swamped with as many as 1,000 calls per hour pouring into the hotline.

There were no killings during the weekend. Residents canceled outdoor events and avoided wooded areas and shopping areas immediately adjacent to main highways and intersections. On Monday at 9:15 P.M. the killing resumed. This time the victim was Linda Franklin, an FBI analyst from Arlington, Virginia, who was shopping with her husband. As they were loading their car she was shot in the head and died instantly. Again roadblocks produced no suspects. One alleged witness, Matthew Dowdy, reported that he saw the shooter, the gun, and the getaway car. It was not until Friday, October 18, that police determined Dowdy had fabricated his story. He was arrested and charged with "knowingly and willfully making a materially false statement to police."

The next shooting took place, for the first time, on a weekend. On Saturday, October 19, shortly before 8:00 A.M., a man was shot in the stomach as he was leaving the Ponderosa Steak House in Ashland, Virginia. He was critically injured but survived extensive abdominal surgery. In searching the area surrounding the restaurant,

(continued)

PROFILE 12.3 (Continued)

police found a note from the sniper. The killer once again claimed that he was God and blamed five of the deaths on police incompetence and for failure by police to respond to his phone calls. In addition, the sniper provided his bank account number, credit card data, and pin number so that authorities could deposit $10 million dollars. He finished the note with the chilling statement, "Your children are not safe anywhere at any time."

On Tuesday, October 22, 2002, Conrad Johnson, a bus driver, stood in the doorway of his empty bus in Aspen Hill, Maryland. A single shot fatally struck his abdomen. While no suspects were found, a bulletin with a composite description had been prepared in Alabama that linked John Allen Muhammad and his young companion John Lee Malvo to the sniper killings in that state. Montgomery County (MD) Police Chief Charles Moose, in turn, released a notice that the two were wanted for questioning in the Beltway killings and that they may be driving a blue Chevrolet Caprice with a New Jersey license plate. At the same time, federal investigators in Washington State examined a tree trunk on the property where Muhammad had once lived. Ballistic evidence linked him to the Beltway cases. A few hours later, at 3:19 A.M. on Thursday, October 24, the two suspects were arrested while asleep in their car at a rest stop in Frederick County, Maryland. They had been noticed by a truck driver, who had reported the sighting to the police. It was the end of 22 days of terror. The toll was 13 dead and 3 wounded. But who were these killers?

John Allen Williams grew up in Baton Rouge, Louisiana. He was raised by his grandmother and his aunts rather than by his biological parents. He joined the Muslim religion in 1988 and changed his name from Williams to Muhammad to honor this choice. His first marriage, in 1982, was to his high school sweetheart with whom he had one child. They divorced in 1988 and he married Mildred that same year. The second marriage produced three children and lasted until 2000. Both divorces were characterized by acrimonious arguments over the custody of the children. His second wife, Mildred, claimed that he was irrational and repeatedly threatened her life. She was worried that if the family continued to live together the children would suffer psychological damage as a result of his abuse.

He served in the Louisiana National Guard from 1978 to 1985; however, his service was not without incident and he was disciplined twice. The most serious offence was for striking a noncommissioned officer in the head. He enlisted in the army in 1985 and was posted to Fort Lewis, Washington State; Germany in 1990; Fort Ord, California, in 1992; and back to Fort Lewis in 1993. He did not receive sniper training in the military but did earn a marksmanship badge with an expert rating in the use of the M-16 rifle. During his military career, he served as a combat engineer, a metal worker, and a water transport specialist. He was discharged in 1994 and then served in the Oregon National Guard until 1995.

Despite his tendency toward violence, his early record is remarkably free of arrests. He was suspected in a shoplifting incident, he was arrested twice for driving without a license, but he never was convicted or served time for any offense. He was not a competent businessman but entered into partnerships in a karate studio and an auto repair business that both failed. In late March 2000, he took his three children and fled to Antigua. He met and lived with a woman who had a son, John Lee Malvo. Muhammad returned to the United States and was joined by the boy and his mother, who entered the United States illegally in 2001 in Washington State. Muhammad formed a close relationship with the boy and they began traveling together, while the mother seemed to drop out of the picture. In August of 2001, they lived in a homeless shelter north of Seattle where John Lee attended school for a few months. They left the area in February 2002 and went to Alabama. They moved from there to Louisiana and finally to Washington, D.C.

John Lee Malvo was a child without a father. His mother brought several men into his life but none with whom he could form a close bond. John's mother was often away working on other Caribbean islands trying to earn enough money to take care of herself and her son. Consequently, as a young teen, he was left on his own to care for himself. By the time John Muhammad came into his life the teen was ready to follow anyone who showed him kindness and attention. The young Malvo had no idea of the motives of his mentor and quickly became his protégé. Muhammad trained John to fire a rifle and eventually introduced him to friends as his sniper. Like other cases of spree and serial murder where more than one assailant is involved, there is usually one offender who serves as the leader. In this case, a 41-year-old man seduced a vulnerable 17-year-old boy into shooting innocent people. Over time the vulnerable Malvo eagerly embraced the sport of killing.

Theories abounded as to the identity of the killer, including the theory of a possible deranged killer from Taliban sleeper cells. Several criminal profilers were consulted and assisted in the investigation, but ultimately no one had it completely right. No one picked two black men, one still a teen, to be the killers. Profiling was criticized as ineffective for failing to figure out who the offenders were in time to save lives. In the end, it was the offenders themselves who made contact with law enforcement and provided clues that eventually led to their capture. Questions were raised because the offenders did not fit the profile of people who commit such crimes. In truth, every case of serial, spree, or mass murder has established profiles that describe general characteristics of offenders who commit such crimes. What made the D.C. Snipers unique was the fact that they were black and that there were two of them. This alone made the case an anomaly even among those who are multiple-homicide offenders. Sometimes, even in best-case scenarios, there are cases that fail to "fit the profile."

The motivations for this case, however, are common to almost all such offenders. John Muhammad had lost his job; Mildred, his wife, had separated from him and filed a restraining order against him. When he abducted his children and left the country, the FBI found him and returned the children to their mother. At 41 he was angry at the American government for taking his children; he had no money and no resources. He was happy that the World Trade Center Towers were destroyed and felt it was justified. In short, he had lost his voice in a society that measures success by one's education, employment, financial resources, and family stability. John Muhammad had lost everything and wanted vengeance. Meeting John Malvo provided him with someone to assist him in that quest. Muhammad was convicted and sentenced to death, while Malvo received life in prison without the possibility of parole (Hickey and Deal, 2003).

Muhammad was executed in 2009. In 2011 Mildred publicly spoke about her relationship with Muhammad. She stated that he had suffered from PTSD and during their time together he had become increasingly reclusive and psychologically abusive. He told Mildred that she was his enemy and that he would kill her. To save herself and her children she went into a federal protection program, changed her name, and relocated. Today she heads an organization to counter domestic violence and is the author of the book *Scared Silent.*

given the manner in which the victims were killed, strongly suggested that this was the work of a lone predator. The suspects were also petty criminals and drug dealers, hardly the types of offenders who suddenly carry out such sadistic sexual murders. Months passed and I continued to maintain that the real offender was still free to kill while these common criminals sat in jail. Then another brutal murder occurred involving a Yosemite Park worker, Joie Armstrong. She had been decapitated. Some investigators still maintained that the men in custody were the killers of the three park tourists. Much of that line of thinking was discarded when Cary Stayner not only confessed to the Armstrong murder but also to the other three killings. It was the manner in which the victims were killed that linked the cases. These were sexual killings where decapitation becomes part of the sexual experience. Certainly this was not the work of petty criminals. I drew my conclusions based on information about how the victims died and, using a psychological profile, determined that the killings were the work of a lone sexual predator. Stayner was sentenced to life in prison, no parole, for the Joie Armstrong case and was convicted in the three tourists' murders (author's files). The profile can be a useful tool but, like any tool, it can be misused. Profiles can complement crime scene investigations and strengthen interagency and interdisciplinary cooperation.

NCAVC AND VICAP

In 1984, the U.S. Department of Justice, composed of the Office of Justice Programs, the National Institute of Justice, and the Office of Juvenile Justice and Delinquency Prevention, along with the Federal Bureau of Investigation in conjunction with the Criminal Justice Center at Sam Houston State University in Huntsville, Texas, established the National Center for the Analysis of Violent Crime (NCAVC). This center serves as a clearing house and resource for law enforcement agencies involved in "unusual, bizarre and/or particularly vicious or repetitive violent crime" (Brooks, Devine, Green, Hart, and Moore, 1987). The NCAVC, at the time of its creation, was composed of four core programs: Research and Development; Training; Profiling and Consultation; and the Violent Criminal Apprehension Program (ViCAP).

ViCAP, now defunct, was located in the Behavioral Science Unit (BSU) in Quantico, Virginia, and served as a national clearing house for reports involving solved or unsolved homicides, attempted homicides, abductions, missing persons where violence is suspected, and unidentified dead bodies involving homicides. In turn, ViCAP provided law enforcement agencies "reporting similar pattern violent crimes with the information necessary to initiate a coordinated multiagency investigation so that they might expeditiously identify and apprehend the offender(s) responsible for the crimes" (Brooks et al., 1987, p. 41). Once patterns were established by ViCAP staff involving victimization, physical evidence, information about the suspect(s), modus operandi, and so on, the multiagency coordination was set into motion. Cavanagh and MacKay (1991, pp. 5–6) point out that criminal profiles are compiled in a variety of cases including those involving postmortem mutilations, torture, child molestations and abductions, bank robberies, serial arson, lust murders, and serial murder.

Ressler and his colleagues (1988) summarized the actual step-by-step process provided by ViCAP: When a new case was entered, the ViCAP computer system simultaneously compared and contrasted over 100 selected modus operandi (MO) categories of that case with all other cases stored in the database. After overnight processing, a printed computer report was returned to the ViCAP crime analyst handling the case. This report listed, in rank order, the top-10 "matches" in the violent crime databank, that is, the 10 cases that were most similar to the new case. This crime pattern analysis technique, called *template pattern matching*, was specifically designed for ViCAP and programmed by the FBI Technical Services Division. The ViCAP computer system also produced selected management information system reports that monitored case activity geographically, with hope that it would eventually trace the travels of serial violent criminals across the United States (Ressler et al., 1988, p. 113).

In June 1985, ViCAP became operational, and within the first year several problems were recognized with the system. More sophisticated computer programs had to be installed to sufficiently manipulate and analyze the large amounts of data and properly develop case matching. In addition, ViCAP received fewer cases than expected, and a good understanding of cases from reported data was more difficult to achieve than anticipated (Ressler et al., 1988, p. 118).

Certainly NCAVC and ViCAP had the potential to move forward in the battle against violent and nonviolent criminals. Even though tracking serial killers was a top priority, other offender data were also being collected and analyzed; for example, Hazelwood and Burgess (1989) conducted research into serial rapists. However, ViCAP was sharply criticized by the media as not having caught any criminals (Allen, 1988). One of the problems was the limited cooperation of other local and state police agencies. Considering that there are over 17,000 law enforcement agencies in the United States, many of which operate on shoestring budgets, it is not surprising that the flow of information to the federally operated control center was less than overwhelming. ViCAP was eventually viewed as a program that could not meet agency expectations. Lack of concern for validity, reliability, and constructing a theoretical basis in the BSU's research brought into question the utility of profiling as articulated by the FBI (Rossmo, 1995).

By 1995, the FBI's Behavioral Science Unit in Quantico, Virginia, had faced severe funding cuts and reorganization. Today, the BSU is now known as the Investigative Support Unit (ISU), part of the Critical Incident Response Group at the FBI Academy. Much of its functions are the same but are more streamlined, more effective.

Fox and Levin (1995) remind us that the ISU becomes involved primarily in the most difficult cases requiring additional investigative techniques and insight. Ressler and his colleagues (1988) also noted, "VICAP's purpose was not to investigate cases but to analyze them" (p. 119). Ressler is correct in his observation. Jackson, van Koppen, and Herbrink (1993) and Jackson, van den Eshd, and de Kleurer (1994) observed that profiles do not directly apprehend offenders because they are a management instrument in assisting specific criminal investigations. During the next several years NCAVC and the ISU will continue to improve the quality and sophistication of computer programs, reporting methods, and analytical procedures. One hopes that, in years to come, those who operate the unit will continue to refine definitions of serial killing, which generally have focused on lust killers who move about the country. Serial killers who are place-specific, those who do not become sexually involved with victims, and female serial offenders all warrant recognition and appropriate inclusion in NCAVC files. We may never have female lust killers in our society, but, as has been presented in this research, women simply choose other methods of murder and have proven they are capable of mass murders and serial killings. The NCAVC program is a developing tool that law enforcement personnel can use to assist in investigations.

The NCAVC is not alone—agencies in Washington have developed a Homicide Investigation Tracking System (HITS); in New York the Homicide Assessment and Lead Tracking (HALT); Homicide Evaluation and Assessment Tracking (HEAT) in New Jersey; in Indiana the Criminal Apprehension Assistance Program (ICAAP); in Canada the RCMP Violent Crime Linkage Analysis System (ViCLAS); and in England the Police Research Group (PRG) of the British Home Office (Rossmo, 1995). Important advances are being made to merge the sciences into a cohesive investigative tool. Rossmo (1995), in his seminal work using geographic profiling, applied geographic concepts in the analysis of criminal target patterns. He analyzed relationships between offender residence and crime-site locations. This applied science of profiling merges both theoretical and structural frameworks into an increasingly useful investigative tool. Additional tools such as DNA profiling play a significant role in connecting samples of semen and blood from crime scenes to offenders. Currently, a national DNA identification index merging federal, state, and local data into the Combined DNA Index System (CODIS) provides a forensic index for unsolved crimes and a convicted offender index for known felons. Other indices such as those for missing persons and unidentified bodies are also in the planning stages. The Automated Fingerprint Identification System (AFIS) used to identify Richard Ramirez, the Night Stalker of Los Angeles, has also become more useful in police investigations (Rossmo, 1995, pp. 83–85). However, we must not forget that tools are for assisting investigations. In the final analysis, it is the police or agents in the cities and towns throughout America who, using the available tools, must track down and apprehend the serial killers.

At the investigation level, Keppel (1989) examined the *solvability factors* involved in serial murder and found the most important ones to be:

1. Quality of police interviews with eyewitnesses
2. Circumstances that led to the initial stop of the murderer
3. Circumstances that established probable cause to search and seize physical evidence
4. Quality of the investigations at the crime scene(s)
5. Quality of the scientific analysis of the physical evidence (p. 4)

This last solvability factor often becomes critical in multiple-homicide investigations because they can include an enormous amount of physical evidence taken from the crime scene(s), from the offender(s) and his or her possessions, and from victims and their possessions. Forensic science has become a valuable tool in linking suspects to the crime scenes and in identifying evidence. Regional labs, such as the Atlanta Crime Laboratory, are used to analyze physical evidence from crime scenes in many states. For example, in the Atlanta child murders, a great deal of hair-fiber evidence was catalogued and eventually used to convict Wayne Williams. Other types of forensic evidence inspection and analysis now performed in crime labs include the following:

1. Glass and soil fragments
2. Organic analysis such as elements, compounds, chromatography, spectrophotometry, and mass spectrometry
3. Inorganic analysis such as atomic absorption spectrophotometry and neutron activation analysis
4. Hair, fibers, and paint analysis including typing and identification
5. Drug analysis such as narcotics, stimulants, depressants, and hallucinogens
6. Toxicological analysis such as alcohol, drugs, poisons
7. Arson analysis including flammable residues and explosives
8. Serological analysis including blood, bloodstains, and semen
9. Fingerprinting analysis including classification, detection, and preservation of prints
10. Firearms and toolmarks including analysis of bullets, gunpowder residue, primer residue, serial number restoration, and so forth
11. Document and voice analysis such as handwriting comparisons, typewriting, alterations, erasures, obliterations, and voice examinations
12. DNA testing and typing, and use of the combined DNA Index System (Saferstein, 2004)

The University of Tennessee Forensic Anthropology Center

Also known internationally as "The Body Farm," this two-acre site has received over hundreds of corpses since its founder, forensic anthropologist Dr. William Bass, opened the facility in 1971. There are currently five such facilities operating in the United States, each connected to a university research center. Researchers in Tennessee study the decomposition of the human body, and with that information crime scene investigators now have another tool in homicide investigations. Researchers focus on two primary areas: to observe bodies decomposing under controlled conditions such as placing the corpse in water, on dry land, buried in shallow versus deep graves, or placed in containers; and to skeletonize the remains in order to add them to the research collection at the center. Families of the deceased donate between 40–50 bodies yearly.

The facility studies the decomposition of bodies in sunlight versus shade, changes in body mass during decomposition, effects of insect activity during decomposition, ground-penetrating radar research of buried remains, and assessments of the early (first two weeks) stages of decomposition. At death two things happen: First the enzymes in the digestive system begin to eat from the body, causing the tissues to liquefy. This process is known as *putrefaction*. Second is insect activity as maggots quickly consume the rotting flesh. The insect activity is critical in determining how long the body has been dead. This research helps homicide investigators identify the actual time of death, which in turn corroborates or discredits alibis of suspects. The FBI also uses the facility for training purposes as agents dig for bodies in simulated crime scenes.

Cold Case Files: Unsolved Murder Series

At the time of this writing serial killers roam the streets of Los Angeles, Chicago, and New York. The killers are going after "strawberries," or prostitutes who sell sex for drugs. Several women will be murdered. Regardless of the motive, offenders who want to kill young women can find easy targets among prostitutes. Dealing with strangers is their trade, and someone who decides to start killing prostitutes can go undetected for years.

One serial-murder case (1988–1989) occurred in the Boston area where at least eight prostitutes were found dumped in woods along the interstate highways. Similar stories can be related about missing and murdered young women in Kansas City, Missouri (1988), and the Washington, D.C., area (1987). A small sampling of other unsolved cases includes the 1983 Joliet, Illinois, murders, 15 victims; the 1976 killings in the Detroit area, 7 victims; the 1974 "Los Angeles Slasher" case, involving 8 victims; the "Texas Strangler" case of 1968–1971, involving 11 victims; the 1967 Kenosha, Wisconsin, murders of 7 victims; the 1956 Chicago serial killings of 5 people; the 1935 "Mad Butcher of Cleveland" case that yielded 12 victims; and the 1906 Chicago, Illinois, murders of at least 20 victims. In 2011 and 2012 a serial killer, Itzcoatl Ocampo, 23, an Iraqi war veteran whose father was homeless, stabbed four homeless men to death in Orange County, California. Often these types of cases may require many years of investigation because there are few if any witnesses and/or there is little physical evidence that can link suspects to the crime scenes.

The Hunt for the Unabomber

Homicide detectives know that their tools for murder investigations are changing with technology. DNA matching and fingerprinting, now computerized, enormously facilitate the ability of investigators to match and locate offenders. The Automated Fingerprint Identification System, or AFIS, codes specific points from crime scene fingerprints and stores them in a memory bank that can be compared to millions of other prints in just moments. Some officers are now resorting to voice-stress analysis in looking for deception when a suspect refuses to answer questions. Others are learning the art of kinetic interviewing, which is the science of reading body language to measure deception. Even though "hunches" will always find a place in law enforcement, those "gut feelings" will increasingly find their origins in forensic science.

This fact has never been clearer than in the case of Ted Kaczynski, the Unabomber, an American serial bomber who eluded capture for 18 years. During the course of this investigation three consecutive UNABOM Task Forces were organized to coordinate interagency cooperation. Several years would pass sometimes before the Unabomber would strike again leaving fresh clues but no arrests. Some agents spent half of their careers hunting for this one offender. Using every available tool, this task force assembled some of the nation's most skilled and insightful investigators. Profile 12.4 is a brief synopsis of the case, including the author's profile of the man referred to as the Unabomber.

Women, of course, are not the only targets. The "Executioner" in Los Angeles (1986) killed at least nine male transients. Vagrants, like prostitutes, are accessible and vulnerable. Occasionally homosexuals, usually males, become the target of someone who has decided it is time to cleanse the Earth of people he or she perceives as wicked. More often it becomes evident that such killers are themselves homosexuals. (However, this does not mean that homosexuals are given any more to violent pathologies than heterosexuals. Although there have been a number of homosexually related serial killings, those figures do not appear to be disproportionate to other types of serial killings.)

When we take into account the fact that serial killers operate in nursing homes, hospitals, and private homes as well as in and around cities and in different states, it is not surprising that we are faced with what appears to be an increasing number of unsolved cases. According to media reports, the United States is being "inundated" with serial killers, most of whom are extremely difficult, if not impossible, to apprehend, and law enforcement and the criminal justice system are unable to effectively stop serial killers. However, such criticism of law enforcement may be premature, if not inappropriate. Law enforcement, in many cases, is doing a much better job than anyone realizes. For example, it is quite plausible that law enforcement personnel actually apprehend many would-be multiple-homicide offenders for one or two murders, thus stopping them before they can commit more. On what can we base this assumption? We know that prison populations comprise an estimated 20% to 30% of psychopathic or antisocial personality types. These types of offenders are considered to be the most dangerous because they are more prone to violent behavior. Certainly not all psychopaths are prone to violent behavior, nor do all those in prison have the propensity to harm others, but many do. We also know that such offenders have the highest rates of recidivism for criminal behavior and time in prison. An argument could then be made that many psychopaths who have been apprehended would have killed if they had not been arrested. Most of them are caught as a result of their own blunders and the good investigative skills of the police.

In 1990, Richard Walter, an American forensic psychologist for the Michigan prison system, cofounded the Philadelphia Vidocq Society along with Frank Bender, a forensic sculptor, and William Fleisher, a U.S. Customs Service agent. (Eugène François Vidocq [1775–1857], a French criminal turned police

PROFILE 12.4 Theodore Kaczynski, the Unabomber, 1978–1996

Starting out as an apparent terrorist bombing, the Unabomber case became the largest and most expensive manhunt in American history, spanning 18 years. The subject of radio talk shows, television documentaries, and hundreds of newspaper articles, the Unabomber attracted worldwide attention. A one million dollar reward was offered for information leading to the arrest of the elusive killer. Code-named "Unabomber" because of the universities and airlines he targeted in his earlier bombings, the Unabomber rose from a relatively obscure criminal status to someone of national recognition. The Unabomber killed three people (two in California and one in New Jersey) and injured 23 others, his attacks spanning nine states. Several victims were university professors or people directly related to technology.

By 1996, over 100 agents from the FBI, the U.S. Postal Service, and the Bureau of Alcohol, Tobacco, and Firearms were working together as the UNABOM Task Force, along with the assistance of local and state law enforcement. Since the first bombing in 1978, this was the third and largest such task force to be assembled. Agent Tony Muljat, working full time on this case for 11 years, waived his retirement in hopes of bringing the case to closure. Staging his first attack in Chicago, the Unabomber appeared to relocate and was thought to be living in Northern California, possibly near Sacramento or San Francisco. Eight of the sixteen bombings either occurred in Northern California or bombs were mailed from that area. From 1993 on, all his letters and bombs were mailed from the San Francisco Bay area. The following list chronicles the Unabomber attacks.

Unabomber Attacks

Place	Date	Number of Victims
1. University of Illinois at Chicago, IL	5/25/78	1 injured
2. Northwestern University, Evanston, IL	5/9/79	1 injured
3. American Airlines Flight 444, Chicago, IL	11/15/79	12 injured
4. President, United Airlines, Chicago, IL	6/10/80	1 injured
5. University of Utah, Salt Lake City, UT	10/8/81	
6. Vanderbilt University, Nashville, TN	5/5/82	1 injured
7. University of California, Berkeley, CA	7/2/82	1 injured
8. Boeing Aircraft, Auburn, WA	5/8/85	
9. University of California, Berkeley, CA	5/15/85	1 injured
10. University of Michigan, Ann Arbor, MI	11/15/85	2 injured
11. Rentech Company, Sacramento, CA	12/11/85	1 death
12. CAAM's Inc., Salt Lake City, UT	2/20/87	1 injured
13. Physician/researcher, Tiburon, CA	6/22/93	1 injured
14. Yale University, New Haven, CT	6/24/93	1 injured
15. Advertising executive, North Caldwell, NJ	12/9/94	1 death
16. Timber lobbyist, Sacramento, CA	4/24/95	1 death

Several physical and psychological profiles were constructed around the Unabomber. The task force believed, for example, that he was a white male probably in his 40s. He was seen once in 1987 by a secretary as he hand-delivered a bomb. Only in the later years of his career did the Unabomber begin to communicate with the public. He increasingly expressed his disdain for law enforcement personnel, while at the same time he appeared to enjoy taunting and challenging them. Although such occurrences are rare, some serial killers, such as the Unabomber and the Zodiac Killer from San Francisco, have enjoyed matching wits with law enforcement. The Unabomber had a history of sending bombs and then remaining silent for periods of time. One hiatus was six years. His bomb-making skills improved markedly in sophistication. The devices were pipe bombs with anti-movement or anti-opening firing switches. He evolved from using smokeless powders to a mixture of ammonium nitrate and aluminum powder. He took time to handcraft his devices using wood and metal components.

He claimed to be part of a clandestine organization named the Freedom Club. The Unabomber signed his letters with the initials "FC" and also carefully inscribed "FC" on his bombs. In 1995 he mailed a 35,000-word "Manifesto" to the *Washington Post* and *New York Times*, demanding that his work be published or the bombings would continue. The Manifesto was a redundant diatribe of denunciations against technology, advocating the dismantling of industrial technology and the redistribution of human society. The Unabomber stated that the evils of technology would eventually destroy our society, and he felt it was his role to bring public attention to pending societal doom. The Unabomber viewed killing a few people in order to get the public's attention as completely justifiable. The task force, along with the media, faced a difficult dilemma: Do we choose not to be held hostage by this killer and run the risk of another attack or submit to his demands in order to save a life and perhaps forestall a near-inevitable bombing? In order to spare another attack and in hopes that someone in the community might recognize the writing, the *Washington Post* published the Manifesto. The Manifesto was also made available on the Internet's World Wide Web.

Investigations focused on several individuals, including a sailor, a handyman, and a career criminal, but they all were eliminated as suspects. Some investigators speculated that James William Kilgore, a fugitive with ties to the Symbionese Liberation Army who went underground after a bombing incident in 1976, could have been the Unabomber. Other investigators dismissed Kilgore as a viable suspect and looked for new leads in the investigation. For example, investigators looked at possible religious connections and the Unabomber's frequent usage of biblical names. Investigators also examined commonalities between the bombings and specific people involved in the technology of developing prosthetic devices.

The final suspect (there were many) in this profile was Theodore Kaczynski. Federal agents near Lincoln, Montana, arrested him in 1996. His brother had read the Manifesto and noticed striking similarities between some letters written by his brother and the manuscript. Ted Kaczynski was living a hermit's life in a 10′ by 12′ shack without electricity or plumbing. Inside, investigators found letters and diaries connected to the bombings, various materials used in bomb construction, several detailed blueprints for bomb making, a partially completed bomb, a completed bomb that had been packaged and partially addressed, a list of potential victims, typewriters (one of which appeared to be the one on which the Manifesto was typed), clothing similar to that worn when the Unabomber was seen delivering a bomb in Salt Lake City, and possibly the original Manifesto manuscript.

(continued)

PROFILE 12.4 (Continued)

Born in 1942, Ted proved to be very intelligent, graduating two years early from high school. At age 16 he started his university studies at Harvard on a scholarship. Throughout his formal education Ted was perceived by others to be a loner who shunned potential friends. In 1967 he earned a doctorate in math from the University of Michigan and began teaching that same year as an assistant professor at the University of California, Berkeley. Three semesters later he suddenly resigned from his position and began living a transient lifestyle. He relocated to Montana and also spent time working at odd jobs in Utah. In 1978, and shortly after the first attack by the Unabomber, his brother David hired him to work in a foam rubber manufacturing company. He tried dating a female coworker but after two dates she ended the relationship. Ted retaliated by posting limericks about her around the office. When confronted by his brother, Ted became angry. The harassment incidents resulted in Ted being fired by his brother. Ted returned to Montana and became more reclusive. In 1990 his father, dying of cancer, committed suicide. Ted did not attend the funeral.

Ted appeared to have harbored much resentment against his family and society in general. He sent a letter to his mother referring to her as a "dog" because of his inability to form lasting relationships. His brother David, with whom he had been close in younger years, married and began a career. In many respects Ted appeared to have perceived himself as rejected or abandoned by those supposedly closest to him. His reclusive lifestyle may well have exacerbated a growing sense of paranoia about people and society.

I served as a consultant to the UNABOM Task Force and profiled the Unabomber to be a man of low self-esteem who thrived on the notoriety he has achieved. The Unabomber did not impress me as a true believer in the evils of technology. His desire to return to a pristine lifestyle appeared to cover a more systemic motivation. He used the issue of technology to promote his own self-interests, frustrations, sense of rejection, and anger. He reconstructed history to justify his behavior. He did not want people to see him as a terrorist but as one who cared for the welfare of his society. The Unabomber appeared to have cared for no one but himself. An intelligent man, the Unabomber probably engaged in jobs requiring little of his intellect. He was more of a thinker than a doer. The only things he ever completed were his

investigator, became legendary at his ability to solve crimes. He is known today as one of the fathers of modern criminal investigations.) The organization is comprised of forensic specialists dedicated to solving cold cases. Walter has also made substantial contributions in developing our current understanding of criminal investigations profiling. A year after the group formed they solved their first case. Today there are over 150 members of this elite group of investigators who focus on solving homicides and some cases of missing persons.

In recent years many police departments, often in tandem with their local district attorneys' office, have developed cold case homicide units. For example, in 2001 the LAPD, with the assistance of the DA's office, established their Cold Case Homicide Unit. Using DNA analysis and CODIS, the unit has solved, by the end of 2011, the murders of 92 victims killed between 1960 and 2005. Of those 92 cases, 67 were solved using DNA analysis. In addition, the unit has arrested seven serial killers responsible for over 40 murders. In 2003, LAPD bombs, and they were all about him. Ted Kaczynski, a man of rationalization and unconscious pretense, "fit" the Unabomber profile.

His need to validate his life may have driven him to seek the limelight. Ted did not appreciate being "upstaged" by other criminals. For example, at the time of the World Trade Center explosion in February 1993, he had been inactive for over six years. Just over four months after the blast, Ted struck again twice. His message was very clear: You may be able to catch those amateurs, but I am still here, after all these years. Then, on April 19, 1995, terrorists struck the Federal Building in Oklahoma City, Oklahoma, killing nearly 168 people. Turning to an associate, I commented that the Unabomber would strike soon because once again he had been upstaged and would no longer be getting the media attention he craved. A few days later a timber lobbyist in Sacramento, California, became the third murder victim of the Unabomber.

Ted Kaczynski, the Unabomber, was a walking facade. His self-pity drove him to envy. Besides his drive for recognition, Ted also found pleasure in depriving others of their talents, skills, and livelihoods by sending devices that would blow off their fingers, hands, faces, or destroy eyesight. Unable to achieve the successes and attention earned by real scientists and scholars, he did not want them to have the rewards either. He rejected technology because he perceived that technology had rejected him. In truth, Kaczynski appears to be a man of many contradictions, frustrations, and self-deceptions. Ultimately, he is nothing more than other serial killers who rear their ugly heads; he just found an innovative way to do it.

The trial was relatively brief. Kaczynski was found to be guilty but a paranoid schizophrenic and confined to federal prison in Florence, Colorado, with no possibility of parole. Ted Kaczynski continues his reclusiveness in the confines of his small prison cell on "bomber row" with other notorious figures, where he continues to vehemently insist that he is neither schizophrenic nor insane. His notoriety has influenced a few living on the fringes of our society to emulate him. Regardless of the eccentric nature of the messenger, the message that Kaczynski was sending appeals to many who feel they cannot compete or be comfortable in a society that is so dominated by fast-paced technology.

investigators picked up a cup of coffee used by Adolph Laudenberg, a suspect in four murder cases between 1972 and 1975. A DNA profile was established from his saliva that matched to the DNA he left when he committed the murders. Chester Turner, another Los Angeles sexual predator, who killed 10 victims between 1987 and 1998, was caught after DNA linked him to the murders. A mentally handicapped janitor who had spent 10 years of his life in prison for those murders was exonerated and released.

Some police departments do not have the resources to have a designated unit but still have detectives who dedicate themselves to solving cold cases. Another approach to handling cold case files is the creation of cold case review teams (CCRT). These teams, similar to a cold case homicide unit, are comprised of investigators who meet periodically to reexamine old cases and how new technologies might be applied to their investigations. These teams select cases based upon solvability factors, resources, and time needed to investigate them.

PROFILE 12.5 Larry DeWayne Hall, 1980–1994

Larry DeWayne Hall, 48, is currently serving a natural life sentence with no possibility of parole in Butner federal psychiatric prison in North Carolina. Larry has been incarcerated for the past 18 years for the abduction and murder of Jessica Roach, 15, in 1994. Unlike other serial killers, Larry is clearly not comfortable doing interviews. He has very low self-esteem and believes that he is not attractive to women. His fraternal twin brother Gary reinforced those feelings of insecurity when they were children. Part Native American, Larry is about 5'5", stocky, with powerful arms, and has a passion for cars and especially Hemming engines. A man with high school education, he has only known manual labor. His graying beard, quiet, controlled monotone voice, and nervous half-smile mask the darkness of allegedly one of America's most prolific serial killers of all time. He does not display the typical narcissism so often found in psychopathic serial killers. Larry wants to be liked by everyone, especially the other inmates. More than anything, he fears death for himself. He expresses concern for his aging and ailing mother, who lives in a nursing home, and fears losing her. These are not the characteristics usually seen in serial killers, but then Larry is no stereotypical murderer.

Larry was contacted by investigators regarding the disappearances of several female college students in northern Indiana. Tricia Reitler disappeared from near her dorm at Indiana Wesleyan University in 1993 and has never been found. Anxious to be cooperative, Larry provided a list of 38 names of young women. Except for two names on the list who were prostitutes, all the rest were college students whose whereabouts are unknown. Of course, if Larry is not a serial killer but wanted to implicate himself he had plenty of time while incarcerated to research these missing persons online. What is compelling to investigators is the fact that Larry was an avid Civil War reenactor, who, with a full Confederate uniform, traveled to many states to participate in these events. He even made it as an extra in the movie *Glory* with Matthew Broderick, a reenactment of Gettysburg. These missing women vanished at approximately the same times Larry was in their area playing soldier. Later Larry added three more names and declared that this one was his "best": three female college students, all roommates, went out to dinner one evening and upon returning home they went to their separate rooms. They were never seen again, nor was there any sign of struggle.

Larry talks about how he killed women without identifying any specific victims. His preference was to stalk the women while driving his van, abduct them using a knife, and take them out into wooded areas. A few victims voluntarily entered his van but most required force. The knife was not as effective as he needed because he

These may be sex crimes cases, homicides, and other crimes of violence. Some of these teams also receive grant money to support their ongoing investigations. Consider the case of Larry Hall, an admitted serial killer currently in prison for the murder of a female college student (see Profile 12.5). He has provided information that links him to dozens of murders of young females who are missing. However, without knowing where the bodies are buried, these cold cases need DNA, witnesses, or specific admissions of guilt to move forward. Wesley Shermantine and Lorenzo Herzog, known as California's "Speed Freak Killers" during the 1980s and 1990s, murdered and buried several victims. Herzog, serving a 77 year to life prison sentence for three murders was released after an appeals also had to tie them up once he got them into the van. Eventually he graduated to using starter fluid with ether to render his victims unconscious enough to get them in his van and under his control. Using a belt or rope, he strangled them from behind while they either laid on the ground or stood or sat against a tree. Larry did not like to see his victims die, but he wanted them dead. He then engaged in postmortem mutilation and sex with the corpse. He liked his last victim because she was a prostitute and offered him free sex. He killed her anyway. Most of his victims he claims were buried in wooded areas where the ground is soft or in areas with water. Larry's father was a gravedigger by trade and Larry learned how and where to dig graves with precision. He remembered digging one grave that he never got to use. Larry, a fan of *True Detective* magazines, was very careful not to leave evidence at the crime scenes.

Larry has always lived in the shadow of his twin brother, Gary. Except for the time he spent with Gary, he was a complete loner, and resented women. Some believe that Gary was involved in the killings, but Larry denies any involvement by him. In 2011 CNN aired a one-hour documentary on the Larry Hall case and interviewed his brother Gary for the documentary. Since that time an estrangement has developed between the two brothers. Larry may eventually tell investigators where the bodies are buried, but with each passing year remembering the exact locations becomes more difficult. Of course, Larry fears that if he cooperates he will be convicted of more murders and sentenced to death. He now works as a prison janitor, has no visitors, and spends much of his time researching cars. Larry is still hopeful that he will one day be released.

This is a cold case spanning many years involving one predator (possibly others), who will only go so far to assist investigators. Those assigned to investigate this case are seasoned homicide investigators who have one mission: to bring the bodies home to their families.

What do you think? Go online and research this case. If you have any information regarding this case, please contact Detective Sgt. David Ellison of the Indianapolis Police Department: Ph. 317-327-3475.

- Is Larry Hall a psychopath or simply a person with some psychopathic characteristics?
- In what ways does Larry fit a serial-killer profile?
- What makes this case different from others you have read about?
- What might investigators do to move this case forward?

court determined that his confesson was obtained illegally. In 2012 his partner Shermantine, on death row for killing 4 women, cut a deal with prosecutors and in return revealed where at least ten bodies were buried, thus implicating Herzog. In response, Herzog killed himself rather than go back to prison.

These are very challenging cases that consume much time and many resources and often involve several jurisdictions. What drives many of these investigators to work on these cases is their desire to help the victims' families find closure and if possible bring those responsible to justice. One investigator worked full time for 11 years on the UNABOM case. He retired the day Kaczynski was arrested.

Serial killers are not indestructible, nor do they have special mystical powers. They are not Hannibal Lecters. I have interviewed and researched enough serial killers to debunk such a myth. They are offenders with grotesquely distorted fantasy systems. They are humans who have acquired certain skills and certain patterns of deviousness that permit some of them to elude police. As discussed in this final chapter, more police agencies have begun to allocate resources specifically for cold case resolution that often includes cases of serial murder. Sometimes, when cold cases are under review, investigators are unaware that the suspect may also have ties to other murders (see Profile 12.6). With the use of DNA and other physical evidence, cases of serial murder can be resolved spanning many years.

Rossmo (2008) in his book *Criminal Investigative Failures* points out that competent investigators sometimes make avoidable mistakes that jeopardize the successful resolution of a case. He offers three main reasons to explain failures in criminal investigations: *Cognitive biases*, such as tunnel vision, that can facilitate errors in reasoning; *organizational traps*, such as groupthink, to which investigators sometimes succumb as a function of working in their agencies; and *probability errors*, such as the "prosecutor's fallacy" where an assumption that the odds of a statistical event points strongly to the odds of a defendant being guilty. Cold case review teams offer a new set of eyes on a case and may be more likely to avoid these types of erros. Roach and Pease (2008) suggest that cold case reviews offer a good place to start. They argue that often a suspect in a cold case may be connected to other crimes not contained within the cold case under investigation. Indeed, criminals are versatile and often engage in crimes of opportunity.

Crime prevention is another matter. Understanding how these offenders think and operate is critical to more effective interventions before they are able to become serial killers. This is certainly a daunting task, and to begin we must first conduct effective interviews that help researchers and investigators understand them.

Interviewing Serial Killers

Scientific researchers have developed several methodologies for data collection and analysis. Typically, data gathered from random-sample surveys or aggregate data collection allow researchers to perform comparative analyses of various social phenomena, based on information gathered from a large number of subjects. Researchers can also gather information from life history analysis. Diaries, autobiographies, and personal interviews can provide particularly insightful information unavailable through more empirically oriented research. The "trade-off," which may not always be equitable, permits researchers to focus exclusively on a few cases to allow in-depth exploration.

OBSTACLES

Obviously, gathering data about serial killers cannot be managed by simply mailing out questionnaires or conducting telephone surveys. Serial killers are not only relatively rare in number, but they also are not easily accessible. The FBI

PROFILE 12.6 Joseph Naso, "The Alphabet Killer," 1977–1994

Also referred to as the "Double Initial Murders," at least 10 women, most of them prostitutes with first and last names beginning with the same letter, were murdered over a 17-year period, including Roxene Roggasch, 1977; Carmen Colon, 1978; Pamela Parsons, 1993; and Tracy Tafoya, 1994. All four had matching initials and were found in Northern California. Joseph Naso is suspected of killing them as well as six other women and underage girls. Three victims were raped and killed in the Rochester, New York, area during the 1970s, but Naso, as of this writing, has not been charged with these murders. Oddly enough, one of these young victims was also named Carmen Colon, along with Wanda Walkowicz and Michelle Maenza. Their bodies were found in towns with names beginning with the same initial as the victim's name. Kenneth Bianchi, who later became known as one of the Hillside Stranglers in Los Angeles, was a suspect in the Rochester, New York, cases but has denied any involvement.

Joseph Naso, now 78, is most recently from Reno, Nevada, but he traveled extensively across the United States as a professional photographer and lived in Rochester, New York, during the 1970s. In 2010 Naso was on probation for a felony larceny conviction in California. A probation officer visiting his home in Reno found a "rape diary" filled with sexually explicit photographs of women appearing unconscious or dead. The diary documented the rapes and assaults of underaged girls and women as well as containing pictures of two murder victims in sexually explicit positions. One of the entries reads: "Girl in North Buffalo woods. She is real pretty. Had to knock her out first." Naso, acting as his own attorney, refers to his diary as his private work.

Investigators also found a "List of Ten" women (including those he is now charged with killing) in his bedroom with details about them. He kept news clippings of the killings and personal items belonging to the murdered women as well as over $150,000 in cash in two safety deposit boxes. The probation officer discovered in a locked bedroom a mannequin covered in a red dress, suitcases full of mannequin parts, mannequin legs clad in hosiery and lingerie stuffed in his dresser drawers. Hidden behind a refrigerator was a box containing knives and guns.

What do you think? Go online and research and follow the Naso case.

- Is there enough evidence to link him to the Rochester murders?
- Naso appears to have acquired and developed some paraphilia. What links do you see, if any, between his interests in pictures of allegedly dead women and the mannequin and mannequin parts.
- Do you think Naso is a necrophile? Why? Why not?
- If Naso is guilty of these murders, how can you explain Naso's interest in killing females having first and last names beginning with the same letter?
- Does his obsession with specific names have any connection to his need to document his "work"?

undoubtedly has the easiest access to serial killers once they have been incarcerated. However, even agents from the Investigative Support Unitin Quantico, Virginia, do not receive cooperation from all multiple-homicide offenders. Some killers confess their crimes, but some serial killers continue to claim they are innocent long after they go to prison and thus refuse to cooperate with police by giving them any information about the murders. In all likelihood, many of the myths associated with serial killers could be dispelled if researchers had greater access to offenders. Indeed, the interview could become a critical tool in understanding serial murder. Interviewing multiple-homicide offenders certainly is not without its limitations and problems. Given the nature of their offenses, offenders are often eager to gain the attention of the researcher, police, or anyone else who will help publicize the crimes. Many of these offenders have led insecure and emotionally truncated lives; they are at last receiving the attention they have so desperately longed for. Sometimes, as in the case of Henry Lee Lucas (see Chapter 8), offenders will confess to many more homicides than they actually committed in order to attract public attention. This, in turn, brings into question the validity of multiple-homicide data. Researchers must be careful not to be drawn into the sensationalism of high victim counts in lieu of investigating the accuracy of those claims.

In addition, certain individuals who are attracted to offenders befriend and follow them through the criminal justice process. Such "groupies" have been common in cases of particular notoriety, including that of Ted Bundy. Several young women, similar in appearance to his victims, attended the court sessions and frequently corresponded with the killer. Some wanted to marry Bundy; others believed they could "help" Ted. "Groupies" are often criticized because they contribute to the killer's notoriety. Similar criticism is sometimes leveled at researchers who spend time interviewing serial offenders, because the information can be easily manipulated and distorted.

In addition, a serial offender may tell interviewers exactly what he or she wants them to hear—or, conversely, what he or she thinks the interviewers want to hear. Some psychiatric units term such behavior *gaming*. Occasionally criminals who have been sent to a psychiatric hospital for evaluation feel a need to live up to the expectation that they are indeed criminally insane. To prove their state of mind, the offenders will "bounce off the walls" for a few days, often in an isolation cell, until they calm down. Inevitably they realize that most people they see on the ward are not acting out and appear rather "normal." To some degree the serial killer, thrust under public scrutiny, may feel a need to fit the typical "mold" of such offenders. Some will articulate their motivations for murder in a way that can be very compelling to the interviewer (see Profile 12.7).

The following is a portion of an interview I conducted with a male serial offender. The interview was audiotaped, reviewed, and then new lines of questioning were developed. Generally, I first followed a rather serendipitous line of questioning based on the offender's responses. The offender, in this instance, does not wish to have any publicity regarding his crimes. Is this because he would face the death penalty for his other murders, or is he simply fabricating his claims to 12 victims in order to create some mystique for himself? Read the interview carefully. Does the interviewer allow the subject to speak freely about his experiences? Does it make sense to follow a logical sequence of topics when interviewing psychopaths? Will the psychopath's brain respond to questioning in the same manner as a non-psychopathic killer? Is it important for the researcher to guide the interview or allow the subject freedom to go on tangents? Remember that the objective of any psychopath, violent or not, is to have control over others, including an interviewer. This was the first face-to-face interview of a serial killer I conducted, many years ago.

Another criticism regarding interviews is that what offenders have to say, even if they believe it, may not reflect a realistic perspective. Hindsight can easily distort reality and mold it to the psychological needs of the offender. How objective, how truthful, can we expect serial murderers to be? One can expect a certain degree of distorted thinking in the mind of an offender who has mutilated 15 or 20 victims. Another critical factor in conducting serial-murder interviews is that most of the murderers are psychopaths. Some may be more psychopathic than others, some are more intelligent than others, and some have greater social skills in manipulating others. Appealing to their sense of guilt, shame, or regret will do nothing to further your interview. They do not think in those terms and they certainly do not feel remorse as a non-psychopathic person might feel. Instead, you might appeal to the costs of their behavior in terms of losing their freedom. They understand the legality of their behavior and subsequent penalties, but they do not fear them as a non-psychopathic person might fear. However, losing privileges does have an impact. Most serial killers make model inmates because they have nothing to gain through traditional prison inmate mentality. Instead, they ingratiate themselves with other inmates or remain isolated. They often see themselves as different from the typical offenders wandering the prison yard and are selective with whom they engage in conversation. As an interviewer you become a connection to the outside world while at the same time they are very wary of your agenda.

Despite the stumbling blocks, interviews can be productive. The interview should be regarded as another source of information, another perspective into the murdering mind. Some offenders have acquired particular insight into their own distorted thinking or the mind-set of other serial killers. For example, serial killers are stereotyped as persons without or incapable of remorse. Although this appears to be true for many such offenders, there are also exceptions. One offender, the killer of five young boys in Utah, apologized to the victims' families and begged their forgiveness. On several occasions he expressed his deep regrets and sorrow. To prove sincerity and to show his willingness to do anything to help right the wrongs he committed, Arthur Gary Bishop stopped his appeals process to allow himself to be executed. Although his remorse appeared to have been sincere, Bishop recognized that what he had become had completely engulfed him. Shortly before his execution, he commented that even though he was deeply sorrowful for his deeds, he knew that if he were released he would continue to kill.

Each murderer has an explanation of what may have caused him or her to commit terrible crimes. Researchers would be neglectful if they did not take every opportunity to gather such information. However, researchers must be cautious about assuming they understand the mind of the serial killer simply because they may have interviewed two or three offenders. Also, some offenders believed to be linked to many deaths may be incarcerated for only one or two homicides and emphatically deny involvement in other killings. Several appear to

PROFILE 12.7 An Interview with Manny

... I was basically living a double life. I was one thing to this person and another thing to that person, all lies. And the reason for that is just a low self-image. You're not happy with who you are. You're not comfortable with who you are. You don't have any self-confidence. I wasn't out committing crimes all the time. One day I'd be fine, and the next time I'd be out, I'd have this compulsion to go out and kill somebody, and so I started looking back at each instance, what was I thinking, and this is what I came up with, and it's kind of a higher-stage process. The first stage is what I call distorted thinking. It's a distorted thought line, and I found that I was God's gift to Earth, I'm the center of the universe. I'm perfect. I'm the smartest guy that ever lived. Nobody's as perceptive as I am. So long as nothing came against that self-image, I was fine. But the problem with that was that it, as I mentioned earlier, was all lies.

Everything was a lie, and you know a lot of times the money that I had was my father's credit cards and it was a lie. I'd go on a date, and be living it up like this was mine. So long as I was living it out, I was all pumped up. I felt very important, just this immense personality, and that couldn't last because it was always based on lies. There was always going to be some challenge to this grandiose self-image. Sometimes it would be a lot of little things, sometimes it would just be the stress of having to live these little lies, having to always be looking over your back, and other times it would be a very definite event, a girlfriend leaves you or something like that. Whenever that happened, then there would be a fall. I was always way up here, and I think that's true of most serial types, serial offenders like I was, arrogant, maybe not outwardly, but at least internally. We're arrogant people, perceiving ourselves as almost godlike beings. All of a sudden we have this fall, psychological fall, and it's very debilitating, very disorienting, confusing, harrowing. It's a very scary feeling. I'm used to being perfect.

I'm not about to put up with anything that tarnishes my own sense of perfection, so that would lead to internal negative response, and that's what I was saying to myself. I'm not gonna have this, and instead of being scared, frightened, knocked off balance, I wheeled into a retaliatory mode. I'm gonna fight this. I'm gonna stand up for my self-importance. The way to deal with that was simply to prove it. You're going to be a somebody, and my means of being a somebody was violence. To me violence had already been reinforced through time as a means of being the star, center stage in this drama. Up to this point I've had a fall, and I felt like I'm not in control. I'm not top dog.

Violence to me had been reinforced as a means of taking control, as a means of getting even, getting even with the world. It's reaffirming that I was all those things, and the actual deed, the victimizing, the brutalizing of another human being, was my proof, a seal, a seal of approval, self-approval, my evidence that I'm really a somebody, and the result of that would be a triumph, a restoration, I'm restored. I'm doing not what other people will, but what I will, and that would restore all those feelings of largeness, power, self-importance that strengthened the overloaded ego that I had in the first stage, and I'd be fine. The act done, it wasn't done so much for fun as it was for restorative gain. As long as I was back in that first stage, there really wasn't any desire to go out and kill. It wasn't like I had an ongoing insatiable lust for murder, and it really wasn't a lust for murder.

have embraced the "Bundy Complex," or complete denial of responsibility despite overwhelming evidence to the contrary. However, these offenders can also provide researchers with insights to their personalities and psychological characteristics.

It was a lust for self-importance at the expense of others, and that's basically the cycle. Sometimes it wouldn't take very much at all. I had a friend who owned a body shop, and I was working for him, and had no car and I get on a bus and I'm just filthy. I was just as filthy as can be, and I'm in distorted thinking. This gal gets on the bus, dressed up real nice and the seat next to me is the only one empty and she comes over and she looks at that seat and then she looks at me—all covered with dust and smelly—and she just turns her nose up in the air, spins around, and walks up and grabs a bar. How can you sit there?

Q: What kind of victims did you select?

A: It was people like kids, usually attractive, just like the ones I was in high school with, and I had felt rejected [by].

Q: Your victims, you say, were primarily white female teenagers.

A: Yes. I like kids. I always did. Back then it was perhaps self-serving. I used to take kids out to the ballpark. I got the praise and adulation of the parents. I enjoyed it, and here I killed two kids because I was in a frenzy—at that time I was in a fall and had been there for long enough and had failed to find somebody that fit the model. And there were these two victims of opportunity, like a wolf stalking.

Q: Hunting humans?

A: Yes.

Q: You say you killed approximately 12 victims. Did they progressively get closer together?

A: It was erratic. I mean, I just killed somebody and I'm infuriated because I didn't get done what I had to do, couldn't act out this ritual that accidentally killed this body, and within a matter of hours I had someone else. With this second victim it involved brutalizing, rape, and then killing. Actually rape ended the episode, killing was just getting rid of the witness. The first killing was not done that way. The first killing, the victim died before I had acted out even.... I did have a pattern and most serial killers do.

Q: There was a sexual component to most of the killings?

A: Yes. Sex was sort of a vehicle. So when that was done, climax was reached. You've already terrorized this person. You've already hurt them, beat them, whatever. But there would be a feeling of letdown. You're excited, and then all of a sudden you come down. Kind of like a ball game. All this had been acted out for years and in particular, it always involved stripping the victim, forcing them to strip themselves, cutting them, making them believe that they were going to be set free if they cooperated, tying them down and then the real viciousness started. The victim's terror and the fact I could cause it to rise at will ... their pain didn't register. All I could relate to was the ritual and the sounds. All this was proof to me that, I'm in control, I am playing the star role here, this person is nothing but a prop. I'm growing and they're becoming smaller. Once both the violence and the sexual aspect were completed, then that was it. That was the end of an episode....

Dr. Candice Skrapec, a criminal psychologist at California State University in Fresno, California, interviewed several Canadian serial killers. In her research (2001) Skrapec explored the method of *empirical phenomenology*. She poses the dictum by Kluckhohn and Murray (1953): "Every man is in certain respects

(a) like all other men, (b) like some other men, (c) like no other man" (p. 53). In understanding what the repeated acts of killing mean to the offender, we can understand the motive forces that drive the behavior. This is empirical phenomenology. It is attention to the killer's words and expressions of emotion or thoughts. The researcher must then "identify the principles that organize his thinking and thus determine his perceptions and feelings and, ultimately, his behavior" (Kluckhohn and Murray, p. 53). This is accomplished through inductive reasoning that comes from understanding the stories or narratives of the offenders, even if they are all lies. Everything has context and subjective meaning. To understand serial murderers we must realize that the "underlying structures of an experience are determined by interpreting an individual's narrative about the situations in which the experience occurs" (Kluckhohn and Murray, p. 55).

Skrapec believes that "learning about a murderer's personal construction of meaning in their own lives positions us to be able to identify the motivations underlying their repeated acts of killing" (p. 46). Indeed, she raises an excellent point: perhaps we are so eager to interpret motives of serial killers that the processes by which we conduct our examinations and draw our conclusions are inherently flawed. She relates the example of Ed Kemper, who challenged a researcher during an interview because she was not asking the right questions. After all, if you, as a reader, could sit with Ed Kemper and ask him anything you wanted, what would you ask? He thinks you might want to know what it feels like to have sex with a corpse or sit on your living room couch and look over and see two decapitated girls' heads on the arms of the couch. Kemper says: "The first time it makes you sick to your stomach" (Skrapec, 2001, p. 48).

Perhaps the reason that we are asking the "wrong" questions is because we are so anxious to have answers—answers to keep the media filled with sensational material. Whether there is merit in the information or not is of little import when the bottom line is selling newspapers and magazines. Let us pause for a moment and consider three vital issues when conducting research:

1. Maintain objectivity.
2. Acknowledge other perspectives.
3. Recognize that asking the "right" questions is more important than finding quick answers.

PROBLEMS IN INTERVIEWING

Many readers have inquired about interviewing serial killers. It is difficult for most people to comprehend what it is like to sit across from someone who has killed 15 to 20 people. In questioning such an individual, certain principles apply: requisite objectivity; a dispassionate search for new perspectives; and, most important, a recognition that the questions asked will be of greater import than any answers obtained. Be cognizant that many of these offenders lie and do it extremely well. Indeed, this is part of their profile. Most of them could not do otherwise, given their careers of killing. Their ability to reconstruct the past in nearly obsessive detail is fascinating. Researchers are not there to judge the offender; nor can you, if you are seeking greater understanding of serial behavior. The offender has already been convicted and sent to prison. We are there to learn and gather information just as any social scientist does in an honest pursuit of understanding. Do not be caught up in the allure of the offender or the sensational nature of the murders. These offenders are not fictional Hannibal Lecters, but distinctively violent offenders who have something to teach us, albeit dark and disturbing, about the nature of violence (see Profile 12.8). What can we learn about the killer from this interview?

Remember that serial murder constitutes a process, not just an act of killing. The offender certainly did not become a serial killer overnight, nor should the researchers' questions be geared toward finding a quick and effortless answer. Answers will take care of themselves if we are able to ask the "right" questions. Monahan and Steadman (1984) noted several problems with researchers in conducting diagnostic work, including the following:

Memory bias—The interview is tainted by the biases of the researcher based on prior experience or knowledge about the offender or case.

False positives or false negatives—False positives means the researcher predicts behavior by the subject but is wrong in his or her prognosis. Conversely, false negatives means that the researcher predicts that certain behaviors will not occur in a subject but they do.

Weighing current factors—Researchers need to examine the case in its entirety. The subject must be examined in his current status as well as where he has come from. Subjects are in transition and need to be viewed as dynamic, not static, entities.

Illusionary correlations—Researchers sometimes are quick to make comparisons in a subject's behaviors and outside events. Often such "correlations" are spurious.

Hindsight bias—The researcher has gained some experience and therefore comes to expect certain responses from the subject. This can be very costly if the researcher begins to over-guide the subject.

Overconfidence—The researcher sometimes fails to connect with the subject because the researcher exudes a sense of superiority, or insight unavailable to the subject. The researcher must remember that prison visits are not visits to the zoo.

Overfocusing—Researchers sometimes are mesmerized by the notoriety of the killer. A Dahmer, or Bundy, or Gacy sometimes causes the researcher to focus on unusual aspects of the case including paraphilia or how victims were killed without understanding the meaning of those behaviors.

Conducting psychological research into the minds of serial killers poses problems when the researcher is not adequately trained or flexible enough to adjust to unusual subjects. Indeed, we must not only be asking the "right" questions as Kemper suggests, but we must also be cognizant of body language, interview settings, and efforts by subjects to control the interview process. That the killer

PROFILE 12.8 Juan Chavez, the MacArthur Park Murderer, 1986–1989

Juan was a 29-year-old Mexican living illegally in California. He was captured in 1994 after a robbery and kidnapping incident in Northern California. Depicted by the prosecution as a very dangerous man deserving harsh punishment, Chavez was given two life sentences and sent to Folsom State Prison. Angrily he remarked that if they (the prosecution) thought what he had done was bad, they were going to be very impressed with what he had done during earlier crimes. Chavez then confessed to killing six white, middle-aged males, all homosexuals whom he met while cruising in MacArthur Park. He would go out by himself into the gay districts of Los Angeles pretending to offer sex to unsuspecting victims. Once victims were undressed, Chavez used a cord to strangle them slowly, so they would suffer as much as possible.

Upon his arrest he insisted the victims themselves were to blame, that they were asking for it because they were spreading AIDS. However, he also forced victims to reveal their ATM personal identification numbers. After murdering them, he stole their jewelry and money. He also committed thefts atypical of serial killers: He stole a VCR and cable box but, instead of unscrewing the cables, Chavez cut them with a knife, suggesting he was in a hurry and afraid of being caught. He stole several vehicles and gave one of them to a friend. One usually does not equate serial murder with such repetitive and ill-concealed property crime.

This case, however, is much more about rage than money. Juan appears soft-spoken, reflective, and very controlled. As I sat at a small table across from the defendant in a super-maximum-security prison, Chavez was clearly agitated. He said he really did not know why he killed his victims, but believed the "devil made me do it." He reiterated that he deserved to die for his crimes. Unlike most serial killers I have interviewed, Chavez was deeply depressed. He spoke quietly and dispassionately, belying the rage that drove him to kill. He would not make eye contact with me but kept his head bowed, speaking in short, often monosyllabic words. For a moment I began to doubt his dangerousness. He was small in stature, but a handsome, almost timid man wanting to be left alone. His demeanor deceptively concealed his capacity for murder.

Juan was having a difficult time looking at me. I decided to move around to his side of the table in order to be closer to him. Just as I moved my hands along the tabletop, Chavez made brief but revealing eye contact with me. I was about to invade his space and he sensed it. The eyes were those of a man in horrible pain, a man living in hell. These were not eyes one would ever wish to encounter alone. Nor were these eyes going to allow me into his space. Chavez was doing all that he could to keep himself under control. Moving to his side of the table would have the same effect as entering a cage with a wild animal. Although I was not afraid, I sensed the danger zone I had nearly entered. I remained where I was, focusing more intently on this man.

I probed him for over an hour. Juan has one brother, whom he loves. His father deserted his family when he was a young boy. He expressed no animosity toward his

manipulates control is not the problem, because in that control he or she will tell the interviewer much. The issue lies in the researcher not being able to effectively adapt to the subject, thereby irritating, boring, or bringing the interview to an abrupt ending. That is the essence of phenomenology or the ability to interpret social and psychological settings without first controlling them.

father yet clearly remembered the day his father left. I learned of Juan's deep hatred for his mother and grandmother. As a child he was frequently beaten and humiliated by his grandmother. She told young Juan that he should never have been born. His beatings became brutal. A beating with a lead pipe left him with serious head injuries. He pointed out the multiple indentations and scars on his head. The beatings appear to have left Juan with some possible brain damage. As an adolescent he was a heavy glue sniffer, which may have also impaired his cognition. I asked him what he would do if either his grandmother or mother were here, at this very moment. He responded: "I would hang them with a rope." The "rope" he was referring to was most likely the one he had used to strangle his victims. If he had been so abused by these two women, why was he not killing women? Chavez's explanation was simple: "I came out of a woman." He also stated that he held women in high esteem.

Juan claims no sexual interest in men. He could not explain why he left all of his victims bound and nude in motel rooms. He says he just wanted their money and that he was not sexually involved with any of them. The autopsy reports, however, indicate that Chavez did engage in homosexual activity with his victims. Juan also expresses no sexual interest in women or men, although his brother remembers him sometimes being with females.

Juan expresses no remorse for his crimes and wants to be executed as soon as possible. He believes God wants him punished for his sins. He wants no media attention and wishes to spare his brother any trouble or pain. Juan is a man of average intelligence who prefers to be alone. He has no friends and his sense of alienation is profound. Other inmates keep their distance from him. Even though he is smaller than some at the prison, inmates are uncomfortable around him. He does not exude machismo; he radiates anger and hate. A man of very low self-esteem and clinically depressed, Juan claims to have attempted suicide.

Juan is a very dangerous man and a very real threat to others, especially males. However, like so many other serial killers, once incarcerated they pose little or no threat to inmates or staff. Juan expresses no anger toward his father, yet he seems to harbor very real feelings of rejection and abandonment. His father was not there to protect him from his mother and grandmother, which may have exacerbated his negative feelings toward men. Juan also denies being attracted to males or having any sexual connection to men, but given his sexual involvement with his victims, he probably has latent homosexual feelings that have caused him considerable dissonance and ambivalence. He is currently serving five life sentences.

You have been exposed to several biological and psychological explanations for violent behavior, in particular, serial murder. Which explanations, in your opinion, best help to explain Juan Chavez's behavior? What other possible motivations do you think he may have had for killing, and for killing only gay men?

A person who has spent the past several years stalking, torturing, killing, and cannibalizing hapless victims probably does not care what the interviewer wants. Every person, however, does have a story to tell (see Profile 12.9). So, the interviewer must be an observer without prejudice or bias. Of course, interviewers are not expected to agree with the killer's perspectives, but they are not there

PROFILE 12.9 Explanations of Serial Killers

The following interview statements are the thoughts and reflections of four serial killers. Each of these offenders was markedly distinct in personality, emotional stability, IQ, attitudes, and types of victims selected.

- Offender has killed over 50 victims, many by poison or suffocation. He considers himself to be a nice, compassionate, caring person and is mean or cruel only when provoked. A homosexual, he remembers (since the age of five) a semihappy childhood during which he was the victim of sexual abuse. The abuse lasted 13 years and involved a male neighbor and an uncle. As a child he was told his mother would be harmed if he did not submit to the sexual advances. Fearing for her safety, he complied. The sexual abuse, he believes, had nothing to do with the killings or his later involvement with homosexuality. He claims a strong belief in a forgiving God and expresses interest in the occult, although he denies that Satan influenced his actions. Some victims he killed as "acts of mercy;" others died at his hands as a result of vengeance, fear, "justice," or anger. The offender claims remorse for some of the murders but would definitely repeat some of them again. He claims that although he was mentally disturbed during some of the killings, he no longer suffers from psychological problems. He portrays himself as a caring person who is at peace with himself and wants to help others avoid becoming murderers. If he can do this, he feels he will have accomplished something.
- Offender has killed at least 10 victims brutally, with extreme mutilation and trophy collecting. He portrays himself living a Jekyll-and-Hyde existence. He also describes a deep love–hate relationship with his mother. He killed out of frustration and his inability to communicate socially or sexually. The offender deeply feared failing in relationships with women. He thought that if he could just kill his mother, the need for murder would stop. He claims regret for not having sought out help earlier and thereby sparing several innocent lives. He now thinks that if he had had the courage, he could have sought help. He believes that if he were now free from prison, he would get married and have children.
- Offender has killed 30–40 victims. Some of his victims were killed to cover up other crimes, but many were women who hitched a ride with him. He believed that women who hitchhiked were prostitutes. He carries a deep aversion to prostitutes because his mother was one. As a child he was subjected to sexual exploitation and constant rejection by his mother. He finally killed her. After he killed several dozen victims, he claimed God helped him have a change of heart. For him, the best way to avoid capture was to be constantly traveling. Now that he is on death row, he expresses remorse for the plight of his victims, including their families. He believes that his home life is primarily to blame for his criminal behavior. Both of his parents were usually drunk and showed no interest in him or his siblings. He believes that a serial killer is someone who bases his or her life on that activity and that is exactly what he thinks he did. A Christian, he firmly believes that he has been saved in God's eyes.
- Offender has killed at least three victims and now resides in an institution for the criminally insane. He claims to have been under the influence of hallucinations that led to the murders. He claims remorse for killing his victims, especially his son, but says that he forgot about the killing after it was done. For this offender it did not matter who his victims were. Inevitably he knew he was going to kill three million people, so it really did not matter where he started. In addition, the offender has a fascination with mutilating sexual organs and claims he will do so again if he ever gets an opportunity. He explains that his hallucinations continue to encourage him to kill. He believes the voice in his hallucinations is that of the devil, which possesses him.

to judge him or her, either. That has already been done. The interviewer's job is to gather information without corrupting it.

And when these murderers are apprehended, interviewed, and convicted, the courts are faced with the determination of appropriate sentencing of these offenders. Sentencing often fails to meet the demands of public outrage or provide necessary treatment facilities and programs for these violent offenders.

DISPOSITION

Once a serial killer is apprehended and interviewed, the disposition of the offender is often very time consuming. Some of the most notorious cases receive extended hearings and go through a morass of legal proceedings. In part, this specialized treatment is due to the complexity of the case as well as to the tendency of such crimes to attract prominent legal figures. Most of these cases end up costing the taxpayers millions of dollars, and many communities are becoming impatient with lengthy legal proceedings. Meanwhile, the offender often assumes celebrity status, attracting reporters and television and radio stations from throughout the country.

Many Americans are apprehensive about giving serial killers anything but a death sentence. However, not all states carry the death penalty, and sometimes (as in the case of Donald Harvey) offenders will enter into a plea bargain to avoid the sentence of death. Indeterminate sentencing, whereby the offender receives a range of years in prison, is occasionally passed down by the judge. In some cases offenders will serve their multiple convictions concurrently, which means, for example, that 180 years in prison for six murders actually becomes 30 years plus time off for good behavior. Some offenders are given life in prison with no possibility of parole. It is unlikely that a serial or mass murderer, once convicted and incarcerated, will ever be free again. Some offenders, such as Edmund Kemper and Charles Manson, do receive periodic parole hearings, but these hearings become little more than a legal formality. No parole board is likely to take the risk of releasing a convicted mass killer back into society.

Although offenders convicted of serial murders are not paroled, some other types of murderers are. Those offenders presently in prison for violent crimes who, if paroled, will eventually go on to become serial offenders are often impossible to identify. We generally cannot incarcerate people for crimes they have yet to commit. The closest we have come to this is through the habitual-offender classification, which involves a person who has been convicted of three or more felonies. Such offenders are considered to be likely candidates for committing future crimes and are given extended sentences in some states. Selective incapacitation (incarcerating chronic offenders for longer periods of time than other offenders) may affect serial-murder rates by unknowingly containing potential offenders. Court records are replete with the names of offenders incarcerated for murder(s) who served time and were then released into the community, where they killed again and again.

In 1939, Louise Peete, convicted of murder, was paroled only to become involved in the murders of several more victims. A similar situation occurred with George Fitzsimmons, who was institutionalized for killing his parents. Upon his early release to his aunt and uncle, he took out insurance policies on them and then stabbed them to death. Frederick Wood had served 17 years in Clinton State Prison for second-degree murder. Following his release, he went on a killing spree and, upon his next arrest, confessed to five more murders. Another killer, Richard Marquette, was paroled after 12 years for the mutilation murder of a woman. He went on to decapitate and mutilate at least two more women before he was apprehended a second time (Brian, 1986).

This does not mean that most people who commit murder and serve time in prison are likely to kill again after their release. Indeed, most do not recidivate. It does suggest, however, that some violent offenders should never be released. What do you think? Consider the Depravity Scale research (see Box 12.1). Now that you have completed reading this book depicting the horrors of mankind, you probably realize that crimes vary enormously in seriousness, depravity, and evil, as does societal response to such acts. Dr. Welner thinks creating a Depravity Scale will help us determine more appropriate responses to crimes. Should punishments differ for sexual predators who rape and murder elderly women compared to a man who shoots and kills a bank teller during a robbery? Safarik and Jarvis (2005) examine the attributes of homicide in their efforts to quantify qualitative values of injury severity of elderly women who were murdered. Does the severity of a crime influence the investigation or punishment? Our criminal justice system provides a plethora of sanctions and punishments ranging from fines to probation to parole to incarceration, to capital punishment in some states. Compared to prison diversion programs for nonviolent offenders that can have positive outcomes (Harris, 2011), serial killers most likely receive death sentences, life without parole, or confinement in state psychiatric facilities.

Capital Punishment

Many proponents of the death penalty argue that punishment for crimes should be gauged according to the seriousness of the criminal offense. The harshest penalty, then, should be reserved for the worst crimes. Modern classical thinkers also point out that capital punishment stands as the last resort to deter people from committing particularly heinous crimes. Obviously someone who is already serving a life sentence with no chance of parole has little to lose by killing a correctional officer or another inmate. However, certain offenders might be less inclined to kill witnesses if they knew a death sentence would likely be imposed. In addition, supporters of the death penalty believe that offenders such as serial killers are so dangerous to other human beings that executing them presents the safest way of protecting society. Others argue, from an economic perspective, that maintaining offenders in prison for life is inevitably much more expensive than executing them.

Victims' rights groups have flourished in the past several years. Some have become particularly outspoken regarding the demise of the usually forgotten victim. The courts are asked to consider, in several states, victim impact statements outlining the devastation of physical, emotional, and financial hardships

BOX 12.1 The Depravity Scale

This is the first project ever developed that invites citizen input to shape a future science instrument for courts, and the first project ever developed in which citizens shape future criminal sentencing standards.

To address an existing arbitrariness in criminal sentencing codes, the Depravity Scale, created by Dr. Michael Welner, a forensic psychiatrist in New York City, is an international research effort that aims to scientifically standardize the definition of legal terms such as "heinous," "atrocious," "evil," and "depraved" according to input from the general public. This multi-phase project's goal is to establish a consistent and fair distinction for the worst of crimes through the development of an instrument that will be used at the sentencing phase of trials. To minimize the arbitrariness of how courts determine the worst of crimes, and to eliminate bias in sentencing, the Depravity Scale research aims to establish societal standards of what makes a crime depraved, and to develop a standardized instrument based on specific characteristics of a crime that must be proven in order to merit more severe sentences. This research will refine into the Depravity Standard, an objective measure based on forensic evidence. **This instrument distinguishes not *who* is depraved but rather *what* aspects of a given crime are depraved and the degree of a specific crime's depravity.** The research will enhance fairness in sentencing, given that it is race, gender, and socioeconomic blind.

The research has already been guided by legal and scientific study. Now, a two-part survey has been developed to involve the general public in establishing societal standards of what makes a crime depraved. The first part enables the general public to shape the specific intents, actions, and attitudes that should be included as items of the Depravity Standard instrument, and the second involves the general public in refining the relative weight of these items. In both surveys, all members of the general public are urged to participate. This is the first project ever developed that invites citizens' direct input to forensic science research, and the first project ever developed in which citizens shape future criminal sentencing standards. **Your perspectives on depraved crime should be included in the Depravity Standard. Therefore, we ask that you participate in this landmark project.**

Go to the www.depravityscale.org and complete the 15-minute survey. If you have any questions please contact us:

By Phone:	**By Fax:**	**By Mail:**	**On the Web:**
(212) 535-9286	(212) 535-3259	The Forensic Panel 224 West 30th Street, Suite 806 New York, NY 10001	www.forensicpanel.com

the victim has suffered. Victims seek restitution, compensation, and a sense of justice. Frank Carrington (1978) observed in the introduction of his book, *Neither Cruel nor Unusual*:

> This book is written from the point of the proponents. It is not objective. It is a defense of the death penalty. In a prior book, *The Victims*, I took the position that it is high time that the rights of the victims of crime were recognized in our criminal justice system. Nowhere is this more true than in the area of capital punishment. Richard Franklin Speck is today contentedly watching television in an Illinois penitentiary

> at the taxpayers' expense. The eight students whom he murdered have been in their graves for ten years, all but forgotten. (p. 14) [Author's note: Speck has since died in prison.]

Efforts are being made by victim coalitions to strike a blow for victims' rights. It seems that the criminal has been afforded all the rights; these groups say that now it is time to create a sense of legal and moral balance. People experience a myriad of emotions once they become victims of crime or their families become victims, especially the families of murdered victims. Revenge, hatred, anger, depression, and anxiety become moving forces in victims' lives and have made stalwart retributionists out of some formerly indifferent people.

Opponents of the death penalty are just as vocal and adamant that state-sponsored executions must never be accepted as a course of punitive action. Indeed, it is argued that adopting capital punishment as a method of expressing social vengeance unalterably impedes our moral progress. Legal scholars, such as Charles Black (1974), argue that arbitrary discretion is found in every case that leads to the chair. In other words, given the same crime of murder, not all offenders sentenced to death will stand the same chance of being executed. Such discretionary factors include race, gender, age, and IQ of the offender.

In the case of Paula Cooper, a black 15-year-old girl in Gary, Indiana, who stabbed an elderly white Bible teacher 33 times, great debates began, and national attention was focused on her death sentence. Even Pope Paul VI sent a message from Rome to intercede on her behalf. Eventually, in 1989, the Indiana Supreme Court removed her from death row. Our nation has decided that people should not be executed for crimes committed at 15. "When a nation does violence to human beings, by conducting wars or executing criminals, it incites its citizens to more criminal violence than they would otherwise commit ... the state can make violence the coin of its own realm" (Wilkes, 1987, pp. 27–28).

Brian (1986) conducted interviews with some of the country's most outspoken and respected opponents to the death penalty. Psychiatrist Karl Menninger, philosopher Hugo Bedau, and sociologist Michael L. Radalet each point out various problems with advocating capital punishment: For example, it discriminates against minorities; innocent people are sometimes mistakenly executed; in our current "pick and choose" mentality there appears to be no rational reasoning in selecting those who should be put to death and those who should be allowed to live; and executions constitute cruel and unusual punishment (Brian, Chapter 22). Jeffrey J. Daughtery, 33, was electrocuted in Florida State Prison in November 1988. In his final statement he criticized the legal system by stating, "I hope with all my heart I will be the last sacrificial lamb of a system that is not just, and all these people know it is not just. The executions serve no purpose." Daughtery had been involved in the serial murders of four young women. In 1996, Utah executed a murderer by firing squad. The last time Utah had used the firing squad was approximately 20 years ago, when it brought back capital punishment by executing Gary Gilmore. In the 1996 execution the condemned man had hoped that by choosing the firing squad over lethal injection people around the nation would be reminded again of the brutality of the death penalty. By 2004 Utah ceased using the firing squad.

Black (1974) expounded on cruelty in capital punishment:

> When we turn from the two usual arguments in favor of capital punishment—retribution and deterrence—to the other side, we find, above all, that the cruelty of it is what its opponents hate—the cruelty of death, the cruelty of the manner of death, the cruelty of waiting for death, and the cruelty to the innocent persons attached by affection to the condemned—unless of course, he has no relatives and no friends, a fairly common condition on death row. (p. 27)

In the matter of serial killers, it seems that people are overwhelmingly in favor of execution. In a sense, it has become a numbers game: The more victims an offender kills, the more people are willing to accept execution as the "best" choice in sentencing. The more victims involved, the more intense is the media coverage. It is not surprising, then, that since the early 1960s, when serial killers began to appear in larger numbers, the general public has been increasingly turning a deaf ear to objections regarding capital punishment. California, for example, which has experienced a proliferation of mass murders, has a special provision for such offenders: In cases of multiple homicides, offenders can be sentenced to death or life in prison without eligibility of parole. Most states appear to use both of these sentences to handle special cases of multiple killings. Consequently, most serial killers in prison today will never have the opportunity to be free again.

Because of the relative rarity of serial-murder cases and the accompanying publicity, there exists a much smaller risk of racial discrimination involving cases of capital punishment. Similarly, it would be extremely unlikely for an innocent person to be executed for seven or eight murders. The issue of intelligence and competency is negated by the fact that most serial offenders possess at least normal, if not above-average, intelligence. Rarely are they found to be insane or incompetent. Consequently, when we are faced with the serial killings of dozens of children, even some people who generally oppose capital punishment agree that exceptions are necessary. Few people have many qualms about executing an offender who has murdered 30 young women. However, one seldom finds such a display of revelry as occurred when Ted Bundy was electrocuted. One anonymous proponent of capital punishment for mass killers wrote the following verse:

> *to a mass murderer*
>
> You know the Judge can send you up
>
> for your remaining years,
>
> And so I send this card to you
>
> to banish all your fears;
>
> No life in prison awaits you, pal.
>
> You won't be rotting there;
>
> The legislators changed the law—
>
> They're bringing back the Chair.

We execute in the name of justice, for revenge, for punishment, for protection, to reduce recidivism, and for a host of other often-emotional reasons. These reasons seem to become clearer when we are faced with a case of multiple homicide. Aside from the moral and philosophical issues surrounding the death sentence, if American society is going to use capital punishment, then serial offenders, who are by far the most dangerous offenders, should be first to qualify for execution. If capital punishment is not to be used, then we must ensure that serial killers remain securely confined.

There is much we could learn about serial killers by studying those now incarcerated. We have already grouped some sex offenders into special programs, often in state hospitals, where they can receive treatment and be studied at the same time.

Treatment

In seeking to interview a serial offender who had murdered between 10 and 12 teenagers and children, I received a personal letter from the warden attempting to explain why such a visit would be unwise. In part, the letter stated: "To permit such a visit would reinforce the inmate's notoriety. It does not assist nor encourage him to become a law-abiding individual and countermands our desire to ultimately integrate him into an open population setting within an institution" (author's files, November 1988).

Implicit in this statement is the assertion that a serial killer can be viewed as a candidate for some form of rehabilitation, even if it is enough to allow him or her to integrate with other inmates. Also implicit is the notion that some form of therapy can assist the offender by increasing his or her willingness to be law-abiding. One usually does not think of serial killers in these terms. Rather, it generally becomes the aim of many to have the offender executed or permanently incarcerated. No treatment strategies are discussed as part of the sentence. Once the offender enters prison, he or she is, for all intents and purposes, forever removed from normal society. Prisons are not managed or operated in such a manner that they are able to provide specialized services.

Dr. Samuel Yochelson, a psychiatrist, served as project director for the Program for the Investigation of Criminal Behavior, funded by the National Institutes of Health. Half of his subjects were psychiatric patients, and the remainder came from the courts and other agencies:

> To his consternation, he found that after several years of intensive treatment, in which they gained many insights, his criminal patients were still committing crimes. However, the crimes were now more sophisticated, and the insights they gained were being used to excuse what they did. Insight became "incite." In following the lead of the therapists, the criminal discovered even more people against whom he was incited. The criminal became skillful in seizing upon any adversity in his life and blaming it for his criminality. Traditional therapy became just one

> more criminal enterprise. The efforts to help him were exploited by the criminal to make himself look good and to substantiate his view of himself and of the outside world. (Samenow, 1978, p. 17)

Treatment, however, may provide researchers opportunities to explore facets of the murdering mind that have yet to be examined. Certainly the prognosis for rehabilitation is not good. It is unrealistic to believe that the psychological complexity of a repetitive killer might ever be completely dismantled.

Considerable work has been conducted in the area of sex-offender research, providing some insight into "lust" killers and the prognosis of treatability. Dr. Liebert, who served as a consulting psychiatrist on the Green River task force, the Atlanta children's murder task force, and the "Ted" (Bundy) task force in Washington, noted:

> The lust murderer has primitive personality abnormalities making him incapable of normal intimacy.... Lust murderers may be able to maintain effective facades as impostors, imitating normal people, but they are not normal enough to tolerate the intensive bonding demands for meaningful psychotherapy.... Lust murder represents the extreme sadomasochistic and sociopathic end of the Borderline-Narcissistic Personality Disorder Spectrum—consequently, the least treatable part of the spectrum. (1985, p. 197)

Our society's continued frustration in dealing with dangerous sex offenders has led to a growing ostracism of these people. In one case, a convicted child molester with an extended history of sexual assaults was ordered by the courts to post a large sign on his door that read "Dangerous Sex Offender—No Children Allowed." Unfortunately, although the intent may be good, such an approach will do little to deter someone who wishes to act out his or her deviant sexual fantasies.

Future Issues and Research

Several issues, focal concerns, and areas of research currently need attention as we explore the phenomenon of serial murder. Some specific needs are as follows:

1. Increased interaction and involvement between academicians and law enforcement agencies in the form of seminars and workshops such as demonstrated in the 2006 FBI San Antonio serial-murder symposium
2. Increased cooperation between law enforcement agencies to improve the circulation of data regarding violent offenders
3. Increased training of local and state law enforcement personnel in respect to serial murder and scientific profiling
4. Increased empirical research into all facets of serial murder to further our understanding of the offenders and victims
5. To debunk and challenge many of the myths and stereotypes that surround serial murderers and their victims

6. To generate and incorporate acceptable operational definitions of serial-murder categories that will inevitably reduce confusion among governmental and private agencies
7. To explore improving methodological issues in data collection and analysis of multiple-homicide offenders
8. To examine prevention strategies using a task force of experts, including law enforcement agencies; social services; and medical, psychiatric, and academic personnel
9. To create public-awareness programs that filter information in a rational and responsible manner
10. To allow for greater accessibility to incarcerated serial killers through the establishment of special research programs and projects
11. To establish projects funded by the federal government specifically for the advancement of multiple-homicide research

CLOSING THOUGHTS

Maxfield (1989), in his examination of homicide categories, stated: "Certain types of homicides are as amenable to prevention as are the events and circumstances with which they are associated.... If propensity to commit violent crimes follows certain patterns, intervention at early stages may truncate a criminal career" (p. 29). His conclusions are based on drug-related homicides, street gangs, and conflict-related murders—but is it possible to create a prevention strategy for serial murder? Currently, we see little hope either of deterring the adult serial offender or of protecting the potential victim. However, members of various communities are singling out what they feel facilitates and stimulates serial offenders. Some groups have increased their war on pornography, alcohol, and drugs, believing that curtailing such vices will inevitably reduce violent criminal behavior. Others are beginning to realize the vulnerability of certain people identified as potential victims. For example, the United States has over 15,000 nursing homes that provide a wide range of quality care. Patient care and safety are growing concerns as more cases of "mercy killing" and angel-of-death attacks begin to surface. Much improved legislation is necessary if we are to protect the elderly and sick.

We must also become more aware of people who create emergencies in order to be rescuers, such as those who work as firefighters and set fires or work as nurses and poison patients. Such people create the opportunities needed to live out their hero fantasies. One glaring example is the case of John Orr, the fire investigator in California connected to a string of arson fires throughout the state. Whenever he attended an arson investigation conference, he would take advantage of the opportunity to set fires. He became legendary in his uncanny ability to assist in the investigations and quickly ascertain the fires' points of origin. California suffered millions of dollars lost in property damage, dozens of injuries, and several deaths. These offenders feel so inadequate that they are willing to jeopardize lives in order to be recognized. Although such people are relatively rare in professions such as firefighting and nursing, it would seem advisable for such professions to implement and adhere to sound psychological testing and screening of potential employees. Of course, every person should use general caution in dealing with strangers and reduce his or her own vulnerability by decreasing unnecessary risk-taking. Walking or jogging alone, hitchhiking, giving rides to total strangers, allowing strangers into one's home—all these activities increase risk potential.

The issue of prevention is really twofold. On one hand, we are trying to detect, apprehend, and incarcerate serial offenders and figure out ways to protect ourselves; on the other hand, we want to identify strategies to prevent individuals from becoming serial killers. People sometimes ask: What is the most important recommendation that should be made from what we currently know about serial murder and our efforts to deter the phenomenon? Actually, there are two approaches to this phenomenon. First is to remember that genetically we can be predisposed to violence. Some offenders may be genetically wired so as to make them void of emotional attachments and impervious to guilt and remorse. If this is true, then we will have to rethink how we try to treat psychopaths, how to identify them when they are young and develop effective treatment strategies. Secondly, we must realize that *reducing violence in the home appears to be the most significant action we can take to affect the circle of violence outside our homes.* This would include reduction/eradication of all forms of child abuse, including neglect, both physical and emotional. It would include reduction/eradication of spouse abuse and a restabilization of the family unit. It would require less divorce and increased bonding between parents and children. It would require parents taking parenting much more seriously. Someone once said that no success can compensate for failure in the home and that the greatest work we will ever do will be within the walls of our own homes. There is more truth to this statement than we realize. Parenting by instinct simply does not work well. Just because people are able to reproduce does not make them fit parents. Effective parenting requires time, commitment, and patience. My wish list would include a requirement that students in junior high school, high school, and in colleges and universities all be required to take parenting classes whether or not they plan on becoming parents. We all deal with children, whether parents ourselves or not, and as the old African saying goes: "It takes a village to raise a child." Our society requires a driver's license in order to drive motorized vehicles. So, too, we should be required to achieve a certain level of understanding of the requisites of fundamental parenting before becoming a parent. However, a solid, happy home does not guarantee the absence of later violence. Nor do I suggest that parents are wholly responsible for the behavior of their children, but, indeed, parents represent a vital part of the puzzle. *We must remember that children may often forget what we, as adults, say or do to them, but children never forget how we make them feel.* If we can alter how people feel about themselves—increase their self-esteem—we might be able to alter how they will feel and respond to others. These recommendations have no particular novelty or originality and may appear idealistic, but they are nonetheless timely. It appears much easier to build hospitals to care for the tens of thousands who die every year of alcoholism, tobacco-related diseases, and diseases caused by pollutants than it does to address the more chronic social ills of our society.

The need for more prisons is also a harbinger of things to come. For example, California's largest growth industry is criminal justice. Billions of dollars are allocated every fiscal year. California has the largest number of incarcerated people in the entire world. California also has the world's largest population of incarcerated female offenders (Chowchilla) as well as the largest institution (Atascadero) for the criminally insane. Although society cannot excuse those who willfully commit crimes, we must also be cognizant of the fact that many offenders have been victims, too. The cycle of violence becomes perpetual. The roots of victimization run deep in our social structure and will only go deeper if we continue to ignore the needs of the family.

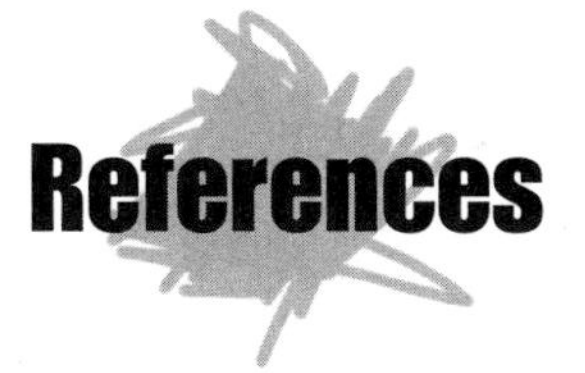

References

Abraham, S. (1984). *Children in the Cross-Fire: The Tragedy of Parental Kidnapping*. New York: Atheneum.

Abrahamsen, D. (1973). *The Murdering Mind*. New York: Harper and Row.

———. (1985). *Confessions of Son of Sam*. New York: Columbia University Press.

Adler, F. (1975). *Sisters in Crime: The Rise of the New Female Criminal*. New York: McGraw-Hill.

Aichorn, A. (1934). *Wayward Youth*. New York: Viking Press.

Aki, K. (2003). Serial Killers: A Cross-Cultural Study between Japan and the United States. Unpublished master's thesis, California State University, Fresno, CA.

Albarus, C. (1996). *Social and Developmental History of Mr. Henry Wallace*. New York: CVA Consulting.

Alexander, M. P., N. D. Kellogg, and P. Thompson. (2005). Community and Mental Health Support of Juvenile Victims of Prostitution. In S. W. Cooper, R. J. Estes, A. P. Giardino, N. D. Kellogg, and V. I. Vieth (Eds.), *Medical, Legal, and Social Science Aspects of Child Sexual Exploitation* (Vol. 1). St. Louis, MO: G. W. Medical Publishing, pp. 397–421.

Alexander, R. (2011). Pathways: Changes in Recruitment for Child Sexual Abuse and Life Course Events. Unpublished dissertation, Kansas State University.

Alexander, S. (1983). *Nutcracker: Money, Madness, Murder: A Family Album*. New York: Dell.

Allen, T. (1988, November 13). Portrait of a Serial Killer. *Statesman Journal*.

Allen, W. (1976). *Starkweather*. Boston, MA: Houghton Mifflin.

American Psychiatric Association. (1988). *Diagnostic and Statistical Manual of Mental Disorders* (3rd ed., rev.). Washington, DC: Author.

———. (1994). *Diagnostic and Statistical Manual of Mental Disorders* (4th ed.). Washington, DC: Author.

———. (2000). *Diagnostic and Statistical Manual of Mental Disorders* (IV-TR). Washington, DC: American Psychological Association.

Anderson, C. A. (2010). Violent Video Games and Other Media Violence (Part I). *Pediatrics for Parents*, 26(1&2), 28–30.

Associated Press. (1989, April 11). Mass Grave Found in Mexico. New York.

Athens, L. H. (1980). *Violent Criminal Acts and Actors*. Cambridge, MA: Routledge and Kegan Paul.

Attewill, F. (2007). *The Animal Lover Who Killed Humans to Let Them into Another World*. United Kingdom: Guardian News and Media Limited.

Bailey, S. (2000). Juvenile Homicide. *Criminal Behavior and Mental Health*, 10(3), 149–208.

Bandura, A. (1973). *Aggression*. Englewood Cliffs, NJ: Prentice Hall.

———. (1974). Behavior Theory and the Models of Man. *American Psychologist*, 29, 861–862.

Bandura, A., and R. H. Walters. (1963). *Social Learning and Personality Development*. New York: Holt, Rinehart and Winston.

Bard, M., and D. Sangrey. (1986). *The Crime Victim's Book* (2nd ed.). New York: Brunner Mazel.

Barnes, B. (1986). FBI Specialist. *Atlanta Journal and Constitution*, 1, 7a.

Bartholow, B. D., and A. Heinz. (2006). Alcohol and Aggression Without Consumption. *Psychological Science*, 17(1), 30–37.

Bartol, C. R., and A. M. Bartol. (1986). *Criminal Behavior: A Psychosocial Approach*. Englewood Cliffs, NJ: Prentice Hall.

———. (1995). *Criminal Behavior: A Psychosocial Approach* (4th ed.). Englewood Cliffs, NJ: Prentice Hall.

Baumann, E. (1987, October 12). When Demons Preyed. *Chicago Tribune*, 1–2.

Beauregard, E., P. Lussier, and J. Proulx. (2004). An Exploration of Developmental Factors Related to Deviant Sexual Preferences among Adult Rapists. *Sexual Abuse: Journal of Research and Treatment*, 16(2), 151–161.

Becker, H. (1963). *Outsiders: Studies in the Sociology of Deviance*. New York: Macmillan, p. 9.

Beine, K. H. (2003). Homicides of Patients in Hospitals and Nursing Homes: A Comparative Analysis of Case Series. *International Journal of Law and Psychiatry*, 26(17), 373–386.

Benezech, M., M. Bourgeois, and J. A. Yesavage. (1981). Cannibalism and Vampirism in Paranoid Schizophrenia. *Journal of Clinical Psychiatry*, 42, 7.

Benning, S. D., C. J. Patrick, B. M. Hicks, D. M. Blonigen, and R. F. Krueger. (2003). Factor Structure of the Psychopathic Personality Inventory: Validity and Implications for Clinical Assessment. *Psychological Assessment*, 15, 340–350.

Benning, S. D., C. J. Patrick, D. M. Blonigen, B. M. Hicks, and W. G. Iacono. (2005a). Estimating Facets of Psychopathy from Normal Personality Traits: A Step toward Community-Epidemiological Investigations. *Assessment*, 12, 3–18.

Benning, S. D., C. J. Patrick, R. T. Salekin, and A. R. Leistico. (2005b). Convergent and Discriminant Validity of Psychopathy Factors Assessed via Self-Report: A Comparison of Three Instruments. *Assessment*, 12, 270–289.

Benning, S. D., C. J. Patrick, and W. G. Iacono. (2005c). Psychopathy, Startle Blink Modulation, and Electrodermal Reactivity in Twin Men. *Psychophysiology*, 42, 753–762.

Bensing, R. C., and O. Schroeder Jr. (1960). *Homicide in an Urban Community*. Springfield, IL: Charles C. Thomas.

Benton, D. (2007). The Impact of Diet on Anti-Social, Violent and Criminal Behavior. *Neuroscience & Biobehavioral Reviews*, 31(5), 752–774.

Berkow, R. (1977). *The Merck Manual* (13th ed.). Rahway, NJ: Merck, Sharp and Dohme Research Laboratories.

Berkowitz, L., and J. Macaulay. (1971, June). The Contagion of Criminal Violence. *Sociometry*, 34, 238–260.

Bierer, J. (1976). Love-Making—An Act of Murder. *International Journal of Social Psychiatry*, 22(3), 197–199.

Bjorklund, L. (2008). Perception of Female Sexual Offenders: The Impact of Misperception. Unpublished doctoral dissertation, California School of Forensic Studies, Alliant International University, Fresno, CA.

Black, C. (1974). *Capital Punishment: The Inevitability of Caprice and Mistake*. New York: Norton.

———. (1980). Objections to S. 1382, a Bill to Establish Rational Criteria for the Imposition of Capital Punishment. *Crime and Delinquency*, 26, 441–453.

Blackburn, R. (1971). Personality Types among Abnormal Homicides. *British Journal of Criminology*, 11, 14–31.

Blagov, P. S., C. J. Patrick, S. O. Lilienfeld, A. D. Powers, J. E. Phifer, N. Venables, D. Herres, M. Hudak, S. C. Garvin Leigh, K. Lieb, and G. Cooper. (2011, October). Personality Constellations in Incarcerated Psychopathic Men. *Personality Disorders: Theory, Research, and Treatment*, 2(4), 293–315.

Blau, J. R., and P. M. Blau. (1982, February). The Cost of Inequality: Metropolitan Structure and Violent Crime. *American Sociological Review*, 47, 114–129.

Blonigen, D. M., B. M. Hicks, C. J. Patrick, R. F. Krueger, W. G. Iacono, and M. K. McGue. (2005). Psychopathic Personality Traits: Heritability and Genetic Overlap with Internalizing and Externalizing Psychopathology. *Psychological Medicine*, 35, 637–648.

Boar, R., and N. Blundell. (1983). *The World's Most Infamous Murders*. New York: Simon and Schuster.

Bogaerts, S., A. Daalder, S. Vanheule, M. Desmet, and F. Leeuw. (2008). Personality Disorders in a Sample of Paraphilic and Nonparaphilic Child Molesters. *International Journal of Offender Therapy and Comparative Criminology*, 52(1), 21–30.

Brewer, N., and G. Wells. (2011). Eyewitness Identification. *Current Directions in Psychological Science*, 20, 24–27.

Brian, D. (1986). *Murderers Die*. New York: St. Martin's Press.

Briar, S., and I. Piliavin. (1965). Delinquency, Situational Inducements, and Commitment to Conformity. *Social Problems*, 13, 35–45.

Briere, J., and M. Runtz. (1989). University Males' Sexual Interest in Children: Predicting Potential Indices of "Pedophilia" in a Nonforensic Sample. *Child Abuse & Neglect*, 13(1), 65–75.

Brodsky, S. L. (Ed.). (1973). *Psychologists in the Criminal Justice System*. Urbana, IL: University of Illinois Press.

Bronswick, A. L. (2001). Using Sexually Related Crime Scene Characteristics to Profile Male Serial Killers: A Question of Motivation. Unpublished dissertation, Alliant International University, Fresno, CA.

Brooks, P. R., M. J. Devine, T. J. Green, B. L. Hart, and M. D. Moore. (1987, June). Serial Murder:

A Criminal Justice Response. *Police Chief*, 54(6), 37–45.

Brophy, J. (1966). *The Meaning of Murder*. New York: Thomas Y. Crowell.

Brown, R., L. Osterman, and C. Barnes. (2009). School Violence and the Culture of Violence. *Psychological Science*, 20, 1400–1405.

Brown, S. E. (1984). Social Class, Child Maltreatment, and Delinquent Behavior. *Criminology*, 22(2), 259–278.

Brownmiller, S. (1975). *Against Our Will: Men, Women, and Rape*. New York: Simon and Schuster.

Bruch, H. (1967). Mass Murder: The Wagner Case. *American Journal of Psychiatry*, 124(5), 693–698.

Bugliosi, V. (1974). *Helter Skelter*. New York: Norton.

Burgess, A., and L. Morgenbesser. (2005). Sexual Violence and Seniors. *Brief Treatment and Crisis Intervention*, 5(2), 193–202.

Busch, K. G., R. Zagar, J. R. Hughes, J. Arbit, and R. E. Bussell. (1990). Adolescents Who Kill. *Journal Clinical Psychology*, 46(4), 472–485.

Bushman, B., and J. Whitaker. (2010). Like a Magnet: Catharsis Beliefs Attract Angry People to Violent Video Games. *Psychological Science*, 21, 790–792.

Bushman, B. J., R. D. Ridge, E. Das, C. W. Key, and G. L. Busath. (2007). When God Sanctions Killing: Effect of Scriptural Violence on Aggression. *Psychological Science*, 18(3), 204–207.

Cameron, D., and E. Frazer. (1987). *The Lust to Kill*. New York: New York University Press.

Campbell, W. K., J. K. Bosson, T. W. Goheen, C. E. Lakey, and M. H. Kernis. (2007). Do Narcissists Dislike Themselves "Deep Down Inside"? *Psychological Science*, 18(3), 227–229.

Canter, D. (1994). *Criminal Shadows*. London: HarperCollins.

———. (2000). Offender Profiling and Criminal Differentiation. *Legal and Criminological Psychology*, 5, 23–46.

———. (2011). Resolving the Offender "Profiling Equations" and the Emergence of an Investigative Psychology. *Current Directions in Psychological Science*, 20, 5–10.

Canter, D., C. Missen, and S. Hodge. (1997). Are Serial Killers Special? *Policing Today*, 2(1), 2–11.

Canter, D., D. Hughes, and S. Kirby. (1998). Pedophilia: Pathology, Criminality, or Both? The Development of a Multivariate Model of Offence Behavior in Child Sexual Abuse. *Journal of Forensic Psychiatry*, 9, 532–555.

Canter, D. V., and L. J. Alison. (2000). *Profiling Rape and Murder* (Offender Profiling series, vol. V). Aldershot: Dartmouth.

Capote, T. (1965). *In Cold Blood*. New York: Random House.

Caputi, J. (1987). *The Age of Sex Crime*. Bowling Green, OH: Bowling Green State University Popular Press.

———. (1989). The Sexual Politics of Murder. *Gender and Society*, 3(4), 437–456.

———. (1990). The New Founding Fathers: The Lure and Lore of the Serial Killer in Contemporary Culture. *Journal of American Culture*, 13(3), 1–12.

Carlson, K. (2010). The Public's Perceptions of Male and Female Sex Offenders. Unpublished dissertation, Alliant International University, Fresno, CA.

Carnagey, N. L., and C. A. Anderson. (2005). The Effects of Reward and Punishment in Violent Video Games on Aggressive Affect, Cognition, and Behavior. *Psychological Science*, 16(11), 882–889.

Carnes, P. (2001). *Out of the Shadows: Understanding Sex Addiction*. Center City, MN: Hazelden.

Carr, C. (1994). *The Alienist*. New York: Random House.

Carrington, F. (1978). *Neither Cruel nor Unusual*. Westport, CT: Arlington House.

Castle, T. (2001). A Case Study Analysis of Serial Killers with Military Experience: Applying Learning Theory to Serial Murder. Unpublished Master's Thesis, Morehead State University.

Castle, T., and C. Hensley. (2002). Serial Killers with Military Experience: Applying Learning Theory to Serial Murder. *International Journal of Offender Therapy and Comparative Criminology*, 46(4), 453–465.

Cavanagh, K., and R. E. MacKay. (1991). Violent Crime Analysis Section. *RCMP Gazette*, 53(1), 5–7.

Centers for Disease Control and Prevention. (2001). *Occupational Violence*. Department of Health and Human Services, National Institute for Occupational Safety and Health.

Chapman, J. (1980). *Economic Realities and the Female Offender*. Lexington, MA: Lexington Books.

Charny, I. W. (1980). A Contribution to the Psychology of Genocide: Sacrificing Others to the Death We Fear Ourselves. *Israel Yearbook on Human Rights*, 90, 90–108.

———. (1982). *How Can We Commit the Unthinkable?* Boulder, CO: Westview Press.

Cheney, M. (1976). *The Co-Ed Killer*. New York: Walker.

Cleary, S., and J. Luxenburg. (1993, October). Serial Murderers: Common Background Characteristics and Their Contribution to Causation. Paper presented at the annual meeting of the American Society of Criminology, Miami, FL.

Cleckley, H. (1976). *The Mask of Sanity* (5th ed.). St. Louis, MO: Mosby.

Clinard, M. B., and R. Quinney. (1986). *Criminal Behavior Systems: A Typology* (2nd ed.). Cincinnati, OH: Anderson.

Cline, V. (1990). Privately published monograph, Department of Psychology, University of Utah, Salt Lake City.

CNN. (1993). *Murder by Number.* Two-hour documentary on the phenomenon of serial murder.

———. (2010). *The Atlanta Child Murders.* Documentary on Wayne Williams and the 1980–1981 serial murders of 22+ children in the Atlanta, GA.

Cohen, L. E., and M. Felson. (1979). Social Change and Crime Rate Trends: A Routine Activity Approach. *American Sociological Review*, 44, 588–605.

Cohen, M. L., T. Seghorn, and S. Calmas. (1969). A Sociometric Study of the Sex Offender. *Journal of Abnormal Psychology*, 71, 249–255.

Cole, R. (1998, January 10). Prosecutors Say Women Seduced, Poisoned Elderly Men for Money. Associated Press.

Coons, P. M. (1988, January 5). LaRue D. Carter Memorial Hospital, personal memo to author.

Copson, G. (1995). Coals to Newcastle? *Part 1: A Study of Offender Profiling (paper 7).* London: Police Research Group Special Interest Series, Home Office.

Corder, B. F., B. C. Ball, T. M. Haizlip, R. Rollins, and R. Beaumont. (1976). Adolescent Parricide: A Comparison with Other Adolescent Murder. *American Journal of Psychiatry*, 133(8), 957–961.

Cormier, B. M., C. C. J. Boyer, R. Boyer, and G. Mersereau. (1972). The Psychodynamics of Homicide Committed in a Semispecific Relationship. *Canadian Journal of Criminology and Corrections*, 14, 335–344.

Coston, C. T. M. (2003). Lives Interrupted!: A Case Study of an African American Serial Murderer in the Bible Belt, Henry Louis Wallace. Unpublished paper, Department of Criminal Justice, University of North Carolina, Charlotte, NC.

Court TV. (2002). *The Elite: The New Profilers.*

Crépault, C., and M. Couture. (1980). Men's Erotic Fantasies. *Archives of Sexual Behavior*, 9(6), 565–581.

Cullen, R. (1993). *The Killer Department.* New York: Pantheon Books.

Cullen, T. (1977). *The Mild Murderer.* Boston, MA: Houghton Mifflin.

Cummings, E. M., and P. Davies. (1994). *Children and Marital Conflict: The Impact of Family Dispute and Resolution.* New York: Guilford.

Cunliffe, T., and C. Gacono. (2005). A Rorschach Investigation of Incarcerated Female Offenders with Antisocial Personality Disorder. *International Journal of Offender Therapy and Comparative Criminology*, 49(5), 530–546.

Cusator, J. (2009). Paraphilic Behavior and the Use of Facilitators in a Serial Murderer Population. Unpublished doctoral dissertation. California School for Forensic Studies, Alliant International University. Irvine, CA.

Dahmer, L. (1994). *A Father's Story.* London: Little, Brown.

Daly, M., and M. Wilson. (1988). *Homicide.* New York: Aldine de Gruyter.

Daniels, S. (1989). Satanic Beliefs, Criminal Actions. *The Training Key.* International Association of Chiefs of Police, p. 390.

Danto, B. (1982). A Psychiatric View of Those Who Kill. In J. Bruhns, K. Bruhns, and H. Austin (Eds.), *The Human Side of Homicide.* New York: Columbia University Press, pp. 3–20.

Darby, P. J., W. D. Allan, J. H. Kashani, K. L. Hartke, and J. C. Reid. (1998). Analysis of 112 Juveniles Who Committed Homicide: Characteristics and a Closer Look at Family Abuse. *Journal of Family Violence*, 13(4), 365–375.

Daubert v. Merrill Dow Pharmaceuticals, Inc., 113 S. Ct. 2786 (1993).

Dean, A. L., M. M. Malik, W. Richards, and S. A. Stringer. (1986). Effects of Parental Maltreatment on Children's Conceptions of Interpersonal Relationships. *Developmental Psychology*, 22(5), 617–626.

DeFronzo, J., A. Ditta, L. Hannon, and J. Prochnow. (2007). Male Serial Homicide: The Influence of Cultural and Structural Variables. *Homicide Studies*, 11(1), 3–14.

Deming, R. (1977). *Women: The New Criminals.* Nashville, TN: Thomas Nelson.

Denov, M. S. (2004). The Long-Term Effects of Child Sexual Abuse by Female Perpetrators: A Qualitative Study of Male and Female Victims. *Journal of Interpersonal Violence*, 19(10), 1137–1156.

De River, J. P. (1949). *The Sexual Criminal.* Springfield, IL: Charles C. Thomas.

Dettlinger, C. (1983). *The List.* Atlanta, GA: Philmay Enterprises.

Devery, C. (2010). Criminal Profiling and Criminal Investigation. *Journal of Contemporary Criminal Justice*, 26, 393–409.

De Young, M. (1982). *The Sexual Victimization of Children.* Jefferson, NC: McFarland, p. 125.

Diamond, M., and A. Uchiyama. (1999). Pornography, Rape, and Sex Crime in Japan. *International Journal of Law and Psychiatry*, 22(1), 1–22.

Dietz, P. (1986). Mass, Serial and Sensational Homicide. *Bulletin of the New England Medical Society*, 62, 477–491.

———. (1994). *To Kill and Kill Again.* London: Optomen Television.

Dietz, P. E., R. R. Hazelwood, and J. Warren. (1990). The Sexually Sadistic Criminal and His Offenses. *Bulletin of American Academy of Psychiatry Law*, 18(2), 163–178.

Dijk, J. M., P. Mayhew, and M. Killias. (1991). *Experiences of Crime across the World: Key Findings of the 1989 International Survey of Crime.* Deventer, The Netherlands: Kluwer.

Dimock, J., and S. Smith. (1997). Necrophilia and Anti-Social Acts. In L. B. Schlesinger and E. Revitch

(Eds.), *Sexual Dynamics of Anti-Social Behavior* (2nd ed.). Springfield, IL: Charles C. Thomas, pp. 241–251.

Dodd, N. J. (1998). Applying Psychology to the Reduction of Insurance Claim Fraud. *Insurance Trends*, 18, 11–16.

Doerner, W. G. (1975, May). A Regional Analysis of Homicide Rates in the United States. *Criminology*, 13, 90–101.

Doerner, W. G., and S. Lab. (1995). *Victimology*. Cincinnati, OH: Anderson.

Doney, R. H. (1990). The Aftermath of the Yorkshire Ripper: The Response of the United Kingdom Police Service. In S. A. Egger (Ed.), *Serial Murder: An Elusive Phenomenon*. New York: Praeger, pp. 95–112.

Donnelly, D., and J. Fraser. (1998). Gender Differences in Sado-Masochistic Arousal among College Students. *Sex Roles*, 39(5–6), 391–407.

Dostoyevsky, F. (1962). *The House of the Dead*. London: Dent.

Douglas, J., and M. Olshaker. (1999). *The Anatomy of Motive*. New York: Scribner.

Drukteinis, A. M. (1992). Serial Murder: The Heart of Darkness. *Psychiatric Annals*, 22, 532–538.

Drzazga, J. (Ed.). (1960). Necrophilia. In *Sex Crimes and Their Legal Aspects*. Springfield, IL: Charles C. Thomas, pp. 199–204.

Dugdale, R. (1910). *The Jukes*. New York: Putnam.

Durham v. United States, 214 F. 2d 862 (D.C. Cir. 1954).

Dussich, J. P. J., P. C. Friday, T. Okada, A. Yamagami, and R. D. Knudten. (2001). *Different Responses to Violence in Japan and America*. New York: Criminal Justice Press.

Dutton, D. (2007). *The Abusive Personality* (2nd ed.). New York: Guilford Press.

Dutton, D. G., and S. D. Hart. (1992). Evidence for Long-Term, Specific Effects of Childhood Abuse and Neglect on Criminal Behavior in Men. *International Journal of Offender Therapy and Comparative Criminology*, 36(2), 129–137.

Egger, K. (1999). Preliminary Database on Serial Killers from 1900–1999. In S. Egger (2001), *The Killers among Us: An Examination of Serial Murder and Its Investigation* (2nd. ed.). Upper Saddle River, NJ: Prentice Hall, 38–73.

Egger, S. A. (1984). A Working Definition of Serial Murder and the Reduction of Linkage Blindness. *Journal of Police Science and Administration*, 12, 348–357.

———. (1985). Serial Murder and the Law Enforcement Response. Unpublished dissertation, College of Criminal Justice, Sam Houston State University, Huntsville, TX.

———. (1986). Utility of the Case Study Approach to Serial Murder Research. Paper presented at the 1986 annual meetings of the American Society of Criminology, Atlanta, GA.

———. (1990). *Serial Murder: An Elusive Phenomenon*. New York: Praeger.

———. (2001). *The Killers among Us: An Examination of Serial Murder and Its Investigation*. Upper Saddle River, NJ: Prentice Hall.

Egger, S., and K. Egger (2001). Victims of Serial Killers: The Less Dead. In J. Sgarzi and J. McDevitt (2003). *Victimology*. Upper Saddle River, NJ: Prentice Hall, pp. 9–32.

Eisler, R. (1951). *Man into Wolf*. New York: Greenwood Press.

Eitzen, D. S., and D. A. Timmer. (1985). *Criminology*. New York: Wiley.

Ellis, A., and J. Gullo. (1971). *Murder and Assassination*. New York: Lyle Stuart.

Ellis, B. E. (1991). *American Psycho*. New York: Vintage Books.

Epstein, S. (1995). The New Mythic Monster. In J. Ferrell and C. Sanders (Eds.), *Cultural Criminology*. Boston, MA: Northeastern Press, pp. 66–79.

Ermer, E., and K. Kiehl. (2010). Psychopaths Are Impaired in Social Exchange and Precautionary Reasoning. *Psychological Science*, 21, 1399–1405.

Estabrook, A. (1916). *The Jukes in 1915*. Washington, DC: Carnegie Institute of Washington.

Eth, S., and R. S. Pynoos. (1985). Developmental Perspective on Psychic Trauma in Childhood. In C. R. Figley (Ed.), *Trauma and Its Wake: The Study and Treatment of Post-Traumatic Stress Disorder*. New York: Brunner and Mazel, pp. 36–52.

Ewing, C. P. (1990). *When Children Kill: The Dynamics of Juvenile Homicide*. Lexington, MA: Lexington Books.

Eysenck, H. J. (1973). *The Inequality of Man*. San Diego, CA: Edits Publishers.

———. (1977). *Crime and Personality* (2nd ed.). London: Routledge and Kegan Paul.

Farrington, D. P. (Ed.). (1998). *Psychological Explanations of Crime*. Aldershot: Ashgate.

Federal Bureau of Investigation. (1984a). *Crime in the U.S., Uniform Crime Reports*. Washington, DC: U.S. Department of Justice, U.S. Government Printing Office.

———. (1984b). *Report to the Nation on Crime and Justice*. Washington, DC: FBI Statistical Department, United States Department of Justice.

———. (1985). *FBI Law Enforcement Bulletin Crime Scene and Profile Characteristics of Organized and Disorganized Murderers* (Vol. 54). Washington, DC: U.S. Government Printing Office, pp. 18–25.

———. (1988). *Crime in the U.S. Adapted from the Uniform Crime Reports*. Washington, DC: U.S. Department of Justice, U.S. Government Printing Office.

———. (1993). *Crime in the U.S. Adapted from the Uniform Crime Reports*. Washington, DC: U.S. Department of Justice, U.S. Government Printing Office.

———. (1995). *Crime in the U.S. Adapted from Uniform Crime Reports*. Washington, DC: U.S. Department of Justice, U.S. Government Printing Office.

———. (2000). *Crime in the U.S., Uniform Crime Reports*. Washington, DC: U.S. Department of Justice, U.S. Government Printing Office.

———. (2008). *Serial Murder: Multi-Disciplinary Perspectives for Investigators*. Behavioral Analysis Unit, National Center for the Analysis of Violent Crime. U.S. Department of Justice, Washington, DC.

———. (2011). *Highway Serial Killing Initiative*. Behavioral Analysis Unit, National Center for the Analysis of Violent Crime. U.S. Department of Justice, Washington, DC.

Felthous, A. R. (1980a). Aggression Against Cats, Dogs and People. *Child Psychiatry and Human Development*, 10(3), 169–177.

Felthous, A. R. (1980b). Childhood Antecedents of Aggressive Behaviors in Male Psychiatric Patients. *Bulletin of the American Academy of Psychiatry and Law*, 8, 104–105.

Felthous, A., and S. Kellert. (1985). America's Abuse Problem. *ASPCA Animal Watch*, Fall/Winter 1992, 10.

Fessenden, F. (2000, April 10). Seething Anger Has Deadly Aim. *New York Times*, 1.

Fezzani, N. (2011). *Mes Tueurs en Serie*. Montreal, QC: Les Editions de L'Homme.

Field, J. (2007). Caring to Death; a Discursive Analysis of Nurses Who Murder Patients. Unpublished doctoral dissertation. University of Adelaide.

Fineman, K. R. (1995). A Model for the Qualitative Analysis of Child and Adult Fire Deviant Behavior. *American Journal of Forensic Psychology*, 13(1), 31–60.

Finkelhor, D. (1979). *Sexually Victimized Children*. New York: Free Press.

———. (1988). *Nursery Crimes*. Newbury Park, CA: Sage.

Finkelhor, D., R. K. Ormrod, H. Turner, and S. L. Hamby. (2005). The Victimization of Children and Youth: A Comprehensive National Survey. *Child Maltreatment*, 10, 5–25.

Fisher, D., and Mair, G. (1998). A Review of Classification Systems for Sex Offenders. Home Office Research and Statistics Directorate.

Forouzan, E., and D. Cooke. (2005). Figuring Out *la Femme Fatale*: Conceptual and Assessment Issues Concerning Psychopathy in Females. *Behavioral Sciences and the Law*, 23, 765–778.

Forrest, A. R. (1995). Deaths from Methadone Use. *Journal of Clinical Forensic Medicine*, 2(3), 143–144.

Fortune, J. (1934). *The Story of Clyde Barrow and Bonnie Parker*. Dallas, TX: Ranger Press.

Fowles, D., and L. Dindo (2009). Temperament and Psychopathy. *Current Directions in Psychological Science*, 18, 179–183.

Fox, C., and D. Harding. (2005). School Shootings as Organizational Deviance. *Sociology of Education*, 78, 69–97.

Fox, J. A., and J. Levin. (1989). Satanism and Mass Murders. *Celebrity Plus*, 49–51.

———. (1994). *Overkill: Mass Murder and Serial Killing Exposed*. New York: Plenum Press.

———. (1995). Serial Murder: A Survey. In T. O'Reilly-Fleming (Ed.), *Serial and Mass Murder: Theory, Research and Policy*. Toronto, ON: Canadian Scholar's Press, pp. 55–76.

———. (2011). *Extreme Killing: Understanding Serial and Mass Murder*. Thousand Oaks, CA: Sage.

Fox, J. A., J. Levin, and K. Quinet. (2011). *The Will to Kill: Making Sense of Senseless Murder*. Boston, MA: Allyn and Bacon Publishers.

Frank, G. (1966). *The Boston Strangler*. New York: The New American Library.

Franke, D. (1975). *The Torture Doctor*. New York: Hawthorn Books.

Franzini, L. R., and J. M. Grossberg. (1995). *Eccentric and Bizarre Behaviors*. New York: John Wiley and Sons, Inc.

Frederick, C. (1981). Violence and Disasters: Immediate and Long-Term Consequences. Paper presented at Psychosocial Consequences of Violence Conference, The Hague, April 6–10.

Freeman, L. (1955). *Before I Kill More*. New York: Crown.

Freeman, N. (2007). Predictors of Rearrest for Rapists and Child Molesters. *Criminal Justice and Behavior*, 34(6), 752–768.

Freiberger, K. (1997). Application of Prominent Typologies to the Female Serial Murderer Phenomenon. Master's thesis, Virginia Commonwealth University, Richmond, VA.

———. (2008). Examining Incidents of Cyberstalking: An Exploration of an Emerging Crime. Unpublished doctoral dissertation, Virginia Commonwealth University, Richmond, VA.

Freud, S. (1936). *The Problem of Anxiety*. New York: Norton.

Freund, K., and R. Watson. (1990). Mapping the Boundaries of Courtship Disorder. *Journal of Sex Research*, 27, 589–606.

Friedman, S. H., S. McCue Horwitz, and P. J. Resnick. (2005). Child Murder by Mothers: A Critical Analysis of the Current State of Knowledge and a Research Agenda. *American Journal of Psychiatry*, 162, 1578–1587.

Fromm, E. (1973). *The Anatomy of Human Destructiveness*. New York: Holt, Rinehart and Winston.

Frye v. United States, 293 F. (D.C. Cir. 1923).

Gaddis, T. E., and J. O. Long. (1970). *Killer: A Journal of Murder*. New York: Macmillan.

Gallagher, B. J., III. (1987). *The Sociology of Mental Illness* (2nd ed.). Englewood Cliffs, NJ: Prentice Hall.

Gastil, R. D. (1971, June). Homicide and a Regional Culture of Violence. *American Sociological Review*, 36, 412–427.

Gaute, J. H. H., and R. O'Dell. (1979). *The Murderers' Who's Who*. New York: Methuen.

Geberth, V. J. (1983). *Practical Homicide Investigation*. New York: Elsevier.

———. (2012, January/February). Black Serial Killers: The Perception vs. Reality. *PI Magazine*, 26, 42–47.

Gebhard, P. H. (1965). *Sex Offenders*. New York: Harper and Row, p. 856.

Gelles, R. J., and C. P. Cornell. (1990). *Intimate Violence in Families* (2nd ed.). Beverley Hills: Sage.

Gibbs, W. W. (1995, March). Seeking the Criminal Element. *Scientific American*, 272(3), 101–107.

Gibson, W. B. (1965). *Murder, the Fine Art*. New York: Grosset and Dunlap.

Gill, E. (1994). Children and Animals: A Clinician's View. *The Animal's Agenda*, March/April, 20–21.

Glaser, B. G., and A. Strauss. (1967). *The Discovery of Grounded Theory: Strategies for Qualitative Research*. Chicago: Aldine.

Glover, J. D., and D. C. Witham. (1989). The Atlanta Serial Murders. *Policing*, 5(1), 2–6.

Goddard, H. H. (1912). *The Kalli Kak Family: A Study in the Heredity of Feeblemindedness*. New York: McMillan.

Godwin, G. M. (1999). *Hunting Serial Predators*. New York: CRC Press.

Godwin, J. (1978). *Murder U.S.A.* New York: Random House.

Goffman, E. (1961). *Asylums*. Garden City, NY: Doubleday.

Golden, C., J. Moses Jr., J. Coffman, W. Miller, and F. Strider. (1983). *Clinical Neuropsychology*. New York: Grune and Stratton.

Goodroe, C. (1987, July). Tracking the Serial Offender. *Law and Order*, 29–33.

Gorby, B. (2000). Serial Murder: A Cross-National Descriptive Study. Master's thesis, California State University, Fresno, Fresno, CA.

Grant, J. E. (2005). Clinical Characteristics and Psychiatric Comorbidity in Males with Exhibitionism. *Journal of Clinical Psychiatry*, 66, 1367–1371.

Gray, G. (1986). Diet, Crime and Delinquency: A Critique. *Nutrition Reviews*, 44, 89–94.

Graysmith, R. (1976). *Zodiac*. New York: Berkeley Books.

Greeley, A. M. (2004). *Priests: A Calling in Crisis*. Chicago: The University of Chicago Press.

Green, R. (2001). (Serious) Sadomasochisim: A Protected Right of Privacy? *Archives of Sexual Behavior*, 30, 543–550.

Greenfeld, L. (1997). Sex Offenses and Offenders: An Analysis of Data on Rape and Sexual Assault. Washington, DC: U.S. Department of Justice, Bureau of Justice Statistics.

Greswell, D. M., and C. Hollin. (1994, Winter). Multiple Murder: A Review. *The British Journal of Criminology*, 34(1), 1–14.

Grombach, J. V. (1980). *The Great Liquidator*. New York: Doubleday.

Groth, A. N., and H. J. Birnbaum. (1978). Adult Sexual Orientation and Attraction to Underage Persons. *Archives of Sexual Behavior*, 7(3), 175–181.

Grubin, D. (1994). Editorial: Sexual Sadism. *Criminal Behavior and Mental Health*, 4, 3–9.

Gudjonsson, G., and J. Pearse. (2011). Suspect Interviews and False Confessions. *Current Directions in Psychological Science*, 20, 33–37.

Gunn, L. (2000). Serial Killers and Their Victims: An Examination of Social Class. Master's thesis, California State University, Fresno, CA.

Guttmacher, M. (1973). *The Mind of the Murderer* (Selected Libraries Reprint series). New York: Arno Press.

Guze, S. B. (1976). *Criminality and Psychiatric Disorders*. New York: Oxford University Press.

Hafner, H., and W. Boker. (1973). Mentally Disordered Violent Offenders. *Social Psychiatry*, 8, 220–229.

Hagan, F. E. (1986). *Introduction to Criminology: Theories, Methods, and Criminal Behavior*. Chicago: Nelson-Hall.

Haggerty, K. (2009). Modern Serial Killers. *Crime Media Culture*, 5(2), 168–187.

Hahn, J. K., and H. C. McKenney. (1972). *Legally Sane*. Chicago: Henry Regnery.

Haizlip, T., B. F. Corder, and B. C. Ball. (1964). The Adolescent Murderer. In C. R. Keith (Ed.), *The Violent Adolescent*. New York: Free Press, pp. 191–208.

Hale, E. (1983, April 18). Startling Discoveries Shed New Light on Enigma of Multiple Personality. *Chicago Tribune*, 1, 5.

Hall, J. R., E. M. Bernat, and C. J. Patrick. (2007). Externalizing Psychopathology and the Error-Related Negativity. *Psychological Science*, 18(4), 326–333.

Hammond, L., and D. Youngs. (2011). Decay Functions and Criminal Spatial Processes: Geographical Offender Profiling of Volume Crime. *Journal of Investigative Psychology and Offender Profiling*, 8(1), 90–102.

Hare, R. D. (1980). A Research Scale for the Assessment of Psychopathy in Criminal Populations. *Personality and Individual Differences*, 1, 111–119.

———. (1991). *The Hare Psychopathy Checklist—Revised*. Toronto, ON: Multi-Health Systems.

———. (2003). *The Hare Psychopathy Checklist—Revised* (2nd ed.) Toronto, ON: Multi-Health Systems.

Hare, R., and J. Jutai. (1959/1983). Criminal History of the Male Psychopath: Some Preliminary Data. In K. T. Van Dusen and S. A. Mednick

(Eds.), *Perspective Studies of Crime and Delinquency.* Boston, MA: Kluwer-Nijhoff, pp. 225–236.

Harris, B. (2011). Aberrant Psychopathy as a Potential Protective Factor Against Posttraumatic Stress Disorder Symptomology. Unpublished doctoral dissertation. California School of Forensic Studies, Alliant International University, Fresno, CA.

Harris, C. (2011). Treatment Outcomes of a Prison Diversion Program. Unpublished doctoral dissertation. California School of Forensic Studies, Alliant International University, Fresno, CA.

Harris, T. (1987). *Red Dragon.* New York: Bantam.

———. (1989). *The Silence of the Lambs.* New York: St. Martin's Press.

Hazelwood, R. R., and A. W. Burgess. (1987, September). An Introduction to the Serial Rapist. *FBI Law Enforcement Bulletin,* 16–24.

———. (1989, February). The Serial Rapist: His Characteristics and Victims. *FBI Law Enforcement Bulletin,* 18–25.

Hazelwood, R. R., and J. Warren. (1989, January). The Serial Rapist: His Characteristics and Victims. *FBI Law Enforcement Bulletin,* 10–17.

Hazelwood, R. R., and J. I. Warren. (2004). (Erratum) Linkage Analysis: Modus Operandi, Ritual, and Signature in Serial Sexual Crime. *Aggression and Violent Behavior,* 9, 307–318.

HBO. (1984). *Murder: No Apparent Motive.* Stamford, CT: Vestron Video.

Healey, J. (2006). Etiology of Paraphilia: A Dichotomous Model. In E. W. Hickey (Ed.), *Sex Crimes and Paraphilia.* Newbury Park, CA: Sage.

Heath, L. (1984, August). Impact of Newspaper Crime on Fear of Crime: A Multimethodological Investigation. *Journal of Personality and Social Psychology,* 47, 263–276.

Heckert, D. M., and M. Ferraiolo. (1996). Social Constructions of Female Serial Murderers. Paper presented at the annual meeting of the American Society of Criminology, Chicago, Illinois.

Heide, K. (1995). *Why Kids Kill Parents: Child Abuse and Adolescent Homicide.* Thousand Oaks: Sage.

_______. (1997). Juvenile Homicide in America: How Can We Stop the Killing? *Behavioral Sciences and the Law,* 15, 203–220.

Hellman, D. S., and N. Blackman. (1966). Enuresis, Fire-setting and Cruelty to Animals: A Triad Predictive of Adult Crime. *The American Journal of Psychiatry,* 122, 1431–1435.

Helpern, M., and B. Knight. (1977). *Autopsy: The Memoirs of Milton Helpern, the World's Greatest Medical Detective.* New York: St. Martin's Press.

Henderson, S. K. (1939). *Psychopathic States.* New York: Norton.

Henn, F. A., M. Herjanic, and R. H. Vanderpearl. (1976). Forensic Psychiatry: Diagnosis of Criminal Responsibility. *Journal of Nervous and Mental Disease,* 162, 423–429.

Hewitt, J. D. (1988). The Victim-Offender Relationship in Homicide Cases: 1960–1984. *Journal of Criminal Justice,* 16(1), 27–38.

Hickey, E. (1985, March). Serial Murderers: Profiles in Psychopathology. Paper presented at the annual meeting of the Academy of Criminal Justice Sciences, Las Vegas, NV.

———. (1986, October). The Female Serial Murderer. *Journal of Police and Criminal Psychology,* 2(2), 72–81.

———. (1990a). The Etiology of Victimization in Serial Murder. In S. A. Egger (Ed.), *Serial Murder: An Elusive Phenomenon.* New York: Praeger, pp. 53–71.

———. (1990b). Missing and Murdered Children in America. In A. R. Roberts (Ed.), *Helping Crime Victims: Research, Policy, and Practice.* Newbury Park, CA: Sage, pp. 158–185.

———. (1996, January). Preliminary Findings in Profiling Juvenile Fire-Setters. Paper presented at the annual meeting of the California Association of Arson Investigators, Fresno, CA.

———. (1997). *Serial Murderers and Their Victims.* Belmont, CA: Wadsworth.

———. (2000). *Application of Domestic and Stranger Stalker-Victim Profiles.* Tel Aviv, Israel: International Security Academy.

———. (2003). *The Encyclopedia of Murder and Violent Crime.* Thousand Oaks, CA: Sage.

———. (2006a). *Sex Crimes and Paraphilia.* Upper Saddle River, NJ: Prentice Hall.

———. (2006b). *Serial Murderers and Their Victims.* Belmont, CA: Wadsworth.

Hickey, E., and M. Deal. (2003). The Beltway Snipers. In E. W. Hickey (Ed.), *The Encyclopedia of Murder and Violent Crime.* Thousand Oaks, CA: Sage, pp. 54–58.

Hickey, E., D. Margulies, and J. Oddie. (1999, February). Victim Profiling in Cases of Stalking and Obsessional Harassment. Paper presented at the American Academy of Forensic Sciences Annual Meeting, Orlando, FL.

Hicks, B. M., E. M. Bernat, S. M. Malone, W. G. Iacono, C. J. Patrick, R. F. Krueger, and M. McGue. (2007). Genes Mediate the Association between P300 Amplitude and Externalizing Psychopathology. *Psychophysiology,* 44, 98–105.

Hicks, B. M., R. F. Krueger, W. G. Iacono, M. K. McGue, and C. J. Patrick. (2004). The Family Transmission and Heritability of Externalizing Disorders. *Archives of General Psychiatry,* 61, 922–928.

Hicks, B. M., K. E. Markon, C. J. Patrick, R. F. Krueger, and J. P. Newman. (2004). Identifying Psychopathy Subtypes Based on Personality Structure. *Psychological Assessment,* 16, 276–288.

Hicks, B. M., U. Vaidyanathan, and C. J. Patrick (2010). Validating Female Psychopathy Subtypes:

Differences in Personality, Antisocial and Violent Behavior, Substance Abuse, Trauma, and Mental Health. *Personality Disorders Theory, Research, and Treatment*, 1, 38–57.

Hill, D., and P. Williams. (1967). *The Supernatural*. New York: Signet Books.

Hill, D., and W. Sargent. (1943). A Case of Matricide. *Lancet*, 244, 526–527.

Hirschi, T. (1969). *Causes of Delinquency*. Berkeley: University of California Press.

Hirst, W. (1982). The Amnesic Syndrome: Descriptions and Explanations. *Psychological Bulletin*, 91, 435–460.

Hoffer, P. C., and N. E. H. Hull. (1981). *Murdering Mothers: Infanticide in England and New England, 1558–1803*. New York: New York University Press.

Hoffman-Bustamante, D. (1973). The Nature of Female Criminality. *Issues in Criminology*, 8, 117–136.

Hollandsworth, S. (1992). Understanding Mass Murder: A Starting Point. *Federal Probation*, 56, 53–61.

———. (1993, May). See No Evil. *Texas Monthly*, 92–140.

Holmes, R., and S. Holmes. (2002). *Profiling Violent Crimes* (3rd ed.). Newbury Park: Sage.

Holmes, R. M. (1990). *Profiling Violent Crimes*. Newbury Park, CA: Sage.

———. (1991). *Sex Crimes*. Newbury Park, CA: Sage.

Holmes, R. M., and J. DeBurger. (1985). Profiles in Terror: The Serial Murderer. *Federal Probation*. U.S. Department of Justice, 49, 29–34.

———. (1988). *Serial Murder*. Newbury Park, CA: Sage.

———. (1994). *Murder in America*. Thousands Oaks, CA: Sage.

Holmes, R. M., and S. T. Holmes. (2000). *Mass Murder in the United States*. Upper Saddle River, NJ: Prentice Hall.

The Holy Bible. (1979). King James Version, Church of Jesus Christ of Latter-Day Saints, Salt Lake City, UT, pp. 1241–1271.

Horney, J. (1978). Menstrual Cycles and Criminal Responsibility. *Law and Human Nature*, 2, 25–36.

Houts, A. C., J. S. Berman, and H. Abramson. (1994). The Effectiveness of Psychological and Pharmacological Treatments for Nocturnal Enuresis. *Journal of Consulting and Clinical Psychology*, 62, 737–745.

Howard, C. (1979). *Zebra: The True Account of the 179 Days of Terror in San Francisco*. New York: Richard Marek.

Howitt, D. (2004). What Is the Role of Fantasy in Sex Offending? *Criminal Behavior and Mental Health*, 14(3), 182–188.

How Many Missing Kids? (1985, October 7). *Newsweek*, 30–35.

Hudson, S. M., and T. Ward. (1997). Rape: Psychopathology and Theory. In D. R. Laws and W. O'Donohue (Eds.), *Sexual Deviance: Theory, Assessment, and Treatment*. New York: Guilford Press, pp. 332–355.

Humane Society of the United States. (2008). 2100 L Street, NW, Washington, DC. 20037.

Inciardi, J. A., and A. E. Pottieger (Eds.). (1978). *Violent Crime: Historical and Contemporary Issues* (Vol. 5). Newbury Park, CA: Sage.

Inglis, R. (1978). *Sins of Fathers: A Study of the Physical and Emotional Abuse of Children*. New York: St. Martin's Press.

Interview with a Vampire: The Vampire Chronicles. (1994). Hollywood, CA: Warner Brothers.

Jackson, J. (1996 Winter). Computer Crimes and Criminals. *American Criminal Justice Association Journal*, 57(1&2), 32–36.

Jackson, J. L., P. van den Eshof, and E. E. de Kleuver. (1994). *Offender Profiling in the Netherlands* (Report NSCR WD94-03). Leiden, The Netherlands: The Netherlands Institute for the Study of Criminality and Law Enforcement.

Jackson, J. L., P. J. van Koppen, and J. C. M. Herbrink. (1993). *Does the Service Meet the Needs? An Evaluation of Consumer Satisfaction with Specific Profile Analysis and Investigative Advice as Offered by the Scientific Research Advisory Unit of the National Criminal Intelligence Division (CRI), The Netherlands* (Report NSCR 93-05). Leiden, The Netherlands: The Netherlands Institute for the Study of Criminality and Law Enforcement.

Jaffe, P., D. Wolfe, S. Wilson, and L. Zak. (1986). Similarities in Behavior and Social Maladjustment among Child Victims and Witnesses to Family Violence. *American Journal of Orthopsychiatry*, 56, 142–146.

James, P. D., and T. A. Critchley. (1986). *The Maul and the Pear Tree*. New York: Mysterious Press.

Jaswal, V., C. Croft, and A. Setia. (2010). Young Children Have a Specific, Highly Robust Bias to Trust Testimony. *Psychological Science*, 21, 1541–1547.

Jeffery, C. R. (1993, Spring). *Journal of Criminal Justice Education*. New York: John Jay College.

Jenkins, P. (1988). Myth and Murder: The Serial Killer Panic of 1983–85. *Criminal Justice Research Bulletin*, 3(11), 1–7.

———. (1993). African Americans and Serial Homicide. *American Journal of Criminal Justice*, 17(2), 47–60.

———. (1994). *Using Murder: The Social Construction of Serial Homicide*. New York: Aldine de Gruyter.

Johansson-Love, J., and W. Fremouw. (2009). Female Sex Offenders: A Controlled Comparison of Offender and Victim/Crime Characteristics. *Journal of Family Violence*, 24, 367–376.

Jones, A. (1980). *Women Who Kill.* New York: Holt, Rinehart, and Winston.

Jones v. United States, 103 S. Ct. 3043 (1983).

Justice, B., R. Justice, and I. Kraft. (1974). Early Warning Signs of Violence: Is a Triad Enough? *American Journal of Psychiatry*, 131, 457–459.

Kadish, S. H., and M. G. Paulsen. (1981). *Criminal Law and Its Processes.* New York: Aspen Publishers, pp. 215–216.

Kafka, M. P., and J. Hennen. (2002). A DSM-IV Axis I Comorbidity Study of Males (n = 120) with Paraphilias and Paraphilia-Related Disorders. *Sexual Abuse: A Journal of Research and Treatment*, 14(4), 349–366.

Kahaner, L. (1988). *Cults That Kill: Probing the Underworld of Occult Crime.* New York: Warner Books.

Kahn, M. (1971). Murderers Who Plead Insanity: A Descriptive Factor-Analytic Study of Personality, Social, and History Variables. *Genetic Psychology Monographs*, 84(2), 275–360.

Karmen, A. (2004). *Crime Victims* (2nd ed.). Belmont, CA: Wadsworth.

Karpman, B. (1954). *The Sexual Offender and His Offenses.* New York: Julian Press.

Kashdan, T. B. and P. E. Knight. (2010). The Darker Side of Social Anxiety: When Aggressive Impulsivity Prevails Over Shy Inhibition. *Current Directions in Psychological Science*, 19, 47–50.

Katz, J. (1988). *Seductions of Crime: Moral and Sensual Attractions in Doing Evil.* New York: Basic Books.

Keeney, B., and K. Heide. (1994). Gender Differences in Serial Murderers: A Preliminary Analysis. *Journal of Interpersonal Violence*, 9(3), 383–398.

———. (1995). Serial Murder: A More Accurate and Inclusive Definition. *International Journal of Offender Therapy and Comparative Criminology*, 39(4), 299–306.

Keppel, R. D. (1989). *Serial Murder: Future Implications for Police Investigations.* Cincinnati, OH: Anderson.

Kerman, S. L. (1962). *The Newgate Calendar.* New York: Capricorn Books.

Keyes, D. (1986). *Unveiling Claudia: A True Story of Serial Murder.* New York: Bantam Books.

Keyes, E. (1976). *The Michigan Murders.* New York: Simon and Schuster.

King, B. (1996). *Lustmord, the Writings and Artifacts of Murderers.* Burbank, CA: Bloat Publisher.

King, G. (1993). *Driven to Kill.* New York: Pinnacle Books.

Kirby, A. (2009). Juvenile Serial Killers: Descriptive Characteristics and Profiles. Unpublished dissertation, California School of Forensic Studies, Alliant International University, Fresno, CA.

Kirby, P. (1998). The Feminization of Serial Killing: A Gender Identity Study of Male and Female Serialists in Female Dominated Occupations. Doctoral dissertation, The American University, Washington, DC.

Kirshner, L. (1973). Dissociative Reactions: A Historical Review and Clinical Study. *Acta Psychiatrica Scandanavica*, 49, 698–711.

Kirwin, B. R. (1997). *The Mad, the Bad, and the Innocent: The Criminal Mind on Trial.* New York: Little, Brown.

Klinesmith, J., T. Kasser, and F. T. McAndrew. (2006). Guns, Testosterone, and Aggression: An Experimental Test of a Mediational Hypothesis. *Psychological Science*, 17(7), 568–571.

Kluckhohn, C., and H. A. Murray. (1953). Personality Formation: The Determinants. In C. Kluckhohn, H. Murray, and D. Schneider (Eds.), *Personality in Nature, Society and Culture.* New York: Knopf, pp. 53–67.

Knight, R. A. (2010). Typologies for Rapists: The Generation of a New Structural Model. In A. Schlank (Ed.), *The Sexual Predator* (Vol. 4). New York: Civic Research Institute, pp. 17-1–17-28.

Kocsis, R. (2006). *Criminal Profiling: Principles and Practices.* New York: Humana Press/Springer Inc.

Kocsis, R., R. Cooksey, and H. Irwin. (2002). Psychological Profiling of Offender Characteristics from Crime Behaviors in Serial Rape Offences. *International Journal of Offender Therapy and Comparative Criminology*, 46, 144–169.

Kocsis, R. N., H. J. Irwin, and A. F. Hayes. (1998). Organized and Disorganized Behavior Syndromes in Arsonists: A Validation Study of a Psychological Profiling Concept. *Psychiatry, Psychology and Law*, 5, 117–130.

Konrath, S., B. J. Bushman, and W. K. Campbell (2006). Attenuating the Link Between Threatened Egotism and Aggression. *Psychological Science*, 17(11), 995–1001.

Kraemer, G., W. Lord, and K. Heilbrun. (2004). Comparing Single and Serial Homicide Offenses. *Behaviorial Science and the Law*, 22, 1–19.

Kramer, E., and A. Lager. (1984). The Use of Art in Assessment of Psychotic Disorders: Changing Perspectives. *Arts in Psychotherapy*, 11(3), 197–201.

Kramer, M. D., C. J. Patrick, M. Gasperi, and R. F. Krueger. (2011). Delineating Physiological Defensive Reactivity in the Domain of Self-Report: Phenotypic and Etiologic Structure of Dispositional Fear. *Psychological Medicine*, 19, 1–16.

Krueger, R. F., B. Hicks, C. J. Patrick, S. Carlson, W. G. Iacono, and M. McGue. (2002). Etiologic Connections among Substance Dependence, Antisocial Behavior, and Personality: Modeling the Externalizing Spectrum. *Journal of Abnormal Psychology*, 111, 411–424.

Krueger, R. F., K. E. Markon, C. J. Patrick, S. D. Benning, and M. Kramer. (2007). Linking

Antisocial Behavior, Substance Use, and Personality: An Integrative Quantitative Model of the Adult Externalizing Spectrum. *Journal of Abnormal Psychology*, 116, 645–666.

Labuschagne, G. (2003). Muti Murder: The Challenges Facing Psychological Investigators. Unpublished paper. Commander of the Investigative Psychology Unit, Serious and Violent Crime Component, Detective Service Head Office, South African Police Service.

Lange, J. E. T., and K. DeWitt Jr. (1990, February). What the FBI Doesn't Know about Serial Killers and Why. Paper presented at the Metropolitan Washington Mensa Regional Gathering, Arlington, VA.

Langlois, J. L. (1985). *Belle Gunnes*. Bloomington, IN: Indiana University Press.

Lansford, J. (2009). Parental Divorce and Children's Adjustment. *Perspectives on Psychological Science*, 4, 140–152.

Larkin, R. (2007). *Comprehending Columbine*. Philadelphia: Temple University Press.

Larson, O. N. (Ed.). (1968). *Violence and the Mass Media*. New York: Harper and Row.

LaVey, A. (1969). *The Satanic Bible*. New York: Avon.

Lawson, C. (1993). Mother-Son Sexual Abuse: Rare or Under-Reported? A Critique of the Research. *Child Abuse & Neglect*, 17(2), 261–269.

Lawson, L. (2008). Female Sex Offenders' Relationship Experiences [Electronic Version]. *Violence and Victims*, 23(3), 331–343.

The Learning Channel. (2001). *Understanding Murder*. Documentary.

Leary, M. R., R. M. Kowalski, L. Smith, and S. Phillips. (2003). Teasing, Rejection, and Violence: Case Studies of School Shootings. *Aggressive Behavior*, 29, 202–214.

Lee, R. A. (1988, July/August). A Motive for Murder. *Police Times*, 6.

Leibman, F. H. (1989). Serial Murderers: Four Case Histories. *Federal Probation*, 53, 41–45.

Leith, R. (1983). *The Prostitute Murders*. New York: Pinnacle Books.

Lemert, E. (1951). *Social Pathology*. New York: McGraw-Hill.

Lester, D. (1979). The Violent Offender. In H. Touch (Ed.), *Psychology of Crime and Criminal Justice*. New York: Holt, Rinehart and Winston, p. 301. (Citing the National Commission on the Causes and Prevention of Violence, to Establish Justice, to Ensure Domestic Tranquility, Washington, DC: U.S. Government Printing Office, 1969.)

———. (1986). *The Murderer and His Murder*. New York: Ams Press.

Lester, D., and G. Lester. (1975). *Crimes of Passion: Murder and the Murderer*. Chicago: Nelson-Hall.

Levin, J., and J. A. Fox. (1985). *Mass Murder: The Growing Menace*. New York: Plenum Press.

Lewis, D. O. (1998). *Guilty by Reason of Insanity: A Psychiatrist Explores the Minds of Killers*. New York: Fawcett Columbine.

Lewis, D. O., B. S. Moy, L. D. Jackson, R. Aaronson, N. Restifo, S. Serra, and A. Simos. (1985, October). Biopsychosocial Characteristics of Children Who Later Murder: A Prospective Study. *American Journal of Psychiatry*, 142, 10.

Leyton, E. (1986a). *Hunting Humans*. Toronto, ON: McClelland and Stewart.

———. (1986b). *Compulsive Killers: The Story of Modern Multiple Murder*. New York: New York University Press.

———. (1993). *Sole Survivor*. Toronto, ON: McClelland-Bantam.

———. (1999). Serial and Mass Murderers. In L. Kurtz (Ed.), *The Encyclopedia of Violence, Peace and Conflict* (3 vols.). New York: Academic Press.

Lieberman, J. (2006). *The Shooting Game: The Making of School Shooters*. Santa Ana, CA: Seven Locks Press.

Liebert, J. A. (1985, December). Contributions of Psychiatric Consultation in the Investigation of Serial Murder. *International Journal of Offender Therapy and Cooperative Criminology*, 29(3), 187–200.

Lifton, R. (1982, November). Medicalized Killing in Auschwitz. *Psychiatry*, 45(4), 283–297.

Lilienfeld, S. O., and B. P. Andrews. (1996). Development and Preliminary Validation of a Self-Report Measure of Psychopathic Personality Traits in Noncriminal Populations. *Journal of Personality Assessment*, 66, 488–524.

Lilienfeld, S. O., and M. R. Widows. (2005). *Psychopathic Personality Inventory—Revised (PPI-R) Professional Manual*. Odessa, FL: Psychological Assessment Resources.

Lindsey, R. (1984, January 21). Killers Who Roam the U.S. *New York Times*, 1, 7.

Linedecker, C. L. (1980). *The Man Who Killed Boys*. New York: St. Martin's Press.

———. (1987). *Thrill Killers*. New York: PaperJacks.

Linnoila, M., M. Virkkunen, M. Scheinin, A. Nuutila, R. Rimon, and F. K. Goodwin. (1983). Low Cerebrospinal Fluid 5-Hydroxyindole Acetic Acid Concentration Differentiates Impulsive from Non-Impulsive Violent Behavior. *Life Sciences*, 33, 2609–2614.

Litton, S. (2006). Characteristics of Child Molesters. In E. W. Hickey (Ed.). *Sex Crimes and Paraphilia*. New Jersey: Pearson, pp. 319–322.

Livsey, C. (1980). *The Manson Women*. New York: Richard Marek.

Locke, J. (1705). Some Thoughts Concerning Education. *The Works of John Locke in Nine Volumes* (12th ed.). London: C & J Rivington, 1968, pp. 112–114.

Lockwood, R., and A. Church. (1996). Deadly Serious: An FBI Perspective on Animal Cruelty. *Humane Society of the United States* (Fall).

Lockwood, R., and F. Ascione (Eds.). (1998). *Cruelty to Animals and Interpersonal Violence*. West Lafayette, IN: Purdue University Press.

Lockwood, R., and G. R. Hodge. (1986). The Tangled Web of Animal Abuse: The Links between Cruelty to Animals and Human Violence. *The Humane Society News* (Summer).

Lombroso, C., and G. Ferrero. (1916). *The Female Offender*. New York: Appleton.

———. (1972). *Criminal Man According to the Classification of Cesare Lombroso*. Montclair, NJ: Patterson Smith, p. 100.

Lord, W. D., M. C. Boudreau, and K. V. Lanning. (2001). Investigating Potential Child Abduction Cases: Developmental Perspectives on the Victimization of Children. *FBI Law Enforcement Bulletin*, 70(4), 1–10.

Lourie, R. (1993). *Hunting the Devil*. London: Grafton.

Lunde, D. T. (1976). *Murder and Madness*. San Francisco, CA: San Francisco Book Company.

Lykken, D. T. (1957). A Study of Anxiety in the Sociopathic Personality. *Journal of Abnormal and Clinical Psychology*, 55, 6–10.

Maas, P. (1975). *King of the Gypsies*. New York: Viking Press.

MacDonald, J. (1963). The Threat to Kill. *American Journal of Psychiatry*, 120, 125–130.

Maier, N. (Ed.). 2002. *The Untold Story. 23 Days of Terror ... The Snipers* (AMI Specials: Volume VI, No. 3). Boca Raton, FL: America Media Inc.

Main, V. (1997). The Changing Image of Serial Killers in Film: A Reflection of Attitudes toward Crime from 1929–1995. Master's thesis, California State University, Fresno, Fresno, CA.

Malmquist, C. P. (1971). Premonitory Signs of Homicidal Aggression in Juveniles. *American Journal of Psychiatry*, 128, 461–465.

———. (1996). *Homicide: A Psychiatric Perspective*. Washington, DC: American Psychiatric Press.

Marron, K. (1988). *Ritual Abuse*. Toronto, ON: McClelland-Bantam.

Marsh, F. H., and J. Katz (Eds.). (1985). *Biology, Crime, and Ethics: A Study of Biological Explanations for Criminal Behavior*. Cincinnati, OH: Anderson.

Marwick, M. (1970). *Witchcraft and Sorcery*. Baltimore, MD: Penguin Books.

Masters, B. (1986). *Killing for Company*. London: Coronet.

Masters, R. E. L., and E. Lea. (1963). *Sex Crimes in History*. New York: Matrix House.

Mathews, R., J. K. Matthews, and K. Speltz. (1989). *Female Sexual Offenders: An Exploratory Study*. Orwell, VT: Safer Society Press.

Matthews, J. (1996). *The Eyeball Killer*. New York: Zebra Publishers.

Matza, D. (1964). *Delinquency and Drift*. New York: Wiley.

Maxfield, M. G. (1989, November). Circumstances in Supplementary Homicide Reports: Variety and Validity. *Criminology*, 27(4), 671–695.

May, R. (1980). *Sex and Fantasy*. New York: Norton, p. 140.

McCarthy, J. B. (1978). Narcissism and the Self in Homicidal Adolescents. *American Journal of Psychoanalysis*, 38, 19–29.

McCrary, G. (2004). Criminal Profiling: The Reality behind the Myth. *Monitor on Psychology*, 35(7), 66.

McDonald, R. R. (1986). *Black Widow*. New York: St. Martin's Press.

McDonald, W. (1970). The Victim: A Social Psychological Study of Criminal Victimization. Unpublished doctoral dissertation. Ann Arbor, MI: University Microfilms.

McGough, M. (2011, November–December). Not Forgotten. *Miller-McCune*, 55–65.

McLeod, M. (1984). Women Against Men: An Examination of Domestic Violence Based on an Analysis of Official Data and National Victimization Data. *Justice Quarterly*, 1, 171–193.

McNamara, J., and R. Morton, (2004). Frequency of Serial Sexual Homicide Victimization in Virginia for a Ten-Year Period. *Journal of Forensic Science*, 49(3), 529–533.

McWilliams, T. (2002). African American Serial Murderers: What Is Behind the Anonymity? Unpublished paper.

Mead, M. (1964). Cultural Factors in the Cause of Pathological Homicide. *Bulletin of Menninger Clinic*, 28, 11–22.

Mednick, S., and J. Volavka. (1980). Biology and Crime. In N. Morris and M. Tonry (Eds.), *Crime and Justice*. Chicago: University of Chicago Press, pp. 85–159.

Mednick, S., G. William, and B. Hutchings. (1983). Genetic Influences in Criminal Behavior: Evidence from an Adoption Cohort. In K. Teilmann, V. Dusen, and S. Mednick (Eds.), *Perspective Studies of Crime and Delinquency*. Boston, MA: Kluwer–Nijhoff, pp. 39–57.

Megargee, E. I., and M. J. Bohn Jr. (1979). *Classifying Criminal Offenders*. Newbury Park, CA: Sage.

Meloy, R. (1988). *The Psychopathic Mind: Origins, Dynamics and Treatment*. London: Jason Aronson.

———. (1993). *Violent Attachments*. New Jersey: Login Bros.

Melton, H. (2007). Predicting the Occurrence of Stalking in Relationships Characterized by Domestic Violence. *Journal of Interpersonal Violence*, 22(1), 3–25.

Messner, S., and K. Tardiff. (1986). Economic Inequality and Levels of Homicide: An Analysis of Urban Neighborhoods. *Criminology*, 24, 297–317.

Messner, S. F., and R. Rosenfeld. (2001). *Crime and the American Dream* (3rd ed.). Belmont, CA: Wadsworth Publishing Company.

Michaud, S. G., and H. Aynesworth. (1983). *The Only Living Witness: A True Account of Homicidal Insanity*. New York: Linden Press, Simon and Schuster.

Miller, A. (1984). *For Your Own Good*. New York: Farrar, Straus, and Giroux.

Miller, D., and J. Looney. (1974). The Prediction of Adolescent Homicide: Episodic Dyscontrol and Dehumanization. *American Journal of Psychoanalysis*, 34(3), 187–198.

Miller, H., K. Turner, and C. Henderson. (2009). Pathology of Sex Offenders Using Latent Profile Analysis. *Journal of Criminal Justice and Behavior*, 36, 778–792.

Milner, J. S., and C. A. Dopke. (1997). Paraphilia Not Otherwise Specified: Psychopathology and Theory. In D. R. Laws and W. O'Donohue (Eds.), *Sexual Deviance: Theory, Assessment, and Treatment*. New York: Guilford Press, pp. 393–423.

Minaar, A. (2001). Witchpurging and Muti Murder in South Africa: The Legislative and Legal Challenges to Combating These Practices with Specific Reference to the Witchcraft Suppression Act (No. 3 of 1957, amended by Act No. 50 of 1970). *African Legal Studies*, 2, 1–21.

M'Naughten. (1843). 10 Clark and Fin. 200, 210, 8 Eng. Rep 718, 722.

Monahan, J., and G. Geis. (1976). Controlling "Dangerous People." *Annals of the American Academy of Political and Social Science*, 423, 142–151.

Monahan, J., and H. Steadman. (1984, September). *Crime and Mental Disorder*. Washington, DC: National Institute of Justice Research in Brief.

Money, J. (1976). Influence of Hormones on Psychosexual Differentiation. *Medical Aspects of Nutrition*, 30, 165.

———. (1984). Paraphilias: Phenomenology and Classification. *American Journal of Psychotherapy*, 38, 164–179.

———. (1990). *Gay, Straight, and In-Between: The Sexology of Erotic Orientation*. New York: Oxford University Press, p. 139.

Money, J., and J. Werlas. (1982). Paraphiliac Sexuality and Child Abuse: The Parents. *Journal of Sex and Marital Therapy*, 8, 57–64.

The Monsters Next Door. (1999, May 3). *TIME*, 20–52.

Montgomery, J. E. (1992, February). Organizational Survival: Continuity or Crisis? Paper presented at the Police Studies Series, Simon Fraser University, Vancouver, British Columbia.

———. (1993). Organizational Survival: Continuity or Crisis? In M. Layton (Ed.), *Policing in the Global Community: The Challenge of Leadership*. Burnaby, BC: Simon Fraser University, pp. 133–142.

Moser, D., and J. Cohen. (1967). *The Pied Piper of Tucson*. New York: The New American Library.

Mother Faces Trial in Child's Death. (1987, June 7). *Atlanta Journal and Constitution*.

Myers, W. C. (2002). *Juvenile Sexual Homicide*. San Diego: Academic Press.

Myers, W. C., D. S. Husted, M. E. Safarik, and M. E. O'Toole. (2006). The Motivation behind Serial Sexual Homicide: Is It Sex, Power, and Control, or Anger? *Journal of Forensic Science*, 51(4), 900–907.

Nash, J. R. (1973). *Bloodletters and Badmen*. New York: M. Evans and Company.

———. (1980). *Murder America*. New York: Simon and Schuster.

———. (1981a). *Almanac of World Crime*. New York: Anchor Press-Doubleday.

———. (1981b). *Look for the Woman*. New York: M. Evans and Company.

———. (1984). *Crime Chronology*. New York: Facts on File.

National Crime Victimization Survey. (2003). *Criminal Victimization*. Washington, DC: Department of Justice.

National School Safety and Security Services. (2009). School Associated Violent Deaths, School Shootings, and High Profile Incidents of School Violence. Cleveland, OH.

Nelson, L. D., C. J. Patrick, and E. M. Bernat. (2011). Operationalizing Proneness to Externalizing Psychopathology as a Multivariate Psychophysiological Phenotype. *Psychophysiology*, 48, 64–72.

Nettler, G. (1982). *Killing One Another*. Cincinnati, OH: Anderson.

Neustatter, L. W. (1957). *The Mind of the Murderer*. London: Christopher Johnson.

Neuwirth, W., and R. Eher. (2003). What Differentiates Anal Rapists from Vaginal Rapists? *International Journal of Offender Therapy and Comparative Criminology*, 47(4), 482–488.

Newsweek. (1985, December 16). The Hunt for the Emotional Rapist, 30.

Ninety-Eighth Congress. (1984). Hearing before the Subcommittee on the Judiciary United States Senate, First Session on Patterns of Murders Committed by One Person, in Large Numbers with No Apparent Rhyme, Reason or Motivation, July 12, 1983. Washington, DC: U.S. Government Printing Office. Serial No. J-98-52.

Nobus, D. (2002). Over My Dead Body: On the Histories and Cultures of Necrophilia. In R. Goodwin (Ed.), *Inappropriate Relationships: The Unconventional, the Disapproved, and the Forbidden*. Mahwah, NJ: Lawrence Publishers, pp. 171–189.

Nolen-Hoeksema, S. (2004). *Abnormal Psychology* (3rd ed.). McGraw-Hill Publishers.

Noll, R. (1992). *Vampires, Werewolves and Demons: Twentieth Century Reports in the Psychiatric Literature*. Brunner/Mazel Publications.

Norris, J. (1988). *Serial Killers*. New York: Doubleday.

Nunberg, H. (1955). *Principles of Psychoanalysis*. New York: International Universities Press.

O'Brien, D. (1985). *Two of a Kind: The Hillside Stranglers*. New York: New American Library.

Oddie, J. (2000). The Prediction of Violence in Stalkers. Doctoral dissertation, California School of Professional Psychology, Fresno, CA.

Office of Juvenile Justice and Delinquency Prevention. (2002). *NISMART, Nonfamily Abducted Children: National Estimates and Characteristics*. Washington, DC: U.S. Department of Justice.

Olsen, J. (1972). *Son: A Psychopath and His Victims*. New York: Dell.

———. (1974). *The Man with the Candy*. New York: Simon and Schuster.

Ondrovik, J., and D. Hamilton. (1991). Credibility of Victims Diagnosed as Multiple Personality: A Case Study. *American Journal of Forensic Psychology*, 9, 13–17.

Optomen Television. (1994). *To Kill and Kill Again*. (British television documentary on serial murder broadcast by the Public Broadcasting Service in the United States and internationally.)

Orne, M. T., D. F. Dinges, and E. C. Orne. (1984). On the Differential Diagnosis of Multiple Personality in the Forensic Context. *International Journal of Clinical and Experimental Hypnosis*, 32, 118–169.

O'Toole, M. E., and A. Bowman (2011). *Dangerous Instincts*. Hudson Street: Penguin.

Ott, J. (1984). The Effects of Light and Radiation on Human Health and Behavior. In L. J. Hippchen (Ed.), *Ecologic-Biochemical Approaches*. New York: Van Nostrand Reinhold, pp. 105–183.

Owen, B. (1998). *In the Mix*. Albany: State University of New York.

Patrick, C. J. (1994). Emotion and Psychopathy: Startling New Insights. *Psychophysiology*, 31, 319–330.

———. (2007). Getting to the Heart of Psychopathy. In H. Hervé and J. C. Yuille (Eds.), *The Psychopath: Theory, Research, and Practice*. Hillsdale, NJ: Lawrence Erlbaum Associates, pp. 207–252.

———. (2008). Psychophysiological Correlates of Aggression and Violence: An Integrative Review. *Philosophical Transactions of the Royal Society B (Biological Sciences)*, 363, 2543–2555.

———. (2010). Conceptualizing Psychopathic Personality: Disinhibited, Bold, or Just Plain Mean? In R. J. Salekin and D. R. Lynam (Eds.), *Handbook of Child and Adolescent Psychopathy*. New York: Guilford Press, pp. 15–48.

Patrick, C. J., B. M. Hicks, P. E. Nichol, and R. F. Krueger. (2007). A Bifactor Approach to Modeling the Structure of the Psychopathy Checklist—Revised. *Journal of Personality Disorders*, 21, 118–141.

Patrick, C. J., B. M. Hicks, R. F. Krueger, and A. R. Lang. (2005). Relations between Psychopathy Facets and Externalizing in a Criminal Offender Sample. *Journal of Personality Disorders*, 19, 339–356.

Patrick, C. J., D. C. Fowles, and R. F. Krueger. (2009). Triarchic Conceptualization of Psychopathy: Developmental Origins of Disinhibition, Boldness, and Meanness. *Development and Psychopathology*, 21, 913–938.

Patrick, C. J., and E. M. Bernat. (2009). Neurobiology of Psychopathy: A Two-Process Theory. In G. G. Berntson and J. T. Cacioppo (Eds.), *Handbook of Neuroscience for the Behavioral Sciences*. New York: John Wiley & Sons, pp. 1110–1131.

Patrick, C. J., E. Bernat, S. M. Malone, W. G. Iacono, R. F. Krueger, and M. K. McGue. (2006). P300 Amplitude as an Indicator of Externalizing in Adolescent Males. *Psychophysiology*, 43, 84–92.

Patrick, C. J., M. M. Bradley, and P. J. Lang. (1993). Emotion in the Criminal Psychopath: Startle Reflex Modulation. *Journal of Abnormal Psychology*, 102, 82–92.

Patrick, C. J., N. C. Venables, and J. L. Skeem. (2012). Psychopathy and Brain Function: Empirical Findings and Legal Implications. In H. Häkkänen-Nyholm and J. Nyholm (Eds.), *Psychopathy and Law*. New York: Wiley, pp. 39–77.

Patrick, C. J., and W. G. Iacono. (1989). Psychopathy, Threat, and Polygraph Test Accuracy. *Journal of Applied Psychology*, 74, 347–355.

Patterson, G. R., B. D. DeBaryshe, and E. Ramsey. (1989). A Developmental Perspective on Antisocial Behavior. *American Psychologist*, 44, 329–335.

Pearson, E. (1936). *More Studies in Murder*. London: Arco.

Pearson, P. (1995, October). Behind Every Successful Psychopath. *Saturday Night*, 50–59.

———. (1997). *When She Was Bad: Violent Women and the Myth of Innocence*. Toronto, ON: Random House Canada.

Peck, M. S. (1983). *People of the Lie*. New York: Simon and Schuster.

Perdue, W., and D. Lester. (1974). Temperamentally Suited to Kill: The Personality of Murderers. *Corrective and Social Psychiatry and Journal of Behavioral Technology, Methods, and Theory*, 20.

Peterson, V. (2005). The Emergence of a New Phenomenon: African American Serial Killers. Unpublished doctoral dissertation. California School of Forensic Studies, Alliant International University, Fresno, CA.

Petherick, W. (Ed.). (2006). *Serial Crime: Theoretical and Practical Issues in Behavioral Profiling*. Burlington, MA: Elsevier/Academic Press.

Peyton, D. (1984, December 16). Henry Lucas Was a Killer at Age 14. *West Virginia Herald-Dispatch*, A5.

Pfeffer, C. (1980). Psychiatric Hospital Treatment of Assaultive Homicidal Children. *American Journal of Psychotherapy*, 2, 197–207.

Piers, M. W. (1978). *Infanticide*. New York: Norton.

Podolsky, E. (1964). The Chemistry of Murder. *Pakistan Medical Journal*, 15, 9–14.

Pokorny, A. D. (1965, December). A Comparison of Homicides in Two Cities. *Journal of Criminal Law, Criminology and Police Science*, 56, 479–487.

Pollak, O. (1950). *The Criminality of Women*. Philadelphia: University of Pennsylvania Press.

Pollock, P. H. (1995). A Case of Spree Serial Murder with Suggested Diagnostic Opinions. *International Journal of Offender Therapy and Comparative Criminology*, 39(3), 258–268.

Porter, S., D. Fairweather, J. Drugge, A. Birt, H. Hervé, and D. Boer. (2000). Profiles of Psychopathy in Incarcerated Sexual Offenders. *Criminal Justice and Behavior*, 27, 216–233.

Porter, S., and K. A. Peace. (2007). The Scars of Memory: A Prospective, Longitudinal Investigation of the Consistency of Traumatic and Positive Emotional Memories in Adulthood. *Psychological Science*, 18(5), 435–441.

Posner, G. L., and J. Ware. (1986). *Mengele*. New York: Dell.

Prentky, R. W., A. W. Burgess, and D. L. Carter. (1986). Victim Responses by Rapist Type: An Empirical and Clinical Analysis. *Journal of Interpersonal Violence*, 1, 73–98.

Price, J. M., and K. A. Dodge. (1989). Peers' Contributions to Children's Social Maladjustment. In T. J. Berndt and G. W. Ladd (Eds.), *Peer Relationships in Child Development*. New York: Wiley Press, pp. 341–370.

Prince, M. (1908). *Dissociation of Personality*. New York: Longman, Green.

Prins, H. (1985). Vampirism: A Clinical Condition. *British Journal of Psychiatry*, 146, 666–668.

Puniskis, M. J., and Anna Gekoski. (2011). Accuracy and Usefulness of Offender Profiling: A Review of the Research. In James M. Peters (Ed.), *Police Psychology* (Psychology Research Progress). Hauppauge, NY: Nova Science Publishers, pp. 89–106.

Purcell, C. (2000). An Investigation of Paraphilias, Lust Murder and the Case of Jeffrey Dahmer: An Integrative Theoretical Model. Doctoral dissertation, California School of Professional Psychology, Fresno, CA.

Purcell, C., and B. Arrigo. (2001). Explaining Paraphilias and Lust Murder: Toward an Integrated Model. *International Journal of Offender Therapy and Comparative Criminology*, 45(1), 6–31.

Quimby, M. J. (1969). *The Devil's Emissaries*. New York: Barnes.

Quinet, K. (2007). The Missing Missing: Toward a Quantification of Serial Murder Victimization in the United States. *Homicide Studies*, 11(4), 319–339.

———. (2011). Prostitutes as Victims of Serial Homicide: Trends and Case Characteristics 1970–2009. *Homicide Studies*, 15(1), 74–100.

Quinsey, V. (1986). Men Who Have Sex with Children. In D. Weisstub (Ed.), *Law and Mental Health: International Perspectives*. New York: Pergammon Press, p. 2.

Rada, R. (1983). Plasma Androgens in Violent and Non-Violent Sex Offenders. *Bulletin of the American Academy of Psychiatry and the Law*, 11, 149–158.

Rada, R. T., D. R. Laws, and R. Kellner. (1976). Plasma Testosterone Levels in the Rapist. *Psychosomatic Medicine*, 38, 257–268.

Ragavan, C., M. Schaffer, R. Dotina, and I. Lobet. (2001). Lost and Found. *U.S. News and World Report*, 131(6), 12–15.

Raine, A. (1993). *The Psychopathy of Crime*. San Diego, CA: Academic Press.

Rajs, J., M. Lundtrom, M. Broberg, L. Lidberg, and O. Linquist. (1998). Criminal Mutilation of the Human Body in Sweden—A Thirty Year Medico-Legal and Forensic Psychiatric Study. *Journal of Forensic Sciences*, 43(3), 580–653.

Ramsland, K. (2005). *The Human Predator: A Historical Chronicle of Serial Murder and Forensic Investigation*. New York: Berkley Publishing Group.

———. (2011). *The Mind of a Murderer: Privileged Access to the Demons That Drive Extreme Violence*. Westport, CT: Praeger Publishers.

Rappaport, D. (1988). *Inside Terrorist Organizations*. New York: Columbia University Press.

Reckless, W. (1967). *The Crime Problem*. New York: Appleton Century Crofts.

Reijntjes, A., S. Thomaes, B. Bushman, P. Boelen, B. Orobio de Castro, and M. Telch (2010). The Outcast-Lash-Out Effect in Youth: Alienation Increases Aggression Following Peer Rejection. *Psychological Science*, 21, 1394–1398.

Reinhardt, J. M. (1960). *The Murderous Trail of Charles Starkweather*. Springfield, IL: Charles C. Thomas.

———. (1962). *The Psychology of Strange Killers*. Springfield, IL: Charles C. Thomas.

Reiss, A., Jr. (1980). Victim Proneness in Repeat Victimization by Type of Crime. In S. Fineberg and A. Reiss Jr. (Eds.), *Indicators of Crime and Criminal Justice: Quantitative Studies*. Washington, DC: U.S. Department of Justice, pp. 41–54.

Reiss, A. J. Jr., and J. A. Roth (Eds.). (1993). *Understanding and Preventing Violence.* Washington, DC: National Academy Press.

Rennie, Y. (1978). *The Search for Criminal Man: A Conceptual History of the Dangerous Offender.* Toronto: Lexington Books.

Resnick, P. (1969). Child Murders by Parents. *American Journal of Psychiatry,* 126, 325–334.

———. (1970). Murder of the Newborn: A Psychiatric View of Neonaticide. *American Journal of Psychiatry,* 126, 58–63.

Ressler, R. K. (1985). *FBI Law Enforcement Bulletin,* 54, 1–43.

Ressler, R. K., A. W. Burgess, and J. E. Douglas. (1988). *Sexual Homicide.* Lexington, MA: Lexington Books.

Ressler, R. K., and T. Shachtman. (1997). *I Have Lived in the Monster.* New York: St. Martin's.

Revitch, E. (1965). Sex Murderer and the Potential Sex Murderer. *Diseases of the Nervous System,* 26, 640–648.

Revitch, E., and L. B. Schlesinger. (1981). *Psychopathology of Homicide.* Springfield, IL: Charles C. Thomas.

Ritzer, G. (1992). *Contemporary Sociological Theory.* New York: McGraw-Hill Publishers.

Roach, J., and K. Pease. (2008). Necropsies and the Cold Case. In D. K. Rossmo (Ed.), *Criminal Investigative Failures.* Boca Raton: CRC Press, pp. 327–348.

Roberts, B., and D. Mroczek. (2008). Personality Trait Change in Adulthood. *Current Directions in Psychological Science,* 17, 31–35.

Robins, L. N. (1966). *Deviant Children Grow Up.* Baltimore, MD: Williams and Wilkins.

Roe-Sepowitz, D. E., and J. Krysik. (2008). Examining the Sexual Offenses of Female Juveniles: The Relevance of Childhood Maltreatment. *The American Journal of Orthopsychiatry: Interdisciplinary Perspectives on Mental Health and Social Justice,* 78, 405–412.

Rosen, I., J. Satten, K. Menninger, and M. Mayman. (1960). Murder without Apparent Motive. *American Journal of Psychiatry,* 117, 48–53.

Rosenblatt, E., and C. Greenland. (1974). Female Crimes of Violence. *Canadian Journal of Criminology and Corrections,* 16, 173–180.

Rosman, J., and P. Resnick. (1989). Necrophilia: An Analysis of 122 Cases Involving Necrophilic Acts and Fantasies. *Bulletin of the American Academy of Psychiatry and the Law,* 17(2), 153–163.

Ross, S. R., S. D. Benning, C. J. Patrick, A. Thompson, and A. Thurston. (2009). Factors of the Psychopathic Personality Inventory: Criterion-Related Validity and Relationship to the BIS/BAS and Five-Factor Models of Personality. *Assessment,* 16, 71–87.

Rossmo, D. K. (1995). Geographic Profiling: Target Patterns of Serial Murderers. Doctoral dissertation, Simon Fraser University, Burnaby, British Columbia.

———. (1999). Geographic Profiling. In J. Jackson and D. Bekerian (Eds.), *Offender Profiling: Theory, Practice and Research.* New York: Wiley, pp. 159–175.

Rowe, D. (1986). Genetic and Environmental Components of Antisocial Behavior: A Study of 265 Twin Pairs. *Criminology,* 24, 513–532.

Rowe, D., and D. W. Osgood. (1984). Heredity and Sociological Theories of Delinquency: A Reconsideration. *American Sociological Review,* 49, 526–540.

Rowley, J. C., C. P. Ewing, and S. I. Singer. (1987). Juvenile Homicide: The Need for an Interdisciplinary Approach. *Behavioral Sciences and the Law,* 5(1), 3–10.

Rozee, P. D. (1993). Forbidden or Forgiven: Rape in Cross Cultural Perspective. *Psychology of Women Quarterly,* 17, 499–514.

Rubin, R. (1987). The Neuroendocrinology and Neurochemistry of Antisocial Behavior. In S. Mednick, T. Moffitt, and S. Stack (Eds.), *The Causes of Crime: New Biological Approaches.* Cambridge, England: Cambridge University Press, pp. 239–262.

Rule, A. (1980). *The Stranger Beside Me.* New York: New American Library.

———. (Stack, A.) (1983). *The Lust Killer.* New York: New American Library.

———. (Stack, A.) (1984). *The I-5 Killer.* New York: New American Library.

———. (1988). *The Want-Ad Killer.* New York: New American Library.

Rumblelow, D. (1979). *The Complete Jack the Ripper.* Bungay, England: Chaucer Press.

Safarik, M., and J. Jarvis. (2005). Examining Attributes of Homicides. *Homicide Studies,* 9(3), 1–21.

Saferstein, R. (2004). *Criminalistics: An Introduction to Forensic Science* (8th ed.). Englewood Cliffs, NJ: Prentice Hall.

Salfati, C. G. (1998) Homicide: A Behavioural Analysis of Crime Scene Actions and Associated Offender Characteristics. Ph.D. thesis, University of Liverpool, UK.

———. (2006). The Homicide Profiling Index (HPI)—A Tool for Measurements of Crime Scene Behaviors, Victim Characteristics, and Offender Characteristics. In C. Gabrielle Salfati (Ed.), *Homicide Research: Past, Present and Future.* Proceedings of the 2005 Meeting of the Homicide Research Working Group. Chicago, IL: Homicide Research Working Group.

———. (2007). "Profiling." *Encyclopedia of Psychology and Law.* Sage. Retrieved October 14, 2010.

———. (2008). Offender Profiling: Psychological and Methodological Issues of Testing for Behavioural Consistency. *Issues in Forensic*

Psychology: Investigative Psychology, 8, 68–81. British Psychological Society, Division of Forensic Psychology Publications.

———. (2011). Research Methods in Offender Profiling Research. In B. Rosenfeld and S. Penrod (Eds.), *Research Methods in Forensic Psychology*. Hoboken, NJ: Wiley, pp. 122–125.

Salfati, C. G., and D. Canter. (1999). Differentiating Stranger Murders: Profiling Offender Characteristics from Behavioral Styles. *Journal of Behavioral Sciences and the Law*, 17, 391–406.

Salfati, C. G., and J. R. Osborne. (2011). The Homicide Profiling Index Revised to Include Rape and Sexual Offenses (HPI-R): The Origin and Next Generation of Homicide Crime Scene Data Collection, Training Protocol, Evaluation & Implementation into Research Practice. Proceedings of the 2011 Meeting of the Homicide Research Working Group, New Orleans, LA.

Samenow, S. E. (1978, September/October). The Criminal Personality: New Concepts and New Procedures for Change. *The Humanist*, 16–19.

———. (1984). *Inside the Criminal Mind*. New York: Time Books.

Sampson, R. (1987). Personal Violence by Strangers: An Extension and Test of the Opportunity Model of Predatory Victimization. *Journal of Criminal Law and Criminology*, 78, 327–356.

Sarason, I., and B. Sarason. (2004). *Abnormal Psychology: The Problem of Maladaptive Behavior* (11th ed.). Upper Saddle River, NJ: Prentice Hall.

Sarrel, P. M., and W. H. Masters. (1982). Sexual Molestation of Men by Women. *Archives of Sexual Behavior*, 11(2), 117–131.

Satten, J., K. Menninger, I. Rosen, and M. Mayman. (1960). Murder without Apparent Motive. *American Journal of Psychiatry*, 117, 48–53.

Schacht, T. E. (1985). *DSM-III* and the Politics of Truth. *American Psychologist*, 40, 513–521.

Schlesinger, L. B. (2004). *Sexual Murder: Catathymic and Compulsive Homicides*. Boca Raton, FL: CRC Press.

———. (2009). Psychological Profiling: Investigative Implications from Crime Scene Analysis. *Journal of Psychiatry & Law*, 37, 73–84.

Schreiber, F. R. (1973). *Sybil*. New York: Warner Books.

———. (1983). *The Shoemaker*. New York: Simon and Schuster.

Schur, E. M. (1972). *Labeling Deviant Behavior*. New York: Harper and Row, p. 21.

———. (1984). *Labeling Women Deviant: Gender, Stigma, and Social Control*. New York: Random House.

Schwarz, T. (1981). *The Hillside Strangler: A Murderer's Mind*. New York: Doubleday.

Scully, D., and J. Marolla. (1985). Riding the Bull at Gilley's: Convicted Rapists Describe the Rewards of Rape. *Social Problems*, 32, 251–263.

Segrave, K. (1992). *Women Serial and Mass Murderers*. North Carolina: McFarland & Company, Inc., Publishers.

Sellbom, M., Y. Ben-Porath, J. K. Graham, S. O. Lilienfeld, and C. J. Patrick. (2005). Assessing Psychopathic Personality Traits with the MMPI-2. *Journal of Personality Assessment*, 85, 334–343.

Sendi, I. B., and P. G. Blomgren. (1975). A Comparative Study of Predictive Criteria in the Predisposition of Homicidal Adolescents. *American Journal of Psychiatry*, 132, 423–427.

Seto, M. (2008). *Pedophilia and Sexual Offending Against Children: Theory, Assessment, and Intervention*. Washington, DC: American Psychological Association, XVI, 303 s.

Sheese, B. E., and W. G. Graziano. (2005). The Effects of Video-Game Violence on Cooperative Behavior. *Psychological Science*, 16(5), 354–357.

Sifakis, C. (1982). *The Encyclopedia of American Crime*. New York: Facts on File.

Silva, J. A., M. M. Ferrari, and G. B. Leong. (2003). Aspergers' Disorder and the Origins of the Unabomber. *American Journal of Forensic Psychiatry*, 24(2), 5–43.

Silvers, J., and T. Hagler. (1997, September 14). In the Name of the Fuhrer. *Sunday Times Magazine* (London), 32–42.

Simons, R. (1983, March). No Ghosts for Killer Gacy. *Toronto Star*.

Singer, S. D., and C. Hensley. (2004). Applying Social Learning Theory to Childhood and Adolescent Firesetting: Can It Lead to Serial Murder? *International Journal of Offender Therapy and Comparative Criminology*, 48(4), 461–476.

Sizemore, C. (1982, August 25). Conversation hour. Annual meeting of the American Psychological Association, Washington, DC.

Skeem, J. L., D. Polaschek, C. J. Patrick, and S. O. Lilienfeld. (2011). Psychopathic Personality: Bridging the Gap between Empirical Evidence and Public Policy. *Psychological Science in the Public Interest*, 12, 95–162.

Skrapec, C. (2001). Phenomenology and Serial Murder. *Homicide Studies*, 5(1), 46–63.

Slovenko, R. (1989). The Multiple Personality: A Challenge to Legal Concepts. *Journal of Psychiatry and Law*, 17, 681–719.

Smallbone, S. W., and R. K. Wortley. (2004). Criminal Versatility and Paraphilic Interests among Adult Males Convicted of Sexual Offences Against Children. *International Journal of Offender Therapy and Comparative Criminology*, 48, 175–188.

Smith, H. E. (1987, January). Serial Killers. *C. J. International*, 3(1), 1–2.

Smith, S. (1965). The Adolescent Murderer: A Psychodynamic Interpretation. *Archives of General Psychiatry*, 13, 310–319.

Smith, S., R. Wampler, J. Jones, and A. Reifman. (2005). Differences in Self-Report Measures by Adolescent Sex Offender Risk Group. *International Journal of Offender Therapy and Comparative Criminology*, 49(1), 82–106.

Snook, B., J. Eastwood, P. Gendreau, C. Goggin, and R. M. Cullen. (2007). Taking Stock of Criminal Profiling: A Narrative Review and Meta-Analysis. *Criminal Justice and Behavior*, 34, 437–453.

Southworth, C., J. Finn, S. Dawson, C. Fraser, and S. Tucker. (2007). Intimate Partner Violence, Technology, and Stalking. *Violence Against Women*, 13(8), 842–856.

Souza, D. C. (2002). Psychopathology and Mass Murder. Unpublished thesis, California State University, Fresno.

Sparrow, G. (1970). *Women Who Murder*. New York: Abelard-Schuman.

Spitzer, R. L. (1985). DSM-III and the Politics-Science Dichotomy Syndrome. *American Psychologist*, 40, 522–526.

Stanley, A. (1983, November 14). Catching a New Breed of Killer. *Time Magazine* (reported by David S. Jackson).

Stark, C., B. Paterson, T. Henderson, B. Kidd, and M. Godwin. (1997). Counting the Dead. *Nursing Times*, 93(46), 34–37.

Stark, C., and D. Sloan. (1994). Murder in the NHS: Audit Critical Incidents in Patients at Risk. *BMJ*, 308, 477.

Steffensmeier, D. J., and M. J. Cobb. (1981, October). Sex Differences in Urban Arrest Patterns, 1934–1979. *Social Problems*, 29, 37–50.

Stinson, J., B. Sales, and J. Becker. (2008). Sex Offending: Causal Theories to Inform Research, Prevention, and Treatment. Washington, DC: American Psychological Association.

Stoker, B. (1897). *Dracula*. (Reprinted 1973). New York: Doubleday.

Stoller, R. F. (1975). *Perversion*. New York: Pantheon Books, p. 128.

Strachey, J. (Ed.). (1961). *The Standard Edition of the Complete Psychological Works of Sigmund Freud* (Vols. 1–20). London: Hogarth.

Strauss, M. A. (1994). *Beating the Devil Out of Them*. New York: Lexington Books.

Strauss, M. A., and L. Baron. (1983). *Sexual Stratification, Pornography, and Rape*. Durham, NH: Family Research Laboratory, University of New Hampshire.

Study Belies Reports of Satanic Network. (1994, October 31). *New York Times*.

Suinn, R. M. (1984). *Fundamentals of Abnormal Psychology*. Chicago: Nelson-Hall.

Swann, W. B., Jr., A. Gomez, J. Dovidio, S. Hart, and J. Jetten (2010). Dying and Killing for One's Group: Identity Fusion Moderates Responses to Intergroup Versions of the Trolley Problem, *Psychological Science*, 21, 1176–1183.

Swanson, C. R., N. C. Chamelin, and L. Territo. (1984). *Criminal Investigation*. New York: Random House.

Sykes, G. (1976). *The Concise Oxford Dictionary* (6th ed.). Oxford: Clarendon Press.

Sykes, G., and D. Matza. (1957). Techniques of Neutralization: A Theory of Delinquency. *American Sociological Review*, 22, 664–770.

Tanay, E. (1976). *The Murderers*. Indianapolis, IN: Bobbs-Merrill.

Terrell, H., B. Terrell, and J. Maredyth. (2009). Case Report of an Adult Female Sex Offender. *American Journal of Forensic Psychiatry*, 30(2), 31–43.

Terry, G., and M. Malone. (1987). The Bobby Joe Long Serial Murder Case: A Study in Cooperation. *FBI Law Enforcement Bulletin*, November, 12–18; December, 7–13.

Terry, K. J. (2007). Sexual Predators: Diversion, Civil Commitment, and Community Reintegration—Challenges and Opportunities. In R. B. Greifinger (Ed.), *Public Health Is Public Safety: Improving Public Health Through Correctional Health Care*. New York: Springer, pp. 478–492.

Thibault, G., and C. Rossier (1992). In Coramae Richey Mann (Ed.), *When Women Kill*. New York: SUNY Press (1996), p. 12.

Thigpen, C., and H. Cleckley. (1957). *The Three Faces of Eve*. New York: McGraw-Hill.

Thomaes, S., B. Bushman, B. Orobio de Castro, G. Cohen, and J. Denissen. (2009). Reducing Narcissistic Aggression by Buttressing Self-Esteem, *Psychological Science*, 20, 1536–1542.

Thomas, W. I. (1907). *Sex and Society*. Boston: Little, Brown.

———. (1923). *The Unadjusted Girl*. New York: Harper and Row.

Thompson, G. N. (1953). *The Psychopathic Delinquent and Criminal*. Springfield, IL: Charles C. Thomas.

Thompson, T. (1979). *Serpentine*. New York: Dell.

Tjaden, P., and N. Thoennes. (2000). *Prevalence, Incidence and Consequences of Violence Against Women Research Report*. Washington, DC: NIJCDC, U.S. Department of Justice.

Torres, A. N., M. T. Boccaccini, and H. A. Miller. (2006). Perceptions of the Validity and Utility of Criminal Profiling among Forensic Psychologists and Psychiatrists. *Professional Psychology: Research and Practice*, 37, 51–58.

Trojan, C., and C. Gabrielle Salfati. (2011). Linking Criminal History to Crime Scene Behavior in Single-Victim and Serial Homicide: Implications for Offender Profiling Research. *Homicide Studies*, 15, 3–31.

Turner, F. J. (Ed.). (1984). *Adult Psychopathology*. New York: Free Press Winston.

Turner, K., H. A. Miller, and C. E. Henderson. (2008). Latent Profile Analyses of Offense and Personality Characteristics in a Sample of Incarcerated Female Sexual Offenders. *Criminal Justice and Behavior*, 35, 879–894.

Turvey, B. (1999). *Criminal Profiling: An Introduction to Behavioral Evidence Analysis*. London: Academic Press.

Ulrich, A. (2000). *Morderisches Mirakel* (Murderous Miracle). Germany: Der Spiegel.

Underwood, R. C. (2000). My Brother's Keeper or My Brother's Killer: An In-Depth Investigation into the Phenomenon of Sibling Homicide. Doctoral dissertation, California School of Professional Psychology, Fresno, CA.

Uniform Crime Report. (2004). Washington, DC: Department of Justice.

United States v. Brawner, 471 F.2d 969 (D.C. Cir. 1972).

U.S. Department of Justice. (1988). Washington, DC: National Center for Missing and Exploited Children, Office of Juvenile Justice and Delinquency Prevention.

———. (1989a). *Missing and Exploited Children: Progress in the 80s*. Washington, DC: Office of Juvenile Justice and Delinquency Prevention, Government Printing Office.

———. (1989b, January). Stranger Abduction Homicides of Children. *Juvenile Justice Bulletin*. Washington, DC: Office of Juvenile Justice and Delinquency Prevention, Government Printing Office.

———. (2002). Child Abductions. Office of Juvenile Justice and Delinquency Prevention, Washington, DC.

———. (2007). Homicide Trends in the U.S.: Multiple Victims and Offenders, Washington, DC.

U.S.: One in Four Children Had a Single Parent. (1988, January 21). *Boston Globe*, 11.

Vaidyanathan, U., C. J. Patrick, and E. M. Bernat. (2009). Startle Reflex Potentiation during Aversive Picture Viewing as an Index of Trait Fear. *Psychophysiology*, 46, 75–85.

Vaidyanathan, U., J. R. Hall, C. J. Patrick, and E. M. Bernat. (2011). Clarifying the Role of Defensive Reactivity Deficits in Psychopathy and Antisocial Personality Using Startle Reflex Methodology. *Journal of Abnormal Psychology*, 12, 253–258.

Vandiver, D., and G. Kercher. (2004). Offender and Victim Characteristics of Registered Female Sexual Offenders in Texas: A Proposed Typology of Female Sexual Offenders. *Sexual Abuse: A Journal of Research and Treatment*, 16, 121–137.

Van Honk, J., and D. J. L. G. Schutter. (2007). Testosterone Reduces Conscious Detection of Signals Serving Social Correction: Implications for Antisocial Behavior. *Psychological Science*, 18(8), 663–667.

Venables, N. C., and C. J. Patrick. (2012). Validity of the Externalizing Spectrum Inventory in a Criminal Offender Sample: Relations with Disinhibitory Psychopathology, Personality, and Psychopathic Features. *Psychological Assessment*, 24(1), 88–100.

Verona, E., C. J. Patrick, J. J. Curtin, M. M. Bradley, and P. J. Lang. (2004). Psychopathy and Physiological Response to Emotionally Evocative Sounds. *Journal of Abnormal Psychology*, 113, 99–108.

Vetter, H. (1990). Dissociation, Psychopathy, and the Serial Murderer. In S. A. Egger (Ed.), *Serial Murder: An Elusive Phenomenon*. New York: Praeger, pp. 73–92.

Virkkunen, M. (1986). Reactive Hypoglycemic Tendency among Habitually Violent Offenders. *Nutrition Reviews Supplement*, 44, 94–103.

Virkkunen, M., A. Nuutila, F. K. Goodwin, and M. Linnoila. (1987). Cerebrospinal Fluid Monoamine Metabolites in Male Arsonists. *Archives of General Psychiatry*, 44, 241–247.

Vitek v. Jones, 445 U.S. 480, 100 S. Ct. 1254(1980).

Volavka, J., D. Martell, and A. Convit. (1991). Psychobiology of the Violent Offender. *Journal of Forensic Sciences*, 37, 237–251.

von Eckartsberg, R. (1986). *Lifeworld Experience: Existential-Phenomenological Research Approaches to Psychology*. Washington, DC: Center for Advanced Research in Phenomenology and University Press of America.

Vorpagel, R. (1998). *Profiles in Murder: An FBI Legend Dissects Killers and Their Crimes*. New York: Plenum.

Vrij, A., S. Mann, S. Leal, and R. Fisher. (2011). Is Anyone There? Drawings as a Tool to Detect Deceit in Occupation Interviews. *Psychology, Crime and Law*. Boca Raton, FL: Taylor and Francis Publishers.

Wallace, H. (2001). *Family Violence: Legal, Medical, and Social Perspectives*. Boston: Allyn and Bacon.

Ward, T., and A. Beech. (2008). An Integrated Theory of Sexual Offending. In R. D. Laws and W. T. O'Donohue (Eds.), *Sexual Deviance—Theory, Assessment and Treatment*. (2nd ed.). New York: Guilford Press, pp. 21–36.

Wasserman, A. (2000). Exploring "Normal" Adolescent Sexual Offenders: An Investigation into Moral Rigidity. Doctoral dissertation, California School of Professional Psychology, Fresno, CA.

Webster-Stratton, C. (1985). Comparison of Abusive and Nonabusive Families with Conduct-Disordered Children. *American Journal of Orthopsychiatry*, 55, 59–69.

WE Channel. (2007). *Black Widows: Explaining Women Who Kill Their Husbands*. Documentary.

Weinberg, M. S., C. J. Williams, and C. Calhan. (1995). "If the Shoe Fits ...": Exploring Male Homosexual Foot Fetishism. *The Journal of Sex Research*, 32, 17–27.

Weisheit, R. A. (1984a). Female Homicide Offenders: Trends over Time in an Institutionalized Population. *Justice Quarterly*, 1(4), 471–489.

———. (1984b). Women and Crime: Issues and Perspectives. *Sex Roles*, 11, 7–8.

———. (1986). When Mothers Kill Their Children. *Social Science Journal*, 23(4), 439–448.

Wertham, F. (1937). The Catathymic Crisis. *Archives of Neurology and Psychiatry*, 37, 974–978.

When Moms Kill Their Infants. (1988, May 26). *The Washington Post*, B17.

White, J. (2007). Evidence of Primary, Secondary, and Collateral Paraphilias Left at Serial Murder and Sex Offender Crime Scenes. *Journal of Forensic Sciences*, 52(5), 1194–1201.

White, L. (2000). Mass Murder and Attempted Mass Murder: An Examination of the Perpetrator and an Empirical Analysis of Typologies. Doctoral dissertation, California School of Professional Psychology, Fresno, CA.

Wijkman, M., C. Bijleveld, and J. Hendriks. (2010). Women Don't Do Such Things! Characteristics of Female Sex Offenders and Offender Types. *Sexual Abuse: A Journal of Research and Treatment*, 22(2), 135–156.

Wilbur, C. (1978). Clinical Considerations in the Evaluation and Treatment of Multiple Personality. Lecture delivered at Multiple Personality Conference, Friends Hospital, Philadelphia.

Wilcox, R. K. (1977). *The Mysterious Deaths of Ann Arbor*. New York: Popular Library Press.

Wilkes, J. (1987, June). Murder in Mind. *Psychology Today*, 27–32.

Wille, W. (1974). *Citizens Who Commit Murder*. St. Louis, MO: Warren Greene.

Wilson, C., and D. Seaman. (1985). *Encyclopedia of Modern Murder 1962–1982*. New York: Putnam.

Wilson, J. Q., and R. J. Herrnstein. (1985). *Crime and Human Nature*. New York: Simon and Schuster.

Wilson, P., and K. Soothill. (1996). Psychological Profiling: Red, Green or Amber? *The Police Journal*, January, 12–20.

Winn, S., and D. Merrill. (1980). *Ted Bundy: The Killer Next Door*. New York: Bantam Books.

Wint, A. V. N. (1998, Spring). There Is Power in the Blood. *Journal of Criminal Justice Education*, 9(1), 169–175.

Wolfe, D. A., P. Jaffe, S. K. Wilson, and L. Zak. (1985). Children of Battered Women: The Relation of Child Behavior to Family Violence and Maternal Stress. *Journal of Consulting and Clinical Psychology*, 53(5), 657–665.

Wolfgang, M. E. (1958). *Patterns in Criminal Homicide*. Philadelphia: University of Pennsylvania Press.

———. (1967). *Criminal Homicide and the Subculture of Violence: Studies in Homicide*. New York: Harper and Row.

Women Who Kill. (1987, March 22). *New York Times*.

Wooden, K. (1984). *Child Lures*. Shelburne, VT: National Coalition for Children's Justice, Child Lures, Inc.

Yallop, D. (1982). *Deliver Us from Evil*. New York: Coward, McCann and Geoghegan.

Yorker, B. C., K. W. Kizer, P. Lampe, A. R. W. Forrest, J. M. Lannan, and D. A. Russell. (2006). Serial Murder by Healthcare Professionals. *Journal of Forensic Sciences*, 51(6), 1362–1371.

Zitrin, A., A. Hardesty, E. Burdock, and A. Drossman. (1975). Crime and Violence among Mental Patients. *Scientific Proceedings of the 128th Annual Meeting of the American Psychiatric Association, Abstracts*, 142, 140–141.

Index

Note: All entries refer to serial murder in the United States unless otherwise noted.

A

B

C

R

S

T

U

Y

Z